REPRESSIVE JURISPRUDENCE IN THE EARLY AMERICAN REPUBLIC

The First Amendment and the Legacy of English Law

This volume will enable readers to understand how the Revolutionary American society dedicated to the noble aspirations of the Declaration of Independence and the Bill of Rights could have adopted one of the most widely deplored statutes in American history, the Sedition Act of 1798. It demonstrates how the wholesale incorporation by the new states in 1776 of the full body of English law into the American law also meant the adoption of the English repressive common-law jurisprudence that had been fashioned to support the English monarchical political system that had been repudiated in the American Revolution. The unhappy result was that in the new nation as well as in England, strong criticism of the executive (King or President), the legislature (Parliament or Congress), the judiciary, and Christianity was criminalized. Despite the First Amendment, freedom of speech and press were dramatically restricted for 150 years as American courts enforced the repressive jurisprudence until well into the 20th century. This book will be of keen interest to all concerned with the Early Republic, freedom of speech, and the evolution of American constitutional jurisprudence. Because it addresses the much-criticized Sedition Act of 1798, one of the most dramatic illustrations of this repressive jurisprudence, the book will also be of interest to Americans concerned with preserving free speech in wartime.

Phillip I. Blumberg is Dean and Professor Emeritus at The University of Connecticut School of Law. After two decades of law practice on Wall Street and service as the CEO of a New York Stock Exchange–listed financial corporation, he turned to legal teaching and scholarship. He is the country's leading authority on corporate groups and the author of path-breaking books including *The Multinational Challenge to Corporation Law* and the magisterial five-volume treatise *Blumberg on Corporate Groups* (2nd edition). Six years ago, he started his study of the early American jurisprudence; this volume is the result.

To my grandchildren, Andrew, Emily, Phillip, Gwen, Sarah, Kathryn, Elizabeth, Christopher, Alexander, and Caroline, and to all the nation's other children who will determine its future

Repressive Jurisprudence in the Early American Republic

THE FIRST AMENDMENT AND THE LEGACY OF ENGLISH LAW

Phillip I. Blumberg

School of Law, The University of Connecticut

CAMBRIDGE
UNIVERSITY PRESS

CAMBRIDGE UNIVERSITY PRESS
Cambridge, New York, Melbourne, Madrid, Cape Town, Singapore,
São Paulo, Delhi, Dubai, Tokyo, Mexico City

Cambridge University Press
32 Avenue of the Americas, New York, NY 10013-2473, USA

www.cambridge.org
Information on this title: www.cambridge.org/9780521191357

First published 2010

Printed in the United States of America

A catalog record for this publication is available from the British Library.

Library of Congress Cataloging in Publication data

Blumberg, Phillip I., 1919–
Repressive jurisprudence in the early American republic : the First amendment and the legacy of
English law / Phillip I. Blumberg.
    p.   cm.
Includes bibliographical references and index.
ISBN 978-0-521-19135-7 (hardback)
1. Seditious libel – United States – History.   2. Trials (Seditious libel) – United States.
3. Freedom of speech – United States – History.   I. Title.
KF9397.B57   2010
345.73′0231–dc22   2010015175

ISBN 978-0-521-19135-7 Hardback

Contents

Acknowledgments

As with all my other books, The University of Connecticut School of Law has made a major contribution to this undertaking. Dean Jeremy Paul and his predecessor, Dean Nell Jessup Newton, have provided continuing interest, encouragement, and support. Law librarian Professor Darcy Kirk and the dedicated members of the library staff, particularly Simon Canick, Lee Sims, Sarah Cox, Janis Fusaro, Andrea Joseph, and Morain Miller; administative staff Lisa Ouellette and Susan Severo, as well as Ann Crawford, Ricardo Mardales, and Christine Dahl of the technological staff, day in and day out over a six-year period were indispensable in their unfailing assistance during the research and writing of the book. Delia Roy, head of the secretarial staff, saw to it that I had unfailingly timely secretarial help, and my devoted secretary, Rosa Colon, cheerfully and conscientiously struggled with the processing and reprocessing, and reprocessing yet again, of the manuscript with its endless revisions. Sandi Browne helped with the preparation of the Table of Cases.

Thomas E. Hemstock, Jr., and Cecil Thomas provided exceptional research assistance during the formative period of writing the book. Numerous other students also provided valuable research help, including Oliver Bowers, Sarah Healey, Peter Hitt, Kellyannna Johnson, Samantha Kenney, Kenneth Kukish, Margaret Sarah Moran, Michael Pohorylo, Jacob Pylman, and Jamalia Wang.

Faculty colleagues, too numerous to mention, were, as always, warm in their support and endlessly helpful when called upon. My dear friend and distinguished colleague, Professor R. Kent Newmyer, was particularly helpful.

Finally, John Berger, senior editor at Cambridge University Press, has been a continuing source of interest, advice, and support. It has been a pleasure to work with him, as well as with my production editor, Regina Paleski, and my copy editor, David Anderson.

I thank them all.

In this as in all other undertakings, I am profoundly grateful to my dear wife, Ellen Ash Peters, superb scholar and distinguished judge, for her continuing inspiration, insightful advice, loving support, and patience.

Phillip I. Blumberg

1

Political and Jurisprudential Worlds in Conflict in the New Republic

The numerous commentators on the Sedition Act of 1798 have typically been so appalled at its role in American history that they have largely neglected to examine its enactment and enforcement in the light of the jurisprudence of which it was an integral part. How was it possible for the generation of the Framers who had so wisely launched this country with the Revolution, the Declaration of Independence, the Constitution, and the Bill of Rights to have adopted this repressive statute? The Act went so far as to criminalize "any false, scandalous, and malicious writing . . . against the [federal] government . . . or either house of the Congress or the President, with intent to defame . . . or to bring . . . either of them, into contempt or disrepute." It was then employed in a determined effort to shut down the opposition Republican press by prosecuting and jailing editors of numerous leading Republican newspapers on the eve of the 1800 presidential election. Truly, it was one of the country's most unattractive political episodes.

This volume seeks to review this deservedly much condemned episode in American legal history in the light of the accepted jurisprudential and constitutional standards of the times. As we will see, it was not a departure from the legal standards of the age. Criminal libel[1] was only one element of the repressive jurisprudence of the times. This is a critical dimension that the discussions of the Sedition Act have failed to take adequately into account. Although this examination will neither rehabilitate the Act nor ease the acute modern discomfort with this episode in American history, it should

---

[1] Common-law criminal libel provided for criminal punishment of persons maliciously defaming the subject (individual or government) and subjecting it to hatred, contempt, disrepute, or ridicule. It was called seditious libel when it involved the government or government officers with respect to their official conduct. Criminal libel so prominent many years ago has virtually faded away.

help explain its unquestionable legitimacy under the legal standards of the period.

Review of the turbulent experience for more than two decades with criminal libel and the Sedition Act in the early days of the New Republic occupies only one portion of this comprehensive examination of the repressive jurisprudence of the times. Allied doctrines included common-law bodies of law criminalizing libel, blasphemy, and out-of-chamber criticism of the courts and the legislature, among others.

Contrary to modern concepts of the sweeping scope of the constitutional guaranties of free speech and press, the constitutionality of the doctrines so dramatically restricting the range of criticism of the established institutions of the society were routinely upheld for more than 150 years, before finally being swept away by an avalanche of revisionist decisions in the middle of the 20th century.

The reality is that the jurisprudence of the Early American Republic was fundamentally incompatible with the political ideals of the Revolution incorporated into the new Constitution. This is the very essence of the problem. In 1776, a political revolution took place. The monarchy was abolished, and its ally, the established church, was abolished in most states. However, the political revolution was not matched by a legal revolution. Far from it; although the English legal system was a jurisprudence that implemented English political institutions, the new states adopted it lock, stock, and barrel.

They did so even though in numerous conceptual areas the established English legal doctrines had been shaped to serve the peculiar needs of that very English political system that had been repudiated in the Revolution. Monarchical rule had developed a rigorous doctrine of criminal libel to reinforce the stability of the Crown. The existence of an established church and Christianity as the prevailing religion had given rise to the law of blasphemy. In the same manner to encourage obedience to the commands of the judiciary and the Parliament, sweeping doctrines of contempt of court and contempt of the legislature flourished that extended as far as to punish critical publications far from the judicial or legislative chamber.

Judicial contempt was a highly useful weapon for those in power because it provided an alternative prosecutorial remedy to criminal libel that was not dependent on a jury. In this manner, relying on criminal libel, Chief Justice Thomas McKean of Pennsylvania, who had been unable to dragoon a grand jury into voting an indictment of a persistent critic, Eleazer Oswald, was enabled to penalize his critic by means of this alternative remedy. He was able to punish the critic without jury participation by holding him in contempt for his critical attacks although they occurred out of the court room.[2]

Still another common-law doctrine reinforced this repressive jurisprudence. This was the "binding over" doctrine empowering courts in their discretion on arraignment for criminal libel to require the defendants to post a "good behavior" bond. The bond would be forfeited in the event of his or her publication of still another criminal libel during the interval between arraignment and trial. This is a dramatic example of "preventive law" resting on the objective of anticipating and preventing "breaches of the peace" and promotion of the "good order" of the established society. In reality, defendants, often newspaper editors, were in effect muzzled *before* their conviction of any criminal offence. It was a survival of the pernicious system of prior restraints that had been abandoned in other respects by the English.

Along with the Alien and Sedition Acts, the busy Federalist Congress in July 1798 enacted a complementary statute expressly authorizing federal judges proceeding under the Sedition Act to require such bonds. They regularly did so. As we will see, "binding over" was one of the legal weapons prominently used along with criminal libel by partisan judges in the New Republic to silence the opposition. Although under the English law, as Blackstone made clear, the courts were required to satisfy themselves of the existence of "probable cause" for concern about repetition of the offence before ordering a "good behavior" bond, the 1798 American statute omitted any reference to such a requirement. Accordingly, "probable cause" played no role in the federal "binding over" cases, and, similarly, it was routinely ignored in practice in the state courts of the period.[3]

In at least two prominent Sedition Act cases, the editors of two leading Republican newspapers, the New York *Time Piece* and the New London *Bee*, ceased publication long before trial for fear that any critical articles would be found to have violated the terms of the bonds they had been required to provide. Further, as in a celebrated "binding over" case under Pennsylvania law involving that scurrilous Federalist William Cobbett, who wrote as "Peter Porcupine," the editor being unsuccessfully attacked under the criminal libel laws when a grand jury refused to indict was, nevertheless, subsequently held

---

[2] Respublica v. Oswald, 1 U.S. (1 Dall.) 319 (1788).
[3] 1 Stat. 609 (1798). *See* 4 William Blackstone, *Commentaries on the Laws of England* 248 (1769, repr. 1992) (hereinafter Blackstone).

to have forfeited his good behavior bond for statements made while awaiting action by the grand jury.[4]

With these doctrines crippling dissenting speech, the English jurisprudence protected the established institutions of the English society, including the monarch, the Parliament, the judiciary, and the Christian church. Although the English common law also protected freedom of speech and press, this extended no further than prohibiting prior restraints. Persons were free to publish whatever they chose, but were subject to criminal penalties under these doctrines in the event their statements were deemed abusive.

As the law of England, this body of jurisprudence had become the law of each of the Colonies. Then, following the Declaration of Independence, when the former Colonies became states, almost all enacted so-called reception laws accepting their Colonial law, which was the English law, virtually *in toto*. In so doing they incorporated into their own law each of these invidious legal doctrines making up the repressive English jurisprudence that had emerged in support of the very political and religious system that had been repudiated by the Revolution.[5]

Thus, the Sedition Act of 1798, criminalizing political speech attacking the reputation of political opponents whenever a jury could be persuaded that it was a "false, scandalous and malicious" statement, made nothing unlawful that was not already unlawful at state common law. Prior to the Act, criminal libel in its rigorous English common-law form had been recognized by federal and state courts alike. The new Act did not go as far. Instead, in several important respects, it was more liberal than the existing American federal and state common law. Evidence of truth, not admissible under the common law, was made admissible, and the highly restricted role of the jury at common law was decisively expanded. Further, proof of "intent" was introduced as an additional element of the crime. Although, as we will see, these statutory

---

[4] Respublica v. William Cobbett, 3 U.S. (3 Dall.) 93, 99 (1800); 1800 Pa. LEXIS 56 (1800). The next year, another editor being prosecuted for criminal libel and bonded to assure his good behavior was similarly found guilty for contempt of court for out-of-court publications violating his bond. United States v. Duane, 25 F. Cas. 920, 1801 U.S. App. LEXIS 271, 1 Wall. Cir. Ct. 102 (C.C.D. Pa. 1801) (No. 14,997).

[5] Connecticut and Rhode Island were the only exceptions. Virginia subsequently adapted a statutory criminal law. The reception laws – sometimes constitutional and sometimes statutory – typically provided that the English law being adopted did not include matter contrary to the statutory and constitutional provisions of the State. *See* Ford W. Hall, The Common Law: An Account of Its Reception in the United States, 4 Vand. L. Rev. 791 (1951).

Moreover, the terms of art in those enactments such as freedom of speech and press also received the same historic common-law meaning. *See generally* 1 Morton Horwitz, *The Transformation of American Law* 4 n.18 (1977, repr. 1992); 1 Oliver Wendell Holmes Devise, *History of the Supreme Court of the United States*; Julius Goebel, Jr., *Antecedents and Beginnings to 1801* 109–118 (1971).

improvements were far from effective in practice, their enactment in the federal jurisprudence encouraged similar changes in the states.

Although the federal government had previously not been impeded in its efforts to punish criminal libel with common-law prosecutions in the federal courts, its jurisdiction to do so had been challenged, albeit unsuccessfully. Thus, from the Federalist point of view, the Act served a useful purpose because it provided a less debatable statutory foundation for federal criminal prosecution. It provided an alternative jurisdictional basis to supplement the federal criminal common-law doctrine under which prosecutions had proceeded before, during, and after the expiration of the Act.[6]

After the Revolution, the various states and in 1791 the new federal government with its adoption of the Bill of Rights incorporated into their Constitutions provisions guaranteeing freedom of speech and press and religion. These seemingly democratized their legal structure to match the revolution in their political structure. However, although these new constitutional provisions – federal and state alike – of freedom of speech and press and of freedom of religion may appear to modern observers to have assured the repudiation of the English repressive doctrines, this did not prove to be the case.

In contrast to the well-established common-law doctrines of English (now American) libel law known to every lawyer of the time, there was virtually no judicial experience with the scope of the free speech and press provisions in the then seven-year-old federal Bill of Rights. Prior to the introduction of the Bill that led to the enactment of the 1798 Act, there had been little consideration of the scope of the free speech provisions of the Bill of Rights adopted a few years earlier. Were they intended to have application to the accepted doctrines of the criminal common law of libel, or were they were intended only to implement the English understanding as set forth by Blackstone that freedom of speech and press meant no more than prohibiting prior governmental restraints of the press, such as government licensing. The English common law had advanced so far and no further.

The opponents of the Act challenged its constitutionality in two important respects. A major source of opposition was the opposition of the "states' rights" Congressmen to the expansion of federal power. Leading opponents, such as Nathaniel Macon of North Carolina, soon to become Speaker of

---

6 With the solitary exception of Justice Chase, all the Supreme Court Justices of the time who addressed the issue in the circuit courts – Federalists to the man – upheld the assertion of federal criminal common-law jurisdiction. However, 12 years later, the Supreme Court, by then under the control of Justices appointed by Presidents Jefferson and Madison, held that federal criminal common-law jurisdiction did not exist. United States v. Hudson & Goodwin, 11 U.S. (7 Cranch) 32 (1812). For discussion of this issue, readers are referred to Ch. 5.

the House after the Jeffersonian triumph in 1800, denounced the Act as an unconstitutional attempt by the national government to enlarge its powers at the expense of the states. There was no express provision in the Constitution supporting the enactment of the Sedition Act, nor was there any express federal power over the press. Its constitutionality had to rest as a "necessary and proper" implied power of some expressly delegated power to the new federal government. Behind their opposition to the Act, the Southerners who headed the opposition to the Act were no doubt fearful of any assertion of the existence of any implied powers for the national government out of concern that it would serve as a precedent that might eventually lead to national efforts to interfere with slavery.

The other important source of opposition rested on the First Amendment and the alleged incompatibility of the Act with the guaranties of free speech and press in the First Amendment. However, while arguing that the Act violated the free speech and press provisions of the federal Constitution, the Jeffersonians did not attempt to explain why, if they were correct, the even more harsh criminal libel law in their own states[7] was not also unconstitutional under the comparable free speech and press provisions of the state constitutions.[8] Quite the contrary, the Republicans attacking the Act argued that the Act was duplicatory and unnecessary because any offenses could be punished under the existing criminal libel laws of the states.[9]

Far from recognizing the constitutional guaranties as a repudiation of English doctrine, as we will see, the American courts when called upon to construe the provisions universally turned to the English law to determine their meaning. The American courts without exception followed Blackstone. They gave the provisions for "free speech" and "free press" no more scope than the cramped meaning that the English law had fashioned to serve the needs of the monarchial system. For more than 150 years, the American courts followed the English law, although as was eloquently argued at the time by such persons as Madison[10] unrestrained freedom of discussion was essential for the free political debate required by a free democratic society.

---

[7] It was a number of years after the Sedition Act of 1798 before the states began expanding the role of truth and the jury in criminal libel cases. During the period discussed, with isolated exceptions, they followed the rigorous English common-law doctrine as enunciated by Blackstone.

[8] Each state except Vermont and Rhode Island had such constitutional or statutory provisions.

[9] See Nathaniel Macon, Annals of the Congress, 5th Cong., 2d. Sess. 2104–2106 (1798) ("the States have complete power on that subject"); Letter, Thomas Jefferson to Abigail Adams (Sept. 11, 1804), 11 Writings of Thomas Jefferson 50–51 (Andrew Lipscomb ed. 1904).

[10] See Majority Report of the Virginia Legislature on the Resolution over the Sedition Act, Jan. 7, 1800 (of which Madison was the author), James Madison, Writings 608–662 (Libr. Am. 1999).

In like manner, the constitutional guaranties did not interfere with the continued judicial enforcement of the wide-ranging English common-law criminal contempt doctrines, empowering both the judiciary and the legislatures to jail their critics for critical publications. These were wide ranging, criminalizing critical publications even when the publication appeared far from the court house or the legislative chamber. They did so even when the publication could not have interfered in any way with the continued ability of the court or the legislature to transact its business. As with speech in the political arena, freedom of speech and a free press when exercised out of the judicial and legislative chambers seemed essential to assure the accountability of the judicial and legislative branches of the government. However, as in the case of criminal libel, constitutional guaranties provided no protection. Finally, there is no instance that can be found that any court using the doctrine of binding over felt it necessary to determine the constitutionality of the practice.

With these English doctrines fully accepted, the law of the New Republic contained an extensive arsenal of jurisprudential doctrines serving to protect the government and all its branches – executive, legislative, and judicial – against critical speech. Of these, the Sedition Act of 1798 and the substantial body of criminal libel litigation are the most prominent and the most important examples, but they represented only a part of the generally accepted contemporary jurisprudence. As for the statute, it was enacted as one of a series of crisis measures to prepare for the war with France that appeared at hand. Hence, it can be readily understood how the Federalist Congress turned to the Act and why it was at the outset enthusiastically embraced by most of the population. Thus, in the 1798 elections, every Congressman who voted for the Act was reelected, and the Federalists increased their margin in the House. Only later with the evaporation of the threat of war with France and the highly partisan nature of the prosecutions under the Sedition Act did the Act and the Federalists become highly unpopular. Then, they were overwhelmingly repudiated by the Republican sweep in the 1800 congressional elections in which the Republicans captured overwhelming control of the House and the Senate, while Jefferson narrowly gained the presidency. Although this was a political revolution, it did not affect the underlying jurisprudence. The repressive jurisprudence continued unchanged, and for more than 150 years, every judicial decision involving any of the doctrines routinely continued to uphold its constitutionality.

The battery of repressive doctrines in the jurisprudence of the times available to punish criticism of each of the branches of government – criminal libel, contempt of court and legislature for out-of-chamber publications, and binding over – were not the only accepted criminal doctrines protecting established institutions against dissenting speech. Still another accepted doctrine was the common-law crime of blasphemy. For centuries, the English law of blasphemy had protected the Christian church. As Blackstone confirmed, "Christianity is part of the laws of England."[11] Following the Revolution and the reception statutes, the English common-law crime of blasphemy similarly became part of the American common law. It was subsequently reinforced by the enactment of statutes criminalizing blasphemy in virtually all the states.

Despite the abolition of the established church in most of the new states, English blasphemy law was American law. Thus, in the Early American Republic, the federal and state constitutional provisions protecting freedom of religion had no more impact on the continued acceptance of the doctrine than the companion guaranties of freedom of speech and press had proved to be barriers to criminal libel, contempt, and binding over.

Finally in the early 19th century, still another peculiarly American doctrine similarly suppressing anti-establishment speech emerged in the jurisprudence of the Early American Republic. With increasing apprehension in the South over the possibility of bloody slave revolts, a concern widely shared in the North as well, every slaveholding state enacted statutes criminalizing speech challenging the legitimacy of slavery.[12] In addition to the criminal cases instituted by state prosecutors, local Postmasters – federal appointees although they were – helped enforce the statutes by intercepting and disposing of abolitionist pamphlets and newspapers in the U.S. mails. Presidents Jackson and Van Buren acquiesced in such actions by U.S. Postmasters censoring the mails and preventing the delivery in Southern states of newspapers and mass mailings of pamphlets challenging the institution of slavery. In similar manner, Presidents Monroe and John Quincy Adams remained inactive in the face of South Carolina's continued enforcement of its free black sailors' act. This provided for the jailing of free black sailors while their ships were in port to prevent their communicating dangerous ideas to South Carolina's black population. They took no action although the Act had been declared unconstitutional in a Circuit Court proceeding conducted by Justice William Johnson. In the very first exercise of its "nullification" policy, South Carolina

---

[11] *See* 4 Blackstone, note 3, at 59.

[12] Although this experience came several decades after the period under review, it serves to show the undeveloped nature of constitutional protection of freedom of speech and press in the Early American Republic.

ignored the decision and Department of State protests and continued to enforce the statute.

In addition to the inertia of these four Presidents, the House of Representatives lent further support to the Southern program of stifling discussion of the emancipation of the slave population. For seven years from 1837 to 1844, the House of Representatives operated under rules rejecting the receipt of anti-slavery petitions. This unhappy development is examined at length in Chapter 8.

Insofar as constitutional guaranties of freedom of speech and press were concerned, in not one of the dozens of cases in these critical areas – criminal libel, contempt of court and of legislature, binding over, blasphemy, and suppression of discussion of slavery – that raised (or could have raised) the issue, did even a single judge challenge the constitutionality of any of these doctrines. It was many, many decades, if not more than a century, later before any one of these repressive doctrines was held unconstitutional or greatly confined in its use. As for Southern suppression of discussion of slavery, it took four years of bloody internecine warfare to bury that doctrine. The same may also be said about the ineffectiveness of the constitutional guaranty of freedom of religion and the doctrine of separation of church and state to end the law of blasphemy.

However, in contrast to the impatience with which the Federalist judges received contentions of unconstitutionality in the Seditious Act litigations, when contentions of unconstitutionality arose with respect to the blasphemy laws some decades later, they received careful and respectful examination from two of the most distinguished state court judges of the time, Chancellor James Kent of New York and Chief Justice Lemuel Shaw of Massachusetts. However, the arguments did not prevail. As with the bulk of the bench and bar, the judges looked to Blackstone for the definitive statement of the English (and hence the American) law. They followed Blackstone and accepted his cramped formulation of the limited scope of free speech and press and freedom of religion.[13]

As construed by the courts of the time, the law of the Early American Republic possessed a very different understanding of the meaning of the constitutional guaranties of freedom of speech and press and religion than the one that ultimately prevailed as the nation developed into a strong, stable, democratic society. Understood as no more than still another repressive legal

---

[13] *See* People v. Croswell, 1 Cai. R. 149, 3 Johns. Cas. 337, 1803 N.Y. LEXIS 1068 (Sup. Ct. 1803), 1804 N.Y. LEXIS 175 (N.Y. 1804) (Kent, Ch.) (common-law criminal libel); Commonweath v. Kneeland, 37 Mass. (20 Pick.) 206, 1838 Mass. LEXIS 35 (1838) (Shaw, C.J.) (blasphemy).

doctrine in a society that was accustomed to a jurisprudence providing for the widespread suppression of dissenting speech, the Sedition Act becomes comprehensible. It was fully compatible with the jurisprudence of the times even if strikingly contrary to the political ideals of the Revolution. Evaluation of the Sedition Act of 1798 through a 20th- or 21st-century lens coupled with distaste for its partisan enforcement by the Adams administration inevitably produces misunderstanding of the legitimacy of its adoption. Set in context, it is no less unattractive, but its legitimacy in the law of the times must be acknowledged.

Legal doctrines useful for the stability of a sociopolitical order resting on a monarchy and an established church had no place in the New Republic. The story of the times is the extended struggle before American constitutional jurisprudence was able to rid itself completely of the repressive doctrines that it had inherited in 1776 from the monarchical English society and to develop more liberal doctrines in keeping with democratic government in a republic. It took 150 years of evolution of an expanding constitutional jurisprudence giving increasingly broader and broader scope to the provisions of the Bill of Rights before the Supreme Court struck down the last of these pernicious doctrines.

Although the repressive nature of the country's jurisprudence is plain, it is striking that along with the dramatic decisions of the courts uniformly upholding its various doctrines, the political society of the day widely ignored "the law in the books." The actual practice featured some of the most vigorous political debate in American history. As Merrill Jensen summarized: "Despite the law, there was freedom in fact. . . . No governmental institution, political faction, or individual was free from attack."[14] Repressive jurisprudence despite its uniform success in the courts when invoked by political leaders did not result in a repressed society.

This volume is a legal scholar's examination of the constitutional jurisprudence of the Early Republic to demonstrate the limited scope of the First Amendment as construed long ago by the judges of the time. This examination also serves to place the Sedition Act and criminal libel in the context of the times and better explain its acceptance by a revolutionary society that had carved out a new country based on fundamentally different political values. Since then, American courts have substantially expanded the scope of American constitutional guaranties, but this is modern law commencing

---

[14] Merrill Jensen, Legacy of Oppression, 75 Harv. L. Rev. 457 (book review), *cited by* Jeffery Alan Smith, *Printers and Press Freedom: The Ideology of American Journalism* 5 (1988).

during the administrations of Franklin D. Roosevelt, not the law of the New Republic. To understand the period, it is essential to avoid the temptation of reading back our modern understanding into those very different earlier times. Although this comprehensive review of the jurisprudence of the era will enable the reader better able to understand why these events developed as they did, such an understanding, of course, does not imply approval of these doctrines so repellant to 20th-century Americans or of the manner of their use in the partisan politics of the time.

Although the Sedition Act stands foremost in any discussion of criminal libel, this chapter in the nation's history does not stand alone. The statutory experience that it represents is only a part, albeit an important part, of the unhappy role that criminal libel played in the partisan politics and the jurisprudence of the Early Republic. The common-law criminal libel cases in the federal and the state courts, in fact, are more than twice the number of those prosecuted under the 1798 Act.

Although several prominent cases of this later period have been widely discussed in the extensive literature, the legal scholars and the historians have typically stopped with the first Jefferson administration in their review of criminal libel in the Early Republic. However, this represents only a small part of the experience in the states with common-law criminal libel. The full story has not been told. This is unfortunate, providing a constricted and misleading review of the full role of criminal libel in the law of the land. Criminal libel as a vital force in American politics did not come to an end with the demise of the Federalists. Quite the contrary: The reality is quite different. The Sedition Act had opened Pandora's box, and after its expiration, criminal libel litigation for partisan purposes did not disappear. For two more decades, Republicans as well as Federalists seized on the usefulness of common-law criminal libel prosecutions in the state courts to harass or silence the opposition press or otherwise to further their partisan interests. In several dozens of cases concentrated in Connecticut, Massachusetts, New York, and Pennsylvania, Federalists, when in power, used the doctrine against Republicans, and Republicans, when in power, used the doctrine against Federalists. Still later as the Federalists faded away, the Republicans in states such as Pennsylvania split, and the Republican faction in power used the doctrine against their Republican opponents.

Thus, criminal libel continued for several decades as a vital feature of American political life. There were many more criminal libel cases after the Sedition Act in the state courts than the federal courts had seen under the Act. In this, as in other matters, the preoccupation of American legal scholarship with the federal courts to the exclusion of the state courts has led to distortion.

The Early American Republic was a revolutionary world with new aspirations reflecting revolutionary constitutional principles and democratic values that over the years since have been widely embraced throughout the world. It was a political society that was new without the institutions, customs, and established doctrines required to implement its revolutionary principles. Worse, in struggling to respond to this challenge, the new society was burdened by the social and political excesses that had developed in the struggle against the British.

These included:

(a) The inheritance of violence from the Colonial period and the Revolutionary War. In the struggle between "Patriots" and "Tories" that accompanied the Revolution, street violence was common. Thus, mob violence shut down numerous Loyalist newspapers.[15] After 1776, this intensified. Dissent over independence was not tolerated. Tories fled or were driven out. In the process, the very idea of rational political debate was seriously undermined.

(b) Mob violence did not end with the end of the war. In the New Republic, mobs physically attacked editors of dissenting newspapers, sacked newspaper offices, and destroyed their printing presses. It was a violent world.

(c) A large segment of the press was highly politicized. Newspapers were widely sponsored and financially supported by leading political figures, and on occasion by the British as well. The parties in power regularly steered public printing contracts to printers that were their vigorous supporters. Much of the press was not "independent."

(d) The press was unrestrained, with a virulence of speech that has not occurred since, even in the most difficult times such as the Vietnam experience. Demonization of opponents was common. As we will see, virtually all political leaders – Federalists and Republicans alike – including Franklin, Washington, Adams, Hamilton, and Jefferson – were at one time or another outraged by brutal, mean-spirited assertions in the press.

---

[15] Buel notes a comment in 1773 from a Maryland Patriot paper: "the liberty of the press... should...be totally at the devotion of the friends of the people." Richard Buel, Jr., Freedom of the Press in Revolutionary America: The Evolution of Libertarianism 1760–1820, in *The Press & The American Revolution* 59, 75 (Bernard Bailyn & John Hench eds. 1980), *citing* Maryland Gazette, Oct. 21, 1773.

The broad departures from the least meager standard of civility extended beyond the newspapers to the clergy, many of whom were engaged in highly politicized sermons.[16] One example may suffice to convey the temper of the times. In 1805, the Reverend Azel Backus was indicted for criminal libel of President Jefferson under the federal criminal common law by the Republican District Attorney for Connecticut. In a sermon to his congregation criticizing President Jefferson, Reverend Backus allegedly let out all the stops. According to the indictment, he called President Jefferson "a liar, whoremaster, debaucher, drunkard, gambler" and "an infidel who only appointed infidels to office."[17]

(e) Notwithstanding the earlier concerns expressed by Madison in No. 10 of *The Federalist Papers*, with the dangers presented by "factions,"[18] the party system had begun to emerge in the first decade after the ratification of the new Constitution. Lacking acceptance of the concept of the "loyal opposition," the groups in power (Federalists at the start, Jeffersonians later) saw the opposition as an illegitimate threat to the stability of the state.

Emerging against this background, the Sedition Act should be seen as a product of the war fever that gripped the Federalists feeling the country on the brink of war with France. The impact on world trade of the protracted struggle for European supremacy between Britain and Revolutionary France and later Napoleon was enormous. As part of the desperate naval war between the British and the French for command of the high seas and the interdiction of neutral trade with their enemies, their navies forcibly took as prizes American ships accused of trading with the enemy. By 1798, the more aggressive French had seized more than 300 American ships on the high seas. Americans all over the country were outraged by such "piracy." With many of the seized ships

---

[16] This was particularly true in Connecticut. The state was the most homogenous in the Union, with Congregationalists constituting 83 percent of the clergy. *See* Christopher Collier, *All Politics Is Local: Family, Friends, and Provincial Interests in the Creation of the Constitution* 79 (2003). Politics was church centered, and Congregationalists were Federalists. They stood for stability and resistance to change. In consequence, Connecticut became known as the land of "steady habits."

Recognizing the partisan role of the Connecticut clergy as allies of the Federalist lawyers, Jefferson referred to the Federalist Congregationalist ministers of Connecticut as "the aristocracy of priests and lawyers." *See* Letter, Thomas Jefferson, to Thomas Seymour (Feb. 11, 1807), 10 Jefferson, *Works* (P. L. Ford ed. 1904).

[17] 1806 indictment in U.S. Circuit Court Records (Boston), III Law Proceedings 218–223 (Apr. 1807); 5 Dumas Malone, *Jefferson and His Time: The President's Second Term, 1805–1809*, 377 n.25 (1974).

[18] *See* Federalist Paper No. 10, *The Federalist or the New Constitution* 62 (intro. Carl van Doren 1945), (attributed to Madison, *id.*, at v, 54).

owned and operated by New Englanders, indignation festered particularly in New England, home of the most rabid Federalists.

The anti-French feeling throughout the country was further inflamed by three provocative French acts: the XYZ Affair with the demands of the French diplomats for bribes; the highly offensive conduct of Citizen Genet, the French minister, with his meddling in American political affairs; and the refusal of the French to receive an American mission seeking the restoration of friendly relations. Xenophobia was rampant. In the overwhelmingly Protestant English population of the time, widespread outspoken hostility was directed at the many thousands of French refugees from the slave insurrections in the French West Indies and "revolutionary" and "anarchic" Irish Catholics fleeing Ireland after the collapse of the Irish Rebellion of 1798.[19] They were viewed as what in more modern vernacular would be termed a treacherous "Fifth Column." The fact that some of the most outspoken Republican editors, including Duane, Cooper, Burk, and Callender – each of whom became a target of criminal prosecutions for seditious libel – were aliens, political refugees from England and Ireland, added to the concern. The vindictive provisions of the Alien Act severely limiting access of aliens to citizenship and providing for deportation (which are beyond the scope of this study) illustrate the depth of the feeling, at least among Federalists.

The Federalists, led by New Englanders, pressed for vigorous measures against the French. Peace hung in the balance; it was a very near thing. Only the tactical concern of some Federalist Congressmen of the advisability of deferring action for a brief period to build more popular support kept them from formally proposing a declaration of war. While deferring that decision, the Federalists moved to arm the country in anticipation. They brushed opposition aside and used their control of the Congress to adopt major measures preparing for the war with France that they expected to break out at any time.

There was no longer any real Army. The concern over the standing Army of British soldiers garrisoned in the Colonies had been one of the prominent grievances leading to the Revolution and denounced in the Declaration of Independence. After the conclusion of hostilities, the victorious Continental Army and Navy had been essentially disbanded. The Congress approved the

---

[19] Samuel Eliot Morison reports that the French consul had estimated that there were 25,000 French émigrés fleeing revolution in France and the Caribbean. Samuel Eliot Morison, *Oxford History of the American People* 353 (1965). Other estimates were higher. *See* John P. Diggins, *John Adams* 113 (2003) (30,000 French refugees); 2 Page Smith, *John Adams* 477 (1962) (30,000 French and "thousands of Irishmen, Englishmen").

establishment of a new Army of 15,500 men[20] and a new Navy to protect the defenseless country from an anticipated French invasion. At the same time, it denounced the 1778 treaty of friendship and alliance with the French. Further, the Congress enacted the Alien Act authorizing the President to deport any aliens he deemed a "danger" to the country.

The Federalists did not stop at this point. In a step foreshadowing comparable responses in American history up to the present day, the wartime climate of the day contributed to the adoption of severe restrictions on permissible public speech in the name of national security. Thus, enactment of the Sedition Act speedily followed, concluding a two-week whirlwind of wartime measures. The pro-French Republicans, who correctly concluded that threats of a French invasion were fantasy, vigorously opposed these statutes. Although the military measures passed handily, the Republicans came very close to defeating the Alien Act in the House. It passed by only four votes.

The gulf between the Federalist and Republican perceptions of the international scene was profound. The Federalists feared France. They were appalled at the bloodshed of the "Terror" and the other excesses of the Jacobins in France. They saw the French seizure of American shipping as a prelude to an imminent French invasion of a demilitarized and defenseless country. They saw the thousands of French and Irish immigrants as the enemy within. In the Federalist view, immediate, drastic measures were required, with the security of the nation at stake.

This contrasted with the Jeffersonian view. The Jeffersonians had identified with France. They had celebrated the French Revolution, its recognition of the Rights of Man, the destruction of the monarchy, and the establishment of a republican system of government. They continued to identify with France notwithstanding the bloody Jacobin Reign of Terror and the seizure of power by the Directory. They did not fear France and dismissed threats of a French invasion as fanciful (as indeed they turned out to be). They looked upon the Federalist response as steps toward the establishment of an alliance with the British and even as the step toward the establishment of a monarchy.

Although Southern discussion of secession seems to have been no more than loose talk, the paranoid Federalists took it more seriously. They looked upon the Jeffersonians at the very least as disloyal sympathizers with "the enemy." Feelings ran high, and the country was as sharply divided as at any

---

[20] The Congress authorized the raising of 12 regiments of infantry and two troops of light dragoons or about 12,000 additional men to the existing minuscule force of 3,000. Act of July 16, 1798, 1 Stat. 604 (1798). Privates were to be paid $5 per month.

time in its history. This was the background against which the Sedition Act was enacted and enforced.

As proposed, the Sedition Act would have codified as part of federal criminal law only the common law of criminal libel that was already the law in the states. This was accepted by the Senate where the Federalists had decisive control. However, in the House, where Federalist control was less firm, the Bill had to be amended to gain approval. Only after the proposed statute had been significantly liberalized to provide more protection for those accused than then available for criminal libel defendants in most of the states did it gain approval by a narrow margin.

Codifying the common-law crime that was part of English common-law jurisprudence, the new Sedition Act criminalized "any false, scandalous, and malicious writing . . . against the [federal] government . . . or either house of the Congress or the President, with intent to defame . . . or to bring . . . either of them, into contempt or disrepute." In order to achieve passage in the House, the Act took two path-breaking steps. It made the truth of the alleged libel admissible in evidence. In contrast, under the English common law, truth was still not a defense. Furthermore, the statute dramatically expanded the role of the jury. Under the common law, the jury was confined to a special verdict determining only two issues of fact: had the defendant made the allegation charged and did the statement have the libelous insinuation charged. The Act transformed the jury's role. It was empowered to respond with a general verdict, determining both the law and the facts, "under the direction of the court, as in other cases." Finally, the Act made proof of "intent" an element of the crime.

Going well beyond the restrictive common law of the time, the liberalized provisions of the Act providing for admission of evidence of truth and expanding the role of the jury soon led to comparable reforms in the criminal libel laws of the states. In brief, the reforms introduced in the Act ultimately changed American jurisprudence throughout the states. Thanks in considerable measure to Alexander Hamilton's brilliant presentation in the *Croswell* case in 1804,[21] the reforms promptly became law in New York and soon thereafter throughout the country.

---

[21] People v. Croswell, 1 Cai. R. 149, 1803, 3 Johns. Cas. 337, 1803 N.Y. LEXIS 1068 (Sup. Ct. 1803), 1804 N.Y. LEXIS 175 (N.Y. 1804).

   Harry Croswell was a Federalist New York editor tried under New York criminal common law by the New York Republican administration. He had asserted that Jefferson had paid a person to denounce Washington as "a traitor, a robber, and a perjurer" and Adams as "a hoary headed perjurer."

Much of the "infamy" attached to the Sedition Act has arisen from the manner in which it was administered. From the outset, the judicial system was partisan, run by politicized Federalist judges and prosecutors. At this time the Secretary of State, not the Attorney General, supervised federal prosecutors. The Secretary of State was Timothy Pickering,[22] a Revolutionary War Colonel,[23] and a leader of the extreme Federalists. With the responsibility for supervising the federal prosecutors, he assiduously read the Republican press and repeatedly referred objectionable passages to the local federal District Attorneys for prosecution.

The criminal libel trials were widely perceived as "political" and "unfair." Not only were the judges and prosecutors all Federalists, but the court clerks and marshals appointed by the judges were Federalist as well. There were repeated complaints about the partisan manner in which they discharged their duties. Thus, it was widely asserted that Federalist marshals and court clerks did not select jurors at random or by lot. Instead, it was asserted that both the grand and petit juries were unfairly chosen consisting solely of Federalists.

Further, it is clear that the charges of the judges, both to the grand and to the petit juries, were also highly partisan. The charges of Justices Chase, Iredell, and Paterson acting as Circuit Court judges provide numerous examples. Similarly, a number of the judges conducted the trials in an impatient, highly partisan manner. Of these, Justice Chase was the worst offender. Justice Chase's irascible, impatient conduct, which led to later Republican efforts to impeach him, made plain his dedication to the governmental program and his impatience with defense counsel and their arguments. In one of the most prominent cases involving one of the very most scurrilous pamphleteers of the time, James Thomson Callender, Chase's abusive conduct was pronounced. It caused defense counsel including William Wirt (later the leading lawyer

[22] Abigail Adams described him as a man "whose manners are forbiding [sic], whose temper is sour and whose resentments are implacable." Letter, Abigail Adams to Mary Cranch (Dec. 11, 1799), *New Letters of Abigail Adams* 219, 221 (Stewart Mitchell ed. 1947). President Adams, who inherited Pickering from the Washington administration, described him as "shifty eyed and ruthless" and "a man in a mask, sometimes of silk, sometimes of iron, and sometimes of brass." Ron Chernow, *Alexander Hamilton* 614 n.54 (2004) *citing* Letter of John Adams to William Cunningham (Correspondence between Hon. John Adams and William Cunningham).

[23] Col. Pickering had distinguished himself during the Revolutionary War, serving as Adjutant General in 1777 and as Quartermaster General in 1780.

   In the new government, he served in Washington's Cabinet, and Adams unwisely continued him in the Cabinet in the interest of continuity of government. He did so although Pickering was closely allied with Alexander Hamilton and other outspoken Federalist critics who despised Adams. After suffering from his disloyal service for years, Adams finally fired him in May 1800 in the last year of his administration.

of his time, Attorney General, and a candidate for President) to refuse to try the case under what they saw as Chase's entirely unacceptable conduct.

Under the Federalists, there were 15 confirmed prosecutions (and about 10 more of which little information is available) under the Sedition Act along with five additional cases under the federal criminal common law. Of these, only one resulted in acquittal, and the explanation for that aberrational result is not clear. A number of indictments never went to trial, several times as a result of the death of the defendant.

The major target was the Republican press. In addition to the celebrated prosecution of Callender, one of the most scurrilous publicists of the time, the Federalists struck at the editors of virtually all the leading Republican papers throughout the North, including papers in Philadelphia, New York, New London, and Boston. As a result of the prosecutions and accompanying "binding over" orders, a number of the defendant editors were no longer able to continue with publication, and their papers shut down. It is hard to escape the conclusion that, as Jefferson anticipated, muzzling the Jeffersonian press during the period before the election of 1800 was a purpose and perhaps even the overriding objective of the Act and its administration.

However, prosecutions under the Act did not stop with the press. They included other targets that illustrate the remarkable extent of Federalist determination to throttle partisan opposition. Three examples will provide some insight into the intensity of the Federalist feelings:

(a) Republican partisans in Massachusetts were prosecuted and imprisoned for erecting a Liberty Pole[24] with Republican slogans.[25]

(b) A Republican legislator in New York, Jedidiah Peck, was indicted for doing no more than circulating a petition that favored the repeal of the Alien and Sedition Acts.[26]

---

[24] During the Revolution, the Patriots regarded the Liberty Poles of the period as symbolizing both liberty and sedition. By the turn of the century, these two strands had separated. The Republicans saw their Poles as symbolizing liberty whereas the Federalists were outraged, viewing the Poles as symbols of sedition.

[25] United States v. David Brown (C.C.D. Mass. 1799), United States v. Benjamin Fairbanks (C.C.D. Mass, 1799). Brown was sentenced to imprisonment for 18 months, but remained in jail after the expiration of his term because of his inability to pay his fine of $480 until pardoned by Jefferson.

These cases are unreported. The fullest descriptions are found in Charles Warren, *Jacobin and Junto, or Early American Politics as Seen in the Diary of Nathaniel Ames, 1758–1822*, 103–112 (1931) and James Morton Smith, *Freedom's Fetters: The Alien and Sedition Acts and American Civil Liberties* 257–270 (1956) (hereinafter J. M. Smith).

[26] United States v. Jedidiah Peck (C.C. S.D.N.Y. 1799), Records of the U.S. Circuit Court, Southern District of N.Y., Sept. 4, 1799, RG 21 (National Archives).

(c) As a final example, among the very first persons convicted under the Act were three drunks in a Newark, N.J., bar who had expressed regret that a welcoming cannonade in honor of President Adams on his way from Washington to Massachusetts had not gone up his rear.[27]

After the expiration of the Act with the end of the Adams administration, criminal libel continued to play an important role for several decades. When Jefferson became President, he speedily pardoned the persons – Republicans all – convicted under the Act and discouraged further prosecutions under the common law. However, he later made exceptions and for a while permitted other prosecutions of Federalists to continue. These were six indictments in Connecticut of Federalists under the federal criminal common law. The cases were instituted by the Republican District Attorney at the instance of the Republican State Chairman and had the support of the Republican District Court judge. The Federalist defendants were a mixed group. They included Federalists of high and low degree. Some were among the most prominent Federalists in the state. These included Barzillai Hudson and George Goodwin, editors of the arch-Federalist *Connecticut Courant*, and Tapping Reeve, state Superior Court judge and founder of the Litchfield Law School. They also included several clergymen of lesser prominence. Apparently instituted without Jefferson's participation, he soon learned about them and acquiesced in the prosecutions for six months.

After a series of mishaps worthy of musical comedy farce, all the Connecticut cases were ultimately dropped except for the one that involved the publishers of the *Courant*. After extended delays, the case, *United States v. Hudson & Goodwin*, ultimately made its way to the Supreme Court. The Court did not act until 1812, when the Court was at last under the control of a Republican majority. Notwithstanding the extensive number of federal judges who had supported the availability of common-law criminal jurisdiction, the Court held that the federal government lacked any common-law

---

[27] United States v. Baldwin, United States v. Clark, United States v. Lespinard (C.C. D.N.J. 1798), Minutes of the U.S. Circuit Court, District of New Jersey, Oct. Sess. 1798, RG 21 (National Archives); New Brunswick Guardian, Nov. 13, 1798; Newark Gazette, Jan. 29, 1799; Trenton Federalist, Apr. 9, 1799; New York Argus, Oct. 12, 15, 1799, Portsmouth Oracle of the Day Oct. 26, 1799. *See* 3 Albert Beveridge, *Life of John Marshall 1801–1826*, 42 (1919) *citing* 1 Jabez Hammond, *History of Political Parties in the State of New York* 130–131 (1852); J. M. Smith, *supra* note 25, at 270–274); Richard N. Rosenfeld, *American Aurora, A Democrat Republican Returns: The Suppressed History of Our Nation's Beginnings and the Heroic Newspaper That Tried to Report It* 200–201, 532, 702 (1997). The defendant received fines ranging from $50 to $150. Contemporary accounts differ as to what was actually said, but all accounts agree that the remarks involved Adams's rear.

criminal jurisdiction. By this time, the Federalists were no longer significant as a national political force, and the issue had lost its highly charged partisan significance. Time had moved on, and the decision was fully accepted.[28]

Criminal libel under state common law, however, continued as a vigorous area in state jurisprudence for decades. The volume of litigation was substantial, overshadowing the level under the Act. As noted, it was widely utilized for partisan purposes by Republicans and Federalists alike. The complaints about packed juries continued. The experience is notable in the uniform rejection by all courts of any concern of unconstitutionality under the state free speech provisions. In view of the insignificant attention thus far given to criminal libel in the Jefferson and Madison administrations, the study undertakes to provide the first comprehensive review of the early decades of this experience.

Along with criminal libel in its full dimensions, including the extensive experience in the states, the variety of concepts contained in the arsenal of the repressive jurisprudence of the period is richly illustrated by the series of cases involving contempt of the legislature and contempt of court for out-of-chamber speech, blasphemy, and finally, in the slaveholding states, discussion of slavery. These doctrines helped shield the executive, legislative, and judicial branches of government, the Christian church, and, later, the institution of slavery from criticism. In their breadth these doctrines demonstrate how much the jurisprudence of the times protected the establishment from dissenting speech on the part of those out of power. Although a review of the Sedition Act and criminal libel must occupy a prominent part in this comprehensive examination, this is not intended as a study solely of the Act. It reviews the experience under the Act as only one of a number of elements in a legal scholar's review of the early jurisprudence and constitutional law of the country and its ultimate demise.

After full acceptance of the entire body of this repressive jurisprudence for 150 years, modern American constitutional law saw in the middle of the 20th century the complete repudiation of the English jurisprudence inherited by the New Republic supporting the suppression of anti-establishment speech. Then, for the first time, American constitutional law in the areas under review was fully in keeping with American traditional political ideals and standards. This drastic change in constitutional law had been facilitated by the increasing reluctance of prosecutors over the decades to actively enforce these restrictive

---

[28] As we will see, Justice Story thought the case was wrongly decided.

doctrines. Although prominent cases did occur and convictions uniformly achieved, they were few indeed. Nevertheless, constitutional law had not changed, and vigorous dissenters continued on occasion to be jailed for their opinions despite the supposed guaranties of freedom of speech and press. Then, at last, after its extensive delay since the times of the New Republic, constitutional law changed with the guaranties of freedom of speech and press at last given a sweeping scope in place of the previous highly restrictive application.

This development is plain with some striking aspects. It illustrates the expansive development of constitutional principles over the ensuing centuries in light of the changing political values of succeeding generations. Thus, these older, very widely accepted limitations on dissenting speech that were so much part of the world of the Early Republic have been swept aside over the years. It also illustrates the length of the time required for the process: This development took 150 years. The definitive decisions expanding the scope of the constitutional protections and striking down the established older law, of which criminal libel and blasphemy provide an excellent example, did not occur until well into the 20th century. Whatever the period required for the evolution of the new jurisprudence, the process represents a triumph for the country and its institutions.

The Early Republic had a very different understanding of the meaning of the constitutional guaranties of freedom of speech and press and religion than the one that ultimately prevailed as the nation developed into a strong, stable, democratic society. Understood as no more than still another repressive legal doctrine in a society that was accustomed to a body of laws providing for the widespread suppression of dissenting speech, the Sedition Act becomes comprehensible. It was fully compatible with the jurisprudence of the times even if strikingly contrary to the political ideals of the Revolution. Evaluation of the Sedition Act of 1798 through a 20th- or 21st-century lens coupled with distaste for its partisan enforcement by the Adams administration inevitably produces misunderstanding of the legitimacy of its adoption. Set in context, it is no less unattractive, but it must be acknowledged that seditious libel was an unchallenged part of the jurisprudence of the time.

In sum, this is a study of the repressive jurisprudence of the Early Republic. It is a legal scholar's analysis of the full legal system of which the Sedition Act and criminal libel were only a part. Although there are a number of splendid accounts of the period by historians, they are not complete from the lawyer's point of view. For a complete understanding of the significance

of the Sedition Act and of common-law criminal libel in the early years of
the Republic, a comprehensive review of the full jurisprudential system of
the country dealing with freedom of discussion is necessary. This volume
seeks to fill this void and to present for the first time a meticulously complete
examination of that jurisprudence as well as a brief review of its eventual
constitutional demise 150 years later.

2

Politics in the New Republic

A. Introduction

American society has changed dramatically from its early days as the New Republic in many ways of which we are instantly aware: extensive change in the ethnic, religious, and immigrant composition as well as explosive growth of the territory, the population, vast changes in its economy, urbanization, and environment, and culture, the emancipation of the enslaved black population, the role of the sexes, and in many other profound respects. It has changed in other major respects that are not so vividly apparent. To understand the role that jurisprudential doctrines used for suppression of dissident speech, particularly criminal libel, played in that very different society, it is essential to understand the political and social context of the times. These too are dramatically different from those in the more mature America that subsequently emerged.

The critical reality is that the New Republic was a very new country in which some of the fundamental political institutions and political culture were still in the process of development. Our examination of the jurisprudence of the times dealing with dissident speech, therefore, is best deferred until readers have identified the key features of the political world in which it evolved and have an understanding of the fundamental departures from the modern experience.

B. The Threat of "Factions," the Rise of Political Parties, and Lack of a Concept of a "Loyal" Opposition

As is well known, in the full flush of the idealism that surrounded the founding of the country and the adoption of the Constitution, the leaders of the day elected by reason of their local prominence naively concluded that the New Republic would similarly be directed by a select group of individuals with government policy determined as a result of their deliberations. Furthermore, many came from an elite society, sharing the view that it would be "the rich" and the "wellborn" who would govern.

The Founding Fathers were gravely concerned by the possibility that organized groups would emerge threatening the integrity of such a deliberative process. Thus, in the celebrated Tenth Paper of the Federalist Papers, attributed to James Madison, "factions" are stigmatized as a destructive force threatening the existence of a new central government. The paper hailed the new Constitution for controlling the effects of "faction." It was seen as accomplishing this on two levels. The introduction of representative government in place of a participatory democracy would place decision-making power in the hands of persons with "enlightened views and virtuous sentiments."[1] In the Thirty-fifth Paper, Hamilton made it plain that the "enlightened views" in an age in which the franchise was highly restricted would be those of "landholders, merchants, and men of the learned professions."[2] Hamilton further observed pragmatically that a federal republic would be vastly larger than any individual state. This, he argued, would substantially increase the diversity of the population and the number of contending interests. In turn, this would render it more difficult for a "faction" composed of a majority to impose its will on the minority.

Hopes for such a world faded fast. Signs of emerging political groupings appeared early, almost before the ink had begun to dry on the Constitution. The political division matched the dispute over the Constitution itself. Supporters of the Constitution called "Federals" are reported to have triumphed in the 1790 election. As John Marshall observes in his five-volume life of Washington, the party opposed to the Constitution (soon joining with others to form the so-called Democrat-Republicans) attacked "supporters of the constitution" (soon to be termed Federalists) as motivated by a desire to establish "a monarchy on the ruins of republican government."[3] This early theme sounded and resounded during the balance of the decade with repeated Republican charges that establishment of a monarchy was the true

---

[1] Paper No. 10, *The Federalist or the New Constitution* 62 (intro. Carl van Doren 1945) (attributed to Madison, *id.* at v, 54).

[2] Paper No. 35, *id.* at 221 (attributed to Hamilton, *id.* at v, 216).

[3] *See* 4 John Marshall, *Life of George Washington* 403, 440 (1926 ed.) (hereinafter Marshall, *Washington*).

objective of both Washington and Adams and the "monarchical" Federalist Party.[4]

Even before Washington had concluded his first administration, the political world was becoming divided with leaders with opposing views on the extent of national power and the continuing role of the states joining with like-minded persons in evaluating and seeking to implement policy. As James Macgregor Burns and Stewart Burns describe it:

> So it was not party theory but personal and ideological rivalry that moved the leaderships of both 'factions' in the later 1790s to build coalitions, reach out to broader electorates, to recruit local and state leaders, to publish tracts and broadsides, to enrol votes – in short to lay the rough foundations of the first nationwide popular parties.[5]

This development occurred both locally and in Philadelphia, then the Capital. It was first marked by increasing differences between Jefferson and Hamilton in Washington's tiny Cabinet over the appropriate objectives for the new federal administration. This division deeply troubled Washington, but his efforts to bridge the divide failed.[6] After Jefferson resigned as Secretary of State in December 1793, the conflict became even more pronounced.

The nascent political parties speedily took form and became better organized. Thanks in part to Jefferson's infinite labors, his regular dining with Republican Congressman while he was still Vice President,[7] and the remarkable volume of his correspondence strengthening ties with like-minded political persons throughout the country, the Republicans came sooner to develop

[4] *See, e.g.,* Letter, Thomas Jefferson to Edmund Randolph (Aug. 18, 1799), 31 *Papers of Thomas Jefferson* 168 (Barbara Oberg ed. 2004); Letter, Thomas Jefferson to Levi Lincoln (Aug. 26, 1801), 4 *Works of Jefferson* 406 (H. Washington ed. 1853); 7 *id.* 389 (H. Washington ed. 1861).

[5] James Macgregor Burns and Stewart Burns, *A People's Charter: The Pursuit of Rights in America* 67 (1991) (hereinafter Burns).

[6] *Compare* Letter, George Washington to Alexander Hamilton (Aug. 26, 1792) (calling for "liberal allowances, mutual forbearance, and temporizing yieldings *on all sides*) (emphasis in orginal), George Washington, *Writings* 818 (Lib. Am. 1997) (hereinafter Washington, *Writings* (Lib. Am.)) and Letter, George Washington to Thomas Jefferson (Aug. 23, 1792) (the partisan "schism" was a subject of "extreme mortification"), 32 *Writings of George Washington* 130–131 (John C. Fitzpatrick ed. 1931); Letter, George Washington to Thomas Jefferson (Oct. 16, 1792), 11 *Papers of George Washington* 238 (John Catanzariti ed. 1990) (hereinafter Washington, *Papers* (Catanzariti)) (I "deeply regret . . . the difference of opinions") *with* Letter, Thomas Jefferson to George Washington (Sept. 9, 1792), 24 *Papers of Thomas Jefferson* 351–359 (John Catanzariti ed. 1990).

[7] *See* Noble E. Cunningham, Jr., *The Jeffersonian Republicans: The Formation of Party Organization, 1789–1801* 132 (1957) (hereinafter Cunningham). (Jefferson conferred and dined regularly with Republican congressmen when in Philadelphia, *i.e.*, the early 1790s. This gave "much unity to the Republican Party which in many states was loosely organized, if at all.")

more formal organization resembling the modern political party. The Federalists took somewhat longer. This was evident in the election of 1800. As Clinton Rossiter has summarized the development:

> by 1800 the [Republicans] were a party in every meaningful sense. . . .
> [T]he Republicans were a tendency in the country from the beginning,
> an identifiable group in the Congress in 1792, a governmental party in
> 1795, an election-fighting alliance in 1796, and an organization functioning
> on a national scale in 1800.[8]

The Federalists lagged behind.

In this very new political world, there was no recognition of the concept of a "Loyal Opposition." Instead, opponents of the administration were seen as enemies of the State, the very personification of those "factions" so much feared in earlier discussions. Distrust hardened into demonization as the French crisis deepened. The Federalists looked upon the Republicans as French Jacobins given to the use of social unrest and violence. Thus, in a charge to a Massachusetts grand jury, Chief Justice Francis Dana of the Suffolk County Court described Vice President Jefferson and the Republicans in the Congress as "apostles of atheism and anarchy, bloodshed, and plunder."[9] As for John Adams, he took very seriously rumors that French sympathizers were thinking of burning down Washington, and he arranged for armed guards to patrol around the presidential residence and the stocking of arms.[10] In turn, the Republicans saw the Federalists and their leaders as monarchists and aristocrats ready to stifle democracy and replace it with a hereditary leader and aristocracy. The vituperative quality of the press carried these opposing descriptions even further. The common ground shared by all Americans was severely narrowed in the process.

As Norman L. Rosenberg has put it: "few Jeffersonians and even fewer Federalists considered their rivals to be members of a legitimate political organization that was committed to republicanism and the constitution of 1787."[11] James Macgregor Burns and Stewart Burns share this view of the

---

[8] *See* Clinton Rossiter, *1787: The Grand Convention* 312 (1966, 1987).

[9] *See* 1 Charles Warren, *The Supreme Court in the History of the United States* 275 (1925).

[10] *See* Ron Chernow, *Alexander Hamilton* 570 (2006) (hereinafter Chernow).
    Abigail Adams, that committed Federalist, provides another insight into the ferocity of Federalist thinking. As she put it in one of her letters to her sister Mary Cranch, "The Jacobins are a very wicked unprincipeld [*sic*] set of Beings." Letter, Abigail Adams to Mary Cranch (Mar. 5, 1800), *New Letters* 236 (Stewart Mitchell ed. 1947) (hereinafter *New Letters*).

[11] *See* Norman L. Rosenberg, *Protecting the Best Men: An Interpretive History of the Law of Libel* 81 (1986) (hereinafter Rosenberg).

struggle between the nascent Federalists and the nascent Republicans in the
infancy of the party system, concluding:

> Both parties shared the conventional wisdom that parties were merely
> large factions and dangerous to order and liberty threatening national
> unity and survival. They did not see themselves as "as alternating parties
> in a two-party system" in Richard Hopfstadter's words. Each side instead
> hoped to eliminate party conflict by persuading and absorbing the more
> acceptable and "innocent" members of the other; either side hoped to
> attach the stigma of foreign allegiance and disloyalty to the intractable
> leaders of the other, and to put them out of business as a party.[12]

C. Corruption of the Press: Financial Support from Political Leaders and Foreign Powers

Two fundamental forces derived from the ugly aspects of the struggle for
Independence visibly shaped the form of development of the press during
the early days of the Republic. The first was the legacy of intense political
identification of many newspapers. During the increasingly unstable days
of the later Colonial administration and even more so during the tumultuous Revolutionary era, there had been no nonpartisan press. Nor was there
any common acceptance of the principles of free discussion of political ideas,
nor any readiness to agree to disagree. Those were times when all had to
choose: Were they Tories or Patriots?[13] The newspapers of the times had
been no exception; each had been strongly identified with one of the contending forces. The contention over the relationship of the Colonies to the
Home Country increasingly become less tolerant and more violent. The
Patriots terrorized Tories, with the Tory press as a prime target. After Independence, matters became worse during the years of of military struggle.
As Pasley puts it, "During the (Revolutionary) War, the Loyalist press was
mobbed, prosecuted, or confiscated out of existence when the British Army
was not around to protect it."[14]

These unhappy aspects surrounding political debate during the pre-
Revolutionary period and the War of Independence largely reappeared as
political divisions became more pronounced in the New Republic. The
Revolutionary atmosphere of intolerance soon reappeared as the increasing

---

[12] *See* Burns, note 5, at 67 ff.
[13] As Shakespeare put it in a much quoted challenge: "Under which King, Bezonian? Speak or die."
Henry IV, Pt. Two, Act V, Scene 3.
[14] See Jeffrey L. Pasley, *"The Tyranny of Printers": Newspaper Politics in the Early American Republic*
34 (2001) (hereinafter Pasley).

division between the Federalists and the Jeffersonian Republicans once again led to intense partisan identification. On each side of the political divide, newspapers were being published by editors with unrestrained, virulent condemnation of political opponents. The virulent calumnies of such violent Federalist editors as Fenno, Cobbett, Coleman, and Dennie were matched by the outrageous prose of Bache, Duane, and Cheetham for the Republican press.

As early as 1789, that icon of the free press, Benjamin Franklin, lamented the state of the press, saying:

> If [liberty of the press] means the liberty of affronting, calumniating and defaming one another, I for my part, own myself willing to part with my share of it, whenever our legislators shall please so to alter the law, and shall cheerfully consent to exchange my *liberty* of abusing others for the *privilege* of not being abused myself.

He went so far as to suggest that, if the legislature failed to act, people could resort to the "power of the cudgel" or mob attacks on offending editors. Franklin concluded by saying that if the proposal "disturb[ed] the public peace," legislators should move to adopt "an explicit law [to] mark their extent and limits."[15]

For an introductory taste of the vituperative invective and near-depraved imagery that demonization of the opposition assumed, William Cobbett and Noah Webster provide some introductory examples. For Federalist Cobbett, who published under the name "Peter Porcupine," his barbed attacks on Republicans included description of them as the "refuse of nations" and as "frog-eating man-eating, blood-drinking cannibals."[16] Federalist Webster similarly indicted Republicans as "the refuse, the sweepings of the most depraved part of mankind."[17] As we will see, the Republican editors were no less restrained.

The partisan climate not only contributed to a proliferation of politically identified newspapers, but also undermined the prospects of a sound economic potential for the industry. Many papers were written for partisan groups, not for the community as whole, and accordingly, their market was significantly shrunken. They desperately required some form of subsidization to

---

[15] Benjamin Franklin, *An Account of the Supremest Court of Judicature in Pennsylvania, viz., The Court or the Press*, Philadelphia Federal Gazette, Sept. 12, 1789 (emphasis in original).

[16] *See* Eric Berns, *Infamous Scribblers: The Founding Fathers and the Rowdy Beginnings of American Journalism* 111 nn.9, 10 (2006) (hereinafter Berns).

[17] Letter, Noah Webster to Timothy Pickering (July 7, 1797), 21 Pickering Papers 173 (Mass. Hist. Soc'y).

stay afloat. Even in earlier times before such political divisions, printers and editors were hard pressed financially.

1. The Politicized Press of the New Republic

During the early days of the new nation and for decades thereafter, most newspapers were strongly identified with either the Federalists or the Republicans, with their very survival often dependent on political financial support. In some cases, the newspapers were even established by political leaders who selected the editors. Financial assistance did not end with contributions. Political patronage in the form of the award of government printing contracts for favored publishers was common. Examples of the linkage between the press and the nascent political parties of the period abound. The following account is no more than a brief series of illustrations.[18]

One of the earliest of the partisan editors was the American Revolutionary poet Philip Morin Freneau.[19] Freneau was the handpicked choice of Jefferson and Madison to establish a Philadelphia paper that would support their policies. After Madison had repeatedly promised support and urged Freneau to forgo his idyllic plans to settle in rural New Jersey and start a country paper and instead come to Philadelphia, Freneau finally acceded in August 1791. As part of the inducements to Freneau, Jefferson, then Secretary of State, provided a sinecure for Freneau. He appointed him a foreign translation clerk in his Department of State at $250 per annum and promised him government printing contracts.[20]

Freneau commenced publication of the *National Gazette* in Philadelphia in 1791 and richly fulfilled Jefferson's and Madison's hopes with his vigorous support. Under Freneau's editorship, the *National Gazette* became a source of unremitting attacks on the Washington administration and along with Benjamin Franklin Bache with his vituperative Philadelphia *Aurora* bitterly offended Washington. Washington lamented: "The publications in Freneau's

---

[18] *See generally* Pasley, note 14; Berns, note 16; Richard N. Rosenfeld, *American Aurora* (1997) (hereinafter Rosenfeld); Donald H. Stewart, *The Opposition Press of the Federalist Period* (1969) (hereinafter Stewart); Kim Tousley Phillips, *William Duane: Radical Journalist in the Age of Jefferson* (1989) (hereinafter Phillips); Robert W. T. Martin, *The Free and Open Press: The Founding of American Democratic Press Liberty, 1640–1800* (2001); Frank L. Mott, *American Journalism* (3rd ed. 1962) (hereinafter Mott, *American Journalism*); Frank L. Mott, *Jefferson and the Press* (1943) (hereinafter Mott, *Jefferson*).

[19] *See generally* Jacob Axelrad, *Philip Freneau: Champion of Democracy* (1967); Samuel E. Forman, *The Political Activities of Philip Freneau* (1902).

[20] Pasley, note 14, at 65–66; Berns, note 16, at 279; Cunningham, note 7, at 15–19, 25–27.

and Beeche's [sic] papers are outrages on common decency."[21] The President urged Jefferson to terminate Freneau's State Department appointment, but Jefferson dragged his feet and never abandoned Freneau.[22]

Soon after Jefferson resigned as Secretary of State and "retired" to Monticello in 1794, Freneau ceased publishing the *Gazette* and moved to New York. His place as the most outspoken Republican editor was soon taken by the fiercely Republican editor Benjamin Franklin Bache. Bache with his newspaper, the Philadelphia *Aurora*, speedily became the most prominent Republican editor in the North, if not the nation. His prose was vituperative, his charges unrestrained, and as we will see, his attacks on the Federalists and their leaders, George Washington and John Adams, brutal. In the process, he infuriated both men. Small wonder, then, that when the High Federalists looked upon ridicule of the national leadership during this period of national crisis as criminal libel, Bache was among the first to be indicted.

Bache was an extreme critic of the Federalists, but was so vituperative that Jefferson tried to maintain some distance from him. However, in 1798, when Bache was in a critical financial condition, Jefferson solicited subscriptions for him and urged Madison to do the same.

After Bache's death, his successor William Duane with "much financial assistance" from Tench Coxe and other wealthy Republicans[23] revived the *Aurora* and continued lambasting the Federalists in the same vituperative vein. Jefferson was unremitting in his support for the Republican press and corresponded with his intimates soliciting subscriptions. As he wrote to Madison, "we should really exert ourselves to procure it [subscriptions] . . . for if these papers fall, Republicanism will be entirely browbeaten."[24] He later reminisced: "I, as well as most other Republicans who were in the way of doing it, contributed what I could afford to the support of Republican papers and printers."[25]

---

[21] Letter, George Washington to Henry Lee (July 21, 1793), Washington, *Writings* (Lib. Am.), note 6, at 840, 842.

[22] *See* Letter, Thomas Jefferson to George Washington (Sept. 9, 1792), Thomas Jefferson, *Writings* 992, 997–999 (Libr. Am. 1984); Thomas Jefferson, The Anas, May 23, 1793 in 9 *Jefferson's Writings* 144, 145 (H. A. Washington ed. 1861). (As to Washington's wish that "I interpose in some way with Freneau, perhaps withdraw his appointment . . . in my office, But I will not do it. His paper has saved our constitution.") Thus, John Catanzariti acidly comments that Jefferson's relationship with Freneau "was far more extensive that the one he portrayed to the President." *See* 24 Washington, *Papers* (Catanzariti), note 6, at 351, 359, ed. note.

[23] Pasley, note 14, at 183.

[24] Letter, Thomas Jefferson to James Madison (Apr. 26, 1798), 10 *Writings of Thomas Jefferson* 32 (Andrew Lipscomb ed. 1904).

[25] *See* Mott, *Jefferson*, note 18, at 35.

The Federalist counterpart to Freneau, Bache, and Duane was John Fenno, editor and publisher of the *Gazette of the United States*. Miller concludes that "in name calling, scurrility, and harshness of tone" Fenno's *Gazette* was an "equal match" for Bache's and Duane's Philadelphia *Aurora*.[26] Matching Jefferson and Madison's role with Freneau, Bache, and Duane, Alexander Hamilton made Fenno's paper possible by raising funds for it, by inducing persons to advertise in it, and by directing Treasury Department printing contracts to it. Later, when Fenno ran into financial difficulties, Hamilton "loaned" substantial funds without expecting repayment. When things became really difficult, Hamilton and Rufus King (a High Federalist and in 1804, the Federalist candidate for Vice President) each gave Fenno $1,000 to keep the paper going.[27]

New York provides a further example. In 1800 Hamilton and the Federalists set up the New York *Evening Post* under William Coleman in New York to battle the Republicans. Hamilton raised over $10,000 for the purpose, selected Coleman to edit it, and got him started with a building and printing press. On their side, the New York Republicans were locked in internal struggle for control between one wing led by George and DeWitt Clinton and the other led by Aaron Burr and Edward Livingston. Henry Adams reports that the Clintons entrusted an English refugee named James Cheetham with a new paper, *The American Citizen*. When Cheetham was not hurling one charge after another at Burr, he was lambasting the Federalists. As for Burr, his friends established the *Morning Chronicle* edited by Dr. Peter Irving, which was used to assail the Clintons.[28]

Pasley provides a cautionary note. Although providing innumerable examples of partisan financial support, he notes that most were episodic and only a few established long-term financial relationships. Start-up loans and assistance in obtaining subscriptions in connection with the start of new journals were a different matter, with such assistance common.[29] Whatever the extent, the relationship between party leaders and newspaper editors was continuing

[26] John C. Miller, *Crisis in Freedom: The Alien and Sedition Acts* 30 (1952) (hereinafter Miller) ("in name calling, scurrility, and harshness of tone," Fenno's *Gazette* was an equal match for Bache's and Duane's *Aurora*, until 1800 the leading Republican paper in the new nation and known for its outrageous prose).

[27] *See* Pasley, note 14, at 58; Berns, note 16, at 267–268.

[28] *See* Mott, *American Journalism*, note 18, at 184–186; Henry Adams, 1 *History of the United States during the First Administration of Thomas Jefferson, 1801–1805*, 84, 225 (Libr. Am. 1982) (hereinafter H. Adams, *Jefferson Administration*).

[29] *See* Pasley, note 14, at 213.

and symbiotic, with printers frequently turning for help when in financial difficulties. In brief, much of the press can only be described as corrupt.

2. Support of the Partisan Press by Political Patronage

In addition to direct loans, contributions, and subsidized subscriptions, political patronage was an important sort of support for the partisan press. Jefferson's early appointment of Philip Freneau as a translation clerk in the Department of State while simultaneously editing his outspoken Republican newspaper proved to be atypical. Instead of this model, which largely faded away, parties in power turned to the partisan awarding of government printing contracts. Without such contracts, survival was not easy.[30]

a. Government Printing Contracts

In the New Republic, public printing contracts became a valued form of patronage that served the ends of the party in power and the partisan press that was supporting them.[31] This symbiotic, corrupting relationship started very soon. Thus, as early as 1792, Freneau's *National Gazette* sardonically observed that outspoken John Fenno, the leading Federalist spokesman with his *Gazette of the United States*, had been designated by the Federalist administration as Official Printer for the Federalist-dominated U.S. Senate for $2,000 or $2,500 per year. The *Gazette* continued: "The natural inference is that" the payment "cannot otherwise have some sort of influence [on him] especially when his avaricious principles are brought into view."[32] This was very early in the period and several years before party divisions became pronounced.

The overshadowing need of most newspaper editors for partisan financial support is well illustrated by William Duane's 1800 experience with the victorious Jeffersonian leadership. As readers have learned, Duane was no ordinary newspaperman. Successor to Benjamin Franklin Bache as editor of the *Aurora*, he made the *Aurora* the outstanding Republican newspaper in the entire country from 1795 to 1800. Duane was further distinguished by his capacity for outrageous prose and the unrestrained nature of his attacks on the Federalists and their leaders.[33] With the success of the Republicans and the election of Jefferson as President in 1800, Duane saw the opportunity

[30] *See* Miller, note 26, at 29.
[31] For a study of this phenomenon in Pennsylvania, *see* Dwight L. Teeter, Press Freedom and the Public Printing: Pennsylvania, 1775–1783, 45 Journalism Q. 445–451 (1968).
[32] *National Gazette* reprinting an article in the *Gazette of the United States*, Aug. 18, 1792.
[33] *See* H. Adams, *Jefferson Administration*, note 28, at 84.

to expand the range of his influence and proposed transferring his base to Washington. However, Duane had gone too far. He had become so notorious that an ungrateful Jefferson, who no longer needed him once elected, sought to distance himself. As Jefferson wrote to Madison in 1803, "Duane is honest, well-intentioned, but over-zealous."[34] When Duane sought public printing contracts from the Jeffersonians to maintain his contemplated Washington enterprise, James Madison and Albert Gallatin acting for Jefferson behind the scenes rebuffed him, and, thereafter, Duane bore a grudge against both.

Instead, Jefferson helped establish a new Republican newspaper in Washington, the *National Intelligencer;* he recruited the more restrained Samuel Harrison Smith to edit it,[35] and saw to it that most lucrative public contracts went to the *Intelligencer* rather than the *Aurora*.[36] In its turn, the *Intelligencer* became "more than the semi-official organ" of the Jefferson administration.[37] Although the Republicans did not completely abandon Duane and gave him some government printing for his Washington print shop, the shop was never successful and ultimately abandoned.[38] Insofar as his newspaper activities were concerned, Duane was obliged to remain in Philadelphia. Although he continued for a while as a major political power on the Pennsylvania scene, his national prominence faded.[39]

Pennsylvania provides several other examples of the use of printing contracts as the reward for support in political struggles. A very early instance involves newspaper editor Eleazor Oswald, whom we will meet again in Chapter 6. In one of the shifting alliances between political partisans and newspaper editors, Oswald was then allied with and financed by printing contracts made available by Robert Morris, then Superintendent of Finance of the Continental Congress.[40]

---

[34] Letter, Thomas Jefferson to James Madison (Aug. 16, 1803), Phillips, note 18, at 129.

[35] Although Samuel Harrison Smith was perceived as more restrained, he was capable of such extreme statements demonizing the *entire* federal judiciary that, as readers will learn in Ch. 5 so outraged two Federalist "midnight" judges of the Circuit Court for the District of Columbia, William Cranch (nephew of Abigail Adams) and James M. Marshall (brother of Chief Justice Marshall), that a few months after Jefferson had assumed the presidency they attempted unsuccessfully to have the District of Columbia grand jury indict him for criminal libel in Oct. 1801. *See* Ch. 5, text accompanying notes 12 to 15.

[36] *See* Phillips, note 18, at 131.

[37] *See* 1 H. Adams, *Jefferson Administration,* note 28, at 160, 223. *See also* Stewart, note 18, at 10, 618, 854; Phillips, note 18, at 131.

[38] *See* Pasley note 14, at 297.

[39] *See* H. Adams, *Jefferson Administration,* note 28, at 160.

[40] Morris was a member of the so-called Republican faction in Pennsylvania politics contending with the opposing "Constitutionalist" faction or Democratic faction who had been responsible for the 1776 Constitution. *See* Gail S. Rowe, *Thomas McKean: The Shaping of an American Republicanism* 93–94 (1978).

Later, after the Federalists had lost ground, the struggle for the control of the Pennsylvania Republican Party provides an unusual example of the award of lucrative state printing contracts for political purposes. In 1806 Republican Governor Thomas McKean had become Governor for his third term, despite the vigorous opposition from the radical Duane-Leib wing of the Republican Party. The McKean wing had triumphed as a result of their alliance with the Federalist remnants in the state. Upon reelection, McKean saw to it that state printing contracts were assigned to Federalist William Dickson, author of the *Quid Mirror*.[41] At the same time, he also rewarded six other editors who had supported him with government printing contracts.[42] As we will see in Chapter 6, political allegiances had their dangers as well as their rewards. Later, when the Duane-Lieb wing gained control, Dickson was prosecuted for criminal libel under Pennsylvania criminal common law.[43]

In Connecticut, still controlled by the Federalists, it should be no surprise to find Barzillai Hudson and George Goodwin, editors of the leading Federalist paper in New England, the *Connecticut Courant*, serving as the official printers of the state.[44] No doubt because of their prominence as leaders of the Federalist press and the bitter invective that they employed, Hudson and Goodwin shortly thereafter were indicted in a Republican-inspired criminal libel prosecution under federal criminal common law.

Complaints over the award of government printing contracts by editors not allied with the party in power and the beneficiaries of its largesse were pronounced but to no avail. Thus, in what was then Federalist New York, the editor of the Republican *Albany Register* complained that although it had underbid all other printers, the official printing always went to Loring Andrews, of the Federalist *Albany Centinel*.[45]

Without government printing contracts, the newspaper partisans of the party out of power, such as the Republicans during the Adams administration, were hard pressed to survive. Financial support from political leaders, including assistance in obtaining paid-up subscriptions, was essential.[46] This was particularly true of the Republican press.

In many instances Republican editors met with financial reverses. As Frank Mott reports, Benjamin Franklin Bache, the editor of the leading Republican

[41] See ibid., at 392.
[42] See ibid., at 363.
[43] *United States Gazette* of Feb. 27, 1806; *Aurora*, Jan., 15, 27, Feb. 20, 22, 26, May 15, 1806; *Sentinel of Freedom*, Feb. 25, 1806; *Spirit of the Press*, Aug. 1, 1806.
[44] See *The Acts and Laws of the State of Connecticut*, 1805, printed by Hudson & Goodwin.
[45] See Miller, note 26, at 30.
[46] See Pasley, note 14, at 99.

newspaper in the country at the time, lost the then-enormous sum of $14,700 during his eight years as editor/publisher.[47] Anthony Haswell, editor of the Republican Bennington *Vermont Gazette*, provides another example. The *Gazette* was a major Republican voice in Vermont and engaged in exchanging invective with the strongly Federalist *Vergennes Gazette*. Prominent publisher or not, Haswell suffered continuing financial difficulties and for a while could not avoid going to jail for debt.[48] Still another Republican editor, Selleck Osborne, editor of the Litchfield, Conn., *Monitor* (whom we will meet in Chapter 6), similarly went to jail for debt.[49]

These factors combined with the unhappy models of the conduct of the press during the late Colonial and Revolutionary eras formed the enveloping climate leading to the violence of the press and the tidal wave of criminal libel prosecutions under federal and state law alike that ultimately ensued.

b. The Flow of Foreign Money

Still another source of corruption of the press was foreign money, particularly British money. There were repeated charges that the British Minister, Robert Liston, and other Englishmen had secretly used English money to support Federalist newspapers and supporters. Thus, as late as the congressional elections of 1802, a Massachusetts Republican paper insinuated that Timothy Pickering, the zealous advocate of the Sedition Act then running for the Congress, had shared in an $500,000 slush fund provided by Liston to British, that is, anti-French, partisans.[50]

Among other occasions, such charges figured prominently in the celebrated *Frothingham* case discussed with other state criminal libel cases in Chapter 6. A prominent feature of that episode was the charge that Alexander Hamilton had attempted to buy the Philadelphia *Aurora* from Mrs. Bache after her husband's death, employing British money supplied by Liston to serve "the corrupt purposes of the British monarch."[51]

In at least the case of William Cobbett ("Peter Porcupine"), the Federalist editor of *Porcupine's Gazette*, the charge is sound. Cobbett's own

[47] *See* Mott, *American Journalism*, note 18, at 128.
[48] *See* John Spargo, *Anthony Haswell: Printer-Patriot-Balladeer* 43–45 (1925).
[49] *See infra* Ch. 6, text accompanying notes 99–112.
[50] Essex Register, Oct. 28, 1802, cited by Hervey P. Prentiss, *Timothy Pickering as the Leader of New England Federalism, 1800–1815*, 7 (1972).
[51] People v. David Frothingham (N.Y. Ct. of Oyer & Terminer, Nov. 21, 1799); Francis Wharton, *State Trials of the United States During the Administrations of Washington and Adams* 649 (1849 repr. 1970) (hereinafter Wharton); James Morton Smith, Alexander Hamilton, the Alien Law, and Criminal Libels, 16 Rev. of Politics 305, 315, 326 (1954); Beatrice Diamond, *An Episode in American Journalism: A History of David Frothingham and His Long Island Herald* 50–67 (1964).

correspondence discloses that Liston had offered to make Cobbett a "stipendiary" of the British Government while he edited the paper. He claims to have refused, and G. D. H. Cole describes Cobbett as an "unpaid British agent."[52] James Morton Smith, however, is less restrained, asserting that British money did in fact flow to Cobbett.[53]

D. Partisan Virulent Speech and the Demonization of Opponents

The deplorable language and tone of the partisan press during this period may properly be included among the very worst instances of this kind in the entire history of the country.[54] For a while during his first administration, President George Washington was universally venerated and above criticism in the press. Soon, however, profound disagreements over the conduct of the new American foreign policy overwhelmed whatever previous civility had existed. The ultimate cause of this conflict was the struggle of Britain and its allies to restore the Bourbons to the French throne.[55] These noxious currents, accordingly, increased and persisted for more than a decade.

A useful way to appreciate the extent of the ugly, unrestrained newspaper war between the contending forces is simply to examine the language employed to denounce the leaders of the day. Let us start with George Washington. As Kent Newmyer observes, by 1793, Washington's efforts to preserve neutrality upon the outbreak of war between England and France rather than supporting the French (as the celebrated 1778 treaty with the French seemed to require the United States to do) for the first time led to open abuse of Washington in the press. This abuse continued for the balance of his presidency.

Freneau in the *National Gazette* was one of the first to criticize Washington, and in John Marshall's words, his paper "soon became a vehicle of

---

[52] *Letters from William Cobbett to Edward Thornton Written in the Years 1797 to 1800* (G. D. H. Cole ed. 1937).

[53] James Morton Smith, *Freedom's Fetters: The Alien and Sedition Acts and American Civil Liberties* 257–270 (1956).

[54] *See* Marshall Smelser, The Federalist Period as an Age of Passion, 10 American Quarterly, No. 4, 391, 396 (winter 1958) ("harshness of partisanship" and "some of the ripest vituperation in American literary history").

[55] The ramifications of the struggle on the American scene included the undeclared naval war with France and such unpopular presidential decisions as the Non-Intercourse Act, the Embargo, and the War of 1812.

calumny."[56] A few years later, Benjamin Franklin Bache took Freneau's place as Washington's leading Republican critic. In the *Aurora*, Bache, even less restrained than Freneau, compared Washington to George III and abused him as "vain and inept with monarchical tendencies" who had managed "to debauch"and "to deceive" the nation. He also denounced him as a "perjured speculator and a wilful assassin."[57] James Thomson Callender, second to none in his scurrility over his professional lifetime, "call[ed] Washington a traitor, a robber, and a perjurer"[58] Others denounced him as a secret traitor.[59] Thomas Paine turned against the President and assailed Washington: "You are treacherous in private friendship, and a hypocrite in public life."[60] Writing to Jefferson in 1796, Washington complained of the press descriptions of him and his administration "in such exaggerated and indecent terms as could scarcely be applied to a Nero, a notorious defaulter, or even a common pickpocket."[61]

In 1797 John Adams succeeded Washington as President and assumed his place as the leading object of Republican abuse. Bache assailed President Adams "as "old, blind, toothless, and decrepid" (*sic*).[62] In her running commentary on the events of the time, Abigail Adams commented to her sister Mary Cranch: "Yet dairingly [*sic*] do the vile incendaries [*sic*] keep up in Baches paper the most wicked and base, voilent [*sic*] & calumniating abuse." She was profoundly offended by the press treatment of her husband and expressed her outrage in letter after letter to her sister.[63] As we will see, she repeatedly called for criminal libel prosecutions to bring such partisan abuse to a close.

That most abusive of Republican polemicists, the notorious James Thomson Callender, among other allegations assailed Adams as a "libeller," a "hoary headed incendiary" "with hands reeking with the blood of a poor friendless Conn sailor," and a liar whose office was a "scene of profligacy

[56] 4 Marshall, *Washington*, note 3, at 448.
[57] See *Gazette of the United States*, Sept. 9, 1799; Rosenfeld, note 18, at 691.
[58] 1 Julius Goebel, Jr., *The Law Practice of Alexander Hamilton: Documents and Commentaries* 775–806 (1964) (hereinafter Goebel, *Hamilton Practice*).
[59] Fawn Brodie, *Thomas Jefferson: An Intimate History* 321 (1974) (hereinafter Brodie).
[60] 2 H. Adams, *Jefferson Administration*, note 28, at 328.
[61] Letter, George Washington to Thomas Jefferson (summer 1796), *cited* in J. Thomas Scharf & Thompson Westcott, *History of Philadelphia, 1609–1884*, 484 (1884) (hereinafter Scharf & Westcott).
[62] *Gazette of the United States*, Sept. 9, 1799; *Aurora*, Sept. 9, 1799; Rosenfeld, note 18, at 691.
[63] Letters of Abigail Adams to Mary Cranch (Apr. 26, 1798, May 10, 1798, May 26, 1798, June 19, 1798, June 23, 1798), *New Letters*, note 10, at 164, 170, 179, 193, 194. The flow of lamentations came to an end with the enactment of the Sedition Act of 1798 on July 14, 1798.

and usury" and whose purpose "was to embroil this country [in a war] with France."[64] Still other Republican editors pilloried Adams as "a ruffian deserving the curses of mankind."[65] For their part, the Federalist editors were no less restrained. The arch-Federalist *Gazette of the United States* assumed an obligation "to watch with eagle eye, the misinterpretations, calumnies, and falsehoods of Jacobinical publications, whose filth and loathsomeness shall no longer screen them from exposure."[66]

However, notwithstanding the revolting calumny incurred by prominent political figures of both parties, they were not free from much the same ugly prose in describing persons who had injured them. Thus, Adams described Benjamin Franklin Bache as "one of the most malicious libelers of me. But the yellow fever arrested him in his detestable career and sent him to his grandfather [Benjamin Franklin] from whom he inherited a dirty, envious, jealous, and revengeful Spight [*sic*] against me."[67] Similarly, he described Alexander Hamilton as "a bastard Bratt [*sic*] of a Scots Pedlar [*sic*]" and as a "Creole Bastard."[68]

Washington was so deeply wounded by the "calumnies" of Freneau and other Republican editors that he deemed it a national problem. Like Washington and Adams, Jefferson was also wounded by the outrageous charges and epithets. In a letter in 1804 to his friend and fellow Virginian John Tyler, he lamented the "direct falsehoods, the misrepresentations of truth, the calumnies and the insults resorted to by a faction to mislead the public mind."[69] Shortly thereafter in his Second Inaugural Address, he bitterly attacked the calumnies of the press and condemned the "licentiousness of the press."[70]

[64] Burns, note 5, at 111.

   The reference to the sailor is to President Adams's controversial decision to surrender a seaman, Jonathan Robbins, of disputed ancestry to the British for alleged desertion from the British Navy after his impressment. The disputed issue was whether Robbins was a British or American citizen. *See* Proceedings in the case of Jonathan Robbins on a Claim for Delivery to the British Government on Charge of Murder (D.S.C. 1789), Wharton, note 51, at 392–457.

[65] Brodie, note 59, at 321.

[66] *Gazette of the United States*, reprinted in the *Connecticut Courant*, Jan. 26, 1801.

[67] Letter, John Adams to Benjamin Rush (June 23, 1807), Rosenfeld, note 18, at 235.

[68] *See* Chernow, note 10, at 522, *citing* Historical Magazine 50–51 (July 1870–1871). For Hamilton's indignant defense of the legitimacy of his birth and the distinction of his Scottish heritage, *see* Letter, Alexander Hamilton to William Jackson (Aug. 26, 1800), Alexander Hamilton, *Writings* 930 (Libr. Am. 2001).

   For her part, Abigail Adams described Albert Gallatin as the "sly, artfull [*sic*], the insidious Gallatin." *See* Letter, Abigail Adams to Mary Cranch (Apr. 4, 1798), *Abigail Adams New Letters*, note 10, at 151.

[69] Letter, Thomas Jefferson to Judge John Tyler (June 28, 1804), Jefferson, *Writings* (Libr. Am.), note 22, at 32.

[70] Thomas Jefferson, Second Inaugural Address, Mar. 5, 1804, *ibid.*, at 518, 521–522 ("whatever its licentiousness could devise or dare").

As Clyde Duniway has concluded, this development of a scurrilous, abusive, partisan press bore bitter fruit. The support of public opinion for freedom of the press

> was largely forfeited by the character of the newspaper press toward the end of the eighteenth century. The violence of the [Revolutionary] war spirit had encourage a habit of intolerance toward political opponents, and vindictive denunciation of all loyalists had been supplemented by rigorous suppression of all publications unfavorable to the Revolutionary movement. Now that the establishment of peace and the organization of settled government gave scope for the development of national parties, the vituperative powers of ardent partisans were employed against each other as domestic antagonists. Coarse personalities, vulgar ribaldry, malicious slanders, were poured forth until it seemed to sober-minded men that unrestrained freedom of discussion was leading to the triumph of anarchy.[71]

When civic temperatures rose with the bitter division of opinion on the likelihood of an outbreak of war with France and over the need for a comprehensive series of defensive measures, the stage was set for consideration of the Alien and Sedition Acts. The war measures and the taxes to support them, the repressive statutes, and the bitter two-year experience of the criminal prosecution and imprisonment of Republican editors and partisans contributed to the election of Jefferson in 1800.

However, the abusive quality of the press not only did not abate with Jefferson in the White House, but grew worse. As Henry Adams observed, the year 1802 saw "an outburst of reciprocal invective and slander such as could not be matched in American history."[72] Indeed, it had become contagious and flavored even legal pleadings. Thus in 1804, when the Republicans had come to control not only the national government but also the state courts in New York, the language employed in the indictment under New York common law of an obscure, upstate Federalist editor, Harry Croswell, illustrates much the same violence of speech as had characterized the earlier exchanges between Federalist and Republican editors. In indicting Croswell for asserting that President Jefferson had paid James T. Callender for his scurrilous comments about President Washington and President Adams, the indictment further stated that Croswell, "being a malicious man and seditious man

---

[71] Clyde A. Duniway, *The Development of Freedom of the Press in Massachusetts* 143 (1906 repr. 1969) (hereinafter Duniway).

[72] *See* 1 H. Adams, *Jefferson Administration*, note 28, at 218–219. For a similar conclusion, *see* Lucius A. Powe, Jr., *The Fourth Estate and the Constitution: Freedom of the Press in America* 53 (1991) ("Probably no period in our history witnessed such an irresponsibly abusive partisan press").

and of a depraved mind and wicked and diabolical disposition . . . contriving and intending . . . to detract from, scandalize, traduce, vilify, and to represent him the said Thomas Jefferson, as unworthy of the confidence, respect, and attachment of the people of the said United States."[73]

E. Partisan Violence in the New Republic: An Inheritance from the Struggles with the British Crown

The remarkable dimensions of partisan virulent speech and partisan violence that characterized the political struggle between the Federalists and the Republicans were an unhappy inheritance from the struggles with the British Crown. The Revolutionary War had been a bitter struggle continuing for five years of protracted warfare. The British were seen by the Patriots as a brutal occupying power. As the fortunes of war waxed and waned and scenes of warfare affected first one and then another portions of the country, loss of life, depredation of property, and enmity increased. Even before the Declaration of Independence, the basis for open discussion of the relations with the British Crown had been fast disappearing. Patriot mob violence, particularly in New England, had become more and more prominent. Tory editors and publishers were assaulted and Tory newspaper offices vandalized and destroyed. Pasley concludes: "During the war, the Loyalist press was mobbed, prosecuted, or confiscated out of existence when the British Army was not around to protect it. Loyalist editors fled for their lives when they were not banished out right." Even in Boston, protected by a British Army, only one Tory paper had survived by the eve of the Revolution.[74]

With the Revolution, matters intensified. Dissent was now viewed as treason. Tories were driven from their homes and their communities. Tories were tarred and feathered, and Tories were even lynched. Thousands fled to Canada. When Washington forced the British to evacuate their occupation of Boston, the fleet that transported the British Army to Halifax squeezed thousands of Tory sympathizers aboard and carried them to safety as well.

This brutal world and the violent pattern of conduct it had legitimated became reincarnated as the increasing differences between the Federalists

---

[73] *See* Goebel, *Hamilton Practice*, note 58, at 791.
[74] Pasley, note 14, at 34; Duniway, note 71, at 131; Leonard W. Levy, *Emergence of the Free Press* 62–88 (1985), Richard Buel, Jr., Freedom of the Press in Revolutionary America: The Evolution of Libertarianism, 1760–1820, in *The Press and The American Revolution* 59, 76–81 (B. Bailyn and J. Hench eds. 1980).

and Republicans sharpened the divide between them. Following the Revolutionary pattern, the New Republic became the scene of mob violence, intolerance, repression of dissenting points of view, and treatment of dissidents as traitors and threats to the stability of the government. Republican editors were personally assaulted by Federalist mobs or militia members, their offices invaded, their printing presses destroyed, and even their homes menaced. There were riotous demonstrations and boycotts, as well as mob violence against politically unpopular editors and authors.[75]

For our purposes, a mere recitation of the barest outlines of such events should suffice. It is perhaps not unexpected to find that Benjamin Franklin Bache and his successor William Duane, two of the most rabid and outspoken of the Republican calumniators, were outstanding victims. As early as 1789, the windows of Bache's house were broken on several occasions, a mob destroyed his office, and Bache was personally assaulted by the son of his arch-rival, John Fenno. This pattern continued as the political conflict worsened. On one occasion, Bache was seriously injured and his assailant fined. Indicative of the temper of the times, Secretary of State Pickering a year later rewarded the perpetrator with a federal appointment to deliver a diplomatic message to the American envoys to France.[76] After replacing Bache, Duane was similarly attacked. He was assaulted, his office pillaged, and his home threatened.[77] In like fashion on no fewer than four occasions, Republican mobs in Philadelphia invaded Federalist editor John Fenno's offices, pillaging and ransacking, and assaulting personnel including Fenno.[78]

Both the Federalists and the Republicans organized gangs flaunting their affiliation with black cockades in the hats of the Federalists and tricolor cockades in the hats of the Republicans. Inevitably, this led to street fighting, with the gangs clashing on various occasions.[79] When Republicans followed the Revolutionary model and erected Liberty Poles carrying Republican sentiments, this also led inevitably to violent clashes. Federalist gangs would attempt to tear down and destroy the poles, with Republican gangs defending them.[80]

[75] *See* Duniway, note 71, at 131.
[76] *See* Berns, note 16, at 335–336, 355; Pasley, note 14, at 98; Rosenfeld, note 18, at 56.
[77] *See* Pasley, note 14, at 189–190.
[78] *See* Scharf & Westcott, note 61, at 497.
[79] *See* Charles Warren, *Jacobin & Junto, or Early American Politics as Seen in the Diary of Nathaniel Ames, 1758–1822*, 81–88 (1931) (hereinafter Warren, *Junto*).
[80] Republican Liberty Poles condemning Federalist policies were torn down by Federalist mobs in numerous states, including Massachusetts, Maine, and Vermont. *See ibid.*, at 103–104.

What appears to have been a typical altercation is described with appropriately partisan touches by the staunchly Federalist *Federal Gazette and Baltimore Advertiser*:

> Symptoms of insurgency occurred. A few days since . . . a number of Vermonters met at Wallingford, erecting a liberty pole, and used abusive language against Congress, the president, etc. A number of true republican federalists assembled soon after – a contest ensued; and the pole was cut down, burnt to ashes and scattered to the wind.[81]

In one of her letters, Abigail Adams vividly describes the street fighting in Philadelphia between Federalists and Republicans wearing their black and tricolor cockades, respectively, in their hats. Writing to her sister Mary Cranch, she laments: "This Bache is cursing and abusing daily. If that fellow and his Agents Chronical [Thomas Adams's Boston *Independent Chronicle*] is [*sic*] not suppressed, we shall come to civil war."[82] Although the sharpness of the division led to ugly near-violent encounters in the streets, there does not appear to have been a single significant outbreak of violence between the two militias. There were other sources of violence. For example, a group of Pennsylvania militia led by Joseph McKean, son of Chief Justice McKean, angry at Duane's comments about the behavior of the militia in the Fries Rebellion, physically attacked Duane, beating and whipping him, and ransacked his office.[83] Still later after Jefferson's election to the presidency, Republican mobs attacked Federalist printers and destroyed their presses.[84]

F. Three Insurrections Threatening the Stability of the New Nation

Let us now review the march of events in the 1790s that ultimately produced the environment that helped shape the direction taken by the political events of the end of the decade.

1. Shays's Rebellion (1787)

Shays's Rebellion was the first of these events. During the later days under the Articles of Confederation, rural discontent with deflated prices for agricultural products, high taxes paid mainly by the poor under the regressive tax system

---

[81] *Federal Gazette and Baltimore Advertiser*, Jan. 1798.
[82] Letter, Abigail Adams to Mary Cranch (May 10, 1798), *New Letters*, note 10, at 170, 172. Abigail Adams interestingly enough was appealing to the classic justification for criminal libel as a legal doctrine designed to prevent breaches of the peace.
[83] *See* Pasley, note 14, at 190.
[84] *See* Pasley, note 14, at 278.

of the times, tight money, and foreclosures of farm mortgages was serious. Farmers with debts to pay and crops they could not sell clamored unsuccessfully to pay their debts in kind. These dire conditions led to the first of three armed revolts over a decade that threatened the stability of the New Republic.

In 1786, in Massachusetts, such discontent exploded with armed farmer mobs led by a Revolutionary hero, Captain Daniel Shays, preventing courts from functioning and thereby preventing the determination of debt collection cases and the issuance of judicial foreclosure orders. A thousand armed farmers prevented the Supreme Judicial Court with Chief Justice Cushing presiding from holding court in Springfield in September 1786 and again in December.

The situation was so serious that the Continental Congress voted to enlist 1,300 men for service in Massachusetts. However, this proved unnecessary when Governor James Bowdoin, who had suspended *habeas corpus*, raised a militia of 4,400 men with "private money." The money variously estimated at £ 4,000 to £6,000 came from 129 Boston merchants who were entreated to provide support with the advice that it was wiser to give a little than risk losing it all.

With two thousand armed men, Shays then attempted to seize the federal arsenal at Springfield with its store of 7,000 muskets and 1,300 barrels of gunpowder. They were repulsed by the arsenal defenders with discharges of grapeshot, with four men killed and more wounded. A week later, the state militia led by Gen. Benjamin Lincoln engaged the insurgents in bitter winter weather and was able to disperse them as an organized armed force. The rebellion was suppressed, and 14 of the ringleaders were arrested, tried, and sentenced to death.[85] With the elimination of the armed threat, the threat to the state faded away, and more equable tempers returned. The Legislature began to address some of the abuses that had led to the Rebellion. The 14 condemned leaders were either pardoned or their sentences reduced to short prison terms.[86]

This outbreak had several important consequences. Samuel Eliot Morison concludes that it alarmed "all Americans leaders," except Thomas Jefferson, and strengthened the case for a stronger federal government. In particular,

---

[85] *See generally* Marion L. Starkey, *A Little Rebellion* (1955) (hereinafter Starkey); David P. Szatmary, *Shays' Rebellion: The Making of an Agrarian Insurrection* (1980); George R. Minot, *History of the Insurrections in Massachusetts in 1786 and of the Rebellion Consequent Thereon* (1971).

[86] See Samuel Elliott Morison, *The Oxford History of the American People* 302–304 (1965); Allan Nevins, *The American States During and After the Revolution 1775–1789*, 534–537 (1927). Jefferson was not concerned. ("I like a little rebellion now and then.") Letter, Thomas Jefferson to Abigail Adams (Feb. 22, 1787), The Adams-Jefferson Letters 173 (L. Cappon ed. 1959).

both President Washington and Secretary of the Treasury Hamilton perceived this as a serious threat to the government. Shaken by the outbreak, they appeared to have exaggerated its significance and overreacted. The episode also incidentally showed the desirability of the use of overwhelming force to deal with such disturbances, a lesson that was learned and applied a few years later in the suppression of the Whiskey Rebellion of 1794 in Western Pennsylvania.

Finally in a prelude to the Sedition Act of 1798, the suppression of Shays's Rebellion was accompanied by four prosecutions for criminal libel in the Massachusetts courts of several editors and a local judge for publications supporting the Rebellion. These are reviewed in Chapter 6.

2. The Whiskey Tax Rebellion (1794)

Shays's Rebellion was followed a few years later by the Whiskey Tax Rebellion in Western Pennsylvania and Kentucky.[87] Corn played an essential role in the local farm economy, but the transportation costs over the mountainous areas to get the corn to market were prohibitive. Conversion of the corn to whiskey reduced the transportation costs sixfold, and the product became highly profitable. Whiskey speedily replaced the corn from which it was made as the marketable product.[88] Thus, nearly every farm had its own still. The federal whiskey tax struck directly home and led to prolonged armed resistance by farmers to the government's efforts to collect the tax.[89] Federal officers were prevented from performing their duties and were subjected to assault, tar and feathering, and in at least one case torture. In Beveridge's summary of the Pennsylvania events, "men had been killed, houses burned, mails pillaged."[90] A series of stormy public meetings adopted what Wharton

---

[87] *See generally* Thomas P. Slaughter, *The Whiskey Rebellion: Frontier Epilogue to the American Revolution* (1986) (hereinafter Slaughter); William Hoagland, *The Whiskey Rebellion* (2006); Mary M. K. Tachau, The Whiskey Rebellion, 73 J. Amer. Hist. 15, 28 n.30 (No. 1, 1986); (hereinafter Tachau, Whiskey Rebellion); Wharton, note 51, at 102–184.

[88] *See* 7 Douglas S. Freeman, *Life of Washington: First in Peace* 183–184 (posthumously completed by John A. Carroll and Mary Wells Ashworth 1957).

[89] In his account of the "Trials of the Western Insurgents," Francis Wharton explains: "the war of the Revolution, by cutting off the trade in foreign spirits, had turned the attention of the grain growing districts . . . to the distillation of rum and whiskey. This soon grew into a very considerable business. . . . [A]lmost the whole local population was connected with it. . . . Not only were whiskey and rum articles of commerce and of consumption, but from the natural deficiency of specie in a wild country, they were also used universally as currency. . . . [T]hey were received in payment of debts. *See* Wharton, note 51, at 102–103.

[90] Albert Beveridge, *The Life of John Marshall, 1801–1827*, 88 (1919) (hereinafter Beveridge).

describes as "some very intemperate resolutions," some of which attacked the government generally.[91] At first, Washington temporized. Then his patience ran out. After three proclamations calling on the insurgents to cease their depredations had been ineffective, Washington responded to the use of force with overwhelming force.[92] He called for 12,000 militia from the states of New Jersey, Pennsylvania, Maryland, and Virginia and designated such revolutionary military heroes as Governor Henry ("Light Horse Harry") Lee of Virginia and Daniel Morgan, as well as Alexander Hamilton[93] to join him in leading this formidable force in the field. Mary Tachau deems the militia army so excessive as to render the military demonstration in Pennsylvania a charade.[94]

In the face of such military power, the Pennsylvania insurrection speedily came to an end. Hamilton as acting Secretary of War characteristically overreacted, recommending the arrest of 150 men for having committed treason.[95] However, the grand jury returned only 51 indictments, of which 31 involved treason. Of the indictments, nine were tried for treason, with John Mitchell and Philip Vigol (Weigel) convicted and condemned to death. Two others, Thomas Wilson and Robert Fulke, were indicted for criminal libel, but it does not appear that these cases ever came to trial.[96] As in the treason trials following the suppression of Shays's Rebellion, Mitchell and Vigol were ultimately pardoned. As for the participants, Washington issued a general amnesty.[97]

---

[91] *See* Wharton, note 51, at 104.

[92] There were political differences between the Federalists and the Democratic-Republicans over the appropriate response of the federal government to the Western Pennsylvania Insurrection. Washington and Hamilton felt that the security of the state was at stake, whereas Democratic-Republicans led by Albert Gallatin were sympathetic to the economic pressures upon the trans-Appalachian farmers and concerned with the use of military might to suppress the farmers.

[93] Hamilton's military role had its less attractive sides. He was vain and ambitious. Thus, glorying in his designation as deputy commander to Washington, Hamilton seized the opportunity to accompany the militia quelling the episode, seizing every opportunity to ride by Washington's side. *See* Tachau, Whiskey Rebellion, note 87, at 25.

[94] Although Tachau concedes that the protest was "increasingly marked by violence," she deprecates the seriousness of the affair, asserting that when Washington left the "triumphal procession . . . after a total absence of any opposition . . . he . . . knew that there was no insurrection to justify the expense of the militia army." *See ibid.*, at 23.

[95] Tachau, *ibid.*, at 27 n.28 *citing* Letter, Alexander Hamilton to George Washington (Nov. 17, 1794), 17 *Papers of Alexander Hamilton* 380–381 (Harold Syrett ed. 1961–1987) (hereinafter Hamilton, *Papers* (Syrett)).

[96] See Dwight Henderson, *Congress, Courts, and Criminals: The Development of Federal Criminal Law, 1801–1829*, 14 (1985) (hereinafter Henderson).

[97] *See* Wharton, note 51, at 175–183; United States v. Vigol, 2 U.S. (2 Dall.) 346, 28 F. Cas. 376 (C.C.D. Pa 1805) (No. 16,621); United States v. Mitchell 2 U.S. (2 Dall.) 348 (C.C.D. Pa. 1795). *See also* Tachau, Whiskey Rebellion, note 87, at 28 n.30; Henderson, note 96, at 14.

Thomas Slaughter reports that the legal response to the insurrection did not end with the treason trials. He observes: "There were individuals who advocated civil war and a separation of West from East.... Robert Lusk (or Luske) was later prosecuted for sending an incendiary letter of support to the Western Pennsylvania rebels. 'As you have begun the good work, ... we wish to have a hand in the fire.'" There is no confirmation of this report, and the outcome of the prosecution is not known.[98]

Indicating the growing gulf between Jefferson and the Federalists even at this early stage, Jefferson writing to Madison about the Whiskey Rebellion dismissed the armed violence as only "riotous" at the worst.[99] He went even further. In a letter, he actually gave his blessings to the outbreak with his well-known hair-raising comment: "The Tree of liberty must be refreshed from time to time with the blood of patriots and tyrants."[100]

President Washington saw things very differently. After the Whiskey Rebellion had been crushed, he wrote "the insurrection was the first *ripe fruit* of the Democratic Societies" and further that "the Democratic Society of this place [Western Pennsylvania] was instituted by Mr. Genet for the express purpose of dissension."[101] The societies were seen as "the fomenters" of the disturbances, which were likened to the violence pursued by the French Jacobins. Indeed, Beveridge relates that when the troops quelling the insurrection reached Harrisburg, they found the French flag flying over the courthouse.[102]

Along with Washington, Alexander Hamilton had strongly reacted to this second populist uprising involving armed resistance to law. He had not only urged President Washington to use military power to put down the resistance, he also sought to impose criminal punishment upon the ringleaders from the start. Singling out a broadside adopted at an August 1792 anti-tax meeting that "we think it our duty to persist in our remonstrances to Congress, and in every other legal measure that may obstruct the operation of the Law until we

---

[98] *See* Slaughter, note 87, at 207.

[99] Letter, Thomas Jefferson to James Madison (Dec. 28, 1794), 8 Jefferson, Works 157 (Paul L. Ford ed. 1895) (hereinafter Jefferson, Works (Ford)).

[100] Letter, Thomas Jefferson to William S. Smith (Nov. 13, 1787), 12 *Papers of Thomas Jefferson* 356 (Julian P. Boyd ed. 1955).

[101] Letter, George Washington to Burges Ball (Sept. 25, 1794), Washington, *Writings* (Libr. Am.), note 6, at 834; George Washington, Address to the Congress, Nov. 19, 1794, *id.*, at 887–893. Jefferson disapproved of Washington's assertion. *See* Letter, Thomas Jefferson to James Madison (Dec. 28, 1794), 6 Jefferson, Works (Ford), note 99, at 516–517.

　　Malone asserts that this episode started the breach between Washington and Jefferson, who had concluded that the President had become a "party" man. *See* 3 Dumas Malone, *Jefferson and His Time* xvii (1962).

[102] *See* 2 Beveridge, note 90, at 88 n.3, *citing* Alexander Graydon, *Memoirs of His Own Time* 374 (John S. Littell ed. 1846, repr. 1969). Other historians do not report such an episode.

are able to obtained its total repeal," Hamilton consulted Attorney General Edmond Randolph. Stating that he had "no doubt" that a "high misdemeanor had been committed," he stressed that the farm leaders had committed an "indictable offense" in the form of a criminal libel against the government.[103] Although Randolph rejected the recommendation so strongly presented by his fellow Cabinet member, he expressed no concern over the existence of federal criminal common-law jurisdiction. Instead, his disinclination to proceed apparently arose from possible constitutional issues involving the constitutional guarantees of freedom of speech and press. Without alluding to the constitutional guaranties, Randolph elliptically distinguished between speech and action where there was no indication of a present threat.[104]

Western Pennsylvania farmers continued to be deeply concerned over access to markets for their crops. This opposition to Federalist policies that they perceived as hostile or uninterested in their impact on their economic problems attracted Jeffersonian support. For example, Albert J. Gallatin (a leading Pennsylvania Republican, later a distinguished Secretary of the Treasury under Jefferson, and briefly Secretary of State under Madison), participated in some of the mass meetings. Although, according to Wharton, he commendably was seeking to introduce a moderating influence on some of the resolutions being considered, the fact is that he was, nevertheless, present and participating in the mutinous assemblies.[105]

The ferment in Pennsylvania and Kentucky over the whiskey tax and the difficulties of the Western farmers in moving their corn to market continued. Thus, the Democratic-Republican Society of Washington County, Pennsylvania, adopted a "petition" attacking the federal government for not taking bold enough action to break Spain's control over the Mississippi River.[106] Again, Hamilton urged the government to prosecute members of the society for the "seditious petition." President Washington solicited advice from the other Cabinet members and suggested instead that he might either "contemptuously" ignore the petition or return it. Against Hamilton's call for criminal prosecution for criminal libel, Postmaster General Knox rejected the recommendation. Relying on expediency as well as on principle, Attorney General William Bradford (former Justice of the Pennsylvania Supreme Court)

---

[103] *See* Letter, Alexander Hamilton to George Washington (Sept. 1, 1792), 12 Hamilton, *Papers* (Syrett), note 95, at 311–312.

[104] *See* Letter, Edmond Randolph to Alexander Hamilton (Sept. 8, 1792), *ibid.*, at 336–337.

[105] *See* Wharton, note 51, at 121–122, 136–137.

[106] This was a sore point in the West because navigation of the Mississippi was necessary to enable Western crops, largely shut off from Eastern markets because of the barrier of the Alleghanies, to find a European market.

and Secretary of State Randolph did the same. Neither, however, challenged Hamilton's view that the federal courts were available as an alternative avenue of response.[107]

As seen by the Federalists, the support of the Democratic-Republican societies for these developments in Western Pennsylvania[108] provided clear proof of the "conspiracy" of the Jeffersonians to destabilize the government in the interests of the French.[109] Even John Marshall, most balanced of the prominent Federalists, shared this belief that the Whiskey Rebellion was aggravated, if not instigated, by bitter attacks in the partisan press against the Washington administration.[110]

From these beginnings, these Federalists linked the "conspiracy" to other serious developments. These included what were perceived as newspaper "lies," vicious attacks on the federal government, the growth of "seditious" political organizations, agitation of immigrant groups, particularly French and Irish Catholics, and the spread of incendiary ideas from revolutionary France now under Jacobin, and later Directorate, domination, and finally to the opposition to the Sedition Act itself. Finally, as we have seen, Virginia hotheads idly talked of secession and forcible resistance in the event of war with France.[111]

Pennsylvania was not the only arena of conflict. Notwithstanding the overwhelming show of force in Pennsylvania, the refusal of Kentuckians to pay the whiskey tax and harassment of federal officials continued but was benignly

---

[107] *See* Rosenberg, note 11, at 72–74 nn.50, 51.

[108] There were about 40 of these societies that emerged between 1793 and 1800, sometimes attributed to Citizen Genet and analogized to the Jacobin clubs of revolutionary France. According to Malone, they became "centers of criticism of government policies." The most important was the Pennsylvania Society, whose constitution was drafted by none other than Alexander J. Dallas. *See* 3 Malone, *Jefferson*, note 101, at 132. They later formed a major constituent of what became the Democratic-Republican political movement.

[109] *See* Rosenberg, note 11, at 74.

[110] R. Faulkner, *The Jurisprudence of John Marshall* 88 (1968).

[111] There is no question that such incendiary statements were made. In Mar. 1799, following the adoption of the Virginia Resolution, John Nicholas, brother of the prominent Republican and intimate of Jefferson Wilson Cary Nicholas, renounced his Republican affiliations. He expressed concern that the Resolution attacked the foundations of the new Republic and if applied would destroy it. He looked upon the store of arms in Richmond authorized by the Virginia Legislature as the first step. *See* Philip G. Davidson, Virginia and the Alien and Sedition Laws 36 Am. Hist. Rev. 336–338 (1931); Adrienne Koch & Harry Ammon, The Virginia and Kentucky Resolutions: An Episode in Jefferson's and Madison's Defense of Civil Liberties, 5 William & Mary Quarterly (3d ser.) No. 2, 145, 163 (Apr. 1948) (hereinafter Koch & Ammon).

Whether the deep concern over the statements was well founded is another matter. Davidson shows that although the facts as to arming were accurate, they were entirely unrelated to the Sedition Act. *See* Davidson, at 336–342. Largely relying on Davidson, Koch and Ammon also conclude that Nicholas's conjectures were "completely unfounded." However, they concede that Nicholas's action demonstrated the wide currency during 1799 of incendiary secessionist remarks by Virginians. *See* Koch & Ammon, *id.*, at 163.

ignored by officials in Washington. Mary Tachau estimates that the opposition to the whiskey tax was as strong in Kentucky as in Pennsylvania. She
concludes that evidence of significant continuing disobedience in Kentucky
was "covered up" and "has remained hidden." Despite the Federalist pretense
that all was well, "the population [was] in fact engaged in massive civil disobedience and occasional violence," including attacks on U.S. marshals, and
that Hamilton and Jefferson both were aware of this. Further, she asserts that
Washington and Marshall pretended that Pennsylvania was an isolated example but knew better. The popular reaction in Kentucky was nearly unanimous
and included the "most respected leaders." All were angered by imposition
of the federal tax on "their most exportable product." To Kentuckians, the
federal government was "remote and seemed unresponsive."

Tachau adds that although it was known not to be the "true situation,"
the Washington administration used the "pretense" that after Washington's
proclamations, resistance to the whiskey tax continued only in Pennsylvania.
The Washington administration did not want to respond to the challenge in
Kentucky and pretended that all was well. Attorney General Randolph was
able to persuade Washington, who had used armed force in Pennsylvania, to
follow a different strategy in the case of Kentucky. At his urging, Washington
sent as special emissary to seek redress of settlers' complaints on navigation
of the Mississippi for their products. Tachau concludes by asserting that
Washington, disappointed by the continued opposition in Kentucky, "retired
to Mount Vernon, exhausted and embittered, leaving the unresolved mistrust
of Kentucky in the hands of his successor." She adds that the whiskey tax and
the Sedition Act were the most controversial issues of the period.[112]

3. The Fries Insurrection (1799)

In the third of the three insurrections that shook the Washington and Adams
administrations, still another armed insurrection broke out in Pennsylvania
in 1799. To finance the new Army and Navy voted by the Federalist Congress
as it prepared for the anticipated war with France, the Federalists had enacted
a direct tax on land and buildings. The tax was highly unpopular, and federal
marshals attempting to examine properties in Pennsylvania for purposes of
the tax were attacked by an armed mob led by John Fries. Although no lives
were lost, the federal officers were assaulted and driven out of the area. With
several hundred armed men, Fries then successfully freed prisoners in federal

---

[112] See Mary K. B. Tachau, *Federal Courts in the New Republic: Kentucky 1789–1816*, 66–71, 92
(1978).

custody without bloodshed. At President Adams's request, Governor Thomas Mifflin of Pennsylvania called out the Pennsylvania militia, who suppressed the insurrection. Fries and others were apprehended and held for trial.[113]

In charging the grand jury considering the *Fries* case, Justice James Iredell charged a grand jury that the federal government had common-law criminal jurisdiction. Fries was promptly indicted and tried for common-law treason. His defense counsel, Republican Alexander J. Dallas, argued that the court lacked common-law criminal jurisdiction, but was overruled by Justice Iredell. As in Shays's Rebellion, the leaders were convicted of treason and sentenced to death. They were eventually pardoned by President Adams, who, according to Dumas Malone, acted against the advice of his Cabinet.[114] These were tumultuous times.[115]

G. Conclusion

This chapter has sought to describe the first decade of the New Republic, a world so dramatically different from the political world of recent times. It was against this violent intolerant world of bitter distrust, demonization, and vilification that the Congress met during the spring and early summer of 1798 to consider the accelerating disintegration of the new country's relationship to its former French ally and the measures to prepare the nation for the expected war with France. In this stressful climate, the Alien and Sedition Acts of 1798 and the other defensive measures were enacted to help the country resist the expected French invasion.

As the crisis worsened, the unrestrained nature of the press became less tolerable on all sides and contributed to a readiness to attempt to apply some restraints on the press. Even persons strongly committed to a free press were appalled at the development. Restraints to curb such abuses by the press became acceptable in the shadow of such deplorable invective. Thus, angered by the calumnies hurled at him, John Adams, author of the 1780 Massachusetts Constitution with its guaranty of a free press, agreed that complete freedom of the press, instead of promoting the cause of liberty, might be used to hasten its destruction.[116]

---

[113] *See* Wharton's 190-page long report of the affair, Wharton, note 51, at 458–648. *See also* 22 Hamilton, *Papers* (Syrett), note 95, at 532.

[114] *See* 3 Malone, *Jefferson*, note 101, at 438.

[115] Morison expressing a detached Federalist point of view loftily dismisses the affair; this occurs on the same page as his attempt to ridicule the Jeffersonian description of the experience under the Sedition Act as a "reign of Terror." *See* Morison, note 86, at 355.

[116] 4 John Adams, *Works* 31–32 (Charles Francis Adams ed., repr. 1969).

As Walter Berns has aptly described the period and its consequences: "With the exception of the Civil War and the periods immediately preceding and succeeding it – and perhaps the contemporary "fascist-pig" era, America probably has not known a time when its politics were conducted with such vehemence and hatred."[117] It is thus not strange that persons in both parties who were the victims of such abuse turned to the criminal law.

The use of criminal libel fueled by partisan motives richly served the purpose. First introduced by the Federalists when they were in power, partisan-motivated criminal libel prosecutions were speedily adopted by the Republicans where they were in power in the various states. The partisan use of criminal libel to suppress the opposition press became a prominent feature of the local political scene in many states, including Massachusetts, New York, and Pennsylvania. We review this unhappy development in Chapters 4 through 6, tracing its role in the federal courts during the Washington, Adams, and Jefferson administrations, and in the state courts during the same period.

---

[117] Walter Berns, Freedom of the Press and the Alien and Sedition Laws: A Reappraisal, 1970 Sup. Ct. Rev. 109, 111 (1970).

3

Criminal Libel in the Colonies, the States, and the Early Republic During the Washington Administration

A. Introduction

An examination of the laws of criminal libel including seditious libel in the early days of the Republic starts with the very roots of American jurisprudence. These are found in the criminal libel doctrines of the English law that governed the American Colonies of Great Britain in the period before the Declaration of Independence in 1776 and their incorporation into the new legal systems of the newly sovereign states. Thereafter, they played a major role in the new jurisprudence of the United States at the close of the 18th century. This chapter reviews this aspect of the new jurisprudence of the Early Republic in the period from the adoption of the Constitution to the outbreak in late 1797 of the undeclared naval war with France and the ensuing enactment of the Sedition Act of July 14, 1798.

At the outset, it is necessary to unbundle the various strands of 18th-century libel law. Libel law was divided into actions for civil libel and prosecutions for criminal libel. Civil actions, with which we are not concerned, include controversies between private parties in which one private party seeks damages from another for allegedly *false* statements leading to disrepute, contempt, or ridicule. In civil libel, evidence of the truth of the challenged allegations was admissible. Except for the judicial branch that provides a forum for the trial of the case, the government was in no way involved. Criminal libels, including seditious libel, were very different. These were criminal prosecutions instituted by an indictment or presentment by a grand jury for statements – *true or false* – maliciously made against a private person, governmental official, the government, or a foreign ambassador that was intended to bring the subject of the statement into disrepute, contempt, or ridicule.

Seditious libel was a subset of criminal libel that protected the government and public officers against such statements relating to acts in their official capacity. In contrast to the monetary damages that were the penalties for civil libel, a conviction for seditious or criminal libel could result in imprisonment, a fine, and a bond to assure good behavior. Thus empowered, the government acting through the prosecuting attorneys possessed the power to imprison political adversaries – whether private individuals or newspaper editors – for statements satisfying the jurisprudential requirement of the doctrine. In brief, the limits of public debate could be determined by politicized decisions made by the local prosecutor whether or not to pursue an indictment. In this manner, the party in power was in a position not only to punish but also in many cases to silence its political critics.

Only the constitutional guaranties of freedom of speech and press – federal and state – and the on-the-ground determinations by the grand juries and petit juries considering the cases stood in the way. As we will see, at this time in American history, neither provided a real barrier. A constitutional jurisprudence that might have effectively restricted such invasive government powers took 150 years to develop. In the late 18th- and early 19th-century cases, the constitutional barriers were held to extend no further than the prevention of licensing and other prior restraints. Nor did state constitutional provisions receive a broader construction. Because the federal judges were all Federalists, one might dismiss the federal constitutional experience as politicized. However, state Constitutions with comparable provisions received the same construction, as we will see. Nor were juries typically a barrier. Juries in the federal courts were composed of panels selected by Federalist court officials and were widely condemned as "packed." For example, under the Sedition Act, only two instances have been reported of grand juries refusing to indict, both involving rebuffs to Justice Chase, and only one instance of a petit jury failing to convict.[1] In the state courts, however, as we will see, refusals by grand juries to indict or by petit juries to convict were much more common, even though complaints of "packed" juries continued.

Above and beyond all this was the problem of prosecutorial discretion. Throughout this period in both the federal and state courts, prosecutors seem almost routinely to have proceeded with seditious libel cases in a highly partisan matter in what can only be perceived as a determined effort to intimidate or even silence the opposition press. Whichever party was in power at the

---

[1] Justice Chase was rebuffed by grand juries in New Castle, Del., and Baltimore in 1800. *See* Ch. 4, note 201. United States v. Shaw (C.C.D. Vt. 1800) was the only acquittal.

turn of the century and for a decade thereafter, its prosecutors concentrated on libel prosecutions directed against the opposition press, while ignoring equivalent conduct by its supporters. It was this unhappy partisan aspect of criminal libel law that helped make the Sedition Act of 1798[2] such a matter of concern over the centuries because it was the law of the land. In this chapter, we review the history of the American law of criminal libel, including seditious libel, commencing with its beginnings in the English law of the late 17th and 18th centuries. The contentious points of the doctrine revolved around the relevance of truth and the role of the jury.

B. English Seditious Libel and Criminal Libel Law: The Law of the American Colonies

1. Eighteenth-Century English Law

Over the centuries, the English Crown had utilized a series of legal measures to control the press and to throttle dissent, including treason, constructive treason, criminal libel including seditious libel, and licensing.[3] As Philip Hamburger has demonstrated in his seminal article, seditious libel in the form with which the American Colonies and the Early American Republic were familiar did not assume its definitive form until the early 18th century. By then, the early system of controlling the press through such prior restraints as licensing and government censorship had come to an end, and the reforms in the Treason Trials Act of 1696 had rendered impractical resort to treason as a method of dealing with printed criticism.[4] The Crown then turned to seditious libel as enunciated by the Star Chamber[5] and subsequently refashioned in a series of decisions by Chief Justice Holt and Lord Mansfield.[6]

---

[2] The Sedition Act has been widely condemned by historians. *See, e.g.,* 3 Dumas Malone, *Jefferson and His Time, Jefferson and the Ordeal of Liberty* 389 (1962); James Morton Smith, *Freedom's Fetters: The Alien and Sedition Laws and American Civil Liberties* (1956); John C. Miller, *Crisis in Freedom: The Alien and Sedition Acts* (1952). However, it has its defenders. *See, e.g.,* 1 William W. Crosskey, *Politics and the Constitution in the History of the United States* 353–354 (1953); Samuel E. Morison, *The Oxford History of the American People* 353 (1965); 2 Page Smith, *John Adams 1784–1826,* 975–976 (1962); and Frank M. Anderson, Alien and Sedition Laws, 1912 Ann. Rep., Am. Hist. Ass'n 115 (1912).

[3] *See* Philip Hamburger, The Development of the Law of Seditious Libel and the Control of the Press, 37 Stan. L. Rev. 661 (1985) (hereinafter Hamburger); R. H. Helmholz and Thomas A. Green, *Juries, Libel, & Justice: The Role of English Juries in Seventeenth- and Eighteenth-Century Trials for Libel and Slander* (1984).

[4] 7 & 8 William III, c. 5 (1695–1696). *See* Hamburger, note 3, at 714–725.

[5] De Libellis Famosis, 5 Coke 125, 77 Eng. Rep. 250 (Star Chamber 1605).

[6] E.g., Chief Justice Holt in: Rex v. Pain, 87 Eng. Rep. 584 (K.B. 1696); Rex v. Bear, 90 Eng. Rep. 1132, 91 Eng. Rep. 363, 1175 (K.B. 1698); and Lord Mansfield in Dean of St. Asaph's Case, 3 Term. Rep. 429, 4 Doug. 73, 100 Eng. Rep. 657 (K.B. 1784).

As Philip Hamburger reports,[7] English prosecutions for seditious libel then became very common. Between 1724 and 1760, at least 115 informations and indictments for seditious libel were filed in the Court of King's Bench alone. It became a prominent part of English criminal law and was the doctrine with which American Colonial and revolutionary lawyers were familiar. However fascinating the historical evolution of the legal doctrines through which the English Crown tried to restrain the press and repress public views critical of the monarchy,[8] it precedes the period with which we are concerned and need not be retraced here.

2. The Colonial Experience

The Colonies operating under the English Crown largely accepted English common law as the law of the Colonies. English common-law criminal libel became the law of the Colonies as well as the law of England. Then, when the Colonies became independent states, the new states adopted the laws of the Colonies, including the common law, as their own.[9]

Studies of the period provide a comprehensive review of the litigation involving criminal libel and related doctrines in the Colonies before the Revolution.[10] Aside from one abortive attempt to reestablish licensing and prepublication censorship in Massachusetts in 1722–1723 notwithstanding its demise in England, as well as isolated resorts to stamp taxes and trials for treason, the arsenal of government weapons to punish dissident political speech typically took three forms: criminal libel, wide-ranging contempt of court, and breach of privilege or contempt of the legislature extending to out-of-chamber publications. As the century progressed with increasing tensions between the Crown and the Colonists, the practical efficacy of criminal libel for suppression of dissent was increasingly impaired; Colonist juries refused to convict. Correspondingly, breach of privilege or contempt of the legislature in

---

[7] Hamburger, note 3, at 725.

[8] *Ibid.*, at 661–762.

[9] *See* 1 Joseph Story, *Commentaries on the Constitution of the United States of America* §§154–158 (5th ed. Melville Bigelow ed. 1891) (hereinafter Story, *Commentaries*).

[10] *See* Harold L. Nelson, Criminal Libel in Colonial America.,3 Am. J. Leg. Hist. 160 (1959) (hereinafter Nelson); Richard Buel, Jr., Freedom of the Press in Revolutionary America: The Evolution of Libertarianism, 1760–1820, in *The Press and the American Revolution* 59 (B. Bailyn and J. Hench eds. 1980) (hereinafter Buel); Clyde A. Duniway, *The Development of Freedom of the Press in Massachusetts* (1906, repr. 1969) (hereinafter Duniway); John Lofton, *The Press as Guardian of the First Amendment* 5 (1980) (hereinafter Lofton); Jeffrey L. Pasley, "*The Tyranny of Printers*": *Newspaper Politics in the Early American Republic* (2001); Livingston R. Schuyler, *The Liberty of the Press in the American Colonies* (1905); Mary P. Clarke, *Parliamentary Privilege in the American Colonies* (1943); Arthur P. Scott, *Criminal Law in Colonial Virginia* (1930).

which the legislature acted as its own judge and jury and Patriot juries played no role increasingly became a more useful vehicle for silencing Colonial critics.

There appear to have been at least 16 attempts by British authorities to employ criminal libel prosecutions during the 18th century. It was an unhappy experience for the Royal authorities. Notwithstanding these persistent attempts, the Crown obtained only *one* conviction in 75 years. Further, the conviction occurred early in the period, in a 1724 Massachusetts case involving one John Checkley, "an Englishman and of the high church party." The jury dutifully followed the court's instruction. Finding that the defendant had made the statement alleged, the jury was content to have the judge determine whether such facts constituted a libel.[11]

In four cases, including the celebrated *Zenger* case in New York in 1735, the jury acquitted the defendant,[12] and in one other, they could not reach a verdict. In most of the cases, the Crown failed on the pleadings[13] or otherwise failed to go to trial. In addition, in a number of cases, it appears that the juries went beyond their instructions, either appearing to decide issues of law or to accept truth as a defense.

From the point of view of the Crown, the experience was highly frustrating. In consequence, after the acquittal in *Zenger* in 1735, the Crown instituted no criminal libel prosecutions during the remaining 40 years of British rule in America. The Crown turned instead to breach of privilege or contempt of the legislature as the doctrine under which to proceed against dissident printers. Even here, however, although it has been suggested that "the chief legal threat to the colonial printer lay in actions by the legislative body,"[14] the cases were few and the number of convictions even less.[15] For a general

---

[11] *See* Nelson, note 10, at 168–172; note 10, at Duniway, 108–111 ("the fate of John Checkley proved that it was still exceedingly dangerous to publish religious opinions that were not in harmony with the predominant sentiment in the province").

[12] Rex v. Zenger, 17 Howell's St. Trials 675, 16 American State Trials 5 (N.Y. 1735), and Rex v. Thomas Maule (Mass. 1695–96) both resulted in acquittals. The jury disagreed in the case of Rex v. William Bradford (Pa. 1692). *See* Nelson, note 10, at 165.

   Without providing any details as to the citation or name of defendant or the jurisdiction, Nelson reports that a German immigrant accused of libeling Governor William Cosby of Virginia was acquitted in 1735. *See* Nelson, *id.*, at 160. *See also* Schuyler, note 10, at 26–27; 1 Isaiah Thomas, *History of Printing in America* 220 (1874).

[13] In the case of Samuel Mulford (N.Y. 1714), the defendant successfully demurred to his indictment on the ground that the court lacked jurisdiction over a charge of an alleged libel of the Royal Governor in a speech before the Assembly. *See* Nelson, note 10, at 166.

[14] *See ibid.*, at 172.

[15] For a full discussion of contempt of the legislature, readers are referred to Ch. 7.

discussion of breach of privilege and contempt of the legislature, readers are referred to Chapter 7.

The reactions of the Colonial legislatures, particularly the lower houses representing the populace, were far from monolithic. Everything turned on the politics of the party in control of the lower house. In Massachusetts, with the Patriots in control of the lower house, it refused to act in 1768 on the charge of the Governor and the Council that the *Boston Gazette* had committed libel, asserting that "liberty of the press is the great bulwark of the liberty of the people." By contrast, in New York, where the Crown controlled the Assembly, Alexander McDougall was indicted and jailed in 1770–1771 for criticizing the New York Assembly.[16]

In summary, the Colonial experience with criminal libel is essentially a record of failure. Harold Nelson and others, accordingly, conclude that criminal libel had ended as serious threat to American Colonial printers in their disputes with the Crown. As explained above, this occurred because in cases involving Patriot printers, Patriot juries identified with the printers and refused to convict or even to respect the instructions of the court. As a matter of jurisprudence, however, the continued acceptance of criminal libel as a firmly established doctrine of the Colonial and later the new federal and state legal system remained unchallenged.

C. Criminal Libel in the States After the Revolution: The English Inheritance and the Role of Blackstone

1. The Reception Statutes

At Independence, the new states moved expeditiously to establish their own new legal systems. Notwithstanding the rejection of English political control, the former Colonies moved almost immediately to adopt the jurisprudence, including the common law, under which they had functioned while Colonies, as the law of the new states. Thus, all states except Connecticut and Rhode Island promptly passed so-called reception statutes. These generally adopted the English and Colonial statutes and common law at a designated date as the law of the state, subject to any inconsistent statutory and constitutional provisions.[17] The New York Constitution is typical, adopting

---

[16] *See* Buel, note 10, at 59; 1 Leonard W. Levy, *Legacy of Suppression* 80–81, 177 (1963) (hereinafter Levy, *Suppression*); Jeffery A. Smith, *Printers and Press Freedom: The Ideology of Early American Republicanism* 144–145 (1988) (hereinafter Jeffery A. Smith).

[17] *See generally* Ford W. Hall, The Common Law: An Account of Its Reception in the United States, 4 Vand. L. Rev. 791 (1951); 1 Morton Horwitz, *The Transformation of American Law* 4 n.18

such of the common law, English statutes, and acts of the New York Assembly "as together did form the law of the colony on April 19, 1775."[18]

In consequence, the English common law as applied during the Colonial period in the respective Colonies now constituted part of the legal systems established by the new states. Criminal libel not only was a part of the law in the books. It again became a doctrine that could be meaningful in practice. Matters had changed with the Revolution. With Patriot prosecutors and judges replacing the former Royalist representatives, Patriot juries no longer had any incentive to play a blocking role. Criminal libel became a formidable legal instrument to serve the needs of those controlling the government – whether state or federal. As we will see, the new federal and state constitutional guaranties of freedom of speech and press made no change in the outcome. In the cases that ensued, the courts unanimously construed these to provide no more than a reaffirmation on the constitutional level of the protection against licensing and other prior restraints already available under the English common-law doctrine that had become part of the common law in every American jurisdiction.

With the Declaration of Independence, the Patriot forces committed to Independence who succeeded the Crown in political power were not faced by antagonistic Patriot juries ready to resist government efforts to invoke the doctrine. In consequence, in the period from Independence to the outbreak of the undeclared naval war with France that led to the enactment of the Sedition Act in July 1798, renewed attempts were made to use criminal libel to deal with dissent. Furthermore, other concepts such as contempt of court or breach of privilege and contempt of the legislature for out-of-chamber publications were also available to serve as an alternative jurisprudential foundation for judicial suppression of opposition. (This is discussed in Chapter 7.)

(1977 repr. 1992) (hereinafter Horwitz); 1 Oliver Wendell Holmes Devise, *History of the Supreme Court of the United States*, Julius Goebel, Jr., *Antecedents and Beginnings to 1801*, 109–118 (1971) (hereinafter Goebel).

[18] E.g., N.Y. Const., art. 35 (1777). Apr. 19, 1775, was the "famous day and year" of the Battles of Lexington and Concord that launched the Revolution and has been celebrated in song and story as well as in the New York law. *See* Henry Wadsworth Longfellow, Tales of a Wayside Inn, Paul Revere's Ride, in *American Poetry: The Nineteenth Century* 173 (Libr. Am. 1993).

Eight other states used various statements referring to the common law among other sources. Massachusetts and New Hampshire used a simpler, all-inclusive formulation. Although they did not refer specifically to the common law, their references, as in the New Hampshire Constitution – "all the laws which have heretofore been adopted, used and approved . . . and usually practiced in the courts" – manifestly included it.

Although there were questions as to the precise content of the common law of the various states, these questions did not relate to criminal libel or the other repressive doctrines.

This is the very essence of the problem. As discussed in Chapter 1, the year 1776 had seen a political revolution. The monarchy was replaced by a republic governed by democratically elected representatives of the people. However, the political revolution was not matched by a legal revolution. Far from it, although the English legal system inevitably had evolved into a jurisprudence that implemented the established English political institutions, such as the monarchy and the established church, the new states adopted it *in toto*. In consequence, the Early Republic was burdened by all the doctrines for suppressing critical speech attacking the English monarchical establishment, including criminal libel, blasphemy, and contempt of court and contempt of the legislature for out-of-chamber speech. These doctrines provided the legal weapons to restrict the unrestrained freedom of discussion required for the electorate to conduct the free political debate required by a free democratic society. It took 150 years of evolution of an expanding constitutional jurisprudence giving increasingly broader and broader scope to the guaranties of the Bill of Rights before the Supreme Court struck down the last of these pernicious doctrines.[19]

A recognition of the failure of the political revolution to be matched by a legal revolution helps explain the great gulf between the views of the press, on the one hand, and the bench, on the other, on the meaning and significance of the constitutional guaranties of freedom of speech and press. As a result of this profound misunderstanding, much of the press relying on the political ideals underlying the Revolution, seemed utterly unprepared for the severity of the reaction of the Federalists to criticism of the Washington and Adams administrations and their readiness to exploit the doctrine of criminal libel to bring it to an end.

2. The Role of Blackstone

For the American lawyers and judges of the late 18th and early 19th centuries, Blackstone's *Commentaries* were universally accepted as the definitive statement of the English law. With the Revolution, Blackstone similarly became the authoritative reference on the contents of the American common-law jurisprudence inherited from the English.

As stated by Blackstone, freedom of speech and press was highly restricted; it meant the absence of licensing or prior restraint and no more.

---

[19] The process was not complete until as late as 1964 with the decisions of the Supreme Court in N.Y. Times Co. v. Sullivan, 376 U.S. 254 (1964) and Garrison v. Louisiana, 379 U.S. 64 (1964).

In . . . the . . . instances . . . where blasphemous, immoral, treasonable, schismatical, seditious, or scandalous libels are punished by the English law, some with a greater, others with a less degree of severity; the *liberty of the press*, properly understood, is by no means infringed or violated. The liberty of the press is indeed essential to the nature of a free state: but this consists in laying no *previous* restraints upon publications, and not in freedom from censure for criminal matter when published. Every freeman has an undoubted right to lay what sentiments he pleases before the public: to forbid this, is to destroy the freedom of the press: but if he publishes what is improper, mischievous, or illegal, he must take the consequence of his own temerity. . . . Thus the will of individuals is still left free; the abuse only of that free will is the object of legal punishment.[20]

For more than 150 years following the Declaration of Independence, the highly limited scope of freedom of speech under the Blackstonian definition was universally accepted by the courts as the law in the United States. Aside from the demise of prior restraint, freedom of speech was no more than rhetoric for this period as far as the courts and their construction of the state and, later, the federal Constitutions were concerned. Although popular attitudes may have differed on the scope of the constitutional guaranties of freedom of speech and press, the more expansive concept so vigorously expressed in the political arena by the Jeffersonians had not yet percolated into the legal system and did not do so for more than 150 years.

For a full understanding of the American legal and constitutional experience with the law of criminal libel and the other repressive jurisprudential doctrines so much at a variance with the principles underlying the new Revolutionary political system, one must fully grasp the overarching influence of Blackstone.[21] Thus, Charles Warren writes of the "almost scriptural

---

[20] *See* 4 William Blackstone, *Commentaries on the Laws of England* 151–152 (1769, repr. 1992) (hereinafter Blackstone) (italics in original).

[21] For a contemporaneous view of Blackstone, *see* 1 Zephaniah Swift, *System of the Laws of the State of Connecticut* 41 (1795, repr. 1972). ("But no writer on law has acquired greater distinction than Sir William Blackstone. He has reduced order out of chaos, and in his commentaries, exhibited a complete system of the laws of England. From this work, the student will obtain a general understanding of this science, in a much shorter time than from any other author. His writings . . . have secured to him a fame that will last as long as the memory of those laws on which he has written will endure.")

  Thus, Francis Wharton referred to him as "The great author of the commentaries of the laws of England. For near thirty years it has been the manual of almost every student of law in the United States." Francis Wharton, *State Trials of the United States During the Administrations of Washington and Adams* 478 (1847).

authority of Blackstone in our early law."[22] Hammond similarly concludes that Blackstone had an "overshadowing influence on the construction of American law."[23] These conclusions are fully supported by the dozens of cases discussed in this volume.

When the American courts in the areas under examination wanted an authoritative reference to the contents of the common law, they typically turned to Blackstone. As readers will see, the law as described by Blackstone repeatedly guides the federal and state courts alike as they apply the doctrines of criminal libel, blasphemy, contempt of court, and contempt of the legislature. The courts, federal and state alike, went further. Blackstone was their guide for constitutional purposes as well. In construing the federal and state constitutional guaranties of freedom of speech and press, they uniformly adopted the narrow view of Blackstone on the meaning of freedom of speech and press[24] and freedom of religion[25] in the English law as the definitive statement of the scope of the comparable guaranties in the new American federal and state Constitutions.

One glowing example illustrates the persistence of Blackstone's preeminence over more than a century of American jurisprudential experience. As late as 1915, in *Patterson v. Colorado*,[26] the Supreme Court of the United States was upholding the expansive common-law doctrine sanctioning the use of contempt of court to punish out-of-court publications critical of judicial conduct. In speaking for the Court on the scope of the First Amendment,

This is the reality of the times. Criticisms by modern scholars of weaknesses in Blackstone's scholarship are irrelevant. The courts in the period under review did not question it.

[22] Charles Warren, *History of the American Bar* 174, 187 (1913).

[23] 1 Jabez Hammond, W. Blackstone, *Commentaries on the Law of England* viii–x, *cited with approval*, Felix Frankfurter & James M. Landis, Power of Congress over Procedure in Criminal Contempts in "Inferior" federal courts – A Study in Separation of Powers, 37 Harv. L. Rev. 1010, 1046 n.128 (1924).

[24] During the first 25 or 30 years of the New Republic, Blackstone was the only commentary available. Thus, Justice Frankfurter and Dean Landis speak of the "Amazing circulation of the Commentaries among American lawyers." *Ibid.*, Story, for example, relied on Blackstone as the definitive statement of criminal libel law and blasphemy law. *See* 2 Joseph Story, *Commentaries on the Constitution of the United States* §1883 (5th ed. Melville Bigelow ed. 1891, repr. 1994).

[25] Examples from the blasphemy experience include Updegraph v. Commonwealth, 11 Serg. & Rawle 394, 1824 Pa. LEXIS 85, 20 Pick. 206 (1824); Commonwealth v. Kneeland. 37 Mass. 206, 213, 1838 Mass. LEXIS 35 (1838). Some of the newspapers of the period did the same. *See, e.g.*, Providence Patriot & Columbian Phoenix, Dec. 15, 1827 (blasphemy in the English common law defined by Blackstone, referring to the quotation in the text.)

[26] Patterson v. Colorado, 205 U.S. 454 (1907). Holmes is reported to have regretted the statement. *See* Ch. 7, note 148.

Justice Oliver Wendell Holmes, Jr., accepted the old common-law doctrine restricting the scope of constitutional guaranties of freedom of speech and press to the prohibition of prior restraints. Speaking in language that could have been borrowed from Blackstone, Holmes echoed that "the main purpose of such [constitutional] provisions is 'to prevent such *previous restraints* upon publications." Although this was Blackstone speaking of criminal libel, Holmes makes clear that he has accepted the law in that area as providing a model for determination of the comparable constitutional issue in contempt, and leaving no doubt as to the origin of the doctrine, he concludes with a citation to Blackstone.[27]

The professional education of lawyers helps explain this continued universal reliance on the English common law and on Blackstone. Without exception, American lawyers through education and training were common lawyers. They were common-law fish swimming in a common-law sea. This was their professional universe. In consequence, all legal questions were typically answered by reference to the common law inherited from the mother country. Finally, English common law meant the common law as articulated by Blackstone.

When a nonlawyer such as Madison attempted to deal with the legal problems, such as freedom of speech, facing the country after the Revolution, he employed a different frame of reference. He not only approached the problem in political, rather than legal, terms, but in political terms that reflected the principles of the Revolution and the new Constitution. He demonstrated that the English doctrines of the common law developed to choke off criticism of the monarchy and the established church did not serve the objectives of the Revolutionary democratic and republican governmental structure. In the New Republic, the need for periodic elections and the conduct of government by elected representatives of the people required a range of freedom for political debate that was anathema under the English system fashioned to serving the needs of a monarchy.[28]

---

[27] 205 U.S. at 462 ("the rule applied to criminal libels applies yet more clearly to contempts").

[28] *See* Report of the Majority Committee on the Virginia Resolution. James Madison, *Writings* 588–591, 608–616 (Libr. Am. 1999). This powerful document attributed to Madison condemned the Sedition Act and its constitutionality. Although drafted by a layman, it was adopted by a legislature containing many lawyers. However, the Resolution was a political document relating to the conduct of new federal government. Although it referred to legal principles, there was no suggestion of any kind that the scathing criticism had any application whatsoever to the identical repressive common-law doctrines under the laws of the various states. Thus, however expedient these comments may have been for political purposes, it destroys their persuasiveness for purposes of federal legal constitutional analysis. *See also* Letter, Thomas Jefferson to James Madison (Feb.

Although Madison rested his argument on political grounds, his views were echoed by some Republican lawyers. As the distinguished legal scholar St. George Tucker put it, in 1799:

> every statute and rule of the common law which were in *derogation* of the *rights of the people,* being founded in the nature of regal government, were consigned to oblivion in America by the *declaration of independence,* whereby *royalty* was *annihilated* in this country and *prerogative* buried under the *equal rights of men* and *citizens.*

He went on to attack Blackstone's definition of freedom of speech as based on decisions of the Star Chamber.[29]

Republican lawyers accepted this analysis, but only as a matter of expediency for political purposes. When it came to state jurisprudence, they were as devoted Blackstonians as the Federalists, fully accepting the same Blackstonian limitations on the constitutional guaranties of free speech and press in their own state Constitutions. Even Jefferson fully accepted traditional criminal libel as valid law in the states, provided only that evidence of truth was admissible.[30]

As noted, notwithstanding the clash between the Revolutionary political values and the traditional legal system, the lawyers raised in the common law applied the law as they knew it. In the federal criminal libel litigations, the courts without exception followed Blackstone. This was not surprising because the federal judges in all these cases were committed Federalists. However, as demonstrated by the extensive examination of criminal libel in the state courts in Chapter 6, the Republican state judges were as zealous in applying English common-law and constitutional doctrines as expounded by Blackstone as their Federalist counterparts. They were all prisoners of their professional education and training.

17, 1826), 10 *Writings of Thomas Jefferson* 376 (P. L. Ford ed. 1899) (hereinafter *Jefferson,* Writings (Ford)).

[29] See St. George Tucker, *A Letter to a Member of Congress respecting the Alien and Sedition Laws* 15, 33 (1799).

[30] *See, e.g.,* 1 Jefferson, *Writings* (Ford ed.), note 28, at 344–345, 353, 363; Letter, Thomas Jefferson to Levi Lincoln (Mar. 24, 1802), 8 *id.,* at 139; Letter, Thomas Jefferson to Thomas McKean, (Feb. 19, 1803), 9 *id.,* at 451–452; Letter, Thomas Jefferson to James Madison (Feb. 26, 1826), 16 Jefferson, *Writings* 156 (A. Lipscomb and Bergh, eds. 1904); Letter, Thomas Jefferson to Abigail Adams (Sept. 11, 1804), *Writings of Thomas Jefferson* 49, 51 (Thomas Jefferson Memorial Ass'n); Letter, Thomas Jefferson to Thomas Seymour (Feb. 11, 1807), 9 Jefferson, *Writings* 25 (Ford). *See also* Jeffery A. Smith, note 16.

What Blackstone had to say on criminal libel was clear. Relying on the relatively modern variations of Holt and Mansfield, Blackstone definitively described the English common-law criminal libel as

> malicious defamations of any person, and especially a magistrate, made public by either printing, writing, signs, or pictures, in order to provoke him to wrath, or expose him to public hatred, contempt, and ridicule. The direct tendency of these libels is the breach of the public peace, by stirring up the objects of them to revenge, and perhaps to blood-shed . . . [I]t is immaterial with respect to the essence of a libel, whether the matter of it be true or false; since the provocation, and not the falsity, is the thing to be punished criminally: though, doubtless, the falsehood of it may aggravate it's [sic] guilt, and enhance it's [sic] punishment . . . in a criminal prosecution, the tendency which all libels have to create animosities, and to disturb the public peace is the sole consideration of the law. . . . [T]he only facts to be considered are, first, the making or publishing of the book or writing; secondly, whether the matter be criminal: and, if both these points are against the defendant, the offense against the public is complete.[31]

In so doing, Blackstone gave the impression that the doctrine had ancient common-law roots.[32] But whether the doctrine was ancient or relatively modern was only of academic concern. Blackstone's statement, as in the case of the other contents of his treatise, was widely accepted as the definitive statement of the common-law doctrine. Although, as we have seen, there was some isolated dissent from American critics, particularly Madison and Tucker, Blackstone's comprehensive statement not only provided a full statement of the English law of the time, but was repeatedly cited by the American decisions of the 18th and early 19th centuries as the prevailing law in the this country as well.[33] Not until well into the 20th century did English and American jurisprudence begin to change. Through the Adams administration, Blackstone represented American law. This is true of the state and federal courts, subject only to

---

[31] See 4 Blackstone, note 20, at 150–151.

[32] Mayton, for example, vigorously attacks Blackstone's scholarship. He contends that the so-called ancient roots of the common law pertained solely to civil libel, and that criminal libel had been invented *ad hoc* by the Star Chamber in the case entitled De Libellis Famosis decided in 1605, which cited no precedents and formulated in a half-dozen later 17th-century decisions. De Libellis Famosis, 5 Coke 125, 77 Eng. Rep, 250 (1605). See William Mayton, Criminal Libel and the Lost Guarantee of a Freedom of Expression, 84 Colum. L. Rev. 91, 102–108 (1984). See also Hamburger, note 3, at 691–714.

[33] E.g. Commonwealth v. Clap, 4 Mass. 163, 166 (1808); State v. Avery, 7 Conn. 266, 268, 1828 Conn. LEXIS 36 (1828); Scharff v. Commonwealth, 2 Binney 514, 517, 1810 Pa. LEXIS 41 (1810).

modifications introduced by the Sedition Act and later incorporated into the law of many states.

As for truth, Blackstone made plain that evidence of truth was not admissible in criminal libel. Libeling the monarch or his government challenged the stability of the state and threatened breach of the peace, if not insurrection, whether the statement was true or not. Hence, in the remark generally attributed to Lord Mansfield but believed to have emanated from the Star Chamber, "The greater the truth, the greater the libel." In civil libel actions, however, matters were very different, with the truth of the allegedly offensive publication a defense.[34]

The final dimension was the role of the jury in implementing the doctrine. As Blackstone noted, it was highly restricted. Under English law at the time of the Revolution (and until its reform in 1792 with the enactment of Fox's Act),[35] the English law severely limited the role of the jury in criminal libel cases to a special verdict on two issues and those alone. As Blackstone emphasized, the jury findings were restricted to whether or not the defendant made the statement alleged and whether the statement had the damaging innuendos alleged. All other issues were reserved to the judge. This was the English law, the law in the Colonies, and, accordingly, the law in the New Republic as well.

---

[34] *See* 4 Blackstone, note 20, at 150 ("for if the charge is true, the plaintiff has received no private injury").

[35] 32 Geo. III, c. 60 (1792) (In trials for criminal libel "the jury sworn to try the issue may give a general verdict of guilty or not guilty upon the entire matter put in issue . . . and shall not be required or directed . . . to find the defendant or defendants guilty, merely on the proof of the publication . . . and of the sense ascribed to the same.) As a practical matter, this enabled the jury not merely to determine elements of law subject to the instructions of the court, but to reject them entirely.

With further evolution with Lord Campbell's Libel Act of 1843, 6 & 7 Vict. c. 96, §6 of 1843, expanding the role of truth as a defense, the English law of criminal libel was vigorously enforced until well into the 20th century, but is now reported to be "very rare." *See Gatley on Libel and Slander* §1.1 n.3 (10th ed. Milmo & Rogers eds. 2004).

Thus in a celebrated case in 1911, *Rex v. Mylius*, the Crown convicted an English republican for libeling King George V. He had published in France an account alleging that the King while an officer in Navy on duty in the Mediterranean had secretly married the sister of the Governor of Malta. The secret bride was, therefore, the Queen of England, the marriage to Princess Mary of Teck called Queen Mary was bigamous, and the heirs to the throne were illegitimate.

The prosecution was personally conducted by the Attorney General, Sir Rufus Isaacs, later Viceroy of India and the Marquess of Reading. The defendant was not defended by counsel. The jury convicted him after "about a minute's deliberation in the box," and the judge condemning the "gross and infamous libels" sentenced Mylius to the maximum sentence of imprisonment for one year, describing it as "wholly inadequate." Winston Churchill, then Home Secretary, was reported to be in the audience. *See The Times*, Feb. 2, 1911; *New York Times*, Feb. 5, 1911, Jan. 14, 1914. *See also* United States *ex rel.* Mylius v. Uhl, 210 F. 860 (2d Cir. 1914) (conviction for criminal libel held not "moral turpitude" barring Mylius from admittance to the United States).

3. The Isolated Cases Before the Adams Administration

After the Declaration of Independence and the triumph of the Revolutionary Army and before the emergence of heated partisan politics, little need was seen for consideration of oppressive prosecutions invoking criminal libel, contempt of court, or contempt of the legislature. The only instance in the federal system occurred during the Revolutionary War. The Continental Congress three times considered the institution of proceedings to punish publications by the press allegedly constituting a breach of its privileges or contempt of the legislature. In each case, the motion failed of adoption after debate in which those opposed made much of the contention that such efforts violated the freedom of the press.[36]

With the complete absence of law reports, scant court records, and news-papers still in their infancy,[37] it is difficult to obtain an accurate and complete identification of the extent of criminal or criminal libel prosecutions in the state courts during the earliest days of the Republic. In the decade before the Adams administration, little evidence has been found of such prosecutions except in Pennsylvania and Massachusetts. A rare item that has survived, for example, is an elliptical account in a 1781 New Jersey newspaper. The Philadelphia *Evening Post* contains a dispatch from Trenton, dated January 3, 1781. Characteristic of the limited information such brief reports conveyed, the report tells us only that the Monmouth County Court of Oyer & Terminer had recently convicted "Peter Parker (Snag Swamp)" for "seditious words."[38] Who Peter Parker or Snag Swamp was, the nature of his "seditious" outburst, and the government against which it was directed are not known.

As described in Chapter 6, Pennsylvania during this period experienced a new development of considerable significance. In what appears to be the first use of seditious libel for partisan political purposes in America, the imperious Chief Justice of the Pennsylvania Supreme Court, Thomas Mc-Kean, attempted to use criminal libel and contempt to silence three fierce critics and political enemies, Eleazer Oswald, the firebrand publisher of

---

[36] 12 *Journals of the Continental Congress, 1774–1789*, 1205–1206 (Worthington C. Ford ed. 1904–1937); 14 *Journals* 588–593, 611, 799–800. *See* Buel, note 10, at 81.

[37] There were only 12 newspapers in the Colonies in 1750, which had increased to about 30 by 1776. With the intensified political debate, this total mounted to reach 239 by 1800. *See* E. Latham, *Chronological Tables of American Newspapers, 1690–1820* (1972); Kim Tousley, *William Duane: Radical Journalist in the Age of Jefferson* 403 (app. 1, chart 27) (1989). Starr adds that in 1800, 85 of the papers were Republican, up from 51 in the spring of 1798. Paul Starr, *The Creation of the Media, Political Origins of Modern Communications* 80 (2004).

[38] *Pennsylvania Evening Post*, Jan. 13, 1781.

the Philadelphia *Independent Gazeteer*; William Cobbett, writing as "Peter Porcupine" in the Philadelphia *Porcupine's Gazette*, and William Duane, editor of the Philadelphia *Aurora*. For further discussion of these series of cases over a decade involving McKean's continued efforts to jail Oswald, Cobbett, and Duane, readers are referred to the Pennsylvania experience with criminal libel, contempt of court for out-of-court statements, contempt of the legislature, and related legal doctrines discussed in Chapter 6 and 8. In all these decisions, the Pennsylvania Constitution with seemingly liberal guaranties of freedom of speech and press was held not to limit in any way the English common-law doctrines.

In Massachusetts, the 1787 demonstrations by impoverished farmers in Western Massachusetts against foreclosures of their mortgaged farms, known as Shays's Rebellion, appeared to challenge the stability of the Early Republic. In this turbulent climate, four outspoken supporters of the Rebellion were indicted under Massachusetts common-law criminal libel for publishing articles and expressing sympathy with the grievances of the farmers and the Rebellion. This episode is discussed more fully in the review of Massachusetts state law in Chapter 6.

These two clusters of cases help demonstrate the accepted place of criminal libel in the jurisprudence of the new states. The adoption of the Sedition Act of 1798 at the federal level did not introduce a novel doctrine into the law of the new country.[39]

In 1780 Massachusetts had adopted a new Constitution largely drafted by John Adams. Among other guaranties, it provided that "The liberty of the press is essential to the security of freedom in a State; it ought not, therefore, to be restrained in this Commonwealth."[40]

What did the constitutional guaranty mean? Did it modify common-law criminal libel in all its draconian rigor or as described by Blackstone? In a historic exchange of private correspondence between two of the most distinguished lawyers in Massachusetts, Chief Justice William Cushing of the Supreme Judicial Court[41] and John Adams, it became quite clear that even these outstanding figures were not sure. This is of particular interest inasmuch

---

[39] *See* Duniway, note 10, at 142n, *citing* Commonwealth v. Brock and Commonwealth v. Pond, Suffolk County Court Records, Nos. 104616, 104618, 106011 (1787); Levy, *Suppression*, note 16, at 207; Lofton, note 10, at 11. *See also* Marion L. Starkey, *A Little Rebellion* 18, 90 (1955) (hereinafter Starkey).

[40] Mass. Const. art. 16 (1780).

[41] Cushing was shortly thereafter appointed a Justice of the U.S. Supreme Court in 1790 and served until 1810. In 1800, Adams nominated him as Chief Justice of the Supreme Court, but he declined for reasons of health. Marshall was thereupon nominated.

as Cushing had served as Chairman of the Massachusetts Constitutional Convention and Adams had been the leading draftsman of the new Constitution.

In February 1789, Chief Justice Cushing wrote to Adams expressing his concern about the sweep of the constitutional guaranty of liberty of the press in view of its "very general and unlimited" provisions. The Chief Justice "confess[ed he] had a difficulty about the construction." Although agreeing that the draconian Blackstone standard of "the liberty of the press as allowed by the law of England" was law in Massachusetts, he inquired as to the effect of the new constitutional provision. Noting that the constitutional provision receiving English common law as the law of Massachusetts excluded doctrines "repugnant" to the Constitution, he inquired whether the guaranty outlawed criminal libel proceedings for publications challenging public officials for the discharge of their official duties when "such charges are supportable by truth."

Adams agreed that "the difficult and important question" was the admissibility of truth, inquiring "whether our Constitution is not at present so different [from the English system] as to render the innovation necessary." Pointing to the election process, he stressed the necessity of discussion of the "character and conduct" of persons running for office. Nevertheless, he temporized, asserting only that he believed that "it would be safest to admit evidence . . . of the Truth of accusations, and if the jury found them true *and that they were published for the Public good*," they would readily acquit. Adams was thus more conservative than Cushing. To constitute a defense to criminal or criminal libel, the charges in issue had not only to be "true," but they had to have been made "for the public good."[42]

But what of the draconian English doctrine? Did the language used in the Constitution strike down criminal punishment where the publication was false? Although neither Cushing nor Adams discussed this issue, their identification of the role of truth as the only issue makes plain that the issue of truth aside, they recognize that the constitutional guaranties in no way prohibited or limited criminal libel proceedings in the historic English model.

In a matter of months, a Massachusetts court answered the question, upholding the constitutionality of the doctrine in *Commonwealth v. Freeman* (1791). Edmund Freeman, editor of *Herald of Freedom*, was indicted in the Massachusetts state courts in 1791 for criminal libel. He had published

---

[42] *See* Letter, John Adams to William Cushing (Mar. 7, 1789), The Early Law of Criminal Libel in Massachusetts, 27 Mass. L.Q. 9, 11, 16 (No. 4, Oct. 1947) (emphasis added).

an article asserting that a state senator, John Gardiner, "had been drunk and a murderer."[43] Unlike so many of these cases, the *Freeman* case went to trial. Attorney General James Sullivan (later the first Republican Governor of Massachusetts), acting for the prosecution, successfully defended the constitutionality of the proceedings, notwithstanding the freedom of press guaranty adopted the year before.[44]

Chief Justice Francis Dana of the Massachusetts Court held that despite the new Massachusetts Constitution, the restrictive English common-law doctrine as stated by Blackstone continued as law in Massachusetts.[45] Accordingly, evidence of truth was inadmissible, and the role of the jury was confined as before to a special verdict on whether the defendant had published the alleged libel and the determination of the meaning of the innuendo. The law had not changed since Chief Justice Hutchinson had ruled to the same effect in 1767 in a much publicized, indeed much criticized, charge to a Massachusetts grand jury.[46]

Notwithstanding its orthodox ruling, the Court in *Freeman* in fact did not apply the law in its full vigor. In separate charges, the judges instructed the jury that evidence of truth was admissible, and the jury was allowed to determine whether or not the publication in the case before them was libelous, that is, to determine the law under the instructions of the court as well as the facts. The jury thereupon found Freeman not guilty.[47]

According to Charles Warren, Dana's ruling constituted a "great shock" to the public and many of the bar. Although Warren does not provide support for his conclusion,[48] it is not inconsistent with the implications of the contemporary Adams-Cushing correspondence indicating their belief that provision for the admissibility of evidence of truth was necessary for the constitutionality of criminal libel.

---

[43] Duniway. note 10, at 143; Levy, Suppression, note 16, at 208–209; Boston *Independent Chronicle*, Feb. 2, 24, 1791, Mar. 17, 24, 1791.

[44] A decade later, Sullivan published a learned monograph building on his arguments in the *Freeman* case. He appears to be unique in his role as a successful Republican political figure defending the constitutionality of criminal libel proceedings in this period. *See* James Sullivan, *A Dissertation upon the Constitutional Freedom of the Press in the United States of America* (1801). This is also available in 2 *American Political Writings During the Founding Era, 1760–1805*, 1126, 1135–36, 1149–50 (1983).

[45] Commonwealth v. Freeman (Mass. 1790) (unreported). *See* Charles Warren, *History of the American Bar* 236–239 (1911) (hereinafter Warren, *American Bar*).

[46] *See* Duniway, note 10 at 124–125, *citing* Quincy, Mass. Rep. 244.

[47] *Independent Chronicle*, Feb. 24, 1791, Mar. 27, 1791. *See* Norman L. Rosenberg *Portecting the Best Man: An Interpretive History of the Law of Libel* 68 (1986).

[48] *See* Warren, *American Bar*, note 45, at 236–239.

However, Judge Dana's decision cannot be dismissed as an aberration. As we will see, Chief Justice McKean of Pennsylvania had already held the same. Nor did Dana and McKean stand alone. Their decisions were only the first of an unbroken line of decisions finding that the constitutional guaranties of freedom and press only assured the prohibition of prior restraints, leaving English common-law criminal libel untouched. Not one of the judges ruling on the issue explained why the constitutional guaranties or freedom of speech and press had been deemed urgently required by the forces pressing for adoption of the Bill of Rights if the guaranties went no further than the existing common law. A number of prominent figures, including Albert Gallatin, made much of this point,[49] but it seems not to have attracted attention in any judicial opinion. The law and much popular feeling were miles apart. Thus, whatever the populace may have thought, for these judges at least, new Constitutions or not, the political revolution of 1776 had not been matched by a comparable revolution in the jurisprudence of the Early Republic.

As the undeclared naval war with France came to present the most challenging issue on the political scene in the spring and summer of 1798, the Federalists used their control of the Congress to enact the Sedition Act on July 14, 1798. With the availability of the new statutory authority, the Federalists led by Secretary of State Pickering[50] proceeded energetically to make partisan use of criminal libel, common law and statutory, in an effort to destroy the Democratic-Republican press on the eve of the 1800 race for the presidency. Although the constitutionality of the statute and the availability of federal criminal common-law jurisdiction were highly disputed

---

[49] *See* Albert Gallatin's speech in opposition to the adoption of the Sedition Act. Annals of Congress, 5th Cong., 2d Sess., 2163 (1798). As was true of so many of the Jeffersonians opposing the Act, of whom Nathaniel Macon is a good example, Gallatin fundamentally weakened his position by going on to argue a separate point: a federal act was unnecessary because state law (based on the common law) already provided relief. However, as with the other Jeffersonians relying on the guaranties of free speech, Gallatin made no effort to attempt to explain why if the federal statute violated the federal free speech guaranty, how it was that the state laws did not violate the comparable free speech guaranties of the state Constitutions?

[50] Pickering (Secretary of State under Washington and Adams from Aug. 1795 to May 1800) was one of the leading figures in the High Federalist wing of the Federalist Party. In the new federal government, supervision of the federal District Attorneys in the various districts was assigned to the Secretary of State. Pickering, thus, had the authority to play a decisive role in enforcing the Sedition Act. In discharge of this responsibility, he assiduously read the Republican press for "libels" and referred instances to the District Attorneys for criminal action. *See infra* Ch. 4.

   When Adams became President, he continued in office each of the members of Washington's Cabinet in an effort to demonstrate the continuity of the federal government. Thus, Pickering continued as Secretary of State for more than three years for a President who came to despise him.

matters in the political forum at the time, neither issue troubled any of the Federalist judges presiding over the 15 trials that ensued under the Sedition Act or the five criminal libel cases instituted under federal criminal common law.

We review this struggle in the next chapter.

4

Federalist Partisan Use of Criminal and Seditious Libel – Statutory and Common Law – During the Tumultuous Adams Administration

A. Collapse of Relations with the French, the Adams Administration Preparing for the Imminent Outbreak of War, and the Bitter Political Climate in the Spring of 1798

For almost two decades after the American Revolution, American relations with the French were very friendly. The two countries were allies by treaty and by national sentiment. After all, French financial support during the dark days of the struggle against Britain and French military and naval power, so prominent in the decisive victory at Yorktown, had been indispensable elements in the American triumph. This warmth began to disappear with the excesses of the French Revolution and the execution of King Louis XVI. Except for Republican zealots such as Jefferson, most Americans were profoundly disturbed by the continuing French excesses. Still, when Citizen Genet, the new French Minister, arrived in Charleston in 1793, relations were still friendly, and Genet received a warm welcome.

The climate soon changed. With France and Great Britain engaged in all-out war, the French Navy commenced seizing American ships on suspicion of trading with Britain. The XYZ Affair involving Talleyrand's apparent solicitation of bribes was viewed as intolerable blackmail and had a "stunning" effect on American public opinion.[1] Matters grew worse when Talleyrand and the Directory refused to receive new American diplomatic representatives. Further, Genet's increasingly intolerable conduct, climaxed by the outfitting of French privateers in American ports and his meddling in American politics with appeals to the American people over the head of President Washington,

---

[1] *See* 7 Douglas S. Freeman, *Life of Washington: First in Peace* 537 (posthumously completed by John A. Carroll and Mary W. Ashworth 1957) (hereinafter D. S. Freeman).

combined with continuing French seizures of American shipping and sea-men at sea[2] to bring matters to a head. Outrage with the French burst into flame.

As noted, the problem was exacerbated by the presence of so many French sympathizers in the country. These included the thousands of French refugees from the West Indies and Irish Catholic immigrants who were flooding into the country. In addition, ardent Republicans, particularly in Virginia, identi-fied with the French and the French Revolution to a surprising degree.

In the late spring of 1798, Federalist outrage with the French mounted with the Federalist "war party" pressing for a formal declaration of war. It was a time of war fever with political passions running high. As Smelser characterizes the scene: "The United States was a scene of fear and hate."[3] At the outset, the Federalists attracted widespread support for their strong anti-French policy. Even as committed a Jeffersonian as Albert Gallatin conceded that the American press of the time overwhelmingly supported the Federalist program.[4] Nevertheless, with Jefferson and the Republicans still vigorously pro-French, the country was bitterly divided.

B. Portent of Future Events: Federalist Partisan Prosecutions of Republicans Under Federal Criminal Common Law Even Before Passage of the Act

1. *United States v. Samuel J. Cabell*, Congressman from Virginia

With the increasingly stormy political scene, the Federalists turned to the federal common-law crime of criminal libel to deal with the Republican opposition. The first case, *United States v. Samuel J. Cabell* (1797), antedated the Sedition Act by almost a year. In contrast to the later Federalist pattern of targeting newspaper editors and printers, many of whom were recent English and Irish immigrants, the Cabell prosecution involved a Virginia Republican Congressman and Revolutionary War hero.[5]

---

[2] David McCullough reports that more than 300 American vessels were seized by the French. *See* David McCullough, *John Adams* 486 (2001).

[3] *See* Marshall Smelser, The Federalist Period as an Age of Passion, 10 Am. Q. 391, 412 (winter 1958).

[4] *See* John C. Miller, *Crisis in Freedom: The Alien and Sedition Acts* 23–26 (1952) (hereinafter Miller).

[5] Cabell left William & Mary College at age 19 to join the Revolutionary Army as early as 1775. Appointed a Captain in 1776, he saw service in the Battles of Trenton, Princeton, Saratoga, and the Siege of Charleston in 1780, where as a Lt. Colonel he was taken prisoner by the British. He served in the Congress for eight years from 1795 to 1803.

In reporting to his constituents in the spring of 1797, Congressman Cabell, who represented Thomas Jefferson's own district, circulated a highly critical commentary condemning the policies of Adams and the Federalists. The Federalist District Attorney for the district, Thomas Nelson, brought the matter to the attention of the federal grand jury. The Circuit Court Justice presiding was James Iredell, one of the most outspoken of all the federal judges on the vital importance of criminal libel prosecutions for strengthening national stability and security. He charged the grand jury on May 22, 1797, giving substantially the same charge as his charges to the Maryland and Pennsylvania grand juries several weeks earlier. Although he did not refer to Cabell directly or indirectly, he expressed his usual concern on the importance of criminal libel prosecutions.[6] The grand jury without dissent promptly returned a presentment[7] charging Cabell with criminal libel for the distribution of the circular letter "endeavoring, at a time of real public danger to disseminate unfounded calumnies against the happy Government of the United States."[8]

In a letter to Bache's Philadelphia *Aurora*, Cabell attacked Justice Iredell for instigating the grand jury action. His accusation was challenged by a grand jury member who asserted that it was the independent work of the grand jury.[9] Justice Iredell flatly denied any responsibility for the grand jury action. In his public statement, he said, "The truth is, that I never knew that Cabell had written any circular at all, until I heard the presentment read in court." In a confidential letter to his wife, he went on to express his approval of the grand jury action.[10]

---

[6] See 3 *Documentary History of the Supreme Court of the United States*, 1789–1800, 173, 181 (Maeva Marcus ed. 1990) (hereinafter Doc. Hist. Sup. Ct.); 2 Griffith J. McRee, *Life and Correspondence of James Iredell* 483, 497–501, 505, 511–513 (1857 repr. 1949).

[7] U.S. Const., Amend. V (1791) provides: "No person shall be held to answer for a capital, or otherwise infamous crime, unless on a presentment or indictment of a Grand Jury."

See S. Brenner & G. Lockhart, *Federal Grand Jury: A Guide to Law and Practice* §2.2. (1996) ("The language of the [constitutional] clause reflects its antecedents in common law practice, which allowed charges to be brought by either an indictment or a presentment. But the federal system no longer uses presentments as a charging instrument so all charges for 'capital or otherwise infamous crime[s]' must be brought by indictment").

Adv. Comm. Note 4, Fed. R. Crim. Proc. 7(a). (Presentments as a method of instituting prosecutions are obsolete, at least as concerns the federal courts.)

[8] See 3 Doc. Hist. Sup Ct, note 6, at 173, 181.

[9] *Compare* Letter, Samuel J. Cabell to the Philadelphia *Aurora* (May 31, 1797), 3 Doc. Hist. Sup Ct, note 6, at 183 *with* Letter, Callohill Minis, a member of the grand jury, to Samuel J. Cabell (June 15, 1797) ("who does not abhore you as a traitor?"). Minnis had been a Captain in the Virginia Line and had served throughout the Revolutionary War.

[10] Letter, James Iredell to the *Virginia Gazette & General Advertiser* (June 21, 1797), 3 Doc. Hist. Sup Ct, note 6, at 197–199; Letter James Iredell to Hannah Iredell (May 25, 1797) (describing the grand jury as "composed of many of the most respectable men in the state" and to the presentment as of "a temper highly suitable to our present situation"), *id.*, at 182. See McRee, note 6, at 511.

The presentment gave rise to a storm of indignation among Virginia Republicans. Jefferson took the lead. As was his wont, he worked behind the scenes. An "anonymous" petition drafted by him was sent to the Virginia House of Delegates. The draft termed the prosecution a violation of the privileges of Congressmen to communicate with constituents, an unconstitutional violation of separation of powers, and a violation of the "natural right" of "free correspondence." It is of particular interest that in his draft Jefferson nowhere challenged the existence of federal criminal common-law jurisdiction. Nor did he invoke the constitutional guaranties of freedom of speech and press.[11] As we will see, this acquiescence in the doctrine of federal criminal common-law jurisdiction as late as the spring of 1797 soon disappeared. A few months later, he had identified the issue of one of supreme importance.[12]

Observing that the Virginia Constitution empowered the House of Delegates to impeach officers "offending against the State," the petition contended that the grand jury's crime was of "that high and extraordinary character" for which the Virginia Constitution provided the extraordinary procedure of impeachment.[13] In a letter to James Monroe, Jefferson explained why the petition had been sent to the Virginia House of Delegates rather than to the Congress: "It is of immense consequence that the states retain as complete authority as possible over their own citizens."[14]

With Jefferson's name kept out of the discussion, the House of Delegates contented itself with adopting a resolution condemning the presentment, but going no further. What happened next is not known, but the outcome is clear. The matter never went to trial. As for Cabell, he was reelected to the Congress in 1800.

Although the proposed Sedition Act moved with speed through the congressional legislative process, it did not move fast enough for the High Federalists that were its sponsors.[15] While the Congress was still discussing the

---

[11] See 9 Writings of Thomas Jefferson 447, 452 (H. Washington ed. 1853); Letter, Thomas Jefferson to James Monroe (Sept. 7, 1797), James Monroe Papers (Libr. Cong.).

[12] See Letter, Thomas Jefferson to Edmond Randolph (Aug. 18, 1799), 10 Writings of Thomas Jefferson 125 (Andrew Lipscomb ed. 1904) (hereinafter Jefferson, Writings (Lipscomb)).

[13] Petition to the House of Delegates, Aug. 1797, 7 Works of Thomas Jefferson 158–164 (P. L. Ford ed. 1904) (hereinafter Jefferson, Works (Ford)). See David N. Mayer, The Constitutional Thought of Thomas Jefferson 199 (1988).

[14] See Letter, Thomas Jefferson to James Monroe (Sept. 7, 1797), 9 Jefferson, Writings (Lipscomb), note 12, at 424.

[15] The High Federalists were the dominant wing of the Federalists, led by the so-called Essex Junto, a group of extreme anti-French partisans based in Massachusetts. It included such figures as Fisher Ames, George Cabot, Francis Dana, Stephen Higginson, Rufus King, John Lowell, Timothy Pickering, and David Strong. See Charles Warren, Jacobin and Junto, or Early American Politics as Seen in the Diary of Nathaniel Ames, 1758–1822, 8, 164 (1931) (hereinafter Warren, Junto).

proposed Act, Secretary of State Pickering saw to it that federal District Attorneys started the immediate prosecution of several Republican newspaper editors in reliance on federal criminal common-law jurisdiction.

At this early stage in the history of the New Republic, the Attorney General was a part-time legal advisor to the President. It was the Secretary of State, not the Attorney General, who had administrative responsibility for the supervision of the federal attorneys in the various judicial districts (then called District Attorneys). Pickering, the Secretary of State, was a leader of the High Federalists and bristled at the outspoken opposition of Republican newspapers to the administration's preparations for war with France including the Sedition Act. He not only urged the District Attorneys to read the local press for seditious statements, but he read the press himself for "seditious" comments and called for prosecutions in a series of cases throughout his term in office.[16]

In this manner, three additional prosecutions for criminal libel resting, as in the *Cabell* case, on federal criminal common-law criminal jurisdiction were started in a matter of weeks against the editors and publishers of some of the most prominent Republican papers in the country. These included the indictment on June 26, 1798, of Benjamin Franklin Bache, publisher of the Philadelphia *Aurora*, and on July 6, 1798, of John Burk, editor and printer of the New York *Time Piece* and of Dr. James Smith, co-publisher of the *Time Piece*.

There may well have been a fourth. On July 17, 1798, three days after the adoption of Act, William Durrell, the Republican publisher of the obscure Mt. Pleasant, N.Y., *Register* was indicted and convicted for criminal libel for reprinting in June 1798 a trial report from another newspaper. However, it is not clear whether the indictment rested on the common law or on the newly adopted Act. Although the indictment was brought after the enactment of the Act, it was for an offense occurring before the Act. In view of the

---

Dana was a Massachusetts judge, and Lowell was the Massachusetts federal District Court judge. Pickering is already known to the reader, and we will encounter the judges when we review criminal libel prosecutions later in the chapter.

[16] Pickering letters calling for prosecutions include: Pickering to Richard Harison (June 28, 1798); Pickering to Harison (July 7, 1798); Pickering to John Adams (Aug. 1, 1799), 9 John Adams, Writings 7 (Charles Francis Adams ed. 1869) and Pickering to John Adams (Jan. 19, 1800). See 8 Pickering Papers 904; 12:82; 25:321–322; 26:10; 37: 315; 40:390, 493, 495. (Mass. Hist. Socy.); Frank M. Anderson, Enforcement of the Alien and Sedition Laws, Ann. Rep. 1912, Am. Hist. Soc'y 115, 119 (1912) (hereinafter Anderson).

Pickering letters urging prosecutors to be on the alert: Pickering to Zebulon Hollingsworth (Aug. 12, 1799); Pickering to Thomas Nelson (Aug. 14, 1799); Pickering to Richard Harison (Aug. 12, 1799); Pickering to William Rawle (Sept. 20, 1799). See 11 Pickering Papers 590, 599, 602–604, 611–612; 12 id. 82–83 (Mass. Hist. Soc'y).

constitutional barrier against *ex post facto* crimes, prosecution under the Act would have faced a major, perhaps insuperable, obstacle. Accordingly, one may reasonably speculate that the case had been brought under the common law, but this is not clear.[17]

With the Sedition Act making its way through the Congress under Federalist control at this time, these four (or five, if *Durrell* is included) proceedings at federal criminal common law eloquently demonstrate the confidence of the Federalists that the federal courts possessed criminal common-law jurisdiction. Whatever the opinions of Republicans may have been, the Federalist Secretary of State, the Federalist District Attorneys, and, as we will see, virtually all the Federalist judges apparently had no concern over its existence.[18] However, the question of the existence of federal criminal common-law jurisprudence soon became hotly disputed on the political level and ultimately became a major constitutional issue. This question is deferred until the next chapter.

We now proceed to examine these three prosecutions in June 1798, 13 months after the *Cabell* case.

2. United States v. Benjamin Franklin Bache, Editor of the Philadelphia Aurora

The grandson of Benjamin Franklin, Benjamin Franklin Bache, was the publisher and editor of the Philadelphia *Aurora*. This was one of the leading, if not the foremost, Republican newspaper in the country. Written without restraint, Bache's violent attacks on Washington, John Adams, and other Federalists made Bache and the *Aurora* a prominent target for Federalist hostility.[19]

Miller trenchantly describes the Federalists' target: "Bache displayed a degree of virulence, vindictiveness, and scurrility that distinguished him even among the journalists of his generation."[20] Bache's abuse of Federalist leaders was fully matched by the vituperative nature of the attacks on Republicans

---

[17] The *Durrell* case is discussed in detail later in the chapter.

[18] Nevertheless, the Federalists in the Congress pressed for enactment of a federal statute criminalizing criminal libel codifying the common law. Some concern over the availability of federal criminal common-law jurisdiction likely had some role in the pressure for the enactment. *See* 2 Oliver Wendell Holmes Devise, *History of the Supreme Court of the United States*, George Lee Haskins & Herbert A. Johnson, *Foundations of Power: John Marshall, 1801–1815*, 638 (1981) (hereinafter Haskins & Johnson).

[19] See James Morton Smith, *Freedom's Fetters: The Alien and Sedition Laws and American Civil Liberties* 188–204 (1956) (hereinafter J. M. Smith).

[20] *See* Miller, note 4, at 27.

by the leading Federalist publishers in Philadelphia, such as John Fenno and later his son John Ward Fenno, and William Cobbett ("Peter Porcupine"). This scurrilous group debased the press and made its so-called licentiousness[21] a matter of general concern. As noted, virtually every political figure of the time bitterly complained of his treatment by the opposition press. In consequence, this gravely undermined the claims of free speech and press.

In the heated wartime atmosphere, the unrestrained criticism of the Adams administration in the publications of Republican editors was perceived by the High Federalists as conduct that bordered on treason and subject to criminal prosecution as criminal libel. Bache had consistently opposed war with France in the aftermath of the Jay Treaty issue and, after Adams was elected, began to attack him regularly. As the crisis with the French escalated, as we have seen, Bache came under increasing physical and editorial attack.[22]

On June 16, 1798, Bache printed a secret state paper that had been "leaked" to him, apparently by two Republican Senators from Rhode Island: Talleyrand's conciliatory letter to Elbridge Gerry, a Republican, who was part of the delegation of three American envoys in France. Ignoring the other two envoys – Federalists John Marshall and Charles C. Pinckney – Gerry forwarded the letter to President Adams. Adams received it two days before the Bache disclosure and had not yet shared it with the Congress. Once the letter was made public by Bache, Adams had little choice and thereupon formally forwarded it to the Congress.

In printing the letter, Bache alleged that Adams had withheld the letter from the Senate to thwart Talleyrand's gesture for peace and cause an unnecessary war with France. In response, Federalist Senators assailed Bache as an agent of the French Directory in treasonable correspondence with Talleyrand.[23] His indictment for criminal libel speedily followed. On June 26, 1798 – the

---

[21] "Licentiousness" was a term repeatedly used during this period to characterize the extreme prose of political opponents. Although criticized by perceptive observers as an utterly useless distinction, the constitutional guaranties were frequently declaimed to protect "liberty" but not "licentiousness." Compare Chief Justic Parker in the celebrated Blanding case. The Massachusetts Constitution of 1780 follows the common law. It protects "The liberty of the press, not its licentiousness." Commonwealth v. Blanding, 20 Mass. (3 Pick.) 304, 1825 Mass. LEXIS 74 (1825), and Justice Vann in People v. Most, 171 N.Y. 423, 431, 64 N.E. 175 (1902) with St. George Tucker: "This word licentiousness as applied to the PRESS, and to writings against the government is a word of the most indefinite signiofication [sic] of any in the English language." Letter to a Member of Congress respecting the Alien and Sedition Laws 35, June 6, 1799.

[22] See Jeffrey Pasley describes him as "France's most vocal defender in the United States." See Jeffery L. Pasley, "The Tyranny of Printers" Newspaper Politics in the Early Republic 97–98 (2001) (hereinafter Pasley); J. M. Smith, note 19, at 193–194.

[23] See J. M. Smith, note 19, at 193.

day that the proposed Sedition Act was introduced in the Senate – Bache was indicted in the federal District Court in Philadelphia for common-law criminal libel of President Adams and the government.[24]

Bache was arrested and arraigned before District Judge Peters. Defense counsel, including the distinguished Republican advocate Alexander J. Dallas, argued that the federal government lacked criminal common-law jurisdiction. Judge Peters, however, refused to dismiss the indictment, noting that Bache could again challenge jurisdiction at the trial before the Circuit Court. Pending trial at the October 1798 Term, Bache was released on posting bail of $4,000.[25]

Awaiting trial, Bache continued his outspoken assault on Adams and the Sedition Act. At the same time, Jefferson reaffirmed his high regard for Bache in a confidential letter to Madison. Speaking of Bache (and his Pennsylvania political ally Dr. Michael Leib), Jefferson described them as "men of abilities, and of principles the most friendly to liberty & our present form of government."[26]

At this point, fate intervened in the form of the return of the yellow fever that had earlier decimated Philadelphia in 1792 and 1793. In the summer of 1798, another yellow fever epidemic swept the city. Bache caught the fever and soon died. Yellow fever did not play politics, for Bache's greatest rival, Federalist editor John Fenno died in the same epidemic.[27]

For several months, the *Aurora*, lacking Bache, ceased publication, but in November 1798, Bache's widow had William Duane, Bache's assistant, take over as editor of the paper. As we will see, Duane had as foul a pen as Bache and matched him for the vigor and pungency of his language, first directed at the Federalists, but soon directed against fellow Republicans such as Chief Justice, and later Governor, Thomas McKean of Pennsylvania. These episodes in Duane's professional life are discussed later in this chapter and in Chapters 6 and 7.

---

[24] The indictment read: "libelling the President & the Executive Government, in a manner tending to excite sedition, and opposition to the laws, by sundry publications and republications." *See* Pasley, note 22, at 98.

[25] United States v. Bache (C.C.D. Pa. 1798), Philadelphia *Aurora*, June 27, 30, 1798. *See* Richard N. Rosenfeld, *American Aurora, A Democratic-Republican Returns* 174–176 (1997) (hereinafter Rosenfeld); Pasley, note 22, at 98; J. M. Smith, note 19, at 282.

[26] Letter, Thomas Jefferson to Samuel Harrison Smith (Aug. 22 1798), Thomas Jefferson, *Writings* 1052 (Libr. Am. 1984) (hereinafter Jefferson, *Writings* (Libr. Am.)).

[27] *See* 1 J. Thomas Scharf & Thompson Westcott, *History of Philadelphia 1609–1884*, 495n. (1884) (hereafter Scharf & Westcott); 7 D. S. Freeman, note 1, at 544.

3. *United States v. John Daly Burk*, Editor of the New York *Time Piece*

The next common-law prosecution was directed at John Daly Burk (occasionally spelled Burke), the editor of the leading Republican newspaper in New York, the New York *Time Piece*, founded by the notable anti-Federalist Philip Morin Freneau. Like so many of the politically active editors of the day, Burk was a recent immigrant. He was an Irish radical who had fled to the United States to avoid prosecution for criminal libel. Becoming editor of the *Time Piece* on June 13, 1798, Burk carried forward Freneau's more genteel criticisms[28] of the Federalists with even more vigorous attacks on the Federalists and their policies. His violent prose attracted an almost immediate response. In a matter of a few weeks, Secretary of State Pickering responded. On July 7, 1798, he instructed the New York District Attorney, Richard Harison, to proceed against Burk for criminal libel. In addition, he ordered the District Attorney to move to deport Burk under the newly enacted Alien Act if, as it seemed likely, he proved to be an alien. Pickering was evidently determined to silence Burk one way or the other.[29]

Burk, along with his co-publisher, Dr. James Smith, were arrested and arraigned before District Judge John Sloss Hobart. They were released on bail of $4,000 for their appearance and good behavior pending trial before Justice Paterson in the Circuit Court. Among the persons standing as sureties for Burk and Smith were such leading Republicans as Aaron Burr. Although Burk and Smith were bound over for good behavior, Burk renewed and intensified his attacks on Adams and the Federalists. At this point, Smith and Burk had a falling out when Burk proceeded with an even more violent attack on Adams over Smith's objection. Smith thereupon withdrew from the *Time Piece*, and a few weeks later, the *Time Piece* ceased publication.

Using Aaron Burr as a go-between, Burk then offered to settle the case. He pledged to leave the United States if the case was dismissed and he and his sureties were released from the bond. Adams approved, and the case was discontinued.[30] Burk, however, did not honor his undertaking. Although

---

[28] One may judge how vituperative Burk must have been in order for Freneau, whose comments Washington found maddening, to be viewed as more genteel. *See* Letter, George Washington to Henry Lee (July 21, 1793) 840, 842, Washington, *Writings* (Libr. Am. 1997).

Abigail Adams describes Burk as "a Hireling wretch, in French pay I doubt not." Letter, Abigail Adams to John Adams (Nov. 27, 1796), *My Dearest Friend: Letters of Abigail Adams and John Adams* 414 (Margaret A. Hogan and C. James Taylor eds., 2007) (hereinafter *My Dearest Friend*).

[29] Letter, Timothy Pickering to Richard Harison (July 7, 1798), 37 Pickering Papers 315 (Mass. Hist. Soc'y).

[30] Letter from Timothy Pickering to Richard Harison (Jan. 1, 1799), 37 Pickering Papers 381 (Mass. Hist. Soc'y). Pickering advises that he finds "very desirable" Harison's suggestion to keep a state prosecution pending, to be resumed in the event Burk violated the terms. *See also* Letter, Jacob

announcing that he was leaving the country, he, instead, went into hiding for almost two years until the expiration of the punitive Alien and Sedition Acts and Jefferson's accession to the presidency.[31] Schachner reports that, with Jefferson's assistance, Burk later wrote "the first good" history of Virginia.[32]

4. *United States v. Dr. James Smith*, Co-Publisher of the New York
Time Piece

As noted, Dr. James Smith was the co-publisher with John Daly Burk of the New York *Time Piece*. It is not clear what his actual role was in the writing and publishing of the issues of the newspaper, but he manifestly was not in control of its contents. After his indictment for criminal libel and the posting of a good conduct bond, he had no appetite for participating in further invective at Adams and his administration and risk forfeiting his bond. Disagreeing with Burk, he withdrew from participation with the paper, and the *Time Piece* soon stopped publication. At this point, proceedings against Smith apparently came to an end.

Although the criminal common-law prosecutions of Bache, Burk, and Smith did not yield a single conviction, they evidently served the purposes of the administration. Both the *Aurora* and the *Time Piece* were silenced, the *Time Piece* permanently, and the *Aurora* briefly until revived by William Duane.

Whatever his earlier views, Jefferson by this time considered the issue of federal criminal common-law criminal jurisdiction a matter of first importance. The highly partisan use of the Act by the Federalist administration to harass or silence the Republican press had transformed the issue. Writing to Edmond Randolph in August 1799, Jefferson expressed himself in the strongest of terms. He denounced it as an

audacious, barefaced and sweeping pretension to a system of law for the US, without the adoption of their legislature, and so infinitely beyond their capacity to adopt.[33]

Wagner (for Pickering) to Edward Dunscomb (May 22, 1799), 37 Pickering Papers 423 (Mass. Hist. Soc'y) (writing on behalf of Pickering requesting that a copy of the indictment and proceedings be sent to the Governor of the Mississippi Territory for the arrest and prosecution of Burk if he appeared).

[31] *See* J. M. Smith, note 19, at 204–20; Rosenfeld, note 25, at 40, 184, 195–197, 225.

[32] *See* Nathan Schachner, *Thomas Jefferson: A Biography* 608 (1951) (hereinafter Schachner, *Jefferson*).

[33] Letter, Thomas Jefferson to Edmund Randolph (Aug. 18, 1799), 7 Jefferson, *Writings* (Lipscomb), note 12, at 125–129.

C. The Enactment of the Sedition Act, July 14, 1798

1. Introduction of the Bill

As relations with France steadily deteriorated during the fall of 1797 and the winter of 1797–1798, the Federalists became convinced that war with France was at hand.[34] The Federalist Congress hastened to prepare for the country's defense, enacting a series of measures in the spring and early summer of 1798. One statute authorized an increase in the token Army of 3,500 by an additional 12,000 officers and men. President Adams promptly appointed former President Washington as its Commander and Alexander Hamilton, ever hungering for a dramatic military career, as Washington's Inspector General and second in command. Other statutes authorized the creation of a new Navy and strengthened the new fleet with the authorization of armed American privateers to harass and seize French shipping, a war loan, and new taxes to pay for the expense of the martial expenditures. In its remarkably comprehensive program, the Congress also terminated the treaties with France providing for amity, commerce, and alliance and banned commerce with France and its colonies.[35]

The Alien and Sedition Acts were the last among the essential "defensive" measures in the Federalist preparations for war. The Alien Act authorizing the President to identify aliens dangerous to the state and to mark them for deportation was adopted on July 6, 1798. Finally, with the adoption of the Sedition Act on July 14, 1798, the Federalist-dominated Congress completed this whirlwind period of emergency legislation preparing for war with France.[36]

All that remained was the adoption of the much expected formal declaration of war with France. Thus, Abigail Adams in her intimate correspondence with her sister Mary Cranch wrote on June 25, 1798: "I expect Congress will decare [sic] war before they rise."[37] It was a very near thing. Jefferson reported that "he had heard" that at a caucus of House Federalists, the more

---

[34] Although it is now apparent that this was a fantasy, some modern historians continue to defend the reality of the Federalists' concern. *See* Samuel Eliot Morison, *Oxford History of the American People* 349 (1965) ("Fears of a French invasion were not unreasonable").

[35] 1 Stat. 578 (1798) (termination of French treaty).

[36] 1 Stat. 577 (1798) (Alien Act); 1 Stat. 596 (1798) (Sedition Act).

[37] Letter, Abigail Adams to Mary Cranch (June 25, 1798), *New Letters of Abigail Adams* 196 (Stewart Mitchell ed. 1947) (hereinafter *New Letters*). Although it is fascinating to speculate whether the letters of Abigal Adams "reflect the private thoughts and feelings of John Adams," as suggested by Mitchell, or instead they represent her own independent thinking that had "great weight" with Adams in formulating his own views," as suggested by Adams's grandson, Charles Francis Adams, they are cited as providing a vivid insight into the unvarnished thinking of at least one prominent

extreme Federalists had come within five votes of carrying the day in the caucus to press for an immediate declaration of war by the Congress.[38] It was against this background that the Congress enacted the Sedition Act on July 14, 1798. Even before this event, as we have seen, the impatient administration had commenced a series of criminal libel prosecutions under federal common law.

Jefferson had seen it all coming. Two months before the introduction of the proposed Sedition Act in the Congress, he wrote to Madison: "There is now only wanting . . . a sedition bill, which we shall certainly see proposed." Nor did he have any illusions as to the partisan use of the measure once enacted, observing: "The object of that is the suppression of the Whig presses."[39]

In the end, however, Congress declined to adopt any declaration of war despite the pressure from the more aggressive Federalists.[40] The door was still open for President Adams to pursue further diplomatic efforts in a last-minute attempt to avoid war. As Abigail Adams wrote to her sister Mary on July 9, 1798: "The Congress are going on very well at the eleventh hour. Though timid they will do all but one thing before they rise [referring to a declaration of war]." In her July 17, 1798, letter to her sister, she became philosophic: "As Congress would not proceed to a declaration of war, they must be answerable for the consequences."[41]

Adams's diplomatic efforts finally were successful and war was averted. Adams's success in accomplishing this objective and snatching peace from the jaws of war is without doubt the outstanding achievement of his presidency.[42] Adams so regarded it, describing the success of his last-ditch peace mission

Federalist of the times. *Compare New Letters*, at xxv, *with* Charles Francis Adams, *Familiar Letters of John Adams and His Wife Abigail Adams During the Revolution* xxvii–xxviii (1875).

[38] *See* 1 Jefferson, *Writings* (Ford), note 13, at 282; 6 *Writings of James Madison* 325, 328 (Gaillard Hunt ed. 1901); Miller, note 4, at 155.

[39] Letter, Thomas Jefferson to James Madison (Apr. 26, 1798), 10 Jefferson, *Writings* (Lipscomb), note 12, at 32.

[40] Abigail Adams tartly commented: "The people throughout the United States, with a few exceptions, would have wholeheartedly joined in the most decided declaration which Congress could have made . . . but the majority in the Congress did not possess the firmness and decision enough to boldly make it." Letter, Abigail Adams to John Quincy Adams (July 20, 1798), 2 Page Smith, *John Adams 1788–1826*, 979 n.4 (1962) (hereinafter Page Smith).

[41] Letters, Abigail Adams to Mary Cranch (July 9, July 17, 1798), *New Letters*, note 37, at 199–201, 205–207.

[42] Morison reports French policy toward the United States changed after Talleyrand learned from Victor DuPont, French consul at Charleston, that the strength of French sympathizers in the United States had been overestimated. The decree ending French depredations on American commerce followed shortly thereafter. With the decree, Adams was encouraged to make still another effort for peace. The renewed negotiations led to peace two years later. *See* Samuel E. Morison, DuPont, Talleyrand, and the French Spoliations, 49 Proc. Mass. Hist. Socy. 63, 78 (1915).

as "the most splendid diamond in my crown" in a letter written years later.[43] In consequence, Adams must be ranked among the outstanding American presidents.

2. The Action of the Congress

In this turbulent period with the High Federalists moving so vigorously to prepare for the war with France that they thought almost immediately upon them, federal action on a criminal libel law had become increasingly likely. Thus, on April 26, 1798, Abigail Adams, that source of such vivid insight into the thinking of some Federalists at the time, wrote to her sister Mary:

> Yet dairingly [sic] do the vile incendaries [sic] keep up in Baches paper [the Philadelphia *Aurora*] the most wicked and base, voilent [sic] & calumniating abuse. . . . But nothing will have an Effect until Congress pass a Sedition Bill, which I assume they will do before they rise – Not a paper from Bache press issues nor from [Thomas] Adams [Boston Independent] Chronicle, [sic] but might have been *prevented cancelled* [sic] [prosecuted?] [sic] as libels upon the President and Congress.[44]

Several weeks later in another letter to Mrs. Cranch, she described street fighting between Federalist mobs with their black cockades and Republican mobs with their French tricolor cockades, adding that the Massachusetts courts should act to suppress the Republican press or "we shall come to a civil war.[45] Similarly, anticipating the introduction of a criminal libel bill in the Congress, Thomas Jefferson saw the country facing a "reign of witches." In his celebrated letter to John Taylor, Jefferson on June 1, 1798, wrote: "A little patience and we shall see the reign of witches pass over, their spells dissolved, and people recovering their true sight, restoring their government to its true principles."[46]

---

[43] Letter, John Adams to James Lloyd (Feb. 6, 1815), 10 John Adams, *Works* 115 (Charles F. Adams ed. 1854) (hereinafter John Adams, *Works* (C. F. Adams)).

[44] Letter, Abigail Adams to Mary Cranch (Apr. 26, 1798), *New Letters* note 37, at 164–165. Two months later, Bache was indicted for criminal libel under the federal criminal common law. Thereafter, Thomas Adams was indicted for criminal libel under the Sedition Act and Massachusetts common law. *See supra* text accompanying notes 19 to 26 (Bache) and *infra* notes 138, 141, 144 (Adams). *See also infra* Ch. 6, text accompanying notes 125–129.

[45] Letter, Abigail Adams to Mary Cranch (May 10, 1798), *New Letters*, note 37, at 170. For other letters of Abigail Adams to Mary Cranch of the same tenor, *see ibid.* (May 26, 1798, June 19, 1798, June 23, 1798).

[46] Letter, Thomas Jefferson to Col. John Taylor of Caroline (June 1, 1798), 8 Jefferson, *Writings* (Ford), note 13, at 265.

Several weeks later, Sen. James Lloyd of Maryland, writing to former President Washington, posted him of the impending events, stating: "We shall very soon declare the Treaty with France void and pass a strong act to punish sedition."[47]

A few days later on June 27, 1798, Sen. Lloyd introduced in the Senate the expected bill providing for the criminal punishment of criminal libel.[48] The bill meticulously followed the English common-law model of criminal libel as described by Blackstone. As readers have seen, this rigorous doctrine was the law in the states in consequence of their general enactment on Independence of "reception statutes" making the law of the colony (that, of course, included the English common law) as the law of the new state.[49] As Blackstone's *Commentaries* had made clear to American lawyers,[50] the English criminal libel doctrine was draconian, providing no role for truth and a highly restricted role for the jury.[51] Further, the Bill ignored the 1792 adoption by the Parliament of Fox's Act with its significant liberalization of the common-law doctrine. The statute greatly increased the role of the jury by empowering it to reach a general verdict and to rule on all issues of law and fact, subject to the instructions of the judge.[52] Thus, as proposed, the Sedition Bill would have enacted the English common-law doctrine in a form that had already been repudiated by the English.

The Federalists had decisive control of the Senate and in a matter of days were able to ram through this bill for the Sedition Act in the very rigid form presented. However, things were very different in the House. Although the Federalists appeared to have had narrow control of the House, the reality was somewhat different on occasion. Party organizations and party discipline

---

[47] Letter, James Lloyd to George Washington (June 18, 1798), 2 *George Washington Papers (Retirement Series)* 341–342 (Dorothy Twohig ed. 1998) 341–342 (1998) (hereinafter Washington, *Papers* (Twohig)).

[48] After the adoption of the Sedition bill by the Senate, Sen. Lloyd wrote immediately to inform former President Washington, then in retirement at Mount Vernon. *See* Letter, James Lloyd to George Washington (July 4, 1798), *ibid.*, at 375.

[49] *See* text accompanying Ch. 3, notes 17 and 18.

[50] *See* 4 William Blackstone, *Commentaries on the Laws of England*, at 150–151 (1769, repr. 1992) (hereinafter Blackstone).

[51] As noted, the role of the jury in criminal libel cases was restricted to a special verdict relating to two issues alone: did the defendant publish the allegedly libelous statement maliciously; did the statement have the innuendos of ridicule and opprobrium required by the doctrine? Every other issue was for the judge.

Proof of malice as a matter of form was an essential element of the American law. *See* James Sullivan, *Dissertation upon the Constitutional Freedom of the Press* 54 (1801). This was in accord with Blackstone. 4 Blackstone, note 50, at 150 ("malicious defamations"). However, "malice" was a legal fiction; it was presumed from the defendant's act in making a defamatory publication.

[52] 32 Geo. III c.60 (1792).

were still in their infancy. Although there were, of course, numerous deeply committed Federalist members, Federalist control in the end depended on the much weaker allegiance of a number of members who tended to vote with them but were not fully committed to the party.[53] At times, the outcome was affected by large-scale absences from the session. Thus, Jefferson had lamented that the Alien Act, which was also adopted by a narrow margin, could have been readily defeated if ten Virginian Republican congressmen had not been absent from Washington.[54]

When the Senate version of the Bill came before the House, it received a hostile reaction. To secure passage, the sponsors of the Bill were forced to liberalize it in two major respects. On truth, the Bill was revised to make evidence of the truth of the allegations admissible, albeit only with respect to the inference it cast on whether the defendant had acted in a malicious manner. On the role of the jury, the Bill was revised to include the reform in Fox's Act granting the jury the power to give a general verdict[55] reflecting its ruling on all questions of law and fact, subject to the instructions of the judge, as in other areas of the law. Even then, the House approved the modified bill only by the narrow vote of 54 to 51.

In the debate, the Federalists argued that the Act was within the constitutional powers of the Congress on a number of grounds. First, it gave the government no powers that it did not already possess under common law[56]; it was a codification, even a liberalization, of its preexisting common-law authority. Second, it was within the implied powers of the Congress supported by the "necessary and proper" clause.

---

[53] In his detailed study of party affiliation in 1798, Manning J. Dauer concludes that there were only 12 "moderates" in the House not firmly committed to either party. Five elected as Republicans and seven as Federalists did not regularly vote the party line. These held the balance of power. Manning J. Dauer, *The Adams Federalists* 170–171, Appdx. 312–317 (Vote Chart No. V, Table No. 19) (1953).

    See also William N. Chambers, *Political Parties in a New Nation: The American Experience,* 1776–1809, 136–138 (1961) (party allegiances were just beginning to become firmly established).

[54] *See* Letter, Thomas Jefferson to James Madison (May 24, 1798), 3p *Papers of Thomas Jefferson* 363 (Barbara Oberg ed. 2003) (hereinafter Jefferson, *Papers* (Oberg)) (the absentees included such prominent members of the Virginia delegation as Representatives Giles, Cabell, and Nicholas).

[55] In a special verdict, the jury determined two specific issues of fact. However, in rendering a general verdict, the jury responded only "guilty" or "not guilty" without any necessity to justify its action. In effect, it was a great liberating process, opening the door to jury nullification with the possibility of a verdict of "not guilty" irrespective of the nature of the prosecutor's proof. However, the reform lacked practical significance when the jury was "packed."

[56] Harrison Otis quoted Blackstone in support. *See* Annals, 5th Cong., 2d. Sess. 1851a, 2147 ff. (1798).

The Republicans not only vigorously attacked the Act as unconstitutional, but went further and asserted that it was unnecessary as well. First, the Act was nowhere authorized by the limited powers granted to the Congress by the Constitution. It was an unwarranted expansion of national power in violation of the rights of the states reserved by the Tenth Amendment. For the South, concerned with any expansion of national power lest it serve as a justification for an attempt to restrict or abolish slavery, this was a matter of first importance. Second, as the Supreme Court held 15 years later, the national government had no common-law powers; there was no federal common law of crimes. Finally, Republicans attacked the Bill as a blatant violation of the constitutional guaranty of freedom of speech and press. Representative Gallatin of Pennsylvania argued eloquently that the Blackstonian concept of freedom of the press, however suitable in a monarchy, was incompatible with the democratic ideals of the New Republic. Representative Nichols of Virginia added that the press had a different role with the entirely different political structure of the Republic and that "a different degree of freedom" was essential.[57] Later, James Madison emphasized this principle in the Majority Report pertaining to the Virginia Resolution denouncing the Act. The Resolution stressed the vital importance of "the right of freely examining public characters and measures and of free communication . . . thereon." Such public criticism was "the only effective guardian of every other right."[58]

By contrast, in his draft of the accompanying Kentucky Resolution, while Jefferson agreed that the Act violated the guaranty of freedom of speech in the federal Constitution, he carefully noted that the states reserved the "right of judging how far the licentiousness of speech and of the press may be abridged without lessening their useful freedom."[59]

Finally, the Republicans also opposed the Bill as a matter of expediency. Republican leaders in the debate such as Representative Nathaniel Macon of North Carolina, (who soon would be Speaker of the House after the Republican triumph in the 1800 elections) pointed to the existence in the various states of criminal libel doctrines fashioned in the rigid Blackstonian model copied in the original bill. They argued that if the federal government encountered criminal libels that required prosecution, it was not defenseless;

---

[57] Annals, 5th Cong., 2d Sess. 2145–2157 (1798).
[58] Majority Report, Virginia Resolution on the Alien and Sedition Acts, James Madison, *Writings*, 588–591, 608–616 (Libr. Am. 1999) (hereinafter Madison, *Writings* (Libr. Am.).
[59] Jefferson, Draft of the Kentucky Resolution, in Jefferson, *Writings* (Libr. Am.), note 26, at 449–451.

the laws of the states already provided a remedy, and a federal statute was unnecessary.[60] Albert Gallatin and Edward Livingson similarly argued that federal law was not only unauthorized by the Constitution, but unnecessary because persons could be prosecuted in the state courts.[61] However, as noted, in making this argument, the Republican speakers in the congressional debate made no effort to explain why the very state doctrines of criminal libel that they were holding out as a demonstration that a federal statute was unnecessary were not also unconstitutional under the guaranties of freedom of speech and press contained in the Constitutions of almost all of the 13 states if the federal criminal libel statute was unconstitutional under the comparable guaranty in the federal Constitution.

Acting behind the scenes as usual, Thomas Jefferson drafted a sweeping response to the Acts for consideration by the Virginia and North Carolina Legislatures. His draft denounced the statutes as unconstitutional by exceeding the powers of the Congress and in violation of the First Amendment. He enlisted the aid of James Madison, who rewrote the Virginia draft, eliminating its more extreme aspects, and obtained its enactment by the Virginia Legislature. The Virginia legislature charged that the Acts were "palpable and alarming infractions of the constitution" and asked the legislatures of the other states to join with it in condemning the Acts as unconstitutional. However, it avoided use of such terms as "null and void" or "nullification."[62]

Jefferson also shared his draft with W. C. Nichols for introduction in the North Carolina Legislature. Apparently feeling that chances of adoption in Kentucky were better, Nichols passed along the draft to another person in Jefferson's confidence, John Breckinridge of Kentucky. Breckinridge succeeded in having the Kentucky Legislature adopt a more extreme statement than that approved in Virginia. The Kentucky Resolution drafted by Jefferson condemned the Acts as "void and of no force" and as "palpably against the Constitution."[63]

These actions badly misread the temper of the country. Virginia and Kentucky were rebuffed by all the other states. Not one supported the Resolutions. On the contrary, virtually all the legislatures of the New England and Mid-Atlantic states adopted resolutions denouncing the Virginia

---

[60] Annals, 5th Cong., 2nd Sess. 2104–2106, 2151 (1798). Gallatin advanced the same argument.
[61] *See* Walter Berns, Freedom of the Press and the Alien and Sedition Laws: A Reappraisal, 1970 Sup. Ct. Rev. 109, 121–125 (1970).
[62] *See* Madison, *Writings* (Libr. Am.), note 58, at 588–593, 608–662.
[63] *See* Jefferson, *Writings*, note 26, at 449–456.

and Kentucky actions. There was no doubt how the public outside of the South felt about the issue at this moment.[64]

As has been widely recognized, the Sedition Act as enacted thanks to the modifications made in the House of Representatives was a significant liberalization of the common law. Thus, under the new federal Act, criminal libel was more liberal than the contemporaneous criminal libel laws in most of the states. Viewed in its context as a substitute for the rigorous Blackstonian criminal common-law doctrine then prevailing,[65] the Sedition Act technically meant more freedom rather than less. In the historic process of incremental improvement of this repressive doctrine of the common law, the Act was a step forward. Although widely noted, this aspect has not fully received the significance it deserves. It paved the way for the states to modify their own common-law doctrines in the same manner, and many did so. However, its impact has been obscured by the indefensible use of the Act by the Federalists for partisan purposes in their efforts to harass or suppress the opposition Jeffersonian press.

Moreover, the liberalizing features of the law made little practical difference. The authorization of the admissibility of evidence of "truth" was unworkable where so many of the contested statements were matters of opinion. Further, the apparently dramatic expansion of the role of the jury lacked practical significance in an age in which "packed" juries were common.

Jefferson's words written a few years after these events demonstrate that the primary Republican concern with the Act arose not from their concern over free speech, but from their concern that it was an expansion of federal power not in keeping with the constitutional concept of a federal government of limited powers, with all nondelegated powers remaining with the states. As for freedom of speech, this was no bar to state criminal libel prosecutions. Thus, in an 1804 letter to Abigail Adams, Jefferson reassured her that his conclusion that the federal statute was unconstitutional would not remove

> all restraint from the overwhelming torrent of slander which is confounding all vice and virtue, all truth and falsehood. . . . The power to do so is fully possessed by the several State legislatures. . . . While we deny that

---

[64] *See* Schachner, *Jefferson*, note 32, at 486–491, 500.

[65] Although a reconstituted Supreme Court under Republican control 14 years later held that the federal government had no criminal common-law jurisdiction, judicial attitudes had been very different. At the time of the enactment of the Act, every judge who had faced the issue, including a majority of the Supreme Court in their capacity as Circuit Court judges, had, with the possible equivocal exception of Justice Chase, accepted its constitutionality. For discussion of this issue, *see infra* Ch. 5.

Congress have [*sic*] a right to control the freedom of the press, we have ever asserted the rights of the states, and their exclusive right to do so.[66]

By contrast, Madison saw very clearly the incompatibility of common-law criminal libel with the republican political principles of the Revolution and the New Republic. He argued in the Virginia Majority Resolution, as Ketcham has pointed out, that "the very nature of the new [American] governments under written constitutions would both be subverted if the common law with all its incongruities, barbarous and bloody maxims [was] saddled 'on the good people of the United States.'"[67] Jefferson and other Republicans saw the issue very differently. Although they argued that the Act violated the First Amendment, this was a secondary argument and contradicted their position that state constitutional guaranties did not bar criminal libel in the state courts. Madison was an exception, apparently never discussing the issue.

3. The Approval of President Adams

The Sedition Act was the product of the High Federalists. Although it does not appear that President Adams had anything to do with its formulation or approval by the Congress, he signed the Bill to enable it to become law. Unwilling to oppose the High Federalists on the issue, he never spoke against it. It is his Act.

The Act was a war measure and made the possibility of war with France even more likely. It, thus, undermined Adams's fundamental objective of peace with France. It sharpened the break with France at a time when Adams was attempting a desperate last effort for peace with the dispatch of still another delegation to negotiate with the French.

Moreover, Adams was one of the country's leading lawyers. As his correspondence with Chief Justice Cushing of the Massachusetts Supreme Judicial Court over the constitutionality of criminal libel under the 1780 Massachusetts Constitution shows,[68] he had a comprehensive grasp of the constitutional issues presented by the Act and the vital need for vigorous debate in a democratic society. Nevertheless, when the Bill came before him, he signed

---

[66] *See* Letter, Thomas Jefferson to Abigail Adams (Sept. 11, 1804), *Writings of Thomas Jefferson*, 49, 51 (Thomas Jefferson Memorial Ass'n); Thomas Jefferson, Second Inaugural Address (Mar. 44, 1805), Jefferson, *Writings* (Libr. Am.), note 26, at 518, 522.

Jefferson had only one limitation on the powers of the States. Borrowing from the Sedition Act, he had one *caveat:* "In those States where they do not admit even the truth of the allegations to protect the printer, they have gone too far." *Id.*, at 51–52.

[67] Ralph Ketcham, *James Madison: A Biography* 402 (1990) (hereinafter Ketcham).

[68] *See* The Early Law of Criminal Libel in Massachusetts, Hitherto Unpublished Correspondence between Chief Justice Cushing and John Adams in 1789, 27 Mass. L. Q. 9, 11 (No.4, Oct. 1942).

it. Further, according to no less an authority than John Marshall, he had no doubts as to its constitutionality.[69] Readers can speculate to what extent his wife's vigorous views may have influenced him. As we have seen, Abigail Adams's correspondence with Mary Cranch leaves no doubt how strongly she felt on the issue.[70] The Act aside, Adams, like Washington and many others, including even Jefferson, bristled at the many personal attacks against him and denounced the "licentiousness" of the press and its "profligacy, falsehood, and malignity in defaming our government."[71]

President Adams left the implementation of the Sedition Act to Secretary of State Pickering and never interfered with Pickering's vigorous use of the penal provisions of the Sedition Act. Although he failed to assume any role in most of the cases, he encouraged the use of the Act against the Republican alien editors who had been particularly aggressive in their personal attacks on him, William Duane and Thomas Cooper.[72]

As for the Alien Act giving Adams as President the unilateral power to order the deportation of persons whom, in the language of the Act, "He shall judge dangerous to the peace and safety of the United States," his record is somewhat better. Adams consistently resisted the pleas of Pickering to exercise his deportation power.[73] Although approving Pickering's harassment of such alien Republican editors as John Daly Burk, William Duane, and William Cooper, Adams's only personal role in the implementation of the Alien Act related to certain French refugees, particularly Gen. Victor Collett and Mery de Moreau, whom he found particularly obnoxious. However, anticipating such action, they had already arranged to leave the country. Notwithstanding the paucity of enforcement, the Alien Act sent a powerful xenophobic message, making it plain to immigrants, particularly the French and Irish refugees, that they were unwelcome.[74] Thus, Jefferson noted that even before the passage of the Act, two ships filled with French refugees

---

[69] *See* Letter, John Marshall to St. George Tucker (Nov. 18, 1800), 6 *Papers of John Marshall* 14 (C. E. Hobson ed. 2006) (hereinafter Marshall, *Papers* (Hobson)). ("The unconstitutionality of the law cannot be urged to the President because he does not think it so. His firm beleif [sic] is that it is warranted by the constitution.")

[70] *See* text accompanying notes 41 to 55.

[71] *See* Letter, John Adams to the Mayor, Aldermen, and Citizens of Philadelphia (Apr. 1798), 9 John Adams, *Works* (C. F. Adams), note 43, at 182.

[72] Letters, John Adams to Timothy Pickering (Aug. 1 and Aug. 17, 1799), 9 John Adams, *Works* (C. F. Adams), note 43, at 5 and 13. *See* J. M. Smith, note 19, at 31.

[73] He also succumbed to xenophobic comments about immigrants. *See* Letter, John Adams to Abigail Adams (Jan. 9, 1797) (We have been opening our Arms wide to all Forreigners [sic] and placing them on a footing with Natives; and now foreigners are dictating to US if not betraying Us.") *My Dearest Friend*, note 28, at 424.

[74] *See* Miller, note 4, at 188–190.

had left the country.[75] With the enactment of the Act, James Morton Smith estimated that as many as 15 shiploads of French refugees fled.[76]

After Adams left the White House, the former President increasingly sought to disassociate himself from the Act and attempted to explain away his approval of the Bill for the rest of his life. At one point, he blamed Alexander Hamilton, asserting that he had received a memorandum from Hamilton urging support for the Act.[77] No such communication appears in either the Adams or Hamilton papers. In an 1809 letter, Adams even tried to deny any responsibility for the Acts, writing:

> I recommended no such thing in my speech. Congress, however, adopted both these measures. I knew there was need enough of both and therefore consented to them. But as they were then considered as war measures and intended altogether against the advocates of the French and peace with France, I was apprehensive that a hurricane of clamour would be raised against them as in truth there was, even more fierce and violent than I anticipated.[78]

A few years later, in his increasingly warm correspondence with Thomas Jefferson long after their withdrawal from active politics, he protested:

> I know not why you are not as responsible for it as I am since [you signed it as Vice President]. . . . Neither of US was concerned in the formation of it. We were then at War with France: French spies then swarmed in our Cities and in the Country. Some of them were intollerably, [sic] turbulent, impure, and seditious. To check these was the design of this law.[79]

D. The Federalists Divided over the Act: The Reaction of Such Federalists as George Washington, Alexander Hamilton, Oliver Ellsworth, and John Marshall

The Act was the product of the High Federalists ready and eager for war with France. It was only one of the numerous measures enacted by the Congress in

[75] *See* Letter, Thomas Jefferson to James Madison (May 3, 1798), 10 Jefferson, *Writings* (Lipscomb), note 12, at 35. *See also* 4 Edward Channing, *History of the United States: Federalists and Republicans 1789–1815*, 223 (1917 repr. 1977) ("many French refugees fled" the country).

[76] *See* J. M. Smith, note 19, at 160.

[77] Ron Chernow, *Alexander Hamilton* 571 (2004).

[78] Boston *Patriot*, May 29, 1809. *See* Letter John Adams to Thomas Jefferson (lacking date) in Correspondence Originally Published in the Boston *Patriot*, 9 John Adams, *Works* (C. F. Adams), note 43, at 289, 291.

[79] *See* Henry Adams, *Life of Gallatin* 203–204 (1879).

anticipation of the conflict. However, it seems clear that not only Adams, but other Federalist leaders including Alexander Hamilton and John Marshall deemed it at best inexpedient. Former President Washington gave the Act his private approval, but always unobtrusively. In brief, the course being taken by the war-hawk High Federalists lacked the solid support of a number of the most respected members of the party.

1. George Washington

Washington was in retirement at the time and characteristically refrained from participation in the public debate. However, he was outspoken in his defense of the Alien Act in his correspondence, speaking out vigorously supporting its use, particularly when directed against the more extreme Republican editors who were aliens. For example, writing to Alexander Spotswood, Jr., Washington vigorously defended the need for the statute with a bitter comment about the press attacks in Republican papers edited by immigrants. Washington exploded: is it

> not time & expedient to resort to protecting Laws against aliens... in many instances are sent among us (as there is the best circumstantial evidence) for the *express purpose* of poisoning the minds of our people; and to sow dissension among them; in order to alienate *their* affections from the Government of their choice, thereby endeavoring to dissolve the Union... [80]

As for the Sedition Act, the historians acknowledge that Washington supported its enactment.[81] At the same time, it is striking to note how circumspect he was in his correspondence pertaining to the Act. For example, he forwarded to Bushrod Washington and John Marshall copies of the grand jury charge of Presiding Judge Alexander Addison of the Pennsylvania Court of

---

[80] Letter, George Washington to Alexander Spottswood, Jr. (Nov. 22, 1798), 3 Washington, *Papers* (Twohig), note 47, at 216. Twohig duly notes that the letter from Spottswood has been denounced as a forgery, *id.* at 217 n.1.

[81] *See, e.g,* Joseph J. Ellis, *His Excellency, George Washington* 249 (2004) ("He cheered the ill-starred Federalist campaign from the sidelines"). *See, e.g.,* 3 George Washington, *Papers: Retirement Series* 216–217, 287 (W. W. Abbot & Edward G. Lengel eds. 1998–1999).

    Washington's typical response was to emphasize the evils that the Alien and Sedition Laws were intended to deal with without expressly endorsing the legislation. His letter to Federalist William Vans Murray provides an excellent example. Letter, George Washington to William Vans Murray (Dec. 26, 1798), 3 Washington, *Papers* (Twohig), note 47, at 297. ("The Alien & Sedition Laws, are now the desiderata [in] the Oppos[it]ion. But anything else would have done, and something there will always be, for them to torture, and to disturb the public mind with their unfounded and ill-favored forebodings.")

Common Plea, a devoted Federalist and one of the nation's most dedicated advocates of the vigorous use of criminal libel against political opponents. In so doing, he seems to have tried meticulously to refrain from making any direct comment about the Act.[82] In this respect, as we will see, John Marshall was equally equivocal in his reply, referring to Addison's charge as "certainly well-written."[83]

2. Alexander Hamilton

Alexander Hamilton firmly supported the punitive purposes of the Sedition Act, as well as the Alien Act.[84] When the Alien Act was being considered, he was concerned by the possible public reaction to some of the extreme provisions of the original proposals and counseled moderation. Writing to Timothy Pickering, Hamilton advised, "Let us not be cruel or violent."[85] Later in the month after the Bills had been introduced, he wrote to Oliver Wolcott (later his successor as Secretary of the Treasury). He criticized provisions that seemed "highly exceptional and such as more than anything else may endanger civil war.... [L]et us not establish tyranny. Energy is a very different thing from violence." He added, "If we push things to an extreme, we shall then give to faction *body* and solidity."[86] In fact, the proponents of the Alien Bill had already recommitted it to committee. A revised bill emerged from the committee, deleting the treason and death penalty provisions. Similarly, the Sedition Bill approved by the Senate had followed the rigid common-law doctrine under which evidence of truth was not admissible and the role of the jury was minimal. As discussed above, the Sedition Act as finally enacted provided for the admissibility of evidence of truth and gave the jury a dramatically strengthened role. Hamilton's influence likely contributed to the outcome.

---

[82] E.g., Letter, George Washington to John Marshall (Dec. 30, 1798), 3 Washington, *Papers* (Twohig), note 47, at 297; Letter, George Washington to Bushrod Washington (Dec. 31, 1798), *id.* at 302; 14 George Washington, *Writings* 134–136 (W. Ford ed. 1893).

[83] Letter, John Marshall to George Washington (Jan. 8, 1799), Washington, *Papers* (Twohig), note 47, at 308.

[84] James Morton Smith provides a comprehensive view of Hamilton and the Alien and Sedition Laws. *See* James Morton Smith, Alexander Hamilton, The Alien Law and Criminal Libels, 16 Rev. of Pol. 305–33 (July 1954) (hereinafter J. M. Smith, Hamilton).

[85] Letter, Alexander Hamilton to Timothy Pickering (June 7, 1798), 22 Pickering Papers, Mass. Hist. Soc'y.; 8 *Hamilton's Works* 490 (Henry Cabot Lodge ed. 1971) (hereinafter *Hamilton's Works* (Lodge)).

[86] Letter, Alexander Hamilton to Oliver Wolcott (June 29, 1798), 21 *Papers of Alexander Hamilton* 522 (Harold Syrett ed. 1961–1987) (hereinafter Hamilton, *Papers* (Syrett)). *See* J. M. Smith, *Hamilton*, note 84, at 307–308.

Once the Alien and Sedition Acts had been adopted, Hamilton repeatedly called for the most energetic enforcement. Outraged by Callender's revelations about his illicit affair with Mrs. Reynolds,[87] Hamilton wrote to Sen. Jonathan Dayton of New Jersey demanding the prosecution of the "foreign born journalists [who were showing] open contempt and defiance of the laws . . . [and who were being permitted to] continue their destructive labours. Why are they not put away?" He was troubled by the limited scope of the Sedition Act that penalized only libels against the President or either House of the Congress. Writing again to Dayton, he urged the adoption of further legislation criminalizing as seditious all publications libelous at common law "if levelled against any officer whatever of the United States."[88] So much for moderation.

3. Chief Justice Oliver Ellsworth

Oliver Ellsworth, then Chief Justice, was another outspoken supporter of the Sedition Act. After its enactment, Secretary of State Pickering consulted him, seeking an advisory opinion on the constitutionality of the Act. Illustrating the very different views of the times as to appropriate judicial conduct, Ellsworth responded. He upheld the constitutionality of the Act, observing that the Act was only codifying what was already federal common law, and that the Act in fact was distinctly more liberal.[89]

4. John Marshall

Of all the prominent Federalists, John Marshall, then a lawyer in Richmond, was the one most troubled by the Sedition Act. Although he made no public comments during the debate in the Congress and the enactment of the Act, he privately expressed his concern to Secretary of State Pickering. Writing in August 1798 shortly after the passage of the law, he reported that in Richmond,

---

[87] Gordon Wood suggests that it was probably John Beckley, whom Jefferson used as a valuable source of potential gossip, who had leaked the Reynolds material to Callender. *See* Gordon Wood, *Empire of Liberty: A History of the Early Republic, 1789–1815*, 237 (2009).

[88] Letter, Alexander Hamilton to Jonathan Dayton (undated 1799), 8 *Hamilton's Works* (Lodge) note 85, at 517–522. *See* J. M. Smith, *Hamilton*, note 84, at 310.

[89] *See* Letter, Oliver Ellsworth to Timothy Pickering (Dec. 12, 1978), 2 Henry Flanders, The Law and Times of the Chief Justices of the Supreme Court of the United States 193–194 (1881 repr. 1971). *See also* William R. Casto, Oliver Ellsworth: "I have sought the felicity and glory of your Administration," in *Seriatim: The Supreme Court Before John Marshall* 292, 309 (Scott D. Gerber ed. 1998); William R. Casto, *Oliver Ellsworth and the Creation of the Federal Republic* 116 (1997).

"those two laws, especially the sedition bill, are viewed by a great many well meaning men, as unwarranted by the Constitution. . . . There are also many who are guided by very different motives [than the partisan Republicans] and who are seriously uneasy on the subject."[90]

A few weeks later, at the repeated urging of former President Washington, Marshall reluctantly became a Federalist candidate for Congress.[91] He then had to take a public stand. Using the occasion of an inquiry purportedly from a voter, an inquiry that some historians, including Beveridge, have suggested was prearranged,[92] he disassociated himself from the Act, without challenging its constitutionality. Nor did he take a public stand on the Virginia and Kentucky resolutions that had vigorously attacked the law.

In his carefully modulated reply in the *Alexandria Times and Virginia Advertiser*, Marshall said

> I am not an advocate for the alien and sedition bills; had I been in Congress, when they passed, I should, unless my judgment could have been changed, certainly have opposed them. Yet I do not think them fraught with all those mischiefs which many gentlemen ascribe to them. I should have opposed them because I think them useless; and because they are calculated to create unnecessary discontents and jealousies at a time when our very existence, as a nation, may depend on our union. . . . [The law by its terms was about to expire and] I shall indubitably oppose their revival.[93]

Marshall's refusal to endorse the Act enraged the High Federalists. Fisher Ames denounced him, saying "excuses may palliate; future zeal in the cause may partially atone; but his character is done for."[94] Other High Federalists

---

[90] *See* Letter, John Marshall to Timothy Pickering (Aug. 11, 1798), 3 *The Papers of John Marshall* 484–486 (William C. Stinchcombe ed. 1979). *See supra* text accompanying note 104 for John Quincy Adams's mistaken understanding of Marshall's position.

[91] Washington invited Marshall to Mt. Vernon and over a several-day period in Sept. 1798 unsuccessfully tried to persuade Marshall to run. Marshall was hardpressed financially and had just returned from his diplomatic responsibilities attempting to negotiate with the French. He wanted to resume his lucrative law practice. At the last moment, appealing to Marshall's patriotism and sense of duty, Washington finally was able to persuade him to do so, notwithstanding the financial sacrifice. *See* 2 Albert J. Beveridge, *Life of John Marshall* 374–378 (1916) (hereinafter Beveridge); R. Kent Newmyer, *John Marshall and the Heroic Age of the Supreme Court* 119–120 (2001).

[92] *See* 2 Beveridge, note 91, at 387 n.1. ("The questions . . . were undoubtedly written with Marshall's knowledge. Indeed, a careful study . . . leads one to suspect that he wrote or suggested them himself").

[93] 2 *ibid.*, at Appdx. III, 574–77 (1916) (containing full text of the Freeholder's questions and Marshall's replies).

[94] Letter, Fisher Ames to Christopher Gore (Dec. 18, 1798). *See* 2 *ibid.*, at 391.

counseled, however, against public denunciation. George Cabot wrote to Rufus King:

> I am ready to join you as well as [Fisher] Ames in reprobating the publication of Marshall's sentiment on the Sedition and Alien Acts, but I still *adhere* to my first opinion that Marshall should not be attacked in the newspapers, nor too severely condemned elsewhere.... [I]t is certain that Marshall at Phila. [i.e., the Congress] would become a most powerful auxiliary to the cause of order and good Govt., and *therefore* we ought not diminish his fame, which wou'd [sic] ultimately be a loss to ourselves.[95]

Abigail Adams, that outspoken sympathizer of the High Federalists at least on the urgent need for the Sedition Act, shared this resentment. Writing to President Adams in January 1799, she confided:

> I have met with Some of the Numbers addrest [sic] to Genll Marshall in the Chronical [sic] [the Boston Independent Chronicle, that arch Republican paper]. They appear to me to be the common place stuff of the party, the same low invective and abuse of the Government for which the Faction are distinguished. They will not injure Marshall so much as he injured himself.[96]

In the Congress, Marshall was the only Federalist to vote for the repeal of the Sedition Act when the Republicans proposed its termination in 1801. Similarly, he was the only Federalist to vote against Sen. Bayard's unsuccessful amendment late in the Adams administration providing that "the offences therein [Sedition Act] specified [to] remain punishable at common law" with the qualification that evidence of truth was admissible in justification.[97]

Nor did Marshall ever take any public stand on the constitutionality of the Act. Although such distinguished historians as Beveridge, Freeman, and James Morton Smith have identified Marshall as the author of the Minority Report in the Virginia Legislature that ably defended the constitutionality of the Act,[98] this is only speculation. More recent studies have indicated

---

[95] Letter, George Cabot to Rufus King (Apr. 2?, 1799). *See* 2 *ibid.*, at 393.

[96] Letter, Abigail Adams to John Adams (Jan. 12, 1799), *My Dearest Friend*, note 28, at 459, 460.

[97] Annals, 6th Cong., 1st Sess. 419, 423 (1800).

[98] *See* 2 Beveridge, note 91, at 401–406; 7 Freeman, *Washington*, note 1, at 539; J. M. Smith, note 19, at 151; Ketcham, note 67, at 397; Robert K. Faulkner, *The Jurisprudence of John Marshall* 88 (1968). Beveridge, for example, states flatly: "Marshall wrote the reply." *See* 2 Beveridge, note 91, at 402.

that Henry Lee might well have been the author.[99] On the other hand, Marshall's subsequent strong interpretation of the "necessary and proper clause" of the Constitution as justifying an expansive recognition of "implied powers" of the Congress is consistent with the arguments of the Federalists in the congressional debate and in the Minority Report on the Virginia Resolution upholding the constitutionality of the Sedition Act.[100] It is similarly consistent with Marshall's later explanation that the Federalist argument on the issue of constitutionality of federal criminal punishment of criminal libel was that the power came not from the common law, but that "the Constitution gave it."[101]

Similarly in his confidential correspondence with former President Washington, Marshall consistently avoided any endorsement of the Act with neutral comments, such as "well-argued" on such impassioned defenses of criminal libel as those contained in Presiding Judge Addison's grand jury charge that Washington had forwarded to him. In his frankest comment, he observes, "However much I may regret the passage of one of the acts complained of, I am firmly persuaded that the tempest has not been raised by them. Its cause lies much deeper and is not to be easily removed."[102] Moreover, in writing to St. George Tucker, he permits himself to refer to "whatever doubts some of us may entertain" on the issue of constitutionality.[103]

A contemporary, High Federalist Theodore Sedgwick, called the Minority Report "a masterly performance for which we are indebted to … Marshall." Letter, Theodore Sedgwick (Mar. 20, 1799) to Rufus King, 2 King's Correspondence 581, cited by J.M. Smith, note 19, at 151 n.40.

　　Baker goes as far as to say the Minority Report "is believed to have been the handiwork of John Marshall," but he carefully notes that "there is no evidence." However, he concludes that most historians have assumed that Marshall was the author. Leonard Baker, John Marshall: A Life in Law 306, 308 (1974) (hereinafter Baker). See e.g., Stephen M. Feldman, Free Expression and Democracy in America – A History 85 (2008) ("probably written by Marshall").

[99] See 3 Papers of John Marshall 494–502 note (William Stinchcombe and Charles Cullen, eds. 1979); 12 Marshall, Papers (Hobson), note 69, at 512–524.

[100] See United States v. Fisher, 6 U.S. (2 Cranch) 358, 396 (1805) (Marshall, C.J.) ("Congress must possess the choice of means, and must be empowered to use any means which are in fact conducive to the exercise of a power granted by the constitution"); McCulloch v. Maryland, 17 U.S. 316, 414–417 (1819) (Marshall, C.J.).

　　However, these decisions rest on an "implied power" to implement the execution of an express provision in the Constitution. It takes a further leap to accept that an "implied power" can be derived from the very existence of the nation and the Constitution.

[101] Letter, John Marshall to Anonymous (Nov. 27, 1800), John Marshall Papers (Libr. Cong.). See Baker, note 98, at 306.

[102] Letter, John Marshall to George Washington (Jan. 8, 1799) in reply to Letter, George Washington (Dec. 30, 1798), 3 Washington, Papers (Twohig), note 47, at 297.

[103] Letter, John Marshall to St. George Tucker (Nov. 18, 1800), 6 Marshall, Papers (Hobson), note 69, at 14.

One Federalist not identified with the High Federalists who strongly supported the Alien and Seditious Laws was John Quincy Adams, then the 32-year-old Minister to Holland appointed by his father. Writing to Federalist William Vans Murray, the younger Adams "heartily approved of the Alien and Sedition Acts." Apparently misinformed, the young Adams also believed that John Marshall had supported the Virginia and Kentucky Resolutions. He described himself as "thoroughly disgusted" by Marshall's supposed action, which, of course, had never occurred.[104]

Preceded by the common-law prosecutions described above, the Sedition Act had become law in mid-July 1798. The Congress promptly adjourned, and the politicians and politics went on vacation for the balance of the summer. This was only a brief interruption in the course of events. In the early fall, the political scene exploded. Led by Secretary of State Pickering, the Federalist administration seized on the availability of the Act and commenced criminal proceedings against a series of Republican critics ranging from a handful of drunks in a Newark, N.J., bar to an outspoken Republican congressman and editor, as well as the editors of the leading Republican papers in the nation.

We turn now to examine the vigorous efforts of the Federalist administration to utilize criminal libel prosecutions under the Sedition Act of 1798 for partisan purposes to harass or even suppress the Republican press on the eve of the crucial 1800 elections.

E. The First Cases Under the Act: Protecting National Security by Prosecuting Three Disorderly Drunks for Vulgar Remarks About President Adams

The very first cases enforcing the Act illustrate vividly how speedily an Act to protect national security at a time when an administration perceives the country to be on the brink of war can be used to suppress freedom of speech. The earliest cases involved the prosecution of three inebriated patrons of a Newark, N.J. bar for a drunken comment, disrespectful of President Adams. Demonstrating the intolerant nature of the times, the conviction of a federal crime for what in calmer times would have been police court behavior, if indeed criminal at all, for a vulgar expression about President Adams appears to be characteristic of a repressive system run by arrogant officials no longer restrained by common sense.

---

[104] Letters, John Quincy Adams to William Vans Murray (Feb. 5, Mar. 12, Apr. 13, 27, 1799), Samuel F. Bemis, *John Quincy Adams and the Foundations of American Foreign Policy* 97 n.41 (1949).

After the enactment of the Act, President and Mrs. Adams left Washington, D.C., for a summer holiday at their home in Quincy, Mass. When the presidential stage coach approached Newark, N.J., on July 27, 1798, the local Federalists made the coach the center of a triumphal procession and civic celebration, complete with parading militia, military bands, mass cheers, and cannonade salutes. Three friends, Luther Baldwin, Brown Clark, and a man known to history only as Lespenard, were in a local bar. As the cannon reports resounded, Baldwin, the "Captain" of a Passaic River garbage scow, made a derogatory comment about the blank wadding in the cannonade and the President's posterior. This is variously reported in bowdlerized terms. Sen. Beveridge's expurgated version will suffice: Baldwin "wished the wadding from the cannon had lodged in the President's backside."[105]

Although neither Clark nor Lespenard is reported to have made any remarks of his own, the three were arrested immediately. The mills of justice ground rapidly. In September 1798, the grand jury in the Circuit Court in Newark at a hearing presided over by Supreme Court Justice William Cushing indicted the three under the Sedition Act for Baldwin's remark. Lespenard pleaded guilty and was immediately fined $40 and court costs. The other two pleaded not guilty, and their trial was postponed to the 1799 spring Term.[106]

At the spring Term in 1799 before the Circuit Court, now consisting of Supreme Court Justice Bushrod Washington and District Judge Robert Morris, Baldwin and Clark withdrew their pleas and pleaded guilty. The Court fined Baldwin $150, Clark $50, and assessed them for court costs and expenses. They were then committed to jail until the fines and costs were paid.[107]

Thus, using an Act to protect the national security when the safety of the nation was deemed to be at stake, the Adams administration had chosen in its first cases to proceed with prosecutions of petty misbehavior involving what was at worst an act of vulgarity. The extreme response seems to illustrate in still another dimension how the Jeffersonians came to their view that the ultimate objective of Adams and his supporters was to refashion the New Republic into a hereditary monarchy.

[105] 3 Beveridge, note 91, at 42 *citing* 1 Jabez Hammond, *History of Political Parties in the State of New York* 130–131 (1852). *See also* Carl E. Price, *New Jersey's Jeffersonian Republicans* 39 (1967) (hereinafter Price).

[106] The Trenton *Federalist*, Apr. 8, 1799, asserts that these cases were at common law, not under the Sedition Act, as falsely stated in some of the "Jacobin" journals.

[107] United States v. Baldwin, Clark, Lespinard, Minutes of the U.S. Circuit Court, District of New Jersey, Oct. Sess. 1798, RG 21 (National Archives); New Brunswick *Guardian*, Nov. 13, 1798; Newark *Gazette*, Jan. 29, 1799; Trenton *Federalist*, Apr. 9, 1799; New York *Argus*, Oct. 12, 1799; Portsmouth *Oracle of the Day*, Oct. 26, 1799. *See* J. M. Smith, note 19, at 270–274; Rosenfeld, note 25, at 200–201, 532, 702. Judge Morris should not be confused with financier Morris.

As ultimately happened with the Act itself, this prosecution of the three drunk and disorderly Newark barflies backfired. It led to widespread ridicule of the Federalists, and in Carl Price's words, Baldwin "became one of the most celebrated victims" of the Act in the country. Republicans everywhere are reported to have kept this miscarriage of justice very much alive and taunted Federalists about it.[108]

Chilling in its implications of what subsequent generations would call the police state, this prelude to the enforcement of the Act also had its comical elements. However, as the Federalist campaign broadened with a major effort to silence the Republican press, matters became very serious indeed.

F. The Major Federalist Onslaught: Nine Cases Against Editors and Publishers of Jeffersonian Newspapers

Commencing almost immediately after the Trenton episode, Federalist District Attorneys in a campaign orchestrated by their supervisor, Secretary of State Timothy Pickering, began to institute proceedings under the Act directed against the editors of the major Republican papers in the major Northern cities, Philadelphia, New York, and Boston, as well as against newspaper editors in Connecticut and Vermont. As such proceedings multiplied and more Jeffersonian editors were indicted, it became plain that silencing the Republican press was the major target of the Federalist administration.

In all, eight of the 15 fully confirmed Sedition Act cases were directed against leading Republican newspapers. As we will see, the early prosecution and conviction of William Durrell, editor of the rural and less important Mt. Pleasant (N.Y.) *Gazette*, adds a ninth case to the suits against the Republican press. Although this was the central aspect of the Federalist campaign, as we have seen, it followed upon the prosecution of three criminal libel prosecutions against the editors and publishers of several major Republican papers brought under federal criminal common law before the enactment of the Act. Finally, three related prosecutions of the editors of major Republican newspapers were brought in the Federalist-dominated Massachusetts and New York state courts under state criminal common law. As a result of such legal intervention, whether by criminal conviction or the heavy burden of defending themselves against such litigation, five Republican papers shut down or ceased publication for a period. The Federalist campaign embracing 15 prosecutions (three at federal common law, nine under the Act, and three under state laws) was tactically a great success, but utterly failed in its

---

[108] *See* Price, note 105, at 39.

stragetic objective of silencing, or even intimidating, the Republican press. In the 1800 elections, the Federalists lost the presidency and were overwhelmed by a Republican congressional sweep.

These were early times in the New Republic. As discussed, official judicial reports for the period are unavailable or regrettably incomplete. Scholars interested in the period have to rely in many cases on secondary accounts of uncertain usefulness. Only 15, or a mere half of the 30 odd cases in issue, have judicial confirmation. Of those with such confirmation, there are only several patchy official reports,[109] and only four more are discussed in some detail in Francis Wharton's invaluable collection of "State Trials" published in 1847.[110] For the rest, scholars must rely on newspaper reports and elliptical formal notations in the sketchy courthouse records that are available. As for the newspapers, it is a question of the reliability of the various accounts and which seem sufficiently confirmed to be accepted. In this volume, all available reports are included, and readers must judge for themselves from the nature, type, and number of the references how credible the report may be. This is manifestly material, relevant evidence and cannot be dismissed out of hand as so many historians have done. The real question, as lawyers would frame it, is, having taken the press reports into account, what is the appropriate weight to be given to them under all the circumstances? From the lawyers' point of view, any attempt to report adequately the extent of the proceedings under the Act without considering the press reports at all would inevitably result in a serious distortion of the record.

Now for the cases.

1. *United States v. Matthew Lyon*, Congressman from Vermont and Editor of the *Vermont Journal*

Matthew Lyon, a particularly outspoken critic of the Federalists both in the Congress[111] and in his newspaper, the *Vermont Journal*, was the first editor

---

[109] Thus, Goebel states that the reports of the earliest of these, Alexander J. Dallas, published as vols. I and II of the *United States Reports* were not complete. *See* 1 Oliver Wendell Holmes Devise, *History of the Supreme Court of the United States*; Julius Goebel, Jr., *Antecedents and Beginnings to 1801*, 664–65 (1972) (hereinafter Goebel).

[110] Francis Wharton, *State Trials of the United States During the Administrations of Washington and Adams* (1847) (hereinafter Wharton). Although Wharton provides detailed accounts of the prosecutions of Lyon (at 333–344), Haswell (at 684–687), Cooper (at 659–681), and Callender (at 688–720), these are in turn based on partisan newspaper and other accounts. Wharton recognizes the possible distortions arising from the nature of his materials and seeks to balance them. *Id.*, at 333n, 344n, 649n.

[111] Lyon was outspoken and uncouth. When Federalist Roger Griswold of Connecticut ridiculed Lyon's war record, Lyon, who had fought at the Battles of Bennington and Saratoga, spat in his

prosecuted of the group of Jeffersonian newspaper editors singled out in the first days after the enactment of the Sedition Act.[112] The proceedings got under way with remarkable speed, taking less than a week from indictment to conviction and sentence.

On October 5, 1798, a Thursday, a grand jury in Rutland, Vt., indicted Lyon for the publication of criminal libels in violation of the Act. Lyon was charged with having acted with intent "to stir up sedition, and to bring the President and government of the United States into contempt." Lyon had allegedly asserted that President Adams had allowed "every consideration of the public welfare [to have been] swallowed up in a continuous grasp for power, in an unbounded thirst for ridiculous pomp, foolish adulation, and a selfish avarice." Further, Lyon had published in the *Journal* diplomatic correspondence between Adams and Joel Barlow, which Adams had refused to make public, and in the process, Lyon had denounced the "bullying speech" of Adams and the "stupid answer" of the Senate. Finally, he "wonder[ed]" that the Congress had not answered with an "order to send [Adams] to the madhouse." The indictment alleged that these comments were "scurrilous, feigned, false, scandalous, seditious and malicious."[113]

Lyon was arrested, held in custody, and arraigned, two days later, on Saturday, October 7. After pleading not guilty, Lyon was released on bail, and on Monday, October 9, four days after his arrest, went on trial before the Circuit Court, consisting of Supreme Court Justice William Paterson and District Judge Samuel Hitchcock. Lyon appeared without his counsel and argued the case himself.[114] Although admitting that he had written and published the letter, he defended on the grounds that the Act was unconstitutional, and that if not, it was, nevertheless, unconstitutional to apply it to a letter written and sent before its enactment.[115] He went further and argued that because

---

face. Griswold responded with a caning. A motion to expel Lyon from the House for the incident failed. His counsel had pointed out that the House was not in session at the time. *See* Stanley Elkins & Eric McKitrick, *The Age of Federalism* 709–710 (1993) (hereinafter Elkins & McKitrick).

[112] For the events of the trial, *see* United States v. Matthew Lyon, 15 F. Cas. 1183, 1798 U.S. App. LEXIS 37 (C.C.D. Vt. 1798) (Case. No. 8646); Wharton, note 110, at 332–344 (detailed report derived from contemporary accounts in the Federalist New York *Spectator* and the Jeffersonian Philadelphia *Aurora*); John Spargo, *Anthony Haswell: Printer-Patriot-Ballader* 56–87 (1925) (hereinafter Spargo) (a very full account based in part on Haswell's own description); J. M. Smith, note 19, at 221–246; Goebel, note 109, at 638–639; Elkins & McKitrick, note 111, at 706–711.

[113] *See* Wharton, note 110, at 334.

[114] Although Lyon did have counsel, they were unable to appear because of the virtual absence of notice. The Court offered a continuance, but Lyon declined. At the trial, however, Chief Justice Israel Smith of the Vermont Supreme Court did appear for Lyon. He declined to respond to the prosecution's closing argument "in consequence of the shortness of time allowed him for preparation, having been called into the case at the bar." *See* Wharton, note 110, at 335.

[115] The allegedly libelous material was indeed contained in a letter dated July 7, 1798, and postmarked that day, before the Sedition Act became law on July 14, 1798. However, the publication did not

the statute, unlike the common law, provided that the jury was to be the judge of the law as well as the facts, just as in other matters, it was for the jury to determine the constitutionality of the Act.[116] Finally, Lyon concluded by contending that the publication was innocent, that is, without malicious intent to defame, as well as truthful.

During the trial Lyon is reported to have repeatedly observed that the jury was "packed" having been brought from towns "inimical" to him. However, Wharton notes that the jurors had been drawn according to a procedure established before the proceedings.[117] Lyon presented no witnesses, but, in an interchange that illustrates the very different judicial practices of the times, he addressed himself to Justice Paterson on the bench. He inquired whether the Justice had not frequently "dined with the President and observed his ridiculous pomp and parade?" Paterson replied that on the "rare" occasions when he had dined with the President, "he had not seen any pomp or parade, [but] on the contrary, a great deal of plainness and simplicity."[118]

Rejecting Lyon's legal arguments. Justice Paterson and Judge Hitchcock refused to allow any challenge to the constitutionality of the Act. They instructed the jury "until this law is declared null and void by a tribunal competent for the purpose, its validity cannot be disputed."[119] The jury was to consider only whether Lyon had published the writing (which had been admitted) and whether he did so seditiously. As to latter issue, which was the sole issue before the jury, the jury was charged: "you will have to consider whether language such as that here complained of could have been uttered with any other intent than that of making odious or contemptible, the President and government, and bringing them both into disrepute." So charged, the jury found Lyon guilty within an hour.

occur until July 23, 1798, after the Act had become law. Publication was, thus, not barred by the *ex post facto* provision of the Constitution. U.S. Const. art. 1, §9, cl. 3. *Cf.* United States v. William Durrell, Minute Book, 1790–1808 (C.C.D. N.Y. 1799) and discussion *infra* accompanying notes 217–220.

[116] Goebel notes that Lyon's contention follows the comment of Senator Bayard of Delaware in the debate over the Act. Bayard, a High Federalist, had opposed the proposed amendment to the original draconian version of the Bill broadening the power of the jury to be judges of law as well as of the fact by observing that such a change would enable a jury to declare the law unconstitutional. *See* Goebel, note 109, at 645–646. Although Bayard had initially prevailed in the Senate, the House voted otherwise and the final Act contained the provision.

[117] *See* Wharton, note 110, at 336. Writing about the partisan influence during this period in the selection of juries generally, Beveridge comments: "the juries were nothing more than machines that registered the will, opinion, or even inclination of the national judges and the United States district attorneys." 3 Beveridge, note 91, at 42. *See also* Miller, note 4, at 235–236.

[118] *See* Wharton, note 110, at 335.

[119] *Ibid.*

The Court sentenced Lyon to four months in jail, a fine of $1,000 and $60.96 costs, and continued commitment until the fine and costs had been paid in full. In so doing, the Court explained that the punishment had been mitigated in the light of Lyon's representation that he was "almost insolvent." From indictment on Thursday, October 5, to conviction on Monday, October 9, a mere five days of Federalist justice sufficed to move from indictment to conviction and sentence in one of the most important cases undertaken under the Act.

When Lyon was unable to pay his fine and costs aggregating $1,060 and obtain his release after serving his term, his Republican allies rallied to his cause. His Vermont supporters headed by Apollo Austin, a wealthy Vermont Republican, and the defendant's son, James Lyon, raised the necessary $1,060 from proceeds of a lottery and contributions. At the same time, Sen. Stevens Thomson Mason of Virginia, a close friend of Jefferson, collected contributions from leading Republicans, including Jefferson, Gallatin, Madison, Monroe, and Taylor. Mason then rode to Vermont on horseback carrying $1,060 in gold in his saddlebags. In the end, the two blocs joined in paying the fine and costs and secured Lyon's release.[120] It is of interest that Mason also helped pay the fines of other Republicans convicted under the Sedition Act, including Cooper, Callender, and Holt.[121]

The conviction and Lyon's claims of maltreatment in prison made him a martyr. He was overwhelmingly reelected to Congress. However, when Lyon returned to Philadelphia, still the nation's capital, for the new Session, he received a different reception. On taking his seat in the new Congress, he was confronted by a Federalist resolution to expel him as having been convicted of "being a notorious and seditious person, and of a depraved mind, and wicked, and diabolical disposition." Although a majority approved the resolution, 49 to 45, it failed, lacking approval of the necessary two-thirds of the members present.

The Federalist *Connecticut Courant* reported with satisfaction in May 1799 the denial of Lyon's application for payment for his "attendance" at the entire session of the Congress, although his actual attendance for most of the session had been prevented by his imprisonment in Vermont following his criminal libel conviction in October 1798. In the same dispatch, the *Courant* reported that two other bills of indictment for sedition were awaiting Lyon in the event

---

[120] Spargo, note 112, at 52–53.
[121] J. M. Smith, note 19, at 243.

of his return to Vermont, but that he had announced his intention to settle in Kentucky.[122]

Lyon subsequently did move. In 1803 he was elected once again to the House of Representatives, now from Kentucky, and reelected four more times. On his return to the Congress, sitting in Washington, Lyon was received as a hero by the new Jeffersonian majority.[123] Over the years, he and his heirs struggled unsuccessfully for vindication in the form of congressional approval of repayment of his fine. In 1833 the House Judiciary Committee paved the way, condemning the Sedition Act as unconstitutional.[124] At last, in 1840 (18 years after his death), the Congress took action. The House Committee Report stated that the Sedition Act had been passed "under a mistaken exercise of undelegated power" and was "null and void." It recommended repayment of the fine with interest in an effort to place beyond question the mandate of the Constitution on abridging the press. The House overwhelmingly approved by a vote of 124 to 15, and the Senate followed suit.[125]

This is not the end of the *Lyon* story. The litigation gave rise to two more instances of the Federalist partisan use of the courts to imprison supporters of Lyon: Rev. John C. Ogden and the Vermont publisher Anthony Haswell.

After the election of Lyon, Rev. John C. Ogden (whom Miller describes as a "noted radical") journeyed to Washington to present a petition from several thousand Vermonters asking Adams to pardon him. President Adams testily refused, saying "penitence must precede pardon." Adams went further and warned Ogden that "your interference in this business will prevent you from receiving any favours from me."[126]

Ogden then set out to return to Vermont. En route, he stopped in his old home town of Litchfield, Ct., a Federalist stronghold. While Ogden lingered in Litchfield, Secretary of the Treasury Wolcott charged that Ogden was delinquent in the payment of an old debt for $200. He was subsequently sentenced to four months imprisonment in December 1798. This was only the first attempt to punish Lyon's supporters. Anthony Haswell was the next target.

---

[122] *Connecticut Courant*, May 20, 1799.

[123] Wharton, note 110, at 343.

[124] H. R. Rep. 218, 22d Cong., 1st Sess. (Jan. 30, 1832). *See* Derek L. Mogck, Connecticut Federalists in President Jefferson's (Republican) Court: *United States v. Hudson and Goodwin*, 41 Conn. Hist. 144 (2002).

[125] Cong. Globe, 26th Sess., 1st Sess. 409 (1840). *See* Michael K. Curtis, *Free Speech: "The People's Darling Privilege"* 84 (2000); Wharton, note 110, at 344n.

[126] *See* Miller, note 4, at 111 n.58; J. M. Smith, note 19, at 242; Rosenfeld, note 25, at 562. *See also* Gordon T. Bell, *Sedition Act of 1798: A Brief History of Arrests, Indictments, Mistreatment Abuse* 6 (hereinafter Bell).

2. *United States v. Anthony Haswell*, Editor of the *Vermont Gazette*

Anthony Haswell was the editor of the Bennington *Vermont Gazette*, which he published for more than 30 years starting in 1783.[127] A deeply committed Republican and editor of the leading Republican paper in Vermont, he worked in close cooperation with other Republican editors, notably with the editor of the Philadelphia *Aurora*. His activities aroused deep indignation among the Federalists. As early as September 8, 1798, a month before the indictment and trial of Representative Lyon, Haswell reported in the *Gazette* that he "has been and is threatened with prosecution under the sedition law, with tarring and feathering, pulling down his house, etc." Similarly shortly after Lyon's conviction and sentence, Haswell asserted in the October 12, 1798, issue of the *Gazette* that he expected to be arrested and prosecuted. However, nothing came of it.[128] After Matthew Lyon's conviction and imprisonment in an unheated Rutland cell, Haswell denounced week by week the ill-treatment of Lyon by his jailor, who was seen as the "tool" of Nathaniel Chipman, the Federalist leader in Vermont.[129]

In the summer of 1799, Haswell published a pamphlet containing the anti-Federalist Independence Day oration of Ezekial Bacon in Williamstown, Mass. The District Attorney attempted to use this publication to support an indictment, but the grand jury refused to indict.[130] Then, in October 1799, Haswell's newspaper, the *Vermont Gazette*, published an appeal from a committee of Lyon's supporters addressed "To the enemies of political persecution." This denounced the imprisonment of Lyon by "the oppressive hand of usurped power in a loathsome prison ... suffering all the indignities which can be heaped upon him by a hard-hearted savage [his jailor]." It then called on sympathizers to "ransom" him by supporting a lottery to raise $1,100 for payment of Lyon's fine and costs. At the same time, the *Gazette* published an extract from the Philadelphia *Aurora* entitled "British Influence" attacking the Federalist administration for asserting that Tories, "men who fought against our independence, who had shared in the destruction of our homes, and the abuse of our wives and daughters were worthy of the confidence

---

[127] United States v. Haswell, 26 Fed. Cas. 218, 1800 U.S. App. LEXIS 67 (C.C.D. Vt. 1800) (No. 15,324). *See generally* Spargo, note 112, at 56–57; Wharton, note 110, at 684–687; J. M. Smith, note 19, at 359–373; Rosenfeld, note 25, at 699, 713, 744, 775, 783–784, 805.

[128] Bennington *Vermont Gazette*, Sept. 8, 1798; Oct. 12, 1798. *See* Spargo, note 112, at 56–57.

[129] *See* Spargo, note 112, at 52–53. The Spargo volume contains a photocopy of the proposed indictment, which the grand jury rejected. Plate xii, at 58.

[130] *Ibid.*, at 63.

of the government," presumably by their appointment to federal office.[131] Haswell was arrested and indicted almost immediately for violation of the Sedition Act. According to a newspaper report in the *Aurora*, another supporter of Congressman Lyon, Judah P. Spooner, editor of *Spooner's Vermont Journal*, was arrested as well.[132] Although judicial confirmation is available on the *Haswell* case, there is no judicial confirmation of the *Aurora* report of Spooner's indictment.

As soon as Haswell's indictment was handed down, a federal Marshal rode on horseback from Rutland to Bennington, Vt., to apprehend him. In his warm and appreciative biography of Haswell largely based on Haswell's papers, John Spargo vividly describes what then transpired.

Early the next morning, the Marshal informed Haswell of the indictment and took him into custody. Although, as Spargo relates, Haswell was "unwell," the Marshal required him to accompany him to the jail in Rutland 56 miles away on horseback in weather that was "raining and chilly." The two men started at 10:00 A.M. and rode all through the "cold and wet" day and part of the night on "muddy" roads. Fifteen hours later, they at last arrived in Rutland at 1:00 A.M., "nearly exhausted"; Haswell was then cast into a chilly cell. On arraignment, he pleaded not guilty and was bound over for trial at the next term of Court. He was required to post a $1,000 bond to assure his appearance and "in the meantime to keep the peace & be of good behavior."[133]

On April 28, 1800, Haswell came for trial before the same judges who had presided the year before in the *Lyon* case, Justice Paterson and District Judge Hitchcock.[134] Haswell was represented by Chief Justice Israel Smith of

---

[131] Philadelphia *Aurora*, Oct. 15, 1799. *See* Wharton, note 110, at 685; Spargo, note 112, at 61; J. M. Smith, note 19, at 361.

[132] Philadelphia *Aurora*, Oct. 24, 1799, Nov. 6, 1799, Oct. 16, 1800. *See* Rosenfeld, note 25, at 699, 704, 705, 712, 860.

[133] Spargo, note 112, at 54–58. Spargo's account was prepared with the benefit of Haswell's own papers and correspondence made available by Haswell descendants. This inevitably colors his description of these events.

[134] United States v. Anthony Haswell, 26 F. Cas. 218, 1800 U.S. App. LEXIS 67 (C.C.D. Vt. 1800) (No. 15,324). It is of interest that Haswell shortly after his trial wrote to President Adams and among other things described the prosecution as having taken place under federal criminal common law. *See* Letter, Anthony Haswell to John Adams (June 3, 1800), 9 *Papers of John Adams*, no. 22 (Mass. Hist. Soc'y). The prosecutor, however, asserted in court that the publications were criminal libels against the government of the United States, the judges of the Circuit Court, and the Vermont federal marshal. *See* J. M. Smith, note 19, at 367. Because the Sedition Act did not protect federal judges and marshals, this creates some plausibility for the assertion. However, truth could serve as a justification under the Act whereas it had no role at common law. As is evident from Haswell's presentation of his case and Justice Paterson's conduct of the trial and charge to the jury, truth was an issue in the case, indicating that the case was, indeed, brought under the Act.

Vermont and Joseph Fay. As readers will recall, Smith had also appeared for Lyon. Their request for a continuance to procure witnesses ready to testify to the Federalist appointment of Tories to office in support of Haswell's charge was rejected,[135] and trial commenced on May 5, 1800.

In a charge that was favorable to the prosecution, Justice Paterson charged the jury that although truth was a defense under the statute, it had to be supported by evidence. The jury had to determine whether the "violent language" applied to the federal jailor's treatment of Lyon was sustained by the evidence. If not, the defense had not been established. As for the allegation about the appointment of Tories, he noted that no justification had been made. Accordingly, if the jury believed beyond reasonable doubt that the intent was defamatory and the publication made, they must convict. Even if Haswell had not written the defamatory matter, he was liable if the objectionable material had appeared in his paper.

Thus, Justice Paterson imposed on the defendant the burden of not only establishing the truth of the offending publication, but establishing it in full. A month later this ruling was followed by an identical ruling of Justice Chase in the *Callender* litigation, discussed below.[136] After a "short deliberation," the jury convicted Haswell, and the Court sentenced him to two months in jail and fined him $200.[137]

The Republicans looked upon Haswell as a political prisoner and welcomed his release after he had served his sentence with an "immense concourse" of nearly 2,000 supporters, a band, and cannonades.[138] He continued to edit the *Vermont Gazette* for the next 15 years. Forty years after the trial, the Congress finally approved refund of his fine, together with interest.[139]

---

[135] The witnesses, Secretary of War McHenry and General Darke, lived in or near Virginia. It has been suggested that at this time, a standard trial tactic for defense counsel was to attempt to obtain the attendance of witnesses far removed from the Court as a means of delaying the trial. Such efforts were made in the Sedition Act cases involving Callender, Duane, and Peck and in the 1805 Republican criminal libel prosecution under federal common law of the Connecticut Federalist minister Azel Backus.

[136] In contrast to the rulings of Justice Paterson and Chase, Chief Justice Marshall snorted at the suggestion. Testifying in 1805 in the *Chase* impeachment *trial*, Marshall testified that, except for the *Callender* trial, he had never heard a court refuse to receive testimony because it went to only a part, not the whole, of a charge. *See* 3 Beveridge, note 91, at 194.

[137] *See* Wharton, note 110, at 686.

[138] *See* Spargo, note 112, at 87. Spargo further reports that in contrast to Lyon's ill-treatment by his jailor in the Rutland jail, Haswell's Bennington jailor was a "personal and political friend" and that his imprisonment "could not have been under conditions less unpleasant." He wrote "regularly" for his paper, and was "freely and frequently visited by his friends." *Id.* at 83.

[139] *See* Wharton, note 110, at 684–687.

3. *United States v. Thomas Adams*; *Commonwealth v. Thomas Adams*
(Mass.); *Commonwealth v. Abijah Adams* (Mass.), Editor and
Bookkeeper, Respectively, of the Boston *Independent Chronicle*

October 1798 saw still another major prosecution under the Sedition Act.
This was directed against Thomas Adams, the editor of the influential Boston
Independent Chronicle, the leading Republican journal in New England. Editor Adams was an implacable critic of President Adams. The vigor and effectiveness of his barbed comments are plain from the exasperation expressed
by Abigail Adams in her confidential correspondence with her sister Mary
Cranch. In a series of letters during April and May 1798, Abigail Adams expos-
tulated over the *Chronicle's* abusive attacks on President Adams. In one, she
expressed the hope that Massachusetts would enact a strong sedition law for
the express purpose of silencing the *Chronicle* along with Benjamin Franklin
Bache of the Philadelphia *Aurora*.[140]

The *Chronicle* criticized Adams for, among other things, his proposals for
a great increase in the size of the Army and the building of a new Navy, his
clumsy handling of the XYZ Affair, removing money from the federal treasury
in the form of pay vouchers over his four-year term and his responsibility for
the pay that John Quincy Adams received as result of Adams's nepotism in
making his son a diplomatic representative of the United States in Europe.
After the passage of the Sedition Act, Thomas Adams continued his attacks,
particularly on the use of the foreign crisis "to further the work of injustice
at home." In addition, Adams accused the Federalists of tyranny in ramming
the Sedition Act through the Congress.[141]

Joining the prosecutions of the three bar room drunks and the prosecution
of Congressman Lyon earlier in the month as the earliest cases under the Act,
Thomas Adams was indicted and in October 1798 arraigned in the federal
Circuit Court in Boston before Justice William Paterson and District Judge
John Lowell. The case was set down for trial at the June 1799 Term. However,
fate intervened; Thomas Adams fell seriously ill. A court-appointed physician
determined that he was too ill to stand trial, and the case was continued.

During the period of Adams's illness while the federal proceedings were
pending, the *Independent Chronicle* had attacked the Massachusetts Legislature for rejecting the Virginia Resolution condemning the Sedition Act. This
speedily led to parallel prosecutions for criminal libel in the Massachusetts

---

[140] Letters, Abigail Adams to Mary Cranch (Apr. 21, 1798, Apr. 26, 1798, May 10, 1798), *New Letters*,
note 37, at 157–159, 164–165, 170–172.
[141] *See* J. M. Smith, note 19, at 250.

courts under Massachusetts common law against Thomas Adams and his brother, Abijah Adams, the bookkeeper of the *Independent Chronicle*. After a charge by Chief Justice Francis Dana of the Court, the Suffolk County grand jury promptly indicted both Adams brothers. Thomas now faced trial in both the federal and state courts, and Abijah in the state.

While the federal prosecution was delayed, matters proceeded apace in the Massachusetts court. With Thomas Adams severely ill, he could not stand trial, and the prosecution concentrated on his brother Abijah. It did so, although Abijah Adams had been only the bookkeeper of the *Chronicle* without editorial responsibility. After trial in March 1799, the jury found Abijah Adams guilty, but only for publishing the libel, not for printing it. The court sentenced him to thirty days in the Suffolk County jail and the costs of prosecution, and required the posting of a $500 surety bond as a security against a similar offense for one year.[142]

As for the ailing Thomas Adams, he still faced trial both in the federal Circuit Court and the Massachusetts Suffolk County Court, but his condition worsened. Severely ill and facing the pending prosecutions, Adams was forced to dispose of the *Independent Chronicle* and sold the paper on May 2, 1799. A week later, he died with his trial date still a few weeks away.[143]

For the moment at least, the Federalists had succeeded in silencing the *Chronicle* and the Thomas Adams family as critics of the administration. The *Adams* litigation was another major success in the campaign of the Federalists to silence the Jeffersonian press. The Federalist campaign launched in the summer of 1798 – first on the eve of the adoption of the Act and then on the heels of its enactment – had silenced at least temporarily three of the leading Republican newspapers in the North: John Daly Burk and Dr. James Smith and the New York *Time Piece*, Matthew Lyon and the *Vermont Journal*, and Thomas and Abijah Adams and the Boston *Independent Chronicle*.[144] As we will see, they soon succeeded in the doing the same with Thomas and Ann Greenleaf and David Frothingham and the New York *Argus*, at least temporarily.

---

[142] *Ibid.*, at 247–256; Rosenfeld, note 25, at 527, 599, 625, 627, 639.

[143] It is singular that illness overtook no fewer than four of the defendants accused under the Sedition Act – Bache, Thomas Greenleaf, Ann Greenleaf, and Thomas Adams. Further, death followed for all except Ann Greenleaf. A few years later, this macabre incidence of illness and death in criminal libel proseutions claimed another editorial victim, William Carleton, editor of the Republican *Salem Gazette*, serving his sentence after conviction by a Federalist Massachusetts state court.

[144] Sickness and death in addition to criminal libel prosecutions helped bring about the silencing – temporary or permanent – of the Philadelphia *Aurora*, New York *Argus*, the Boston *Independent Centinel* and the *Salem (Mass.) Gazette*.

However, the Federalist triumph over Abijah Adams and the *Independent Chronicle* was short-lived. After the election of Jefferson, Massachusetts Republicans were able to regenerate the *Independent Chronicle*. With Abijah Adams now acting as editor for at least a decade thereafter, it continued in its former role as one of the leading Republican papers in Massachusetts. Nevertheless, as we will see in Chapter 6, a decade later found the Federalists once again prosecuting Abijah Adams for criminal libel in the still Federalist-dominated Massachusetts state courts.[145]

After their triumphs in the judicial arena in the fall of 1798 and the spring of 1799, the Federalists led by Pickering paused for a time in their campaign of extermination of the Republican press. Then, commencing in the summer of 1799 and continuing on into the spring of 1800, they caused the institution of a number of important prosecutions against other Republican papers and pamphleteers. The summer of 1799 saw the indictments of Charles Holt, editor of the New London *Bee*, William Duane, by then editor of the Philadelphia *Aurora*, and Thomas Greenleaf, Ann Greenleaf, and David Frothingham of the *Argus*. A few months later in April 1800, prosecutions were instituted against Thomas Cooper, editor of the *Sunsbury and Northumberland Gazette* (Pennsylvania) and early in May 1800 against Anthony Haswell of the *Vermont Gazette*, which has already been discussed, and later in May 1800 against James Thomson Callender, an editor of the Richmond *Examiner* and, along with Duane, one of the most scurrilous editors and pamphleteers of the time.

4. *United States v. Charles Holt*, Editor of the New London *Bee*

Charles Holt was the editor of the New London *Bee*, the leading Republican newspaper in heavily Federalist Connecticut.[146] As the undeclared naval war with France intensified, Holt was unremitting in his attacks on President Adams, his conduct of relations with the French, and the military and naval measures being taken to defend against the anticipated invasion by the French. In the May 8, 1799, issue, he published a letter from a reader condemning the military steps as the establishment of a "standing army" and urged citizens to consider the evils of military life before permitting their sons to participate. George Goodwin and Barzillai Hudson, publishers of the *Connecticut Courant*, the leading Federalist newspaper in the state, forwarded

---

[145] *See infra* Ch. 6, text accompanying notes 125–129, 149.
[146] *See* 2 H. G. Randall, *Life of Thomas Jefferson* 418 (1856); Rosenfeld, note 25, at 665, 695–698, 704–705, 753, 769, 775, 779; J. M. Smith, note 19, at 373–384.

thereafter largely confined himself to Republican state affairs. Allied with the radical Republican faction headed by Dr. Michael Leib, Duane bitterly fought Governor Thomas McKean, Alexander J. Dallas, and Albert Gallatin for control of the Pennsylvania Republican Party. By 1808, Duane and Leib triumphed and assumed control of the party. They elected their candidate, Samuel Snyder, as Governor, replacing McKean and driving him into enforced retirement. By this time, Gallatin had moved onto the national scene. He became Secretary of the Treasury in the Jefferson and Madison administrations, one of the most able Treasury Secretaries in the history of the nation.

7. *United States v. Thomas Cooper*, Editor of the *Sunsbury and Northumberland Gazette*

In April 1800, still another leading Republican editor, Thomas Cooper, editor of the *Sunsbury and Northumberland Gazette*, was indicted for violation of the Sedition Act.[181] Cooper was a man for all seasons who led a remarkably diversified life. At one time or another, he was a chemist, a lawyer, a judge, and a physician before concluding his career as a college president. He was a person of outspoken views. Like so many of the Republican editors who ran afoul of the Federalists, Cooper was an English émigré run out of England for his political writings.[182]

He was also a political turncoat. With the support of his close friend, the renowned English chemist Dr. Joseph Priestly, a friend of Adams, Cooper applied to President Adams for a federal job. He sought appointment as an American representative on the British Claims Commission, evaluating American claims under the provisions of the Jay Treaty. Only when Adams passed over him did he became a political enemy. In his newspaper, the *Sunsbury and Northumberland Gazette*, and in pamphlets, he thereafter repeatedly attacked Adams and his administration. On June 29, 1799, in the *Gazette*, he attacked Adams's arrogance, "seizure" of the treaty-making power, and the Alien and Sedition Acts. Secretary of State Pickering passed this information along to President Adams. Adams was incensed, replying to Pickering in heated terms: "A meaner, a more artful, or a more malicious libel [has not

---

[181] United States v. Thomas Cooper, 25 F. Cas. 631, 1800 U.S. App. LEXIS 56 (C.C.D. Pa. 1800) (No. 14,865); Thomas Cooper, *An Account of the Trial of Thomas Cooper, of Northumberland on a Charge of Libel against the President of the United States* (1830); Wharton, note 110, at 659–681; J. M. Smith, note 19, at 307–333.

[182] See Dumas Malone, The Public Life of Thomas Cooper, 1783–1839 (1961).

the offending issue to the Federalist District Attorney.[147] The District Attorney was Pierpont Edwards, who six years later played such a prominent role in the most celebrated criminal libel prosecutions instituted during the Jefferson administration.[148]

In September 1799, the grand jury indicted Holt for publishing the May 8 letter. The indictment also cited his articles in the *Bee*, as having the tendency to oppose and encourage resistance to Army recruiting efforts. The grand jury described Holt as "a wicked, malicious, seditious, and ill-disposed person" who was "'greatly disaffected' from the government and was contriving to stir up and excite discontent and sedition among the citizenry." Holt pleaded not guilty and was held over for trial. In the seven months before trial, Holt continued to publish with unabated vigor.

In April 1800, Justice Bushrod Washington and District Judge Richard Law presided at Holt's trial in the New Haven Circuit Court. Counsel for Holt did not contest the charge that Holt had published the offending letter. They first contended that the Act was beyond the limited powers of the national government and unconstitutional. They further asserted that the facts asserted in the letter were true, and in any event, they did not constitute an offense because they were mere expressions of opinion. According to an account in the *Connecticut Journal*, Justice Washington's charge concluded that the publication was libelous and rejected the contention of the defense that the Act was unconstitutional.[149] The jury thereupon found Holt guilty, and the court sentenced him to three months in prison and a $200 fine.[150] While Holt was serving his sentence, the *Bee* discontinued publication.

Thus, in the bitter 1800 campaign for the presidency, one of the few Republican outlets in Connecticut was silenced for a critical period. By the time Holt was released and the *Bee* resumed publication, Connecticut had already cast its votes and elected nine Federalist electors pledged to vote for Adams and Pinckney. Although a few critical states, including New York,

---

[147] *See* J. M. Smith, note 19, at 375–377.
   It is ironic that a few years later, tables had reversed. Jefferson had then assumed control of the federal government, and the courts were being directed by Jeffersonian appointees. In 1805, a Republican District Attorney guided by a Republican judge caused Hudson and Goodwin to be indicted for criminal libel under federal criminal common law, the very doctrine that had only a few years before been so bitterly assailed by Jefferson himself.

[148] *See* Ch. 5.

[149] *Connecticut Journal*, Apr. 24, 1800, *cited by* J. M. Smith, note 19, at 381.

[150] A group of Republicans collected funds to pay Holt's $200 fine. Sen. Stevens Thomson Mason of Virginia approached Jefferson, and Jefferson sent him a $10 contribution. *See* Letter, Thomas Jefferson to Stevens Thomson Mason (Oct. 11, 1798), 32 Jefferson, *Papers* (Oberg), note 54, at 49n. As noted, Mason undertook similar collections for the payment of the fines imposed under the Sedition Act on Lyon, Cooper, and Callender.

South Carolina, and Georgia, still had to choose their electors, who would in the end determine which candidate had won the presidency, for Connecticut the election was over.

Upon release, Holt resumed publication of the *Bee* until 1802. He then moved to Hudson, New York. With the aid of local Republicans, he commenced publishing the Hudson *Bee*. At this point, he reentered the stage of history as a result of his confrontation with Federalist Harry Croswell, publisher of the Hudson *Wasp*. It is a sign of the temper of the times that Holt, victim of criminal libel proceedings instituted by Federalists during the Adams administration, played a major role in having a Republican prosecutor pursue Croswell for criminal libel under New York law during the Jefferson administration. The celebrated *Croswell* case is discussed with other state common-law cases during the Jefferson administration in Chapter 6.[151]

5. *United States v. Ann Greenleaf; People v. David Frothingham* (N.Y.), Editor and Employee, Respectively, of the New York *Argus*

After the demise of the New York *Time Piece* following the federal common-law criminal libel prosecutions of John Daly Burk and Dr. James Smith, the New York *Argus* was the only Republican paper in New York City. As we have seen in the discussions of common-law criminal libel proceedings, Thomas Greenleaf was unrestrained in his political comments. Twice before, he had been indicted under federal criminal common law for libels of the British Minister, once in 1795 and again in 1797.[152] Staunch defender of the French and an abusive critic of the British, Greenleaf was a determined opponent of the Federalists. As early as the spring of 1797, President Adams had singled him out as one of his three leading critics.[153] As the domestic political scene became heated in the summer of 1798 with the deterioration of relations with the French, the Federalists pilloried the *Argus* and Greenleaf as centers of sedition. Thus, the Federalist *Commercial Advertiser* held them responsible for the appearance of Liberty Poles, those "wooden Gods of sedition" in upstate New York symbolizing Republican opposition to the administration's war program.[154] To Federalists, Greenleaf was an obvious candidate for prosecution.

[151] *See infra* Ch. 6, text accompanying notes 55–75.

[152] Although the 1795 indictment never came to trial, the 1797 indictment led to Greenleaf's trial and conviction. *See* Goebel, note 109, at 629.

[153] *See* Letter, John Adams to Abigail Adams (Apr. 24, 1797), *Letters of John Adams Addressed to His Wife* 254 (Charles F. Adams ed. 1841). *See* J. M. Smith, note 19, at 398.

[154] Commercial *Advertiser*, Aug. 11, 1798, reprinted in Albany *Centinel*, Aug. 17, 1798. *See* J. M. Smith, note 19, at 398–399.

However, as happened repeatedly in those unhappy times, fate intervened. We have already seen how Benjamin Franklin Bache, another prominent newspaper opponent of the Adams administration, had escaped Federalist prosecution for criminal libel by succumbing to yellow fever in the epidemic that swept Philadelphia in the summer of 1798. A few months later, Thomas Greenleaf similarly came down with yellow fever and died before an indictment could be considered. Like Bache, he had been silenced, but by yellow fever, not by the Federalist administration.

When Greenleaf could no longer continue as editor and publisher of the *Argus*, his wife, Ann Greenleaf, replaced him. The *Argus* continued as before, vigorous in its attacks on the administration. Thomas Greenleaf had escaped prosecution, but Ann did not. In August 12, 1799, Secretary of State Pickering wrote to District Attorney Harison to scrutinize the *Argus* for any "audacious calumnies against the government." Harison obtained an indictment against Ann Greenleaf for articles in the *Argus* supporting the right of Americans to erect Liberty Poles, denouncing the Alien and Sedition Act, and accusing the federal government of being corrupt and inimical to the preservation of liberty. However, she, too, then fell ill, and her trial was postponed until April 1800.[155]

With Thomas Greenleaf dead and beyond the range of prosecution and Ann Greenleaf ill, the attack on the *Argus* entered a new stage. David Frothingham, variously described as a journeyman printer, managing editor, and foreman of the *Argus*,[156] assumed responsibility for the paper and continued its publication. At this point, Alexander Hamilton took over the assault on the *Argus*.[157] Outraged by a personal attack, Hamilton pressed the Federalist Attorney General of New York, Josiah Ogden Hoffman, to institute criminal libel proceedings against Frothingham in the New York state courts. As will be reviewed in Chapter 6, Frothingham was speedily tried, convicted, and jailed for four months, fined $100, and required to post a bond for his good behavior.

Like the cases involving the *Adams* brothers in the Massachusetts state courts, the *Frothingham* case in the New York state courts involved parallel litigations that provide an insight into Federalist political power and resolve.

---

[155] Letter, Timothy Pickering to Richard Harison (Aug. 12, 1799), 11 Timothy Pickering Papers 599 (Mass. Hist. Socy.); Letter, Richard Harison to Timothy Pickering (Apr. 10, 1800), 26 Timothy Pickering Papers 78 (Mass. Hist. Soc'y.) *See* J. M. Smith, note 19, at 399–400.

[156] *Compare* Wharton, note 110, at 651 ("journeyman") *with* Schachner, *Jefferson*, note 32, at 468 and Beatrice Diamond, *An Episode in American Journalism: A History of David Frothingham and His Long Island Herald* 50–67 (1964) ("managing editor"). Greenleaf's own *New York Journal and Patriotic Register* described him as "the office foreman."

[157] *See* Wharton, note 110, at 648–651; J. M. Smith, *Hamilton*, note 84, at 305–333.

Whether the fatal blow was delivered under federal law – statutory or common law – or state criminal libel law was immaterial.

With the indictment of Frothingham under New York law, the *Argus* ceased publication, and the proceedings against Ann Greenleaf were brought to an end. At the direction of President Adams, District Attorney Harison filed a plea of *nolle prosequi* in the case against Ann Greenleaf.[158] The prosecutions instituted first against Thomas Greenleaf, then Ann Greenleaf, and finally against Frothingham had borne fruit. Mrs. Greenleaf was forced to sell the *Argus*. She was able to find a Republican, David Denniston, to purchase it. However, Denniston promptly discontinued it and replaced it with the *Republican Watchtower*.[159] This was in the spring of 1800, on the eve of the critical presidential election of 1800 in which New York proved to be a pivotal state.

6. *United States v. William Duane*, Editor of the Philadelphia *Aurora*

After Benjamin Franklin Bache's death from yellow fever in 1798 while awaiting trial for criminal libel under federal criminal common law, William Duane soon married Bache's widow and succeeded him as editor of the Philadelphia *Aurora*. As noted, like Bache, Duane was a highly partisan Jeffersonian journalist given to violent and vituperative prose. Under his direction, the *Aurora* continued in its role for several years as one of the most outspoken Republican newspapers in the country.[160]

Duane's unrestrained attacks on the Federalists made him one of the principal enemies of the administration, which sought to use all the powers of government against him. After passage of the Alien and Sedition Acts in the summer of 1798, Duane became embroiled in continual legal conflicts with the Federalists. For a period in 1799 and the crucial election year 1800, Duane had the remarkable experience of being faced with five separate criminal prosecutions in the federal and Pennsylvania courts under a notable spectrum of legal doctrines. He faced indictments for riot under Pennsylvania criminal common law, criminal libel under the Sedition Act, contempt of the U.S. Senate, and then twice again for criminal libel under the Sedition Act. Indicative of his political adeptness, personal energy and agility, and

---

[158] Letter, Timothy Pickering to Richard Harison (Apr. 22, 1800), 13 Pickering Papers 406 (Mass. Hist. Soc'y.). *See* Rosenfeld, note 25, at 689, 715–716, 719, 752–754.

[159] *See* J. M. Smith, Hamilton, note 84, at 331.

[160] Henry Adams described it as "the leading newspaper in the United States" between 1795 and 1800. See Henry Adams, *History of the United States During the Administrations of Jefferson* 84 (Libr. Am. 1986).

what Elkins and McKitrick characterize as "the almost comic clumsiness, the sheer political ineptitude with which the Federalists went about their work of trying to silence the opposition press,"[161] Duane managed to publish the *Aurora* throughout his travail while avoiding punishment despite these determined efforts to silence him.

The first of the five prosecutions involved the common law crime of riot, gratuitously characterized by Wharton as "seditious riot."[162] Like so many of the most rabid Jeffersonian newspaper critics of President Adams, including John Daly Burk, Thomas Cooper, and James Thomson Callender, Duane, an English resident when young, was accused of being an alien.[163] He was a Catholic, and his religion led to his participation in a political rally that turned into a riot and his indictment and trial for riot.

As Wharton reports the episode, on Sunday morning, February 9, 1799, Duane and three allies – Dr. James Reynolds, Robert Moore, and Samuel Cuming – joined in the churchyard of St. Mary's Catholic Church in Philadelphia. Without the approval of the pastor, they posted signs addressed to "The natives of Ireland, who worship at this church." The parishioners were exhorted to remain in the churchyard after the divine service and to sign their names to a memorial to the Congress calling for the repeal of the Alien Act. Trustees of the church tore down the placards. They were replaced and once again torn down. As persons were signing the petition after the service, someone in the crowd yelled "Turn him out." Dr. Reynolds was pushed and pulled a gun to defend himself. The doctor was knocked down, disarmed, and kicked, and the rally broke up.

The Federalist papers denounced the event as an "United Irish riot." Duane, Reynolds, Moore, and Cuming were promptly arrested and charged

---

[161] *See* Elkins & McKitrick, note 111, at 704.

[162] *See* Wharton, note 110, at 345.

[163] Duane claimed to have been born near Lake Champlain, N.Y. However, in a procedural proceeding on a motion raised in one of the libel actions in which he was involved, Duane was found to be an alien. Hollingsworth v. Duane, 12 F. Cas. 355, 4 U.S. (4 Dall.) 353, 1801 U.S. LEXIS 114 (C.C.D. Pa. 1801) (No. 6614); Hollingsworth v. Duane, 12 F. Cas. 356, 1801 U.S. App. LEXIS 240 (C.C.D. Pa. 1801) (No. 6615); United States v. Duane, 25 F. Cas. 920, 1801 U.S. App. LEXIS 278 (C.C.D. Pa.1801) (No. 14,997). It is undisputed that as a boy he served an apprenticeship in England, was active in India before being expelled by the Governor General, returned to England, became active in radical politics, and ultimately fled to the United States in 1795. *See* Wharton, note 110, at 389–391.

As on other matters, Abigail Adams expressed herself strongly on alien editors. Writing to her sister Mary Cranch, she said: "The greater part of [our *cancelled*] the abuse leveld [*sic*] at the Government is from foreigners. Every Jacobin paper in the United States is Edited by a Foreigner." In an uncharacteristically detached view, she added: "and John Fenno [the prominent Federalist editor] is become a coppiest [*sic*] of them. What a disgrace to the country." Letter, Abigail Adams to Mary Cranch (Nov. 26, 1799), *New Letters*, note 37, at 215–216.

under Pennsylvania common law with assault and riot. Dr. Reynolds was separately charged with intent to kill with a deadly weapon. After trial in the Philadelphia Court of Oyer and Terminer on February 21, 1799, less than two weeks later, all defendants were acquitted on the riot charge after a mere half hour's deliberation. Duane had escaped reprisal.[164] As for Dr. Reynolds and his gun, he was convicted of assault. Seven other participants were indicted for assault, tried after a two-year delay, and ultimately convicted.[165]

Undaunted, Duane continued the assault on the Adams administration. The *Aurora* charged that the administration was under corrupt British influence, implying that Adams's foreign policy had been influenced by British bribes. Secretary of State Pickering, assiduously monitoring the Republican press, noted the charges and referred the matter to Federalist District Attorney William Rawle for prosecution under the Act.[166] In one of the few occasions in which Adams personally interested himself in the enforcement of the Sedition Act, the President expressed his approval of the prosecution.[167] George Washington, who had been previously wounded by attacks in the *Aurora*, similarly approved.[168] Duane was thereupon indicted for violation of the Sedition Act on July 24, 1799, and arraigned in the federal Circuit Court in Philadelphia on August 2, 1799, before Supreme Court Justice Bushrod Washington and District Judge Peters. He was held on $2,000 bail, required to have two others as surety for $1,000 each, and was bound over for trial at the October 1799 Term.[169]

Duane, nevertheless, continued his violent attacks on the Federalists in the *Aurora*. His offensive remarks on the conduct of federal Army officers on the very day of his indictment speedily led to a second indictment under the Sedition Act.[170] At the October trial on the July indictment, Duane's counsel defended by relying on the truth of Duane's allegations, asserting that he had charged nothing that he could not prove. When they attempted to present an authenticated letter from President Adams discussing British influences in the administration, a debate over the admissibility of the document arose. At the same time, three prominent material witnesses – Timothy Pickering,

---

[164] *See* Wharton, note 110, at 344–391; J.M. Smith, note 19, at 165.

[165] *See* Scharff & Westcott, note 27, at 497.

[166] Letters, Timothy Pickering to William Rawle (July 24 and 25, 1799), 11 Pickering Papers 486, 495 (Mass. Hist. Soc'y.). *See* 2 Page Smith, note 40, at 1008.

[167] Letter, John Adams to Timothy Pickering (Aug. 1, 1799), 9 John Adams, *Works* (C. F. Adams), note 43, at 5.

[168] Letter, George Washington to Timothy Pickering (Aug. 4, 1799), 37 Washington, *Writings* 322 (Fitzpatrick ed.).

[169] *See* Rosenfeld, note 25, at 707; Philadelphia *Aurora*, Oct. 22, 1799.

[170] *See* Philadelphia *Aurora*, Aug. 2, 1799 ("These military officers seem to consider themselves above all law but that of their own free will"); Rosenfeld, note 25, at 670; J. M. Smith, note 19, at 285.

James Monroe, and Tench Coxe, as well as a "General Clark of Georgia" – called by the defense failed to be in attendance. The trial was thereupon postponed and ultimately dropped.[171]

Free on bail and awaiting trial under the August indictment, Duane continued to publish the *Aurora* and to attack the Federalists and the conduct of the U.S. Senate. As the country commenced the election of a President during 1800, he seized on the series of prosecutions directed against him as a campaign issue, charging that they represented a Federalist plot to throttle a free press.[172]

At this point, he became involved in a third major legal controversy. With the presidential elections about to proceed,[173] a senior Federalist, Sen. James Ross of Pennsylvania, introduced an extraordinary bill that would have effectively superseded the Electoral College. Under the bill, the Federalist-controlled Congress would have been authorized to establish a "Grand Committee" with jurisdiction to determine the "validity" of the electoral vote being cast in the forthcoming election. The Committee would have possessed the final power to determine which electoral votes to count and which to reject. Three Republican Senators "leaked" a copy of the Ross Bill to Duane, who made it public in the *Aurora*. In his inflammatory commentary, Duane got some of his facts wrong.

Upset at the premature disclosure of the Bill, the Federalist-controlled Senate sought to retaliate. It proposed the establishment of a Committee on Privilege to consider criminal proceedings against Duane for breach of privilege or contempt of the legislature. These doctrines were part of the repressive English law that is discussed at greater length in Chapter 7 along with other doctrines derived from English law under which the institutions of the establishment – the monarchy, the Parliament, the courts, and the established church – could punish their critics. Without a hearing, the Federalist-dominated committee concluded that in making the Ross bill public before it was enacted Duane had committed an illegal breach of the "privilege" of the Senate. It further found that Duane's editorial had contained false, defamatory, scandalous, and malicious assertions intended to bring the Senate into contempt.

---

[171] J. M. Smith, note 19, at 282–88; Elkins & McKitrick, note 111, at 704 n.32. *See also Connecticut Courant*, Oct. 28, 1799.

[172] Philadelphia *Aurora*, Mar. 13 and 17, 1800.

[173] At this time, there was no fixed national election day. Each state determined when and how its electors would be chosen. The process proceeded state by state with the outcome in doubt but Adams leading until the last state, Georgia, chose its four electors. As expected, they were all for Jefferson and provided the narrow margin for his 73 to 66 victory.

Duane was summoned to appear before the Senate to respond to the charges. When he demanded counsel, the Senate acceded, but ruled that his counsel would not be permitted to challenge the Senate's jurisdiction, to call witnesses, or to prove the truth of Duane's statements. Counsel for Duane – Republicans Alexander J. Dallas and Thomas Cooper – refused to serve under the circumstances, and Duane then refused to appear. The Senate held him in contempt and a warrant was issued for his arrest. As President of the Senate, Vice President Jefferson found himself in the awkward position of having to sign the warrant.

Duane then went into hiding for several months, successfully evading service of process until the Congress adjourned, and the warrant became ineffective. Once again, legal proceedings had failed to prevent Duane from continuing to publish the *Aurora*, to continue to attack the administration, and to broadcast the details of the onslaught against him. With all the publicity, the Ross bill did not survive, closing a particularly unsavory episode in the country's political history.[174]

In its frustration, the Senate attacked Duane on still another front. With adjournment looming, the Senate in May 1800 requested President Adams to cause the institution of still another criminal libel action under the Sedition Act. Duane was thereupon indicted for the third time for violation of the Sedition Act on October 17, 1800, for the *Aurora* article on February 19, 1800, about the Ross Bill.[175] However, the Adams administration was in its final months. Although the case was initially set for prompt trial, it was postponed, and then postponed again to the October Term 1801 to permit the attendance of absent witnesses.[176] In the interval, Jefferson became President in March 1801 and ordered the prosecution discontinued.[177] A *nolle prosequi* disposed of the case.

---

[174] Annals, 6th Cong., 1st Sess, 68–69, 104–105, 111–124. *See* Guy Padula, *Madison v. Marshall: Popular Sovereignty, Natural Law, and the United States Constitution* 88–89 nn. 154, 155 (2001); J. M. Smith, note 19, at 289–300.

[175] Philadelphia *Aurora*, Oct. 17, 1800. Duane proclaimed: "Today at the Circuit Court in Philadelphia, I am indicted under the instructions of John Adams for libeling the Senate of the United States." *See* Rosenfeld, note 25, at 869.

[176] As we have seen and will continue to see, a continuance to permit the attendance of absent witnesses almost inevitably resulted in the cases ultimately never going to trial.

[177] *See* Letter, Levi Lincoln to Alexander J. Dallas (Mar. 25, 1801); Letter of Thomas Jefferson to William Duane (May 23, 1801); Letter of Thomas Jefferson to James Monroe (May 26, 1801), 9 Jefferson, *Writings* (Ford), note 13, at 259; Letter, James Madison to Thomas Jefferson, July 17, 1801; Letter, Thomas Jefferson to Edward Livingston (Nov. 1, 1801), *ibid.*, explaining the reasons for the *nolle prosequi* for Duane); Letter, Thomas Jefferson to William Cary Nicholas (June 13, 1809), 11 Jefferson, *Papers* (Oberg), note 54, at 101.

A few months later, Jefferson found it necessary to explain his action. Writing to Albert Gallatin, he expressed his views on the "Senatorial complaint" against Duane:

> My idea of a new prosecution was not that our Attorney shall ever be heard to urge the common law of England as in force otherwise than so far as adopted in any particular State, but that, 1st, he should renew it in the Federal courts if he supposed there was any Congressional statute which provided for the case (other than the Sedition Act) or if he thought he could show that the Senate had made or adopted such a *lex parliamentaria* as might reach the case, or 2d under Pennsylvania statute, or statutory adoption of English common law had made the office punishable.[178]

This concluded a remarkable episode in American history. Duane, assailed by five Federalist criminal prosecutions over a period of two years, managed to escape them all.[179] Equally surprising, notwithstanding Duane's participation in the defense of the five cases, his repeated court appearances, and his enforced life in hiding during much of this period, the *Aurora* continued to publish without missing a day with its bitter attacks on Adams and the Federalists.

Although Duane emerged as a Republican hero for a while, his influence on the national scene soon dwindled. After 1800, when the Jeffersonians had achieved national power, they distanced themselves from Duane and his extreme brand of journalism. A new Washington newspaper, the *National Intelligencer*, organized by Jefferson and Madison, assumed the place previously occupied by Duane and the *Aurora*. With Jefferson's election, Duane had wanted to move to Washington and publish from the new Capital. As noted, when he turned to the new administration for financial support in the form of governmental printing contracts, he was rebuffed by Madison and Gallatin. The bulk of the lucrative contracts went to the *National Intelligencer* and its handpicked editor, Samuel Harrison Smith. Although some minor patronage scraps did go to Duane, they proved insufficient to enable him to maintain a Washington base.[180] He remained in Pennsylvania and

---

[178] Letter, Thomas Jefferson to Albert Gallatin (Nov. 12, 1801), Jefferson, *Writings* (Ford), note 13, at 57.

[179] Duane's agility in avoiding legal sanctions is further illustrated by Pasley's reports that he managed to continue publishing throughout his career notwithstanding dozens of suits for libel and numerous judgments totalling thousand of dollars. *See* Pasley, note 22, at 278.

[180] *See* Frank Mott, *Jefferson and the Press* 47–48 (1943) (hereinafter Mott); Nobel E. Cunningham, *The Jeffersonian Republicans: The Foundation of Party Organization, 1789–1801*, 260 (1957); Henry Adams, 1 *History of the United States During the First Administration of Thomas Jefferson* 160 (Libr. Am. 1986).

thereafter largely confined himself to Republican state affairs. Allied with the radical Republican faction headed by Dr. Michael Leib, Duane bitterly fought Governor Thomas McKean, Alexander J. Dallas, and Albert Gallatin for control of the Pennsylvania Republican Party. By 1808, Duane and Leib triumphed and assumed control of the party. They elected their candidate, Samuel Snyder, as Governor, replacing McKean and driving him into enforced retirement. By this time, Gallatin had moved onto the national scene. He became Secretary of the Treasury in the Jefferson and Madison administrations, one of the most able Treasury Secretaries in the history of the nation.

7. *United States v. Thomas Cooper*, Editor of the *Sunsbury and Northumberland Gazette*

In April 1800, still another leading Republican editor, Thomas Cooper, editor of the *Sunsbury and Northumberland Gazette,* was indicted for violation of the Sedition Act.[181] Cooper was a man for all seasons who led a remarkably diversified life. At one time or another, he was a chemist, a lawyer, a judge, and a physician before concluding his career as a college president. He was a person of outspoken views. Like so many of the Republican editors who ran afoul of the Federalists, Cooper was an English émigré run out of England for his political writings.[182]

He was also a political turncoat. With the support of his close friend, the renowned English chemist Dr. Joseph Priestly, a friend of Adams, Cooper applied to President Adams for a federal job. He sought appointment as an American representative on the British Claims Commission, evaluating American claims under the provisions of the Jay Treaty. Only when Adams passed over him did he became a political enemy. In his newspaper, the *Sunsbury and Northumberland Gazette,* and in pamphlets, he thereafter repeatedly attacked Adams and his administration. On June 29, 1799, in the *Gazette,* he attacked Adams's arrogance, "seizure" of the treaty-making power, and the Alien and Sedition Acts. Secretary of State Pickering passed this information along to President Adams. Adams was incensed, replying to Pickering in heated terms: "A meaner, a more artful, or a more malicious libel [has not

---

[181] United States v. Thomas Cooper, 25 F. Cas. 631, 1800 U.S. App. LEXIS 56 (C.C.D. Pa. 1800) (No. 14,865); Thomas Cooper, *An Account of the Trial of Thomas Cooper, of Northumberland on a Charge of Libel against the President of the United States* (1830); Wharton, note 110, at 659–681; J. M. Smith, note 19, at 307–333.

[182] See Dumas Malone, The Public Life of Thomas Cooper, 1783–1839 (1961).

appeared].... As far as it alludes to me, I despise it, but I have no doubt it isn't a libel against the whole government, and as such ought to be prosecuted."[183]

This was an unusual outburst on Adams's part. He personally approved only one other prosecution under the Sedition Act – the prosecution of Duane – while distancing himself from the others. Nevertheless, no action was taken against Cooper. Then, in November 1799, Cooper issued a handbill, defending his application to Adams for appointment and continuing his attacks on him. This, too, was forwarded to Adams. Still no action was taken against Cooper. With Cooper continuing to inveigh against Adams. Abigail Adams, writing again to her sister Mary Cranch, condemned Cooper for his "Mad, democratic Stile [sic]," noting that he had again "abused the President, and I presume subjected himself to the penalty of the Sedition act."

Shortly thereafter, Cooper appeared as counsel for William Duane in the U.S. Senate proceedings to punish Duane for "breach of privilege," and, as we have seen, he had written an unyielding letter about the Senate's limitations on the conduct of the hearing that had led him and his co-counsel to withdraw. In a highly critical review of the conduct of Duane and his counsel, the Federalist *National Gazette* called for even "severer" action against Cooper.[184] The Federalist District Attorney, William Rawle, finally acted. On April 11, 1800, he secured the indictment of Cooper, "a person of wicked and turbulent disposition," for criminal libel under the Act, citing the contents of his November 1799 handbill. Cooper was charged with tending to "incite insurrection against the government" and for having published a "false, scandalous and malicious libel upon the President of the United States, with intent to bring him into contempt and disrepute, and to excite against him the hatred of the good people of the United States." The indictment further cited Cooper's charges that the President was capable of making mistakes, that he had maintained a standing Army and Navy, established expensive embassies in European countries, caused the government to borrow at the usurious interest rate of 8 percent on government loans, and had employed violent expressions against France.[185]

Cooper came to trial in April 1800 in the Circuit Court in Philadelphia before Supreme Court Justice Samuel Chase and District Judge Richard Peters. He appeared without counsel, denied the charge, and pleaded truth as a defense. He sought to subpoena President Adams, Secretary of State

[183] *See* J. M. Smith, note 19, at 311. *See also* 9 John Adams, *Works* (C. F. Adams), note 43, at 5–7.
[184] Philadelphia *Gazette*, Mar. 27, 1800; *see* J. M. Smith, note 19, at 316.
[185] *See* Wharton, note 110, at 658–681.

Pickering, and other witnesses to prove the truth of his charges. But Chase was at his intemperate worst. In what Wharton reports was a "rage," Chase angrily refused to issue the writ. It is of note that a few years later in the tempestuous treason trial of Aaron Burr, Chief Marshall was bitterly criticized by the Jeffersonians for approving the issuance of such a subpoena upon President Jefferson.[186]

In his instructions to the jury, Justice Chase properly noted the need for the prosecution to establish both proof of the publication of the alleged libel and that Cooper had acted maliciously with bad intent. However, Chase then added that by showing his handbill to a Justice of the Peace, Cooper had evidenced a "bad intent . . . to dare and defy the government." As for the implications of Cooper's charge about Adams and the establishment of a standing Army, Chase explained, "There is no subject on which the people of American feel alarm, than the establishment of a standing army." He then went so far as to comment that in the publication cited in the indictment, Cooper " intended to mislead the ignorant and inflame their minds against the President, and . . . influence their votes in the next election." Further, he described the publication as "the boldest attempt I have known to poison the mind of the people."[187] Cooper was convicted and received one of the heavier sentences imposed under the Act. He was sentenced to prison for six months, fined $400, and required to post a $1,000 bond for himself with two sureties for $500 each to assure his good behavior.

Surprisingly in view of his earlier vehement approval of the prosecution, President Adams, who had refused to intervene in any other criminal libel case except that of *Durrell*, later offered Cooper a pardon. Cooper refused because it would not be accompanied by an apology for the prosecution.[188] Forty years later, as in the case of Representative Matthew Lyon and editor Anthony Haswell, the Congress finally authorized repayment of his fine with interest.[189]

A final note about Cooper: The climactic stage of the 1800 election campaign saw an entertaining development. Alexander Hamilton, the leading Federalist in the crucial state of New York and one of the most prominent Federalists in the country, bitterly attacked President Adams, the Federalist

---

[186] For Jefferson's hostile attitude toward the subpoena, *see* Letter, Thomas Jefferson to George Hay (June 20, 1807), Jefferson, *Writings* (Libr. Am.), note 26, at 1179.
[187] *See* Wharton, note 110, at 670–677.
[188] *See* Goebel, note 109, at 640.
[189] 26th Cong., 1st Sess., H.R. Doc. 86. *See* Wharton, note 110, at 679.

presidential candidate.[190] Blinded by his antipathy for Adams and preferring Jefferson to Adams,[191] Hamilton urged Federalist electors to desert Adams and instead cast their ballots for President for Charles C. Pinckney, the Federalist candidate for Vice President. With the New York Federalists in such schismatic disarray, Jefferson, then running behind Adams in the Electoral College vote, carried New York and gained the margin ultimately required to secure the presidency. Cooper seized upon Hamilton's invective and, using the Federalist model as his guide, tongue in cheek urged Hamilton's indictment under the Sedition Act. This was political theater at its best.[192]

Cooper remained in public life. After serving on the bench in Pennsylvania from 1804 to 1811, he moved to South Carolina, where he became a leader in the states' rights movement, as well as serving as President of South Carolina College.[193]

8. *United States v. James Thomson Callender*, Polemicist

Cooper's indictment, trial, and conviction was followed the next month by the indictment and trial of still another leading Republican critic of the administration, James Thomson Callender.[194] Callender, perhaps the most violent and vituperative journalist of the time, was the author of a series of unrestrained polemics attacking Washington, Adams, and the Federalists generally.[195]

---

[190] Alexander Hamilton, The Public Conduct and Character of John Adams, Esq. President of the United States," Alexander Hamilton, *Writings*, 934–971 (Oct. 24, 1800) (Libr. Am. 2001) (hereinafter Hamilton, *Writings* (Libr. Am.)).

[191] *See* Letter, Alexander Hamilton to Theodore Sedgwick (May 10, 1800), Alexander Hamilton, *Writings* (Libr. Am.), note 190, at 925–926 (He is "a very *unfit* and *incapable* character. . . . I will never more be responsible for him by my direct support – even if though the consequence should be the election of *Jefferson*.")

[192] *See* Dumas Malone, The Threatened Prosecution of Alexander Hamilton under the Sedition Act by Thomas Cooper, 29 Am. Hist. Rev. 76–81 (Oct. 1923); J. M. Smith, *Hamilton*, note 84, at 305, 319.

[193] See William W. Freehling, *Prelude to Civil War: The Nullification Controversy in South Carolina 1816–1836*, 128–130 (1966).

[194] 25 F. Cas. 239 (C.C.D. Va. 1800) (No. 14,709). *See generally* Wharton, note 110, at 688–721; J. M. Smith, note 19, at 334–358; Goebel, note 109, at 641; Katherine Preyer, U.S. v. Callender, Judge and Jury in a Republican Society, in *Origins of the Federal Judiciary: Essays on the Judiciary Act of 1789*, 173 (Maeva Marcus ed. 1992); Rosenfeld, note 25, at 737, 799–800, 804–805, 810; 3 Beveridge, note 91, at 36–41.

[195] Throughout Callender's career, Jefferson made repeatedly financial contributions to Callender, a circumstance that Jefferson's admirers, like Jefferson himself, have been hard-pressed to justify. Jefferson defended the payments as "charities." Letter, Thomas Jefferson to Abigail Adams (July 22, 1804) (repeatedly using the terms "charities" and "contributions"), Jefferson, *Writings* (Ford), note 13, at 42.

Like three other outspoken Republican spokesmen prosecuted under the Sedition Act – John Daly Burk, William Duane, and Thomas Cooper – Callender was an English political refugee. He had the distinction of having been convicted of criminal libel in England before his flight to America. In his *History of the United States for 1796*, he accused Alexander Hamilton of corrupt financial dealings and uncovered some of his intimate personal affairs. By 1798, Callender had moved to the Philadelphia *Aurora*, where he assisted Bache and Duane in their work. Callender became a citizen to avoid the Alien Act. When Bache was arrested, Callender moved south to Virginia, which proved a congenial location with its strong local opposition to the Sedition Act. After a brief hiatus on arriving in Richmond, Callender joined the staff of the Richmond *Examiner* and resumed his attacks on the Federalists. His outpourings soon caused Secretary of State Pickering to instruct Richmond District Attorney Thomas Nelson to examine every issue of the *Examiner* for Callender's seditious material.[196]

At this time, Callender published his pamphlet *The Prospect Before Us*, an unrestrained pro-Jefferson election piece. There can be no question that it was published with Jefferson's support. In his letter to Callender of October 6, 1798, Jefferson made plain that he had read and approved the proofs, saying "such papers cannot fail to produce the best effect."[197]

Attacking without any bounds, Callender denounced Adams and his administration as "a tempest of malignant passions," his system had been "a French war, an American Navy, a large standing Army, an additional load of taxes and all the other symptoms of debt and despotism," his "reign . . . has hitherto been one continued tempest." Adams was a "professed aristocrat and he had proved faithful and serviceable to the British interest." By sending Marshall and his associates to France, "Adams and his British faction designed to do nothing but mischief." This "hoary headed incendiary . . . bawls out

For an unsympathetic account of the relationship *see* Worthington C. Ford, *Jefferson and Callender* (1897). As we will see, their relationship came to an end when Jefferson became President and rebuffed Callender in his aspirations for appointment as Postmaster of Richmond. Callender then turned on Jefferson and took after him as viciously as he had earlier pursued Washington and Adams.

[196] *See* J. M. Smith, note 19, at 338–341.

[197] *See* Letter, Thomas Jefferson to James T. Callender (Oct. 6, 1799), Jefferson, *Writings* (Lipscomb), note 12, at 10. *See also* Letter, Thomas Jefferson to James T. Callender (Sept. 6, 1799), 9 Jefferson, *Writings* (Ford), note 13, at 81–82; Letter, Timothy Pickering to Stephen Higginson (Jan. 6, 1804), Pickering Papers (Mass. Hist. Soc'y).

    It is of interest that the co-publisher of *The Prospect Before Us* was none other than James Lyon, son of Rep. Matthew Lyon, one of the first Republican critics to be prosecuted and convicted under the Sedition Act. The press accounts of the time report that James Lyon himself had also been indicted under the Act; however, judicial confirmation is lacking. *See* text accompanying Ch. 4, notes 245–250.

to arms! the call to arms." Callender referred to the "scene of profligacy and usury" accompanied by the "grossness of [Adams's] prejudice" and "the violence of his passions."[198]

According to Sen. Beveridge and Clyde Anderson,[199] the *Callender* case has the distinction of having been instituted by Justice Chase himself, rather than by Secretary of State Pickering as had occurred in so many other cases of moment. En route to Richmond fresh from presiding over the conviction of Cooper in Philadelphia, Chase met the prominent Maryland lawyer Luther Martin,[200] who presented him with a copy of Callender's pamphlet, "with the offensive pages underscored."

After reading the pamphlet, Justice Chase continued on to Richmond. Shortly thereafter, Callender was indicted on May 24, 1800, by the Richmond grand jury for violation of the Sedition Act[201] and arrested shortly. Jefferson rushed to Callender's support. Within two days, he wrote to James Monroe: "I think it essentially just and necessary that Callender should be substantially defended." Jefferson then went on to make the extraordinary suggestion that the financing of the defense should be presented to the Virginia Legislature so that it could decide whether this was best accomplished "by publick interference or proviate contribution."[202]

Callender was indicted on May 24, 1800, and confronted by 23 counts, each consisting of a passage from the pamphlet. Trial commenced four days later in

---

[198] Callender's subsequent indictment cites these passages as violations of the Act.

[199] *See* Beveridge, note 91, at 37; Anderson, note 16, at 119–120.

In fact, of the 15 confirmed cases, about half arose locally. These included the cases of the three Newark drunks – Baldwin, Clark, and Lespenard – Callender, the Dedham Liberty Pole enthusiasts – Brown and Fairbanks – Peck, and Shaw. The balance all stemmed from Washington.

[200] Luther Martin, Attorney General of Maryland for 30 years, was widely acknowledged as being one of the great advocates of the period, serving as Attorney General of Maryland for about two decades and as chief counsel for Aaron Burr in the celebrated treason trial. *See* 3 Beveridge, note 91, at 186n.

He was also an alcoholic. Beveridge reports that this formidable leader of the American bar was the "heaviest drinker of that period of heavy drinking." Brodie describes him as "coarse, vituperative, and frequently drunk." She added that he habitually was sipping brandy from a flask during his court appearances. *See* Fawn Brodie, *Thomas Jefferson: An Intimate History* 409 (1974) (hereinafter Brodie).

[201] Although Chase's Richmond efforts to cause the indictment of Callender were successful, he was unsuccessful in his efforts to obtain indictment of Republican editors while on circuit in New Castle, Del. and Baltimore. Baltimore *American*, June 4, 1800, reprinted in the Charleston *City Gazette and General Advertiser*, June 20, 1800. *See* Anderson, note 16, at 120; 3 Beveridge, note 91, at 37, 41.

The Philadelphia *Aurora* published a report from an unidentified contributor that addressing the New Castle, Del., grand jury, Justic Chase expressed surprise that they had voted no indictments and ordered the prosecutor and jury "to go in search of sedition and report tomorrow." Philadelphia *Aurora*, June 28, 1800.

[202] Letter, Thomas Jefferson to James Monroe (May 26, 1800), 31 Jefferson, *Papers* (Oberg), note 54, at 590. *See* Mott, note 180, at 32.

the Circuit Court in Richmond before Justice Chase and District Judge Cyrus Griffin.[203] The case was unique. It was the only Sedition Act prosecution of a Southern journalist and the only case to be heard in a Southern federal court. As with so many other Sedition Act cases, there were charges that the Callender jury was composed solely of Federalists. Indeed, Miller asserts flatly: "it can be proved positively that the trial jury was Federalist to the man."[204] Callender's counsel requested a continuance to permit the attendance of material witnesses and documents deemed material. Justice Chase, however, imperiously insisted that there was no justification of a delay because all publishers of libels should have the documents on hand to prove the truth of their assertions, if required. He grudgingly granted a postponement for five days, subsequently generously adding one additional day.

Callender was defended by three young lawyers, each of whom soon achieved prominence: William Wirt (later Attorney General from 1817 to 1829 under Presidents James Monroe and John Quincy Adams and unsuccessful candidate for President in 1832), George Hay (later co-counsel for Aaron Burr in the *Burr* treason trial), and Philip Nicholas (later Attorney General of Virginia.)

Justice Chase gave the defense counsel little opportunity to present whatever case they had. When, for example, the defense called a distinguished Virginian and former U.S. Senator, Col. John Taylor, to offer evidence of the truth of some of Callender's numerous charges about Adams and his administration, Chase refused to allow him to testify. As Justice Paterson had ruled in the *Haswell* case, Chase ruled out Col. Taylor's proffered testimony

---

[203] United States v. Callender, 25 F. Cas. 239, 1800 U.S. App. LEXIS 58 (C.C.D. Va. 1800) (No. 14,709).

[204] *See* Miller, note 4, at 423. After the *Callender* trial, there were further Republican charges that the jury had been "packed." Finally, there was some testimony to that effect at the Chase impeachment trial.

John Heath, a Richmond attorney, testified at the Chase impeachment proceedings that in his presence, Chase had asked the U.S. Marshal, David M. Randolph, "if he had any of those creatures or people called democrats on the panel of the jury to try Callender" and that when the Marshal replied that he had "made no discrimination," Chase told him "to look over the panel and if there were any of that description, strike them off."

However, William Marshall (John Marshall's brother, who was then clerk of the District Court) testified that Chase told him that he hoped even Giles [a prominent Virginian Republican Congressman] would serve on the jury – "Nay, he wished that Callender be tried by a jury of his own politics." Randolph testified that he had never seen Heath in the judge's chambers, that Chase "never at any time or any place" said anything to him about striking names from the jury panel, and that he never received "any instructions, verbal, or by letter, from Judge Chase in relation to the grand jury." *See* Annals, 8th Cong. 2d Sess. 251–262; Chase Impeachment Trial 65–69. Beveridge subsequently concluded that Heath's account was "entirely false." *See* 3 Beveridge, note 91, at 191–192; J. M. Smith, note 19, at 348n.

as inadmissible, holding that no evidence was inadmissible that did not prove the entire charge. District Judge Cyrus Griffin agreed.[205] In addition, Chase interrupted Callender's counsel to deny that the charges in the indictments were merely opinions and not facts falsely stated.

At this point, the proceedings took a dramatic turn. One of the defense counsel, William Wirt, had intended to make the unconstitutionality of the Act and the power of the jury to decide for itself whether or not the Act was constitutional the central features of the defense. He chose to do so, although, as we have seen, Justice Paterson and District Judge Hitchcock in the *Lyon* case had previously ruled against this very contention. However, Justice Chase would have none of it. He interrupted Wirt and directed him to sit down, summarily rejecting his contention that the issue of unconstitutionality was for the jury. Chase then "read part of a long opinion" in support of his ruling.[206] When Wirt attempted to continue to argue the issue, Chase again interrupted him, terming his argument a "non sequitur." At this point, Wirt gave up.

Nicholas also unsuccessfully sought to argue the same point. He was followed by Hay, but Chase stopped him as well and restated his opinion of the law. "Mr. Hay folded up and put away his papers," seeming to decline any further argument. When Chase urged him to continue, assuring him that he would not be interrupted further, Hay refused to proceed.[207] Throughout the trial, Chase was brutally contemptuous of the defense lawyers, repeatedly interrupting them and sneering at them as "young gentlemen."[208] As noted, this led to their refusal to participate further with the case, much like the defense counsel appearing before Justice Chase in the *Fries* case a few months before.

In his charge, Justice Chase condemned the suggestion that the jury had the power to determine the constitutionality of a statute "as not only new, but very absurd and dangerous, in direct opposition to, and a breach of the Constitution." He concluded with the pious statement that it was his duty

---

[205] As noted, in the Chase impeachment proceedings, Chief Justice John Marshall testified that he had, never, except in the *Callender* trial, heard a court refuse to receive testimony because it went to only a part, not the whole of a charge. However, as we have seen, it had escaped Marshall's attention that in the *Lyon* case, Justice Paterson had ruled the same as Chase.

[206] *See* Wharton, note 110, at 700.

[207] *See ibid.*, at 712.

Hay subsequently published his views on freedom of speech in two carefully argued, well-received essays published under the pseudonym Hortensius, *An Essay on the Liberty of the Press* (1799), *An Essay on the Liberty of the Press* (1803 repr.).

[208] *See* Wharton, note 110, at 708.

to "execute the laws of the United States with justice and impartiality, with firmness and decision."[209]

The trial had lasted only part of one brief and stormy day. The case then went to the jury, who returned a verdict of guilty in two hours. The Court immediately sentenced Callender to nine months in jail and a $200 fine, and required him to post a $1,200 bond of good behavior for two years. According to James Morton Smith, Chase expressed his satisfaction with the conviction because it "shewed [sic] that the laws of the United States could be enforced in Virginia, the principal object of this prosecution."[210] Callender remained in prison until the statute expired.

Justice Chase's conduct of the case with only five days elapsing between indictment and conviction and the matter heard and determined in less than a single day outraged Jefferson and his supporters. A report of the trial was printed and distributed in pamphlet form, and in Fawn Brodie's words became a "national sensation."[211] Wharton similarly concludes: "The tempest which this trial excited can now hardly be understood. . . . Virginia was in a flame."[212]

Jefferson's association with Callender soon backfired. After Jefferson became President, he not only promptly pardoned Callender and all others convicted under the Act, but sought to arrange for remission of Callender's fine. When this met with some delay, Callender complained to Jefferson, who received him at the White House. As we have seen, Callender sought his reward, seeking money and a federal appointment. Jefferson rebuffed him while giving him $50. Jefferson then deemed it wise to sever the relationship. Writing to James Monroe, Jefferson commented that Callender's "scurrilities" have begun "evidently to do mischief. As to myself, no man wished more to see his pen stopped, but [seeking to explain the $50 payment] I considered him still a proper object for benevolence."[213]

Relations cooling, Callender soon became an implacable enemy of Jefferson and sought not merely to blacken, but to destroy, his standing by smearing his reputation indelibly.[214] Referring to her as "sooty Sal,"

---

[209] Ibid., at 718.

[210] Richmond Examiner, June 6, 1790; Albany Register, June 17, 1800. See J. M. Smith, note 19, at 356.

[211] Brodie, Jefferson, note 200, at 322.

[212] See Wharton, note 110, at 718n.

[213] Letter, Thomas Jefferson to James Monroe (July 15, 1802), 9 Jefferson, Writings (Ford), note 13, at 387.

[214] See 2 Page Smith, note 40, at 49.

Callender so effectively exposed Jefferson's alleged liaison with his domestic slave Sally Hemings that it has reverberated to the present day.

After the dust on the 1800 Election had thoroughly settled, Abigail Adams and Jefferson maintained a prolific correspondence. Writing in 1804, Abigail Adams scolded Jefferson over his pardon of Callender. She noted that he had been convicted for "his crimes for writing and publishing the basest libel, the lowest and vilest Slander, which malice could invent, or calumny exhibit against the Character and reputation of your predecessor." In reply, Jefferson defended his support of his payment to Callender as "charities," not "rewards for calumnies" as Abigail Adams had suggested. He added:

> My charities to him were no more meant as encouragement to his scurrilities, than those I gave to the beggar at my door, are meant as rewards for the vices of his life.... With respect to the calumnies of writers and printers at large, published against Mr. Adams, I was as far as stooping to any concern or probation of them as Mr. Adams was respecting those of Porcupine, Fenno, or Russell, who published volumes against me for every sentence rendered against their opponents against Mr. Adams.[215]

For Justice Chase, the reverberations of the case did not cease. In 1805 he was impeached and tried before the Senate. Among the charges on which the impeachment was based, there were no fewer than five that attacked aspects of his conduct in the *Callender* case. Although some of these attracted only limited support, two charges – his misconduct in refusing to allow Col. John Taylor to testify and his "rude, contemptuous, and indecent conduct during the trial" – were approved by a vote of 18 to 16, but failed of adoption, lacking the necessary two-thirds vote.[216]

9. *United States v. William Durrell*, Editor of the Mt. Pleasant *Register*

During June 1798, the Republican editor of a small rural newspaper in upstate New York, William Durrell of the Mt. Pleasant *Register*, republished a highly critical account of President Adams that had appeared in another rural newspaper, the New Windsor *Gazette*. As happened so often during this period,

---

[215] *Compare* Letter, Abigail Adams to Thomas Jefferson, (July 1, 1804), 1 *The Adams-Jefferson Letters: The Complete Correspondence between Thomas Jefferson and John and Abigail Adams* 273 (Lester Cappon ed. 1959) *with* Letter, Thomas Jefferson to Abigail Adams (July 22, 1804) 8 Jefferson, *Writings* (Ford), note 13, at 306–308. For a further attempt by Jefferson to explain his support of Callender over the years, *see* Letter, Thomas Jefferson to James Monroe (July 15, 1802), 10 *Jefferson* (Lipscomb), note 12, at 331–332.

[216] *See* Wharton, note 110, at 719.

Secretary of State Pickering noted the entry in his readings of the Republican press. Forwarding the *Register* to District Attorney Harison on June 28, 1798, Pickering advised Harison to prosecute the editors of both the *Register* and the *Gazette* if he determined that the matter was libelous. This was some weeks before the July 14, 1798, enactment of the Sedition Act.

On July 17, 1798, three days after the enactment of the Sedition Act, Durrell was arrested and indicted for libeling Adams in the *Register* by republishing the account in the *Gazette*. He was released on posting a $2,000 bond to assure good behavior with two additional sureties for $1,000 each. Durrell ceased publication immediately, apparently for fear of inadvertently forfeiting the bond. The indictment and copies of the news item for which Durrell had been arrested are unavailable.

After a year's delay, the judicial processes began to move. On September 5, 1799, Durrell pleaded not guilty before the U.S. Circuit Court in New York. Harison requested postponement of the trial, and Durrell was released until the next term of the Circuit Court upon posting a reduced bond of $3,000. Procuring the bond reduced Durrell to poverty, and his real and personal property were foreclosed. In the spring of 1800, almost two years after his arrest, Durrell was finally tried before Justice Bushrod Washington and District Judge John Sloss Hobart.

Without any testimony presented by the defense, Justice Washington delivered his charge to the jury, and it returned a verdict of guilty. Durrell made a plea for clemency, claiming ignorance that reprinting was a criminal offense and stressed his poverty and his concern for his family's welfare. He was sentenced to four months imprisonment and a $50 fine, and was required to remain in prison until the fine was paid. In addition, Durrell was required to post a $2,000 bond to assure his good behavior for two years. It is of interest that no prosecution was ever brought against the New Windsor *Gazette* in which the offending story had first appeared.[217]

The Court recommended executive clemency, urging remission of the sentence except for the bond. Joining in the recommendation, Harison noted that Durrell was a very poor man, had discontinued the paper, had expressed regret, and had not been the original source of the libel.[218] President Adams accepted the recommendation and pardoned Durrell, except for the bond.[219]

---

[217] United States v. William Durrell, Minute Book, 1790–1808, (C.C.D. N.Y 1799) 176, RG 21 (National Archives). *See* J. M. Smith, note 19, at 388 (1953); Rosenfeld, note 25, at 193, 690, 768, 781.

[218] *See* J. M. Smith, note 19, at 389.

[219] *See* Letter, Timothy Pickering to Richard Harison (Apr. 22, 1800), 13 Pickering Papers 406 (Mass. Hist. Soc'y.).

This was the only pardon issued by Adams of the dozen persons convicted for criminal libel during his administration.

The *Durrell* case is puzzling on a number of levels. First, it is not clear whether this prosecution was brought under the Sedition Act or in reliance on federal criminal common-law jurisdiction. The case is not reported, and the available records do not contain copies of the indictment or records of the proceedings. As James Morton Smith notes, Durrell was indicted after the adoption of the Act for acts committed *prior to* the Act. Because indictment under the Act would have been unconstitutional under the *ex post facto* clause, it seems likely that Durrell was tried at common law. If so, *Durrell* would be the sixth of the series of cases making up the substantial body of federal common-law criminal libel actions of the period.[220] The others include the 1797 *Greenleaf* conviction for libel of the British Minister, the *Cabell* case, and the *Bache, Burk,* and *Smith* cases on the eve of passage of the Sedition Act.

Second, it is far from clear why the enormous might of federal power was directed at such a minor publisher. After all, Durrell was a relatively obscure figure editing an obscure rural newspaper of limited influence. Third, the cause of the indictment – that Durrell had republished a report first appearing in another newspaper that was not prosecuted – seems tame compared to the vituperative statements giving rise to most of the other criminal libel cases of the period. Why, then, did such a relatively innocuous republication by a far from prominent Republican editor lead to his indictment? No answer appears to be available.

This concludes the review of the nine partisan prosecutions under the Act directed at the Republican press. These prosecutions represented an immediate, but only a short-term, success for the Federalists. At a critical period before the 1800 presidential election, they had succeeded in shutting down temporarily or permanently four leading Republican newspapers in New York City, Boston, and New London. These included the New York *Time Piece* and the New York *Argus,* the Boston *Independent Chronicle,* and the New London *Bee.*

The Federalist partisan use of the Sedition Act and federal criminal common-law jurisdiction to silence criticism in the Republican press, if not the newspapers themselves, constituted the great majority of the prosecutions. However, there were other prosecutions that did not involve the Republican

---

[220] James Morton Smith provides the most detailed account of the *Durrell* case. *See* J. M. Smith, note 19, at 385–90.

press. These included not only the prosecution of the three Newark drunks already discussed, but at least four additional prosecutions of Republicans of little prominence for reasons that are far from clear. These cases are relatively few in number and episodic, and lack the indicia of the coordinated campaign that seems so evident in the numerous cases against the editors of the Republican press. Although these additional targets were all Republican activists, there is no indication why these particular individuals were singled out for prosecution and who was responsible. Much is known about three of these cases: the successful prosecution of two Massachusetts Republican activists – David Brown and Benjamin Fairbanks – and the abortive prosecution of Jedidiah Peck, a New York legislator. Unlike so many other cases, these three cases are reasonably well reported. Virtually nothing is known about the fourth case other than the bare facts of the indictment and acquittal of a man known to history as Dr. Shaw of Castleton, Vt.

G. Three Cases Involving Republican Activists

1. *United States v. David Brown; United States v. Benjamin Fairbanks*, the Dedham, Mass., Liberty Pole Activists

David Brown and Benjamin Fairbanks were staunch Republicans in Federalist Dedham, Mass., who found themselves indicted under the Sedition Act[221] for following the Revolutionary War practice of the erection of Liberty Poles to symbolize the democratic struggle for both freedom of speech and for independence. As we have seen, by the time of the Adams administration, Federalists for their part looked at the latter day Liberty Poles as "emblems of sedition" and as "a rallying point of insurrection and civil war,"[222] while

---

[221] Charles Warren and J. M. Smith provide the fullest accounts of the Brown and Fairbanks episode. *See* Warren, *Junto*, note 15, at 103–112; J. M. Smith, note 19, at 257–270.

[222] *See* Warren, *Junto*, note 15, at 103–105. Although the Dedham, Mass., Liberty Pole incident is the only one that led to litigation under the Sedition Act, there were numerous other instances of Republicans erecting Poles and provoking violent reaction from Federalists. Such confrontations occurred during this period in Reading, Pa., Newburgh, N.Y., Blockley, Pa., and Wallingford, Vt. *See* Bell, note 126, at 9; Rosenfeld, note 25, at 199, 579–580, 615–616, 620–621. The Liberty Pole erected in Wallingford, Vt., was in protest against the Federalist-sponsored Stamp Tax. It was seen as a result of the poison of Lyon's efforts. *See* William A. Robinson, *Jeffersonian Democracy in New England* 21 (1916); *United States Chronicle*, Apr. 25, 1799; Columbia *Centinel*, Jan. 24, 1798; *Federal Gazette* and Baltimore *Advertiser*, Jan. 1789; Hartford *American Mercury*, Jan. 29, 1798 ("Many high words past but no killing, wrongdoing or fighting, as has been reported"). However, the Pole was cut down "burnt...and the ashes scattered to the wind." Other Poles were reported in New York, some with the inscription *Liberty or Death*, no Stamp Act Duties. Republicans erected still other poles in upstate New York. *See* J. M. Smith, note 19, at 398–399.

to the Republicans they were symbols of free speech. Of course, during the Revolution, they had been symbols of both.

As we have seen, encouragement of the erection of Liberty Poles had been part of the complaints against Thomas Adams and Ann Greenleaf. Still earlier, at the time of the Whiskey Rebellion, a Justice of the Peace had been ordered to show cause why an information for a misdemeanor for malfeasance of office for not actively assisting in suppressing a riot over a Liberty Pole. The Court explained:

> The setting up of a pole at any time, in a tumultuous manner, with arms, is a riot; but such an erection, when the army were known to have been on their march in support of the constitution and the laws, could only be attributed to an avowed design of giving aid to the insurgents, and intimidating the executives of government.[223]

Led by David Brown, an itinerant Republican activist stumping Massachusetts "inveighing" against the Sedition Act,[224] Dedham Republicans erected a Liberty Pole in October 1798. The Dedham Pole called for:

> . . .
> No Stamp Tax, No Sedition, No Alien Bills, No Land Tax
> Downfall to the Tyrants of America
> Peace and Retirement to the President
> Long Live the Vice President and the Minority
> May Moral Virtue be the Basis of Civil Government[225]

The Federalist governmental machinery went into action. A federal marshal promptly obtained an order from District Judge Lowell "to demolish the . . . symbol of sedition." Before the marshal could do so, however, local Federalists cut the Pole down.

A hunt for those responsible for the construction of the Pole commenced. Brown, the leader, fled the area. However, Benjamin Fairbanks, one of those involved in the erection of the pole, was promptly arrested on November 6, 1798, and charged with "being an accessory in erecting this rallying point of insurrection and civil war." He was bound over for trial for violation of the Sedition Act at the June 1799 Term of the US. Circuit Court in Boston. Fairbanks, a man of means, was able to raise his $4,000 bail and escaped confinement before trial.

---

[223] Respublica v. Daniel Montgomery, 1 Yeates 419, 422, 1795 LEXIS 5 *4 (1795).
[224] See 3 Doc. Hist. Sup. Ct., note 6, at 320.
[225] Boston *Independent Chronicle*, Nov. 12, 1798. See J. M. Smith, note 19, at 260.

Brown managed to escape arrest for several months, but was at last apprehended in March 1799, with "seditious" publications in his possession. Brown, a poor man, was unable to post the $4,000 bail required and remained in jail. The two defendants were very different people. Brown, a Revolutionary War veteran, has been described as a common laborer with little schooling and little money, who toured Massachusetts speaking on politics. Benjamin Fairbanks, a supporter, was a wealthy farmer, a former Selectman, and a devoted Republican.[226]

Trial took place at the June 1799 Term of the U.S. Circuit Court in Boston before Supreme Court Justice Samuel Chase and District Judge John Lowell. Although Brown changed his original plea of not guilty to guilty, he utterly refused to cooperate with the prosecution or to disclose the names of his associates or supporters.[227] Justice Chase and Judge Lowell responded with the most severe sentence of imprisonment imposed on any person convicted under the Act. They vindictively sentenced Brown to jail for 18 months and fined him $480, an enormous sum for a poor man, with the imprisonment to continue until the fine was paid. Brown served his full term. However, unable to pay the fine, he remained in jail. Adams twice refused to pardon him.[228] Thus, Brown was not released until Jefferson became President and finally pardoned him along with all the others convicted under the Act. Jefferson went further and was one of the group who contributed to the payment of Brown's fine.[229]

In contrast to Brown's defiant position, Fairbanks humbled himself before the Court. On changing his not guilty plea to guilty, he admitted his presence at the raising of the Pole and apologized to the Court. Claiming that he had been misled, he appealed for clemency. He was supported by Congressman Fisher Ames, a prominent High Federalist and a fellow resident of Dedham, who appeared to request leniency for him.[230] Ames was successful, and Fairbanks benefited from the influence brought to bear. Whereas Brown, a poor man, received the heaviest sentence under the Act, Justice Chase and Judge

---

[226] See J. M. Smith, note 19, at 261, 265; Miller, note 4, at 119.

[227] See J. M. Smith, note 19, at 267.

[228] Letter, John Adams to Timothy Pickering (June 19, 1800), *Miscellaneous Letters of John Adams, 1800*, Dep't. of State. See Anderson, note 16, at 125; J. M. Smith, note 19, at 268.

[229] See note 149.

[230] There is a further link between the Ames family and the trials of Brown and Fairbanks. Fisher Ames, the ardent Federalist, had a Republican brother, Dr. Nathaniel Ames, who had been subpoenaed to testify at the Brown trial. He failed to appear and was arrested. Before Supreme Court Justice William Cushing and District Judge Lowell in the Circuit Court, he defended alleging that the service had been defective. Like wealthy Fairbanks, he, too, received a slap on the wrist, being fined $8.00. See J. M. Smith, note 19, at 269–270.

Lowell gave Fairbanks, a wealthy property owner, the lightest sentence of any, letting him off with six hours imprisonment and a fine of $5.00 with costs of $10.60. This was a sorry contrast to the harsh treatment of Brown.

2. *United States v. Jedidiah Peck*, New York Legislator

Later in 1799, proceedings instituted against a relatively minor New York legislator, Jedidiah Peck, a Revolutionary War veteran, demonstrated the limits of governmental power in the face of fierce public resentment.[231] While serving as a judge of the state Court of Common Pleas, Peck had been elected to the Legislature as a Federalist. Breaking with the party over the Sedition Act, he publicly opposed a Federalist motion in the Legislature to reject the Virginia and Kentucky Resolutions and supported the unsuccessful Republican motions to declare the Act unconstitutional. He later supported another Republican proposal to adopt popular election for the New York electors of the Electoral College. In reprisal, the Federalists were successful in removing him as a judge and opposed his reelection to the Legislature. Nevertheless, he was reelected as a "Democratic-Republican."

In the summer of 1799, Peck sent to Congress a petition calling for the repeal of the Sedition Act and began to circulate it among his constituents, soliciting their signatures. In a lamentable loss of judgment that illustrates the extreme partisan feeling of the times, a Federalist local county judge, William Cooper, considered even the mere circulation of the petition to be a violation of the Sedition Act and recommended that he be indicted.[232] Federalist District Attorney Harison promptly obtained the indictment for violation of the Sedition Act.[233] After Peck's arrest (allegedly at midnight according to his supporters) and arraignment in Albany, N.Y., in September 1799, trial was set for New York City at the April 1800 Term of the Circuit Court. Still in custody, Peck was forced to travel to New York City to await trial, while manacled and under armed guard. The trip to New York City took five days and, according to historian Jabez Hammond, turned into a "triumphal" procession. Hammond wrote: "A hundred missionaries in the cause of democracy stationed between New York and Cooperstown could

---

[231] For accounts of the Peck affair, *see* J. M. Smith, note 19, at 390–398; Elkins & McKitrick, note 111, at 705; Rosenfeld, note 25, at 689–690, 700, 704; 3 Beveridge, note 91, at 42.

[232] Thus, Peck was one of the few cases under the Sedition Act that developed from local pressures.

[233] United States v. Jedidiah Peck, Records of the U.S. Circuit Court, Southern District of N.Y., Sept. 4, 1799, RG 21 (National Archives); 15 Oliver Wolcott Papers 60 (Conn. Hist. Soc'y.) (containing broadside about the proceeding).

not have done so much for the Republican cause as this journey of Judge Peck, a public exhibition of the suffering of a martyr for the freedom of speech and press."[234]

Although trial had been set for April 1800, the prosecution and defense both ran into difficulties in securing the attendance of upstate witnesses in New York City to testify, and the trial had to be postponed. As the case dragged on, Harison advised Secretary of State Pickering that the case would be too expensive for a relatively minor figure. At the instruction of President Adams, Pickering left the matter for decision at Harison's discretion.[235] That was the end of the case. It had accomplished nothing but to serve as a rallying point for opponents of the Adminstration. The indictment and treatment of Peck had made him a popular figure, and he was again reelected to the Legislature as a Democrat-Republican. There he achieved lasting distinction for his leadership in establishing the New York system of public education.[236]

3. United States v. Dr. Samuel Shaw

There are numerous references in the contemporary press to the 1799 arrest for violation of the Sedition Act, the 1800 trial, and the acquittal of Dr. Samuel Shaw of Castleton, Vt. Shaw was a Republican activist known for his denunciations of the Adams administration. After his acquittal, he was elected to the Vermont Legislature; serving several terms, he was later elected to the Congress.[237] With none of the details of the prosecution and trial known and the absence of judicial confirmation, however, the leading historians of the Act, led by Frank Anderson (publishing in 1912) and James Morton Smith (publishing in 1955), refused to acknowledge the case.[238] However, a third outstanding historian, Julius Goebel, Jr. (publishing in 1972) was subsequently able to find confirmation in the federal archives. Dr. Shaw had, indeed, been tried and acquitted under the Act, just as had been reported in the press of the time.[239] Accordingly, the Shaw litigation must be accepted as an established part of the Sedition Act history.

---

[234] 1 Jabez Hammond, Political Parties in the State of New York 89 (1852); see J. M. Smith, note 19, at 390.

[235] See Letter, Richard Harison to Timothy Pickering (Apr. 10, 1800), 26 Pickering Papers 77 (Mass. Hist. Soc'y.) and Letter, Timothy Pickering to Richard Harison (Apr. 22, 1800), 13 Pickering Papers 406 (Mass. Hist. Soc'y.).

[236] See Sherman Williams, Jedidiah Peck, The Father of the Public School System of the State of New York, 1 N.Y. State Hist. Ass'n Q. J. 219–240 (1920); J. M. Smith, note 19, at 390.

[237] See 74 Vermont History 174 (Lynn Bonfield et al. eds. 2006).

[238] See J. M. Smith, note 19, at 185; Anderson, note 16, at 120.

[239] Ms. Docket No. 26, Oct. Term 1799 (C.C.D. Vt.). See Goebel, note 109, at 638 n.107.

The episode further illustrates the desirability of the historians taking the newspaper evidence more seriously. After all, no fewer than five New England newspapers, including both Federalist and Democratic-Republican journals, had published references, summary references to be sure, to the *Shaw* trial and its outcome.[240] Unfortunately, neither the press accounts nor Professor Goebel share with us any details of the case. However, the one fact that they do underscore is of paramount importance. The *Shaw* case provides the only example of an acquittal in the entire history of the Sedition Act.

At this point, this volume has examined all cases under the Act confirmed to the satisfaction of the historians. However, restricting one's examination of the litigation to these cases does not do justice to the full extent of the impact of the Sedition Act. One cannot escape the reality that the Federalist press of the time was alive with reports of further criminal libel cases directed with partisan venom against Republican newspaper editors and adherents. Lacking confirmation in the scant judicial records available, these accounts, of course, must be received with reservations.[241] In addition to the cases discussed, there were reports in the press of a number of additional cases, mostly involving newspaper editors, for which satisfactory judicial confirmation is not available and about which little is known.

H. Unconfirmed Cases

1. *United States or New Jersey v. Daniel Dodge; United States or New Jersey v. Aaron Pennington*

Carl E. Price has reported the arrest and indictment in 1798 under the Sedition Act of Daniel Dodge and Aaron Pennington, editors of the Republican

---

[240] The *Connecticut Gazette and Commercial Intelligencer* (New London) May 21, 1800, reports that at the very term of the Circuit Court ended May 13, 1800, in which Haswell was convicted of violation of the 1798 Act, Doctor Shaw of Castleton [of Vt] was "likewise tried for sedition, and acquitted"; *Spooner's Vermont Journal* (Windsor), May 13, 1800; *Connecticut Courant*, May 26, 1800. *See also* New York *Spectator*, Oct. 19, 26, 1799; Newport *Mercury*, Oct. 29, 1799, and Newburyport *Herald*, Nov. 5, 1799, reporting the filing of an information against Dr. Shaw of Castleton for "sedition"; and Philadelphia *Aurora*, Jan. 16, 1800.

[241] In his pathbreaking 1912 study of the Sedition Act, Anderson observes that most of the reports of proceedings under the Sedition Act and United States criminal common law "come from the newspapers. For many of the newspapers of the time, no files have been preserved. Those which remain are incomplete and so widely scattered that some part of the newspaper material is almost certain to be overlooked.... Great difficulties arise from the meagerness and conflicting chracter of the reports." He concludes without providing any identification of the particular cases that there were 24 or 25 arrests, 15 and perhaps several more indictments, only 10 or perhaps 11 went to trial. Ten were convicted and perhaps one acquitted. *See* Anderson, note 16, at 120. In fact, there were 12 convictions.

Newark *Centinel* for their attacks on Federalist Governor Richard Howell. However, because a state, not a federal, officer was involved, these prosecutions were most likely brought under New Jersey criminal common law and, hence, are discussed in Chapter 6.[242]

2. *United States v. Judah P. Spooner; United States v. James Lyon*

A series of newspaper accounts in October 1798 and then again in October 1799 report the arrest and indictment at the U.S. Circuit Court in Rutland, Vt., under the Sedition Act of Judah P. Spooner, of Fair Haven, Vt., editor of the *Vermont Journal* and a former printer of Congressman Lyon's *Scourge of Aristocracy*.[243] Because the accounts typically discuss the Spooner indictment along with the simultaneous indictments of Anthony Haswell, editor of the *Vermont Gazette*, and James Lyon, they are discussed together.

In these accounts, Judah P. Spooner is uniformly described as a printer and editor of the *Vermont Journal*, based in Fair Haven, Vt. (16 miles west of Rutland), but the nature of the libels for which he was allegedly indicted, was not disclosed. However, in one of the reports, a Federalist paper describes him as "the particular friend and tool of [Matthew] Lyon."[244] A number of the October 1799 reports also include references to the indictments at this time of Anthony Haswell and James Lyon, editor/son of Representative Matthew Lyon.[245] Finally there are reports of two additional indictments of Matthew Lyon following his release from prison. However, as we have seen, he successfully avoided arrest and safely made his way to Kentucky, where he was five times elected to the Congress.

It is significant that Haswell's own newspaper, the Bennington *Gazette*, reported his 1799 indictment, which, as discussed, led to his 1800 trial, and any suggestion that such an account lacks credibility is unpersuasive. If, then,

---

[242] Price, note 105, at 38, *citing* Woods, *National Gazette*, Aug. 9, 1798, Newark *Centinel*, Aug. 7, 14, 21, 28, 1798, New Brunswick *Guardian*, Aug. 28, 1798.

[243] (C.C.D. Vt. 1798 and 1799). Reports of the indictment of Spooner and James Lyon in Oct. 1798: Bennington *Vermont Gazette* (Oct. 12, 1798); Boston *Independent Chronicle* (Oct. 22, 1798).

   Reports of arrest and indictment of Spooner in Oct. 1799: New York *Spectator*, Oct. 19, 26, 1799; Philadelphia *Aurora*, Oct. 24, 1799 *citing* the Vermont *Northern Budget*; Philadelphia *Aurora* Nov. 6, 1799, *citing Gazette of the United States*, Nov. 6, 1799; *Federal Gazette & Baltimore Advertiser*, Oct. 19, 1799; Providence *Gazette*, Oct. 19, 1799; Middlesex *Gazette* Oct. 25, 1799; Windham *Herald*, Oct. 31, 1799. *See* J. M. Smith, note 19, at 185 n.86; Rosenfeld, note 25, at 708, 713, 869.

   An Oct. 16, 1799, report from Troy reprinted in the *Connecticut Courant* reports that "Mr. Spooner" was discharged. *Connecticut Courant*, Nov. 4, 1799.

[244] *Newburyport Herald*, Oct. 30, 1798.

[245] *Federal Gazette & Baltimore Advertiser*, Oct. 19, 1799; Providence *Gazette*, Oct. 19, 1799; Middlesex *Gazette* Oct. 25, 1799; Windham *Herald*, Oct. 31, 1799; *Connecticut Courant*, Nov. 4, 1799.

we are constrained to accept the accuracy of the newspaper report of the Haswell indictment, it argues for the accuracy of the accompanying accounts about the indictments of Spooner and James Lyon as well. However, Anderson does not trouble to mention these accounts, and Smith rejects them out of hand.[246]

It is apparent that Spooner and James Lyon as well as Haswell were closely identified with Matthew Lyon, who was the center of the major Vermont prosecution at this time, and this makes reports of their indictment entirely plausible. According to one account, Spooner, unlike Haswell and Lyon, had been promptly released.[247] As we have seen, Haswell was bound for trial at the April 1800 Term, at which he was convicted and fined and served a term of imprisonment. As for James Lyon, he was reported to have evaded service of the indictment and fled first to Virginia and then to Kentucky.[248] While he was in Virginia, James Lyon had the distinction of being the co-publisher along with James Thomson Callender of the scurrilous pamphlet *The Prospect Before Us*, which, as we have seen, led to Callender's arrest and conviction under the Act. It is possible that these matters may have involved a second set of proceedings against Spooner, James Lyon, and Anthony Haswell. They had earlier been reported to have been arrested the previous year in October 1798, along with Congressman Matthew Lyon, but there is no report of their indictment at the time.[249] Although Spargo's authoritative account confirms that although there had been talk at this time of Haswell's indictment, an indictment did not actually occur until the following year.[250]

Fair Haven, Vt. (home of Spooner), Castleton, Vt. (home of Dr. Shaw), Windsor, Vt. (home of Matthew and James Lyon), and Bennington, Vt. (home of Haswell) all are clustered within a 60 mile radius of Rutland, Vt., site of the U.S. Circuit Court. The various indictments are evidently the result of the energetic enforcement of the Act by the local District Attorney. Although indictments were voted in Rutland, only Dr. Shaw was tried in Rutland; the trials of Lyon and Haswell took place 42 miles to the east in Windsor, Vt.

---

[246] *See* J. M. Smith, note 19, at 229 n.22 ("there seems no basis for these assertions").

[247] New York *Spectator*, Oct. 26, 1799.

[248] Windham *Herald*, Oct. 31, 1799. This reports gain credibility from the later history of his father. After Congressman Lyon had completed his second term as a Vermont Representative, he, too, resettled in Kentucky, where he was five times reelected to the Congress. *See* Wharton, note 110, at 343.

[249] Boston *Independent Chronicle*, Oct. 22, 1798; Newburyport *Herald*, Oct. 30, 1798. Philadelphia *Aurora*, Oct. 24, 1798 *citing* the Vermont *Northern Budget*; Bennington *Vermont Gazette*, Oct. 12, 1798; Boston *Independent Chronicle*, Oct. 22, 1798; Newburyport *Herald*, Oct. 22, 30, 1798.

[250] *See* Spargo, note 112, at 56–57; Bennington *Vermont Gazette*, Oct. 12, 1798.

3. United States v. Conrad Fahnestock; United States v. Benjamin Moyer or Mayer

In the 18th century, numerous German immigrants were settled in Western Pennsylvania, and a German-language press existed for some time.[251] Conrad Fahnestock and Benjamin Moyer, co-editors of one of these papers, the *Harrisburger Morgenrothe*, were widely reported to have been arrested in August 1799 and indicted for publishing seditious statements against the laws and government of the United States. They were bound over for trial at the U.S. Circuit Court in Philadelphia on October 11, 1799. Bail was set at $2,000 each, together with four sureties for $1,000 each.[252] What subsequently transpired before the Circuit Court is not known; no account of either a trial or dismissal of the charges is available. Three years later, there were newspaper reports that *The Farmer's Instructor*, a "democratic" paper printed by Benjamin Mayer [*sic*] of Harrisburg had ceased publication.[253]

Still another German-language newspaper editor, Jacob Schneider (or Schneyder), the editor of the Reading, Pa., *Readinger Adler* (or *Reading Eagle*), barely escaped prosecution in the Federalist 1799 assault against the Republican press. The *Adler* had urged Pennsylvania voters to vote against Sen. James Ross, the Federalist candidate, in the 1800 Pennsylvania gubernatorial race. As readers will recall, Sen. Ross was a High Federalist and author of the Bill to supersede the Electoral College with a Federalist-packed Select Committee. Writing in the *Adler*, Schneider had condemned Ross for his support of the Sedition Act, a "dreadful shameless and destroying attempt" against the Constitution; and as "one of the political murderers of our liberty." The attack came to the attention of Secretary of State Timothy Pickering, who promptly instructed the Federalist District Attorney for Pennsylvania, William Rawle, to indict Schneider for violation of the Sedition Act. However, there is no report that Rawle, who had prosecuted Duane and Cooper for violations of the Act, took action against Schneider.[254]

---

[251] *Gazette of the United States*, Sept. 6, 1799; New London *Bee*, Sept. 18, 1799; Salem *Gazette*, Sept. 20, 1799; *City Gazette and Daily Advertiser*, Sept. 24, 1799; *Spooner's Vermont Journal*, Oct. 1, 1799; *Columbian Museum and Savannah Advertiser*, Oct. 1, 1799; Frankfort, Ky., *Palladium*, Oct. 3, 1799. In some of the accounts, Fahnestock and Moyer (Mayer) are described as the editors of a "Dutch [*i.e.*, German] Aurora." *See* Rosenfeld, note 25, at 690; J. M. Smith, note 19, at 185; Donald H. Stewart, The Opposition Press of the Federalist Period 476 (1969) (hereinafter Stewart).

[252] Salem *Gazette*, May 18, 1802.

[253] *See* Philadelphia *Aurora*, July 30, 1799; Letter, Timothy Pickering to William Rawle (July 5, 1799), 11 Pickering Papers 390 (Mass. Hist. Soc'y.); Stewart, note 251, at 476.

[254] *See* Rosenfeld, note 25, at 620, 622, 737.

Subsequently, however, a Federalist mob outraged by Schneider's attacks on the Adams administration sacked Schneider's printing press and office and physically assaulted Schneider.[255] Following the model of the Patriot mob attacks on Tory newspapers during the Revolution, this was a repetition of the earlier Federalist mob attacks on Bache, Duane, and other leaders of the Republican press in their misguided efforts to stifle the opposition. This was what Benjamin Franklin meant in his unhappy remark, which has been dismissed as jocular, when he spoke of "the law of the cudgel."[256]

4. United States or Commonwealth v. James Bell

The prosecution of James Bell is reported to have occurred while the Sedition Act was still under consideration by the Congress. The accounts in two Maryland newspapers and the Boston *Independent Chronicle* are elliptical, and details of the nature of the case are lacking. It is not even clear whether the case was brought under the Act, federal criminal common law, or even state common law. From the accounts, it appears that on July 3, 1798, James Bell of Stoney Ridge, Md., was apprehended on a warrant for "treasonable expressions" in Carlisle, Pa. He was arraigned before "William Levis and James McCormick, Esquiries" and bound over on their recognizance of $600.[257] Unfortunately, further details of the proceedings are lacking.

5. Dr. John Tyler; Dr. John Vaughan

In the correspondence of James Madison and Thomas Jefferson are found two summary references to the attempted prosecution under the Sedition Act of Dr. John Tyler, a Maryland optometrist and candidate for Elector, and Dr. John Vaughan of Wilmington.[258] There is no description of the facts and

---

[255] Benjamin Franklin, An Account of the Supremest Court of Judicature in Pennsylvania, viz. The Court of the Press, *Federal Gazette*, Sept. 12, 1789. *See also* Ch. 2, note 15.

[256] Boston *Independent Chronicle*, July 30, 1798. *See* J. M. Smith, note 19, at 185 n.87; Charles Warren, *The Supreme Court in United States History* (rev. ed. 1928), *citing* a Jan. 10, 1799, Carlisle newspaper as his source.

[257] Letter, Charles P. Polk to James Madison (June 20, 1800), 17 *Madison Papers* 394 (David Mattern ed. 1962) (Libr. Cong.) (without providing any detail, Polk's letter advises that a letter written by Tyler had been forwarded to the General Government in the hope of having him prosecuted under the Sedition Act; Letter, Dr. John Vaughn to Thomas Jefferson (Jan. 10, 1801), 32 Jefferson, *Papers* (Oberg), note 54, at 441, 442. *See* J. M. Smith, note 19, at 185n.

[258] Annals, 5th Cong. 3d Sess. 1851b, 916, 975 (1801).

Although the Republicans at the time sneered that the Federalists were eager to protect President Adams, but not his possible successor, Thomas Jefferson, against such libels, they later blocked

circumstances of the prosecutions, and no other information available about their disposition.

A final note: In May 1800, long-suffering President Adams at last fired Secretary of State Timothy Pickering. As we have seen, Pickering, an arch-Federalist, had been a supremely vigorous source of prosecutions under the Sedition Act. With his departure, further indictments seem to have come to an end. Although there may have been some, there are none that have judicial confirmation. Then, in a surprising move at the twilight of the Adams administration in January 1801, the Federalists proposed the continuation of the Sedition Act, scheduled to expire in less than two months. Although the Republicans on the passage of the Act had sneered that the Federalists were eager to protect President Adams, but not his possible successor, Thomas Jefferson, against such libels, they blocked the Federalist proposal. After several favorable votes in the earlier stages of the proposed legislation, the House narrowly rejected the Bill, and the Sedition Act came to an end on the eve of the Jefferson administration.[259]

I. Judicial Consideration of the Constitutionality of the Sedition Act

The question of constitutionality was raised in only three of the cases. In the *Lyon* case, one of the earliest, Lyon, arguing *pro se*, attacked the constitutionality of the Act and contended that it was for the jury to determine the issue. He quoted the Act's provision that "the jury was to be the judge of the law as well as the facts, just as in other matters." Justice Paterson and Judge Hitchcock rejected his claim and instructed the jury to ignore the issue. The issue next arose in the *Holt* case. When counsel for Holt argued the question, Justice Washington and Judge Law ruled on the issue, holding the Act constitutional and so charged the jury. Finally, in the *Callender* case, counsel repeatedly sought to argue both that unconstitutionality was a question for the jury and that the Act was unconstitutional. As we have seen, Justice Chase presiding would have none of it and summarily ruled to the contrary.

a late attempt by Federalists in 1801 a few months before the expiration of the Act to repeal the sunset provision. 6 *Annals of the Congress* 975–976 (1800) *See* Miller, note 4, at 227–228.

[259] *See* Wharton, note 110, at 335–336 (*Lyon*) and 709–710 (*Callender*); J. M. Smith, note 19, at 375–377 (*Holt*).

In addition, Chief Justice Ellsworth in response to a request for an opinion from Secretary of State Pickering had responded with an Advisory Opinion that the Act was constitutional.[260]

Thus, these seven judges, including Chief Justice Ellsworth, Justices Paterson, Washington, and Chase of the Supreme Court, and three District Court judges, agreed that the statute was constitutional and and all but Ellsworth had in fact also ruled that the judges, not the jury, were to decide the issue.[261] It took more than 150 years before the Supreme Court in *New York Times Co. v. Sullivan* and *Garrison v. Louisiana* at last outlawed both criminal and civil libel, except in very limited circumstances. However, during that very lengthy period, the views of the early judges were uniformly accepted as the law of the land.[262]

J. Conclusion

The Federalist criminal libel prosecutions were brought by Federalist prosecutors in courts presided over by Federalist judges who typically saw their responsibilities to include support for the Federalist administration and its attempts to build a powerful national government. This array of prosecutions largely directed at the Republican press achieved great temporary tactical success. No fewer than eight prominent Republican papers that were spokesmen for the Republicans in the most important metropolitan centers in the North in the New Republic were distracted, harassed, and in a number of instances driven out of business on the eve of the critical 1800 presidential election. A ninth prosecution silenced an obscure rural New York publisher of little prominence. In addition, there are the less well-supported reports in the press of at least four additional prosecutions against Republican editors, of which the outcomes are unknown. Finally, there are the widely scattered episodic instances of a number of prosecutions that seem to reflect aberrational selections by the local prosecutors. These include the prosecutions of

---

[260] Letter, Olive Ellsworth to Timothy Pickering (Dec. 12, 1798), 2 Henry Flanders, *Lives and Times of the Chief Justices of the Supreme Court of the United States* 193–194 (1875).

[261] Although reference to foreign law in connection with American constitutional issues has recently come under severe attack, the dictum of an outstanding English judge with respect to a similar issue under European law will be of interest. Fifteen years after *N.Y. Times Co. v. Sullivan*, Lord Diplock expressed his concern that it was "difficult to reconcile" English libel law with art. 10 §2 of the European Convention for the Protection of Human Rights and Fundamental Freedoms (1950). *See* Gleaves v. Deakin, [1980] A.C. 477, [1979] 2 All. Eng. Rep. 497, 498 (H.L. 1979).

[262] *See* Warren, *Junto*, note 15, at 75.

such anti-Federalists as the three Newark drunks, the Dedham, Mass., Liberty Pole enthusiasts, and Assemblyman Peck in New York.

Initially, the vigorous response of President Adams and his administration to the French threat met with wide approval. As noted, Citizen Genet's misconduct, the XYZ Affair with its intolerable demand for bribes to induce the American peace representatives to negotiate, and the subsequent refusal of the French Ministry to meet with them had swung public opinion sharply against the French. With his call for a new Army and a new Navy to resist the anticipated French invasion and the passage of the Alien and Sedition Acts themselves, the popularity of Adams and his administration attained an all-time high during the summer of 1798. Charles Warren thus advises that "the country became stirred to a white heat in the support of the administration."[263]

In the congressional elections of that year, the Federalists, already in the control of the Congress, gained additional seats in the House and the Senate. Although the Republicans strenuously attacked the Act in and out of the Congress as unconstitutional, the courts made up of Federalist judges unanimously upheld the law. As we have seen, not a single judge dissented. As Story asserts, it was "deliberately affirmed by the courts of law."[264]

However, as we will see, this popularity did not last long. As the threat of immediate war with France seemed less and less credible, popular opinion increasingly swung the other way.[265] Legislation that could be justified only by the likelihood of war and invasion and that had seemed so prudent in the time of crisis now seemed misguided. Worse, the measures were expensive and involved unpopular new taxes to pay the bill. With the new armaments recognized as unnecessary, the financial burdens in paying for the new Army and Navy became unacceptable.[266] The final straw was the partisan abuse of the Sedition Act, using it to silence leading voices of the Republican opposition. Although briefly popular, the prosecutions in the end led to deep public disapproval, and the effort backfired. The prosecutions ultimately proved a strategic disaster. The Republican triumph in the 1800 congressional

---

[263] See 2 Joseph Story, *Commentaries on the Constitution of the United States* §1892 (5th ed. Melville Bigelow ed. 1891, repr. 1994).

[264] Page Smith, one of the few historians endorsing the necessity of the Sedition Act, reports that President Adams was unhappy with the cost of maintaining the naval and military establishment. When Secretary of State Pickering pressed him to authorize an additional six companies of cavalry, Adams rejected the suggestion, exclaiming that debts and taxes were leveling all Europe and "we must inevitably go the same way." *See* 2 Page Smith, note 40, at 98.

[265] In contrast to the immediate impact of the Act, the number of Republican papers almost doubled between 1798 and 1800. See Pasley, note 22, at 126.

[266] *See* Stephen Kurtz, The French Mission of 1799–1800: Concluding Chapter in the Statecraft of John Adams, 80 Pol. Sci. 543 (1965).

elections was overwhelming, but the presidential election was another matter. Fresh from the triumph of achieving peace with France,[267] Adams was not directly associated with the Act, and his popularity hardly suffered. In the 1800 presidential election, he actually increased his number of electoral votes, ultimately losing with 68 electoral votes to 73 electoral votes for Jefferson. Adams's defeat stemmed from the loss of the votes of New York, which he had received in 1796. Hamilton's treacherous pamphlet[268] and lobbying with the High Federalists had proved fatal. Preferring Jefferson to Adams, Hamilton, the perverse Federalist, had achieved his objective of defeating Adams.

Notwithstanding the loss in New York, Adams might still have squeaked through and been reelected if he had gained three of South Carolina's eight electors. Along with North Carolina, South Carolina was viewed as the most Federalist of all the Southern states. In addition, South Carolina was the home of Charles C. Pinckney, the Federalist candidate for Vice President. However, Jefferson carried each of the decisive districts by narrow margins. In the end, the 1800 election was decided by a small number of South Carolina voters.

The expiration of the Sedition Act did not mean the end of criminal libel. There were isolated recurrences under federal common-law criminal jurisdiction under the Jefferson and Madison administrations as reviewed in Chapter 5, and it flourished for decades thereafter in the state courts as reviewed in Chapter 6.

---

[267] Alexander Hamilton, The Public Conduct and Character of John Adams, Esq. President of the United States, Hamilton, *Writings* (Libr. Am.), note 190, at 934–971 (Oct. 24, 1800).

[268] *See* Letter, Alexander Hamilton to Theodore Sedgwick (May 10, 1800) ("I will never more be responsible for him [Adams] by my direct support – even though the consequence should be the election of Jefferson"), *ibid.*, at 925; Letter, Alexander Hamilton to Charles Carroll of Carrollton (July 1800), *id.*, at 926.

5

Criminal Libel During the Jefferson and Madison Administrations, 1800–1816

A. Introduction

With the 1800 elections, a dramatic change had transformed the government. There was a Republican President, a Republican House, and a Republican Senate. With the Republicans firmly in control of the government, the country was on the brink of vigorous change.

On the commencement of his administration, President Jefferson took vigorous steps to undo the remaining consequences of the Sedition Act, which had expired in accordance with its terms. He immediately ordered the discontinuance and dismissal of all pending federal seditious libel prosecutions and pardoned all persons convicted under the Act who were still in jail. In his view the Act had been unconstitutional, and he moved to expunge its lingering traces.[1]

The dramatic change commencing with the 1800 elections was only the beginning of the Federalist decline. The Republicans built on their narrow 1800 triumph. Jefferson, a narrow victor in 1800, with 73 electoral votes against 68 votes for Adams, won an overwhelming victory in 1804 over the Federalist candidates, Charles C. Pinckney and Rufus King, with 162 electoral votes to a mere 14 for the Federalists. With the 1804 elections, the Republicans had increased their control of the Senate to an overwhelming margin with 27 Republicans and a token 7 Federalists; the House consisted of 117 Republicans with only a handful of 25 Federalists.[2]

---

[1] *See* James Morton Smith, *Freedom's Fetters: The Alien and Sedition Laws and American Civil Liberties* 204 (1956) (hereinafter J. M. Smith).

[2] *See* William N. Chambers, *Political Parties in a New Nation: The American Experience* 1776–1809, 182–183 (1963); Ralph Ketcham, *James Madison: A Biography* 433 (1971 repr. 1990).

With the triumph of the Republicans, the arena for criminal libel prosecutions was fast becoming a matter of state law. There was no longer any federal criminal libel statute with the expiration of the Sedition Act, and the Republicans had opposed the very concept of federal criminal common-law crimes. However, inconsistencies were to be found, and in this chapter, we review the quickly dwindling appearance of criminal libel in the federal courts.

B. Ambivalence of the Jeffersonians: The Federal Government

1. The Accession of Jefferson to the Presidency, 1801

The expiration of the Sedition Act with the end of the Adams administration brought to a close a deplorable episode in American history. The High Federalists led by Pickering had discovered a serious weakness in the jurisprudential structure of the Early American Republic. The doctrine of common-law seditious libel inherited from the English permitted the political party in power to suppress political opponents so long as the judiciary chose to follow Blackstone as its guide in determining the limited scope of the constitutional guaranties of freedom of speech and press.

Moreover, when the Federalists lost national power in 1800, the evil they had introduced did not die with them. They left a corrupted political scene. They continued to employ criminal libel for partisan purposes in the states where they were still in power. The pressures on Republicans to do the same in retaliation were well-nigh irresistible. Even Jefferson, who had so strongly condemned the process, was ready to accept it in exceptional cases. Aroused by the vituperative attacks of the Federalist press and with the partisan usefulness of the doctrine so prominently before them, the Republicans now embraced the doctrine. In the states under their control, such as New York and Pennsylvania, they readily invoked the doctrine for partisan purposes, and on one celebrated occasion did so with a cluster of six prosecutions of Connecticut Federalists in the Connecticut federal courts as well. In brief, although historians have typically busied themselves with the 15 cases prosecuted under the Sedition Act and have virtually ignored the subsequent evolution of the doctrine,[3] the reality is that criminal libel played a continuing role of considerable importance in the party politics of the time for another 15 years. These cases involved not only the continuing political rivalry between

---

[3] Although a few celebrated cases – the *Croswell* case in New York and the *Dennie, Duane,* and *Cobbett* litigations in Pennsylvania – have attracted a full measure of attention, the two dozen or so other cases have been virtually ignored.

the Federalists and Republicans, but were also prominent in the Republican internecine warfare in Pennsylvania and New York between two wings of the Republican Party struggling for control. In all, at least as many as 30 criminal libel cases – a half dozen federal, the balance state – have been reported during the Jefferson and Madison administrations, or twice as many as had occurred under the Sedition Act.

These 30-odd cases lack the chilling drama of the earlier effort of the Federalists seeking to cripple, if not destroy, the Republican press on the eve of the 1800 presidential election. However, they illustrate two vital points. First, the thoroughly politicized press of the time – whether allied to Federalists or Republicans – was more vituperative and scurrilous than ever in its characterization of its political opponents. Henry Adams observed that "the summer of 1802 was marked by an outburst of reciprocal invective and slander such as could not be matched in American history."[4] As noted, leading newspapers had been organized with political or even foreign funding and continued to receive financial support from persons active in the party that the editors supported. Further, as we have seen, when in power, Federalist and Republican leaders regularly saw to it that government printing contracts were awarded to their editorial supporters.[5] Second, criminal-libel litigation continued to be a hotly pursued vehicle for parties in power to attempt to tilt the political scales by jailing editors allied with their political opponents. This chapter of American history did not come to a close until the Federalists virtually disappeared as a political force. It had taken almost a quarter century for the new American political system and party politics to mature to the point where attempts to destroy one's political enemies by partisan prosecutions faded away. This welcome evolution mirrored a corresponding change. The vituperative nature of the political press gradually moderated, and this provocation for resort to partisan criminal libel lost its power.

2. The Demise of Criminal Libel and Federal Criminal Common Law
in the Jefferson and Madison Administrations

When Jefferson became President, federal policy changed abruptly on two related matters of grave jurisprudential importance: criminal libel and federal

---

[4] 1 Henry Adams, *The History of the United States During the First Administration of Thomas Jefferson* 219 (Libr. Am. 1986) (hereinafter H. Adams, *Jefferson Administration*).

[5] As noted, the *National Intelligencer* illustrates the process. Thus, Jefferson had provided financial assistance to start the *National Intelligencer* and had personally selected Samuel Harrison Smith to be its editor.

criminal common-law jurisdiction. Jefferson wrote to his Attorney General, Levi Lincoln, early in his administration, "I would wish more to see the experiment tried of getting along without public prosecutions for libel."[6] Thus, with the exception of one episode, neither Jefferson nor Madison resorted to the use of prosecutions for criminal libel to harass or silence political opponents. Although Jefferson was prepared to acquiesce in the occasional use of such prosecutions to deal with a particularly offensive critic, he never participated in or encouraged such actions except on one occasion in the Pennsylvania state courts.[7]

Nevertheless, on isolated occasions federal officials during the Jefferson and Madison administrations used or seriously contemplated the resort to federal common-law criminal prosecutions. However, with one glaring exception, these involved litigation in implementation of federal programs, not criminal libel to harass or silence Federalist newspapers or critics. The exception occurred during the winter of 1805–1806 during the Jefferson administration. At the instance of the Connecticut Republican State Chairman, a zealous Connecticut Republican District Attorney and District Court Judge proceeded to indict six Connecticut Federalists (including such prominent persons as Tapping Reeve and the publishers of the leading Federalist newspaper in the state) for seditious libel under federal criminal common-law jurisdiction. As far as is known, the litigation arose without the encouragement or knowledge of Jefferson. However, as we will see, Jefferson soon learned of the prosecutions and acquiesced for months before intervening, so he cannot escape responsibility.[8] Let us review this record and the final moments of federal criminal common-law jurisprudence.

When Jefferson assumed office, there were still persons – Republicans all – still in jail, serving sentences under the Sedition Act. One of Jefferson's first actions was to pardon them.[9] He also considered whether to remit their fines on the theory that the Act was unconstitutional. However, he ultimately

---

[6] Letter, Thomas Jefferson to Levi Lincoln (Mar. 24, 1802), 8 Jefferson, *Writings* 139 (Paul L. Ford ed. 1897) (hereinafter Jefferson, *Writings* (Ford)).

[7] As we will see, he gave his approval to Governor McKean of Pennsylvania when McKean expressed his distress at the vituperative nature of certain newspaper criticisms and proposed prosecution of Pennsylvania critics under Pennsylvania law. Jefferson went further and forwarded a newspaper that he found particularly offensive. *See* Letter, Thomas Jefferson to Thomas McKean (Feb. 19, 1803), *ibid.*, at 218. The prosecution of William Dennie, editor of the Philadelphia *Port Folio* in the Pennsylvania courts promptly followed. *See infra* Ch. 6, text accompanying notes 15–21.

[8] As we will see, his intervention did not occur for months after he first learned of the prosecutions, and when it did occur, it was to prevent disclosure of a highly discreditable personal matter, rather than because of his views on federal criminal common-law prosecutions.

[9] *See* Letter, Thomas Jefferson to Abigail Adams (July 22, 1804), 11 *Writings of Thomas Jefferson* 43 (A. Lipscomb ed. 1904) (hereinafter Jefferson, *Writings* (Lipscomb)) ("I discharged every person

decided against it. The remission issue thereupon faded away for a while. Some years later, one of those convicted, Matthew Lyon (who had been a member of Congress from Vermont and subsequently became a member from Kentucky), sought to re-open the issue. After repeated failures, Lyon's heirs were at last successful in persuading the Congress to remit the fine with interest in 1840. Haswell's heirs were similarly successful in 1844. In the earlier stages of this campaign, a bill for remission of Lyon's fine was accompanied by a declaration that the Act had been unconstitutional, but this addition had been dropped by the time remission was finally approved in 1840.[10]

A second important episode in the first months of the Jefferson administration illustrates the Jeffersonian readiness to block or undermine Federalist use of seditious libel against Republican editors. In the spring of 1801, two of the new Federalist Circuit Court Judges in the District of Columbia,[11] James M. Marshall (brother of the Chief Justice) and William Cranch (later Reporter of the Supreme Court opinions),[12] were responsible for the adoption of a resolution by the three-man Circuit Court, instructing the District Attorney for the District of Columbia to institute a common-law criminal libel prosecution against Samuel Harrison Smith, Jefferson's handpicked editor of the nation's leading Republican newspaper, the *National Intelligencer*. The Chief Judge of the Court, William Kilty, a Jefferson appointee,[13] disagreed but was outvoted.

Harrison had condemned the federal judiciary *in toto*, charging in a broadside attack that the courts had "been prompt to seize *every* occasion of aggrandizing Executive power, of destroying all freedom of opinion, of executing unconstitutional laws."[14] Even an editor admired for his moderation could at times be an extremist in these heated times.

under punishment or prosecution under the Sedition Act because I considered, and now consider, that law to be a nullity").

[10] *See* Francis Wharton, *State Trials of the United States During the Administrations of Washington and Adams* 344n., 686 (1849 repr. 1970) (hereinafter Wharton).

[11] They were among the so-called midnight judges appointed by Adams in the twilight of his administration. As to these, Jefferson wrote to Dr. Benjamin Rush a decade later "those scenes of midnight appointment, which have been condemned by all men. The last day of his political power, the last hours, and even beyond the midnight, were employed in filling all offices, and especially permanent ones [*i.e.*, judges] with the bitter interest federalists." *Letter*, Thomas Jefferson to Dr. Benjamin Rush (Jan. 16, 1811). 13 Jefferson, *Writings* (Lipscomb), note 9, at 7.

[12] William Cranch was on the fringes of President Adams's extended family. His brother Richard was married to Mary Cranch, sister of Abigail Adams.

[13] Adams had nominated a Federalist, Judge Thomas Johnson of Maryland, to be Chief Judge. However, Johnson declined, and Adams had no time to nominate a successor.

[14] Jeffrey B. Morris, *Calmly to Poise the Scales of Justice: A History of the Courts of the District of Columbia* 13–14 (2001) (hereinafter Morris). Emphasis added.

The matter moved to the District Attorney, who as a result of Jefferson's accession was a Republican. He balked. Although he did present the resolution to the grand jury, he carefully noted the dissent of Chief Judge Kilty and did not recommend that the jury take any action. Although the jury initially returned a presentment, it considered the matter again and refused to approve an indictment, and the matter was dropped.[15]

A little-known episode in Kentucky in 1802 illustrates some minor ambivalence of the Jefferson administration with respect to federal criminal common-law prosecutions. John Williams and two other settlers in the Kentucky Territory had murdered three Indians. After Williams had been apprehended and taken into custody, a mob led by William Hardin overpowered the jailor, freed Williams, and subsequently blocked attempts to reapprehend him. Informed of these developments, Jefferson's Attorney General, Levi Lincoln, issued instructions to Gen. Dearborn, Governor of the Territory, to prosecute Hardin and his followers in the federal courts under its criminal common-law jurisdiction. Although, as we have seen, Jefferson had made clear to Lincoln his hostility to federal common-law prosecution for seditious libel, he had not expanded his statement to include federal criminal common-law prosecutions generally.[16]

Gen. Dearborn forwarded Lincoln's instructions to the federal District Attorney in Kentucky, Joseph H. Daviess (brother-in-law of Chief Justice Marshall).[17] Before acting, Daviess, albeit a Federalist, reminded Gen. Dearborn, a Republican, "of the public heat his party had raised about the common law." Not receiving any reply,[18] Daviess went ahead and succeeded in having the grand jury issue a presentment against William Hardin, leader of the rescue mob, and three of his accomplices.

> The *National Intelligencer* was more restrained in its prose and was in a different class than the vituperative press of such editors as Bache, Duane, Fenno, Cobbett, or Cooper. Nevertheless, as this incident illustrates, even the *Intelligencer* had its extreme moments.

[15] *National Intelligencer*, June 12, 1801. See Morris, note 14, at 14; 2 Oliver Wendell Holmes Devise, *History of the Supreme Court of the United States*, George Lee Haskins & Herbert A. Johnson, *Foundations of Power: John Marshall, 1801–1815*, 161–162 (1981) (hereinafter Haskins & Johnson); 1 Charles Warren, *The Supreme Court in United States History* 195–197 (rev. ed. 1928) (hereinafter Warren, *History*).

[16] *See* Letter, Thomas Jefferson to Levi Lincoln (Mar. 24, 1802), 8 Jefferson, *Writings* (Ford), note 6, at 139.

[17] *See* 5 Dumas Malone, *Jefferson and His Time: Jefferson the President: Second Term 1805–1809*, 355 (2003) (hereinafter 5 Malone).

[18] Daviess stated that he later received General Dearborn's order forbidding him from proceeding on the ground that the offense was a common law matter. *See* Haskins & Johnson, note 15, at 435 n.9.

However, the matter was soon dropped. When the matter came before the Court, Daviess, mindful of the Republican position on federal criminal common-law jurisdiction, raised the question with District Judge Harry Innes. Judge Innes promptly quashed the charge and dismissed the case. Mary Tachau provides a possible explanation. She notes that it is "possible that the whole case was a smokescreen to enable [Indian Territory] Governor Harrison to negotiate the new series of treaties with the Indians."[19] Such speculation that it was a "sham trial" is fortified by Daviess's later role as a leader of inflamed settlers seeking to destroy the Indian presence in the area; Henry Adams, in fact, describes Daviess as sabotaging the efforts of the administration to maintain peace with Tecumseh and helping precipitate the massacre at Tippecanoe.[20]

United States v. Hardin was not the only development in 1802 in Kentucky involving the federal law of crimes discussed by Tachau in her study of the federal courts in Kentucky during this period. Later the same year, the Kentucky federal grand jury issued presentments for the prosecution of Asa Combs and Stephen, Robert, and Daniel Kennedy for having counterfeited notes of the Bank of the United States. Although a 1790 federal statute made counterfeiting of U.S. certificates or securities a capital crime,[21] the Bank of the United States, albeit incorporated by an act of Congress, was a private bank not included under the statute. Tachau accordingly suggests that in view of the lack of statutory authority, the case must have been brought under federal criminal common-law jurisdiction. However, the Congress had enacted in June 1798 a statute criminalizing the counterfeiting of the notes of the Bank of the United States.[22] The *Combs* and *Kennedy* cases most likely

---

[19] *See* Mary K. B. Tachau, *Federal Courts in the Early Republic: Kentucky 1789–1816*, 128–133 (1978) (hereinafter Tachau, *Kentucky*).

   Jefferson a decade later used the *Hardin* case as the framework for a complex discussion of the interrelationship of overlapping federal and state law and the unavailability of federal criminal common-law jurisdiction. Thomas Jefferson, Miscellaneous Paper, Observations on the force and obligation in the United States, on the occasion of Hardin's case, in Kentucky, Nov. 11, 1812. 9 Jefferson, *Writings* (Ford), note 6, at 485–489.

[20] *See* 2 H. Adams, *The First Jefferson Administration*, note 4, at 365, 368.

[21] 1 Stat. 115 (1790). This provided: "And be it [further] enacted, that if any person or persons shall . . . counterfeit, or cause or procure to be . . . or counterfeited, or willingly act or assist in . . . counterfeiting any certificate, indent, or other public security of the United States, or shall . . . counterfeited certificate, indent or other public security, with intention to defraud any person, knowing the same to be . . . counterfeited, and shall be thereof convicted, every such person shall suffer death."

[22] 1 Stat. 573 (1798). It is of interest that in the heresies of the Federalist administration condemned in Jefferson's draft of the Kentucky Resolution, Jefferson denounces this very statute as unconstitutional and along with the Alien and Sedition Acts was "altogether void, and no force." In Jefferson's

had been brought under the new statute. In any case, as with the defendants in *Hardin*, the cases faltered. Combs was acquitted. The suits against the Kennedy brothers were continued, but eventually abated.[23]

Tachau further reports another Jeffersonian effort to use a federal criminal action to silence a Federalist editor, Francis Flourney. Flourney had published an article criticizing the alliance with France and Monroe's mission to negotiate what became the Louisiana Purchase as well as advocating Kentucky's secession from the Union. In view of the strong Jeffersonian position that the federal courts had no federal common-law criminal jurisdiction, the administration did not invoke common-law seditious libel. Although alleging that the publication tended "to execute a spirit of discord, seditious discontent, or schism," the federal grand jury's presentation relied on Flourney's alleged violation of the Logan Act for "unlawfully commencing a written correspondence, indirectly, with the French." However, with Napoleon's sudden readiness to consummate the sale of the entire Louisiana Territory, the matter became no longer contentious, and the federal attorney had the case dismissed.[24]

Still another interesting development involving the prominent Republican Alexander J. Dallas (then the United States District Attorney in Pennsylvania and later Secretary of Treasury under Madison) occurred in 1804. As we will see, during the earlier Federalist administrations, Dallas had challenged the constitutionality of federal prosecutions under federal criminal common law in several leading cases.[25] However, now acting as U.S. District Attorney in *United States v. Passmore*, he defended the use of federal criminal common-law jurisdiction to prosecute Passmore for alleged perjury in a bankruptcy proceeding.[26]

The Embargo and Non-Intercourse Acts provided the final occasion for the Jefferson and Madison administrations to consider reliance on federal criminal common-law prosecutions. These Acts were notably ineffective with

---

view, the federal government lacked the power to create federal crimes "other than those so enumerated in the Constitution." *See* Draft of the Kentucky Resolutions, Jefferson, *Writings* 449–450 (Libr. Am. 1984) (hereinafter Jefferson, *Writings* (Libr. Am.)).

[23] *See* Tachau, *Kentucky*, note 19, at 133–134.

[24] United States v. Flourney, (D.C. Ky. 1803), D.C O.S.D. Ky., Mar.14,1803, 94–102. Tachau, *Federal Courts in the Early Republic*, 136–137 (1978).

[25] E.g., United States v. Henfield, 11 F. Cas. 1099, 27 F. Cas. 713, 1793 U.S. App. LEXIS 16, 713 (C.C.D. Pa. 1793) (No. 6360); United States v. Worrall, 2 U.S. (2 Dall.) 384, 28 F. Cas. 774, 1798 LEXIS 39 (C.C.D. Pa. 1798 (No. 16,766).

[26] United States v. Passmore, 4 U.S. (4 Dall.) 372, 27 F. Cas. 458 (C.C.D. Pa. 1804) (No. 16005). (B. Washington, J.) Judgment went to the defendant because of repeal of the statute, not on the issue of jurisdiction.

New England commerce struggling to survive by widespread smuggling. Haskins and Johnson report a number of common-law criminal indictments in Richmond, Virginia, for violation of these enactments.[27]

One of the embargo cases, *United States v. William Smith*, came before Chief Justice Marshall when he was sitting as a Circuit Court Judge in Richmond. Marshall artfully avoided having to decide the fundamental question of whether there was a federal common law of crimes and federal criminal common-law jurisdiction. He ruled that by providing only for civil penalties in the statute, the Congress had indicated its intention that violations were not criminal. He expressly noted that there was, therefore, no occasion to rule on whether federal jurisdiction over common-law crimes existed.[28] Then, as we will see in the following section, the Supreme Court finally ruled in 1812 in *United States v. Hudson & Goodwin*[29] that federal courts lacked criminal common-law jurisdiction.

Surprisingly, this did not immediately dispose of the issue once and for all. Thus notwithstanding Marshall's decision in *United States v. Smith* and the Supreme Court's decision in *Hudson & Goodwin*, the Madison administration continued to give consideration to the use of federal criminal common-law prosecutions to end flagrant violations of the Embargo Act. However, when pressures developed in 1814 to seek such indictments, Attorney General Richard Rush firmly disapproved, noting that his own view of the unavailability of federal criminal common-law jurisdiction had been adopted, "partially at least," by the Supreme Court.[30]

3. Supping with the Devil: Republican Partisan Use of Criminal Libel Against Federalist Critics in the Connecticut Federal Courts Under Federal Criminal Common Law

United States v. Tapping Reeve, United States v. Hudson & Goodwin, and three other prosecutions in Connecticut in Jefferson's second administration

[27] *See* Haskins & Johnson, note 15, at 638 n.111; Letter, Thomas Jefferson to Albert Gallatin (Aug. 11, 1808), 12 Jefferson, *Writings* (Lipscomb), note 9, at 121–123; Richmond *Enquirer*, June 2, 1809.

[28] United States v. William Smith, (C.C.D. Va.1808) (Order Book No. 7, June 2, 1809, 265; Richmond *Enquirer*, June 2, 1809. *See* Katherine Preyer, Jurisdiction to Punish: Federal Authority. Federalism, and the Common Law of Crimes in the Early Republic, 4 Law & Hist. Rev. 223, 246 (1986) (hereinafter Preyer).

[29] United States v. Hudson & Goodwin, 11 U.S. (7 Cranch) 32, 1812 U.S. LEXIS 365 (1812).

[30] Letter, Richard Rush to the United States District Attorney, Boston, Mass. (July 28, 1814), 1 Warren, note 15, at 439. It is noteworthy that the Attorney General was not ready to assert that the Supreme Court had stripped the federal courts of *all* criminal common-law jurisdiction. He may have been concerned about the possible existence of such jurisdiction for crimes under the law of nations or in admiralty.

represent the dramatic use for partisan purposes by a Republican District Attorney and a Republican judge of federal criminal common-law jurisdiction to harass Federalist critics with seditious libel prosecutions.[31] The institution of these prosecutions seemed to have been driven by Connecticut factors and instituted by Connecticut Republicans without any prompting or cooperation with the national administration.

Following the death of the Federalist federal District Court judge Richard Law, President Jefferson appointed Pierpont Edwards, son of Jonathan Edwards and uncle of Aaron Burr, as Connecticut's first Republican District Court judge.[32] Shortly thereafter in April 1806 at the New Haven Term of the Court, probably the first term of court conducted by Judge Edwards, Hezikiah Huntington, Connecticut's first Republican District Attorney, presented to the grand jury the first and only attempt at federal seditious libel prosecutions undertaken under the Jefferson administration. The Sedition Act having expired by its terms with the close of the Adams administration, the actions were at common law.

Instructing the grand jury with a vehemence that any Federalist judge might have envied, Judge Edwards stated that it was their duty to consider the authors and publishers against the government as serious criminal offenders: "Such publications, if the authors of them may not be restrained, but are permitted to continue them with impunity will more effectually undermine and sap the foundation of our Constitution, and Government, than any kind of treason." He then went on to state that the jury had the power to proceed under federal common law and that this view was also the sentiment of a "great majority" of the Justices of the Supreme Court.

---

[31] See generally J. M. Smith, note 1, at 373–384.

There is a rich Connecticut literature on these events. See, e.g., Robert Wetmore, Seditious Libel Prosecutions in 1806 in the Federal Court in Connecticut: United States v. Tapping Reeve and Companion Cases, 57 Conn. B. J. 196, 204 (1983) (hereinafter Wetmore); Derek L. Mocgk, Connecticut Federalists in President Jefferson's (Republican) Court: United States v. Hudson and Goodwin, 41 Conn. Hist. 144 (2002); Charles A. Heckman, A Jeffersonian Lawyer and Judge in Federalist Connecticut: The Career of Pierpont Edwards, 28 Conn. L. Rev. 669 (1992) (hereinafter Heckman).

[32] Edwards had previously served as District Attorney under the Federalists. Six months after Edwards had been appointed to the bench, Madison, on Aug. 4, 1806, forwarded to Jefferson two letters received from Edwards. These related to the prosecution against Smith and Ogden for their roles in the Miranda Affair in which Edwards had served as special counsel. The Miranda affair involved the expeditionary force raised by Gen. Francisco de Miranda for the invasion and "liberation" of Spanish possessions in the Americas. Madison assured Jefferson that Edwards's letters "give a very favorable idea . . . of his own honest and steadfast attachment to the administration." See Letter, James Madison to Thomas Jefferson (Aug. 4, 1806), 3 Republic of Letters: The Correspondence Between Thomas Jefferson and James Madison 1776–1826, 1432–1433 (J. M. Smith ed. 1995) (hereinafter Republic of Letters). Heckman reports that, among other achievements, "For decades after his death, Edwards was known as the "Great Connecticut Adulterer." See Heckman, note 31, at 669.

The grand jury responded by voting indictments under federal criminal common law for seditious libel of President Jefferson against three defendants, Tapping Reeve, Thomas Collier, and Thaddeus Osgood.[33] In the following month at the Hartford Term of the court, a second grand jury voted comparable indictments against three additional defendants, Barzillai Hudson, George Goodwin, and Azel Backus.

All six defendants were Federalist critics of Jefferson and included four prominent Federalists in the state. Judge Tapping Reeve, a staunch Federalist allied to the Essex Junto, was a state court judge, one of the leading Connecticut lawyers of the time, and founder of the Litchfield Law School, America's first law school. Using pen names borrowed from Classical Rome – Asdrubal, Marcellus, and Phocion – Reeve had bitterly attacked Jefferson and the Republicans in a series of articles in the Federalist *Litchfield Monitor*. He was indicted for an article published in the *Monitor* more than four years earlier on December 2, 1801, under the name "Phocion." This assailed Jefferson for "abolishing the Constitution, destroying the judiciary and depriving the people of the right to trial by jury . . . and attempting to establish a despotic government."[34]

Hudson and Goodwin were the editors and publishers of the aggressively Federalist *Connecticut Courant*. Thomas Collier was editor of another prominent Federalist paper, the Litchfield *Monitor*, who was then engaged in a vicious struggle with its Jeffersonian local rival, the Litchfield *Eye-Witness* edited by Selleck Osborne and Thomas Ashley. The other two defendants were Congregationalist ministers, Rev. Azel Backus and Rev. Thaddeus Osgood. They were indicted for vituperative attacks on Jefferson in their sermons. As we will see, the violence of their comments was remarkable.

All officers of the Court were now Republicans. In addition to the Judge and the District Attorney, the Court Marshal was a Republican stalwart, Joseph Willcox, and the Clerk of Court was the Judge's son, Henry Waggaman Edwards.[35] Following the model of the Federalists in administering the 1798 Act, the Republican court personnel appear to have selected grand juries consisting of handpicked Republicans that voted the indictments.[36] According to

---

[33] Richard J. Purcell, *Connecticut in Transition: 1775–1818*, 277 (1918) (hereinafter Purcell).

[34] *See* Wetmore, note 31, at 204.

[35] *Connecticut Courant*, May 21, 1806. Crosskey, a Federalist sympathizer, asserts that the appointment of his son as Court Clerk was Edwards "very first act as judge." *See* 2 William A. Crosskey, *Politics and the Constitution in the History of the United States* 771 (1953) (hereinafter Crosskey). Henry Waggaman Edwards subsequently became a U.S. Senator and Governor of Connecticut.

[36] Thus, in a triumphal letter to President Jefferson reporting on the prosecutions. Thomas Seymour, a prominent Connecticut Republican, confirmed that the indictment had been voted by a grand jury "of the most intelligent of our citizens, attached to the principles which uniformly guided the

Dumas Malone, the distinguished admiring biographer of Thomas Jefferson, the prosecutions were prompted and guided by the Connecticut Republican State Chairman, Alexander Wolcott. Malone adds that when the cases were called, Wolcott had been seen in court consulting "frequently" with the District Attorney, Huntington.[37] There does not appear to be any available evidence indicating consultation with the Republican national administration as well. However, as we will see, Jefferson soon learned of the prosecutions and acquiesced for months.

Jefferson subsequently sought to excuse this Republican partisan campaign,[38] commenting that the Republican "spirit of indignation and retaliation" was an understandable reaction to the prosecutions for libel brought earlier by Federalist prosecutors against Republicans in the Connecticut state courts. For Republicans, the cause célèbre was the libel conviction by a Federalist state court judge and jury of Selleck Osborne, editor of the strongly Republican newspaper, the *Eye-Witness*, in the Federalist stronghold of Litchfield. The Republicans were particularly indignant because of Osborne's "confinement in a dark, damp, noisome jungle, with maniacs and felons." The Federalists denied the charges of ill-treatment. They charged that Osborne was only in confinement because he had declined to pay his $400 fine for civil libel of a Connecticut Federalist, Julius Deming. They claimed that Osborne preferred to play the role of martyr to free speech and ill-treatment at the hands of a Federalist judge, an allegedly packed Federalist jury, and an inhumane Federalist jailor.[39]

---

administration." *See* Letter, Thomas Seymour to Thomas Jefferson (Dec. 20, 1806) (William K. Bixby Collection). *See also* Purcell, note 33, at 175. Jefferson responded. Letter, Thomas Jefferson to Thomas Seymour (Feb. 11, 1807), 11 Jefferson, *Writings* (Lipscomb), note 9, at 155.

That the jury had been packed with Republicans was ultimately conceded, even by Jefferson. *See* Letter, Thomas Jefferson to Wilson Cary Nicholas (June 13, 1809), 12 Jefferson, *Writings* (Lipscomb), note 9, at 287, 290 ("the marshals being republicans had summoned a grand jury partly or wholly republican"). The person selecting the jurors was the Republican Marshal, Joseph Willcox.

[37] Jefferson had appointed Wolcott as the Collector of the Port of Middletown, yielding a rich harvest of $3,000 per year in fees. This was a rich plum. Supreme Court Justices earned only $3,500 per year at this time. *See* 5 Malone, note 17, at 373–374; 1 Warren, *History*, note 15, at 416 n.1. In 1813 President Madison appointed Wolcott to the Supreme Court, but he failed badly of confirmation, by a vote of 9 to 24. Warren dismisses Wolcott as a man "of somewhat mediocre legal ability." *Id.*, at 410–413.

[38] *See* Letter, Thomas Jefferson to Thomas Seymour (Feb. 11, 1807), 11 Jefferson, *Writings* (Lipscomb), note 9, at 155.

[39] *See generally* 2 Crosskey, note 35, at 766–784 (1953); 5 Malone, note 17, at 376–377; J. McNulty, *Older than the Nation: The Story of the Hartford* Courant 37–38 (1966) (hereinafter McNulty). The press comment was extensive. *See*, *e.g.*, Hartford *American Mercury*, Aug. 14, 1806; *United States Gazette*, Apr. 24, 1806; *Connecticut Courant*, Oct. 1, 1806; *United States Gazette*, Oct. 7, 1806; Richmond *Enquirer*, Oct. 17, 1806; *United States Gazette*, May 9, 1807.

Even if Jefferson had not learned of the indictments at the time of the grand jury action in April 1806, a series of communications soon brought them forcibly to his attention. On October 9, 1806, Gideon Granger, his Postmaster General, wrote to express his concern: "where will be the liberty of future generations if the dreadful doctrines maintained by Federalists . . . are to be sanctioned by precedents given by the Republican Administration?" Like Hamilton shaking his head when he first learned of the High Federalist proposals leading to the Sedition Act, Granger also advised that they were politically inexpedient. A week later, the Richmond *Enquirer*, the paper regularly read by Jefferson according to Leonard W. Levy, reported the criminal libel indictments by the grand jury.[40] Then, in December 1806, Thomas Seymour, a leading Connecticut Republican, wrote in detail, reporting on the prosecutions.[41]

The following month, January 1807, Federalist Congressman Samuel W. Dana – later Senator from Connecticut – raised the problem of criminal libel in the Congress. Seeking the enactment of a bill moderating the harsh standards of the common-law doctrine by specifying the role of truth and the jury in federal common-law criminal libel litigation, Dana did not mention the Connecticut litigations by name. However, they were the only pending seditious libel prosecutions in the federal system, and the reference was unmistakable. Dana further discussed the prosecutions with Granger, the Connecticut member of the Cabinet, and urged him to intervene with the President.[42]

There is a further circumstance to be considered. Tapping Reeve and Judge Edwards were related by marriage. Reeve, one of the defendants in the cases before Edwards, had been married to Sarah (Sally) Burr, sister of Aaron Burr. Sarah was the Judge's niece, making Reeve the Judge's nephew by marriage. Edwards is said to have recused himself because of the relationship. However, Sally had died on March 30, 1797, and Edwards had remarried in 1799, years before the prosecution. At best, the relationship had significantly faded away.[43] Whatever the explanation for the Judge's conduct, the facts are plain. Judge

---

[40] Letter, Gideon Granger to Thomas Jefferson (Oct. 9, 1806) (Libr. Cong. 28,332–28,334); Richmond *Enquirer*, Oct. 17, 1806. *See* Levy, *The Emergence of a Free Press* 344 (1985); 5 Malone, note 17, at 380.

[41] Letter, Thomas Seymour to Thomas Jefferson (Dec. 20, 1806) (William K. Bixby Collection, to which Jefferson responded. Letter, Thomas Jefferson to Thomas Seymour (Feb. 11, 1807), 9 Jefferson, *Writings* (Ford), note 6, at 137–140).

[42] 19 Annals, at 1327–1328; 20 *id.*, at 78–80, 83–84.

[43] *See* Heckman, note 31, at 700.

Edwards at no time took any action of any kind in connection with the *Reeve* case, other than to approve continuances. Nor did the District Attorney or counsel for Reeve take any step that would have required a decision of any nature from the Judge, other than to have the case continued to another term. Throughout the years of the litigation of the accompanying cases, the *Reeve* case remained in limbo. In view of the unreadiness of Judge Edwards and District Attorney Huntington to prosecute Reeve, it is not clear why he was indicted in the first place.

Two other defendants, Barzillai Hudson and George Goodwin, were the editors of the leading Federalist paper in the state, the *Connecticut Courant*. They were indicted for an article in the *Courant* boldly asserting that President Jefferson and the Congress having sat two months in secret conclave had voted two million dollars, a present to Bonaparte, for "leave to make a treaty with Spain" for acquisition of West Florida and that 60 tons of silver had been delivered to Napoleon as a bribe to stop French seizure of American ships.[44]

Hudson and Goodwin were longtime political enemies of Jefferson. During the 1800 presidential campaign, they had bitterly attacked him. Thus, in the June 20, 1800, issue of the *Connecticut Courant*, they charged that Jefferson had "long felt a spirit of deadly hostility against the Federal Constitution" and that if elected President, "the Constitution will inevitably fall a sacrifice to Jacobinism.... The result will be dreadful to the people of the United States."[45]

The remaining three defendants were less prominent people. One was Thomas Collier, editor of the Litchfield *Monitor* in which Reeve's offending articles had appeared. The other two were clergymen apparently selected for indictment because of the extreme nature of their comments about President Jefferson in their sermons. Rev. Azel Backus was indicted for a particularly vituperative attack on the President. In a sermon in Bethlehem, Conn., he had denounced Jefferson as "a liar, whoremaster, debaucher, drunkard, gambler, and infidel [who] keeps a black wench as his whore and brings up in his family black females for that purpose"[46] Rev. Thaddeus Osgood was an aspiring minister, indicted for allegedly calling Jefferson a "base, traitorous infidel, debaucher and liar" in his sermon to a congregation on Thanksgiving Day, 1805.[47]

---

[44] *Connecticut Courant*, May 7, 1806.
[45] *Connecticut Courant*, June 20, 1800. *See* McNulty, note 39, at 38.
[46] *See* 3 *Republic of Letters*, note 32, at 1479–1480 n.39.
[47] 5 Malone, note 17, at 376.

After the arraignment of the defendants at which all pleaded not guilty, the cases were held over for the September 1806 Term. Five of the defendants posted bail and were released. Rev. Thaddeus Osgood, the ministry candidate, was unable to post bail or find sureties. Although commentators including William W. Crosskey simply leave Osgood languishing in jail awaiting trial, Malone reports that after two days, two prominent Federalists – David Daggett (later Chief Justice of the Connecticut Supreme Court) and Reeve himself – posted bail, and he was released.[48] The cases were marked for trial at the April 1807 Term.

When the cases came for trial at the April 1807 Term, things did not go well. At the outset, Edwards sat alone; Justice Brockhurst Livingston, the designated Circuit Justice, was not qualified under the empowering statute to sit in Connecticut because he was not a Connecticut resident. Counsel for several of the defendants objected to going to trial because they intended to challenge the criminal common-law jurisdiction of the Court and wanted Justice Livingston to participate in the decision. Edwards noted that the statute had to be amended before Livingston could participate, that this would take a year, and that trial should not be deferred so long. He assured counsel that the jurisdictional issue could be raised after trial on a motion in arrest of judgment.

Nevertheless, the cases did not go to trial. The District Attorney, Huntington, explained that the indictments contained defects and that the trials could not proceed. As Huntington explained this to Judge Edwards case by case, the judge became increasingly angry. The *Osgood* case was the last case to be heard. When the indictment in that case also proved defective, and, further, when Huntington acknowledged that he would not have been prepared to proceed even if the indictment had been in order, the proceedings bordered on the ridiculous. Judge Edward then became very angry indeed. He threw out the indictment and dismissed the *Osgood* case. Trial of the remaining five cases was deferred to the September 1807 Term while new indictments were prepared and substituted for the earlier indictments.[49]

At the September 1807 Term, counsel for the three publishers – Hudson, Goodwin, and Collier – filed demurrers, pleading the absence of criminal common-law jurisdiction in the federal courts. Judge Edwards, who had been eager for trial at the April Term, reversed course and abandoned his efforts to have them go to trial. This time he postponed matters until Justice Livingston could join him in determining the matter.

---

[48] *Compare* 2 Crosskey, note 35, at 771 *with* Malone, note 17, at 376.
[49] *Connecticut Courant*, May 13, 1807.

Although Edwards urged that the remaining cases also go over until the jurisdictional issue had been determined, counsel for Backus insisted on trial. They stated that they had been ready to proceed immediately, but that the witnesses they had subpoenaed from Virginia to prove the truth of Backus's charges had been told by the President of the United States, Thomas Jefferson, to disregard the summons; their appearance was no longer necessary because the cases would be dismissed.[50] In view of the unavailability of the witnesses, both Edwards and Huntington sought to defer matters until the underlying issue of the availability of federal jurisdiction had been determined. Counsel for Backus refused. Instead, he gave notice of his intention to go to trial at the next term.

Backstage events of great import were seemingly afoot. Judge Edwards, in the past so urgent in pressing for immediate trial, had abruptly changed his mind. The President of the United States had been instructing witnesses who were under federal subpoena to ignore a court order. What was going on? Counsel for Backus had taken their gloves off. They were evidently ready to back up the truth of the defendant's alleged libel that Jefferson was a "whoremaster."

To consider the impact of this tactic it is necessary to understand fully the role of truth in these common-law criminal libel cases in Connecticut federal courts. Because the prosecutions relied on the federal common law of criminal libel, it would have seemed that the trials were to be conducted under the rigorous common-law rules with respect to the role of truth and the jury. As readers will recall, at common law, evidence of truth was not admissible and the role of the jury was severely restricted, all as described in Blackstone.

However, this was no longer the case in Connecticut. In May 1804, the Connecticut Legislature, still controlled by Federalists, had liberalized the Connecticut law of criminal libel. It adopted in *haec verba* the more liberal standards with respect to the admissibility of evidence of truth and the greatly expanded role for the jury that had been such striking, albeit anomalous, provisions of the Sedition Act.[51]

Although the new statutory rule now governed libel prosecutions in the Connecticut state courts, these cases were in federal court. However, the federal Judiciary Act of 1789 stated that such state rules of procedure would

---

[50] The subpoena to Madison (July 29, 1807), 3 *Republic of Letters*, note 32, at 1479, signed by Chief Justice Marshall was forwarded by Madison to Jefferson by an undated letter received by Jefferson on Aug. 24, 1807. Jefferson replied the next day. *See* Letter, Thomas Jefferson to James Madison (Sept. 18, 1807), *id.*, at 1497–1498.

[51] Conn. Pub. Stat. Laws 355 (1808).

apply to trials at common law in the federal courts of the state.[52] Hence, Judge Edwards ruled that the trials of the six defendants would be conducted according to the more liberal Connecticut state practice.[53] It was this ruling that provided counsel for Backus with their opportunity.

Relying on the ruling, counsel for Backus were plainly determined to present the details of Jefferson's infatuation and attempted seduction of Betsy Walker, wife of one of Jefferson's friends, neighbor, and intimate, John Walker.[54] In 1768 Walker was on a four-month government mission to Fort Stanwix, N.Y. Before his departure, he made a new will, naming Jefferson one of his executors and leaving his young wife and infant son in Jefferson's charge. Then, while Walker was away on government service, Jefferson, 25 and unmarried, proved faithless to his trust and ardently pursued Mrs. Walker.

After he returned and heard his wife's account of the incident, Walker was outraged. He demanded that Jefferson exonerate his wife and protect her reputation. Gen. Henry Lee, father of Robert E. Lee, acted for Walker, and ultimately Jefferson confessed his role to a selected group, including Lee, James Monroe, and David Randolph.[55] However, although Jefferson may have achieved an uneasy peace with Walker, he had not put the matter behind him.

Three decades later, the sordid affair had leaked out. It was 1802, and Jefferson was now President. He had at last broken with that notorious master of calumny, James Thomson Callender, who had earlier been so useful politically with his poisonous attacks against Adams. Callender then turned on Jefferson and took his revenge. Along with other distasteful charges against Jefferson, such as insinuations about Sally Hemings, whom Callender made famous as "Dusky Sally" and "Sooty Sal," Callender learned of Jefferson's role in the Walker affair and reported it with relish.[56] Aware of the matter, counsel for Backus subpoenaed Walker, Madison, and the peacemakers – Lee, Monroe, and Randolph – as witnesses to prove the truth of the alleged

[52] Section 2, 1 Stat. 73 (1789).

[53] Judge Edwards's construction of the Judiciary Act did not survive. Shortly thereafter in the *Burr* trial the judges, including Chief Justice Marshall, ruled that this provision in the Judiciary Act did not apply to federal cases involving criminal prosecutions for crimes against the United States. *See* 2 Crosskey, note 35, at 774, *citing* 2 Burr's Trial 481–482 (1808).

[54] This discussion of the Walker affair rests substantially on the accounts in 4 Dumas Malone, *Jefferson and His Time: Jefferson the President; First Term, 1801–1805*, 216–223 (1970) (hereinafter 4 Malone); 5 Malone, note 17 at 14–15, 386–387; and 1 Crosskey, note 35, at 779.

[55] *See* 1 Dumas Malone, *Jefferson and His Time: Jefferson the Virginian* 153–155, Appdx. III (1948), *citing* Letter, Thomas Jefferson to Robert Smith (July 11, 1805). Jefferson acknowledged: "when young and single, I offered love to a handsome lady. I acknowledge its incorrectness." *See* 3 *Republic of Letters*, note 32, at 1491 n.51.

[56] *See* 4 Malone, note 54, at 212–216.

libel of Jefferson. Thus, it was apparent to all that the *Backus* trial was going to revolve around the Walker affair and whether Jefferson's conduct with Mrs. Walker justified the use of the term "whoremaster."

For Jefferson, this was intolerable. As described in his letter to Madison dated August 25, 1807:

> I had never any information of the [Backus] case, its parties or subject, until that I had read in the newspapers some time ago.... I accordingly wrote to Mr. Granger [Postmaster General and Jefferson's Connecticut liaison], who is at home, recommending in general an endeavor to have the whole prosecution dropped if it could be done.[57]

At the same time, Jefferson advised the three witnesses that it would not be necessary to attend in response to the subpoena, and that "if they [the summoned witnesses] do not attend, the cause will certainly be laid over until the spring term."[58]

Three weeks after his letter to Madison, Jefferson wrote again to him on September 18, 1807, reassuring him: "I have a letter from Connecticut. The prosecution there will be dismissed this term on the ground that the case is not cognizable by the courts of the U.S. Perhaps you intimate this where it will give tranquillity."[59] Before the next term, the Congress finally amended the Judiciary Act deleting the provision that a Circuit Court Justice could only sit in a state in which he was a resident, at last enabling Justice Livingston to take up his assignment as a Circuit Judge in Connecticut.[60] It

---

[57] Letter, Thomas Jefferson to James Madison (Aug. 25, 1807), 3 *Republic of Letters*, note 32, at 1490.

Jefferson's statements about his knowledge of the Connecticut cases is less than candid. As we have seen, Jefferson learned of the cases in Oct. 1806, if not earlier, when Postmaster General Granger wrote to advise that the cases were "contrary to Republican principles" and should be withdrawn, and likely from the story at the same time in the Richmond *Enquirer*, his favorite newspaper. Letter, Gideon Granger to Thomas Jefferson (Oct. 9, 1806) (Libr. Cong. 28,332–28,334); Richmond *Enquirer* Oct. 17, 1806. *See* 5 Malone, note 17, at 380. This was ten months before his letter to Madison.

Jefferson maintained the pretense that he acted as soon as he learned of the Connecticut prosecutions. Thus, in 1809 Jefferson was still claiming that the Connecticut prosecutions "were disapproved by me as soon as known, and directed to be discontinued." Thomas Jefferson, Letter to Wilson Cary Nicholas (June 13, 1809). 12 Jefferson, *Writings* (Lipscomb), note 9, at 287, 289, 290 (Jefferson claimed to have acted "because the federal courts had no jurisdiction over libels").

[58] Letter, Thomas Jefferson to James Madison (Aug. 25, 1807) *See* 3 *Republic of Letters*, note 32, at 1490; *See also* 11 Jefferson, *Writings* (Lipscomb), note 9, at 108–110. *But see* Jefferson's letter a few years later to Wilson Cary Nicholas (June 13, 1809) trying to explain away the earlier letter. *Id.*, at 108.

[59] Letter, Thomas Jefferson to James Madison (Sept. 18, 1807), 3 *Republic of Letters*, note 32, at 1497–1498.

[60] 2 Stat. 471 (1808).

had taken the Congress 19 years to correct the deficiency in the statute.[61] When Court resumed in 1808, Justice Livingston finally joined Judge Edwards, and matters began to move to a conclusion. The two judges heard the demurrer to jurisdiction in the *Hudson & Goodwin* case and predictably divided on the issue. The matter was certified to the Supreme Court for decision,[62] and the remaining cases were dismissed. These included not only the case against Judge Reeve, in which no action of any kind other than continuance had taken place since his arraignment, but the cases against Thomas Collier and Rev. Azel Backus as well. Whether or not counsel for Backus wanted to proceed with the trial and rub the Walker affair once again in Jefferson's face, they were helpless. Once Jefferson wrote to Granger, Granger visited with the District Attorney, and the District Attorney promptly entered plea of *nolle prosequi*.

The events in Connecticut reverberated in Washington for some time. In 1809 John Randolph, a prominent Virginia Republican who had become increasingly eccentric and alienated from Jefferson, moved in the House of Representatives for an investigation of the Connecticut prosecutions. However, Jefferson's supporters in the House were able to throttle the threat of investigation.[63]

4. The Constitutional Issue: Did the Federal Courts Have Criminal Common-Law Jurisdiction?

a. The Experience in the First 25 Years of the Early American Republic

From the earliest days of the new nation, the federal judiciary was repeatedly confronted with the issue of whether the federal courts possessed federal criminal common-law jurisdiction. By the end of the last decade of the 18th century, the federal courts staffed with Federalist judges had repeatedly

---

[61] It may be that the statutory limitation had simply been ignored during the Federalist administrations. As we have seen in developments reviewed in the previous chapters, numerous justices are described as participating as Circuit Court judges in more than one state in delivering charges to the grand jury (Iredell, Ellsworth) or presiding in criminal libel trials (Chase, Paterson).

[62] United States v. Hudson & Goodwin, 11 U.S. (7 Cranch) 32, 1812 U.S. LEXIS 365 (1812). In the Judiciary Act of 1802, the statute was amended to permit either party to certify the matter to the Supreme Court, 2 Stat. 156, 159–161 (1802). In *Hudson & Goodwin*, however, neither party would certify, and the judges did so. The propriety of such a departure from the literal terms of the statute was not discussed by the Court; perhaps the judges concluded that they had inherent power to do so. At any rate, the ability of the judges to certify *sua sponte* was subsequently upheld *sub silentio* in *Hudson & Goodwin* and again in United States v. Daniel, 19 U.S. (10 Wheat.) 542, 547–548 (1821) (Marshall, C.J.).

[63] *See* Warren, *History*, note 15, at 437 n.1.

upheld such jurisdiction. During the Washington and Adams administrations, there were nine cases involving common-law criminal libel and even more involving offenses against the federal government or its officers or the implementation of federal statutory policies. Some of the cases were prominent and received national attention, but many were obscure. Numerous cases went no further than the indictment stage. In as many more, however, they went to conclusion. However, the law was plain. In 1800 there could be no question to the legal observer of the time. The Federalist-dominated Circuit Courts had overwhelmingly accepted and were routinely applying the concept of a federal common law of crimes. Although this was the law as seen by the judges, Federalists all, it lacked acceptance by the society as a whole. On the contrary, it was being hotly disputed in the political arena, and law that fails to receive general acceptance, particularly politicized law, does not survive. And so it proved in this case.

With their defeat in the 1800 elections, the Federalists went into a rapid decline, and the country fell under Republican hegemony for the ensuing two decades. With Jefferson's election, Republican rule became immediately effective in the Executive and Legislative branches, but only very slowly percolated into the Judiciary. As the aging Federalist judges died or retired, they were replaced by Republican judges who did not share their views. As the judges changed, so did constitutional interpretation. By 1812 with a Republican majority on the Supreme Court, the law changed with the Court's decision in *United States v. Hudson & Goodwin*, the Connecticut criminal libel case.[64] Notwithstanding the virtually unbroken chain of lower court authority, Justice Johnson, speaking for the majority of the Court, held that the federal courts had no criminal common-law jurisdiction. The minority,[65] and it is not clear who they were, did not trouble to dissent formally.[66]

---

[64] As we have seen, this was one of six seditious libel cases instituted in 1806 in Connecticut against Federalists, some prominent, some obscure, for bitter attacks on Jefferson.

[65] It is not clear which justices were in the minority. Most likely, it included Justice Story. Although some historians have also included Bushrod Washington, Cranch's report states that he was not present. 11 U.S. (7 Cranch) at 32. As for Marshall, whether or not he would have voted to uphold federal jurisdiction had the issue arisen a decade or so earlier, the historians disagree whether he in fact was still ready to press the issue in 1812 and vote to uphold the doctrine. *Compare* R. Kent Newmyer, *Joseph Story: Statesman of the Republic* 101 (1985) (hereinafter Newmyer) (with the majority) *with* 2 Crosskey, note 35, at 783 (with the dissent along wth Bushrod Washington and Story).

[66] Justice Story was not daunted. In *United States v. Coolidge*, an admiralty case, Justice Story sitting as Circuit Court Justice sought to revive federal criminal common-law jurisdiction, but could not persuade District Court Judge Davis who was also sitting to join him. United States v. Coolidge, 25 Fed. Cas. 619, 621, 622, 1815 U.S. App. LEXIS 260 (C.C.D. Mass. 1815) (No. 14,857). In light of the division of the Court, the judges certified the question to the Supreme Court. The Supreme

Decided more than a decade after the Republicans had assumed power and with the Federalists fading away, the decision was fully in keeping with the rushing tide of political events. This striking manifestation of the interlocking nature of law and politics reappeared a century later with the decisions in the 1930s upsetting the constitutional jurisprudence of the previous decades. Although the movement is still in its early stages, the country seems to be experiencing a similar reversal of constitutional jurisprudence in the early 21st century.

Unlike the other constitutional issues in criminal libel prosecutions, the federal courts considering the threshold constitutional issue of the existence of federal criminal common-law jurisdiction for prosecutions for criminal libel had numerous federal judicial precedents to guide them. When the first common-law criminal libel case involving domestic partisan political concerns arose in 1798, federal courts had already faced the jurisdictional issue in other areas involving the implementation of federal authority. They had uniformly upheld the availability of federal jurisdiction over other common-law crimes in eight other cases. The legal problem was whether criminal libel could be distinguished from those other cases.

Starting with the unreported 1790 decision in *United States v. Hopkins* (murder at sea),[67] the 1792 decision in *United States v. Smith* (counterfeiting of bills of the Bank of the United States,[68] and the 1793 decision in *United States v. Rivers* (violation of American neutrality),[69] the federal courts without exception accepted federal criminal jurisdiction[70] to punish crimes involving

Court, however, refused to overrule *Hudson & Goodwin*, putting the issue finally to bed. United States v. Coolidge, 14 U.S. (1 Wheat.) 415, 1816 U.S. LEXIS 336 (1816). *See* 1 William W. Story, *Life and Letters of Joseph Story* 243–245, 247 (1851 repr. 1971).

[67] Four years before *Henfield*, in United States v. Hopkins, two sailors were tried at common law before Chief Justice Jay, Justice Cushing and District Judge James Duane for the crime of conspiracy to seize a ship and murder its captain. Apparently, the jurisdiction of the Court was not challenged. The Court took jurisdiction and convicted the defendants. United States v. Hopkins (C.C.D. N.Y. Apr. 12, 1790) (unreported). *See* Letter, William Cushing to John Lowell (Apr. 4, 1790), 2 *Documentary History of the Supreme Court* 21–22 (Maeva Marcus ed. 1990) (hereinafter Doc. Hist. Sup. Ct.).

　　See William R. Casto, *The Supreme Court in the Early Republic: The Chief Justiceships of John Jay and Oliver Ellsworth* 130 (1995) (hereinafter Casto, *Supreme Court*), *citing* Wythe Holt, The First Meeting of the Circuit Court in New York: A Federal Common Law of Crimes? in *Second Circuit Redbook 1990–1991* Supp. 119 (V. Alexander ed. 1990).

[68] United States v. Smith, 27 F. Cas. 1147, 1792 U.S. App. LEXIS 23 (C.C.D. Mass. 1792) (No. 16323).

[69] United States v. Rivers, (C.C.D. Ga. 1793); see Casto, *Supreme Court*, note 67, at 135n.

[70] While a few of these cases did not proceed beyond the indictment stage, most went to trial with one acquittal (*Henfield*) and numerous convictions.

such matters as federal maritime issues, the law of nations, and interferences with federal officers before the first of the partisan criminal libel cases came before the courts in 1798.

This earlier body of jurisprudence also included *United States v. Ravara* (1793; attempted extortion of a British Minister); *United States v. Henfield* (1793) and *United States v. The Roland* (1793; serving on a French privateer in violation of the nation's obligations under treaty); *United States v. Thomas Greenleaf* (1794); Greenleaf I (libel of British Minister); *United States v. Thomas Greenleaf* (1797); Greenleaf II (libel of British Minister); and *United States v. Cobbett* (1797; libel of the King of Spain and the Spanish Minister).[71] The failure of any judge to challenge its availability confirms its acceptance as part of the jurisprudence of the time.[72] In addition, no fewer than seven Justices of the Supreme Court in performing official duties in their charges to grand and petit juries similarly upheld the availability of federal criminal common-law jurisdiction. These included Chief Justice Oliver Ellsworth, who elaborately defended the existence of federal common-law crimes in his charge to the South Carolina grand jury in May 1799 that was reprinted in newspapers based in at least eight different states.[73]

Although the Supreme Court had not yet been faced with the issue, the virtual unanimity of the decisions and views of the Federalist justices and judges in this extensive body of litigation made it clear that under their view of the new federal system, the federal courts had common-law criminal jurisdiction, at least over crimes involving the law of nations, the treaty power, or federal officers. This was also the official opinion of each of three Attorneys General who had to rule formally on the issue.

Before the *Henfield*, *Greenleaf* (I), and *Cobbett* cases were commenced, the Secretaries of State involved (Jefferson, Randolph, and Pickering) requested

---

[71] United States v. Hopkins (C.C.D. N.Y. Apr. 12, 1790) (unreported); United States v. Ravara, 2 U.S. 297, 27 F. Cas. 713, 1793 U.S. LEXIS 245, (C.C.D. Pa. 1793); United States v. Henfield, 11 F. Cas 1099, 1793 U.S. App. LEXIS 16 (C.C.D. Pa. 1793) (No. 6,360) and United States v. The Roland, (C.C.D. 1793) (unreported); United States v. Thomas Greenleaf (C.C.D. N.Y. 1795) (unreported); United States v. Thomas Greenleaf (C.C.D. N.Y. 1797) (Greenleaf II) (unreported). Although the *Greenleaf* cases involved alleged libels, jurisdiction was supported by the recognized obligation of a nation to protect foreign ambassadors under the law of nations and did not have to rest on a general federal common law of crimes.

[72] Although some historians attempt to dismiss the significance of these cases, by asserting that the issue of jurisdiction was not before the court. However, as every lawyer knows, lack of subject matter jurisdiction cannot be waived, and courts have the duty to challenge their jurisdiction, even if they have to raise the issue *sua sponte*.

[73] *See* 3 Doc. Hist. Sup. Ct. 357, note 67, at 357; Casto, *Supreme Court*, note 67, at 116.

the opinions of the Attorney General. Each of the Attorneys General (Randolph, Bradford, and Lee) recommended prosecution. They unanimously agreed that the federal courts had jurisdiction.

Henfield[74] involved a violation of treaties with England and allied powers providing for peace between the subjects of the signatories. Randolph noted that "treaties are the supreme law of the land" and that the courts had common-law jurisdiction because the violation was "disturbing the peace of the United States."[75] *Greenleaf* (I) involved a libelous publication about the British Minister. In Bradford's opinion, this was criminal, and in the case of Ministers, the municipal law was strengthened by the law of nations. He stopped at this point, leaving it to the reader to assume that federal jurisdiction flowed automatically.[76]

Cobbett similarly involved libelous publications about the King of Spain and the Spanish Ambassador. Lee relied on the obligation of nations, presumably under the law of nations to punish insults to foreign ambassadors. Lee went further and quoting Lord Mansfield volunteered that "no infringement of the liberty of the press" was involved.[77] When the Adams administration was considering the advisability of prosecuting William Blount in 1797 for recruiting for the invasion of West Florida, then under Spanish sovereignty, Lee again counseled that prosecution could proceed under federal criminal common-law jurisdiction. Although Blount was expelled from the Senate, he was not punished further.[78] On still another offence involving conduct of an American in retrieving property from Spanish-held Florida, Lee found the offence a violation of the law of nations and one that could be punished in federal courts as a common-law misdemeanor, Congress having enacted no statute. Lee explained: "The common law has adopted the law of nations in its fullest extent, and made it a part of the law of the land."[79]

---

[74] Henfield's Case, 11 F. Cas. 1099, 1793 U.S. App. LEXIS 16 (C.C.D. Pa. 1793) (No. 6,360). *See* Casto, *Supreme Court*, note 67, at 130–135.

[75] Edmund Randolph, Opinion, May 30, 1793, 1 Doc. Legisl. & Exec. of the Congress of the U.S. 152 (1833).

[76] William Bradford, Opinion, Sept. 17, 1794, 1 Op. Att'y Gen. 52 (1791–1825).

[77] Charles Lee, Opinion, July 27, 1797, 1 Op. Att'y Gen. 71 (1791–1825).

[78] Charles Lee, Opinion, July 28, 1797, 1 Op. Att'y Gen. 75.

[79] Charles Lee, Opinion, Jan. 26, 1797, 1 Op, Att'y Gen. 68.

    Lee was likely following Chief Justice McKean's dictum in Respublica v. De Longchamps, 1 U.S. (1 Dall.) 111, 116 (Pa. Oyer & Term. 1784) ("This law [the law of nations] in its fullest extent is part of the law of this State"). In turn, this rested on a comment by Lord Mansfield. Triquet et al. v. Bath, 3 Burrow 148 (K.B. 1748).

    Justice Iredell had also echoed the dictum. In his charges to the grand jury in 1792, 1794, and 1796 upholding federal jurisdiction to punish violations of American neutrality Mansfield quoted the "clear opinion" of Lord Talbot in Buvol V. Barbut (Barbuit's Case), Talbot's Cases in Equity 281 (July 16, 1736; 2d ed. 1753). However, the quotation appears in The Reporter's Note,

As this body of jurisprudence began to develop, it attracted little public attention and seemingly appeared to be no more than a technical legal issue. However, as difficulties with the French multiplied, party lines and allegiances firmed up, cases began to take on political dimensions, and the atmosphere soon changed. Then, when the Federalist government began to make partisan use of the doctrine commencing with the *Cabell* presentment in 1797, the situation exploded. As happened throughout this period, Jefferson played an important role behind the scenes. At his urging, the Virginia Legislature adopted a resolution condemning the *Cabell* presentment and subsequently in its famous resolution condemning the Sedition Act as unconstitutional, it again asserted its opposition.[80] It went on to instruct the two Virginia Senators to oppose any law pertaining to federal common-law jurisdiction.[81]

Until the prosecution of Robert Worrall in 1798 for attempted bribery of a federal official, the Commissioner of Revenue, every one of the many judges who had considered the issue had upheld the availability of federal common-law jurisdiction. Then in *Worrall*, Justice Samuel Chase acting as a Circuit Justice vigorously challenged the doctrine.

Counsel for Worrall included the prominent Republican lawyer Alexander J. Dallas, whom we have already met on several occasions. In his earlier defense of *Henfield*, Dallas had unsuccessfully argued against the constitutionality of federal criminal common-law prosecution. In *Worrall*, he repeated the argument. Although he conceded that the Congress could criminalize bribery or the attempted bribery of federal officials, Dallas argued that it was not a crime until it had done so. He then unsuccessfully tried to distinguish the earlier convictions under federal criminal common-law jurisdiction. In arguing that the Constitution nowhere contemplated federal criminal common-law jurisdiction, he contended that jurisdiction in the *Henfield* case involving conduct allegedly in violation of the country's treaties with the

---

not in Talbot's opinion. Mansfield is echoed by Balckstone, 4 W. Balckstone, Commentaries on the Laws of England 67 (1769 repr. 1992). Justice Iredell asserted that the law of nations was part of the laws of the United States "in the same manner and upon the same principle as any other offence committed against the common law." 3 Doc. Hist. Sup. Ct., note 67, 106, 111; 2 Griffith J. McRee, *Life and Correspondence of James Iredell* 423, 467–474 (1857) (hereinafter McRee).

    But see Philip Hamburger, Law and Judicial Duty 350 n.43 (asserting that the dictum was overbroad, that the law of nations was always subject to "the law of the land," and referring to Art. I, sec. 8 of the Constitution authorizing the Congress "to define and punish . . . Offences against the Law of Nations"). *Compare* Sosa v. Alvarez-Machain, 542 U.S. 692, 714 (2004) (Souter, J.).

[80] Majority Report on the Virginia Resolutions, in James Madison, *Writings* 608–662 (Libr. Am. 1999).

[81] *See* 4 Madison, *Letters and Other Writings* 533–539 (1865).

Dutch and British rested on the express recognition in the Constitution of the federal government's treaty power. Similarly, he sought to distinguish the decision in *Ravara*, as sustained by the defendant's "official character as a consul."

When U.S. District Attorney William Rawle, who prosecuted so many of these cases, started to respond, Justice Chase brusquely interrupted him and flatly asserted that "the indictment cannot be sustained": the United States had no common-law jurisdiction. Not troubling to discuss the views of the other judges and justices, Chase ridiculed the suggestion, pointing out that the common law of the various states differed but nowhere was it the entire common law of England. He inquired: What then did the federal common law consist of? Further, how did it become part of the federal system since neither Constitution nor Congress had enacted it?

Chase's outburst did not end matters. District Judge Peters who was also sitting did not agree. Having the support of the unanimous decisions of all the previous judges and Attorneys General who had considered the issue of federal criminal common-law jurisdiction, Peters spoke out vigorously. He contended that the inherent powers of the federal government to preserve itself provided the constitutional basis for the prosecution. In his view, the defendant had committed an offence against the well-being of the government. It was a misdemeanor that the government had the common-law power to punish.[82]

With the two-person Court divided on this critical issue of jurisdiction, the judges attempted to have counsel refer matters in the Supreme Court, but counsel declined. However, an extraordinary event then occurred. After what the Dallas report describes as a "brief consultation," Justice Chase, notwithstanding his earlier expression of opinion, joined Peters in convicting Worrall.[83] The two judges sentenced Worrall to three months in jail and fined him $200. This could not have occurred unless Chase had changed his mind on jurisdiction. In his notes on the case, Wharton speculates that Justice Chase "had used this 'short consultation' to learn the views of so many of his brethren on the supreme bench, about which, after *Henfield's* case, there could then have been no doubt."[84]

---

[82] United States v. Worrall, 2 U.S. (2 Dall.) 384, 28 F. Cas. 774, 1798 U.S. App. LEXIS 39 (C.C.D. Pa. 1798) (No. 16,766). *See* Casto, *Supreme Court*, note 67, at 141–147.

[83] 2 U.S. (2 Dall.) 384, 401–402 (1798).

[84] *See* Wharton, note 10, at 199n. One may also speculate that the light sentence may indicate that the outcome was a rough and ready compromise, what in a jury trial would be called a quotient-verdict and did not reflect any change in Chase's constitutional views.

There is some support for the contention that Justice Chase had changed his mind. First, Levy, Presser, Marcus, and Tachau assert that in 1799 Chase presided over *United States v. Sylvester*, a case they describe as a federal criminal common-law prosecution for counterfeiting. Sylvester was not only convicted by Chase but also received the heavy sentence of imprisonment for a year in jail in addition to a fine of $100. However, Jay and Preyer disagree. They conclude that the *Sylvester* case was conducted under a 1798 statute.[85] Second, in the *Fries* case involving the 1799 Pennsylvania armed insurrection,[86] Justice Iredell cited the decision in *Worrall* as authority for the availability of federal criminal common-law jurisdiction, ignoring Chase's earlier comment.

Finally, there is the little noted change of face by Dallas, who had strenuously challenged the constitutionality of federal criminal common-law jurisdiction in *Henfield* and *Worrall*. In 1804, acting as U.S. District Attorney in the common-law prosecution of Thomas Passmore for perjury in bankruptcy, Dallas cited *Worrall* and *Henfield* as authority for the availability of federal jurisdiction.[87] Readers should not be misled. The significant aspect of this development is not that Dallas was arguing for a position contrary to the one he had taken when acting for the defense in *Henfield* and *Worrall*.[88] That is not unusual for an advocate. What is significant is that this participant in the *Worrall* case in his 1804 review of the law in *Passmore* acknowledged that *Worrall* stood for the availability of federal jurisdiction. No doubt he was

---

[85] United States v. Sylvester (unreported) (1799), 1 Final Records of the U.S. Circuit Courts of Massachusetts for 1790–1799 at 303. *See* Letter, William Paterson to Tench Coxe (Oct. 16, 1797) (Pennsylvania Hist. Soc'y).

Leonard W. Levy, Stephen Presser, and Maeva Marcus agree that this was a common-law prosecution. Presser, A Tale of Two Judges: Richard Peters and Samuel Chase, and the Broken Promise of Federal Jurisdiction, 78 Nw. L. Rev. 48, 69 (1978); 3 Doc. Hist. Sup. Ct., note 67, at 322 n.29 ("By 1799, Chase had apparently abandoned his heretical views... presiding over a common law prosecution that ended in conviction"); Leonard W. Levy, *Emergence of a Free Press* 278 (1985).

However, Stuart Jay and Katherine Preyer disagree. Jay asserts that "it seems likely that the case was brought under the Act to Punish Frauds Committed on the Bank of the United States, enacted on June 27, 1798 before *Sylvester*." 1 Stat. 573 (1798) (providing for criminal punishment for persons counterfeiting bills of the Bank of the United States). *See* Stewart Jay, Origins of Federal Common Law, pt. 1, 133 U. Pa. L. Rev. 1070 n.332 (1985) (hereafter Jay); Preyer, note 28, at 231. Apparently, the date of the indictment is not available.

[86] *See* Ch. 2, text accompanying notes 114–116.

[87] United States v. Passmore, 4 U.S. (4 Dall.) 372, 27 Fed. Cas. 458 (C.C.D. Pa. 1804) (No. 16,005). This appears to be the same case as Anonymous, 1 Fed. Cas. 1032 (C.C.D. Pa. 1804) (No. 475). *See* Preyer, note 28, at 239 n.55.

[88] *See* page 171.

encouraged to do so by the fact that Judge Peters, who had upheld federal jurisdiction in *Worrall*, was one of the judges sitting on the case.

In rejecting the contention that Chase changed his position in *Worrall*, Preyer points to an unnamed 1806 case involving a common-law prosecution of a murder at sea of a cabin boy. She reports that in this case, Chase reasserted the view that the federal courts lacked criminal common-law jurisdiction and that there was no federal law of crimes.[89] With these exceptions, the historians generally have not pursued the question of Justice Chase's possible ambivalence. Led by Chancellor Kent in his *Commentaries*, they have instead cited Chase's uncompromising statement in *Worrall* before the "consultation" that the federal courts had no criminal common-law jurisdiction as a demonstration that the judges were divided on the issue.[90]

However, even if Chase had persisted in his view, he stood alone. No other judge considering the issue during this decade of critical concern agreed with him. It was a solitary lightning bolt in the sky. Moreover, as noted, Republican prosecutors installed after Jefferson's triumph in 1800 themselves instituted prosecutions relying on the doctrine.

Worrall was decided in April 1798. This was a time of growing war fever, with the Federalist Congress just commencing the enactment of a series of urgent defense measures in preparation for the war that they anticipated with France. Among other responses to the French challenge, the Adams administration, a mere two months after *Worrall*, ignored Chase and began a series of criminal libel prosecutions in the federal courts at common law against Jeffersonian critics of the President and Federalist policies. As discussed in Chapter 4, six of these cases, involving the prosecutions of Republican Congressman Samuel Cabel, four prominent Republican editors or publishers – Bache, Burk, Smith, and Cobbett – and one obscure Republican editor, William Durrell, were instituted under federal criminal common-law jurisdiction during the Adams administration.[91]

This is the record. For an understanding of the jurisprudence of the time, scholars can be guided only by the actions of the judges and public officials of the time charged with the responsibility for law enforcement. A wealth of insight into their views and actions is available from the available reports

---

[89] *See* Preyer, note 28, at 240–241, *citing* Letter, Richard Peters to Timothy Pickering (Dec. 8, 1806) 27 Pickering Papers 334 (Mass. Hist. Soc'y).

[90] 1 James Kent, *Commentaries on the Constitution of the United States* 355–356, 360 (11th ed. 1866) ("This case settled nothing as the Court were [*sic*] divided").

[91] *See* Ch. 4, notes 5–31, 217–20. The *Cabell* presentment following Justice Iredell's charge upholding jurisdiction occurred a year before *Worrall*, but Chase chose to ignore it. The other federal prosecutions for common-law criminal libel occurred a few weeks after *Worrall*.

of the official acts, judicial decisions, formal opinions of the various Attorneys General, and opinions of other Cabinet ministers who were lawyers. This is the direct window into the contemporary opinion of the persons with official responsibility – Federalists to the man. In any such recapitulation, the evidence is uniform that in the relatively quiet period before the outbreak of the undeclared naval war with France, judges and public officials alike proceeded on the assumption that the federal courts did possess extensive criminal common-law jurisdiction. This unbroken chain of support was interrupted only by Justice Chase's contrary, but ambivalent, position in 1798 in *Worrall*. Thereafter, in a series of cases, judges and prosecutors alike continued to assert such jurisdiction without further judicial dissent until the decision of the Supreme Court in *United States v. Hudson & Goodwin*.

In sum, neither in the 11 federal common-law prosecutions before *Worrall* (*Hopkins, Henfield, Ravara, Williams, Smith, The Roland, Greenleaf (I), Greenleaf (II), Cobbett, Cabell, Fries*) nor in the 12 federal common-law prosecutions between the time of *Worrall* and 1808 (*Bache, Burk, Smith, Durrell, Hudson, Goodwin, Reeve, Collier, Backus, Osgood, Passmore,* and *McGill*), an impressive total of 23 cases, did a single case fail to proceed because of constitutional objection to jurisdiction.[92] In the process, many of the most prominent members of the Bench accepted and applied federal criminal common-law jurisdiction in their charges to grand juries, charges to petit juries, rulings, and commentary in their opinions. These included seven Supreme Court Justices: Chief Justices Jay[93] and Ellsworth,[94] Justices

---

[92] In addition, there was the abortive effort of Circuit Court Judges James M. Marshall and William Cranch in the early days of the Jefferson administration to indict Samuel Harrison Smith, editor of the *National Intelligencer* for an alleged libel of the entire federal judiciary. *See* text accompanying notes 11–13.

[93] United States v. Hopkins, (C.C.D. Mass. 1790) (unreported); United States v. Henfield, 11 F. Cas. 1099, 1793 U.S. App. LEXIS 16 (C.C.D. Pa. 1793) (No. 6360); United States v. Ravara, 2 U.S. 297, 1793 U.S. LEXIS 245, 27 F. Cas. 713 (C.C.D. Pa. 1793); Williams' Case, 29 F. Cas. 1330, 1331, 1799 U.S. App. LEXIS 39 (C.C.D. Conn. 1799) (No. 17,708), reported in Wharton, note 10, at 652–658.

[94] United States v. Greenleaf (II) (unreported); United States v. Pardon (unreported), United States v. Naire Smith (unreported); charge in Williams' Case 29 F. Cas. 1330, 1331, 1799 U.S. App. LEXIS 39 (C.C.D. Conn. 1799) (No. 17,708); charge to the South Carolina Grand Jury (1799).

   In his charge to the South Carolina grand jury in 1791, Ellsworth ruled that "the common law remains the same as it was before the Revolution" and endorsed federal criminal common-law jurisdiction over "acts manifestly subversive of the national government or of some of its powers specified in the Constitution," *reprinted in* Boston *Independent Chronicle*, June 6, 10–13 (1799); 3 Doc. Hist. Sup. Ct., note 67, at 322–323. *See* William R. Casto, Oliver Ellsworth, in *Seriatim: The Supreme Court before John Marshall* 309–10 (S. Gerber ed. 1996) (Casto, *Seriatim*).

Iredell,[95] Wilson,[96] Bushrod Washington,[97] William Cushing,[98] and William Paterson;[99] two Circuit Court Justices: James M. Marshall and William

[95] United States v. Henfield, 11 F. Cas. 1099, 1793 U.S. LEXIS 16 (C.C.D. Pa. 1793) (No. 6,360), see Wharton, note 10, at 49–89; United States v. Cabell (C.C.D. Va. 1797) (unreported); United States v. Fries, 3 U.S. (3 Dall.) 515 (C.C.D. Mass. 1799). See also Wharton, note 10, at 87nn.

See also the 1796 and 1797 charges of Justice Iredell to the South Carolina grand jury. Griffith McRee suggests that the vigor of Justice Iredell's jury charges reflected his concern with criminal libel and led to his impassioned defense of the Sedition Act. 2 McRee, note 79, at 485, 497–502, 505–509, 551–570; 3 Doc. Hist. Sup. Ct., note 67, at 106, 113, 163; Willis P. Whichard, James Iredell: Revolutionist, Constitutionalist, Jurist, in Seriatim: The Supreme Court Before John Marshall 309–10 (S. Gerber ed. 1996), at 198, 211.

The Trenton Federalist, Apr. 8, 1799, reports that in his charge to the grand jury, Justice Iredell defended the Alien and Sedition Acts and "proved them . . . to be perfectly consistent with the principles of the constitution." Moving from the law to politics, he added that they were "founded on the wisest maxims of policy." Trenton Federalist, Apr. 8, 1799, reprinted in 3 Doc. Hist. Sup. Ct., note 67, at 328.

Similarly, in other charges to the grand jury in 1792, 1794, and 1796 upholding federal jurisdiction to punish violations of American neutrality in the absence of any statute criminalizing such behavior. Justice Iredell asserted that the law of nations was part of the laws of the United States "in the same manner and upon the same principle as any other offence committed against the common law." 3 Doc. Hist. Sup. Ct., note 67, 106, 111; 2 McRee, note 79, at 423, 467–474; Preyer, note 28, at 228.

[96] United States v. Henfield, 11 F. Cas. 1099, 1793 U.S. LEXIS 16 (C.C.D. Pa. 1793) (No. 6,360); United States v. Ravara, 2 U.S. 297, 1793 U.S. App. LEXIS 245, 27 F. Cas. 713 (C.C.D. Pa. 1793).

In his grand jury charge to the Philadelphia and Richmond grand juries in early 1791, Justice Wilson noted that the 1790 Federal Crimes Act punished murder and manslaughter but did not define the offenses. Justice Wilson held that reference to common law crimes for the meaning of the crimes was necessary. See Preyer, note 28, at 227.

[97] See United States v. M'Gill, 4 U.S. (4 Dall.) 426, 429 (1806) (Washington, B., J.) ("I have often decided that the federal Courts have a common-law jurisdiction in criminal cases"). See James R. Stoner, Heir Apparent: Bushrod Washington and Federal Justice, in Casto, Seriatim, note 94, at 322, 330–331.

Numerous historians record Justice Bushrod Washington as dissenting from the majority opinion in United States v. Hudson & Goodwin rejecting federal criminal common-law jurisdiction. However, as noted, the Cranch's report of the case records Washington as absent. 11 U.S. (7 Cranch) at 32. The LEXIS report of the case is incomplete.

[98] Letter, William Cushing to John Lowell (Apr 4, 1790), 2 Doc. Hist. Sup. Ct., note 67, at 21–22; United States v. Hopkins (C.C.D. N.Y. Apr. 12, 1790) (unreported).

[99] United States v. Hopkins (C.C.D. N.Y 1790) (unreported).

Memoranda of draft charges by William Paterson warning of the danger of seditious statements and implying a readiness for common-law prosecution are also available. See 3 Doc. Hist. Sup. Ct., note 67, at 228–229.

Paterson's biographer, concludes that the evidence "gives us every reason to believe" that Paterson would have supported federal criminal common-law jurisdiction. He relies on Paterson's "broad interpretation of federal authority in his grand jury addresses" and his defense of the common law in New Jersey. Apparently unaware of Paterson's action in United States v. Hopkins, he was unnecessarily ready to concede that there is no "incontrovertible proof" of Justice Paterson's view of the issue. See John E. O'Connor, William Paterson: Lawyer and Statesman 1745–1806, 220 n.55, 330 (1979).

Cranch;[100] and District Court judges: Robert Troup,[101] Richard Peters,[102] John Sloss Hobart,[103] and Pierpont Edwards.[104]

Although it must be recognized that the available historical record, incomplete as it is, does not include all the Circuit Court and District Court decisions of the period, the richness and near unanimity of the materials available buttressed by the contemporary views of a scholar of the eminence of Justice Story should render unpersuasive any assertion that the record, because limited, is also inconclusive.[105]

In the author's view, the conclusion is clear. It is indisputable, according to the voluminous evidence available, that the judges of the time construing and applying the Constitution as they read it in the absence of a Supreme Court decision viewed federal criminal common-law jurisdiction as the law of the land.[106] Although the Supreme Court had not formally considered the issue, it is clear that seven Justices, two Circuit Court judges, six District Court judges, and three Attorneys General had officially endorsed this view. Of course, all were Federalists acting at a time when the Federalists were in national ascendancy. Their actions can well be criticized as politically motivated, but is that relevant? As Chief Justice Hughes observed, "the Constitution is what the judges say it is," echoing Justice Holmes's earlier admonition that was much the same about the law generally: "The prophecies of what the courts will do in fact, and nothing more pretensious [*sic*], are what I mean about the law."[107]

---

[100] Order in 1801 to the District Attorney of the District of Columbia to request indictment for criminal libel by the District of Columbia grand jury of Republican editor Samuel Harrison Smith for his article in the Jefferson "semi-official" house organ, the *National Intelligencer*, condemning the entire Federal judiciary for its conduct during the Adams administration. *See* Morris, note 14, at 14; 1 Warren, *History*, note 15, at 195–197.

[101] United States v. Greenleaf, (C.C.D. N.Y. 1797) (Greenleaf II).

[102] United States v. Henfield, 11 F. Cas. 1099, 1793 U.S. App. LEXIS 16 (C.C.D. Pa. 1793) (No. 6360), Wharton, note 10, at 49, 87n.; United States v. Ravara, 2 U.S. 297, 1793, 27 F. Cas. 713, 1793 App. LEXIS 245 C.C.D. Pa. 1793), *id.*, at 90–92; United States v. Worrall, 2 U.S. (2 Dall.) 384, 1798 U.S. App. LEXIS 158, 28 F. Cas. 774 (C.C.D. Pa. 1798) (No. 16,766), *id.* at 189–199; United States v. Burk (C.C.D. N.Y. 1798) (unreported).

[103] United States v. Burk (C.C.D. N.Y. 1798) (seditious libel) (unreported).

[104] (United States v. Barzillai Hudson & George Goodwin, (C.C.D. Conn. 1808); United States v. Azel Backus (C.C.D. Conn. 1808); United States v. Thomas Collier (C.C.D. Conn. 1808; United States v. Thaddeus Osgood (C.C.D. Conn. 1807); United States v. Tapping Reeve (C.C.D. Conn. 1808) (all unreported).

[105] However, the distinguished historian R. Kent Newmyer, for example, simply concludes that "Because district court cases were not generally reported, no generalizations about the state of the common law can be made." *See* Newmyer, note 65, at 408 n.96.

[106] *See* Jay, note 85, at 1016.

[107] *See Addresses and Papers of Charles Evans Hughes, Governor of New York 1906–1908*, 139 (1908) (address at Elmira, N.Y., May 1907); Oliver Wendell Holmes, Jr., *The Path of the Law* 9 (dedication of building at Boston University School of Law, Jan. 6, 1897).

And the judges had spoken. However, whether of high or low degree, the judges had spoken in the lower courts, and the final definitive decision remained with the Supreme Court when it belatedly addressed the issue in 1812 in *Hudson & Goodwin*. It could ignore such near unanimous expression of opinion and, as we will see, so it did.

Notwithstanding such virtual unanimity on the availability of jurisdiction prior to the decision in *Hudson & Goodwin*, the fundamental issue of the scope of such jurisdiction, assuming it existed, was unclear. Some of the judges spoke in such general terms that it appeared that they were referring to the existence in the federal system of a comprehensive common-law jurisprudence existing either as an inherent aspect of sovereignty or inherited from the British, fully as extensive as the common law that was an integral part of the law of the states. Because the common law in the various states differed from one another and from the English common law in some areas, it was far from clear what the precise content of such a federal common law might be, as Jefferson, Chase, and others pointed out. Similarly, such a comprehensive body of jurisprudence seemed fundamentally incompatible with the concept of a federal government of limited, delegated powers. It was this sweeping doctrine that so frightened Jefferson when he exclaimed in his well-known letter to Edmund Randolph:

> Of all the doctrines which have ever been broached by the federal government, the novel one, of the common law being in force & cognizable as an existing law in their courts, is to me the most formidable. All their other assumptions of un-given powers have been in the detail. The bank law, the treaty doctrine, the sedition act, alien act, the undertaking to change the state laws of evidence in the state courts by certain parts of the stamp act, etc., etc., have been solitary, unconsequential, timid things, in comparison with the audacious, barefaced and sweeping pretension to a system of law for the U.S., without the adoption of their legislature, and so infinitely beyond their power to adopt.[108]

Writing to Gideon Granger, soon to become his Postmaster General, Jefferson again warned "that if the principle were to prevail, of a common law being in force in the United States (which principle possesses the General Government at once of all the powers of the State governments, and reduces

---

[108] Letter, Thomas Jefferson to Edmund Randolph (Aug. 18, 1799), 10 Jefferson, *Writings* (Libr. Am.), note 22, at 1066.

us to a single consolidated government), it would become the most corrupt government on the earth."[109]

Jefferson's and Madison's concern was misplaced. Most of the judges upholding the assertion of federal criminal common-law jurisdiction had a very different, and much more limited, doctrine in mind than the open-ended version Jefferson was fighting against. These judges spoke in much more measured terms. For example, Chief Justice Ellsworth and Justice Story made it plain that the scope of the doctrine of federal criminal common-law jurisdiction that they supported was instead quite limited, extending only to matters involving federal powers, express or implied, under the Constitution. Ellsworth, for example, had instructed the South Carolina grand jury that the doctrine of federal common-law jurisdiction was limited to "acts manifestly subversive of the national government."[110] The prominent Republican James Sullivan, soon to be elected as the first Republican Governor of Massachusetts, similarly asserted in his learned disquisition on freedom of speech and press that federal criminal common-law jurisdiction extended to all crimes *over which the Congress had legislative power.*[111]

Finally, writing a decade later in 1813, Justice Story, one of the strongest protagonists for federal criminal common-law jurisdiction, did not argue for a general common-law jurisdiction. As he said in 1813 in *United States v. Coolidge*, "all offenses against the sovereignty, the public rights, the public justice, the public peace, the public trade, and the public police of the United States" were punishable in the federal courts under federal common law.[112] To qualify under this carefully delimited view, a case had to involve the federal government or its officers in the discharge of their constitutional duties. In fact, this had occurred in each of the cases described above upholding such jurisdiction.

The state common-law system rested on the reception statutes, but there was no provision in the Constitution or federal statute that provided a similar basis in the federal legal system. Thus, Chief Justice Marshall characterized the contention that the Constitution had adopted English common law as the common law of the United States as "strange and absurd."[113] Hence,

---

[109] Letter, Thomas Jefferson to Gideon Granger (Aug. 13, 1800), Jefferson, *Writings* (Libr. Am.), note 22, at 1079.

[110] 3 Doc. Hist. Sup. Ct., note 67, at 357. *See* Casto, *Supreme Court*, note 67, at 150–151.

[111] *See* James Sullivan, *Dissertation on the Constitutional Freedom of the Press* 30, 40–41, 48–54 (1801).

[112] *See* United States v. Coolidge, 25 Fed. Cas. 619, 620 (C.C.D. Mass. 1813) (Story, J.).

[113] Letter, John Marshall to St. George Tucker (Nov. 27, 1800), Marshall Papers Ac. 2354 (Libr. Cong.).

the constitutional standard formulated by Chief Justice Ellsworth and Justice Story was carefully circumscribed.

As Marshall had stressed, federal power had to rest either on the Constitution or on statute.[114] This was also Justice Story's view.[115] However, such a view did not necessarily rule out the existence of inherent powers of the federal government under the Constitution. This is the jurisprudential basis for the view that the federal government by virtue of its sovereign creation as a result of the adoption of the Constitution by the States was subject to the law of nations. Similarly, it provided support for Justice Peters's contention in the *Worrall* case that the federal government had the powers deemed necessary for its survival simply as a matter of self-defense.[116]

Thus, every one of the 24 cases in which the Federalist judges recognized the existence of federal criminal common-law jurisdiction and a federal law of crimes has to be explained in these terms. Examined over the gap of two centuries, the argument is not without its problems. It rests on the contention that a sovereign country has certain inherent authority and responsibilities. However plausible this contention, it is manifestly limited to matters of the greatest importance. Without some such limitation, the doctrine would leave little of the concept that the federal government was a government of limited and delegated power.

There was a further pragmatic problem, one of great significance. With the adoption of the Constitution, a new nation had been created. It was a nation of delegated powers. Was it a nation that was to be utterly impotent to punish criminally behavior impairing its exercise of its constitutional powers in the hiatus before the new nation had adopted a comprehensive statutory code of jurisprudence expressly punishing the particular offense, no matter how destructive of the government or the exercise of its delegated powers? Did considerations such as these lead to the ready acceptance by virtually all the judges of federal jurisdiction in the specific cases before them? By the same token with the passage of time, was it the gradual enactment of federal statutes punishing particular crimes, as well as the decline of the Federalists by 1812, that had so reduced the importance of the

---

[114] *Ex Parte* Bollman, 8 U.S. (4 Cranch) 75, 93 (1807).

[115] United States v. Coolidge, 25 Fed. Cas. 619, 619 (C.C.D. Mass. 1813) (No. 14,857) (Story, J.) ("courts of the United States are courts of limited jurisdiction, and cannot exercise any authorities, which are not confided to them by the constitution and laws made in pursuance thereof").

[116] 28 F. Cas. at 779 ("Whenever a government has been established, I have always supposed, that a power to preserve itself was a necessary and inseparable concomitant").

issue when it was at last considered by the Supreme Court in *Hudson & Goodwin?*

These views must be sharply distinguished from still another possible role of the common law in federal jurisprudence. At the very least, resort to the common law was essential for an understanding of the legal and constitutional terms of the time. As was suggested earlier, lawyers drafting documents inevitably employed terms with a well-defined meaning in the common law. Thus, as Justice James Wilson had early explained and other judges had echoed, the common law played an invaluable interstitial role in filling lacunae in the law. He pointed out, for example, that the Crimes Act of 1790 expressly punished such crimes as murder and manslaughter, but failed to define them. Wilson pointed out that resort to the common law was required for this purpose. Similarly, this is what Chief Justice Marshall was referring to in the *Burr* trial when he observed that the common law was "the substratum of law of the country."[117] However, such interstitial reliance on the common law to explain legal terms or fill in lacunae could have no application in resolving the fundamental question of the subject matter jurisdiction of the federal courts under the Constitution.

b. The Constitutional Issue Resolved: Hudson & Goodwin *(1812)*

After the Circuit Court decision in 1808, *Hudson & Goodwin* moved on to the Supreme Court for decision. However, the curious delay that attended so many stages of this litigation occurred once again. The continuing pattern of professional incompetence, real or pretended, that had been so evident earlier in the conduct of the District Attorney in these cases now infected the Clerk of the Court, Henry Waggaman Edwards, son of the judge. He "forgot" to file the certified question with the Supreme Court to enable the case to be heard at its next term in 1809, and it had to go over to the 1810 Term. At the 1810 Term, it was continued. Then, by congressional vote, there was no session of Court at all in 1811.

In all, it was four years after the decision in the Circuit Court and six and a half years after the institution of the cases before the Supreme Court at its 1812 Term finally heard the case. With the extended delay – whatever its cause – the Court at last had a firm Republican majority. In the eyes of Federalist Crosskey, these repeated delays were part of an underlying conspiracy on

---

[117] *See* 2 Works of James Wilson 802–223 (Robert G. McCloskey ed. 1967); United States v. Burr, 2 Burr's Trial 402, 482 (1808) (Marshall, C.J.); Casto, *Supreme Court*, note 67, at 154–155; Preyer, note 28, at 227–228; 1 Crosskey, note 35, at 636, 2 *id.*, at 1346 n.39.

the part of "the Republicans" to delay matters until Jeffersonian appointees achieved a majority on the Supreme Court.[118]

In the Supreme Court, the curious events that had attended the prior stages of the prosecution persisted. In this case, instituted on behalf of the United States for a crime allegedly committed against the government, the Attorney General of the United States, William Pinkney, refused to appear to argue on behalf of the constitutionality of the prosecution that Wheaton reports that he had previously supported.[119] Thus, no one presented the case for the constitutionality of jurisdiction, which, as we have seen, had previously been recognized by seven Supreme Court Justices and seven Circuit Court and District Court judges and upheld by three Attorneys General. The government had all but defaulted.[120]

In an opinion for the Court, Justice William Johnson, who had been Jefferson's first appointee to the Supreme Court, stated: "Although this question is brought up now for the first time to be decided by this Court, we consider it as having been long since settled in public opinion."[121] Although he recognized that the Congress had power to enact criminal legislation, Johnson refused to have such jurisdiction exercised by the federal courts without express statutory authorization. The Congress had enacted criminal statutes punishing such crimes as bribery of federal judges and counterfeiting of national currency as within powers implied from the constitutional grant of such essential governmental functions. However, this did not extend to recognizing an implied power of the federal courts to exercise criminal jurisdiction of their own.

In reality, the issue had been decisively determined at the polls and in public opinion. The Federalists had been overwhelmed in the federal elections of 1804 and 1808 and were in visible decline. As Johnson himself explained in 1813, a year after the decision in his Circuit Court opinion in *United States v. William Butler:* "It is true [that *Hudson*] was not argued, but the true reason was, the universal conviction prevailing at the bar, that opinion

---

[118] *See* 2 Crosskey, note 35, at 775–782. Professor Ackerman finds this suggestion "utterly implausible" noting that until the appointment of Justice Duval in late 1811, a Federalist majority disposed to recognized federal criminal common-law jurisdiction existed on the Court. *See* Bruce Ackerman, *Before the Next Attack: Preserving Civil Liberties in an Age of Terrorism* 361–362 n.42 (2006).

[119] Henry Wheaton, *Some Accounts of the Life, Writings, and Speeches of William Pinkney* 114 (1826) *quoted in* Jay, note 85, at pt. 1, 1015 n.42. *See also* Gary D. Rowe, The Sound of Silence: United States v. Hudson & Goodwin, The Jeffersonian Ascendancy, and the Abolition of Federal Common Law Crimes, 101 Yale L.J. 919, 926 n.32 (1992) (hereinafter G. D. Rowe).

[120] No one appeared for the defendants either. The default of the government on this pivotal issue was entirely satisfactory to counsel for the defendants since a finding of lack of jurisdiction would uphold their demurrer and free their clients.

[121] United States v. Hudson & Goodwin, 11 U.S. (7 Cranch) 32, 32 (1812).

had, in every department, settled down against" federal common-law criminal jurisdiction.[122]

No dissent was published. However, Justice Story leaves no doubt that the Court had divided on the issue.[123] It is safe to assume that the four Republicans – Justices Livingston, Todd, Duval, and Johnson – had voted that the federal government had no criminal common-law jurisdiction. Justice Story was clearly opposed but may not have felt free to have himself recorded in dissent less than a month after he first sat on the Court.[124] Justice Bushrod Washington, who had left no doubt that in his view the judicial courts possessed criminal common-law jurisdiction,[125] did not participate.[126] As for Chief Justice Marshall, time had moved on, and whatever his position on the issue might have been a decade earlier, he no longer appeared disposed to take on a lost cause. The historians are not in agreement on the issue.[127]

In this manner, the first decade of Republican political supremacy saw what had been one of most hotly contested political issues of its time become ancient history.[128] The firestorm of the past was now cold ashes. This was the background when the issue at last came before the Supreme Court in 1812 in *United States v. Hudson and Goodwin*. The issue was of such little interest that neither counsel bothered to appear, and the Federalist judges opposed to the change did not trouble to dissent. In rejecting the concept of federal criminal common-law jurisdiction, the Supreme Court was only

---

[122] Trial of William Butler for Piracy 12 (C.C.D. S.C. 1813) (memorandum from Johnson to President Madison), Beinecke Library, Yale, *quoted by* G. D. Rowe, note 119, at 926.

[123] *See* United States v. Coolidge, 25 F. Cas. 619, 621, 1813 U.S. App. LEXIS 260 (C.C.D. Mass. 1813) (No. 14,857). (Justice Story refers to the decision in *Hudson* as having been made "without argument, and by a majority only of the court.")

[124] Story had been confirmed on Nov. 15, 1811, and first took his seat on the Court on Feb. 3, 1812. *See* 1 Warren, *History*, note 15, at 423.

[125] *See* note 98.

[126] 11 U.S. (7 Cranch) at 33.

[127] *Compare* Newmyer, note 65, at 101, 105 (Marshall ultimately came to reject federal criminal common-law jurisdiction); James McClellan, *Joseph Story and the American Constitution* 174 (1971) (Marshall's position was one of "the great mysteries of his constitutionalism"); and 2 Crosskey, note 35, at 782 (Marshall supported federal criminal common-law jurisdiction).

G. Edward White has still another view. *See* 3 and 4 Oliver Wendell Holmes Devise, *History of the Supreme Court of the United States*, G. Edward White, *The Marshall Court and Cultural Change, 1815–1835*, 865 (1988) (hereinafter White) ("Marshall, previously a supporter of a federal common law of crimes soft pedaled that position by 1809 and kept a distinctly low profile" in *Hudson* and *Coolidge*).

[128] Newmyer asserts that seditious libel litigation, both common law and statutory, were among the issues dominating the political discussion of the time. "Certainly no other issue of that period was more explosive." *See* Newmyer, note 65, at 102. Another leading legal historian, G. Edward White, describes it as "one of the major political and jurisprudential controversies" of its time. *See* White, note 127, at 120.

ratifying what had become the new reality at the polls. As Gary D. Rowe put it so well: "Few major controversies have ended with as slight a whimper."[129]

c. Jefferson and Criminal Libel

Before Jefferson became President, he was one of the country's leading defenders of freedom of speech and press, including bitter criticism of the government. At the same time, he recognized the importance of protecting reputation against personal attacks on character. Although he was ready to make much of the remedy provided by common-law *civil* libel as the preferred solution, he recognized that in isolated cases, *criminal* libel was appropriate. Rather than looking upon his limited toleration for criminal libel as his "darker side,"[130] one should appreciate that his view, a view he maintained consistently during his time in power, was a balanced response, reflecting the inherent difficulties presented by the established jurisprudence of the times.

From Jefferson's draft for the Virginia Constitution in 1776 to a statement of his views shortly before his death 50 years later in 1826, he left no doubt that he did not approve of unlimited freedom of speech. He repeatedly acknowledged that it did not preclude civil action for private personal injury from false statements. Nor did it preclude "occasional" prosecutions for criminal libel in appropriate cases.

He had two concerns. Recognizing the dangers of restricting debate, he wanted to avoid its use except in extreme cases. On the jurisprudential level, he did not challenge the legitimacy and constitutionality of criminal libel. That was difficult, if not impossible, for any lawyer grounded in the English common law. Instead, like John Adams and Chief Justice Cushing, he was concerned with the desirability, if not the necessity, of modifying the Blackstonian doctrine of the common law to provide a role for the admissibility of truth as a defense. Libelous speech could be punished, but only if it was false; this condition for punishment appears throughout his correspondence.[131] Paradoxically, admission of the evidence of truth was a reform introduced by the much detested Sedition Act.

Although he condemned the actions of the Adams administration, Jefferson did not entirely rule out the use by his own administration of criminal libel prosecutions in the federal courts under common-law jurisdiction. Thus, as noted, one year after he became President, he instructed his Attorney General,

---

[129] *See* G. D. Rowe, note 119, at 919.
[130] *See* Leonard W. Levy, *Jefferson and Civil Liberties: The Darker Side* (1973).
[131] *See* Ch. 3, note 14.

Levi Lincoln, as follows: "While a full range is proper for actions by individuals, either public or private, for slanders affecting them, I would wish much to see the experiment trying of getting along without public prosecution for libels."[132] In short, he was reluctant to see such prosecutions, but recognized not only that the remedy existed but that its use conceivably might be useful under appropriate circumstances. What, then, was the difference between his view and that of Adams, except over the circumstances that might render governmental reliance on the doctrine appropriate? Thus, as a hurricane of extreme personal attacks by the Federalist press continued to harass him, Jefferson – like President Washington and President Adams before him – became increasingly sensitive and at last irate about the abusive use of freedom of the press. Not too long after his letter to Lincoln, Jefferson assumed a much more aggressive stance in his correspondence with Governor (formerly Chief Justice) McKean of Pennsylvania. As discussed elsewhere in this book, in response to McKean's request for guidance, he encouraged McKean to proceed with the use of selected criminal libel prosecutions as a way of "restoring the integrity of the presses."[133]

Although Jefferson had the full details of the six prosecutions in Connecticut of Federalists under federal criminal common law in April 1806 and was fully aware that the Connecticut Republicans were making the same partisan use of seditious libel to silence their political opponents for which he had so bitterly condemned the Federalists, Jefferson made no effort to bring the prosecutions to a close. Quite the contrary: Jefferson gave his blessings to the prosecutions, asserting that "confined to an appeal to truth only, it [the group of prosecutions] could not lessen the usual freedom of the press."[134] With Jefferson declining to intervene, the prosecutions, now having Jefferson's approval, went forward for months until counsel for *Backus* threatened to involve the President in personal scandal.

During the Adams administration, the Republicans had brushed aside as ineffective the provisions of the Act liberalizing the harsh limitations of the common law by making evidence of truth admissible and expanding the role of the jury. However, in sanctioning the Connecticut prosecutions, Jefferson found that the provision for the admissibility of truth rendered even partisan use of criminal libel acceptable. This should not have been a surprise.

---

[132] Letter, Thomas Jefferson to Levi Lincoln (Mar. 24 1802), 8 *Writings* (Ford), note 6, at 139.

[133] Letter, Thomas Jefferson to Thomas McKean (Feb. 19, 1803), 8 *ibid.*, at 218–219. This correspondence is discussed at greater length in the discussion in Ch. 6 of Governor McKean's repeated use of criminal and civil libel suits for partisan purposes in Pennsylvania.

[134] Letter, Thomas Jefferson to Abigail Adams (June 13, 1804), 8 *ibid.*, at 307.

Throughout his career, Jefferson repeatedly asserted that so long as proof of truth was admissible, criminal libel carefully and sparingly used was sound policy and, of course, constitutional.[135] It is striking how Jefferson persisted in this position, although in fighting the Sedition Act, his very own leading supporters had eloquently demonstrated the very limited usefulness of such a requirement as a practical matter.[136]

In summary, with the victory of Jefferson in 1800, notwithstanding occasional aberrational departures under federal criminal common law, criminal libel ceased to exist as a significant part of federal criminal jurisprudence. The issue no longer was a prominent matter on the political or legal scene. Although federal prosecutors during the Jefferson administration obtained indictments resting on federal criminal common law from grand juries on no fewer than 14 occasions,[137] the doctrine of federal jurisdiction was fast fading away. Finally, a decade later, federal criminal common law, a doctrine that was nearing its demise, at last came to its formal end with the decision in 1812 in *Hudson & Goodwin* after the Republicans had gained control of the federal judiciary. This was the end of federal criminal common law, and federal statutory seditious libel did not reappear for more than a century until the enactment of the Sedition Act of 1917 with American participation in World War I.

Although this unhappy chapter had dwindled away so substantially in the federal courts with the 1800 defeat of the Federalists, it was a very different matter insofar as the states were concerned. In fact, there were more prosecutions in the states than had occurred in the entire period of federal recognition of the crime. We now turn in Chapter 6 to review this resurgence of the use of criminal libel for partisan purposes under state criminal common law in the first decade of the 19th century. This was a very different matter. Criminal libel was universally accepted as an established part of state law, and partisan use of the doctrine by Federalists and Republicans alike was extensive.

---

[135] *See* Ch. 4, at 36.

[136] For a latter-day critic, *see* J. M. Smith, note 1, at 421–422.

[137] Eleven of these indictments were obtained in connection with the Connecticut prosecutions where defective drafting of five original indictments made superseding indictments necessary.

6

Partisan Prosecutions for Criminal Libel in the State Courts

Federalists Against Republicans, Republicans Against Federalists, and Republicans Against Dissident Republicans in Struggles for Party Control

A. Introduction

During the Jefferson and Madison administrations, the use of criminal libel prosecutions for partisan political purposes flourished in the courts in four important states. The Federalists still clung to power in Connecticut and for some time in Massachusetts, and there they used the pernicious doctrine where they could to harass Republican editors. The Republicans had attained power in New York and Pennsylvania and later in Massachusetts as well. In their turn, they seized on criminal libel prosecutions as a tool to silence Federalist editors. Still later in celebrated cases in both Pennsylvania and New York, Republican judges used repressive doctrines – criminal libel in Pennsylvania and contempt of court in New York – against opposition Republicans in the internecine warfare that emerged between the contending wings of the bitterly divided Republican parties in those states. The earlier Federalist use of criminal libel for partisan political purposes had legitimated the use of the doctrines for all. Once the political advantages that could be captured by the partisan use of criminal libel had been demonstrated, it infected the political process generally. Notwithstanding their pious, psalm-singing abhorrence of the doctrines when used by Federalists, Republicans seized on their political usefulness as they moved into power. Indeed, they went beyond the Federalists and used them against dissident factions in their own party in two of the country's most important states.

B. Republican Use of Repressive Doctrines Against Federalists and Dissident Republicans Alike

1. Pennsylvania

The Republicans who had bitterly criticized the Federalist use of the Sedition Act of 1798 to silence Republican editors found the usefulness of criminal and civil libel for partisan purposes too appealing to resist. In Pennsylvania much of this history revolves around the litigious Thomas McKean, Chief Justice from 1777 to 1799 and Governor from 1800 to 1808. As early as 1788, McKean was seeking to use criminal libel to silence critics and political opponents, and he repeatedly turned to the doctrine for the following two decades. During this period under McKean's direction or with his encouragement, Republican prosecutors throughout the state instituted criminal libel actions against the most outspoken Federalist editors. As Federalists faded in popular support, the triumphant Republican Party in Pennsylvania split into two bitterly opposed wings in 1805 – one led by Governor McKean, Alexander Dallas, and Alexander Gallatin, the other by Michael Leib and William Duane. Against this background emerged a new development. McKean shifted his target from pestiferous Federalist editors to his now even more pestiferous Republican opponent, William Duane. This use of criminal and civil libel for partisan purposes by one wing of the Republicans against the other highlights the full extent of the corruption of the political process unleashed by the Federalists with the 1798 Sedition Act.

This unhappy period began long before the Sedition Act, in 1788 when Thomas McKean, then Chief Justice, was conducting a personal political vendetta against a bitter critic, editor Eleazer Oswald. As the decades unfolded, he had similar run-ins with such outspoken Federalist editors as John Fenno, Thomas Cobbett ("Peter Porcupine"), and Joseph Dennie. Ultimately, he became embroiled with a Republican political rival, the scurrilous Republican editor William Duane. These struggles took the form not only of numerous prosecutions for criminal libel, which are the subject of this chapter, but prosecutions for contempt of court and suits for violation of bonds to keep the peace as well. The latter topics are subjects of the succeeding chapter.

a. Republicans Against Federalists

The conduct of Chief Justice McKean in office was most vigorously attacked by two outspoken editors, first, Eleazer Oswald and, later, Thomas Cobbett (writing as "Peter Porcupine") whom we have already encountered. Mc-Kean attempted to strike back with criminal punishment of both. His first attempts at criminal punishment through criminal libel proceedings in the state courts, first against Oswald in 1788 and then Cobbett in 1797, foundered. The Pennsylvania grand juries refused to indict. At the same time as the 1797 assault on Cobbett, according to Wharton, a comparable effort was made to indict Cobbett in the federal court, but the federal grand jury also refused to indict.[1]

McKean was undaunted. He subsequently turned to the institution of proceedings for contempt of court for out-of-court publications and the imposition of forfeiture proceedings on bonds for good behavior to achieve his objective of punishing these highly critical editors. Readers may refer to Chapter 7 for an extended discussion of these cases along with the other materials relating to contempt of court and bonds for good behavior, but certain aspects of the Cobbett litigation are relevant here because of their interrelationship to the abortive state criminal libel litigation of 1797.

Following the arrest of Cobbett for criminal libel in August 1797, McKean had required Cobbett to post a bond of $2,000 to assure his appearance and good behavior until his appearance at the November Term of the Court of Oyer and Terminer. When, as mentioned, the grand jury then failed to indict, the criminal libel litigation came to an end, but McKean persisted. At his urging, the Commonwealth sued Cobbett in debt for forfeiture of his good behavior bond. It alleged that in the three-month interval between the posting of the $2,000 bond and the grand jury's rejection of the indictment, Cobbett had grossly violated the terms of his bond. In the trial on the bond, the jury found for the Commonwealth, and the bond was forfeited. Cobbett, who had defeated the criminal libel charge, fell victim to the binding over procedure. A full account of the episode appears in the discussion of good behavior bonds in Chapter 7.

The *Cobbett* criminal libel and good behavior bond litigations did not stand alone. A companion civil libel proceeding was instituted by a prominent Republican, Dr. Benjamin Rush, the distinguished physician and friend of Jefferson. After counsel for Cobbett unsuccessfully tried to get the case away from the Pennsylvania courts, seeking to remove the proceeding to the federal

---

[1] See Francis Wharton, *State Trials of the United States During the Administrations of Washington and Adams,* 329 (1849 repr. 1970) (hereinafter Wharton).

court,[2] the case went to trial. Dr. Rush prevailed and was awarded the then enormous sum of $5,000 in damages.

Cobbett was crushed. Unable to pay the judgment, he fled the state and settled in New York. He started a new paper, *The Rush-Light*, and hastened to even scores with Rush. Pointing to Dr. Rush's standard regimen of violent purges and copious bleeding for patients stricken with yellow fever, Cobbett in the February 28, 1800, edition of the *Rush-Light* sardonically described Rush's procedures as "one of the great discoveries . . . which have contributed to the depopulation of the earth."

However, Cobbett could not stay long in New York. After a few months, he disappeared from the American scene. Moving to England in June 1800, he resumed his scurrilous journalistic career.[3] Prominent Republicans McKean and Rush had successfully managed to use legal proceedings as the weapon to drive one of the most outspoken Federalist editors in Pennsylvania out of the country. The *Cobbett* litigation was not the only partisan libel proceeding by leading Pennsylvania Republicans against Federalist editors at the close of the 18th century. Still another outspoken Federalist editor, John Fenno, was the defendant in partisan criminal libel proceedings in Pennsylvania at the same time that Federalist prosecutors were still bringing cases under the 1798 Act. Fenno was one of the most vituperative Federalist editors. As Miller describes him, "in name calling, scurrility, and harshness of tone" Fenno's *Gazette* was an "equal match" for the extreme Republican *Aurora*,[4] known for its outrageous prose.

As with so many other of the editors of the time, Fenno (and his son John Ward Fenno who succeeded him) were supported financially by one of the contending political parties or by a foreign power, such as Britain. Corrupted by their acceptance of such financial support, the papers tended to support their sponsor's interests without restraint. In Fenno's case, he was on the Federalist payroll. He had an appointment as the Official Printer of the U.S. Senate reported to be worth $2,000 or $2,500 per annum.[5] John Ward Fenno was later subsidized by Alexander Hamilton and other prominent Federalists.

The Republican McKean was not the only imperious Pennsylvania judge who sought to use his judicial office to punish newspaper critics who were political opponents. He may be paired with Alexander Addison, Presiding

---

[2] Benjamin Rush v. William Cobbett, 2 Yeates 275, 276; 1798 Pa. LEXIS 7 (1798). *See* T. Carpenter, *A Report of an Action for Libel Brought by Dr. Benjamin Rush Against William Cobbett* (1800).
[3] *See* John C. Miller, *Crisis in Freedom: The Alien and Sedition Acts* 229 (1952) (hereinafter Miller).
[4] *Ibid.*, at 30.
[5] *Gazette of the United States*, Aug. 8, 1792, reprinted in the *National Gazette*.

Judge of the Sixth Pennsylvania Common Pleas Court.[6] A dedicated Federalist, Addison is best known today for his outspoken defense of the Sedition Act.[7] Like McKean and his unremitting campaign to punish, first, Oswald and then Cobbett, Addison conducted a feud with John Israel, publisher of the Washington *Herald of Liberty* and the Pittsburgh *Tree of Liberty*. Israel was a leader of Western Pennsylvania Republicans. Closely allied with Gallatin, Israel played a prominent role in Gallatin's first successful run for the Congress.

Addison sought no fewer than three indictments for criminal libel against Israel in two years. The grand jury twice refused to vote indictments, but Addison persisted and was at last successful the third time. However, at the trial, Israel was acquitted. Not content with these criminal prosecutions, Addison joined two other Federalists and sued Israel for civil libel; the outcome of that suit is unknown.

During this period, Addison's Federalist press allies, such as John Scull of the Pittsburgh *Gazette*, waged a press campaign against Israel that in one respect was unique for the time. It was not only vicious, but also anti-Semitic. Scull drew nasty insinuations from the fact that Israel, an Episcopalian, had a Jewish grandfather.[8]

Several newspaper accounts report a *civil* libel action instituted about this time by the distinguished Republican lawyer Alexander J. Dallas against Fenno in the Pennsylvania courts for an article in Fenno's paper, the *United States Gazette*. They report that in the last week of November 1800, the Pennsylvania Supreme Court decided Dallas's civil action by default and that the jury brought in a verdict, variously reported as $2,500 and $2,000. These newspaper accounts agree that as a result of a clerical error in the jury report, the award was to be reduced to $1,000.[9] A subsequent account asserts that the Supreme Court had *fined* Fenno $1,000 in the suit brought by Dallas.[10] Compounding the confusion, a fourth newspaper report, describing the action as criminal, asserts that Fenno was convicted and fined $2,500.[11]

---

[6] In politicized Pennsylvania, Federalist Addison was impeached in 1803 and removed from office by a Republican-dominated Legislature. *See* Gail S. Rowe, *Thomas McKean: The Shaping of an American Republicanism* 339 (1978) (hereinafter G. S. Rowe).

[7] *See* Ch. 4, text accompanying note 52.

[8] See Jeffrey L. Pasley, *"The Tyranny of Printers": Newspaper Politics in the Early American Republic* 170–171, 437 n.12 (2001) (hereinafter Pasley).

[9] *Commercial Advertiser*, Dec. 1, 1800 ($2,000); Jenks's *Portland Gazette*, Dec. 5, 1800 ($2,500).

[10] New London *Bee*, Dec. 17, 1800.

[11] *Gazette of the United States*, Dec. 15, 1800. *See* Miller, note 3, at 229. The conflicting reports in the press highlights the difficulties of relying on newspaper accounts for precise details of any cases not officially reported. However, the reports cannot be ignored. Whatever the precise nature of

Whether the action was criminal or civil, the Federalists bitterly criticized the result. They contrasted the heavy damages or fine with the $200 fine imposed on Republican editor Abijah Adams at much the same time by a Massachusetts court for a like offense against President Adams[12] and bemoaned the lack of equal justice.[13] In the states where Federalists were in power, Republicans similarly lamented the disproportionately heavy sentences on Republican editors convicted in libel cases.[14] In sum, the courts had lost credibility. It made no difference which party was in power. In the institution and conduct of these cases, the prosecution and the judges – and, in particular, the sentence after conviction – were all perceived by their political opponents as highly partisan. The complaints were typically accompanied by charges that the juries, grand and petit, had been politically selected and had been "packed" with supporters of the prosecuting party.

As noted, a little more than a year after the close of the Fenno prosecution, Governor McKean and President Jefferson exchanged important letters that may help explain the subsequent march of events. McKean wrote to Jefferson on February 3, 1803, finding "intolerable" the "infamous & criminal libels, punished almost daily in our newspapers" and wondered whether a "few prosecutions" might ease the problem. Writing for Jefferson's "advice and consent" before he proceeded, he characterized the situation as a national vice that "call[ed] aloud for redress."[15]

Jefferson, like Washington and Adams before him, had been sickened by the vituperative comments about him and his conduct in office. Jefferson promptly responded to McKean, readily agreeing on the "licentiousness [of the press] and its lying," and sending along an unidentified paper to "make

the proccedings may have been, it would seem clear that there had been a libel proceeding, that Dallas had been upheld and that Fenno had lost, and that a penalty ranging from $1,000 to $2,500 had been imposed on Fenno.

[12] *See* Ch. 5, text accompanying notes 128–129. The sentence imposed on Adams was one month's imprisonment, a good behavior bond, and costs.

[13] The Nov. 28, 1800, *Gazette of the United States* reported that the Fenno case involved a libel of Dallas "a foreigner" and "for this he is to pay *two thousand five hundred* !!!!!!!!!!!!!!!! [*sic*] How much better is a foreigner than an American? Had we not better all turn foreigners, says Pat." Readers will note the xenophobic slur on Irish immigrants. *See also Gazette of the United States*, Dec. 15, 1800.

[14] When the publisher of the Republican Hartford *American Mercury* was convicted of criminal libel and fined $1,000 in the Federalist-dominated state court, the newspaper protested: "We live in a conquered country." Hartford *American Mercury*, Jan. 3, 1806.

[15] Letter, Thomas McKean to Thomas Jefferson (Feb. 7, 1803), 4 Dumas Malone, *Jefferson the President: First Term, 1801–1805*, 229 (1970) (hereinafter 4 Malone), *See also* G. S. Rowe, note 6, at 337.

an example of." McKean had asked for his approval of the prosecutions, and Jefferson expressly assented, writing:

> This is a dangerous state of things, and the press ought to be restored to its credibility if possible. The restraints provided by the laws of the states are sufficient for this if applied. And I have therefore long thought that a few prosecutions of the most prominent offenders would have a wholesome effect in restoring the integrity of the presses. [Not a] general prosecution, for that would look like persecution: but a selected one.[16]

This is the letter that is prominently cited by Jefferson's critics intent on showing that whatever his professed allegiance of freedom of speech, he, too, had his "darker side," in Leonard W. Levy's phrase, and was prepared on occasion to attempt to suppress dissent.[17] These critics fail to recognize that in the light of the jurisprudence of the day, Jefferson was one of the most moderate political figures. Instead, they hold him out as a hypocrite by contrasting his restrained response with their perception of him as a person posing as a modern absolutist on the unlimited scope of freedom of speech two hundred years ahead of his time.

It is not known which was the "unidentified paper" to which Jefferson referred. There is some basis for supposing that it was the Philadelphia *Port Folio*[18] published by the rabid Federalist editor Joseph Dennie, who was as scurrilous on his side of the political divide as his political ally William Cobbett ("Peter Porcupine"), had been before him, and as his political rival William Duane was on the other.[19]

In the issues of the *Port Folio* in the period immediately before Jefferson's letter, Dennie had ridiculed Jefferson and his relationship with Sally

[16] Letter, Thomas Jefferson to Thomas McKean (Feb. 19, 1803), 9 Jefferson, *Writings* 449 (Paul L. Ford ed. 1904) (hereinafter Jefferson (Ford)).

[17] Leonard W. Levy, *Jefferson and Civil Liberties: The Darker Side* (1963); 2 William W. Crosskey, *Politics and the Constitution in the History of the United States* 776–784, 1356–1358 (1953).

[18] Among those suggesting that this is likely are the biographers of Jefferson and McKean. *See* 4 Malone, note 15, at 230–231; G. S. Rowe, note 6, at 337–338.

[19] Dennie had previously been private secretary to Secretary of State Pickering and an editor of the *Gazette of the United States*, another High Federalist organ. *See* James M. Smith, *Freedom's Fetters: The Alien and Sedition Laws and American Civil Liberties* 329 n.47 (1956) (hereinafter J. M. Smith).

He was a complex individual. Henry Adams noted that Dennie's paper, the Philadelphia *Port Folio*, was also the "sole source of light literature in the country at the turn of the century." *See* Henry Adams, *History of the United States During the Second Madison Administration* 1317 (Libr. Am. 1986). Moreover, Adams's father, John Quincy Adams, a prolific author, in this period regularly published his own literary attempts in the *Port Folio*. *See* Paul Nagle, *John Quincy Adams: A Public Life, A Personal Life* 122, 220 (1991).

Hemings. Dennie referred to "the indulgence of Sally, the sable, and the auspicious arrival of Tom Paine, the pious." A week later Dennie borrowed from Callender and mocked Jefferson's "tricks with sooty Sal."[20]

Whether that was the contributing event or not, the fact is that at the July 1803 Term, at McKean's instigation, Attorney General William McKean (the Governor's son) successfully obtained an indictment against Dennie for criminal libel under Pennsylvania criminal common law. The comments on Jefferson were not the basis of the indictment. Instead, the indictment cited Dennie's denunciation of democracy, citing examples from Athens, Sparta, Rome, France, and England in the *Port Folio* of April 23, 1803.[21] The case was postponed a number of times. Before it came to trial, it was joined by a number of other political libel cases, all but one of which had been instituted by Governor McKean.

b. Republicans Against Republicans
During the summer of 1805, the struggle in the Republican Party over the 1806 nomination for Governor provoked an outpouring of litigation. The radical wing of the Republicans led by Dr. Michael Leib and William Duane[22] was seeking to block McKean's renomination. In the struggle that followed,

---

[20] *Port Folio*, Jan. 15, 1803, Jan. 22, 1803. *See* 4 Malone, note 15, at 230–231; G. S. Rowe, note 6, at 338.

[21] *See Port Folio*, Apr. 23, 1803. The temper of the times is apparent in the description of Dennie in the indictment. Justice Yeates's charge instructed the jury that the indictment described Dennie as

> a factious and seditious person, of a wicked mind, and unquiet and turbulent disposition and conversation, seditiously, maliciously and wilfully intending, as much as in him lay, to bring into contempt and hatred, the independence of the United States, the constitution of this commonwealth and of the United States, to excite popular discontent and dissatisfaction against the scheme of polity instituted and upon trial in the said United States, and in the said commonwealth, to molest, disturb and destroy the peace and public tranquility of the said United States, and of the said commonwealth, to condemn the principles of the revolution, and revile, depreciate and scandalize the characters of the revolutionary Patriots and statesmen, to endanger, subvert and totally destroy the republican constitutions and free governments of the said United States, and this commonwealth, to involve the said United States, and this commonwealth in civil war, desolation and anarchy, and to procure by art and force, a radical change and alteration in the principles and forms of the said constitutions and governments, without the free will, wish and concurrence of the people of the said United States, and this commonwealth respectively.

> Respublica v. Joseph Dennie, 4 Yeates 267, 1805 Pa. LEXIS 38, *2–4 (1805).

[22] An oddity of the period may be found in the *Connecticut Courant*, Aug. 14, 1805, containing an undated dispatch from the *Freeman's Journal*. The *Journal* contained a collection of letters written by most of the defendants, including Leiper, Leib, Lawler, and Duane as well as by two others named Clay and Ferguson on the subject of public office.

McKean and his allies made flagrant use of libel actions against his Republican opponents, as well as against his traditional enemy, the Federalist editors. There are reports of a virtual flood of criminal and civil libel proceedings instituted by McKean and his allies against the dissident Republican political figures and editors who were fighting his renomination.

In August 1805, McKean's staunch ally in this political struggle, Alexander J. Dallas, was responsible for still another libel action. As reported in satiric vein by the Federalist *New Hampshire Centinel*, Dallas pronounced an electioneering address by Matthew Lawler, Mayor of Philadelphia, "an infamous libel" and an "outrage" and that it was Dallas's duty as a faithful citizen to prosecute and punish him. The *Centinel* mocks the participants, sneering that it involved " merely Democrat versus Democrat – of very little moment we hope, to honest men."[23]

Other proceedings instituted by McKean included *civil* libel suits against his Republican opponents, Leib and Duane. Other defendants included Lawler again, Thomas Leiper (former President of the Philadelphia City Council), and Jacob Mitchell (former member of the Pennsylvania Legislature). Along with others still not identified, McKean accused the defendants of charging him falsely with "opposing the Louisiana Purchase," and for asserting that he headed a "monstrous combination . . . against principles and people."[24] Further information about the outcome of these suits is not available.

Numerous newspapers report that McKean proceeded with two other civil libel suits in October 1805. He instituted one action against two Lancaster, Pa., anti-McKean figures, Republican John Steele and Federalist William

---

[23] *New Hampshire Centinel*, Aug. 17, 1805 contains a dispatch headed Philadelphia, Aug. 5, 1805; Newburyport *Herald*, Aug. 13, 1805.

    In fact, the *United States Gazette*, Aug. 3, 1805, had printed a letter from Dallas dated more than a month previously addressed to Lawler. He advised Lawler that an item bearing Lawler's name and published in the June 27, 1805, Philadelphia *Aurora* was an infamous libel upon his reputation and demanded to know whether the signature was genuine. The *Gazette* also printed a letter from Dallas dated July 1, 1806, advising that it was the "duty of a faithful citizen to prosecute and punish him" together with advertisement of $100 reward for evidence that Lawler subscribed to the paper bearing his name as published in the *Aurora* of the previous week.

    See also The Massachusetts Spy and Worcester *Gazette*, Aug. 14, 1805, containing a dispatch from the Philadelphia's *Freeman's Journal* of Aug. 2 referring to the litigation between Dallas and Lawler, and the political allegiances of the parties; *United States Gazette*, Aug. 21, 1805, defending Lawler.

[24] *United States Gazette*, Oct. 14, 1805, Nov. 6, 1805, *Evening Post*, Nov. 7, 1805, and *American Citizen*, Nov. 8, 1805 *reprinting* a dispatch from the Philadelphia *Aurora*, Sept. 6, 1806, Jan. 1, 1806.

    See G. S. Rowe, note 6, at 361; George M. Dallas, *Alexander James Dallas* 226 ff. (1871) (hereinafter Dallas).

Dickson. Steele was the Speaker of the Pennsylvania Senate and the chairman of the anti-McKean Leib/Duane "democratic caucus" that had proposed Simon Snyder to run against McKean for the Republican nomination for Governor. McKean charged that Steele had circulated a scurrilous pamphlet during the Republican nomination procedures. Dickson was the Federalist editor and printer of the *Lancaster Intelligencer and Weekly Advertiser* but allied with dissident Republicans Steele and Duane in opposing McKean for Governor.[25] McKean also brought a second suit against Dickson alone.[26] Finally, there was still a third action apparently allied to these two, instituted against Dickson by one Samuel Cochran, details of which are lacking.[27]

Reflecting the temper and the journalism of the times, another Federalist paper joined the fray. The *Philadelphia Evening Post* of August 8, 1805, reprinted a story from the *United States Gazette* explaining that Dallas and a Dr. Logan[28] were supporters of Governor McKean and that Lawler was an ally of his opponents, Duane and Leib. The *Evening Post* then pointed out that Dallas and Logan were only allies of the moment. It asserted gleefully that according to Duane's *Aurora*, Dr. Logan had in the past accused Dallas of cheating the public by improperly retaining $6,000 of public funds.[29] The Philadelphia *Aurora*, edited by McKean's arch-rival William Duane, described this wave of litigation as instituting a "new reign of terror," using Jefferson's old description of the 1798 Sedition Act.[30] These were *civil* libel suits, but this was not the end of the wave of litigation. The wave of civil libel suits was soon overtaken by a series of criminal libel prosecutions.

McKean was also instrumental in the institution of still another criminal libel proceeding against Duane in 1805 for allegedly libelous attacks on McKean and his nephew and secretary, Thomas McKean Thompson. Duane had made sinister insinuations about their relationship to McKean's son-in-law, the Spanish Minister, Marquis Carlos de Yrujo. This much delayed prosecution did not go to trial for several years.

---

[25] *United States Gazette*, Oct. 14, 1805; *American Citizen*, Oct. 14, 1805; *Evening Post*, Oct. 17, 1805; *Postboy & Vermont and New-Hampshire Federal Courier*, Nov. 5, 1805. *See* G. S. Rowe, note 6, at 361; Dallas, note 24, at 226 ff.

[26] *American Citizen*, Oct. 14, 1805.

[27] *United States Gazette*, Oct. 14, 1805.

[28] Likely, this was Dr. George Logan, a Republican who went as a private citizen to France in an attempt to negotiate peace with France. In consequence, the Congress in 1799 passed a statute criminalizing such attempts at private diplomacy. 1 Stat. 613 (1799). The statute known as the Logan Act is still in force. *See* 18 U.S.C. 953 (2008).

[29] Philadelphia *Evening Post*, Aug. 8, 1805 reprinting report of the *United States Gazette*.

[30] *See Evening Post*, Oct. 17, 1805, mocking Duane's use of the Jeffersonian phrase.

Not all the criminal libel actions had political significance. As an example, William McCorkle, editor of the Philadelphia *Freeman's Journal*, published in his May 27, 1805 issue an account of Thomas Passmore that led to a criminal libel prosecution prompted by Passmore against McCorkle for publication of a "malicious, false, and scandalous libel against his character and reputation." McCorkle was arrested and required to post a bond of $500 with two sureties for $250 each to assure his appearance in the Mayor's Court of June 29, 1805, and to keep the peace and be of good behavior in the meantime. Unfortunately, the outcome is not known.[31]

These few months in 1805 may well have been one of the busiest periods for libel litigation that ever occurred in the United States. After this avalanche of cases, the much delayed prosecution of Joseph Dennie for criminal libel eventually came to trial in the November Term of 1805 with Attorney General William McKean still acting for the prosecution.[32] Justice Jasper Yeates charged the jury. Citing the liberal provisions of the Pennsylvania Constitution of 1790 dealing with freedom of speech and imposing restrictions on the conduct of criminal libel cases[33] and Alexander Hamilton's argument in *Croswell* (discussed later in this chapter), Justice Yeates established a new liberal standard for Pennsylvania libel law.

He started with the provisions of Art. 9, §7 of the Constitution stating that persons "may freely speak, write, or print on any subject while remaining responsible for the abuse of that liberty." So far, this was Blackstone. However, Yeates then instructed the jury that Art. 9, §7 further provided that in matters involving the

> publication of papers, investigating the official conduct of officers or men in a public capacity, or where the matter published is proper for public information, the truth thereof may be given in evidence and, in all indictments for libels the jury shall have the right to determine the law and the facts, under the direction of the court, as in other cases.

Judge Yeates then charged that truth was a defense when published from "good motives" and "for a justifiable end" even though it reflected on government or on magistrates.

---

[31] *United States Gazette*, June 5, 1805, *reprinted in the Connecticut Courant*, Aug. 14, 1805.

[32] Respublica v. Dennie, 4 Yeates 267, 271, 1805 Pa. LEXIS 38 (1805) (report describes the proceedings of the case but contains no opinion).

[33] Penn. Const. Art. 9, §7 (1790).

He concluded:

> if the consciences of the jury shall be clearly satisfied that the publication
> was seditiously, maliciously, and wilfully aimed at the independence of
> the United States, the constitution thereof, or of this state, they should
> convict the defendant. If on the other hand, the production was honestly
> meant to inform the public mind, and warn them against supposed dan-
> gers in society, though the subject may have been treated erroneously, or
> that the censures on democracy were bestowed on pure unmixed democ-
> racy, where the people en masse execute the sovereign power without the
> medium of their representatives (agreeably to our forms of government)
> as have occurred at different times in Athens, Sparta, Rome, France,
> and England, then however the judgments of the jury may incline them
> to think individually, they should acquit the defendant.... If the jury
> should doubt of the criminal intention, then also the law pronounces
> that he should be acquitted.[34]

Almost instructed to find Dennie not guilty, the jury brought in a verdict of
not guilty on December 2, 1805.[35]

Two months later, Governor McKean, ever relentlessly pursuing his critics,
dealt with still another political enemy, Federalist William Dickson, editor
of the Lancaster *Intelligencer and Weekly Advertiser*, against whom he had
earlier brought a civil libel action. Unlike the *Dennie* case, the *Dickson* case
proceeded at breakneck speed. On Tuesday, February 11, 1806, Dickson's
Intelligencer and Weekly Advertiser had denounced Governor McKean as "a
man who had basely prosecuted his official station" with "corruption."[36] The
Court of Oyer and Terminer being in session, Attorney General William
McKean obtained an indictment from a unanimous grand jury two days
later on Thursday, February 13, 1806.[37] Trial commenced another two days
later on Saturday and continued on Sunday, February 15 and 16. Although

---

[34] 4 Yeates at 271, 1805 Pa. LEXIS 38, at *10–11.

[35] Philadelphia *Evening Post*, Dec. 4, 1805; Philadelphia *Commercial Advertiser*, Dec. 4, 1805. *See also* G. S. Rowe, note 6, at 467 n.12.

[36] In her biography of McKean, Rowe provides some further detail. She asserts that the alleged libel involved an accusation against McKean's secretary and nephew, Thomas McKean Thompson, of attempted bribery of a state senator to obtain his vote on approval of an appointment. Chief Justice McKean was the subject of great ridicule and criticism because of his energetic practice of nepotism. Rowe lists no fewer than 10 members of his family including relations by marriage who held government positions in the Pennsylvania state and local administrations. *See* G. S. Rowe, note 6, at 321.

[37] With so much criticism of trials during this period for allegedly "packed" juries, it may be of interest that this grand jury is reported to have been drawn by lot pursuant to the Pennsylvania statute of Mar. 29, 1795. *United States Gazette* of Feb. 27, 1806 (also containing a report from Lancaster publishing the names of the members of the grand and petit juries).

Dickson, like Dennie, had invoked the Pennsylvania constitutional guarantee of freedom of speech, the jury convicted him on Monday, February 17, 1806, a mere six days after the offending publication. He was sentenced to three months imprisonment, a $500 fine, and costs.[38] Taking no more than a week from offense to sentence, the pace of the *Dickson* prosecution contrasts vividly with the extensive delays in so many of the criminal libel litigations of this period.[39]

These cases were followed in 1807 and 1808 by a further series of politically related libel proceedings against William Duane for libelous publications in the *Aurora*. February 1807 saw a newspaper report of a prosecution by George Rogers Clark for a libelous publication accusing Clark at being head of a conspiracy to effect a separation of the United States.[40] Clark had become a national hero during the Revolutionary War after his successful campaigns against the British in what became the Northwest Territory. After the war, Clark's reputation lost most of its luster with his participation in several abortive plans for military expeditions involving the seizure of the then Spanish-held Mississippi River. The newspaper account that led to the prosecution seems to be related to one of these episodes. Like so many of these litigations, the outcome is not known. In the following month, there was still another criminal prosecution against Dr. Leib and William Duane in which the hand of Governor McKean is evident. They are reported to have been indicted in February 1807 by the Philadelphia grand jury. The charge was

[38] *United States Gazette* of Feb. 27, 1806; Philadelphia *Aurora*, Jan. 15, 27, Feb. 20, 22, 26, May 15, 1806; *Sentinel of Freedom*, Feb. 25, 1806; *Spirit of the Press*, Aug. 1, 1806 (challenging contention that the jury was packed, asserting that it had been selected before the action had been instituted).
    Another newspaper similarly ridicules Duane's defense of Dickson. It asserts that Dickson's fine had been paid by his political allies and that he remained in jail only because he refused to acknowledge the offence and apologize. See *Spirit of the Press*, Aug. 1, 1806. *Compare* the Connecticut Federalist disparagement of the Republican claims about the inhumane imprisonment of Selleck Osborne. *See* text accompanying note 112.

[39] Haskins and Johnson similarly relate that Governor McKean in 1806 had been instrumental in having a criminal libel brought against a "William *Dickenson*, a federalist editor" (*sic*) for publishing an accusation that Governor. McKean's secretary and nephew, Thomas McKean Thompson, had attempted to bribe a state senator to obtain his vote on approval of an appointment. *See* 2 Oliver Wendell Holmes Devise, *History of the Supreme Court of the United States*, George Lee Haskins & Herbert A. Johnson, *Foundations of Power: John Marshall, 1801–1835*, 638 n.110 (1982).
    This is reported to have occurred in May 1806, relying on a newspaper account of that month. Philadelphia *Aurora*, May 17, 1806). In view of the similarity of name, the identical nature of the libel, and the identical punishment, these appear to be one and the same prosecution. However, the first accounts are Feb. 1806 reports of the event as just occurring and the May 1806 accounts read as if the event had just occurred in May.

[40] The *Centinel*, Feb. 4, 1807. *See* J. Thomas Scharf & Thompson Westcott, *History of Philadelphia 1609–1884*, 529 (1884) (hereinafter Scharf & Westcott).

criminal conspiracy, alleging that they made unlawful threats and promises to influence the official conduct of Governor McKean in his inquiry into the legality of the election for the Philadelphia Sheriff.[41] The Attorney General then moved for a warrant summoning Dr. Leib to answer the charge of conspiracy. The Lancaster *Journal* interviewed Duane on the development, and it quoted a blustering Duane as stating that if the warrant had been granted and the Sheriff had attempted to execute it, violence would have ensued. Duane is quoted as saying that "in less time than twice 24 hours, I would have had 700 men at Lancaster. We would have made the cartridges and cast the balls on the wagons coming up [from Philadelphia]."[42]

During the same year, as reported by Scharf and Westcott in their *History of Philadelphia*, "Duane had his usual crop of libel suits." These involved Daniel, Marquis de Urujo, Joseph Lloyd, and, as reported, George Rogers Clark.[43]

One thing is clear. Commencing with Oswald in 1782, Chief Justice McKean was indefatigable in his determination to use the libel laws – seditious, criminal, and civil – to punish opponents, Federalists or radical Republicans alike. Nor can his fierce preoccupation be explained simply as a campaign against libelous publications generally. Although the actions and prosecutions for which he was responsible were for the most part directed against Federalists, he also resorted to numerous civil libel actions against Republican political allies of William Duane and Michael Leib and a series of criminal prosecutions against Duane himself.[44] What makes this pattern so significant is McKean's stature in the public life of the era. McKean had been Chairman of the Continental Congress under the Articles of Confederacy, President of Delaware before the adoption of the Constitution, Chief Justice of Pennsylvania for two decades, and three times elected Governor of Pennsylvania.

In response to the conspiracy charge instigated by McKean, Dr. Leib struck back, resurrecting an episode that allegedly had happened six months earlier.

[41] Commonwealth v. William Duane and Michael Leib (Pa. 1807) (unreported); *Connecticut Herald*, Feb. 24, 1807; Litchfield *Monitor*, Apr. 1, 1807.

[42] *United States Gazette*, Mar. 30, 1807 contain the report from the Lancaster *Journal*.

[43] Scharf & Westcott, note 40, at 529.

[44] As early as 1802, the Federalists had "virtually disappeared" in Pennsylvania, with the Republicans soon disintegrating into the McKean-Gallatin-Dallas and Leib-Duane factions. *See* Ronald P. Formisano, Deferential Participant Politics: The Early Republic's Political Culture, 1789–1840, 68 Am. Pol. Sci. Rev. 473, 477 (1974); Kim Tousley Phillips, *William Duane: Radical Journalist in the Age of Jefferson* 167–168 (hereinafter Phillips).

    After the debacle of 1800, the Federalists continued to lose ground in Pennsylvania as elsewhere. In the 1802 Pennsylvania elections, the Federalists put up only "nominal" opposition to the reelection of Governor McKean. In the 1804 Pennsylvania elections, the Federalists did not even nominate their own candidates. *See* Phillips, at 167–168, 171.

He swore to a warrant that William McKean, the Governor's son and former Attorney General of Pennsylvania, had challenged him to a duel with pistols. The younger McKean was arrested and convicted. Pending trial, he was ordered to post a bond in the amount of $3,000 with a surety for an additional $3,000 to assure his appearance and that he would not further breach the peace.

With suit and counter-suits threatening all concerned, there were abortive peace negotiations. Dr Leib is reported have filed a deposition dated March 23, 1807, in the Lancaster, Pa., court describing the negotiations. He retraced the history. As described above, Leib had been a surety for $1,000 for Duane's good behavior while awaiting trial in Duane's 1799 prosecution for criminal libel. Although Duane was ultimately acquitted of the libel charge, the state brought a second action seeking forfeiture of the bonds posted by Duane and his surety, Leib.[45] While the suit on the bonds was pending, McKean had become Governor. A mutual friend then intervened to negotiate a discontinuance of all the pending litigation. Although Leib had been told that the litigation would be discontinued, the suits continued. The trial of the action on the bonds neared in 1804. After receipt of a special jury list for the trial, Leib waited upon Governor McKean and requested discontinuance. McKean responded that it would be better that all suits be dropped, referring to the suits against his son and others as well as those against Duane and Leib. He assured Leib that if Duane would drop those actions, the suit for forfeiture of the bonds and the prosecution of Duane for rioting and assault in the fracas at the Philadelphia Catholic Church (discussed in Chapter 4) would be dropped. Governor McKean suggested that Dr. Leib transmit the proposal to Duane. Leib did so, although asserting that he had advised Duane against acceptance. Duane then rejected the proposed settlement, and the cases proceeded.[46] Then in November 1808, near the end of McKean's third and final term as Governor, the long-delayed libel prosecution of Duane for his comments about McKean, his nephew/secretary, and son-in-law at last went to trial, three years after Duane had been indicted. After several days of deliberation, the jury found Duane guilty on one count.[47] Duane appealed.

While the appeal was pending, the Legislature, now controlled by the Leib-Duane wing of the Republican Party, enacted a statute on March 16, 1809, virtually eliminating criminal libel. The Act prohibited any prosecution by indictment for publications examining legislative proceedings or any branch

---

[45] McKean's similar pursuit of Cobbett in 1797–1800 had repeated itself.

[46] *Kline's Carlisle Weekly Gazette*, May 1, 1807.

[47] Commonwealth v. William Duane, 1 Binney (Pa.) 601, 605, 1809 Pa. LEXIS 12 (1809); Newburyport *Herald*, Dec. 1, 1808. *See* G. S. Rowe, note 6, at 367–369.

of government, of official conduct of officers or men in public capacity. It further provided that in all libel actions or criminal prosecutions, truth could be pleaded in justification or offered into evidence.

One matter, however, was not clear: Was the statute enacted by Duane's allies so soon after his conviction retroactive? On the appeal, the Supreme Court held that the statute was indeed retroactive and threw out the Duane conviction.[48] Duane had escaped punishment once again. In all, Duane had been the defendant in libel actions – criminal and civil – several dozen times. Although he lost only occasionally, he was continuously in the courts, and as he wrote to Jefferson: "I am disposed I fear to live out my life in the law courts."[49]

At this point, the saga of the struggle between the McKeans – father and son – and Dr. Leib and his ally William Duane comes to an end. With an abortive impeachment movement in the Legislature having been defeated with some difficulty and his third term as Governor at an end, McKean withdrew from politics after holding the highest public offices for almost 30 years. He died in 1817. Dr. Leib served in the U.S. Senate until his term expired in 1814. Duane's influence dwindled, and he at last abandoned the *Aurora* in 1822 and moved for a while to South America. He returned to Philadelphia, where he served as an Alderman and later as Prothonotary of the Pennsylvania Supreme Court for the Eastern District.[50]

At this point, libel litigation for political purposes subsided in Pennsylvania. However, the 1815 decision of the Pennsylvania Supreme Court in *Gray v. Pentland* is instructive on the contours of the doctrine and deserves mention. In the *Gray* case,[51] Pentland had sent to the Governor an affidavit that Gray, the Prothonotary of the Court of Common Pleas, was frequently intoxicated and unfit for performing his duty. Gray thereupon promptly sued Pentland for civil libel. At the trial, Pentland asked the judge to rule that if his complaint to the Governor had been sent for the purpose of an investigation of the plaintiff's official conduct and his continued fitness for office, his statements were not actionable. The trial judge refused, ruling instead that if the communication had "originated in malice" and was "destitute of probable cause," the plaintiff's suit could be maintained.

On appeal, the Supreme Court reversed. There were several opinions. Chief Justice William Tilghman held that the defendant did not have to

[48] Commonwealth v. William Duane, 1 Binney (Pa.) 601, 605, 1809 Pa. LEXIS 12 (1809).
[49] Letter, William Duane to Thomas Jefferson (Feb. 11, 1809), Phillips, note 40, at 242.
[50] *See* the biographical sketch of Duane in Wharton, note 1, at 389–391, Phillips, note 40, *passim*.
[51] *Gray v. Pentland*, 2 Serg. & Rawle, 23, 1815 Pa. LEXIS 66 (1815).

prove the truth of the statements. He would be excused if he could show that the allegedly libelous statements did not originate in malice and without probable cause. The trial judge had committed no error in so ruling. However, reversal was necessary on other grounds. Justices Yeates and Brackenbridge concurred (relying on other grounds).

2. New York

Lacking the hair-trigger, litigious Thomas McKean, New York did not have the same explosive use of criminal and civil libel for partisan purposes that characterized Pennsylvania politics and jurisprudence at this time. Nevertheless, New York experienced a series of politically prominent criminal libel prosecutions.

a. The Federalist Interlude

As described in Chapters 4 and 5, the first wave of New York partisan libel litigations was instituted by the Federalists when they were in power. Using federal and state law, the Federalists aggressively pursued criminal libel litigations to harass the two Republican newspaper editors in New York City.

As we have seen, the New York *Time Piece* ceased publication after its editor, John Daly Burk, and its publisher, James Smith, were indicted for criminal libel under federal criminal common-law jurisdiction and were required to post bonds to assure their good behavior during the period before trial. Similarly, Thomas Greenleaf, editor of the other Republican paper in the city, the New York *Argus*, was ardently pro-French and twice indicted under New York common law for libels on the British Minister. The first indictment in 1795 does not seem to have gone to trial. However, he was indicted a second time under New York law in 1797 and convicted. When Greenleaf continued to attack Federalist policies, he was among the first group of Republican editors to be indicted under the federal Sedition Act in 1798. However, as we have seen, he escaped trial, falling victim to the yellow fever epidemic that swept New York that year.

With his death, his wife, after a brief interval, resumed the publication of the paper. Then she too was indicted under the Sedition Act.[52] With the *Argus* continuing to attack the Federalists, David Frothingham, a printer

---

[52] After Frothingham was indicted, President Adams instructed Pickering in Apr. 1800 to discontinue the prosecution of Mrs. Greenleaf, and the case was brought to an end. Letter, John Adams to Timothy Pickering (Apr. 21, 1800); Letter, Timothy Pickering to Richard Harison (Apr. 22, 1800), 13 Pickering Papers 406 (Mass. Hist. Soc'y).

who had assumed responsibility for the *Argus*, was indicted under New York law. As described in Chapter 4, he was convicted and imprisoned with the requirement of a bond to assure his good behavior after his release.[53] With this development, Mrs. Greenleaf was forced to sell the *Argus*. Although she was able to find a Republican, David Denniston, to purchase it, Denniston promptly discontinued the paper and replaced it with the much more restrained *Republican Watchtower*.[54] The Federalist triumph was complete. The most aggressive New York Republican papers, the *Port Folio* and the *Argus*, were both driven out of existence on the eve of the 1800 election.

b. The Republican Era

Although the Federalists had been responsible for the first wave of partisan libel litigation, the political balance changed. In the 1800 elections that had elevated Jefferson to the White House, Republican George Clinton had been elected Governor of New York. As in Pennsylvania, Republican domination in New York did not mean abandonment of criminal libel prosecutions in partisan politics. Only the targets changed. Federalist newspaper editors were now attacked in the state criminal courts, rather than the Republicans as before.

Thus, when the next major criminal libel arose in New York, it was a prosecution of a Federalist editor instituted by a Republican prosecutor. This was the celebrated *Croswell* case in the General Sessions Court, Columbia County, upstate New York.[55] It arose in consequence of an intense political controversy between Harry Croswell, a fervent Federalist editor, and a prominent Republican editor, Charles Holt. As readers will recall, Holt had been among the Republican editors convicted under the Sedition Act.[56] Several years after his release from prison, Holt closed down his New London newspaper, the New London *Bee*, and moved to Hudson, N.Y.

The leading Hudson newspaper was the Federalist *Balance and Columbian Repository*, of which Harry Croswell was the printer and an editor. To counter this Federalist voice, Columbia County Republicans helped Holt commence

---

[53] *See* Richard W. Rosenfeld, *American Aurora: A Democratic-Republican Returns* 719, 724 (1997) (hereinafter Rosenfeld); Beatrice Diamond, *An Episode in American Journalism: A History of David Frothingham and His* Long Island Herald 50–67 (1964).

[54] *See* James Morton Smith, Alexander Hamilton, the Alien Law and Criminal Libels, 16 Rev. of Pol. 305, 331 (July 1954).

[55] *See* People v. Croswell, 1 Cai. R. 149, 3 Johns. Cas. 337, 1803 N.Y. LEXIS 169, 175 (1803); 3 Johns. Cas. 337 (N.Y. 1804); 1 Julius Goebel, Jr., *Law Practice of Alexander Hamilton* 775–884 (1964) (hereinafter Goebel, *Hamilton*).

[56] For discussion of Holt's conviction under the Sedition Act, see Ch. 4, text accompanying notes 146–149.

publication of the Hudson *Bee*. With political warfare intensifying, Croswell established an additional Federalist journal, a four-page flyer, the Hudson *Wasp*, to further harass the Republicans. Tempers were running high. The invective flowed. As Malone puts it, the *Wasp* was "a symbol of unrestrained scurrility."[57]

Croswell in the *Wasp* charged that Jefferson had paid James Thomson Callender to call George Washington a "traitor, a robber, and a perjurer" and John Adams "a hoary-headed incendiary."[58] The Republican District Attorney, Ebenezer Foote, then saw to it that Croswell was indicted for criminal libel under New York common law in January 1803. The indictment asserted that Croswell with "scandalous, malicious and seditious intent" had attempted to bring President Jefferson "into the great contempt of the people."

Surprisingly, it was none other than Ambrose Spencer, Attorney General of the State of New York and later Chief Justice of the Court of Appeals, who undertook the prosecution. Croswell had lampooned Spencer severely in *The Wasp*. In fact, there was a satirical article mocking Spencer in the very issue containing one of the articles about Jefferson for which Croswell was subsequently indicted. Goebel suggests that the attacks on Spencer may explain Spencer's participation and his rancorous personal attitude toward Croswell. They may also explain why this minor upstate editor was prosecuted in the first place.[59]

At the trial in the circuit court in July 1803, Chief Justice Morgan Lewis charged the jury that English libel law as laid down by Lord Mansfield in the *Dean of St. Asaph's* case[60] was the law of New York.[61] Accordingly, the sole role of the jury was to determine whether the defendant was the publisher of the offending article and whether the alleged innuendos had defamed and held Jefferson up to ridicule and hatred. This was the law of criminal libel as formulated by Blackstone. When counsel for Croswell sought a continuance to obtain the testimony of Callender to enable him to prove the truth of his

---

[57] *See* 4 Malone, note 15, at 232.
[58] Goebel asserts that these attacks had been in response to Holt's defense of Jefferson in the *Bee*. Goebel, *Hamilton*, note 55, at 777.
[59] One of Croswell's wounding comments about Spencer was: "The Attorney General too was drunk but not with grog – Power and pride had set his head agog." *The Wasp*, Sept. 9, 1802. *See* Goebel, *Hamilton*, note 55, at 779; Nathan Schachner, *Alexander Hamilton* 414 (1946) (hereinafter Schachner, *Hamilton*).
[60] Dean of St. Asaph's Case, 3 Term. Rep. 428, 4 Doug. 73, 100 Eng. Rep. 657 (K.B. 1784) (Mansfield, J.).
[61] Like most states at the time, New York had no statute dealing with criminal libel, nor did it have any statutory provision defining the role of jury or the role of the truth of the alleged libels. Under the reception statute, English common law prevailed.

allegations, the Court refused. Evidence of truth was not admissible according to Blackstone, and this was the New York common law.[62]

Croswell was convicted. He appealed, seeking a new trial.[63] On argument of the appeal in February 1804, Alexander Hamilton appeared for the defendant. Although Hamilton conceded that the English common law was the guiding standard in New York, he challenged the Blackstonian statement of the content of the English common-law doctrine as inaccurate.

Hamilton spoke brilliantly, leading Chancellor Kent to observe later that "a more able and eloquent argument was perhaps never heard in any court."[64] In attacking Croswell's conviction, Hamilton based his presentation on the contention that Chief Justice Lewis following Blackstone had not properly applied the English common law. In an extensive review of English common-law libel said to have been six hours long spread over two days,[65] he argued that the decision in the *Dean of St. Asaph's* case and inferentially Blackstone[66] were in error. They were based on 17th-century decisions in the proceedings conducted in the infamous Star Chamber that had disregarded binding precedent and were wrongly decided. Instead, the English common law was properly found in still earlier English decisions, and it was on these that Hamilton rested his case. Caine, his fellow counsel, added that both Fox's Act of 1792 in England and the provisions on the admissibility of truth and the role of the jury in the Sedition Act should be viewed as declaratory of the true English common law.

In brief, Hamilton and Caine contended that under the earlier and binding English decisions, evidence of truth was admissible, that truth was a defense

---

[62] Ironically, in the interval between New York's reception of the English common law as a part of the law of the state and the trial of Croswell, the English law had changed. As we have seen, Parliament's enactment of Fox's Act in 1792 had modified the Blackstonian common-law doctrine. 32 Geo. III c.60 of 1792. However, the Act only went as far as to provide that the jury could give a general verdict, thereby enabling it to determine not only the facts but the law, subject to the instructions of the judge. It was not until Lord Campbell's Libel Act of 1843 that the defendant in the English courts in criminal libel cases could introduce evidence of the truth of the assertions in issue in justification for his or her statements when made "for the public benefit." 6 & 7 Vict. c.92, §6 (1843).

[63] People v. Croswell, 1 Cai. R. 149, 1803 N.Y. LEXIS 169 (1803); 3 Johns. Cas. 337, 1804 N.Y. LEXIS 175 (1804). Goebel provides the most extensive discussion of the *Croswell* case. *See* Goebel, *Hamilton*, note 55, at 775–848. See also Schachner, *Hamilton*, note 59, at 413–418 and Morris Forkosch, Freedom of the Press: Croswell's Case, 33 Fordham L. Rev. 415 (1965) (hereinafter Forkosch).

[64] Reports of the Proceedings and Debates of the Convention of 1821, 488. *See* Goebel, *Hamilton*, note 55, at 848 n.130. *See also* Schachner, *Hamilton*, note 59, at 416–417 (James Kent noted that Hamilton "was sublimely eloquent").

[65] *See* Forkosch, note 63, at 438.

[66] Because Blackstone and the decision in *St. Asaph's Case* were identical, Hamilton was staking a position contrary to Blackstone. *See* 4 William Blackstone, *Commentaries on the Law of England* 150 (1769, repr. 1992).

if presented with "good motives" and for "justifiable ends," and that the jury was able to bring in a general verdict, and, accordingly, was the judge of the law and the facts, subject to the instructions of the judge, as in other criminal cases.[67]

The four judges sitting on the case[68] divided two to two. Federalist Chancellor Kent and Justice Smith Thompson (later Secretary of the Navy under Monroe and Justice of the U.S. Supreme Court) sided with Hamilton and Croswell; Republican Chief Justice Morgan Lewis[69] (hearing the appeal from his own order in the trial court) and Justice Brockholst Livingston (two years later appointed Justice of the U.S. Supreme Court by Jefferson) voted to uphold the prosecution. With the tie vote, Croswell's motion for a new trial, accordingly, failed.

Promptly after the *Croswell* trial, the New York Legislature, which had been considering a bill to admit truth as evidence in criminal libel cases, enacted a statute codifying the Hamiltonian view, but the Council of Revision (which then had the power to override the Legislature) sent the Bill back for further consideration. The following year, the New York Legislature unanimously adopted the liberalized standard advanced by Hamilton and supported by Chancellor Kent. Hamilton may have lost the battle, but he posthumously won the war.

The new statute provided:

(1) the jury . . . shall have a right to determine the law and the fact, under the direction of the court, in like manner as in other criminal cases . . . ;

(2) the defendant may "give in evidence, in his defense, the truth of the matter . . . ; provided . . . that the matter charged as libelous, was published with good motives and for justifiable ends;

(3) any person . . . convicted . . . shall not be sentenced to an imprisonment exceeding . . . eighteen months, or to pay a fine exceeding . . . five thousand dollars.

On remand of the *Croswell* case to the trial court, it turned out that the prosecutor had still not moved for judgment on the earlier verdict of guilty. In consequence, the new statute governed the case. Faced by the momentous

---

[67] *See* Goebel, *Hamilton*, note 55, at 808–844.

[68] The Court had five members. Attorney General Spencer had been appointed to the fifth seat on Feb. 3, 1804. Instead of sitting, however, he helped argue the case for the prosecution.

[69] Shortly after the trial, Chief Justice Lewis, a Republican, was nominated for Governor. After a bitter campaign against another Republican, Aaron Burr, Lewis was elected Governor in the 1804 elections. This episode highlights the rapid decline of the Federalists in New York. As early as 1804, the battle for Governor involved two fiercely contending wings of the Republican Party.

changes made by the statute, the Supreme Court at its August 1805 Term granted Croswell's motion for a new trial.[70]

However, matters did not stop at this point. Reflecting the bad feelings between the parties, Attorney General Spencer and his associate, District Attorney Ebenezer Foote, thereupon both instituted actions for civil libel against Croswell. In form, they both won, but whether they felt that the actions were worthwhile is another matter. Spencer obtained a judgment of only $100, and Foote was for practical purposes repulsed, being awarded a mere six cents.[71]

Hamilton's professional triumph in the appeal of the *Croswell* case and the prompt enactment by the New York Legislature of Hamilton's position not only changed the law in New York. It became a national model with many other states following suit. In 1821 the New York Constitution was similarly amended to provide: "in all prosecutions or indictments for libels, the truth may be given in evidence to the jury, if it be made to appear to the jury that the matter charged as libellous was published from good motives, and for justifiable ends, the party shall be acquitted."[72] As Justice Frankfurter has pointed out, Hamilton's restatement of the law of criminal libel was adopted not only in the 1821 New York Constitution but subsequently in the Constitutions of more than a dozen states.[73] In what must be considered one of Hamilton's greatest contributions to American law and politics, the

---

[70] People v. Croswell, 1 Cai, R. 149, 3 Johns. Cas. 337, 1804 N.Y. LEXIS 175 (1804).

The overlapping timetables of the legislative and judicial proceedings are of interest. The Legislature approved the first Act on Apr. 9, 1804, and it was before the Council of Revision (of which the Supreme Court judges were members) when the Supreme Court was considering its decision; it was announced on Apr. 30, 1804. After rejection by the Council of Revision in Nov. 1804, the Legislature at its next session unanimously passed a modified Act on Apr. 6, 1805, months before the Supreme Court granted the new trial on Feb. 13, 1804.

This inevitably prompts several questions for which there is no available answer: Did the Apr. 9, 1804, action of the New York Legislature and its submission that date to the Council of Revision influence the Supreme Court's decision on Apr. 30, 1804? Does the Legislature's action and the delay until Nov. 1804 before the Council of Revision rejected the law explain the Attorney General's decision not to press for judgment on the verdict in the extended interval between the verdict and the enactment of the modified act on Apr. 6, 1805?

[71] Spencer v. Croswell (N.Y. Columbia Cty. Cir. Ct. 1804). *See* Goebel, *Hamilton*, note 55, at 844 *citing The Balance*, July 17, 1804, July 24, 1804, containing a full account of the trial.

In preliminary proceedings, the court ruled that Foote's allegations did not call for a "struck" jury. Although Foote was, indeed, a public officer instituting the libel action and thereby qualifying for a "struck" jury, his complaint had failed to include the necessary allegation. Foot [sic] v. Croswell, 1 Cai. R. 498, 1804 N.Y. LEXIS 180 (Feb. 1804).

[72] *See* Reports of the Proceedings and Debates of the New York Constitutional Convention of 1821 487, *cited by* 1 Goebel, *Hamilton*, note 55, at 847–848; N.Y. Const., Art. VII, §8 (1821). It has since been successively incorporated in later Constitutions. *See* N.Y. Const., Art. I, §8 (2009).

[73] *See* Beauharnais v. Illinois, 343 U.S. 250, 293 (1952) (Frankfurter, J.).

draconian Blackstonian model of English criminal libel law with only a few states excepted no longer governed libel prosecutions in the new nation.

However, it should not escape attention that Hamilton's definition of the rules of admissibility did not make truth the absolute standard. Truth was, indeed, made a defense, but only if the publication was made with "good motives" and for "justifiable ends." This limitation echoes the conclusion of the 1789 correspondence between John Adams and Chief Justice Cushing with respect to common-law criminal libel in Massachusetts. To assure constitutionality, they too would have made truth a defense, only in the case of statements made for "good purposes."[74] The English ultimately moved in a similar direction. Lord Campbell's Libel Act of 1843 permitting evidence of truth as a defense required that the publication had been made "for the public benefit."[75]

The *Croswell* litigation had its reverberations. A newspaper account of the *Croswell* case in the *Ulster Gazette* led to a contempt proceeding of the Federalist editor Samuel S. Freer discussed in Chapter 7. At the same time, another Federalist editor, Gardner Tracy of the *Lansingburg Gazette*, who had republished the account in the *Ulster Gazette*, was indicted for criminal libel of Chief Justice Lewis and District Attorney Foote.[76] The doctrines of contempt, on the one hand, and criminal libel, on the other, were both available for the courts to punish opposition editors.

Whether there were still other prosecutions of newspaper editors for this affair is not entirely clear. On the one hand, one newspaper account in October 1803 asserted that the Rensellaer County grand jury had indicted five persons (three Federalists and two Republicans) for newspaper libels.[77] The Federalist *New Hampshire Centinel* published a different account some months later. It asserted that five or six "democratic" newspapers had similarly published an account of this phase of the *Croswell* case, but that only the editors of the two Federalist papers (presumably Freer and Tracy) had been indicted.[78]

Back in New York City during this period, James Cheetham, editor of the *American Citizen* and allied with the Clinton wing of the New York

[74] *See* Ch. 3, text accompanying notes 40 to 42.
[75] 6 & 7 Vict. c.96, §6 (1843).
[76] Hudson *Balance*, Mar. 16, 1804.
[77] New York *Evening Sun*, Nov. 14, 1803.
[78] *New-Hampshire Centinel*, Dec. 31, 1803. Still another newspaper account of this period reports that two others – James Dole and David Allen – who were otherwise not identified were also indicted for criminal libels of Ebenezer Foote. Albany *Centinel*, Oct. 18, 1803, reprinting an item from the Lansingburg *Gazette*. Unfortunately further details of these prosecutions are not available.

Republican Party, achieved notoriety as one of the most scurrilous and litigious editors of the period, ranking with Bache, Fenno, Cobbett, and Duane.
Like his predecessors, Cheetham's unrestrained prose repeatedly embroiled
him in libel litigation. In 1803 there was an unconfirmed report that Aaron
Burr, then Vice President of the United States, had ordered the institution of
a libel prosecution against Cheetham, as editor of the *American Citizen*, but
further details are lacking.[79] In 1806, following an altercation with Stanley,
the editor of the New York *Morning Chronicle*, Cheetham was able to instigate the prosecution of Stanley for criminal libel for printing the following
assertion in the *Morning Chronicle*:

> James Cheetham has the effrontery to offer $50 for the discovery of
> the proprietor or editor of the Morning Chronicle. But none of our
> employees are "Judas's" nor would they for thirty or fifty of Cheetham's
> pieces of silver betray their masters. Any one of our *carriers* will pay a
> reward of *one cent* who will declare "on oath if required" that he believes
> the captain [Cheetham] to possess one particle of honesty or truth. . . . All
> newly imported *wild* Irishmen are expressly included.[80]

Although there is considerable information on the outcome of a number of
other actions for contempt and libel in which Cheetham was involved, the
outcome of the proceedings against Stanley is not known.

In the same year, Cheetham charged in his *American Citizen* that rampant
corruption in the New York Senate had secured the passage of a controversial banking bill. As reviewed in Chapter 8 dealing with contempt of the
legislature, the Senate unsuccessfully tried to prosecute Cheetham for the
allegation, as constituting criminal contempt of the legislature, but the grand
jury refused to indict.[81] When Cheetham continued to print his charges,
several State Senators thereupon brought civil suits for libel. Of these, Sen.
Tillotson brought two suits and was successful in each. He obtained judgments of $400 in the first action and $800 in the second. On appeal in the
second suit, Cheetham contended that the two articles were part of a single
publication and that the $400 damages awarded in the earlier action should
be taken into account. In rejecting the argument, Chancellor Kent seized

[79] A member of the Clinton wing of the Republican Party, Cheetham has been described as the
leading editorial enemy of Aaron Burr. *See* Henry Adams, *History of the United States During the
First Jefferson Administration* 225 (1982).

[80] *American Citizen*, Jan. 16, 18, 20, 1806. In its Jan. 18, 1806, issue, the *American Citizen* accuses
Stanley of being hired "by his Excellency or his friends."

[81] It is not clear why the legislature turned to the courts. Under the common-law doctrine of breach
of the privileges or contempt of the legislature, the legislature could act on its own.

the opportunity to assail the "licentiousness" of the press and called for an increase in damages for libels of public officials.[82]

With the decline and ultimate disappearance of the Federalists, debate in New York partisan politics thereafter lost its criminal dimensions. Criminal libels became a matter of the past, and as illustrated in the *Tillotson* affair, civil libel was replacing criminal libel. However, for a time, criminal proceedings for contempt of court for out-of-court publications and contempt of the legislature to a limited degree served much the same purpose.

Thus, at this time, New York followed in the path of Pennsylvania and experienced the same attempted use of criminal process – in this case, contempt of court – by a Republican Governor to harass the leaders of a Republican faction trying to deprive him of renomination. The political struggle between McKean and Duane in Pennsylvania was replayed in New York in 1807. Republican Governor Morgan Lewis, like McKean, turned to a repressive legal doctrine to punish supporters of his Republican opponent for the nomination, Daniel D. Tompkins (later Vice President of the United States). As in Pennsylvania, the New York Republican Party was badly divided. The Livingston faction supporting Lewis was fighting for control against the Clinton faction supporting Tompkins. As in Pennsylvania, both vied for the support of the declining Federalists.

People ex rel. *Lewis v. Farmer* followed by *People* ex rel. *Lewis v. Few* must be read against this background. These cases involved the very essence of free public political debate. In *Farmer*, Governor Lewis had instigated a prosecution for criminal libel action against Thomas Farmer, who had been the Chairman at a public political rally that had adopted anti-Lewis resolutions.[83] While the *Farmer* case was pending, another public meeting nominating Tompkins to oppose Lewis for Governor adopted resolutions criticizing the institution of the *Farmer* litigation, The resolution asserted that the prosecution was

> an unwarrantable attempt to suppress and destroy one of our dearest
> and most valuable privileges, that of assembling together openly and
> publicly; of discussing freely the conduct of public men and public
> measures; ... and that, therefore, such prosecution evinces an intolerant
> spirit, unbecoming the chief magistrate of a free State, disgraceful in a

---

[82] Tillotson v. Cheetham, 2 Johns. Cas. 64 (N.Y. 1806); 3 Johns. Cas. 56 (1808). *See* Norman L. Rosenberg, *Protecting the Best Men: An Interpretive History of the Law of Libel* 126–128 (1986) (hereinafter Rosenberg).

[83] People *ex rel.* Lewis v. Farmer (N.Y. Sup. Ct. 1807) (unreported) is reviewed in People *ex rel.* Lewis v. Few, 2 Johns. Cas. 290, 1807 N.Y. LEXIS 58 (N.Y. Sup. Ct. 1807).

free government, and insulting to the feelings of every citizen who was present at that meeting.

Following the meeting, at which William Few acted as chairman and James Townsend had acted as secretary, the resolutions under Few's and Townsend's names were printed in Cheetham's *American Citizen* on March 6, 1807. The next issue of the *American Citizen* published further resolutions signed by Few as Chairman and Pierre C. Van Wyck as Secretary that characterized the suit against Farmer in similar terms.

Counsel for Governor Lewis in the *Farmer* litigation then moved to cite Few, Van Wyck, and Townsend for contempt of court. In their affidavits the defendants disclaimed any intention to commit any contempt of court or to influence the administration of justice. They also informed the Court that Lewis had published a letter in the *Morning Chronicle* characterizing Farmer's assertions for which the plaintiff had brought his suit as "a base, villainous, and slanderous falsehood."

In *People* ex rel. *Lewis v. Few*,[84] the Court *per curiam* declined to attach the defendants for contempt. The opinion noted that the affidavits had shown the absence of any intentional disrespect or intention to influence or affect the course of justice. It also observed that "the first impropriety was on the part of the plaintiff [Lewis] in appealing to the public, in regard to the subject matter of his suit, at the time when he had commenced it." Under the circumstances, the Court declined to exercise its discretionary power to impose any punishment for contempt.[85] (Tompkins, who was a member of the Court, did not participate.)

Repulsing the former Chief Justice of the Supreme Court in his bid to punish political opponents through the use of the Court's contempt power and doing so by a summary *per curiam* opinion, the Court in *Lewis v. Few* seems to be reflecting a changing attitude and an increased recognition of the value of public debate in the political forum. Two other prominent cases of this period – *Spencer v. Southwick*, and *Root v. King* – may also illustrate such a change.

In 1814 when Solomon Southwick, editor of an Albany newspaper, insinuated without providing details that Justice Ambrose Spencer of the Supreme Court (whom readers may recall as the Attorney General who prosecuted the *Croswell* case) was corrupt, Justice Spencer brought a civil libel suit, rather

---

[84] People *ex rel.* Lewis v. Few, 2 Johns. Cas. 290, 1807 N.Y. LEXIS 58 (N.Y. Sup. Ct. 1807).

[85] As discussed in the next chapter, the contempt power of the courts for out-of-court publications in pending cases such as *Freer* rested on a concern that publication would improperly influence courts and juries and affect the administration of justice.

than seeking to instigate a criminal libel prosecution. Reflecting less receptive attitudes by the bench, the suit was dismissed because of the lack of specificity in Southwick's allegations that left it to Southwick's readers to draw whatever inferences they chose.[86] Martin van Buren is reported to have lamented that the decision left the reputation of the judges at the mercy of the press.[87]

In *Root v. King*, 15 years later, when the *New York American* asserted that Lt. Governor Erastus Root had presided over the state Senate while intoxicated, Root brought a civil libel action. He prevailed and won a judgment of $1,400 when the defense could not prove the truth of the assertion, and the Court inferred the maliciousness of the charge from its falsity. On appeal, the Supreme Court upheld the judgment. The Court refused to adopt more liberal libel standards for the press.[88]

As illustrated by *Southwick v. Spencer* and *Root v. King*, civil libel suits were replacing criminal libel when political figures turned to libel litigation to settle campaign scores. In his splendid study of the early American press, Pasley reports that around 1804, one of the most virulent of the Federalist editors, William Coleman of the New York *Evening Post*, "called for Federalists to file private defamation actions whenever Republican editors criticized them. 'There is no method so likely to bring them down from their daring flights of effrontery in slander . . . as for the injured constantly to appeal to the law of the land for redress.'" Pasley continues:

> Given the sorry financial state of most Republican newspapers, the legal costs alone might be enough to put them out of business. The *Evening Post's* advice was followed, and private lawsuits became the approach of choice for gentlemen interested in punishing troublesome newspaper editors. . . . In an age when people were imprisoned for debt, private [i.e., civil] libel suits against an impecunious printer could result in jail time even more easily than criminal libel prosecutions. . . . [T]he private libel approach was also much harder on Republicans than Federalists. Republican politicians filed private libel suits against Federalist editors but never found the method an effectual check, because Federalists

---

[86] Spencer v. Southwick, 11 Johns. Cas. 573, 593, 1814 N.Y. LEXIS 16 (1814).

[87] *See* Phillips, note 44, at 127.

[88] Root v. King, 7 Cowen 613, 1827 N.Y. LEXIS 274 (1827); King & Verplank v. Root, 4 Wend. 113, 1829 N.Y. LEXIS 310 (1829).

Describing this period after the constitutional reform in 1805, Rosenberg concludes: "Libel decisions such as *Lewis v. Few* and *Root v. King* were designed to help maintain the balance of democratic and elitist impulses in American political life. Although judges and lawmakers rejected the Blackstonian doctrine that the law should proscribe virtually all political criticism, they still hoped to protect the reputation of public officials, using civil rather than criminal libel as their main line of legal defense." *See* Rosenberg, note 82, at 129.

typically had courts, money, and the finest available legal talent in their corner.[89]

Thus, the volume of civil libel suits instituted against prominent Republican editors reached staggering dimensions. Pasley further reports that by 1806 William Duane had been the defendant in 60 to 70 suits. A wit of the time commented that this sufficed to make Duane judgment-proof, stating, "Duane's own reputation is so bad that his slanders no longer injure his targets."[90] In New York, James Cheetham faced judgments aggregating "tens of thousands of dollars."[91]

3. Other Jurisdictions

In contrast to the extensive experience with criminal libel litigation in such Republican-dominated states as New York and Pennsylvania and in such Federalist-dominated states as Connecticut and Massachusetts, there are only minimal references to such cases in other jurisdictions.

One of the isolated exceptions occurred in Maryland. In 1808 the radical Republican editor Baptis Irvine of the Baltimore *Whig* was convicted in 1808 for contempt of court for criticizing the conviction of one of his employees for assault.[92]

Then in July, Irvine was convicted of criminal libel in charging a city official for corruption. The report described his conduct as "A FALSE, SCANDALOUS AND MALICIOUS LIBEL" (capitals in the original). It continued: "Who is this that thus violates the sober decorum that your laws enjoin. An emigrant wretch who has been six months among you, a part of which time, he spent in gaol, as a punishment for his outrageous conduct."[93] He was sentenced to 60 days' imprisonment and a $200 fine. In response, another Republican newspaper sarcastically commented: "Tell us of an instance of a federal printer being convicted in a court of justice, if you can, and we'll answer you three to one."[94]

Another is the report of the *Newburyport Herald* of March 24, 1807, that John Wood, editor of the Washington *Atlantic World*, was prosecuted for an

[89] Philadelphia *Aurora*, Aug. 12, 1806.
[90] *See* Rosenberg, note 82 at 107 n.18.
[91] *See* Pasley, note 7, at 278.
[92] *See* A. C. Hanson, An Accurate Report of the Argument on a Motion for Attachment against Baptis Irvine, editor of *The Whig*, for a Contempt (1808) (hereinafter Hanson).
[93] State v. Irvine, 1 Am. L. J. 298 (Ct. of Oyer & Terminer, Baltimore City July 1808). It is not clear from the report whether the words are those of the reporter or of the Court.
[94] *See* Pasley, note 7, at 284; Baltimore *Federal Republican*, July 29, 1808.

alleged libel of the prominent Republican John Beckley, twice chosen as Clerk of the House of Representatives, the first Librarian of Congress, and a steady source of "inside" gossip for Jefferson.[95] In view of the activities of the defendant and the complainant, it seems likely that the prosecution was in the Federal District Court in the District of Columbia. However, this is only surmise. Information about the jurisdiction, the court, the details of the indictment, and the outcome of the case is not available.

In the next section, readers will have an opportunity to review the Federalist use of criminal libel and other repressive legal doctrines against Republicans in such states as Connecticut and Massachusetts in which they still retained remnants of their fading political power.

C. Federalist Use of Repressive Doctrines Against Republicans

With the election of Thomas Jefferson as President in 1800, the Federalist Party went into decline. It never regained national power and progressively lost control of the states that it had previously dominated. For a while, Massachusetts and Connecticut were exceptions, and we see in these states frequent partisan invocation of criminal libel by Federalists upheld by Federalist judges in the first decade of the 19th century.[96]

1. Connecticut

Following the expiration of the Sedition Act in March 1801, criminal libel briefly came to an end in the federal courts. However, for at least a decade, criminal libel played a prominent role in Connecticut, punctuating the growing struggle between the dominant Federalists and the emerging Republican Party. Alone among the states of the New Republic, Connecticut along with Rhode Island had no Constitution. Although Connecticut operated under the Fundamental Orders of 1639 and the Convention of 1687, these did not begin to resemble the post-1776 Constitutions of the other states. Among other omissions, they had no express constitutional guaranties of freedom of speech and press. Although Connecticut did not adopt a reception statute until much

---

[95] Newburyport *Herald*, Mar. 24, 1807. For Jefferson, Beckley, although useful, had his limitations. "Beckley is a man of perfect truth as to what he affirms of his own knowledge but too credulous as to what he hears from others." *See* 4 Malone, note 15, at 18–19.

[96] Although Republicans in Massachusetts elected their first Governor, James Sullivan, in 1806, Federalist judges with lengthy terms continued to sit for years on the bench.

later, Connecticut courts followed the rigorous criminal libel doctrine of the English criminal common law until 1804. Connecticut then adopted a statute entitled "An Act to Secure Freedom of the Press" that significantly liberalized the common-law doctrine. Adopting the reforms in the Sedition Act of 1798, it provided that the defendant could introduce into evidence the truth of the matters contained in the alleged libel, and that the jury had the right to determine the law and the facts, subject to the direction of the court, as in other cases. In so doing, Connecticut, "the land of steady habits," of all the states, was a year ahead of New York and 20 years ahead of Massachusetts in modifying its rigid common-law criminal libel laws.

After the Jeffersonian triumph of 1800, Litchfield, Conn., under Federalist domination appears to have been the scene of the first skirmishes in the state courts between the Federalists and Republican spokesmen and editors. As reported by the Republican Litchfield *Monitor*, Major Seth Wetmore had been indicted in September 1802 for "wickedly and maliciously intending and contriving to defame and bring into contempt the laws and government of this state by publishing the "following false, scandalous, and malicious words, of and concerning the General Assembly of this state and the acts and laws thereof, viz: 'Every man who is twenty-one years of age, and pays taxes, has a natural right to vote.'"

In moss-bound Federalist/Congregationalist-dominated Connecticut, this was political heresy. Although it is reported that there were "two of Major Wetmore's political sentiments" (that is, Republicans) on the jury, he was convicted. The Court imposed a $100 fine and costs.[97] The Republican New London *Bee* reported a month later that Wetmore, so "lately honored by a prosecution and fine for *sedition* by the federal party," had been elected by his townsmen to represent them in the Legislature.[98]

After an apparently peaceful three-year interval, partisan use of criminal and civil libel became pandemic in Connecticut in 1806. In the state courts, there are reports of no fewer than seven different litigations in which Federalist judges imposed penalties on Republican defendants. In the same year, as we have already seen, the Republicans responded and used their control of the federal courts to institute six criminal libel cases against Federalists.

This assault of suit and countersuit continued for several years, and then resort to criminal prosecutions of this nature faded away. As we have already

---

[97] Litchfield *Monitor*, Sept. 8, 1802, *reprinted* by the *Federal Gazette*, Oct. 11, 1802, and Albany *Centinel*, Oct. 12, 1802.

[98] New London *Bee*, Oct. 5, 1802. The *Bee* mistakenly used the term "sedition" to describe the case. The offense was criminal libel.

seen, none of the cases in the federal courts ever went to trial before the Supreme Court ultimately held that the federal courts lacked common-law criminal jurisdiction. As the political and legal systems of the New Republic matured, the repressive doctrines inherited from the English monarchial system gradually fell into disuse.

A brief review of the litigation in 1806 will illustrate the extent and the vigor of the prosecutions. During this unhappy period, Federalist prosecutors instituted criminal proceedings against the editors of almost all the major Republican papers in the state. These included the editors of Osborne's Litchfield *Citizen*, Babcock's Hartford *American Mercury*, and Osborne and Ashley's Litchfield *Witness*. In addition, as noted, Charles Holt of the New London *Bee*, following his conviction under the Sedition Act, had ceased publishing the *Bee* in Connecticut, left the state, and as we have seen commencing publishing another Republican newspaper, also called the *Bee*, in Hudson, N.Y.

Much of the litigation arose in Litchfield, Conn., where the vicious struggle between the Federalists and Republicans continued unabated. On January 8, 1806, the Republican Litchfield *Citizen* contained a report written in the first person that the editor, Selleck Osborne, and the printer, Thomas Ashley (who were also editor and printer of the Republican Litchfield *Eye Witness* or simply *Witness*) had been tried for criminal libel of a prominent Federalist, Julius Deming. They had been indicted for asserting in the *Witness* that at a public meeting in the Meeting House while a vote before the divided Town Board was pending, Deming crossed the floor and reminded a Republican member (Simmons) that he was past due on repayment of his indebtedness of about $12 to $15 to Deming, and that in dunning Simmons, Deming acted with a view to influence his vote on the appointment of a Republican to a vacancy. Simmons ultimately acknowledged that Deming had finally said that he would not sue him if Simmons paid $10 by Saturday and that he had done so.[99]

At the trial, the defendants' counsel relied on the 1804 Connecticut statute. However, the jury divided, voting 11 to 1 for conviction. The dissenting juror for a while refused to give up the papers pertaining to the trial, but eventually did so.[100] The matter then went over to the March 1806 Term, but the outcome of the litigation is not known.

---

[99] *Republican Watch-Tower*, Sept. 19, 1806 in article entitled "Reign of Terror."

[100] Litchfield *Citizen*, Jan. 8, 1806; Litchfield *Watch-Tower*, Jan. 18, 1806; Hartford *American Mercury*, Apr. 10, 1806.

At this point, in early 1806, another Republican newspaper editor, Major Elisha Babcock of the Hartford *American Mercury*, was brought to court in Litchfield on a criminal libel charge instituted by a Federalist clergyman, Dan Huntington. As described in his own account in his *American Mercury*, Babcock was charged with a "wilful falsehood" for a statement that he believed to be correct and in violation of no law. Further, he complained that the jury rejected testimony of 10 to 12 witnesses:

> It does not hurt character nor feelings nor the Law to declare of certain republican clergy-men that they are ideots [*sic*] and apastates [*sic*], nor to charge other republicans with swindling, forgery, burglary, murder. So far from it law and religion are glorified by the very slanders. But turn the tables and a federal court and jury will discover that society is on the precipice of anarchy.

Babcock was convicted by what the *American Mercury* denounced as a Federalist-controlled jury and fined $1,000. The *American Mercury* lamented: "We live in a conquered country."[101]

At the March 1806 Term, over the protests of the Republican press who denounced it as a second trial for the same offence,[102] the Osborne/Ashley case in which the jury had disagreed 11 to 1 for conviction at the first trial was called for trial a second time. After the defendants refused to plead, the Court without further evidence pronounced "the defendants" guilty. They were subsequently fined $100 plus costs and required to post bonds of $500 each to assure "good and peaceable behavior." They were ordered imprisoned until they complied with the judgment.

In addition to the two prosecutions of Osborne and Ashley and the action against Major Babcock described above, Federalists in Litchfield successfully proceeded against Gen. Hart, the Republican candidate for Governor.[103] The trial of Hart led to a still another trial and conviction of Osborne and Ashley for criminal libel. They were convicted for publishing in the Litchfield *Witness* what, according to a sister Republican newspaper, Babcock's Hartford *American Mercury*, they believed to be an accurate account of the *Hart*

---

[101] Hartford *American Mercury*, Apr. 3, 1806. *See* Robert Wetmore, Seditious Libel Prosecutions in 1806 in the Federal Court in Connecticut: *United States v. Tapping Reeve* and Companion Cases, 57 Conn. B. J. 199 (1983).

[102] Hartford *American Mercury*, Apr. 10, 1806; *Sun*, Apr. 21, 1806.

[103] The *Sun*, Apr. 21, 1806 reprinting Hartford dispatch dated Apr. 10, 1806; Hartford *American Mercury*, Sept. 4, 1806. The accounts do not make it plain whether this was a criminal or civil libel action. Nor do they state what punishment or damages were awarded.

trial.[104] Sentence was deferred until the September 1806 Term when the court imposed a fine of $250 each and costs.

The Republican press denounced this series of prosecutions. Describing these five libel actions against Republicans as "proceedings to subvert and annihilate the Freedom of the Press" and appealing to "moderate and candid federalists," the *American Mercury* stated: "The public are well acquainted with the unremitting exertions of federalists in Litchfield county to elect exclusively federal Jurymen and to prostitute Courts and Juries, the Palladiums of our Liberties, to party purposes . . . [condemning] the unprecedented conduct of the federalists in prosecuting Printers."[105]

In its account, entitled the "Reign of Terror," the Republican *Watch-Tower* condemned the trial and its aftermath. It charged that the jury were "unanimously thorough going Federalists of the same stamp which had decided the case of Huntington and Babcock." The *Watch-Tower* added that after being unable originally to pay the fine, Ashley sold his interest in the Litchfield papers, satisfied the fine and costs, and posted the bond for good behavior. On the other hand, Osborne "feeling a strong wish for the continuance of the business and not willing to transfer the editorial department to 'any class of men' has ever since continued in close confinement, where he is now for an uncertain duration."[106] In his biography of Jefferson, Malone describes the Osborne prosecutions as a "determined effort of the local establishment to crush his paper."[107]

Osborne chose to remain in jail, and his supporters claimed that he was receiving inhumane treatment at the hands of a brutal Federalist jailor. The case became a cause célèbre. Even Jefferson defended the prosecutions of Tapping Reeve, Barzilai Hudson, and George Goodwin and the three other Federalists by the Republican District Attorney in the Connecticut federal Court as a readily understandable reaction to the brutality suffered by Osborne.[108]

The Federalists derided the charge and mocked the affair. The *Connecticut Courant* indignantly exclaimed that "in Litchfield, there was a great and

---

[104]   Hartford *American Mercury*, Apr. 10, 1806.

[105]   The *Sun*, Apr. 21, 1806, *reprinting* Hartford *American Mercury*, Apr. 10, 1806.

[106]   *Watch-Tower*, Sept. 19, 1806.

[107]   4 Malone, note 15, at 374; Hartford *American Mercury*, July 14, 1806; *Connecticut Courant*, Apr. 23, 1806. *See also* Letter, Thomas Seymour to Thomas Jefferson (Dec. 20, 1806) (William K. Bixby Collection) to which Jefferson responded. Letter, Thomas Jefferson to Thomas Seymour (Feb. 11, 1807), 9 Jefferson, *Writings* (Ford), note 16, at 137–140.

[108]   *See* Letter, Thomas Jefferson to Gideon Granger (Oct. 9, 1806) (Libr. Cong. 28,332–28,334). *See* 5 Malone, note 15, at 380.

grand collection to sympathize with Selleck Osborne who was imprisoned for publishing a criminal libel on the government of this state." Another Federalist paper, the *Connecticut Gazette and Commercial Intelligencer*, ridiculed complaints about Osborne's imprisonment: "The whole of this noise about Osborn's imprisonment is an unprincipled farce." It noted that Osborne's imprisonment had occurred only because of his refusal to post bail and further asserted that he had refused the Sheriff's offer, without bail, to have the liberty of the yard.[109]

The furor continued. On August 6, 1806, the Republicans conducted a festival in Litchfield to honor Osborne, with a procession of approximately 1,000 supporters parading past and saluting Osborne as he stood looking out from his jail window. After the parade, the procession marched to a meeting house. At this point, a local Republican lawyer, Joseph L. Smith, seized a 77-year-old minister and ordered him out of the meeting house.[110] The Litchfield community condemned the action, and Smith as a result lost most of his law practice and finally left the state.[111]

The Federalist public pamphlet describing the affair as Federalists saw it provides a keen insight into the vituperative nature of the debate. The Federalists charged:

> "10: That Seleck Osborne came to Litchfield without property and esteemed only for his impudence and blackguardism.
>
> 11. That Seleck Osborne is the instrument of certain furious and unprincipled jacobins.
>
> 12. That The Witness is notoriously the most foul and scurrilous paper printed in the United States.
>
> 13. That Osborne practices a daily butchery of character and has published an atrocious libel on Julius Deming, a man of great worth.
>
> 14. That Sheriff Landon practiced no cruelty toward Osborne, but showed him more lenity than such an unprincipled offender could expect.[112]

---

[109] *Connecticut Courant*, Mar. 2, 1806; *Connecticut Gazette & Commercial Intelligencer*, July 30, 1806.

[110] Litchfield *Monitor*, Aug. 13, 1806; *Connecticut Courant*, Aug. 20, 1806.

[111] Dwight C. Kilbourn, *Biographical Sketches of Bench and Bar of Litchfield County 1709–1909*, 290 (1909). Smith served in the War of 1812 in which he became a major, emigrated to Florida, and finally sat as the federal judge for the District of Florida from 1823 to 1827. He was married to the daughter of Ephraim Kirby, a well-known Republican. Kirby's *Connecticut Reports* with cases commencing in 1792 along with Dallas's report of Pennsylvania cases commencing in 1798 are among the earliest of the reports of American state courts.

[112] *See* Hartford *American Mercury*, Sept. 18, 1806. It also claimed to contain a "refutation of many of the lies contained" in the pamphlet.

The Republican press continued its assault on the Federalist conduct. The Litchfield *Witness* derided Federalist Governor Trumbull's appeal of the year before calling for "harmony, peace, and unity," contrasting it with the $1,000 judgment against Major Babcock, publisher of the Hartford *American Mercury*, "by the aid of a jury composed of men the most strongly affected with the "asperities of political opinions.""[113] Another Republican newspaper contrasted the prompt convictions of these Republican editors with the slow-paced, Republican-directed prosecution in the federal courts of Thomas Collier, Federalist publisher of the Litchfield *Monitor*. It noted that Collier's prosecution was still pending although he had "printed more abuse and gross calumny against the Republicans than any other printer in the State, (the printers of the *Connecticut Courant* excepted.)"[114]

There were still other partisan libel proceedings in the Federalist campaign against the Republican press and leadership. In September 1806, the Hartford *American Mercury* reported that convictions or judgments had been obtained not only against Gen. Hart but also against Gen. Wilcox and Col. Tilden. Other than the circumstances that the three defendants apparently came from Lebanon, Conn., details on these suits are not available.[115]

In March 1807, the Newburyport *Herald* reported that Thomas Collier, printer of the Litchfield *Monitor*,[116] obtained a verdict of $400 against "Selleck Osborne & Co.," printers of the *Witness*.[117]

After 1806 this tidal wave of libel litigation in Connecticut seems to have come to an end. There are no further reports of Federalist prosecutions in the state courts. Although the Republican prosecutions in the federal courts remained pending for some time, all were dismissed by 1808, except for the prosecutions of Hudson and Goodwin. After hanging fire for several years, those fizzled as well when the Supreme Court held that the federal courts lacked common-law criminal jurisdiction.

It is not clear why this unhappy chapter in Connecticut history had come to such an abrupt end. The struggle between the Federalists and Republicans for control of the state had clearly not gone away. Although the Republicans were steadily growing in strength, they did not elect their candidate for Governor until 1818. Nor did they secure control of the Legislature as well until 1818.

[113] *American Mercury*, July 31, 1806, *reprinting* dispatch from *The Witness*.
[114] Hartford *American Mercury*, Apr. 4, 1806, reprinted in the Hartford *Weekly Times*, Jan. 14, 1865.
[115] Hartford *American Mercury*, Sept. 4, 1806.
[116] Readers will recall that Collier was one of the six Connecticut Federalists indicted in the previous year by a Republican prosecutor and Republican Judge in the Federal District Court for common-law criminal libel.
[117] Newburyport *Herald*, Mar. 24, 1807.

2. Massachusetts

As we have seen, Section XVI of the 1780 Massachusetts Constitution drafted by John Adams provided that "The liberty of the press is essential to the security of freedom in a state; it ought not, therefore, to be restrained in this Commonwealth."[118] A few years later, no fewer than four prosecutions for seditious libel of supporters of Shays's Rebellion demonstrated that the constitutional provision did not eliminate the traditional common-law crime. Two prominent Western Massachusetts publishers, George Brock and Gideon Pond, had given editorial support to the Rebellion and were indicted for seditious libel. In the post-Rebellion amnesty, they were never brought to trial and, indeed, were pardoned. However, a Captain Moses Harvey was convicted of "seditious and inflammatory words" and Dr. William Whiting, a lower court judge, was also convicted for criticizing unjust laws and urging citizens lacking redress of grievance to "disturb the government."[119]

As discussed in Chapter 3, Chief Justice William Cushing and John Adams, principal draftsman of the Massachusetts 1780 Constitution, two years later discussed the impact of the Constitution's guaranties of free speech and press on the existing common-law criminal jurisprudence. They assumed that seditious libel continued without referring to any of the four prosecutions two years earlier. Cushing's letter had argued for the "liberty of publishing truth," and Adams agreed that "it would be safest" to permit the admission of evidence to the jury of truth when the publication had been made "for the public good."[120]

However, this did not become the Massachusetts law. On the contrary, when the issue arose shortly thereafter in the Suffolk County Court in *Commonwealth v. Freeman*, the prosecutor James Sullivan (later the first Republican Governor of Massachusetts) quoting from Blackstone "at interminable length" argued that the constitutional provisions did not bar common-law prosecutions based on the old Blackstonian model and, accordingly, that evidence of truth was not admissible. The defense did not press the issue, and the court so charged the jury. The jury, nevertheless, acquitted Freeman.[121]

---

[118] *See* 1 Bernard Schwartz, *The Bill of Rights: A Documentary History* 337, 342 (1971).

[119] Clyde A. Duniway, *The Development of Freedom of the Press in Massachusetts* 142 n.1 (1906, repr. 1969) (hereinafter Duniway); Leonard W. Levy, *The Emergence of a Free Press* 214–215 (1985).

[120] *See* The Early Law of Criminal Libel in Massachusetts, 27 Mass. L. Q. 9, 12 (No. 4, Oct. 1947).

[121] Commonwealth v. Freeman (Suffolk Cty. Ct. Mass.1790). Boston *Independent Chronicle*, Feb. 24, 1791. *See* Duniway, note 118, at 142; 1 Charles Warren, *History of the American Bar* 236–239 (1911).

This was the 1790 Massachusetts law, a law based on the rigorous Blackstone model, that substantially persisted for 36 years insofar as nongovernmental officials were concerned until finally changed by statute. In 1804 a bill to make evidence of truth admissible and to enlarge the role of the jury to permit a general verdict passed the Senate, but failed of adoption in the House. Not until 1826 was the law finally changed.[122]

However, starting in 1804 with the decision in *Commonwealth v. Clap*, the law did change insofar as public officials and candidates for office were concerned. Although *Clap* upheld the Blackstonian model for matters not involving public conduct, it recognized the admissibility of truth in *public* matters upon a showing that "the publication was for a justifiable purpose, and not malicious, nor with the intent to defame any man." Adams's view had triumphed at least in part; moreover, because he had failed to distinguish between public and nonpublic matters, this may well have been all that he had in mind. Two decades later, the Supreme Court in *Common-wealth v. Blanding* reaffirmed the ruling in *Clap*. Truth was not admissible except in cases of public conduct when published with "an absence of malicious motives." Similarly, the role of the jury was confined within its historic common-law limitations.[123]

Along with Federalist Connecticut, Massachusetts was a bastion of the Federalists. In the Massachusetts state courts, the same self-righteous extremism evident in the enactment of the Alien and Sedition Acts gave rise to a more vigorous series of Federalist-inspired partisan prosecutions of Republicans, particularly Republican editors and printers, for criminal libel than was experienced in any other state, including Connecticut. This continuing feature of Massachusetts political life commenced in 1798 and lasted almost until 1815.

Although, as we have seen, criminal libel had been an accepted part of Massachusetts law, it assumed a much more significant role with the development of political parties and vituperative political debate. The story of partisan criminal libel in the Massachusetts state courts starts with Thomas and Abijah Adams, the Republican editor and printer of the Boston *Independent Chronicle*, the leading Republican paper in New England and a bitter foe of John Adams and the Federalists. As described in Chapter 4, Thomas Adams unrelentingly attacked President Adams and the Federalist use of the

---

[122] Mass. Acts of 1826, ch. 107 §1 (publication must have been with "good motives and for justifiable ends").
[123] Commonwealth v. Clap, 4 Mass. 163, 169, 1808 Mass. LEXIS 38 (1808) (Parsons, C.J., Commonwealth v. Blanding, 20 Mass. (3 Pick.) 304, 1825 Mass. LEXIS 74 (1825) (Parker, C.J.).

French crisis "to further the work of injustice at home" and for the "tyranny" of the Sedition Act. He compared them to an "invader" and a "criminal" that would be brought to justice.[124]

As we have seen, the *Chronicle*'s attacks on President Adams severely provoked Abigail Adams. In writing to her sister Mary Cranch in March 1798, she called for the adoption by Massachusetts of a strong sedition law to silence the *Chronicle*.[125] She apparently did not recognize that with the availability of the common-law doctrine, no statute was required.

Thomas and Abijah Adams were indicted in Massachusetts federal District Court under the Sedition Act and arraigned in October 1798 with the trial set for the June Term 1799. Notwithstanding the indictment, Thomas Adams not only continued to attack the Federalist national administration but also attacked the Massachusetts Legislature for rejecting the Virginia and Kentucky Resolutions. He and Abijah Adams were, thereupon, indicted in the Massachusetts state courts for violation of the Massachusetts criminal common law.

At this point, the earlier federal proceedings came to an unhappy end. As with two other prominent Republican editors facing trial for criminal libel – Benjamin Franklin Bache of the Philadelphia *Aurora* and Thomas Greenleaf of the New York *Argus* – fate in the form of the bad sanitation of the post-Revolutionary Era intervened. Thomas Adams fell seriously ill. In May 1798, a few weeks before his trial on the federal indictment, Adams died of his illness after selling the *Chronicle* the week before.[126]

After Thomas Adams's death, Abijah was tried in the Massachusetts courts for criminal libel for the *Chronicle*'s attack on the Legislature's rejection of the Virginia and Kentucky Resolutions. Chief Justice Dana presided. The *Massachusetts Mercury* a few weeks earlier had reported that Dana on receiving a copy of the *Chronicle* by accident had commented that if he had been a subscriber, his conscience would charge himself as assisting to support a traitorous enmity to the government and the United States.[127]

---

[124] J. M. Smith, note 19, at 251.

[125] *See* Letter, Abigail Adams to Mary Cranch (May 10, 1798), *New Letters of Abigail Adams* 170–172 (Stewart Mitchill ed. 1947).

[126] *See* Rosenfeld, note 53, at 627.

In this unhappy necrology, it is of interest that a fourth Republican editor died in jail while serving a sentence for criminal libel under Massachusetts common law. This was William Carleton, editor of the Salem *Register*, convicted for charging Pickering with accepting a British bribe during the hurly burly of Pickering's unsuccessful race in 1802 for the Congress. *See infra* text accompanying notes 132–133.

[127] *Massachusetts Mercury*, Feb. 22, 1799.

With Republican James Sullivan, the Attorney General, again acting as prosecutor, the jury convicted Abijah Adams for *publication* of the libel after a trial that lasted three days.[128] However, he had been only the bookkeeper of the *Chronicle*, and the jury refused to find him guilty of *printing* the libel. In pronouncing sentence, Dana noted that Abijah was neither publisher nor editor of the *Chronicle* but "the only person the public could look to for retribution." Accordingly, he sentenced Adams only to one month's imprisonment, but required sureties for his good behavior for a year and for payment of the costs.[129]

The conviction of Abijah Adams for criminal libel was only the first of a lengthy series of politically inspired criminal libel proceedings against Republican publishers in the Massachusetts state courts. After Adams's conviction, at least six more partisan prosecutions for criminal libel soon followed.

In 1801 and 1802, there were two related prosecutions involving articles in the Boston *Constitutional Telegraph* and the Boston *Independent Chronicle*. John S. Lillie, described as the editor of the offending publication, was indicted for publishing an article calling Chief Justice Dana "a tyrant judge" who administered "that execrable engine of tyrants the Common Law of England in criminal prosecutions." The indictment alleged that Lillie had used terms to bring Dana into "great hatred, contempt and disgrace" and into danger of impeachment and prosecution for "bribery and corruption." The first prosecution was against Lillie as the editor. He pleaded guilty and stated that he did not know who had been the author of the article but would make every effort to discover his identity. He was sentenced to three months' imprisonment and $100 fine and costs. In the second case, John Vinal was indicted as the author of the libelous matter published by Lillie. However, Vinal was acquitted for lack of proof.[130] Remarking on the mixed results of the two cases, Pasley points out that the printer or editor named in the masthead of a journal could easily be linked to an article in the journal, but "typically there was no way to legally document the identity of an anonymous contributor."[131]

---

[128] *Connecticut Courant*, Mar. 18, 1799.

[129] *See Columbian Sentinel*, Mar. 27, 1799; Boston *Independent Chronicle*, Apr. 11 to May 2, 1799; Apr. 8 to 29, 1801. *See also* J. M. Smith, note 19, at 247–255; Rosenfeld, note 53, at 599.

[130] Commonwealth v. J. S. Lillie (not offically reported) (Suffolk Cty. Ct. Mass. 1802); Commonwealth v. Vinal (not officially reported) (Suffolk Cty. Ct. Mass. 1802); *See* Duniway, note 118, at 146 n.1, *citing* Records, Supreme Judicial Court, 1800–1802 pp. 228–233; Suffolk Court files, 1802; 2 Joseph T. Buckingham, *Reminiscences* 312–314 (1850) (hereinafter Buckingham); Pasley, note 8, at 141; *Mercury and New-England Palladium*, Mar. 16, 1802; *American Citizen and General Advertiser*, Mar. 22, 1802.

[131] Pasley, note 8, at 141.

In the 1802 elections, that arch-Federalist Timothy Pickering was running for Congress against the Republican Crowninshield. Supporting Crowninshield, the Republican Salem *Register* edited by William Carleton accused Pickering of accepting a bribe in the form of a pension from the British Minister Robert Liston and of spreading $500,000 among British partisans in the United States. Carleton was promptly indicted for criminal libel. As has been noted, evidence of truth in criminal libel matters was not admissible under Massachusetts law until 1827. Nevertheless, although contrary to law, Solicitor General Davis consented as a special indulgence to the admission of any evidence on truth of the alleged libelous charges. Carleton, who had denounced the prosecution as "persecution," was unable to prove the truth of the allegations. Convicted, he was sentenced to two months in jail, a fine of $100 and costs, and required to post a bond of $800 to keep peace for two years.[132] Unfortunately, in the brief interval while Carleton was in jail, he too contracted a disease and subsequently died. However much of a coincidence it may be, one cannot help observing that the mortality rate among Republican newspaper editors indicted for criminal libel was remarkably high.[133]

As for the congressional race in 1802, it will be of interest that in Massachusetts, the stronghold of High Federalism, Timothy Pickering – the former Secretary of State – was defeated, 1,400 to 1,293. The Federalist Salem *Gazette* had an explanation for the defeat. It explained that Crowninshield owed his triumph to the extension of the suffrage. He had built up a lead in the seaport towns supported by "the sailors and lower classes" that Pickering, who led in the rest of the district, could not overcome.[134] Despite his defeat, the Federalists still controlled the Legislature and the following year elected Pickering as a U.S. Senator; he served in the Senate from 1803 to 1811.[135]

The Republican Salem *City Gazette and Daily Advertiser* denounced the Carleton prosecution as a partisan use of Federalist prosecutorial discretion. It asserted that the grand jury that had indicted Carleton had before them issues

---

[132] *City Gazette and Daily Advertiser*, Oct. 18, 1806. *See* Hervey Putnam Prentiss, *Timothy Pickering as the Leader of New England Federalism 1800–1815*, 7 (1972): Pasley, note 8, at 277. Duniway, note 118, at 146; 2 Buckingham, note 130, at 334–335.

[133] In addition to Carleton, Benjamin Franklin Bache, Thomas Greenleaf, and Thomas Adams, died after indictment for criminal libel.

[134] Salem *Gazette*, Nov. 2, 1802.

[135] See Josiah H. Benton, Jr., *A Notable Libel Case: The Criminal Prosecution of Theodore Lyman, Jr. by Daniel Webster* (1904) (hereinafter Benton).

of the Federalist Salem *Gazette* published by Cushing containing calumnies against President Jefferson. Nevertheless, while indicting Carleton, the grand jury did not indict Cushing. As Republican editors had done so often before in this era of attacks by Federalist prosecutors against the Republican press, the *City Gazette and Daily Gazette* lamented: "Should not federal printers be prosecuted as well as the republicans?"[136]

In September 1806, Andrew Wright, printer of the Northampton *Republican Spy*, was convicted of two criminal libels against Federalist Caleb Strong, who served as Governor from 1800 to 1807 and from 1813 to 1816. The case involved local issues, not national politics. The *Spy* had charged Strong with financial misconduct and improper actions with respect to appointments, particularly the appointment of his son as clerk of a local court. Although the Attorney General refused to take the case, Wright was convicted on both counts. He was sentenced to six months imprisonment and required to provide sureties for $600 for his good behavior for two years more.

As has been so common, the account in the *City Gazette and Daily Advertiser* reporting these events went on to complain of Federalist abuse of the criminal process. It pointed out that the grand jury that indicted Andrew Wright had also considered and refused to indict one Butler, editor of the Federalist Northampton paper. The account asserted that the paper had reprinted numerous libels against President Jefferson published by the Massachusetts Federalist press, including the *Repertory Gazette*, the *Palladium*, the *Centinel*, and others. The *City Gazette and Daily Advertiser* sarcastically concluded by observing "Thus the scales of justice are held even.[137]

Although the three newspaper accounts of the trial and conviction of Wright, the *printer* of the *Spy*, do not refer to any associate or companion proceedings, the Republican New London *Bee* during this period printed an account entitled "Federal liberty of the press." This reported that Thomas Ashley, *publisher* of the *Spy*,[138] had also been indicted for publishing libels of Governor Caleb Strong, presumably the same libels for which Wright had been convicted. The *Bee* further lamented that complaints about libels

<hr />

[136] *City Gazette and Daily Advertiser*, Oct. 18, 1806.

[137] *City Gazette and Daily Advertiser*, Oct. 16, 1806; Hartford *American Mercury*, Oct. 9, 1806. In reporting the indictment, the Newburyport *Herald*, May 21, 1805, asserted on response that there were four Democrats on the jury.

[138] In the following year, Ashley was again embroiled in still another criminal prosecution, this time in Connecticut. He was also the printer of the Republican Litchfield, Conn., *Monitor*. He was tried in Litchfield along with Selleck Osborne, editor of the *Monitor*, for libel of Julius Deming in Jan. and Mar. 1806. *See* text accompanying notes 99 and 100.

in a Federalist paper were before the grand jury, but that the grand jury, composed of 14 Federalists and four Republicans, had chosen only to indict the Republican paper. The paper added: "In Massachusetts, where sauce for the goose is not always sauce for the gander."[139]

The next reported partisan political libel litigation in Massachusetts took a very different turn. Following much the same pattern as in the internecine struggles in Pennsylvania and New York between the radical and conservative wings of the Republican Party, a confusing account in the Newburyport *Herald* in the fall of 1806 reports the conviction of the editor of the Portland *Eastern Argus*, allied with the radical or "democratic" wing of the Republican Party, for the libel of Joseph Bartlett, who is described as a "moderate democrat," apparently too moderate for the *Eastern Argus*. The account does not make it clear whether this is a case of *criminal* or *civil* libel. On the one hand, the proceeding is listed under "Indictments" and the outcome is a "conviction." However, the punishment is described as a jury award of "$500 damages."[140]

The Newburyport *Herald* account is included in a report from Boston entitled "Trying Times," describing the series of politically inspired criminal libel prosecutions. In a noteworthy departure, the account is nonpartisan and does not stop at this point. It also lists the prosecution of the editors of the Federalist *Connecticut Courant* and of a Connecticut clergyman for speaking "disrespectfully" against Thomas Jefferson. It editorialized: "The newspaper editors in the U. States are passing a very severe *ordeal*. Some of them are in prison; others paying smart money. Those of the Aurora, Citizen, Morning Chronicle, &c. &c. have actions by dozens pending against them."[141]

It is not entirely clear whether the next reported Massachusetts criminal libel litigation had political significance. As reported in an account in the Northampton *Republican Spy*, one Charles Shepherd was indicted in the December 1805 Term of the Hampshire County grand jury for three libels: one of the bar of Hampshire County, another of the "Supreme Court,"[142] and the third of one Samuel Henshaw. In the May 1807 Term, the jury acquitted Shepherd of the libels against the county bar and against Henshaw. At this

---

[139] New London *Bee*, June 4, 1805.

[140] Newburyport *Herald*, Oct. 4, 1806.

[141] *Ibid*.

[142] Pittsfield *Sun*, June 28, 1806, reprinting account in the *Republican Spy*; Pittsfield *Sun*, May 6, 1807. The reference is most likely to the Supreme Judicial Court of Massachusetts rather than the U.S. Supreme Court, but this is not at all clear.

point, the prosecution moved to quash the indictment of the libel against the Supreme Court.[143]

After a puzzling absence of almost five years in which the available materials do not disclose any cases, Massachusetts experienced another wave of litigation involving politically inspired criminal libel cases. The first case involved the fifth politically inspired indictment for criminal libel brought against Abijah Adams for publications in the *Independent Chronicle*. Adams, now editor rather than mere bookkeeper, of the *Independent Chronicle*, was indicted yet again at the November 1811 Term for comments on the official conduct of Chief Justice Parsons. Before the trial, Parsons, seeking vindication, requested that no objection be made at the trial to the admissibility of any evidence offered by Adams to prove the truth of any publication against him. Although the trial was conducted on this basis, Adams was convicted. Adams applied for a pardon from Republican Governor Gerry, in which Parsons joined.[144]

As reported in the Newburyport *Herald*, of May 15, 1812, the next case involved a criminal libel proceeding against one Timothy Medar Joy for a "scandalous tale respecting Col. [Timothy] Pickering for the gratification of the democrats of Haverill." He pleaded guilty. "In view of his penitence, infirm health, and having already suffered imprisonment a considerable time," the court sentenced him to only one month's imprisonment, a $50 fine, and costs. The account claimed that the prosecution commenced the proceedings without Pickering's knowledge.[145]

After reporting the *Joy* case, the *Herald* went on to observe that Cushing, editor of the *Salem Gazette*, had been indicted for a libel on the former selectmen of Salem. Although further details on the *Cushing* case are lacking, there was apparently a second trial for libels of the Salem selectmen. Thus, the Salem *City Gazette and Daily Advertiser* of June 3, 1812, citing the *Register*, printed an account of the trial of the printer "of this paper" (presumably the Salem *Register*) for an alleged libel on the selectmen. The account asserted that the printer pleaded truth as a defense. When the trial resulted in a jury disagreement, the defendant was bound over for appearance at the next term of court in November. Further details are unavailable. Although the above dispatch does not give the name of the printer defendant, it would appear from the text and the reference at the end of the account in the *Register*

---

[143] Pittsfield *Sun*, May 6, 1807.
[144] Duniway, note 118, at 153.
[145] Newburyport *Herald* of May 5, 1812, *citing* the "Register."

that the *Gazette* is reprinting an item from the *Register* and that the printer of "this paper" was the printer of the Salem *Register*, who was unidentified. Pasley reports that Warwick Palfray, Jr., was the editor and printer of the Salem *Register* at the time.[146] Similarly, the Newburyport *Herald* of May 15, 1812, contains a further account from the Salem *Gazette* that in the case of "Palfrey," printer of the Salem *Register*, for a libel on the selectmen, the jury did not agree.

The reference to the plea of truth in a number of these cases requires explanation. As discussed at greater length below,[147] truth was not generally admissible as evidence in Massachusetts criminal libel cases until 1826. Although the newspaper account refers to an indictment, the litigation perhaps involved a *civil* libel proceeding, in which truth had always been available as a defense at common law. Alternatively, the prosecutor may have acceded to the liberalized practice as had occurred in the *Carleton* trial and the *Abijah Adams* trial in 1811.

Governor Elbridge Gerry's Message to the Legislature in February 1812 brought the conduct of the Massachusetts press and criminal libel briefly to the center of the Massachusetts stage.[148] Like so many political figures before him,[149] Gerry was appalled by the "licentiousness" of the press and the use of libelous allegations for political advantage. Although he paid the traditional Republican respect to the paramount importance of freedom of press, he, like Governor McKean in Pennsylvania in 1805, urgently recommended to the Legislature that the libel laws be strengthened so that the prevalent "licentiousness" could be checked.

Governor Gerry appended to his Message a lengthy study of libels in the "metropolitan" newspapers from June 1811 to February 1812 prepared by the state Attorney General and Solicitor General. The study under the direction of these Republican officials reported to have found 236 libels in the Federalist press against only 17 libels in the Republican press during that period.

The Message also reported four indictments for criminal libel in Suffolk County against the unidentified printer of the *Scourge*, whom the study had identified as the leading Federalist offender. After pleading guilty in each case, he was severely punished with a sentence of six months' imprisonment. There were four additional indictments of the vendor who had sold the offending

---

[146] *See* Pasley, note 8, at 221.
[147] *See infra* text accompanyng notes 160–165.
[148] Message of Governor Elbridge Gerry to the Legislature, Feb. 27, 1812.
[149] The list is long. It includes Benjamin Franklin, George Washington, John Adams, and Thomas Jefferson.

issues of the *Scourge*. Although the vendor pleaded not guilty, he was also convicted. In sharp contrast to the drastic sentence imposed on the editor, the vendor was fined only $50 and ordered to keep the peace for 12 months.

The Message further reported criminal libel convictions of the editors and publishers of the Republican *Independent Chronicle*. These defendants, not otherwise identified, were reported to have been sentenced to imprisonment for two months. Abijah Adams was editor of the *Chronicle* during this period, and this reference is likely to his 1812 conviction previously discussed. The Message also noted that although presentments in other cases had been issued against the editors and publishers of the Federalist *Columbian Centinel, New England Palladium, and Repertory and General Advertiser*, Boston *Gazette*, and the *Scourge*, indictments had not followed. It concluded with the report that two editors (identified only as the editor of the *Scourge* and as one of the editors of the *Independent Chronicle*) had been pardoned for health reasons.[150]

The Governor pointed out that although Massachusetts had no statute dealing with libel, libels were subject to punishment as common-law crimes. This was the English criminal common law, which had become part of Massachusetts law subject to the Massachusetts Constitution.[151] As authority for the Massachusetts doctrine that truth was not admissible in evidence and that the jury had a very limited role in criminal libel prosecutions, the Governor pointed to the 1804 decision of the Supreme Judicial Court in *Commonwealth v. Clap* and to the charge of Judge Isaac Parker to the grand jury in the previous term of court.[152]

In his valuable study of Massachusetts law during this period,[153] Clyde Duniway comments that the widespread litigation and public discussion of the issue provided Governor Gerry with the opportunity to take partisan advantage of the situation. In response, the House passed a libel statute providing that in all public prosecutions for libel of persons holding office by appointment of the Governor and the Council, evidence of the truth was admissible, provided it had a tendency to show the unfitness of an individual for appointment or continued service in office. The Senate advised that it

---

[150] The reference to the *Chronicle* editor is likely to Abijah Adams. *See* text accompanying notes 144.

[151] Pt. 2, sec. VI, art. VI of the Massachusetts Constitution of 1780 provided: "All the laws which have heretofore been adopted, used, and approved in the province, colony, or State of Massachusetts Bay, and usually practiced on in the courts of law, shall remain and be in full force . . . such parts only excepted as are repugnant to the rights and liberties contained in this constitution."

[152] Commonwealth v. Clap, 4 Mass.163, 169, 1808 Mass. LEXIS 38 (1808) (Parsons, C.J.); Charge to the Grand Jury, Sup. Jud'l. Ct., 1811 (Parker, C.J.); Boston *Patriot*, Dec. 28, 1811, *cited by* Rosenberg, note 82, at 301 n.42.

[153] Duniway, note 118, at 153–154; Suffolk Court Files Nov. Term 1811.

had insufficient time to act, while adopting a resolution sympathizing with Gerry's recommendations. This was the end of the matter. No legislation was ultimately voted, but the wave of prosecutions soon came to an end with the increasing decline of the Federalists and the eventual disappearance of a virulent politicized press.

Then, in 1828, came a reprise of the earlier resort to criminal libel as a political weapon.[154] In the 1828 presidential election with John Quincy Adams running for reelection against Andrew Jackson, most of the surviving Federalists supported Adams. However, an unreconciled group of High Federalists were so bitter over what they regarded as the turncoat policies of Adams and his support of the Republican embargo policies at high cost to New England merchants that they were supporting Jackson. In the process, the group including Theodore Lyman, Jr., a "leading citizen" and member of the "Federal Oligarchy" and Boston Brahmin elite, and a one-time legislator, organized a newspaper called the *Jackson Republican* to attack Adams more effectively.[155] The surviving Federalists who supported Adams bitterly resented the defection by Lyman and the others.

In the October 29, 1828, issue of the paper, an article written by Lyman bitterly attacked Adams. It reported a recent disclosure that 20 years earlier during the controversy over the embargo laws, Adams had "unequivocal evidence" that charged that a group of High Federalists, including such well-known figures as Harrison Gray Otis, Samuel Dexter, Josiah Quincy, and Daniel Webster, had been "engaged in a plot to dissolve the Union and to re-annex New England to Great Britain." It enquired why this had been concealed and released only on the eve of the election. It further denounced Adams for relying on Webster as a counselor whom he had called a "traitor." The newspaper also published a letter written by Jefferson at the same time stating that Adams had called upon him with "information of the most unquestionable certainty that certain citizens of the Eastern States . . . were in negotiation with the agents of the British Government" for withdrawal of the New England States from the war and would "withdraw from all aid and obedience" to the Union of the States.[156]

By now a U.S. Senator and a national figure supporting Adams, Webster was "highly incensed" by the story describing him as a "traitor" and presented the article as a criminal libel to the grand jury. Within two weeks of the publication, the grand jury approved the indictment of Lyman for insinuating

---

[154] This account is based entirely on the account of Benton, note 135.
[155] *Ibid.*, at 36–37.
[156] *Ibid.*, at 6–11.

that Webster had been "engaged in an atrocious, and treasonable plot to dissolve the Union" and that Adams "had denounced . . . Webster as a traitor to his country." The indictment was verbose and repetitive, using what Benton in his account accurately describes as "harsh and unnecessarily vituperative" terms.

The trial took place in a few weeks in the Supreme Judicial Court with Chief Justice Isaac Parker presiding. Boston was strongly for Adams,[157] and the atmosphere was "hostile" to Lyman. The jury disagreed, with a newspaper account reporting that it stood for 10 to 2 for conviction.[158] The District Attorney declined to retry the case and ultimately filed a *nolle prosequi*. In the election, Jackson won, and the case became ancient history. Lyman was later elected Mayor of Boston, and a contemporary account reports that he and Webster were ultimately reconciled and became close friends.

With this celebrated case, the utilization of criminal libel as a political tactic seems at last to have come to an end in Massachusetts.

3. New Jersey

In his history of the New Jersey Republican press during this period, Carl E. Price, relying on a series of August 1798 newspaper accounts, reports two criminal libel cases not mentioned by any other historian. He states that as a result of their "unrelenting public criticism" of New Jersey's Federalist Governor Richard Howell, the editors of the Republican Newark *Centinel*, Daniel Dodge and Aaron Pennington, were "early but by no means singular victims of the Sedition Act." Price adds that "both were arrested and like so many other Republican newspapermen charged with seditious libel for failing to divulge the name of the author of an article attacking the Governor" that they had published. Like many such accounts, nothing appears to be known of the outcome of these cases.

Although Price describes these indictments as being brought under the Sedition Act, this reflects a misunderstanding. The person allegedly libeled was the state Governor and, thus, not one of the one of the public officers protected by the federal enactment. The prosecutions more likely were brought under New Jersey common-law criminal jurisprudence.[159]

---

[157] In the election, Adams swept Boston, 3,113 to 846. *Ibid.*, at 62.

[158] The jury division is reported in the Boston *Daily Advertiser*, Dec. 22, 1829, but Benton observes that the information "is probably not very reliable." *See* Benton, note 135, at 102n.

[159] Carl E. Price, *New Jersey's Jeffersonian Republicans* 38 (1967), *citing Woods' Newark Gazette*, Aug. 9, 1798; Newark *Centinel*, Aug. 7, 14, 21, 28, 1798; New Brunswick *Guardian*, Aug. 28, 1798.

D. Liberalization of Massachusetts Criminal Libel Law

The American society slowly responded to the inherent conflict between the English common law dealing with criminal libel and the American constitutional guaranties of freedom of speech and press. As we have seen, the English criminal common law that was shaped to serve the ends of not only a monarchy but a monarchy not fully subservient to parliamentary power was ill-suited to the democratic principles of the Revolution and the New Republic. The inadmissibility of evidence of the truth of the alleged libel seemed to strike at the very foundations of the free-ranging political debate so indispensable in a democracy. Further, under the older common law, the role of the jury had been severely restricted to determining whether the defendant had indeed published the alleged libel and that its innuendo served to ridicule or defame or bring the plaintiff into the hatred or contempt of the community. All other questions were reserved for the judge.

As noted, the historic criminal common law of libel as stated by Blackstone was the American common law when the catastrophic decline in relations with France brought the country to the brink of war in 1797 and 1798. Taking advantage of this repressive jurisprudence, the Federalist use of criminal libel prosecutions to suppress the Republican newspaper opposition flourished.

Paradoxically, the reform of the draconian aspects of the common-law doctrine of criminal libel commenced with the Sedition Act itself, dramatically liberalizing both the role of truth and the rule of the jury. Although the issue of the role of truth occupied the primary place among the reform proposals, its impact was more theoretical than effective in the actual hurly-burly of criminal prosecution. Similarly, broadening the role of the jury had the capacity to provide an additional barrier against governmental repression, as the experience of the Crown during the Colonial Era had demonstrated. However, the effectiveness of the barrier depended on still another factor: the absence of political control of the process for selection of the jury.

1. The Role of Truth

When the Congress was considering the Sedition Act in 1798, the Senate had approved a bill that made no change in the existing American common law. However, when the sweeping bill ran into opposition in the more closely divided House, the Bill was amended in two major respects to provide for the admissibility of truth and to transform the role of the jury. Section 3 of the Act, accordingly, provided:

it shall be lawful for the defendant, upon the trial of the cause, to give in evidence in his defence, the truth of the matter contained in the publication charged as a libel. And the jury who shall try the cause, shall have the right to determine the law and the fact, under the direction of the court, as in other cases.[160]

As enacted, the much criticized Sedition Act was more liberal than the seditious and criminal libel law in every state of the Union except Pennsylvania, Delaware, and Kentucky. With the amendments, federal law on the surface was distinctly less repressive than the Blackstonian common-law doctrine still largely typical of state law. The reality was quite different. As the prosecution record under the Act demonstrates, the reforms provided little protection to the Republicans harassed under the Act.

Statements in political controversies such as those involved in the cases arising under the Act were most often expressions of opinion. In many cases, proof of their truth was very difficult, if not near-impossible. Opponents of the law, accordingly, were little mollified by the provision. Their fears were largely justified. In not one of the Sedition Act prosecutions did attempted proof of the truth of the offending allegation achieve significant success.[161]

Further, in practice as administered by some Federalist judges, the opportunity to establish truth as a defense was realistically simply not available. As Justice Chase held in *Callender* and Justice Paterson held in *Haswell*,[162] a witness could not testify as to truth at all unless he could fully establish the entire truth of the matter. These two Justices refused to permit collective proof of truth by several witnesses. As a result, defense counsel in these cases had to abandon the attempt.[163] These decisions barring collective proof are very difficult to understand. Chief Justice Marshall, for example, was unequivocal in his disagreement.[164]

Although Jefferson bitterly opposed the Act, he, too, placed considerable importance on the admissibility of evidence of truth. As noted, on each of the occasions in which he expressed approval of criminal libel prosecutions,

[160] 1 Stat. 596 §3 (1798).
[161] Anderson agrees that the provision had been deprived of "all value." *See* Frank M. Anderson, Enforcement of the Alien and Sedition Laws, Ann. Rep. 1912, Am. Hist. Soc. 126 (1912). The *Shaw* prosecution ending in the only acquittal of all the Sedition Act cases may have been an exception, but unfortunately the facts of the litigation are not available.
[162] United States v. Callender, 25 F. Cas. 239, 1800 U.S. App. LEXIS 58 (C.C.D. Va. 1800) (No.14,709); United States v. Haswell, 26 Fed. Cas. 218, 1800 U.S. App. LEXIS 67 (C.C.D Vt. 1800) (No. 15,328).
[163] *See also* Wharton, note 1, at 676–677, 686, 707.
[164] John Marshall, Chase Trial 60.

he carefully conditioned his approval on the availability of truth.[165] However, it is notable that although Jefferson had studied law with George Wythe and had practiced law for seven years, albeit without distinction or success, he never addressed any of the practical problems involved in proof of the truth.

However, the availability of truth as a defense indirectly did provide defense counsel with a valuable tactical alternative. It enabled a defendant to seek a continuance to permit the attendance of witnesses located in distant areas. As noted, in numerous criminal libel prosecutions, such continuances resulted in such delays or other problems so that the cases never went to trial. Indeed, Goebel asserts that a motion for discontinuance became a recognized dilatory tactic.[166]

2. The Scope of the Jury's Role

As with truth, the role of the jury was a significant moderating feature of the Sedition Act. However, as with the admissibility of evidence of truth, the substantial expansion of the role of jury in the Act as enacted had little practical impact.

As the courts were administered by the Federalist clerks and marshals under the supervision of Federalist judges, the reform never had a chance to show what difference it could make. The numerous Republican complaints that Federalist Court clerks and marshals had deprived defendants of a fair trial by providing jury panels composed only of Federalists[167] seem well established. Amid widespread complaints of "court packing," Sedition Act juries virtually unanimously followed the comments of the judges on proof of the guilt of the defendants and dutifully brought in verdicts of guilty, often after notably brief deliberation. As we have seen, only one acquittal emerged in all of the indictments under the Act. This was the acquittal of Dr. Samuel Shaw of Castleton in a case in which none of the details other than the fact of acquittal is known. Thus, despite the ostensible safeguards in the liberalized statute, the credibility of the proceedings was gravely suspect.[168]

In sum, the reforms introduced by the Act had little significance in practice so long as the partisan passions of the times flamed high. However, as time

---

[165] See Letter, Thomas Jefferson to Abigail Adams (June 13, 1804), 8 Jefferson, Writings (Ford), note 16, at 307.

[166] See Goebel, Hamilton, note 55, at 617.

[167] See Letter, Thomas Jefferson to T. N. Randolph (Feb. 19, 1801), 33 Writings of Thomas Jefferson 21 (Barbara Oberg ed. 2006) ("the prostration of justice by packing of juries cannot be passed over").

[168] The "rubber stamp" role of the petit juries may be contrasted with the greater independence of the grand juries. As we have seen, there were numerous cases in which state grand juries rejected the efforts of judges or prosecutors to obtain indictments under common-law criminal libel.

moved on with the surprisingly speedy disappearance of the Federalists, the reforms established a model for comparable action on the state level.

3. The Requirement of Proof of "Intent"

There was still a third respect in which the Sedition Act liberalized the common law. The common law had not required proof that the offending statement was intentional.

As defined in the Act, the crime required proof of a libelous statement that the publication was false and had been made intentionally and maliciously to defame or bring the government or the President into ridicule, hatred, or contempt. This aspect of the criminal libel jurisprudence has led to considerable misunderstanding because of the confusion between "intent" and "malice." "Malice" is sometimes mistakenly understood to involve a subjective state of mind. This is an error. The "malice" component of common-law criminal libel is a legal fiction and is unrelated to any subjective state of mind of the defendant. "Malice" is a legal construct meaning no more than the performance of an unlawful act (whether intentionally or unintentionally) without justification or excuse.[169] It is a conclusory term resting on circular reasoning. By contrast, "intentional" is an issue of fact on the state of mind of the defendant.

Thus, in the common-law tradition, Justice Chase in *Cooper* and Chancellor Kent in *Croswell* had no difficulty in finding the necessary proof of malice from the manner of publication of the libelous handbill or newspaper. Thus, Chancellor Kent in his opinion in *Croswell* spoke of "the presumption of malice drawn from the fact of publication."[170] Bleecker writing in 1818 observed that the requirement of proof of "malice" was ineffective. The prosecutor had

---

[169] As Chief Justice Parker said in *Commonwealth v. Blanding*, "When the publication complained of is of a libellous nature, it must be taken to be of a malicious character." Commonwealth v. Blanding, 20 Mass. (3 Pick.) 304, 1825 Mass. LEXIS *74 (1825). *See also* Justice Thompson: "The accusation being false, the *prima facie* presumption of law is that the publication was malicious." People *ex rel.* Lewis v. Few, 5 Johns. Cas. 1, 37, 189 N.Y. LEXIS 92 *56 (1809). The burden was on the defendant to rebut. Commonwealth v. Blanding, 20 Mass. (3 Pick.) at 311; 1825 Mass. LEXIS 74 at *14–15.

"Actual malice" is another matter. *Cf.* N.Y. Times Co. v. Sullivan, 376 U.S. 254, 280 (1964) ("knowledge that it was false or with reckless disregard of whether it was false or not essential").

[170] United States v. Thomas Cooper, 25 F. Cas. 631, 641, 1800 U.S. App. LEXIS 56 (C.C.C.D. Pa. 1800) (No. 14,865); People v. Croswell, 1 Cai. R. 149, 3 Johns. Cas. 337, 1803 N.Y. LEXIS 169 (1803).

Kent added that it was the need to provide the defendant with an opportunity to rebut the presumption that rendered the right of the defendant to introduce evidence of the truth of the challenged allegation essential. *See also* Commonwealth v. Clap, 4 Mass. 163, 169, 1808 Mass. LEXIS 28 (1808) (Parker, C.J.) ("Although . . . truth . . . is no justification, . . . yet the defendant

only to show that a statement tending to defame or hold out in ridicule and contempt had been willful.[171]

Although the introduction of "intent" in the Sedition Act was another theoretical step forward, the significance of the requirement of proof of was undermined in practice. Like the reforms of the roles of truth and the jury, this higher level of proof had little meaning in practice as result of the construction of the provisions by judges. As held by such judges as Chase in the *Cooper* case,[172] proof that an allegedly libelous statement had a "bad tendency" was sufficient; it would then be presumed that it was "intentional." In consequence, the issue of "intent" did not play a role in any of the cases under the Act.[173] In the 20th century, the "bad tendency" doctrine became an important target for those arguing for vigorous expansion of the constitutional protection of free speech and press.

James Madison had immediately recognized the limited implications of the requirement of proof of intent. He pointed out: "It is manifestly impossible to punish the intent to bring those who administer the government into disrepute or contempt, without striking freely at the right of freely discussing public characters and measures."[174]

4. Reform in the States

With all its practical limitations, the liberalization of the common-law doctrine contained in the Sedition Act, nevertheless, stimulated reform in the states. Starting with Connecticut and New York, the other states gradually caught up with liberal statutes of their own, typically providing a role for truth and broadening the role of the jury in the criminal libel trials. Thus, as early as 1804, Federalist Connecticut enacted its own statute. Using the Sedition Act as its model, the Connecticut statute provided that the defendant could introduce into evidence the truth of the matters contained in the alleged

---

may defend by proving that the publication was for a justifiable purpose and not malicious nor with the intent to defame anybody").

[171] *See* Francis Ludlow Holt, *The Law of Libel* 57 (1st Am. ed. Anthony Bleecker ed. 1818).

[172] United States v. Thomas Cooper, 25 F. Cas. 631, 1800 U.S. App. LEXIS 56 (C.C.D. Pa. 1800) (No. 14,865).

[173] *See* 2 Henry Schofield, *Essays on Constitutional Law and Equity and Other Subjects*, ch. 2, Freedom of the Press in the United States 512, 534 (1921) ("The judges reduced the test of intent...to a fiction by inferring bad intent from the tendency of the publications as opinion makers").

[174] *See* James Madison, *Writings* 396 (Libr. Am. 1999); Miller, note 3, at 85.

libel. It also gave the jury the right to determine the law and the facts, under the direction of the court, as in other cases.[175]

During the same year, the celebrated argument of Alexander Hamilton and its adoption by Chancellor Kent in the ensuing divided Court in *State v. Croswell* led immediately to a fundamental reconsideration in New York of the role of the old English common-law rule that truth was not admissible in criminal libel matters. Within a year, the New York Legislature substantially enacted Hamilton's contentions, liberalizing the New York law of libel.

The 1805 New York statute first empowered the jury, authorizing it to submit a general verdict making it the judge of both law and facts. It went further and provided that evidence of truth was admissible in cases where the allegedly libelous statement had been asserted with "good motives" and for "justifiable ends," as Hamilton had argued in *Croswell*. This modification echoes Chief Justice McKean's 1788 decision in *Browne v. Oswald* in Pennsylvania. McKean had asserted that truth was not a justification even under the advanced Pennsylvania Constitution of 1790 unless the statement had been made with "good motives" and "upright intentions."[176] The 1805 New York statute with its similar qualification became part of the 1821 New York Constitution. It thereafter was followed by similar provisions in the Constitutions or statutes of almost one-third of the states.[177]

Although in form a limitation of the Sedition Act standard with respect to the role of "truth," the qualification requiring "good motives" and "justifiable ends" was not as significant as it might seem. It appears to be little more than a restatement of the requirement in the Sedition Act itself that the alleged libel be "malicious" and "intentional." Thus, in his opinion in *Croswell*, Chancellor Kent noted that truth was admissible to explain the absence of "intent."[178]

As we have seen, the criminal libel conviction of William Duane in 1808–1809 led promptly to a further reform in the Pennsylvania law by the

---

[175] *See* Act entitled "An Act to Secure Freedom of the Press," Conn. Acts of 1804.

[176] *See* Browne v. Oswald (Pa. 1798). This aspect of the prosecutions involving Eleazer Oswald is discussed in the text in Ch. 6 accompanying notes 26, 29.

[177] *See* Beauharnais v. Illinois, 343 U.S. 250, 293 (1952) (Jackson, J., concurring). This requirement has its counterpart in the English law. Thus, speaking of discussion of the public conduct of persons in public life including public officers, and politicians, including judges, Chief Justice Cockburn in Seymour v. Butterworth in 1862 said that it was not disputed "that such public conduct might be discussed with the fullest freedom . . . provided the language of the writer was kept within the limits of an honest intention to discharge a public duty, and was not made a means of promulgating slanderous and malicious observations." 3 F. & F. 372, 375, 176 Eng. Rep. 166 (1862).

[178] State v. Croswell, 1 Cai. 149, 377–378, 3 Johns. Cas. 337, 377–378, 1803 N.Y. LEXIS 169 *21 (1803).

Pennsylvania Legislature, then controlled by Duane's close ally Dr. Michael Leib. The statute of March 16, 1809, had two objectives. First, it significantly restricted the scope of criminal libel prosecutions, providing that "no person shall be subject to prosecution . . . for the publication of papers examining the proceedings of the legislature or any branch of government, or for investigating the official conduct of officers or men in a public capacity." In addition, it substantially liberalized the role of truth in all criminal libel prosecutions, by providing that "in all actions or criminal prosecutions of a libel, the defendant may plead the truth thereof in justification, or give the same in evidence."[179] Alone among the reforms in the various states during this period, the statute surprisingly did not liberalize the role of the jury. However, it successfully accomplished its other objective, to set aside the conviction of Duane several months earlier.

As we have seen, the experience in in Massachusetts was very different. In *Commonealth v. Clap* in 1804 and *Commonwealth v. Blanding* in 1825, the Massachusetts Supreme Judicial Court reaffirmed the earlier ruling in *Commonwealth v. Freeman* that the Massachusetts common law governing criminal libel followed the rigorous English common law. At the same time, however, *Clap* and *Blanding* did accept a tangential role for admission of evidence of truth. Consistent with the views of Adams and Cushing in their celebrated 1789 correspondence, the defendant was permitted in cases involving public officials to introduce evidence of truth for the limited purpose of "proving that the publication was for a justifiable purpose and not malicious nor with the intent to defame any man."[180] It was not until 1826 that Massachusetts abandoned the Blackstonian common-law form of the doctrine and followed the reform path set by New York and Connecticut 20 years earlier.[181]

Although American law was slowly emancipating itself from the clutch of the monarchic English system, the English themselves were moving in the same direction. With the adoption of Fox's Act in 1792 empowering the jury and Lord Campbell's Libel Act of 1843 making truth a defense when the

---

[179] Holding the statute retroactive, the Pennsylvania Supreme Court overrode the conviction for criminal libel of William Duane a few months earlier. *See* text accompanying note 48.

[180] Commonwealth v. Clap, 4 Mass. 163, 169, 1808 Mass. LEXIS 38 (1808) (Parsons, C.J.); Commonwealth v. Blanding, 20 Mass. (3 Pick.) 304, 1825 Mass. LEXIS 74 (1825); Commonwealth v. Buckingham, Mass. Munic. Ct. 1824, 14 John D. Lawson, American State Trials 505, 519 (1914–1936, repr. 1972). *Cf.* People v. Croswell, 1 Cai. R. 149, 1803 N.Y. LEXIS 169 (1803); 3 Johns. Cas. 337, 1804 N.Y. LEXIS 175 (1804) (Kent, Ch.) ("good motives and for justifiable ends").

[181] 1826 Laws of Massachusetts ch. 109 (1826).

publication was "for the public benefit," England had also eliminated the worse aspects of its legal inheritance.[182]

With these modifications, criminal libel persisted in the states. State constitutional guaranties of freedom of speech and press provided no further restrictions on the doctrine. As for the federal constitutional guaranties, as we have seen, it was not until the decision in *People v. Gitlow* in 1925 before the Supreme Court held that the federal constitutional guaranties of free speech and freedom of the press extended to the states. It took another 20 years before the Supreme Court held in *Garrison v. Louisiana* that the high federal constitutional barriers to civil libel actions decided in its momentous decision in *N.Y. Times Co. v. Sullivan* were also applicable to criminal libel.[183]

Thus, 150 years after the adoption of the Constitution, libel was finally confined to statements that were knowingly false.

E. Conclusion

Virtually all the histories of this period gloss lightly over the prominence of criminal libel litigation under the two decades of Republican domination following the turn of the century. Aside from recognizing the role of the *Croswell* case in New York, the *Dennie* case in Pennsylvania, and the federal prosecutions of Hudson, Goodwin, and Reeve in Connecticut, this rich history has been largely neglected.

The growing accumulation of cases during the post–Sedition Act period indicates that criminal libel was, at least judging from the number of cases, a potential threat to the press comparable to the Federalist "reign of terror" during its heyday under the Sedition Act. With these cases spread among various states, particularly Connecticut, Massachusetts, New York, and Pennsylvania, rather than concentrated in the federal government, the litigation during this period may not have been as great a menace. However, from the jurisprudential point of view, it is now beyond argument that criminal libel flourished under the Jeffersonians as much as it had under the Federalists in the preceding era. It confirms that the doctrine, however pernicious and unconstitutional it may have come to be viewed in subsequent years, was very much part of the accepted jurisprudence of the times, pursued for political

---

[182] 32 Geo. III c. 60 (1792); 6 & 7 Vict., c.92, §6 (1843). See *Gatley on Libel and Slander* A2.4 (10th ed. 2004).

[183] Gitlow v. People, 268 U.S. 652 (1925) (holding the First Amendment applicable to the states by reason of the 14th Amendment) rendering obsolete Barron v. Baltimore, 32 U.S. 243, 1833 U.S. LEXIS 346 (1833) (the Bill of Rights not applicable to the states).

advantage by the particular party in the power. State or federal government, Democratic-Republican or Federalist, seemed to have made little difference.

This was the jurisprudence, the "law in the books." The reality was very different. The wave of criminal libel litigation did not restrain the vigor of public debate. Although the jurisprudence was repressive, free discussion flourished hardly diminished in the political arena.

7

Established Jurisprudential Doctrines (Other than Criminal Libel) Available in the New Republic for Suppression of Anti-Establishment Speech

A. Introduction

The early American experience with criminal libel represented only one of a number of established criminal common-law doctrines available in the Early American Republic for the partisan suppression of critical speech. There were a series of other repressive common-law doctrines inherited from English law widely used to protect other institutions of the established society against vigorous critics. Supplementing criminal libel reviewed in the preceding chapters, the additional repressive doctrines reviewed in this chapter include such criminal remedies for suppression of dissenting speech as contempt of court for out-of-court criticism of judicial decision or conduct, contempt of the legislature for out-of-chamber critical publications, and pre-trial binding over for good behavior (i.e., no more offending statements).

These additional repressive doctrines did not stand alone. In addition, two other areas of suppression of dissenting speech existed that did not involve the partisan suppression of opposition political speech. One was the state statutory and common law criminalizing blasphemous religious commentary. The other was the body of state law criminalizing discussion of slavery. These are reviewed in the next chapter. The slavery statutes, although arising later, are very much closer to criminal libel than the blasphemy cases. Both involve sensitive political areas in which political/moral concerns run deep, human passions run high, the potential for violent aftermath is strong, and the security of the state may be at stake.

Along with criminal libel, these supplemental doctrines illustrate the surprising extent of the legal doctrines of the times available for the suppression of what may be termed anti-establishment speech. In the light they cast on the jurisprudence of the times, these doctrines provide a fuller understanding of the widespread acceptance of criminal libel by the 18th- and early 19th-century American political society. Although Republicans did attack the federal use of criminal libel, they fully accepted criminal libel and all the other repressive doctrines as an established part of state jurisprudence.

All these doctrines were alive and strong in the early 19th century and persisted for decades before fading away over the years. As with criminal libel, the constitutional provisions regarding freedom of speech and press or religion in the federal or state Constitutions were ineffective to prevent any of these unfortunate developments. Moreover, they were not outlawed as a practical matter until well into the 20th century, when the U.S. Supreme Court progressively expanded the sweep of the federal constitutional guaranties of freedom of speech and press.

B. Criminal Contempt of Court for Out-of-Court Speech

For decades the power of judges to punish conduct interfering with the orderly processes of the Court through sanctions for contempt extended far beyond conduct in the judicial chamber or courthouse. Until the middle of the 20th century, judges had the power under the common law to punish critics of their conduct and decisions, even when expressed away from the courtroom. Critical statements published in newspapers were subject to the imposition of criminal penalties imposed by the judge who was the subject of the criticism.[1] At the outset, it should be understood that contempt is not simply a matter of an offense giving rise to punishment. It also relates to the process. Criminal conduct is involved, but unlike other criminal punishment that can proceed only in accordance with the historic protections of the rights of the accused, punishment for contempt is summary. The judge commences

---

[1] *See generally* Sir John Fox, *History of Contempt of Court* (1927) (hereinafter Fox); R. Goldfarb, *The Contempt Power* (1963) (hereinafter Goldfarb); C. Holmes, *Problems of Contempt of Court: A Study in Law and Public Policy*, ch. 4 (1934) (hereinafter Holmes); H. Sullivan, *Contempts by Publication: The Law of Trial by Newspaper* (3d ed. 1941) (hereinafter Sullivan); C. Thomas, *Problems of Contempt of Court: A Study in Law and Policy* 22 (1934) (hereinafter C. Thomas); John T. Thomas, *The Law of Constructive Contempt: The Shepherd Case Reviewed* (1904 repr. 1980) (hereinafter J. Thomas); F. Frankfurter & J. M. Landis, Power of Congress over Procedure in Criminal Contempt in "Inferior" Federal Courts: A Study in Separation of Powers, 37 Harv. L. Rev. 1010 (1934) (hereinafter Frankfurter & Landis); W. Nelles & C. W. King, Contempt by Publication in the United States, 28 Colum. L. Rev. 401, 525 (1928) (hereinafter Nelles & King); E. Linenthal, Freedom of Speech and the Power of Courts and Congress to Punish for Contempt (Ph.D. dissertation, Cornell Univ. 1956) (hereinafter Linenthal).

the proceeding unilaterally with issuance of an order called an attachment, directing a court officer to arrest the individual and bring him or her before the Court. In contrast, in most criminal actions, proceedings can be instituted only after a grand jury votes in favor of an indictment.

In contempt matters, the judge then not only sits as the judge and jury in what may be seen as his or her own case, but decides the case unilaterally. This contrasts with other criminal cases. In those, one disinterested agency – the grand jury – must find probable cause and vote an indictment. Another disinterested agency – the petit jury – must find the crime established beyond a reasonable doubt. Thus, in many respects, the contempt process seems to depart from everyday concepts of a fair trial and manifestly presents the potential for serious abuse.

Only very serious countervailing considerations suffice to justify such procedures in a democratic legal system. Criminal contempt involving such unusual features, thus, rests on a demonstrated need for only such judicial punitive powers as are indispensable to protect the very administration of the system of justice against intolerable obstruction and interference. Where, however, *out-of-court* publications criticizing the court and its conduct are involved, these countervailing considerations are at their very weakest. This is the background against which the American experience with contempt for out-of-court publications must be evaluated.

Like other legal doctrines that flourished in the Early Republic and were used to punish anti-establishment speech, the contempt power of judges including the exercise of the power over out-of-court critical publications was derived from the English law.

In his *Commentaries* so widely accepted in the new nation as the authoritative exposition of the English common law,[2] Blackstone advised:

> The process of attachments for...contempts, must necessarily be as antient [*sic*] as the laws themselves. For laws, without a competent authority to secure their administration from disobedience and contempt, would be vain and nugatory. A power, therefore, in the supreme courts of justice, to suppress such contempts, by an immediate attachment of the offender, results from the first principles of judicial establishments, and must be an inseparable attendant upon every superior tribunal. Accordingly, we find it actually exercised as early as the annals of...law extend.[3]

---

[2] *See* Ch. 3, note 21–27.
[3] 4 W. Blackstone, *Commentaries on the Law of England* 282–283 (1769, repr. 1992) (hereinafter Blackstone).

In describing the various types of contempts, he lists "speaking or writing contemptuously of the court or judges, acting in their judicial capacity."[4]

Writing in 1767, Blackstone had relied substantially on the still unpublished draft opinion of Justice Wilmot in *Almon's* case two years before,[5] in which appears the oft-quoted characterization of the power and its summary nature as resting upon "immemorial usage."[6] However, Wilmot's scholarship has been more recently questioned in failing to recognize that "immemorial usage" rested on a long line of cases involving punishment after trial by jury or cases in equity where no jury was available. Further, *Almon's* case had never gone to judgment. In fact, Wilmot's so-called opinion in *Almon's* case had never been delivered and was only a draft. It did not represent a judicial action at all, and, finally, the draft did not become public for 37 years.[7] Scholars led by Sir John Fox[8] have, accordingly, questioned the validity of Wilmot's analysis of English history, the usefulness of an unpublished draft opinion never actually delivered, and Blackstone's exposition based on it.[9]

This, however, is merely an academic whirlwind. All agree that whether Blackstone's summary accurately reflected the English precedents or not, the law of contempt as he outlined it became accepted as the established law in both England and the Colonies and, with the reception statutes following the Revolution, became part of the law of the states in the New Republic.[10]

All courts agreed that they possessed the inherent power to punish contumacious conduct and publications interfering with the work of the courts or the administration of justice, whether in court or out-of-court. This was a

---

[4] *Id.*, at 282.

[5] Rex v. Almon, (K.B. 1765) (case abandoned and opinion never delivered). The proposed opinion was posthumously printed in J. Wilmot, *Notes, Opinions and Judgments* 243 (1802). However, Wilmot's view was extolled by Justice Holroyd in Rex v. Davison, 4 B. & Ald. 329, 338 (1821) and ultimately became English law. In Roach v. Garvan, Lord Hardwicke had earlier upheld the application of the summary contempt power to out-of-court publications, Roach v. Garvan, 2 Atkyns 469, 26 Eng. Rep. 683 (1742) (Lord Hardwick, J.).

[6] *See* Fox, note 1, at 5–6. Blackstone echoes the conclusion, stating "by long and immemorial usage is now become the law of the land." Blackstone, note 4, at 285.

[7] Although the "opinion" did not become public until 1802, Blackstone decades earlier was privity to it as a result of correspondence with Wilmot. As Sir John Fox points out: "some resemblances both in phrase and matter will be noticed, and it is not improbable that Blackstone received advice from Wilmot on the subject." *See* Fox, note 1, at 21.

[8] Fox's *History of Contempt of Court*, is the path-breaking work of scholarship on which the subsequent discussion rests. *See also* Frankfurter & Landis, note 1, at 1011–1012 ("exploded history"); Nelles & King, note 1, at 524 (1928).

[9] The earliest American discussion of the limitations of the decision in *Almon's* case appears to be a critical note in 1902 by an anonymous author in the Virginia Law Register. Note, Contempt: Libelous Publication After Decision Rendered, 7 Va. L. Reg. 652 (1902).

[10] *See, e.g.,* 2 Joseph Story, *Commentaries on the Constitution of the United States* §1774 (5th ed. Melville Bigelow ed. 1891, repr. 1994).

matter of judicial "self defense and self preservation."[11] As counsel in *Yates v. Lansing* decided in New York in 1811 explained:

> This law as to the powers of courts to punish for contempts, is the settled law of England [citing Blackstone], grounded upon immemorable usage and confirmed by Magna Carta. By the thirty-fifth article of our [New York] Constitution, it is also the common law of this State: for no statute has been passed to abrogate this law.[12]

In many jurisdictions to boot, the legislatures and the Congress passed statutes confirming such power.[13] Although the unrestrained contempt power of the courts was fully accepted in the earliest days of the New Republic, the dangerous potential of the scope of the doctrine in a democratic society was widely recognized. Many states, led by Pennsylvania in 1809 and New York in 1827, and the Congress in the Act of March 2, 1831, enacted statutes severely limiting the scope of the judicial contempt power over out-of-court publications.

At the outset, one must recognize that contempts of court may take many forms. This chapter considers only contempt for out-of-court *publications*. Other forms of contempt occurring in the courtroom or directly interfering with the work of the Court[14] do not present problems of the suppression of dissenting speech and are beyond the scope of this discussion.[15]

This discussion examines the historic use of criminal contempt of court as a technique to punish out-of-court speech or out-of-court publications critical of judges or of judicial proceedings. It bears a close relationship to the other doctrines of the period used for suppression of dissenting speech that are discussed in this chapter. As will be seen, many of the cases involve clashes between the judges and the newspapers and thereby present issues of the utmost importance to a free society.

---

[11] *See* Burdett v. Commonwealth, 103 Va. 838, 841, 45 S.E. 878 (1904).

[12] *See* Yates v. Lansing, 9 Johns. 395, 1811 N.Y. LEXIS 211 N.Y. 1811) (argument of counsel).

[13] *E.g.*, The Federal Judiciary Act of 1789, 1 Stat. 73 §17 (1789).

[14] These include such forms of contempt as contumacious speech and contumacious conduct in the courtroom or the courthouse, disobedience to lawful orders of the court, and conduct interfering with the administration of justice such as jury or witness tampering or bribery.

[15] When a member of the bar is guilty of contumacious speech or conduct, he or she is subject to punishment under the contempt powers of the court like any other person. The court may also choose the alternative route of disciplining the offender as an attorney, such as disbarment or otherwise.

A federal District Court has recently upheld the constitutionality of punishment of a lawyer for professional misconduct for his critical comments of the court on the Internet. United States v. Flieger, 2008 U.S. Dist. LEXIS 18473 (E.D. Mich. 2008). *See* Tresa Baldas, Bloggers Pay Price for Criticizing Judges, *Conn. Law Tribune*, Mar. 16, 2009, at 5 (referring to two similar unreported decisions as well).

1. Contempt in the Early Republic During the Late 18th Century
and Early 19th Century

Although isolated, the early litigations involving contempt of court for out-of-court criticism of judges and courts take on added interest because they involve no fewer than three of the most prominent editors hotly engaged in the partisan struggles of the day. The initial cases arose in Pennsylvania and involved Chief Judge Thomas McKean of the Pennsylvania Supreme Court and his bitter adversaries in the press, Eleazer Oswald and William Cobbett, whom we have encountered in the earlier examination of criminal libel.[16] Subsequently, the Pennsylvania federal District Court assumed the center of the stage with litigations involving William Duane, whose unrestrained comments on public and private persons repeatedly brought him into the courts.[17] At the same time, New York saw the development of a different type of litigation in which judges continued their vigorous use of the contempt power, but without partisan political motivations. As the century moved on, partisan use of the contempt power that was so apparent in the earliest cases faded away. It no longer played a role in the continuing litigation testing the outer scope of the judicial contempt power for out-of-court speech.

a. The Early Pennsylvania Experience

The story of the clash between the extent of the judicial contempt authority and freedom of press in the state and federal courts in the New Republic begins in Pennsylvania and involves Eleazer Oswald, editor of the Philadelphia *Independent Gazetteer*, and one of the most prominent figures of the period, Thomas McKean. The antagonists were formidable foes.

Oswald had been a Lt. Colonel in the Continental Army and a military hero during the early days of the Revolutionary War.[18] He was a prominent

---

[16] For general discussion of these controversies and their participants, *see* William Cobbett (writing as "Peter Porcupine"), *The Democratic Judge or the Equal Liberty of the Press* (1788 repr. 1970) (hereinafter Cobbett); Gail S. Rowe, *Thomas McKean: The Shaping of an American Republicanism* 183–188 (1978) (hereinafter G. S. Rowe); J. Wheeler, *The Maryland Press 1777–1790*, 20–34 (1938) (hereinafter Wheeler); Dwight Teeter, The Printer and the Chief Justice, 45 Journalism Q. 235–242 (1968) (hereinafter Teeter).

[17] *See generally* Kim Tousley Phillips, *William Duane: Radical Journalist in the Age of Jefferson* (1989) (hereinafter Phillips). Duane was sued repeatedly for alleged libels.

[18] Oswald had served with distinction at Fort Ticonderoga in 1775 and served with Arnold at the battle for Quebec later in the year. As a Lt. Colonel in the Artillery, he played a significant role in the Battle of Monmouth in 1778. *See* Wheeler, note 16, at 20–23; Teeter, note 16, at 235.

editor given to the unrestrained, even abusive, speech that marked so much of the journalism of the period.

As we have seen, McKean was one of the most distinguished Americans of his time. After his distinguished earlier career, he occupied the highest offices in Pennsylvania for three decades, acting as Chief Justice of the Supreme Court from 1777 to 1799 and Governor from 1800 to 1808. Notwithstanding this distinguished record, he was also one of the most contentious. He has been described as an "imperious man" with "strong will and personality" and with his judicial actions "oftentimes considered arbitrary."[19] Others were even less kind, seeing him as "irascible" or "combative" or without "patience to bear contradiction" and "an uncontrollable temper."[20] William Rawle, U.S. District Attorney for Pennsylvania, said of him "all epithets would fall short of describing his badness."[21]

As we have already seen, McKean's imperious conduct in the courtroom and later in the political arena as Governor made him a major figure in a series of major litigations commencing with Oswald.[22] Precipitated by Oswald's attacks on McKean in the Philadelphia *Independent Gazetteer*, two major confrontations between the two erupted in which McKean, then Chief Justice, sought first to use criminal libel, then forfeiture of good behavior bonds, and subsequently contempt of court to punish, and perhaps silence, Oswald.

The first of these arose in 1782.[23] Oswald, the former Army officer turned editor, used his *Independent Gazetteer* to criticize Chief Justice McKean's conduct in fining and lecturing two Army officers for military arrogance, and for hearing only one side. In response, McKean is reported to have said: "You gentlemen of the army hold your heads too high; but I will teach you how to behave."[24] He then immediately ordered Oswald arrested for a "seditious, scandalous, and infamous libel." Oswald was required to post a £750 bond for his " good behavior" until the trial. This did not silence him. He continued to attack McKean, alleging that McKean had been a "noted speculator" in

---

[19] *See* J. Thomas, note 1, at 115–116.

[20] *See* G. S. Rowe, note 16, at xii–xiii, 3, 40.

[21] Letter, William Rawle to Mary Rawle (May 3, 1780) *cited by* Thomas R. Meehan, The Pennsylvania Supreme Court in the Law and Politics of the Commonwealth 1796–1790, 135 (Ph.D. dissertation, Univ. Wis. 1960); Steven R. Boyd, *Political Choice: The Case of the Pennsylvania Loyalists in American Political Trials* 45, 49 (Michael Belknap ed. 1994 rev. ed.).

[22] *See* Rosenberg, note 17, at 62–68; Lucius A. S. Powe, *The Fourth Estate and the Constitution: Freedom of the Press in America* 34–35, 40–42 (1991).

[23] For fuller accounts of the confrontation, *see* G. S. Rowe, note 16, at 182–187; Wheeler, note 16, at 28; Teeter, note 16, at 238–241; and J. Thomas Scharf & Thompson Westcott, 1 *History of Philadelphia*, 1609–1884, 46 (1884).

[24] *See* Wheeler, note 16, at 28; Teeter, note 16, at 237.

distressed soldiers' certificates. Oswald was thereupon arrested a second time and required to post a £1,000 bond for his appearance at the next term of court, and the matter was referred to the grand jury.

The day the grand jury met, the *Gazetteer* published "A Hint to the Grand Jury" advising on the doctrine of libel. The grand jury, thereupon, refused to indict Oswald for criminal libel by a vote of 16 to 3.[25] McKean was infuriated and instructed the grand jury to reconsider. However, the jury dug its heels in and once again refused to indict, this time by a vote of 17 to 2.

Angered by the outcome, McKean asserted that the grand jury had been biased by party affiliation and that Oswald had met with the jurors. In a public response, 16 members of the grand jury defended their action, denied any tampering, and responded that they had maintained "their unshaken zeal for the liberties of their country." At the same time, however, they also expressed their "abhorence and detestation of all such defamatory publications, as have a tendency wantonly to expose public characters to censure or contempt – or private ones to abuse and obloquy."[26]

As noted, the comparable experience during the struggle between Patriots and the Crown in Colonial times had shown the difficulties of persons in authority in getting juries to indict or convict. Just as the Crown had then turned to contempt of the Royal Colonial legislatures, a doctrine not requiring jury trial, as the preferred route for dealing with anti-establishment dissent, McKean similarly turned to contempt of court rather than criminal libel in his subsequent attempts to silence such political enemies such as Eleazer Oswald and later William Cobbett.

A number of litigations in the Pennsylvania courts in which persons were punished for "offensive" speech by use of such alternative remedies as contempt of court and breach of pre-trial "good behavior" bonds, rather than by prosecution for criminal libel, soon followed. These are the second *Oswald* case and the *Passmore* case involving contempt of court discussed below, and

---

[25]   Rosenberg asserts that Oswald and his supporters openly lobbied with the grand jurors. Rosenberg, note 17, at 60. He relies on Teeter, note 16, 235–242, 260 and G. S. Rowe, note 16, at 184–187. However, the lobbying apparently refers to Oswald's comments published in the *Gazetteer* as noted above.

   Oswald's rallying cry that freedom of speech was at stake had reverberations in the Pennsylvania Constitutional Convention that followed shortly thereafter. After much debate, the new Constitution significantly liberalized the common law of criminal libel. Foreshadowing the liberalized features of the Sedition Act, the Constitution provided that contrary to the common law, evidence of the truth could be introduced into evidence. Further the jury was to be the judge of the law and the facts. *See* Rosenberg, note 17, at 65.

[26]   *See* Jeffrey A. Smith, *Printers and Press Freedom* 155–156 (1988) (hereinafter J. A. Smith, *Printers*) citing *Freeman's Journal*, Oct. 30, 1782, Jan. 1, 15, 1783; *Pennsylvania Gazette*, Jan. 8, 15, 22 (1783).

the *Cobbett* litigation reviewed in the discussion of bonding over later in this chapter.

The second Oswald-McKean controversy[27] arose six years later in 1788 as a result of litigation in Pennsylvania, once again involving Oswald's articles in the *Independent Gazetteer*. Oswald had a vituperative pen. Among other sallies, he called Benjamin Franklin a feeble-minded fool and denounced George Washington as a dupe for supporting the Constitution.[28] His unrestrained prose inevitably led to libel litigation, such as the one that led to his second confrontation with McKean. Andrew Browne, a teacher, whose character was allegedly assailed in the *Independent Gazetteer*, instituted the action, and his counsel sought $1,000 bail to assure Oswald's appearance. After a hearing in his chambers, Justice Bryan of the Supreme Court ordered Oswald's release on "common bail."

Oswald thereupon published "An Address to the Public." The article described the suit as an effort "to please the malicious dispositions of old and permanent enemies." In an article attacking the suit and libel law as incompatible "with "law and liberty," he denounced Browne as "the hand maid of some of my enemies among the federalists," including "his great patron, Doctor Rush"[29] (whose brother, Richard Rush, was a Justice of the Pennsylvania Supreme Court). He further observed that "it may perhaps add to the hopes of malignity, that this action is instituted in the Supreme Court." Browne's counsel promptly moved for an attachment of Oswald for contempt of court because the publication tended to interrupt the course of justice, attempted to prejudice the minds of the people, and to stigmatize the judiciary.

Relying on English law, Chief Justice McKean first upheld the application of the contempt power to publications out of court, notwithstanding the freedom of press provision in the Pennsylvania Constitution. He concluded that the address had the "object and tendency . . . to dishonor the administration of justice." He held Oswald in contempt imposing a fine of "101" (*sic*) and imprisonment for one month and afterwards until the fine and costs were paid.[30]

---

[27] Respublica v. Oswald, 1 U.S. (1 Dall.) 319 (Pa. 1788).

[28] *See* J. A. Smith, *Printers*, note 26, at 150.

[29] This was Dr. Benjamin Rush, prominent in Pennsylvania public affairs and medicine alike. For a time during the Revolutionary War, he served as Surgeon-General of the armies of the Middle Department, but got into an altercation with Washington over what he asserted were deplorable medical conditions. He was not a Federalist, but a Republican and a correspondent of Jefferson.

[30] 1 U.S. at 326, 329. It is difficult to ascertain from the report whether this is a fine of £10 or $101 from the opinion. However, the historians widely accept £10 as the fine. *See, e.g.,* C. Thomas, note 1, at 22 (1934); Wheeler, note 16, at 32; Rosenberg, note 17, at 63.

Bruised by Oswald's brutal comments the previous year, Benjamin Franklin, generally ready to defend freedom of the press, showed him little sympathy.[31]

Relying on his allies in the Leib-Duane wing of the Pennsylvania Republican Party in the Legislature, Oswald submitted a memorial to the Legislature calling upon it to impeach McKean for his conduct in the *Browne* case. Although he attracted some support, the lower house of the Legislature rejected a motion to impeach, 23 to 34.[32]

In much the same fashion as his continuing efforts to respond to attacks by Eleazer Oswald, McKean's next target was William Cobbett, one of the most outspoken Federalist editors.[33] The *Cobbett* cases turn on the doctrine of bonding over, rather than contempt of court, and thus they are discussed later in the chapter with the discussion of that doctrine. However, they rank with the litigations against Oswald as episodes in McKean's continuing use of repressive doctrines of the law to punish his critics. The *Oswald* and *Cobbett* litigations illustrate the impressive number of remedies available for use to silence establishment critics

State v. Passmore is another case of the use of judicial contempt by Pennsylvania judges to punish out-of-chamber critical speech, but, unlike the preceding litigations, lacked any political dimensions. Passmore had obtained a judgment against the underwriters of his insurance policy and was outraged when the underwriters were successful in obtaining a stay of execution by filing a bill of particulars. He posted a public notice accusing one of the underwriters of false swearing to obtain the stay and calling the other a "liar, a rascal, and a coward" and describing his action as "mean and dirty."

The Court held Passmore in contempt for the publication in a case that was pending.[34] Although counsel for the prosecution had cited the *Oswald* case as authority, Chief Justice Shippen ignored the decision and instead turned to the English common law and the decision of Lord Hardwicke in *Rex v. Atkyns* to uphold the use of the summary contempt power in cases of out-of-court publications. He emphasized: "If the minds of the public can be prejudiced by such improper publications before a cause is heard, justice cannot be administered." Passmore was fined $50 and ordered imprisoned for 30 days and afterwards until the fine and costs were paid.[35]

---

[31] *See* J. A. Smith, *Printers*, note 26, at 151.

[32] *See* J. Thomas, note 1, at 25.

[33] For general discussions of Cobbett and McKean and their clashes. *see* Cobbett, note 16; G. S. Rowe, note 16, at 295–306.

[34] State v. Passmore, 3 Yeates 441, 1802 Pa. LEXIS 25 (1802). The report gives an inadequate description of the litigation. The description given above is based on the account in Linenthal, note 1, at 90–91.

[35] Roach v. Garvan, 2 Atkyns 469, 26 Eng. Rep. 683 (1742) (Lord Hardwicke, J.).

Like Oswald, Passmore pressed for intervention by the Legislature. He was successful in persuading the committee of the House considering the memorial to report that "the judges have exercised a stretch of power in this case, not warranted by the constitution and laws of our country."[36] The lower house approved the impeachment of Chief Justice Shippen and Associate Justices Yeates and Smith overwhelmingly, 65 to 16. After trial in January 1805, the Senate voted to uphold the charges by 13 to 11. The impeachment failed, however, because it did not receive the necessary two-thirds vote.[37] One commentator has asserted that the impeachment was a "malicious partisan attack upon the Federalist members of the court, and the entire bar of the State refused to assist in the prosecution."[38] Thus, the Senate ultimately went out of state and engaged a Delaware lawyer, Caesar A. Rodney of Constitutional Convention fame, to serve as prosecutor.[39]

In Chapter 6, readers learned of the repeated attempts of McKean, both while Chief Justice and as Governor, to punish William Duane for his bitter attacks in the Philadelphia *Aurora*. When he was at last successful in finally obtaining Duane's conviction for criminal libel in 1809, Duane's allies in the Legislature, as we have seen, rescued him by enacting a sweeping reform statute, which was held to be retroactive. Although the statute was directed at criminal libel, it also dealt with contempt and "publications out of court."

Section 2 of the new Pennsylvania statute provided:

All publications out of court respecting the conduct of the judges, officers of the court, jurors, witnesses, parties . . . in or concerning any cause pending before any court of this Commonwealth shall not be construed into a contempt of the said court, so as to render the author, printer, or publisher . . . liable to attachment and summary punishment.[40]

---

[36] He was less successful with an additional proposal recommending a statute defining the power of the courts to punish for contempt. The recommendation failed of adoption in committee by a tie vote. Phillips, note 17, at 177.

[37] W. Hamilton, *Report of the Trial and Acquittal of Justices of the Supreme Court of Pennsylvania* 8 (1805) (hereinafter Hamilton) *cited by* Linenthal, note 1, at 92–94.

[38] William S. Carpenter, *Judicial Tenure in the United States* 112 (1918) *cited by* Holmes, note 1, at 22.

[39] *See* Phillips, note 17, at 175.

[40] 1808–1809 Pa. Acts, c. 78, p. 146, reenacted by the Act of 1836, Pa. Laws 784, §23. For the history leading up to the Pennsylvania legislation, see Respublica v. Oswald, 1 Dall. 319 (1788), particularly note beginning at 329; Respublica v. Passmore, 3 Yeates (Pa.) 441; Hamilton, note 37. *Cf.* Hollingsworth v. Duane, 12 F. Cas. 359, 1 Wall. Cir. Ct. 7 (C.C.D. Pa. 1801); United States v. Duane, 25 F. Cas. 920, 1801 U.S. App. LEXIS 278, 1 Wall. Cir. Ct. 102 (C.C.D. Pa. 1801) (No. 14,997).

See also Foster v. Commonwealth, 8 Watts & Serg. 77 (Pa. 1844), 1844 Pa. LEXIS 148 (1844). ("The framers of the Statute thought they were not dealing with the Law of Libel or the liberty of the press at all; for there is not a word in it about either. The end in view was to abolish the

In this way, Pennsylvania had led the nation in prohibiting the use of criminal contempt by its judiciary to punish critics for out-of-court publications. Two decades later, the Congress enacted a statute purporting to do much the same. Although the 1809 Pennsylvania statute provided for expiration in 1812, Pennsylvania has continued until this day under a substantially similar statute severely restricting the permissible scope of judicial contempt.[41]

b. The Early New York Experience

In addition to the Pennsylvania litigations involving Oswald and Duane, two New York cases related to the celebrated *Croswell* case shortly after the turn of the century further illustrate the use of the contempt power to subordinate the press to the courts. Samuel S. Freer, the Federalist editor of the Ulster *Gazette*, published an apparently premature account of the *Croswell* proceedings including a report that "the Judge [Lewis] refused Mr. Croswell the privilege of producing his witnesses." Freer, was, thereupon, promptly indicted for contempt of court. The case was removed to the Supreme Court, where Freer, who was represented by Alexander Hamilton, was adjudged guilty of contempt and fined a token $10.[42] At much the same time, a second Federalist editor, Gardner Tracy of the Lansingburg *Gazette*, was indicted for criminal libel for reprinting in the Lansingburg *Gazette* the account in the Ulster *Gazette* that had led to Freer's indictment. In a striking indication of the equivalent usefulness of the different repressive doctrines of the time, Tracy was indicted for criminal libel of Chief Justice Lewis and District Attorney Foote, while Freer was punished for contempt for virtually the same offense.

In another early New York lower court contempt case, *In re Spooner*, the court acknowledged in dictum:

> It has not been, and could not with propriety be questioned, but that this court has power not only to punish by this summary process of attachment, such contempts as are committed in the face of the court

obnoxious process of attachment for contempt, in all but a few specified cases; not to narrow a libeller's liability punishment, by interdicting any procedure which allows him the benefit of trial by jury. The Legislature were stimulated to action. The public mind had been roused, by what was thought at the time to be an arbitrary and unconstitutional conviction of that person, though he had certainly earned the common law punishment due to a contempt of court, by placarding a gentlemen of great respectability, for his defence of a cause depending in the court.")

[41] See Penn. Stat. tit. 17, §§2041–2055 (1936).

[42] People v. Freer, 1 Cai. R. 485, 518, 1803 N.Y. LEXIS 234 (N.Y. 1803) (*per curiam*) Albany *Centinel*, Oct. 18, 1803, Mar. 2, 1804; *New-Hampshire Centinel*, Dec. 31, 1803; *Columbian Repository* (1802–1807) June 26, 1804. The *Freer* case was removed by certiorari to the Supreme Court, as was the associated *Tracy* case. The Hudson *Balance*, Mar. 6, 1804.

or which openly insult or resist its authority, which are called direct contempts, but it had been conceded that it may also punish, by this process, consequential or implied contempts, among which are speaking or writing contemptuously of the Court.[43]

The judicial contempt power continued as a matter of concern in New York. This led to the adoption in 1829 of a statute restricting the scope of the power.[44] The New York statute limited punishment of speech or publications to specified behavior "committed during its sitting, in its immediate view and presence, and directly tending to interrupt its proceedings or to impair the respect due to its authority" or to the "publication of a false and grossly inaccurate report of its proceedings." Contempt for critical out-of-court commentary had been outlawed.

c. Other Early Developments

During the early days of the 19th century, several other reported state cases involved the application of the contempt power to out-of-court publications. Two of these occurred in Maryland. In 1808, Baptis Irvine, editor of the Baltimore *Whig*, printed a "most outrageous attack" on the jurors in a case in which he was interested. The Baltimore Criminal Court found him in contempt and sentenced him to 30 days' imprisonment. On review under the ancient Maryland procedure, the judgment was upheld by the Maryland Legislature.[45] Reflecting the partisan nature of the case, another newspaper, the Baltimore *Federal Gazette*, commended the Governor of Maryland for refusing to remit the sentence of the Court. The Governor was reported as supporting the "constitutional right of the court to punish for contempt in a summary way" and "condemns, in strong terms, the publications which the court deems in contempt."[46] In *Spooner*, discussed above, the New York Court relied on *Irvine* as support for its action.[47]

In 1811 a judge of the Baltimore County Court punished the jailer and turnkey of the Baltimore County jail, John Bentley and Isaiah Green, for publishing false copies of the orders of another judge of the Court. The judge not only rejected the arguments of Luther Martin, one of the outstanding lawyers of the time and longtime Attorney General of Maryland, based on

---

[43] In re Spooner, N.Y. Gen. Sess. Ct. Sept. 4, 1820, 5 N.Y. *City-Hall Recorder* No. 9, 109 (Sept. 1820).

[44] N.Y. Rev. Stat., ch. 3, §10 (1829).

[45] *See* Baltimore *Federal Gazette* and *Poulson's American Daily Advertiser*, Mar. 8, 1808.

[46] Poulson's *American Daily Advertiser*, Mar. 8, 1808.

[47] *See* In re Spooner, N.Y. Gen. Sess. Ct. Sept. 4, 1820, 5 N.Y. *City-Hall Recorder*, 109, 111 (Sept. 1820).

the "sacred" right of trial by jury, but suspended Martin from practice for his conduct as counsel.[48]

In addition to these early contempt cases involving out-of-court publications, many contempt cases dealt with other types of contempts. These were cases in which state courts upheld the use of a state court's inherent contempt power to punish contumacious conduct obstructing the administration of justice that did not involve issues of free speech and press. These included conduct in the physical presence of the judge or in the court, violation or refusal to obey court orders, and conduct obstructing the judicial process such as tampering with witnesses or jurors.[49] As noted, these latter cases are beyond the scope of our inquiry.

In Louisiana in 1815, federal District Court Judge Hall cited Gen. Andrew Jackson, fresh from his victory in the Battle of New Orleans, for contempt for his conduct in refusing to obey court orders and subsequently for refusing to respond to interrogatories. Jackson was fined $1,000. After Jackson became President, the Congress refunded the fine with interest at 6 percent compounded semiannually.[50]

Although Louisiana a few years later adopted a statute severely restricting the scope of summary punishment for contempt, punishment for out-of-court publications by attorneys was not among the areas eliminated.[51] The following year, Edward Livingstone (a New Yorker turned Louisianan who had been the unsuccessful counsel for Jackson and was later his Secretary of State from 1830 to 1832), published a model Criminal Code for Louisiana. Although it generally followed the statute, it ended the continued availability of contempt for out-of-chamber publications.[52] Livingston's code did not become law in Louisiana, but a watered-down version may be seen in the New York statute of 1828.[53]

---

[48] *See* C. Thomas, note 1, at 23. Martin collaborated in writing a pamphlet about the case. W. Dorsey & L. Martin, *An Inroad upon the Sacred Trial by Jury* (1811). The result of the case could be supported not only by the contempt power but also by the positions of the defendants as officers of the court.

[49] For early examples, *see* Yates v. Lansing, 9 Johns. 395, 1811 N.Y. LEXIS 211 (N.Y. 1811) (imprisonment of a master in chancery for filing a bill to which he had forged the name of a solicitor); Hiss v. Bartlett, 69 Mass. (3 Gray) 468, 1855 Mass. LEXIS 315 (1855); Johnston v. Commonwealth, 4 Ky. (1 Bibb) 598, 1809 Ky. LEXIS 159 (1809); Burnham v. Morrisey, 80 Mass. (14 Gray) 226, 1959 Mass. LEXIS (1859).

[50] *See* C. Thomas, note 1, at 24–25; E. P. Deutsch, Liberty of Expression and Contempt of Court, 27 Minn. L. Rev. 296, 303 (1942) (hereinafter Deutsch).

[51] La. Act of Mar. 27, 1823. Its modern counterpart may be found in La. Rev. Stat. §§124, 125.

[52] E. Livingston, *System of Penal Law* (1824). It may also be found in 2 E. Livingston, *Complete Works on Criminal Jurisprudence* 59–60 (1873).

[53] N.Y. Rev. Stat. 1829, pt. iii, ch. iii, tit. 2, §10.

By this time, the Federalist Party had disappeared, and partisan use of the judicial contempt power to punish critical out-of-court speech had come to an end. Nevertheless, the use of contempt to suppress out-of-court criticism of judicial conduct in the state courts continued for more than another century.

The absolute nature of the judicial power in which judges acting summarily and unilaterally imposed criminal punishment on their critics for publications outside the courtroom or courthouse provoked continuing political controversy. The absence of any procedure for indictment by a grand jury or subsequent trial by jury and the other customary protections of a defendant facing a criminal trial became increasingly unacceptable. Thus, as noted, both in Pennsylvania and New York, the litigations described above led to the early passage of restrictive statutes severely limiting the scope of the judicial contempt power in their state courts. As we will see, similar concerns arose in the federal judicial system, culminating in the 1831 enactment of a federal statute governing the use of contempt in cases involving out-of-court publications.

2. Federal Statutory and Constitutional Limitations of the Judicial Contempt Power

a. The "Duane" Prelude (1800) and the Congressional Contempt Power

While Chief Justice McKean was testing the use of the judicial contempt power to silence Duane and other critics in the Pennsylvania courts, Duane was under siege in the federal courts as well. In fact, just as Chief Justice McKean provides a continuous thread in the series of Pennsylvania cases involving the contempt power during this period, so too does William Duane, the outspoken editor of the Philadelphia *Aurora*. Duane's vituperative prose plunged him into an astonishing legal maelstrom. At various times, he was the defendant in dozens of civil libel actions and numerous criminal prosecutions under the Sedition Act, common-law criminal libel prosecutions in the federal courts as well as in Pennsylvania, contempt of the Congress, and contempt of court in Pennsylvania.

In May 1801, Duane's involvement in the federal Circuit Court in Philadelphia came to a boil. He or his counsel was in court on no fewer than seven days out of 11 continuous court days involving four separate matters. He was the defendant in a prominent civil libel case involving Federalist Levi Hollingsworth, the defendant in a federal criminal libel proceeding for libels of the Federalist-controlled U.S. Senate, the defendant in an attachment for contempt of court for hostile articles in the *Aurora* on the proceedings in the *Hollingsworth* case, and the moving party in an attempted attachment for contempt of court for comments on the *Hollingsworth* litigation on the part of Caleb Wayne, an associate of Hollingsworth.

He was besieged on other legal fronts as well. Duane was also under indictment in three other pending federal criminal libel suits. Indictments had been handed down against him for publishing stolen letters of the British Ambassador, Robert Liston, and for asserting that Timothy Pickering while Secretary of State had encouraged separating France from its rebellious colony Santo Domingo. Finally, he was the defendant in a pending contempt proceeding brought by the U.S. Senate. (We review this parallel episode below with the other contempt of Congress or legislature cases.)

Matters became most intense for Duane during the second and third weeks in May 1801. On Tuesday, May 12, in the libel case involving the Senate, the Circuit Court reluctantly granted him a continuance but set the case down for peremptory trial at the next term.[54] On the following Monday, May 18, Duane was again in Circuit Court involved in a civil libel suit, *Hollingsworth v. Duane*. His distinguished counsel, Alexander J. Dallas, challenged the jurisdiction of the federal District Court. He argued that Duane and Hollingsworth were both citizens of Pennsylvania and, accordingly, that diversity jurisdiction did not exist. Hollingsworth's counsel, however, contended that Duane was a citizen of Great Britain, thereby satisfying the requirements for diversity jurisdiction. Dallas sought to delay the trial by moving for a continuance in order to obtain the testimony of an absent witness. The Court denied the motion[55] and proceeded to hear Dallas's attack on jurisdiction. After the Court had expressed its unanimous view that Duane was an alien and a subject of Great Britain, the jury so held in "two minutes."[56]

Duane, thereupon, dropped the challenge to jurisdiction, and counsel for the parties agreed that damages should be assessed by a special, or "struck," jury. The jury assessed the damages at $600. Duane then challenged one of the jurors as an alien. However, the Court held that while the challenge might have been upheld if made before the verdict, it came too late.[57] However, on

---

[54] United States v. Duane, 25 F. Cas. 917, 1801 U.S. App. LEXIS 277, 1 Wall. Cir. Ct. 5 (C.C.D. Pa. 1801) (No. 14,996).

[55] Hollingsworth v. Duane, 12 F. Cas. 355, 1801 U.S. App. LEXIS 239, 1 Wall. Cir. Ct. 46 (C.C.D Pa. 1801) (No. 6,614).

[56] Hollingsworth v. Duane, 12 F. Cas. 356, 1801 U.S. App. LEXIS 240, 1 Wall. Cir. Ct. 51 (C.C.D. Pa. 1801 (6,615). One commentator suggests that this was the whole point of the *Hollingsworth* suit, to establish that Duane was foreign so that he would be subject to being deported. *See* Phillips, note 17, at 125.

[57] Hollingsworth v. Duane, 4 U.S. (4 Dall.) 353, 1801 U.S. LEXIS 114 (C.C.D Pa. 1801).

Duane's application, it issued a rule for Hollingsworth to show cause why the verdict should not be set aside for that reason.

On the same day, May 18, the Court heard a further attack on Duane by Hollingsworth. In earlier stages of the *Hollingsworth* litigation, Duane had continued to use the Philadelphia *Aurora* to attack Hollingsworth. He represented him "as a man who had been guilty of treason, and saved from the gallows by the lenity" of former Chief Justice McKean, now Governor of Pennsylvania. Further, Duane had asserted that the jury had given a most infamous verdict and insinuated that no justice could be expected for citizens of Republican principles in a trial by "struck jury."[58] Hollingsworth now moved to have Duane cited for contempt for these comments. The Court granted the motion and set the matter for hearing on May 21. Duane's counsel then moved for a continuance to prepare for the hearing, but this was denied.[59] At the hearing on Friday, May 22, before Judges Tilghman and Griffin, the Court upheld the contentions of Hollingsworth's counsel, and it held Duane in contempt of court. Pointing to the "gross falsities and unprincipled tendency of the publication," the Court stated with some heat: "They were, indeed, sorry to find that any man should be so lost to decency and truth, as to publish . . . such flagrant calumnies upon the administration of justice." The Court found it irrelevant that the judges had not been attacked nor that they had not known of the publication until the motion was brought. They concluded that "It was equally a contempt when pending a cause, the party, his witnesses, or the jurors are reflected upon; or . . . only calculated to influence the decision."[60]

This action presented the federal courts with their very first opportunity to consider the extent of the contempt power of federal judges to punish critics for attacks in out-of-chamber publications. As we have seen, the Pennsylvania Supreme Court had earlier held the same under Pennsylvania law in the second *Oswald* case in 1788. While sentencing Duane, Judge Tilghman reviewed the proceedings and then added further observations about the Court's conclusions. He noted that "the evident tendency" of the comment was "to vilify and degrade the character of the plaintiff, and thereby to lessen his damages . . . to deter counsel, the clerk of the court, and the future jury from doing their duty; and to intimidate the court themselves. . . . [C]ourts of

---

[58] Philadelphia *Aurora*, May 20, 1801.

[59] Hollingsworth v. Duane, 12 F. Cas. 355, 1801 U.S. App. LEXIS 239, 1 Wall. Cir. Ct. 46 (C.C.D. Pa. 1801) (No. 6,614).

[60] Hollingsworth v. Duane, 12 F. Cas. 359, 1801 U.S. App. LEXIS 241, 1 Wall. Cir. Ct. 77 (C.C.D. Pa. 1801) (No. 6,616).

justice must prevent all discussions, all interference, or reflections in newspapers, *while causes are depending*.[61] As to the power of the courts to punish by contempt summarily, the Court pointed to the 1788 decision in the *Oswald* case under Pennsylvania law upholding the power of judges to exercise criminal jurisdiction in contempt cases.[62] He then observed that principles of the *Oswald* decision "are too strongly founded to be shaken" and have been considered "as the undoubted law of Pennsylvania."[63] There was no right to trial by jury. Finally, the Court rejected Dallas's argument in extenuation that Duane's comments had been provoked by an "abusive" publication in Caleb Wayne's antagonistic newspaper. It sentenced Duane to 30 days' imprisonment and costs, and to remain committed until costs were paid.

Notwithstanding Duane's conviction and jail sentence, his counsel, Alexander J. Dallas, that same day, Saturday, May 23, 1801, counterattacked. He then moved for a rule for Wayne to show cause why he should not be cited for contempt of court for his comments about Duane in the *Hollingsworth* case while the earlier proceeding was proceeding. The rule was entered "rather as of course," and Dallas commenced prosecution on Monday, May 25, 1801. Finding that the matter had been wrongly entitled by Dallas, the Court dismissed the motion for a technical deficiency and discharged the rule with costs to Wayne.[64]

On the following Tuesday, May 26, Dallas attempted to proceed on his motion to make the rule against Wayne absolute. However, he had failed to make personal service and had left it "at his house, with his housekeeper." The Court held this insufficient in the absence of a showing that Wayne was evading service. Dallas thereupon successfully moved for a rule on Wayne to show cause on the first day of the October Term with an order that service at the party's last abode be deemed sufficient, which was granted.[65] At this point in the checkered Duane legal history, developments temporarily came

---

[61] Emphasis added. The distinction between publications involving *pending* causes and cases that had come to an end is critical. It was accepted even during these times that the judicial contempt power extended to out-of-chamber publications only in pending cases.

[62] *See* text accompanying notes 27–30.

[63] United States v. Duane, 25 F. Cas. 920, 1801 U.S. App. LEXIS 278, 1Wall. Cir. Ct. 102 (C.C.D. Pa. 1801) (No. 14,997).

[64] United States v. Wayne, 28 F. Cas. 504, 1 Wall Cir. Ct. 134 (C.C.D. Pa. 1801) (No. 16,654). When a party commences proceedings for contempt of court against another party, the matter is civil and should be so entitled. Until the rule is made absolute or an attachment is issued, there is no suit between the United States and the person charged. Once the party is adjudged in contempt, the court will direct an attachment, and at this point, the litigation becomes a criminal matter involving the United States and the accused.

[65] Hollingsworth v. Duane, 12 F. Cas. 367, 1801 U.S. App. LEXIS 242, 1 Wall. Cir. Ct.141 (C.C.E.D. Pa. 1801) (No. 6,617).

to a halt, except, of course, for the 30 days' imprisonment for Duane, the payment of costs in the contempt proceeding, and the $600 judgment in the *Hollingsworth* matter. Jefferson considered whether to pardon Duane and consulted Robert H. Livingston. After conferring with Dallas and Duponceau, Livingston advised against it, and Duane served his term.[66]

Fundamental threshold issues faced the Court in *Hollingworth v. Duane* on the scope of the contempt power in the federal courts. The existence of the contempt power was beyond challenge. Notwithstanding the silence of the Constitution, the courts and the commentators agreed that the courts had the inherent power to punish summarily persons for conduct, speech, or publications that threatened the administration of justice. This had been recognized at common law for "time immemorial" according to Blackstone[67] and in the Judiciary Act of 1789.

Although the existence of the power was conceded, the problem was its scope. As to this, the Judiciary Act gave no clue. It provided merely that the courts of the United States "shall have power ... to punish by fine or imprisonment, at the discretion of said courts, all contempts of authority in any cause or hearing before the same."[68] The vital issues of the scope of the contempt power remained open, whether one was considering the common law, or the Act of 1789, or the federal and state Constitutions. Little guidance was available on such fundamental distinctions as contempts in court and contempts out of court, or between contempts in cases pending in the trial courts, contempts in cases determined in the trial court but with an appeal pending, and contempts in cases in which all proceedings had come to an end. These all remained for future determination.

---

[66] Letter, Thomas Jefferson to Robert H. Livingston (May 31, 1801), 9 Jefferson, *Writings* 757 (P. L. Ford ed. 1804); Letter, Robert H. Livingston to Thomas Jefferson (May 31, 1801). *See* Phillips, note 17, at 119–31 for a description of Duane's unsuccessful negotiations with Jefferson for a pardon of his various cases involving criminal libel.

[67] 4 Blackstone, note 3, at 284. As we will see, Blackstone appears to have been mistaken, but his views were accepted at the time as an authoritative statement of the English law.

The American courts had no doubt of the matter. "Certain implied powers must necessarily result to our Courts of justice from the nature of their institution.... To fine for contempt – imprison for contumacy – enforce the observance of order, &c. are powers which cannot be dispensed with in a Court, because they are necessary to the exercise of all others." United States Hudson & Goodwin, 11 U.S. (7 Cranch) 32, 34 (1812); Anderson v. Dunn, 19 U.S. (6 Wheat.) 204, 227 (1821).

In Bridges v. California, 314 U.S. 252, 286 (1941) (Frankfurter, J., dissenting along with Stone, C.J., Roberts, and Byrnes, J.) Justice Frankfurter quoted *Hudson & Goodwin* and continued: "it was expounded and supported by the great Commentaries that so largely influenced the shaping of our law in the late 18th and early 19th centuries, those of Blackstone, Kent and Story." 314 U.S. at 285–286.

[68] 1 Stat. 73, 83 (1789).

For two decades following the *Duane* litigation, the federal reporters are silent. However, we do not really know whether the federal judges during this period were actually exercising their criminal contempt power to deal with contempt in general or in out-of-court publications. Although there are no reported decisions, that does not always provide an accurate insight into the jurisprudential reality of the times in the early days of the Republic.

Then, in 1826 came *United States v. Lawless*, in which District Court Judge Peck used the contempt power to punish a disappointed lawyer for criticizing the judge's opinion in a newspaper.[69] As described in the next section, the decision in *Lawless* had dramatic consequences.

b. The Act of March 2, 1831

Two decades after *Duane*, the federal law of contempts changed dramatically. The question of criminal contempt for out-of-court speech was catapulted into national prominence by the actions of Judge James H. Peck, federal Judge for the District of Missouri.[70] Thomas Lawless, a disappointed lawyer, strongly criticized one of Judge Peck's decisions in the *Soulard* case that Lawless was then appealing. He cited 18 propositions on which he supposed Judge Peck to be wrong on the law or the facts.[71] Peck held him in contempt, imprisoned him for 24 hours, and suspended him from practice for 18 months. Lawless presented a memorial in 1826 to the Congress but there was no response. Not for several years until after the election in 1830 of a new administration and a new Congress did the Congress move. After receiving the Report of the Judiciary Committee of which James Buchanan, the future President, was chairman, the House of Representatives voted to impeach Judge Peck by a vote of 123 to 49.

The trial before the Senate was conducted by some of the leading lawyers of the day including Buchanan (for the prosecution) and William Wirt (for the defense). The argument of counsel is reported to have been chiefly concerned with the "liberty of the press and the right to publish comments on questions pending in the courts, and to the limitations upon the power of courts to

---

[69] United States v. Lawless (C.C.D. Mo. 1826) (unreported).

[70] *See* Arthur J. Stansbury, *Report of the Trial of James H. Peck* (1833, repr. 1972) (hereinafter Stansbury); 2 John P. Kennedy, *Memoirs of the Life of William Wirt* 311–312 (1849) (repr. 20 *Classics of Legal History* (R. Mersky & J. Jacobstein eds. 1975). Kennedy characterizes William Wirt's speech for Judge Peck as "remarkable for its power and beauty and will always be regarded as one of the best in the literature to which it belongs."

[71] Judge Thomas added an historical footnote to Lawless's contention. He states that in *Soulard v. United States*, 29 U.S. (4 Pet.) 511 (1830), the Supreme Court subsequently reversed Peck's reasoning, vindicating Lawless's opinion. *See* J. Thomas, note 1, at 26 n.36.

punish for contempts." Frankfurter and Landis assert that Peck's conduct was "defended chiefly upon his good faith in following what purported to be the staunch precedents of the common law."[72] Judge Peck, described as an ailing blind man, was acquitted by a vote of 22 for conviction to 21 for acquittal, failing to obtain the necessary two-thirds vote.[73]

Although impeachment and removal of Judge Peck had failed, the Congress recognized that the open-ended nature of the Judiciary Act of 1789 led to serious abuse. The next day, the Congress began proceedings to consider "the expediency of defining by statute" offenses that could be punished by the judicial contempt power.[74] A month later, it enacted the Act of March 2, 1831, which appeared to limit drastically the power of the courts to punish out-of-court publications, such as had been involved in the *Lawless* case.[75] The first section of the Act provided:

> The said courts shall have power to . . . punish, by fine or imprisonment, at the discretion of the court, that such power to punish contempts shall not be construed to extend to any cases except the misbehavior of any person *in their presence, or so near thereto as to obstruct the administration of justice,* the misbehavior of any of the officers of said courts in their official transactions, and the disobedience or resistance by any such officer, or by any party, juror, witness, or other person to any lawful writ, process, order, rule, decree, or command of the said courts."[76]

Most of the states adopted comparable statutes. Seven states – Alabama, Georgia, Maryland, North Carolina, Ohio, Tennessee, and Virginia – copied

---

[72] *See* Frankfurter & Landis, note 1, at 1,025.

[73] Among the Senators voting for conviction was Sen. Edward Livingston of Louisiana, who had years before resisted the application of the contempt power as counsel for Gen. Andrew Jackson. *See* text accompanying note 50.

Five years later, Judge Peck again appears on the pages of American history in a chilling episode. Russel B. Nye reports that in 1836, a mulatto, Francis McIntosh, who had killed an officer while resisting arrest had been lynched and slowly burned to death. Judge Peck presiding over the grand jury investigating the matter directed a verdict to take no action. The celebrated abolitionist Elijah Lovejoy bitterly excoriated the lynching and attacked Judge Lawless's action, resulting in his expulsion from St. Louis. Lovejoy then settled across the Mississippi River in Alton, Illinois, where anti-abolitionist mobs destroyed his printing presses and ultimately murdered him defending his fourth replacement press. *See* Russell B. Nye, *Fetters and Freedom: Civil Liberties and the Slavery Controversy, 1830–1860,* 146–148 (1963).

[74] 7 Cong. Debates, 21st Cong, 2d Sess., Feb. 1, 1831.

[75] Frankfurter & Landis, note 1, at 1037 assert that it was modeled after the Pennsylvania Act of 1809. However, the language of the 1831 Act is very different. The Pennsylvania Act flatly banned "all publications out of court respecting the conduct of judges . . . concerning any cause pending. *See* note 40. Chief Justice White tried to support his construction of the 1831 Act in *Toledo Publishing* by pointing to the differences. Frankfurter & Landis, however, assert that his commentary was based on an incomplete quotation from the Pennsylvania Act. *Id.* at 1037.

[76] 4 Stat. 487 (1831). Emphasis added.

the 1831 Act.[77] Goldfarb reports that by 1860 no fewer than two-thirds of the states had enacted statutes restricting the scope of the judicial contempt power.[78]

The Act of 1831 seems clear enough, but as we will see, it took more than a century and no fewer than five decisions before the Supreme Court finally declared that the Act meant what it literally said. This lengthy episode in which judges appeared to be stubbornly insisting on their unlimited powers of contempt, notwithstanding the Act, is not one of the most creditable in the history of the federal judiciary.

The judicial contempt power presented several fundamental problems. The first was an issue of statutory construction: what did the Act of 1831 mean? Another was the constitutional issue. Did the constitutional protection of freedom of speech and press limit the exercise of the contempt power, and if so, what were the limits? Finally, to what extent were the issues affected by the procedural posture of the underlying litigation: whether it was still pending in the trial court, or on appeal, or whether it had come to an end?

c. *The Century-Long Struggle in the Federal Courts over the Meaning of the Act of 1831*

Although there was general agreement on the inherent power of the American courts to punish for contempt, the Judiciary Act of 1789 provided express statutory power for the federal courts to exercise contempt powers, but, as we have seen, without any guidance as to its scope. The question of the outer perimeters of the contempt power took more than a century to resolve.

With the enactment of the Act of 1831, the issue became one of statutory construction.[79] Did the Act mean what it literally said when, on the heels of

---

[77] *See* Nelles & King, note 1, at 533 n.30.

[78] He also reports that in a number of these states, state courts had subsequently declared the statutes unconstitutional. Goldfarb, note 1, at 91. Such a decision was State *ex rel.* Crow v. Shepherd, 177 Mo. 205, 238–239 (1904). This was an extreme decision in which the court blustered: "Nowhere in the Constitution is the Legislature given any power to meddle with the the inherent powers of the courts.... [T]his court has an inherent and constitutional right to punish contempt summarily, which can not be taken away, abridged, limited or regulated by the Legislature."

    A number of courts substantially followed suit, finding that the inherent power of the state courts to punish for contempts was beyond the powers of the legislature to restrict. *E.g.*, State v. Morrill, 16 Ark. 384, 1855 Ark. LEXIS 73 (1855). Still other courts rejected such an extreme view. They accepted moderate regulation, and when they did act, they restricted their determination of unconstitutionality to specified sections of the statute rather than to the statute generally. *See, e.g.*, Bradley v. State, 111 Ga. 168 (1900); Carter v. Commonwealth, 96 Va. 791 (1899). This, of course, was a matter of separation of powers. It had nothing to do with such constitutional guaranties as freedom of speech or due process.

[79] Although certain interpretations might present constitutional issues, none of the Supreme Court decisions considering the issue of statutory construction found it necessary to introduce any constitutional dimension in considering the powers of the federal judges under the Act.

the *Peck* impeachment trial, it restricted exercise of contempt powers of the federal courts to events in the "presence" of the court "or so near thereto so as to obstruct the administration of justice"? Although the language seems clear enough, it ultimately presented a profound difficulty.

With the hindsight of history, it is apparent that the draftsmen were myopic. With the *Peck* case providing the immediate impetus for the drafting and passage of the Act, the structure of the Act suggests that it was drafted to limit the use of the contempt power to deal with out-of-courtroom speech, as in the episode that led to the impeachment of Judge Peck. Although this, of course, was the type of contempt of immediate concern, there were many other, and more serious, types of contempt. What of jury or witness tampering? disobedience of court orders? bribery? and other acts going well beyond speech obstructing the administration of justice? Did the Congress also intend to place such contumacious conduct beyond the contempt power if it did not occur in the courthouse? Indeed, why would the Congress have so intended? The venality of such obstructive contumacious conduct in no way depended on the location of where it took place. For example, was bribery outlawed only if took place in the courthouse?

Nor is there a substantial body of reported cases that gives us any clue how the Act was construed. Although one case did occur within months of the passage of the Act, *United States v. Emerson*, it dealt with the easiest of cases, holding that the exercise of the contempt power in a case of speech occurring in the entrance of the courthouse[80] satisfied the "so near thereto" standard.

Over the next 75 years, little litigation involved the availability of the contempt power to punish out-of-court publications. There were five decisions: holdings in two cases and dicta in an additional three. Each gave the Act a literal, geographical construction.[81] As Justice Field put it in dictum, "the power of these courts in the punishment of contempts *can only be exercised to insure order and decorum in their presence*."[82]

Each of these decisions involved out-of-court publications. But what of cases involving contumacious conduct, not merely publication? Did the statutory reference to "interference to the administration of justice" broaden the

---

[80]   United States v. Emerson, 25 F. Cas. 1012, 1831 U.S. App. LEXIS 319 (C.C.C. 1831).

[81]   The cases construing the statute to impose a geographical restriction include *Ex Parte* Poulson, 19 F. Cas. 1205 (C.C.E.D. Pa. 1835); Cuyler v. Atlantic & N.C.R., 131 F. 95 (C.C.E.D.N.C. 1904).

[82]   *See Ex Parte* Robinson, 86 U.S. (19 Wall.) 505, 511 (1873) (Field, J.). Emphasis added. For similar dicta, *see In re* May, 1 F. 737 (E.D. Mich. 1880), Morse v. Montana Ore-Purchasing Co., 105 F. 337, 347 (C.C.D. Mont. 1900) (newspaper article reaching jurors in pending case held to require granting motion for new trial, but "extremely doubtful" whether contempt power was available in view of the Act of 1831). Similarly, in another Supreme Court decision, there is a passing reference to the Act that could be read as suggesting a geographical standard. *See In re* Savin, 131 U.S. 267, 276 (1889).

available scope of the contempt power to deal with contumacious conduct without regard to the geographical limitation posed by the reference to the "presence, or so near thereto"? On this, there was no judicial answer whatever for 50 years after the passage of the Act. Then, starting in 1880, there was a dramatic change with at least 11 cases involving contumacious conduct arising in the next few decades. Every one upheld the use of the use of the contempt power to punish such contumacious conduct notwithstanding its occurrence far from the courtroom. It is apparent that when these federal courts were faced with such conduct as tampering with jurors or witnesses or related misconduct, they refused to give the Act a literal construction and make the contempt power unavailable.

These unanimous decisions were supported by the lack of logic in a contrary construction of the statute. Contumacious conduct of this nature threatened the integrity of the judicial system wherever it occurred. The effect on the obstruction of the administration of justice was the same. In attempting to decide what the Congress intended, these courts must have asked themselves whether the Congress could really have intended to prohibit use of summary contempt in such cases as jury or witness tampering or bribery, for example, that occurred at locations remote from the courthouse. In cases of contumacious conduct, the judges, thus, uniformly refused to give the Act a geographical construction. Instead of emphasizing "presence or so near thereto," they emphasized "as to obstruct the administration of justice" to include contumacious acts with a "direct, causal impact on the proceeding so as to obstruct the administration of justice" wherever they occurred.[83]

The opinion in *Ex Parte* McLeod decided in 1903 involving an assault on a court officer expresses the rationale of these judges:

> What is meant by the words "so near thereto" has not been defined by judicial decision. In view of the evil [intended] to be suppressed, they mean not the place where the "misbehavior" is committed, but

---

[83] The contumacious conduct cases applying a "causal" or "functional" standard of the statute and upholding the use of contempt in cases not including speech include: *In re* May, 1 F. 737 (E.D. Mich. 1880) (juror discussing case outside of the jury room); United States v. Anonymous, 21 F. 761 (C.C.W.D. Tenn. 1884) (violent speech and conduct in out-of-court examination); *In re* Brule, 71 F. 943 (D. Nev. 1895) (preventing attendance of witness); *Ex Parte* McLeod, 120 F. 130 (N.D. Ala. 1903) (assault on commissioner); McCaully v. United States, 25 App. D.C. 404, 1905 U.S, App. LEXIS 5294 (1905) (corrupt influence on juryman); United States v. Carroll, 147 F. 947 (D. Mont. 1906); United States v. Zavelo, 177 F. 536 (N.D. Ala. 1910) (serving foreign witness while in state to testify in another matter); Kirk v. United States, 192 F. 273, 277–278 (9th Cir. 1911) (corrupt solicitation of prospective juror three blocks from courthouse); *In re* Steiner, 195 F. 299, 1912 U.S. Dist. LEXIS 1638 (S.D.N.Y. 1912) (perjury in affidavits before notary public); United States v. Sanders, 290 F. 428 (D. Tenn. 1923); United States v. Sullens, 36 F.2d 230 (S.D. Miss. 1929). *Cf.* Francis v. People of Virgin Islands, 11 F.2d 860 (3d Cir. 1926).

the power of the "misbehavior" to harm the administration of justice. If the force put in motion by the "misbehavior," at whatever place it is committed, assails or threatens the authority and independence of the court, then the "misbehavior" is "so near thereto" as to be punishable under this section.[84]

Similarly, the court in *McCaulley v. United States*, a jury tampering case, asserted: "the question is not one of geography or topography, or propinquity or remoteness, but one of direct influence upon the administration of justice."[85]

If the jurisprudence implementing the Act of 1831 is examined as a whole in all its applications at this stage of its evolution, it would appear at first that there were two opposing lines of cases on its proper construction. The courts had divided on the issue of whether the judicial contempt power could apply to conduct not occurring "in the presence of the court... or nearby." However, if the 17 decisions are unbundled, with the five out-of-chamber speech cases separated from the 12 contumacious conduct cases interfering with the administration of justice, a very different impression emerges. When the focus is on the decisions, not the theory on which the decision was reached, no conflict is seen between the cases. Each of the reported decisions of the judges in cases involving out-of-court publications applied the plain-text geographical standard, while each of the reported decisions of the judges considering cases involving contumacious conduct applied a functional, causal construction.

Thus, matters stood for 75 years until a cluster of cases involving out-of-courtroom speech arose just before World War I. The first of these was *United States v. Huff*, decided by an Alabama District Judge in 1913. This involved an offensive letter to the judge delivered to him at his home, not the court. Relying on the cases applying the "causal construction" standard to the statute in the case of contumacious conduct and disregarding the cases involving out-of-chamber speech, the judge held the letter writer in contempt. For the first time in the 80 years after the passage of the Act, a federal court held that the statutory limitation did not establish a geographical standard in a case involving offensive out-of-court publications.

Huff was soon followed by the *Toledo Newspaper* litigation, which went to the Supreme Court.[86] This case grew out of the highly divisive 1913 municipal election in Toledo, Ohio. This turned on the street transit franchises that were

---

[84] *Ex Parte* McLeod, 120 F. 130, 141 (N.D. Ala. 1903).
[85] McCaully v. United States, 25 App. D.C. 404, 413, 1905 U.S App. LEXIS 5294 *15 (Sup. Ct. D.C. 1905).
[86] United States v. Toledo Newspaper Co., 220 F. 458 (N.D. Ohio 1915), *aff'd*, 237 F.2d 986 (6th Cir. 1916), *aff'd*, 247 U.S. 402 (1918).

being operated by a private transit company. One slate of candidates supported by the *Toledo Bee* pressed for municipal ownership and a three cent fare, while the other slate, condemning socialism, was committed to continuation of private ownership and operation. When the municipal ownership candidates favored by the *Bee* prevailed in the election, the lame duck outgoing council favoring private ownership took decisive action in the interval before the winning candidates assumed office. It adopted a resolution requiring the transit company to operate with a three cent fare and to pay rent to the city for the use of the streets. The existing franchise did not expire for at least another four months, and the transit company, which had been newly acquired by a New York investment firm, refused to comply and filed for injunctive relief.

The Toledo *Bee*, which was playing a leading role in the campaign for municipal ownership, sharply criticized the acts of the local federal District Judge in his preliminary orders on the injunction application. It was then cited for contempt. In his 56-page opinion, the judge made it plain that he viewed the underlying conflict in apocalyptic terms. He condemned the *Bee*'s editorial role as incendiary in an inherently dangerous confrontation, referring to the "great public excitement" and to a proposed "mass meeting" "with an anarchistic afterpriece" (*sic*). In addition, he made references to the "curious fact" that the *Bee*'s editorials were interconnected with "socialist thought" that gave inspiration to the outbursts of "both the Socialists and the labor agitator." It concluded by noting that later publications by the *Bee* "offer[ed] additional fuel . . . to a situation already highly inflamed."[87]

The court then held the paper and one of its editors in contempt for attempting to interfere with the administration of justice in a pending matter. In its lengthy opinion, the court collected and reviewed the precedents and concluded that notwithstanding its language, the Act of 1831 had not eliminated the power of the federal courts to use the contempt power to punish offensive out-of-court speech wherever it occurred.

On appeal, the Court of Appeals for the Sixth Circuit affirmed. It found that the publications referred to a pending judicial action tended to provoke public resistance to an injunction order, if one should be made, and constituted an attempt to intimidate or at least unduly influence the district judge with regard to the matter pending before him.[88]

The matter moved on to the Supreme Court and provided the first opportunity for the Court to determine what the Act meant. The Supreme Court had

---

[87] 220 Fed. at 498–499.
[88] Toledo Publishing Co. v. United States, 237 F. 986 (6th Cir. 1916), *aff'd*, 247 U.S. 402 (1918).

not had an opportunity to rule on the matter for almost a century. However, as we will see, the question had to come before the Court on no fewer than four occasions before all issues were finally resolved.

In *Toledo Newspaper Publishing Co. v. United States*,[89] Chief Justice White led four other members of the Court to uphold the two lower courts and emasculate the 1831 Act. Ignoring the history of its enactment,[90] the Court held, Holmes and Brandeis dissenting, that the Act had not been intended to limit the inherent power of the judiciary. White contended that the Act "conferred no power not already granted and imposed no limitations not already existing."[91] The majority adopted a "causal" construction of the statutory term "in the presence of the said courts or so near thereto." It held that the statute granted the courts the power to restrain acts that tended to obstruct and prevent the untrammeled and unprejudiced exercise of the judicial power.

In *Toledo Newspaper Co.*, the case was still pending. Thus, it threw no light on the majority's view whether the contempt power could also extend to publications about a case that had fully come to an end.

The next case was *Craig v. Hecht*, decided by the Court five years later. This involved the publication of a letter by a New York City official criticizing the action of a federal District Court judge for certain decisions made in a pending receivership proceeding. Relying on *Toledo Newspaper Co.* and without any discussion of the Act of 1831, Justice McReynolds writing for the Court in this case, also involving a pending matter, brusquely held the contempt order to be within the power of the District Court.[92] His opinion adds little, if anything, to an understanding of the statute.

In the 15 years following *Toledo Newspaper Co.* and before the Court again dealt with the contempt power of federal judges in *Nye*, there were at least seven cases in which federal trial court judges bound by *Toledo Newspaper Co.* used their contempt powers to punish newspaper editors for out-of-court

---

[89] Toledo Newspaper Co. v. United States, 247 U.S. 402, 418 (1918) (only seven justices participated in the decision).

[90] Frankfurter and Landis excoriated the opinion: "Abuse of power furnished a great 'public grievance,' the country became deeply aroused, a remedy was deliberately 'applied by the legislature, it was widely followed in the State legislation, it became imbedded in the practice and decisions of Federal courts – yet three generations later the Chief Justice finds that nothing had really happened." Frankfurter & Landis, note 1, at 1029.

[91] The 1809 Pennsylvania Act had dealt specifically with these questions that plagued the federal courts. It expressly referred both to "pending" litigation and to "all publications out of court." In its decision in *Toledo Newspaper Co.*, the court contended that the omission of such references in the federal act indicated the Congress's intent not to go so far in limiting the contempt power.

[92] Craig v. Hecht, 263 U.S. 255 (1923).

publication of comments critical of their decisions and conduct. All seven involved pending cases.[93]

Then the tide decisively turned. In *Nye v. United States*, decided in 1941, the Supreme Court overruled its decision in *Toledo Newspaper* and finally resolved the disputed issue of the meaning of the statutory term in the Act of 1831 "in the presence of the said courts or so near thereto as to obstruct the administration of justice." *Nye* involved the "reprehensible" conduct of counsel in using improper influence over an illiterate person to obtain dismissal of his lawsuit. Although the conduct clearly related to a pending matter, the acts in question took place far from the courtroom. Justice Douglas, speaking for the Court, ended the controversy over the meaning of the statute. The Court construed the critical statutory provision "misbehaviour of any person or persons *in the presence of the said courts, or so near thereto* as to obstruct the administration of justice" as "geographical terms." As Justice Douglas recognized, "the previously undefined power of the courts was substantially curtailed" by the statute.[94]

Although the offending counsel could not be punished under the contempt power, Justice Douglas made clear in *Nye* that a decision that certain contumacious conduct "which corrupts the judicial process and impedes the administration of justice" was beyond the contempt power did not mean that it escaped the law. Although "not reachable through the summary procedure of contempt," the provisions of the Criminal Code might apply. However, the defendant would then have the full protection of the criminal law.

---

[93] Cornish v. United States, 299 F. 283 (6th Cir. 1924); *In re* Independent Publishing Co., 240 F. 849 (9th Cir. 1917); United States v. Sullens, 36 F.2d 230 (S.D. Miss. 1929); United States v. Sanders, 290 F. 428 (D. Tenn. 1923); United States v. Markewich, 261 F. 537 (S.D.N.Y. 1919) (case appears to be still pending, but not clear); United States v. Providence Tribune Co., 241 F. 524 (D.R.I. 1917).

    In a case arising under Virgin Islands law to which the Act of 1831 was not applicable, the Court of Appeals for the Third Circuit upheld the use of the contempt power by a Virgin Islands court under its inherent powers to punish a newspaper for critical comments about a case that was no longer still pending. Francis v. People of Virgin Islands, 11 F.2d 860 (3d Cir. 1926). Because the decision in *Toledo Newspaper Co.* had rendered the Act surplusage, *Francis* is regarded as fully comparable to the other federal decisons.

[94] Nye v. United States, 313 U.S. 33, 47–48 (1941). Emphasis added. Before concluding the discussion of the 1831 Act, one should note that in 1948, Section 401 of the new Federal Criminal Code substantially reenacted the Act of 1831 (by then codified as section 365 of Title 28). Section 401 provided:

    A court of the United States shall have the power to punish by fine or imprisonment, at its discretion, such contempt of its authority, *and none other*, as –
    (1) Misbehavior of any person in its presence or so near thereto as to obstruct the administration of justice; . . .

This made no substantive change in the statute.

Nye involved a pending matter. It did not address the remaining issue whether such critical publications could "obstruct the administration of justice" when the cause was no longer pending. However, this remaining open question was undecided only as a matter of form. If the contempt power as so construed could not constitutionally be applied to a pending cause, it would seem all the more clear that it would not be available where the cause had come to an end. In fact, many years earlier in *Craig v. Hecht*, perhaps stimulated, perhaps provoked, by Justice McReynolds's unenlightening opinion in the case, Chief Justice Taft, concurring, and Justice Holmes, dissenting, discussed this very element not presented by the case before them.

Chief Justice Taft made plain that the contempt power for out-of-court publications criticizing the court or the judges extended only to pending matters. When the matter

> has been finally adjudicated and the proceedings are ended so that the carrying out of the court's judgment can not be thereby obstructed, the publication is not contempt and cannot be summarily punished by the court however false, malicious, or unjust it may be. The remedy of the judge is by action [*i.e.*, civil] or by prosecution [*i.e.*, criminal] for libel.[95]

After emphasizing that no cause was pending, Justice Holmes agreed:

> Suppose the petitioner falsely and unjustly charged the judge with having excluded him from knowledge of the facts, how can it be pretended that the charge obstructed the administration of justice.[96]

Chief Justice Stone in dictum in *Nye v. United States*, almost two decades later, agreed on the inapplicability of contempt in cases that were no longer pending.[97] However, these conclusions were only dicta. The Supreme Court still had not definitively ruled on the issue.

During this hiatus, the lower federal courts appeared to be in substantial agreement. Two Court of Appeals decisions agreed that the contempt power was not available when the offending out-of-courtroom publication did not relate to a pending case. In *Cornish v. United States*, the Court of Appeals for the Sixth Circuit in 1924 held that not only did actions for contempt have to comply with the Act of 1831 but that there was still another hurdle as well. The Court said flatly: "When the conduct complained of is a newspaper

---

[95] Craig v. Hecht, 263 U.S. 255, 278 (1923).
[96] Craig v. Hecht, 263 U.S. 255, 281 (1923).
[97] Nye v. United States, 313 U.S. 33, 56 (1941) (Stone, J. dissenting).

publication, defamatory of the trial judge, it is also necessary that the publication relate to a matter pending, and not to one that is past."[98] Similarly, in *Independent Publishing Co.*, decided in 1917, the Ninth Circuit relied on the statutory history surrounding the enactment of the Act of 1831 to reach the same conclusion. The Court concluded that enacted promptly after the unsuccessful impeachment trial of Judge Peck, the Act was intended to prohibit the use of the contempt power only in causes that had been concluded, the type of conduct that had led to the impeachment proceedings.[99]

Other federal cases involving the contempt power seemed with one exception to have involved out-of-court critical publications in pending matters and did not present the issue.[100] The sole exception arose in the Virgin Islands, to which the 1831 Act did not apply. In *Francis v. People of the Virgin Islands*, the District Court upheld the application of contempt under the Virgin Islands Code, although the proceeding had come to an end.[101]

With *Nye* turning on the interpretation of the 1831 statute, the federal *constitutional* limits on the application of the contempt power by federal and state judges still remained to be determined. Before reviewing the evolution of the federal constitutional doctrines in this area in the 20th century, we must review the 19th-century evolution of the judicial contempt power in the states.

3. The Judicial Contempt Power in the States

a. Statutory and Other Issues

Notwithstanding the general recognition of the inherent common-law power of the courts to protect the administration of justice from obstruction in general and by out-of-court publications in particular, the judicial powers resting on the doctrine raised serious questions. The penalties were criminal. With the process controlled by the very judge at whom the critical commentary had been addressed, any semblance of objectivity was lacking. The process was summary, lacking checks and balances. The judge possessed the power to proceed unilaterally without the sanction of a grand jury or a petit jury and the other protections afforded to the defendant in the ordinary criminal

---

[98] Cornish v. United States, 299 F. 283, 284 (6th Cir. 1924) (*per curiam*).

[99] *In re* Independent Pub. Co., 240 F. 849 (9th Cir. 1917).

[100] United States v. Sullens, 36 F.2d 230 (S.D. Miss. 1929); United States v. Sanders, 290 F. 428 (W.D. Tenn. 1923); United States v. Providence Tribune Co., 241 F. 524 (D.R.I. 1917). *Quaere* United States v. Markewich, 261 F. 537 (S.D.N.Y. 1919).

[101] Francis v. People of Virgin Islands, 11 F.2d 860 (3d Cir. 1926). For more on *Francis, see* note 83.

proceedings.[102] Finally, as noted, most of the defendants were newspapers and newspaper editors. Thus, profound issues of the value of public discussion and the role of the press in a democratic society were presented.

As we have seen in the preceding review, the judicial contempt process was widely perceived as having serious potential for abuse. The Congress acted first with the enactment of the Act of March 2, 1831. Indeed, as noted, well before the Congress acted, Pennsylvania and New York had enacted statutes restricting the scope of the application of the doctrine. In the wake of the 1831 federal statute, numerous states adopted the provisions of the federal Act in restraint of their own judicial systems.[103] Still other states subsequently proceeded with their own restrictive statutes. The Mississippi statute, for example, restricted the judicial contempt power to contempts "while sitting, either in the presence or hearing of the court."[104] In all, Ronald Goldfarb has reported that by 1860, 23 of the then 33 states had enacted statutes restricting the imposition of judicial contempt.[105] However, as the years moved on, a counter-tide set in, and a significant number of states backtracked and substantially reaffirmed the traditional contempt powers of the courts.

In contrast to the federal experience with various courts contending over "geographical" and "causal" interpretations of the 1831 statute, there seems to have been little litigation in the states on the interpretation of the restrictive state statutes. However, outstanding exceptions are seen in Mississippi and Ohio.

As noted, the Mississippi statute had restricted the contempt power to libels in "the presence or hearing" of the judge, thereby apparently banning its application to out-of-court publications entirely. For such publications, the statute transformed what had been a criminal contempt into a "mere libel" that was subject only to the common-law punishment for libels.

Ex Parte Hickey involved a newspaper publisher whose newspaper accused the judge of releasing a murderer and called for the judge to be "brought as a criminal abettor of murder to the bar, to answer for his crimes."[106] The judge imposed a contempt citation calling for five months' imprisonment and a fine of $500 and costs. On a writ of *habeas corpus*, the Supreme Court

---

[102] This is what is meant in the distinction between proceedings by attachment (summary contempt) and proceedings by indictment (criminal process including action by the grand jury and verdict by the petit jury).

[103] *See* Frankfurter & Landis, note 1, at 1027 n.77.

[104] 26 Miss. Code 436 (How. & Hutch.), *cited in Ex Parte* Hickey.

[105] Goldfarb, note 1, at 91.

[106] *Ex Parte* Hickey, 12 Miss. 751, 772–782 (1840), 1840 Miss. LEXIS 104. While the reporter states that the date of the case is 1840, the opinion refers to events occurring in 1844.

of Mississippi held that the acts did not constitute a contempt under the statute and ordered the defendant released. In so doing, the Court criticized the draconic English common-law doctrine, noting that the common-law contempt power was "irresponsible" and might be "despotic." In support of the Mississippi policy of restricting the contempt power, the Court pointed to a series of statutes – federal and state – purporting to restrict the application of the contempt power to out-of-court publications. In the end, the Mississippi court's enforcement of the plain meaning of the statutory text dictated the outcome.

The experience in Ohio was very different. Like the 1831 Act, the Ohio enactment authorized application of the power of contempt only over "misbehavior in the presence of or so near the court or judge as to obstruct the administration of justice." In a striking contrast to the Mississippi decision construing a comparable statute, the Ohio Supreme Court in its 1889 decision, *Myers v. State*, upheld the application of the contempt power to punish the author of a newspaper article published 150 miles from the courthouse.[107]

In *Myers*, the Supreme Court of Ohio ignored the plain language and apparent meaning of the statute. It upheld the power of a Columbus, Ohio, judge to hold in contempt the author of a Cincinnati newspaper article criticizing the judge's conduct for "packing" the jury in a pending case, resulting in the indictment of the author "by rascally and infamous methods."[108]

Bowing to the text of the statute, the Court gave the appearance of accepting a geographical standard for the statute. However, in applying the standard to the case, the Court made a mockery of the plain text of the statute. Although the offending commentary had occurred 150 miles from the courtroom, the Court found that was sufficiently "near thereto" to satisfy the statute. It concluded:

> the publication was in the courtroom, as well as elsewhere. It was intended to have effect, and did have effect, in the courthouse, at Columbus, and the writer was just as responsible for that effect as though he had been in the courtroom itself, and while the trial was progressing, circulated and read aloud the article, or uttered the libelous words verbally.[109]

---

[107] Myers v. State, 46 Ohio St. 473; 22 N.E. 43, 43; 1889 Ohio LEXIS 93 *2 (1889).

[108] Ohio Rev. Stat. §5639 (originally enacted in 1834) making applicable in Ohio the 1831 Act of the Congress that so provided. Act of Mar. 1, 1831, 4 Stat. 587 (1831).

[109] 46 Ohio St. at 490.
   An odd circumstance in the official report is worthy of note. The case syllabus states that the offending publication in the Cincinnati newspaper was done: "with knowledge . . . that such newspaper has a large circulation in the county where the trial is in progress, and with reasonable ground to believe that the same will, when published, be circulated in the court room and about the court-house during the said trial, and there read, which was, afterward, during the trial,

The Court's rejection of a "geographical" test in applying the statute modeled after the 1831 Act was fully consistent with the long line of lower court federal decisions that applied a "causal" reading of the statute. Thus, when the Supreme Court 29 years later in *Toledo Newspaper Co.* construed the federal Act on which the Ohio statute was based to authorize the use of the contempt power over an offensive article in a newspaper published remote from the court, *Myers v. State* was one of the decisions it advanced in support of its construction of the statute.

A quarter century later, the U.S. Supreme Court at last overruled *Toledo Newspaper* in *Nye v. United States*. As far as the federal Act of 1831 was concerned, the Court had finally accepted a literal construction, giving the statute an unyielding geographical construction. This ended the matter as far as federal statutory jurisprudence was concerned. Although influential, this decision on a federal *statutory* level did not control the Ohio courts in their construction of the Ohio statute.

b. State Constitutional Limitations

The exercise of the judicial contempt power by the state judges presented no fewer than four fundamental issues under state constitutional law: separation of powers, freedom of speech and the press, trial by jury, and due process. Of these, separation of powers played the most prominent role. As we have seen, federal constitutional guaranties in these areas were not applicable to the states until well into the 20th century. Until then, state law was unchallenged. We review the state constitutional history as the last preliminary matter before reviewing the current status of the American law of judicial contempt in the light of the dramatic expansion of federal constitutional law in this area.

c. Separation of Powers

All state courts agreed that the contempt power rested on the inherent power of the courts to prevent obstruction of the court's administration of justice. However, if the power was indeed inherent in the judicial branch, did this not mean that the power was by definition beyond the power of the legislature to prohibit or limit its use? Thus, a number of courts upheld the use of the contempt power under the inherent power doctrine and brushed aside the state restrictive statute either as unconstitutional or as irrelevant.[110]

circulated and read therein." However, these "facts" do not appear in the opinion. Nor does the syllabus indicate the basis for its statements or indicate who was the author of the syllabus. 1889 Ohio LEXIS 93, *4 (1889).

[110] State v. Morrill, 16 Ark. 384, 1855 Ark. LEXIS 73 (1855); In re Woolley, 74 Ky. 95, 11 Bush 95 (1875); Hale v. State, 55 Ohio St. 210, 45 N.E. 199 (1896); McDougall v. Sheridan, 23 Idaho 191, 223, 128 P. 954 (1913); Carter v. Commonwealth, 96 Va. 791, 32 S.E. 780 (1899).

In *State v. Morrill*,[111] the Supreme Court of Arkansas, faced by its statute providing that the judicial contempt power could be used "only" to punish conduct specified in the statute, argued:

> The Legislature may regulate the exercise of, but cannot abridge the express or necessarily implied powers, granted to this court by the constitution. If it could, it might encroach upon both the judicial and executive departments, and draw to itself all the powers of government: and thereby destroy that admirable system of checks and balances to be found in the organic frame-work of both the Federal and State institutions, and a favorite theory in the governments of the American people.

The Court, thereupon, upheld the exercise of the judicial contempt power on an out-of-court publication, although punishment for such an offence was not included in the Arkansas statute.

Similarly, in *McDougall v. Sheridan*,[112] the Supreme Court of Idaho held: "The legislature has not the authority to restrict the inherent power of the court to punish for contempt, for if it has the power to restrict such right, where will the line be drawn? If it could abridge the right, it could so minimize it as to make it ineffective for any purpose." The Supreme Courts of Kentucky, Ohio, and Virginia joined the Arkansas and Idaho courts in a series of decisions illustrating their concern.[113]

Nevertheless, in other jurisdictions, courts were less rigid, seeking to avoid confrontation with the legislature. These courts upheld the reform legislation restricting the use of the contempt power in the cases before them while noting that in view of the inherent nature of the power, there were limits on how far the legislature could proceed.[114]

Thus, in *In re Oldham*, the Supreme Court of North Carolina observed:

> The courts must... "have the power by summary remedies to preserve order during their session, control the action of the officers and enforce their mandates and decrees" and this power is "inherent in the court and essential to the exercise of its jurisdiction and the maintenance of its authority." . . .

---

[111] State v. Morrill, 16 Ark. 384, 390, 1855 Ark. LEXIS 73, *10 (1855).

[112] McDougall v. Sheridan, 23 Idaho 191, 223, 128 P. 954 (1913).

[113] In re Woolley, 74 Ky. 95, 11 Bush 95 (1875); Hale v. State, 55 Ohio St. 210, 45 N.E. 199 (1896); Carter v. Commonwealth, 96 Va. 791, 32 S.E. 780 (1899). *See* Nelles & King, note 1, at 537–538, 554–562.

[114] *See* Note, Statutory Restrictions on the Power of Courts to Punish for Contempt, 13 Yale L.J. 90 (1903); Note, Contempt – Statements Regarding Concluded Cause – When Punishable Summarily as Contempt, 9 Va. L. Rev. 467–471 (1923) (hereinafter Note, Contempt).

It cannot be doubted that the withdrawal of the power to punish for contempt would be to cripple it in the exercise of its functions and impair its essential attributes; and that legislation attempting to do this would be wholly inoperative and void. . . .

But short of this, the legislature may define the acts which shall be treated as contempts, and designate the final consequences incurred in committing them. . . . [O]ur province is limited in enforcing constitutional limitations and seeing that the court is not deprived of its just and necessary prerogatives in the performance of judicial duties.[115]

In *Drady v. District Court of Polk County*, the Supreme Court of Iowa similarly recognized the potential conflict between the inherent power doctrine and legislative reform of the contempt process. It temporized, managing to uphold the legislative action in question while deferring resolution of the issue to a more sweeping restrictive statute of another day. For these courts, the acid test was whether the legislation attempted "either to take away the power, or under the guise of regulation, render it ineffective."[116]

Thus in 1899, after the Virginia Legislature had provided for the right of trial by jury in cases of indirect contempts,[117] the Virginia Supreme Court in *Carter v. Commonwealth* held the provision unconstitutional on the ground that the legislature could not constitutionally take away the court's inherent power to punish summarily contempts, whether direct or indirect.[118] When the Legislature then amended the statute to provide for summary power in the case of "obscene, contemptuous, or insulting language addressed to a judge" for any official act, the Court upheld the revised statute. The contempt power could be regulated but not destroyed.[119]

d. Free Speech and Press

Not a single court in all the state jurisprudence considering the application of the contempt power to out-of-court publications held the application of the contempt power unconstitutional under the guaranties of free speech and press in their state Constitutions. The courts unanimously concluded that the inherent contempt power resting on what mistakably was seen "as its immemorial usage" long preceded the constitutional guaranties and that

---

[115] In re Oldham, 89 N.C. 23, 1883 N.C. LEXIS 167 (1883).

[116] Drady v. District Court of Polk County, 126 Iowa 345, 352, 102 N.W. 115 118 (1905).

[117] *See* Saunders, at 281 (1898) (supporting the constitutionality of the statute).

[118] Carter v. Commonwealth, 96 Va. 791, 32 S.E. 791 (1899).

[119] Yoder v. Commonwealth, 107 Va. 823, 57 S.E. 581 (1907) (newspaper libel held not addressed to the judge and therefore not a contempt); Boorde v. Commonwealth, 134 Va. 625, 114 S.E. 731 (1922) (contempt upheld though cause concluded). *See* Note, Contempt, 114, at 467–471.

the constitutional doctrines were not intended to restrict the doctrine. In this, the courts were simply following a pattern identical with the judicial experience in such comparable areas of repression of dissenting speech as criminal libel or blasphemy. In upholding the constitutionality of the exercise of the judicial contempt power in the face of the constitutional guaranty, the courts treated judicial contempt as inherent in the judicial system and dismissed the relevancy of the constitutional provisions. In this, they did not differ from the federal courts. Not until years later than the cases discussed did the U.S. Supreme Court rule that the federal constitutional guaranties of freedom of speech and press took constitutional priority and so severely restricted the judicial contempt power that it has lost practical significance insofar as out-of-chamber publications are concerned.

Respublica v. Oswald,[120] which readers may recall from its prominent discussion in Chapter 4, appears to be the very first decision considering the constitutional dimensions of the judicial contempt power. Addressing the issue in 1788, Chief Justice McKean had to determine whether the contempt power was limited by the Pennsylvania constitutional guaranties of free speech and press.[121]

McKean had little difficulty in concluding that these constitutional provisions in no way limited the scope of the judicial contempt power. Following Blackstone, he stated that the provisions were intended only to prohibit any prior licensing of the press. They did not protect speech that was libelous or sought "to bias and intimidate with respect to [legislative and judicial] matters still in suspense."[122]

Typical of a number of state supreme court decisions, the Supreme Court of Missouri in *State* ex rel. *Crow v. Shepherd* upheld the application of the contempt power over out-of-court publications, rejecting all constitutional claims whether based on freedom of speech, the right of trial by jury, or due process. Citing Chief Justice McKean in *Oswald* along with Cooley's *Constitutional Limitations*,[123] the Court expounded what readers will recognize as the Blackstonian formulation of the limited scope of freedom of speech and press:

> The liberty of the press means that anyone can publish anything he pleases, but he is liable for abuse of this liberty. If he does this by scandalizing the courts of his country, he is liable to be punished for contempt.

---

[120] Respublica v. Oswald, 1 U.S. (1 Dall.) 319 (Pa. 1788).
[121] Penn. Decl. of Rights §12 (1776); Penn. Const. §35 (1776).
[122] Respublica v. Oswald, 1 U.S. (1 Dall.) 319, 325–326 (1788).
[123] Thomas Cooley, *Constitutional Limitations* 518 (6th ed. 1890) (hereinafter Cooley).

If he slanders his fellowmen, he is liable to a criminal prosecution for libel, and to respond, civilly, in damages.[124]

e. Trial by Jury

As with all other courts examining the issue including the U.S. Supreme Court,[125] the Arkansas Supreme Court in *State v. Morrill* held the right of trial by jury inapplicable to contempt proceedings. The Court explained its result: "this right existed at common law, by immemorial usage in harmony with the power of courts to punish for contempts by attachment, each applying to its appropriate class of cases."[126] In *State ex rel. Crow v. Shepherd*, the Missouri Supreme Court similarly held that the Missouri constitutional provision protecting the "right of trial by jury, as heretofore enjoyed" did not include contempt cases because the right to trial by jury in contempt cases had never existed at common law. Other courts,[127] including the Louisiana court punishing Gen. Andrew Jackson for contempt, reached a comparable result.[128]

f. Due Process

The *Crow* case appears to be the only contempt case confronted with a claim that the summary nature of contempt violated the state due process clause. Citing *Cooley*,[129] the court rejected out of hand the due process claim, noting blandly that the defendant "has had his day in court."[130]

In brief, the judicial contempt power in the states, as in the federal courts, flourished unrestrained by federal or state constitutional or statutory guaranties for 150 years. During this lengthy period before federal constitutional intervention when state law reigned supreme in this area, there does not appear to be a single state decision that imposed constitutional limitations based on its state Constitution on the exercise of the judicial contempt power.

---

124 State *ex rel.* Crow v. Shepherd, 177 Mo. 205, 253, 76 S.W. 79, 94 (1903).

125 ICC v. Brimson, 154 U.S. 447 (1894); Ellenbecher v. District Ct., 134 U.S. 31 (1890). *See also In re* Fellerman, 149 F. 244 (2d Cir. 1906).

126 State v. Morrill, 16 Ark. 384, 400, 1855 Ark. LEXIS 73, *28 (1855).

127 *E.g.*, State *ex rel.* Crow v. Shepherd, 177 Mo. 205, 242, 76 S.W. 79 (1903); McDougall v. Sheridan, 23 Idaho 191, 128 P. 954 (1913).

128 *See* Deutsch, note 50, at 296, 303 (1942). There is no official report of the *Jackson* case, but Deutsch states that the record in the court's docket (Proc. No. 791) contains minute entries citing counsel's plea resting on the Sixth Amendment.

129 State *ex rel.* Crow v. Shepherd, 177 Mo. 205, 244, 76 S.W. 79, 89–90 (1903); Thomas Cooley, note 123, at 431.

130 McDougall v. Sheridan, 23 Idaho 191, 128 P. 954 (1913) (holding that trial by jury not required to satisfy due process).

The inapplicability of constitutional guaranties to the exercise of the contempt powers of the state judges then came to an end with the expansion by
the U.S. Supreme Court of the applicability of *federal* constitutional guaranties of freedom of speech and press to the states. In *Gitlow* in 1925 and in
Bridges v. California, Pennekamp v. Florida, and *Craig v. Harney*[131] in 1945
and thereafter, the Supreme Court severely narrowed the constitutional area
for the exercise of judicial contempt of American courts – state as well as federal – by subjecting judicial contempt to the strict constitutional limitations
of the freedom of speech and press clause of the federal Constitution, including the "clear and present danger" test. As a practical matter, this meant that
the courts could no longer punish out-of-court critical publications, however
abusive, through their contempt power, barring only the most exceptional
cases meeting the very demanding "clear and present danger" standard. With
such an effective barrier now available to defense counsel, the need to invoke
the application of constitutional trial by jury or due process clauses to restrict
the use of the contempt power has also come to an end as a practical matter.
These are now dead issues.

*g. State Law in Conflict: Was Contempt Available After the Case Had Come
to an End?*
While the federal courts were struggling for more than a century over the scope
of their contempt powers in the light of the 1831 Act, the state courts were
experiencing their own difficulties in developing a coherent jurisprudence
in this area.

The state common-law doctrines pertaining to the judicial contempt power
were well established. State courts without exception agreed that they had
inherent power to use the contempt power to impose criminal punishment of
critical speech or publications intended to interfere with the administration of
justice. This was the accepted principle, applying to speech and publications
out of court as well as to speech and publications in or about the court or the
courthouse.[132]

The only issue that concerned the state courts on the scope of the contempt
power was whether they could act under their inherent common-law powers
to punish contempts in cases that were no longer pending. On this, they
were very badly divided. When a case had been finally decided and concern

---

[131] Gitlow v. People, 268 U.S. 652 (1925); Bridges v. California, 314 U.S. 252 (1941); Pennekamp v.
   Florida, 328 U.S. 331 (1946); Craig v. Harney, 331 U.S. 367 (1947).
[132] *See* decisions collected *supra* in notes 110 and 119.

that the out-of-court publication could influence a pending decision was no longer present, the courts could not agree whether the remedy was available at all. The conflict between these two camps arose from a disagreement on the fundamental objective of the contempt power. Did the doctrine rest on the need of a court to protect itself and its process against publications that might influence the outcome? The basis for contempt resting on this objective ended when the cause had come to an end. On the other hand, did the contempt power also rest on the need to protect the reputation of the courts and the judicial system, and their credibility, and prevent the undermining of their public support? If so, it would be as necessary after the cause ended as before.

Most state courts held that the judicial contempt power over out-of-court publications existed only so long the case was pending. Once the cause was finally concluded, these courts[133] reasoned that the contempt power no longer existed when the possibility that the out-of-court publication could influence the outcome of the proceedings and thereby affect the administration of justice came to an end.[134]

This has been described as the American rule. Thus, in *Ex Parte* Green, the Texas court stated:

> the rule announced in the great majority of cases, and it may be considered the American doctrine, is, that no matter how defamatory of the court or judge, a publication may be, it can not be regarded as a contempt of court unless it is written and published with reference to a case then pending before the court.[135]

In addition to the numerous cases sharing this conclusion, it is striking how courts in still other cases upholding the contempt power over out-of-court publications in cases that were still pending emphasized the pending

[133] *Ex Parte* Barry, 85 Cal. 603 (1890); Storey v. People, 79 Ill. 45 (1875); *Ex Parte* Anderson & Canfield, 34 Chicago Legal News 132 (Dec. 7, 1901, Ill. Cir. Ct.), *cited in* Note Contempt – Libelous Publication after Decision Rendered, 7 Va. L. Reg. 652 (1901); Cheadle v. State, 110 Ind. 301 (1887); Zuver v. State, 188 Ind. 60, 121 N.E. 828 (1919); State v. Anderson, 40 Iowa 207, 1875 Iowa Sup. LEXIS 9 (1875); State *ex rel.* Grice v. District Court, 37 Mont. 590, 97 P. 1032 (1908); Rosewater v. State, 47 Neb. 630 (1896); Dugan v. State, 34 Ohio Cir. Ct. (NS) 42 (1915); State v. Kiser, 20 Ore. 50 (1890); Bayard v. Passmore, 3 Yeates 438 (Pa. 1802); *In re* Cottingham, 182 P. 2 (Pa. 1919); Ex Parte Green, 46 Tex. Crim. 576, 81 S.W. 723 (1904). *See In re* Sturoc, 48 N.H. 428 (1869).

[134] The unavailability of contempt did not mean that the defendant would escape punishment. The out-of-court publication might constitute a criminal libel, but such a proceeding would afford the defendant all the protections of the criminal law.

[135] *Ex Parte* Green, 46 Tex. Crim. 576, 581, 81 S.W. 723, 725–726 (1904).

nature of the case before them.[136] Although this can be read as a demonstration of their acceptance of the general principle, it may alternatively be no more than an acknowledgment that the instant case did not present this complexity.

Similarly in his *Commentaries*, Blackstone is careful to include "in pending cases" in his description of the judicial contempt power in the English common law.[137] Other commentators do the same.[138] Still other commentators go further and assert directly that the contempt power in the particular case comes to an end once the matter is no longer pending.[139]

However, these conclusions were not universally accepted. The state courts were, in fact, badly divided. Notwithstanding the substantial judicial and academic authority upholding the so-called American rule,[140] the American experience was not that clear. Numerous jurisdictions, including courts in Arkansas, Georgia, Michigan, Missouri, North Carolina, Vermont, and Virginia,[141] rejected the so-called American Rule. Instead, they held that whether or not the matter in question had ended and whether or not the remarks or publication were in the presence of the court, the courts retained the power to impose punishment under their inherent contempt powers. In their view, contumacious speech or press attacking the reputation, conduct, or integrity of the court and the judicial system constituted an interference with the administration of justice and, accordingly, was subject to the contempt power.

In effect, there was no "American rule." The courts of the country were sharply divided, with only a few more states holding that the contempt power was no longer available when the cause had come to an end than those holding to the contrary. It may be of interest that Sir John Fox in his classic

---

[136] *See, e.g.,* Globe Newspaper Co. v. Commonwealth, 188 Mass. 449, 449–450, 74 N.E. 682, 683 (1905).

[137] *See* 4 Blackstone, note 3, at 286.

[138] *See, e.g.,* Joel P. Bishop, *Bishop on Criminal Law* §216 (9th ed., John Zane and Carl Zollman ed. 1923).

[139] *See e.g.,* 7 Am. & Eng. Encyc. of Law 59 (2d ed.). ("A slanderous and libelous publication concerning the judge in relation to an act already done, or a decision rendered, cannot be punished by the court as contempt. However criminal the publication may be, it lacks that necessary ingredient to contempt of tending to prejudice the cause, or impede its progress when it relates to a matter that is no longer pending.")

[140] *See* notes 133 and 134.

[141] *E.g.,* McDougall v. Sheridan, 23 Idaho 191, 221, 128 P. 954 (1913); *In re* Chadwick, 109 Mich. 588, 67 N.W. 1071 (1896); State v. Hildreth, 82 Vt. 382, 74 A. 71 (1909); State *ex rel.* Crow v. Shepherd, 177 Mo. 205, 76 S.W. 79 (1903); Burdett v. Commonwealth, 103 Va. 838, 48 S.E. 878 (1904); Commonwealth v. Dandridge, 4 Va. 408; 1824 Va. LEXIS 59 (1824); State v. Morrill, 16 Ark. 384, 1855 Ark. LEXIS 73(1855); *In re* Fite, 11 Ga. App. 665, 76 S.E. 397 (1912). *See* Note, Contempt, note 114, at 467–471.

study of contempt refers to two 20th-century English cases upholding contempt in cases that had been finally determined because the contumacious speech is "an obstruction to justice generally."[142] For a comparative American dimension, he refers to the similar decisions in *Morrill* and *Crow*.

In all the cases considering the problem, whatever their outcome on the critical issue, there appears to be little discussion or controversy addressing the threshold issue: At what point does a proceeding cease to be still pending? The courts seem to have generally acted on the principle that, for purposes of contempt, a case may be said to be pending so long as a court still has jurisdiction and is able to take some action with respect to it. Under such circumstances, the critical speech or publication may conceivably influence the action and thus interfere with the administration of justice. Thus, a matter may have been "decided" in the court of last resort with the opinion published. However, it still may still be said to be "pending" so long as the court retains the power to grant a motion for reargument or rehearing or even to modify its opinion.[143]

There was no suggestion in any case during this period that the freedom of speech provisions in the state Constitutions might provide outer limits on the exercise of the contempt power of the state courts. Similarly, not until well into the middle of the 20th century, did the expansion of federal constitutional powers change the law of the previous 150 years and apply the principles of the Bill of Rights, including the First Amendment, to the states. During this period, which did not end until after World War II, state law with respect to the judicial contempt power was supreme.

After *Gitlow* decided in 1925 that the Fourteenth Amendment rendered the states subject to the limitations of the First Amendment, state court use of the contempt power had to comply not only with state constitutional and statutory provisions and judge-made law, it now had to pass federal constitutional scrutiny as well. However, it took about 20 years before the first case testing the extent of federal constitutional limitations of the contempt powers of state judges reached the Supreme Court. The next section reviews the evolution of the *federal* constitutional jurisprudence and its eventual transformation of the American law of judicial contempts.

---

[142] Reg. v. Gray, [1900] 2 Q.B. 36 (1900); Rex v. Vidal, [1922] Times (Oct. 14, 1922). *See* Fox, note 1, at 32–33; 218–220, *citing State v. Morrill* and *Commonwealth v. Dandridge*, two of the American decisions upholding the use of contempt in settled causes.

[143] E.g., McDougall v. Sheridan, 23 Idaho 191, 221, 128 P. 954 (1913); State v. Faulds, 17 Mont. 140, 42 P. 285 (1895) (pending until remittitur issued); *In re* Tugwell, 19 Wash. 238, 52 P. 1056 (1878). *See* Sullivan, note 1, at 35.

4. Federal Constitutional Limits of the Contempt Power of State Judges

The U.S. Supreme Court did not address the constitutional limitations of the contempt power until its 1907 decision in *Patterson v. Colorado*.[144] In *Patterson*, arising under Colorado law, the Supreme Court of Colorado had held the publisher of a major newspaper in contempt. The publisher had published several articles and a cartoon allegedly reflecting on the motives and conduct of the Colorado Supreme Court in cases still pending[145] and intended to embarrass the Court in the impartial administration of justice. The defendants had unsuccessfully moved to quash, contending the action was unconstitutional under the state Constitution and the Fourteenth Amendment of the federal constitution.[146]

The Supreme Court affirmed. Justice Holmes, writing for the Court, made it clear that the Court was leaving "undecided the question whether there is to be found in the Fourteenth Amendment a prohibition similar to that in the First." However, he ruled that even if one assumed that freedom of speech and press were protected from abridgment on the part of the states as well as the United States, it would not support the defendants. As previously noted, he then went on to construe the constitutional provision to protect only against previous restraints.[147] This, of course, was pure Blackstone, whom Holmes cited along with the well-known *Oswald* case in Pennsylvania and the decision of the Supreme Judicial Court of Massachusetts in *Commonwealth v. Blanding*.[148]

[144] Patterson v. Colorado, 205 U.S. 454 (1907) (Holmes, J.).

[145] The defendants had unsuccessfully contended that because the case had been decided, it should no longer be regarded as still pending even though the time for filing a motion for rehearing had not yet expired.

[146] This was almost two decades before the decision in Gitlow v. People, 268 U.S. 652 (1925) holding for the first time that the First Amendment was binding on the states through the Fourteenth Amendment. Counsel in *Patterson* chose not to enter into that thicket and relied on the Fourteenth Amendment alone.

[147] 205 U.S. at 462. Rabban states that in subsequent correspondence in 1922 with Zechariah Chafee, Holmes acknowledged that in *Patterson* "I had taken Blackstone and Parker of Mass.[author of *Blanding*] as unrefuted, wrongly. I was simply ignorant." *See* Rabban, The Emergence of Modern First Amendment Doctrine, 50 U. Chi. L. Rev 1207, 1265–1266 (1983).

In *Schenck v. United States*, decided in 1919, Holmes had only gone as far as to state: "It may well be that the prohibition of laws abridging the freedom of speech is not confined to previous restraints, although to prevent them may have been its main purpose, as intimated in *Patterson*." 249 U.S. 47, 51–52 (1919). A few months later, in *Abrams v. United States*, Holmes' thinking had advanced. He stated: "I wholly disagree . . . that the First Amendment left the common law as to seditious libel in force. History seems to me against the notion." 250 U.S. 616 at 630 (1919).

[148] 4 Blackstone, note 3, at 150; Respublica v. Oswald, 1 U.S. (1 Dallas) 319, 325 (1788); Commonwealth v. Blanding, 20 Mass. (3 Pick.) 304, 313–314 (1825).

There matters stood for almost 35 years. After the Court had at last resolved the *statutory construction* issue of the Act of 1831 in its decision in *Nye*, the Court soon definitively decided the *constitutional* issue as well.[149]

In three decisions over the next five years, the Court delineated the constitutional dimensions of proceedings for contempt in three cases involving the constitutional validity of the exercise of contempt by state judges: *Bridges v. California*,[150] *Pennekamp v. Florida*,[151] and *Craig v. Harney*.[152]

In each, the Court invoked federal constitutional principles to reverse decisions by the Supreme Courts of California, Florida, and Texas upholding the use of the contempt power by lower court state judges. Because these all concerned state court judges, the Act of 1831 was irrelevant. The issue was constitutional: whether state courts had the constitutional power under the First Amendment (binding on the states under the Fourteenth Amendment) to punish journalists for articles and editorials criticizing the Court's decisions in pending matters.[153]

Bridges v. California involved the conviction of a newspaper and the radical labor leader Harry Bridges for contempt for statements out of court with respect to pending litigation. The newspaper articles had criticized the actions of the court, and Bridges had threatened a strike. Ruling for the first time on the constitutional dimensions of contempt, the Supreme Court by a vote of 5 to 4 concluded that the citations for contempt were unconstitutional under the First Amendment made applicable to the states by the Fourteenth Amendment.

The Court set aside the contempt orders because of a failure of proof that they met the "clear and present danger" standard. Justice Black, speaking for the majority, went on to add that the "clear and present danger" standard is "a working principle that the substantive evil must be extremely serious and the degree of imminence extremely high before utterances can be punished.[154]

As for the Court's decision in *Patterson*, which had been written by Justice Holmes, Justice Black merely noted that Holmes had made it clear that the decision "cannot not be taken as a decision squarely on this point." He pointed to Holmes's caution that the Court was leaving the constitutional question

---

[149] *See generally*, Goldfarb, note 1, at 89–100.
[150] Bridges v. California, 314 U.S. 252 (1941).
[151] Pennekamp v. Florida, 328 U.S. 331 (1946).
[152] Craig v. Hornay, 331 U.S. 367 (1947).
[153] In *Bridges* and *Craig*, the matters were pending before a judge. In *Pennekamp*, matters were pending before a jury.
[154] Bridges v. California, 314 U.S. 252, 263 (1941).

undecided. As for Holmes's Blackstonian dictum limiting the constitutional protection of freedom of speech and press to a prohibition of prior restraints, Black simply buried it in silence.

The Court was badly divided. Justice Frankfurter speaking for the minority, which included Chief Justice Stone and Justices Roberts and Byrnes, strongly dissented. Although cast in the language of federalism and the rights of the states, Frankfurter's underlying concern was with what he saw as the overriding importance of the judicial contempt power as a means of assuring the "administration of justice by an impartial judiciary" in pending cases. In the majority opinion, Justice Black was speaking in absolutist terms, as was not uncommon in his First Amendment opinions. He did not discuss the significance of the pending nature of the case in striking down the district judge's contempt citation.

Although expressing allegiance to the importance of free discussion and criticism of the courts, Justice Frankfurter, nevertheless, saw the comments by the leading paper in Los Angeles about the appropriate sentence in a matter of great public interest as "coercive interference" with a pending matter. The most powerful newspaper in the area had admonished the judge that a mild sentence for Bridges would be "a serious matter." With the judge facing reelection within the year, such a comment was unmistakably an attempt to influence the judge's decision. Frankfurter, accordingly, contended:

> We cannot say that the state court was out of bounds in concluding that such conduct offends the true course of justice. Comment after the imposition of sentence – criticism, however unrestrained, of its severity or lenience or disparity [English citation omitted] is an exercise of the right of free discussion. But to deny the states power to check a serious attempt at dictating from without, the sentence to be imposed *in a pending case*, is to deny the right to impartial justice. . . . [155]

It is of interest that Justice Frankfurter did not discuss whether in the federal courts parties were being "den[ied] the right to impartial justice" by the provisions of the Act of 1831 construed in *Nye v. United States* to bar the use of the contempt power in the very same type of case as *Bridges*.

Shortly after *Bridges*, the Court decided two more contempt cases: *Pennekamp v. Florida* and *Craig v. Harney*.[156] The issue once again was whether state courts had the constitutional power under the First Amendment to punish journalists for newspaper articles and editorials criticizing the court's

---

[155] 314 U.S. at 300. Emphasis added.
[156] Pennekamp v. Florida, 328 U.S. 331 (1946); Craig v. Harney, 331 U.S. 367, 376 (1947).

conduct or decisions in pending matters. In both cases, the Court turned to its decision in *Bridges v. California* for the guiding principle. In each, the Court reversed the lower court decisions upholding the use of the contempt power because of their failure to comply with the standard introduced by *Bridges*. Under the First Amendment, courts were barred from attempting to punish contumacious speech or publications as contempt even in pending cases in the absence of a showing that the utterances created a "clear and present danger" to the administration of justice. In *Craig v. Harney*, Justice Douglas emphasized: "The fires which [the language] kindles must constitute an imminent, not merely a likely threat to the administration of justice. The danger must not be remote or even probable; it must immediately imperil."[157] Justice Frankfurter, dissenting, persisted in his view that the historic powers of courts to protect the administration of justice was of paramount importance to which freedom of speech, as important as it was, had to yield.[158]

Frankfurter took the Court's rejection of his view on the primacy of the contempt power very hard. Several years later in *Shepherd v. Florida*, he and Justice Jackson took the remarkable step of writing a separate opinion concurring in the Court's unanimous *per curiam* reversal, lamenting: "The Court has recently gone a long way to disable a trial judge from dealing with press interference with the trial process," citing *Craig, Pennekamp*, and *Bridges*.[159]

In addition in *Craig*, Justice Douglas again speaking for the Court repeated that *Nye* had disapproved the rule of *Toledo Newspaper Co.* that "comment on a pending case in a federal court was punishable by contempt if it had a 'reasonable tendency' to obstruct the administration of justice." This also was now dead. In the light of the Court's decision involving the extreme limitation of the contempt power in pending cases, it became all the more clear that except when the allegedly contemptuous conduct occurred in or "nearby" the court room, punishment by the contempt power would rarely, if ever, survive.

As for cases that were no longer pending, it was all the more clear that the contempt power was subject to the constitutional limitation. In the light

---

[157] Craig v. Harney, 331 U.S. 367, 376 (1947).

[158] Pennekamp v. Florida, 328 U.S. 331, 350, 354–355 (1946) (Frankfurter, J., dissenting) ("Without a free press, there can be no free society. Freedom of the press, however, is not an end in itself but a means to the end of a free society"); Craig v. Harney, 331 U.S. 367, 384) (1947) (Frankfurter, J. dissenting).

[159] Shepherd v. Florida, 341 U.S. 50, 52 (1951) (*per curiam*) (Frankfurter, J. concurring), *Shepherd* involved four black men sentenced to death for rape of a 17-year-old white girl in an atmosphere of mob violence. The Court's opinion was four words: "The judgment is reversed."

of the Court's decisions establishing a severe restriction on the exercise of the contempt power by requiring compliance with the "clear and present danger" standard even in pending cases, it became all the more clear that the contempt power did not apply to cases that were no longer before the court.

Writing 60 years earlier in *Patterson v. Colorado*, Justice Holmes had recognized the inevitability of such a rule with respect to cases no longer before the court. Thus, speaking in 1907 for the Court in *Patterson*, Holmes first decided the issue before the Court and enunciated what was then the constitutional standard for contempt in pending cases. He then added in dictum: "When a case is finished, courts are subject to the same criticism as other people."[160]

Even Justice Frankfurter conceded the point. Thus, in his dissent in *Bridges*, he agreed: "The litigation must be immediately pending."[161] Similarly, it is not without interest that Justice Frankfurter in *Pennekamp* noted that whatever the technicalities, the litigation was no longer "actively pending."[162]

Thus, after repeated review of the matter over a period of 150 years, the statutory limitations under the 1831 Act and the constitutional limits on the federal judicial contempt power were at last determined. In this manner, the near-unrestrained power of the judiciary to criminalize out-of-chamber speech critical of a judge or the courts that had been available for more than a half century after the Revolution was sharply circumscribed, if not eliminated entirely as a practical matter. In all the courts of the country – federal and state – the offending speech must pertain to a pending cause and must present a "clear and present danger" to the administration of justice of an "extremely serious substantive evil" of which the degree of imminence was extremely high." In addition, in the federal courts and many state courts, the offending speech must be in the presence of the court or "nearby" in the geographical sense.

In sum, starting with the classic Pennsylvania decision in *Oswald* in 1788, the cases – state and federal – frequently involved clashes between newspapers

---

[160] Patterson v. Colorado, 205 U.S. 454, 463 (1907).

[161] 314 U.S. at 303–304.

[162] 328 U.S. at 369. Justice Reed in the opinion of the Court described the cases as "then pending." 328 U.S. at 333. The case involved the judge's decision to quash certain indictments in a rape case. The grand jury promptly reindicted the defendants, and in its findings in the contempt matter, the trial court found that the reindictments were then pending. In his assignment of error, counsel for the defendant newpaper challenged the ruling that the matters in the offending editorials were pending. The Supreme Court of Florida ruled that the cases were pending, while noting that under "the general rule" and the Florida statute, "publications about a case that is closed, no matter how scandalous, are not punishable as contempt." 156 Fla. 227, 241, 22 So. 2d 875 (1945); Fla. Stat. 1941 §§38.23, 932.04; *cited in* Pennekamp v. Florida, 328 U.S. 331, 342 (1945).

and their editors reporting or making editorial comment on the events in court and the judges. Fundamental interests of the courts and the press were in deep conflict[163] and make American jurisprudence in this area a subject of profound interest. However, as we have seen, not until well into the 20th century did a divided U.S. Supreme Court finally conclude that the values associated with the constitutional assurances of free speech and a free press outweighed those concerned with the reputation and credibility of the judicial system insofar as the contempt power was concerned.

This review of the state and federal judicial contempt power over out-of-court publications is, of course, today mostly of historical interest. With the evolution of the federal constitutional doctrine, as we have seen, the application of the state, as well as federal, judicial contempt power to out-of-court publications has vanished as a practical matter. Under the newer jurisprudence, contempt may be applied only in the very unusual case where the publication presented a "clear and present danger" threatening the obstruction of the administration of justice. Punishment of false and malicious attacks on judges is still possible, but only through the institution of traditional libel remedies.

With these decisions, no federal constitutional or statutory issue with respect to the application of the judicial contempt power remains.[164] The evolution of the federal doctrine appears to have come to an end as a matter of jurisprudence.

C. Criminal Contempt of the Legislature

1. The English and Colonial Inheritance

Inherited from English law and Colonial experience, still another area of jurisprudential repression of the press in the Early American Republic was

---

[163] E.g., State v. Morrill, 16 Ark. 384, 1855 Ark. LEXIS 73 (1855); McDougall v. Sheridan, Broxon, & Cruzen, 23 Idaho 191, 128 P. 954 (1913); People v. Wilson, 64 Ill. 195, 1872 Ill. LEXIS 256 (1872); Stuart v. Illinois, 4 Ill. 395, 1842 Ill. LEXIS 18 (1842); Telegram Newspaper Co. v. Commonwealth, 172 Mass. 294, 52 N.E. 445 (1899); Ex Parte Hickey, 12 Miss. 751, 1840 Miss. LEXIS 104 (1840); Missouri v. Shepherd, 177 Mo. 205, 76 S.W. 79 (1903); In re Sturoc, 48 N.H. 428, 1869 N.H. LEXIS 55 (1869); People v. Freer, 1 Cai. R. 518, 1804 N.Y. LEXIS 200 (1804); Respublica v. Oswald, 1 U.S. (1 Dallas) 319 (Sup. Ct. Pa. 1788); Burdett v. Commonwealth, 103 Va. 838, 48 S.E. 878 (1904); West Virginia v. Frew & Hart, 24 W.Va. 416, 1884 W. Va. LEXIS 72 (1884). See State v. Magee Pub. Co., 29 N.M. 455, 224 P. 1028 (1924).

[164] As noted, there is still an unresolved issue with respect to the use of the professional code governing lawyers to punish out-of-court publications criticizing judges. See Tresa Baldas, Bloggers Pay Price for Criticizing Judges, Conn. L. Trib., Mar. 2, 2009, at 5.

the accepted doctrine of legislative contempt, including so-called breach of privilege, punishing critical speech and publications out of the legislative chamber.[165] Similar in purpose and effect to criminal libel for political speech and criminal contempt for out-of-court critical publications, the doctrine of contempt of the legislature[166] protected still another branch of the government. Furthermore, like contempt of court, it provided an avenue for criminal punishment that sidestepped the protective features of the criminal law, such as the participation of grand and petit juries.

Under the English common law, the Parliament and its members were protected in numerous respects. The Parliament's power of contempt to punish persons interfering with the Legislature's conduct of its affairs or the capability of its members to discharge their duties extended well beyond disobedience to the legislative orders and the members' freedom from molestation during the legislative sessions, such as arrest or assault or affront. It extended to freedom from insults and libels, the area of our particular concern. The power of the Legislature to use its common-law power of contempt to punish out-of-chamber critical comments and publications was uniformly recognized.[167]

With the doctrine of criminal contempt of the Parliament accepted as a part of the common law in the English jurisprudence,[168] whatever the explanation for its origin and development may be, it became an important part of Colonial law as well. As we have seen, with the increasing tension arising between the Crown's Colonial government and the rising Patriot movement, the Crown found that it could not rely any longer on prosecution for criminal libel as the legal instrument to criminalize dissent. As early as 1735 with the *Zenger* case,[169] it had become apparent that Patriot juries would not convict persons publishing attacks condemning the Crown or its policies. Under these circumstances, Crown lawyers were forced to rely on

---

[165] *See generally* Potts, Power of Legislative Bodies to Punish for Contempt, 74 U. Pa. L. Rev. 691 (1926) (hereinafter Potts).

[166] References to "contempt of the legislature" should be read to include "breach of privilege" as well.

[167] *See* Potts, note 165, at 703.

[168] Although all scholars agreed on the existence of Parliament's power to punish for contempt, there is disagreement on whether it is derived from the view that Parliament is a form of court or whether it exists as an inherent attribute of a legislature essential for its proper functioning. Further, there is disagreement on whether or not the Parliamentary experience is indeed relevant. Justice Miller in *Kilbourn v. Thompson*, 103 U.S. 168, 184, 189 (1880), for example, found it irrelevant. *See* Potts, note 165, at 692. This is of only academic interest because it is agreed that the power exists, supported as an inherent power, if not by its historical roots.

[169] Zenger's Case, 17 Howell's *State Trials* 626 (1735).

such doctrines as contempt of the Royal Colonial councils and assemblies to muzzle Patriot critics.[170]

The outstanding example of the use of legislative contempt to punish Patriot opinion before the Revolution was the *McDougall* affair. This was the jailing of Alexander McDougall, a prominent Patriot before the Revolution and a military hero during the Revolutionary War. As reported by Jeffery Alan Smith, a broadside had charged that the New York General Assembly had betrayed the colony in voting supplies for British troops stationed in New York. When a witness identified McDougall as the one responsible, he was charged with criminal libel, indicted in April 1770, and jailed. When the witness died, the Assembly was no longer able to support the charge of criminal libel, and it was dropped. Instead, McDougall was then cited for contempt of the Assembly for conduct characterized as a "scandalous Reflection on the Conduct, Honor, and Dignity of this House." McDougall was again arrested and remained in jail for 81 days until the Assembly ended its session in March 1771.[171]

Similarly, in 1757 the Pennsylvania Assembly took affront at an assertion by a man named Moore that the Quaker Party had fraudulently procured the election of his opponent to the Assembly and condemned the publication. When Moore persisted, the Assembly punished him with imprisonment for "breach of privilege." After his release, he was later involved in another series of comments about the Assembly. The Assembly ordered Moore's rearrest, but he had fled the area.[172]

Jeffrey Alan Smith reports that before the Revolution, at least 20 persons were brought before one house or another of the Colonial legislatures because of their publications and that journalists were occasionally jailed for contempt.[173] In Potts's review of the early history of contempt of the legislature in the Colonies and the New Republic, he, too, reports several instances of contempt proceedings involving out-of-chamber critical publications about

---

[170] *See*, e.g., Harold L. Nelson, Criminal Libel in Colonial America, 3 Am. J. Legal. Hist. 160 (1959) (hereinafter Nelson); Jeffery A. Smith, A Reappraisal of Legislative Privilege and American Colonial Journalism, 61 Journalism Quar. 97 (1984) (hereinafter J. A. Smith, Legislative Privilege).

[171] *See* Potts note 165, at 705; J. A. Smith, Legislative Privilege, note 170, at 144–45; Nelson, note 170, at 169–70; Leonard W. Levy, *Emergence of a Free Press* 76–81 (1985).

McDougall was a Patriot, not an editor devoted to freedom of the press. Five years later, he led a band of armed men to destroy the press of a New York Tory printer, James Rivington. *See* J. Lofton, *The Press as Guardian of the First Amendment* 5 (1980).

During the Revolutionary War, McDougall rose to the rank of Major General. Washington demonstrated his great confidence in McDougall by assigning him command of West Point after Arnold's treachery and unsuccessful attempt to surrender the fortress to the British.

[172] Linenthal, note 1, ch. 2, at 64.

[173] J. A. Smith, Legislative Privilege, note 170, at 98, 144–45.

the legislature or members. In addition, there were even more cases in which the Colonial legislatures exercised their contempt power to punish various types of contumacious behavior, including disregard of legislative orders, bribery of legislators, and assaults and affronts against legislators.[174]

Thus, as a jurisprudential matter, the inherent power of the legislature to punish for contempt was well established in Colonial America. However, as a practical matter, the impact of the doctrine was limited. The instances of its application were limited and episodic, hotly resisted by printers and Patriot elements of the population, and generally ineffective. Thus, Smith concludes that exercise of the legislative contempt power was, in fact, "typically capricious, confused, and futile"[175] or "sporadic, inconsistent, and largely ineffectual."[176] Similarly, Buel brushes aside the entire area, asserting flatly that Colonial legislatures seldom exercised their power to punish for breach of privilege. However, these authors and historians generally have conceded that, as a matter of legal doctrine, there was general acceptance of the power[177] and have attributed its limited effectiveness to the turbulent political climate and the strong popular opposition to the Crown.[178]

Writing in 1833, Justice Story had no doubt about the matter. Speaking of the common-law contempt powers of Colonial Assemblies (and inferentially of state legislatures by reason of the reception statutes), he wrote in his *Commentary*: "No man ever doubted, or denied its existence, as to our colonial assemblies in general, whatever may have been thought, as to particular exercises of it."[179]

After Independence, the doctrine of legislative contempt established during the Colonial Era became part of the law of the new states. The common-law doctrine of the contempt powers of the legislature was still another part of the legal inheritance from English law and the Colonial experience that provided the legislatures in the new states with still another powerful legal weapon for the suppression of dissenting speech.[180] Eleven of the new states went further and enacted statutes reinforcing the common-law legislative powers to punish contumacious conduct or speech as constituting a criminal

---

[174] *See* Potts, note 165, at 715.

[175] J. A. Smith, Legislative Privilege, note 170, at 83–84.

[176] *Ibid.*, at 103.

[177] *See also* Linenthal, note 1, at ch. 2.

[178] Richard Buel, Jr., Freedom of the Press in Revolutionary America: The Evolution of Libertarianism, 1760–1860 in *The Press & the American Revolution* 59, 75 (Bernard Bailyn and John Hench eds. 1980).

[179] *See* Joseph Story, 3 *Commentaries on the Constitution of the United States* 306–307 (1833 repr. 1970) (hereinafter Story, *Commentaries*).

[180] *See* Jurney v. MacCracken, 294 U.S. 125, 148–149 (1935) (Brandeis, J.); Potts, note 165, at 780.

contempt of the legislature. Two of these – Maryland and Massachusetts – acted before the adoption of the federal Constitution.[181] In the federal system, the Congress had similar inherent contempt powers.

The doctrine rested on pragmatic consideration The legislative contempt power was seen as essential to enable the state legislatures and the new Congress, too, to perform their constitutional duties. However effectively this consideration may have served as a justification for the punishment of obtrusive contumacious conduct, such as a refusal to respond to lawful congressional directions with respect to such matters as appearance, answering questions, or producing documents, it still left open the question of the justification for the punishment of out-of-chamber critical publications. That aspect of the doctrine rested on the English Parliamentary tradition that contempt of the legislature also included the defense of parliamentary "privileges," which extended to the capacity to punish any "clear violation of the undoubted right of the assembly to be treated with dignity," extending even to out-of-chamber publications.[182]

Although this historical development may provide an explanation why the power to punish for contempt power or "breach of privilege" came to be regarded as an inherent power of the Parliament, it does not provide a satisfying jurisprudential basis for the power in the face of constitutional guaranties of free speech and press where critical political speech is concerned. May offensive out-of-chamber criticism really be said to obstruct the legislature's ability to perform its constitutional functions?

2. The Federal Experience

With the Revolution and the accompanying reception statutes, this repressive English doctrine, along with comparable repressive doctrines such as criminal libel, contempt of court for out-of-court speech, and blasphemy, became part of the American legal structure. As with the question of the scope of judicial power to punish for out-of-court critical speech, definitive judicial determination of all the issues presented by three doctrines in the jurisprudence of the New Republic – the interrelationships of the constitutional protections of freedom of speech and press, state as well as federal, the fundamental doctrine of separation of powers, and the historic common-law recognition of

---

[181] See Marshall v. Gordon, 243 U.S. 521, 534–535 (1917).

[182] See C. Beck, Contempt of Congress, 2–3 (1959) (hereinafter Beck). See also G. Campion, *Introduction to the Procedure of the House of Commons* 73 (2d ed. rev. 1950); M. Clarke, *Parliamentary Privilege in the American Colonies* 206 (1943).

the legislative power to punish for out-of-chamber criticism – took more than a century. The Supreme Court was confronted by no fewer than five cases involving the contempt powers of the houses of the Congress before it finally determined the outer constitutional perimeters of the doctrine. This section reviews the history of this protracted development.

The federal Constitution has a series of provisions dealing with the powers, rights, and duties of each house of the Congress, including provisions dealing with the punishment, and even the expulsion, of members. However, as Justice Story commented, "It is remarkable, that no power is conferred for any contempts committed against either house." Story adds: "yet it is obvious, that, unless such a power, to some extent, exists by implication, it is utterly impossible for either house to perform its constitutional functions."[183]

a. The First Quarter Century of the Early Republic

As early as 1795, the House of Representatives in the new Congress moved to exercise its contempt powers. Robert Randall was charged with the attempted bribery of a member of the House. After a trial in which Randall had had the right of counsel and an opportunity to prepare his defense, he was found guilty for attempted bribery of members of the House and incarcerated briefly.[184]

As we have seen, William Duane, the unbridled editor of the arch Republican Philadelphia *Aurora*, was one of the most unrestrained journalists in the Adams and Jefferson administrations. His slashing criticism of Federalist conduct provoked repeated Federalist efforts to muzzle him through prosecutions for criminal libel and for contempt of court for out-of-court publications.[185] The Federalists did not rely on these doctrines alone. They also invoked the doctrine of contempt of the legislature in their attempts to silence him. This continuing struggle between Duane and the Federalist Government led to the first attempt in the New Republic by the controlling party in the New Congress to respond to partisan considerations by resorting to the use of the doctrine of contempt of the legislature to silence out-of-chamber criticism by a political opponents.

Duane ran afoul of the Federalist Senate early in 1800 as the country was advancing to the crucial presidential election. As we have seen, Sen. James Ross of Pennsylvania, a dedicated Federalist, had introduced a bill that, if enacted, could have had a profound effect on the outcome of the forthcoming election. Appropriately described by James Morton Smith as a

---

[183] *See* 2 Story, *Commentaries*, note 179, at §842.
[184] *See* Beck, note 182, at 3.
[185] *See* Ch. 4, notes 162–165.

"thoroughly vicious measure,"[186] the Bill would have transformed the process for determining the winner of the 1800 and subsequent presidential elections. It would have subordinated the Electoral College to a Committee, comprising six Senators, six Representatives, and the Chief Justice. The Committee was to meet in secret and review the Electoral College balloting for President and Vice President. It would then have the final power to determine which electoral votes to count or disallow, to throw out electoral ballots deemed illegal, and thus to determine which candidate had been elected President. This Committee determination was to be final and beyond review; there was to be no appeal.[187]

The Federalists controlling the Senate had tried to keep the contents of the Bill secret by distributing copies of the Bill only to members of the Senate. In an episode reminiscent of contemporary America, a copy was leaked to Duane. He promptly published the full text in the *Aurora* and vigorously attacked the Federalist conduct. The Senate promptly approved the appointment of a special Committee on Privileges and directed the Committee to ascertain how Duane got possession of the Bill. The Committee adopted a resolution finding him in contempt for the publication, characterizing it as "false, defamatory, scandalous, and malicious; tending to defame the Senate . . . and to bring them into contempt and disrepute."[188]

The Senate also summoned Duane to appear before it and defend his conduct in attacking the Senate and one of its committees. He appeared and requested counsel. This was approved, and Duane arranged for two prominent Republicans – Alexander James Dallas and Thomas Cooper – to represent him. However, when Duane's counsel were denied the opportunity to challenge the Senate's jurisdiction or to provide justification by demonstrating the truth of his assertions, they withdrew.

Duane thereupon wrote to Thomas Jefferson, then Vice President, that the lawyers he desired would not appear because of the restrictions on their defense and informed the Senate that he would not further attend the proceedings. On March 26, 1800, the Senate by a largely partisan vote of 16 to 12 held him guilty of contempt for violation of the *order to appear* (not the underlying libel). It approved the issuance of a warrant, duly signed by Thomas Jefferson as Vice President, for a marshal to take him into custody. However, as noted, Duane went into hiding and successfully evaded service

---

[186] James Morton Smith, *Freedom Fetters: The Alien and Sedition Laws and American Civil Liberties* 289 (1956) (hereinafter J. M. Smith).

[187] 6C Annals of the Congress, 6th Cong., 1st Sess. 124 (1800).

[188] See *supra* ch. 4, at 119–120.

by the process server until the end of the session. Failing to apprehend Duane before adjournment, the Senate was impotent. However, the Federalists also controlled the White House. Thus, just before Congress adjourned in May 1800, the Senate Federalist leadership turned to President Adams for help. It called upon him to take the necessary steps to have Duane indicted, and Adams did so. Duane was promptly indicted for a criminal libel of the Senate. However, the case did not come to trial before the 1800 election, and, after the election, the victorious Jefferson ordered the case discontinued. (This episode in the Duane story has been previously reviewed in Chapter 4 of the prosecutions under the Sedition Act.)[189]

Reviewing the judicial experience in this early period of the Republic, Story, writing in 1831, concluded that recognition of the inherent power of the legislature to punish contempts had been upheld by the highest courts in both the United States and England, citing *Anderson v. Dunn*, among other cases. He also reviewed the cases in the New Republic[190] in which the House of Representatives had punished "contempt[s] committed within the walls of the house." Although Justice Story also referred to the attempted punishment of Duane by the Senate for his out-of-chamber contemptuous publications, he does not discuss whether this very different type of contempt presented a different issue.[191]

b. The Evolution of the Doctrine in the Federal Courts

Twenty years after the *Duane* episode, a House of the Congress in 1818 was again confronted by the attempted bribery of a member and had to consider the use of its powers of contempt. A lobbyist, Col. John Anderson, representing people in Michigan, allegedly offered a $500 bribe to a Representative. A storm of outrage broke out, with the House debating for several days whether it had the inherent power to punish for contempt. After agreeing by a vote of 119 to 47 that it had the "power to arrest, examine, and punish" the offender, it conducted a trial. After hearing testimony by Gen. William Henry Harrison (later President) and others that Anderson had an "unblemished character" and "displayed during the war much courage and zeal in defense of his

---

[189] See Ch. 4, notes 172–175.

[190] In addition to the 1795 imprisonment of Randall for an attempt to corrupt a member (1 St. G. Tucker, *Blackstone's Commentaries* App. 200–205 note), these included the 1796 imprisonment of an unidentified person for challenging a member to a duel (T. Jefferson, Manual §3); Anderson v. Dunn, 19 U.S. (6 Wheat.) 204 (1821), 1821 U.S. LEXIS 358 (attempted bribery)); and the 1832 reprimand of Sam Houston for an assault upon a member for words reflecting on Houston's character. See 2 Story, *Commentaries*, note 179, at §845.

[191] See 2 Story, *Commentaries*, note 179, at §845.

country," the Speaker (Henry Clay) restricted his punishment to a reprimand and discharged him.[192]

In *Anderson v. Dunn* in 1821, the Supreme Court upheld the House's power to compel Anderson's appearance. Justice Johnson for the Court faced for the first time the question of the power of the House to apprehend a person accused of contempt. He attempted to dispose of the entire issue and confirmed the inherent power of the houses of the Congress[193] to impose criminal punishment for contempt. He explained that the power was inherent, arising from necessity: It was a matter of self-preservation.[194] Finally, Justice Johnson commented on the extent of the inherent contempt power. He suggested that it supported only "the least possible power adequate to the end proposed." He further noted that because the legislative body ceased to exist on the moment of its adjournment or "periodical dissolution," imprisonment terminated with that adjournment.[195]

It was not until a quarter century later that another contempt of the Congress case came before the federal courts. In *Ex Parte* Nugent, decided in 1848,[196] the Circuit Court for the District of Columbia, as in the *Duane* case, was concerned with the use of the contempt power for violation of the leak of the contents of a treaty. At this stage of its history, the Senate was operating under a rule that all treaties submitted to it should be kept secret until release to the public had been approved. The rule had been violated, and the Senate

---

[192] For a journalistic review of the congressional debate and action, *see* Baltimore *Patriot & Mercantile Advertiser*, Jan. 9, 1818; Boston *Gazette*, Jan. 15, 1818; *Columbian Centinel*, Jan. 21, 1818; Washington *Gazette*, Jan. 21, 1818; Boston *Weekly Messenger*, Jan. 22, 1818; *Vermont Intelligencer and Bellows Falls Advertiser*, Jan. 26, 1818; *The Star of Freedom, a Congressional & Legislative Journal*, Jan. 28, 1818; Alexandria *Herald*, Jan. 26 (1818); Newport *Mercury*, Jan. 24, 1818; *Rhode-Island American and General Advertiser*, Feb. 3, 1818.

[193] It was not until 1857 that the Congress enacted a statute dealing with the congressional contempt power, 11 Stat. 155 (1857). This dealt solely with contempt citations for contumacious conduct for failing to appear or answer questions. It provided that such offenses were misdemeanors and subject to prosecution as a statutory criminal offense. The ultimate power of adjudication moved from the Congress to the courts. However, the inherent power of the Congress to deal with contempt for out-of-chamber publications, subject to constitutional limitations, apparently remained unaffected. The Supreme Court's decision in *Marshall v. Gordon* did not suggest to the contrary. *See* Marshall v. Gordon, 243 U.S. 521 (1917). *See also* Beck, note 182, at 5–7.

[194] Anderson v. Dunn, 19 U.S. (6 Wheat.) 204 (1821).

[195] 19 U.S. at 231.

[196] *Ex Parte* Nugent, 18 F. Cas. 471 (C.C.D. D.C. 1848) (No. 10,375). Judge Cranch was not content to dispose of the case by reference to the Supreme Court pronouncements in *Anderson v. Dunn* on the congressional power of contempt and *Ex Parte* Kearney, 20 U.S. (7 Wheat.) 38 (1822) on the inappropriateness of habeas corpus as the method of review. He continued on for as many as 11 pages in the Wheaton reports to support the outcome with a lengthy review of no fewer than 16 English cases complete with lengthy quotations. Two Supreme Court decisions were apparently insufficient.

was investigating. Nugent had refused to answer a question in its inquiry, and the Senate found him in contempt. He was arrested and confined. The Circuit Court refused to release him on *habeas corpus*, holding that *habeas corpus* was not available, that the Senate and the House of Representatives had inherent power to punish by contempt and were "the sole judge of its contempts." Following *Anderson v. Dunn*, it added that no other court had "the right to inquire directly into the propriety or correctness or propriety of the commitment."[197]

Thirty years later, the Supreme Court in *Kilbourn v. Thompson* revisited this area of the law and introduced fundamental limitations in the standards enunciated by *Anderson v. Dunn* and affirmed in *Ex Parte* Nugent. The Court assumed for sake of argument that, as upheld in *Anderson*, the Senate had the inherent power to arrest and imprison a witness before a Senate committee for refusal to answer questions and produce documents. Overruling *Anderson*, the Court then held that the federal courts had both the obligation and the jurisdiction to review whether the Congress was exercising its power over a matter "beyond their legitimate cognizance" and beyond their constitutional duties. Finding on the facts that in the case before it the House was acting without authority, the Court held that its order for arrest of Kilbourn was void. It, accordingly, ruled that Kilbourn's suit for false imprisonment would lie.[198]

Three decades later in *Marshall v. Gordon* (1916), the Supreme Court for the first time dealt with the use of the congressional contempt power to punish critical publications out of the legislative chamber.[199] Although it upheld the constitutional power of either House of the Congress to punish critics for out-of-chamber publications, it introduced restrictions on the scope of its authority. Building on *Kilbourn v. Thompson*, the Court confirmed that the Houses of Congress had implied powers to deal directly with contempts that inherently prevented or obstructed the discharge of its legislative duties and to compel the doing of things essential to the performance of its legislative

---

[197] "Directly" meant a remedy other than appeal.

[198] Kilbourn v. Thompson, 103 U. S. 168 (1881). The Supreme Court considered the legislative contempt power again in *In re* Chapman, 166 U.S. 661 (1897). This decision, however, throws no light on our immediate concern. The *Chapman* case involved the punishment by the Senate of a witness refusing to answer questions in an inquiry into allegations of corruption in the Senate in the consideration of a tariff act. It upheld the constitutionality of the congressional statute authorizing either house to impose criminal punishment on a witness for willful failure to answer questions. R.S. §§12–104, 859.

[199] Marshall v. Gordon, 243 U.S. 521 (1917). The Court collected no fewer than 18 cases involving contempts of the Congress. Of these only the *Duane* case involved criticism of the House or Senate. The others involved contumacious witnesses or assaults on members of one House or the other. 243 U.S. at 543 n.1.

functions. However, the congressional contempt power stopped there. The Court stated that the Congress had no power for infliction of punishment that did not involve its inherent power to take steps necessary "to preserve itself" by using contempt to prevent "*direct* obstructions to its legislative duties" (emphasis added). The theoretical power to punish out-of-chamber criticism could be exercised only in the case, if ever, where the publication could be said to constitute a "direct obstruction."

Marshall v. Gordon involved the arrest of the U.S. Attorney for the Southern District of New York by the Sergeant-at-Arms of the House. The U.S. Attorney was conducting a grand jury investigation of the alleged illegal conduct under the Sherman Antitrust Act of a member of the House and of an organization to which the member belonged. At the instance of the member, a subcommittee was considering the impeachment of the U.S. Attorney when the latter wrote to the press charging that the subcommittee was acting to frustrate the grand jury. The House thereupon adopted a resolution characterizing his statement as defamatory and insulting and tending to bring the House into contempt and ridicule and adjudging him to be in contempt. The House marshal thereupon arrested him. On a writ of *habeas corpus*, Chief Justice White speaking for a unanimous Court ordered his discharge. The Court held that the House had no power to punish for contempt because its powers rested only on self-preservation.

Although, as the Court recognized, 11 federal decisions had recognized the existence of the contempt power of the Houses of the Congress, it is striking that *Marshall v. Gordon* along with *Ex Parte* Nugent decided 75 years earlier are the only federal decisions to have involved out-of-chamber offensive publications. The others all related to contumacious conduct. With the *Marshall v. Gordon* standard of self-preservation accepted as a constitutional prerequisite for implementation of the legislative contempt power, the question arises when, if ever, an offensive out-of-chamber publication may so threaten the legislative process as to satisfy this prerequisite for application of the doctrine.

In *Jurney v. MacCracken*, decided in 1935, the Supreme Court once again addressed the issue of the outer constitutional scope of the contempt power of a house of the Congress over out-of-chamber publications. Speaking for the Court, Justice Brandeis flatly reaffirmed the constitutional limitation introduced by *Marshall v. Gordon:* "It is true that the scope of the [contempt power] [of the Houses of the Congress] is narrow. No act is so punishable unless it is of a nature to obstruct the performance of the duties of the legislature." Citing *Marshall v. Gordon*, he thereupon reaffirmed that "the power to punish for contempt may not be extended to slanderous attacks which present no immediate obstruction to legislative processes."[200]

However, this apparent ruling was only dictum. *Jurney* involved a different issue. Counsel had allowed persons to destroy papers that had been subpoenaed by the Senate. Justice Brandeis held that such destruction of subpoenaed matter obstructed the legislative process and, accordingly, was within the Senate's contempt power. It was a vindication "of the established and essential privilege of requiring the production of evidence." However, like Chief Justice White in *Marshall v. Gordon*, he made it clear in the dictum that the contempt power of the Congress did not extend beyond conduct that interfered with the performance by the Congress of its constitutional duties.[201]

Dictum or not, Justice Brandeis's statement at last ended the matter. Although *Jurney v. MacCracken* has not been followed by a complementary Supreme Court decision applying the doctrine to state courts in the same way as *Bridges v. California* was followed by *Craig v. Harney* and *Pennekamp v. Florida* in the case of the contempt powers of state judges,[202] it should be clear that contempt of the legislature for out-of-chamber critical publications has for practical purposes almost come to an end. It will require quite remarkable circumstances to satisfy the constitutional standard held out by the Court.

Thus, a doctrine so out of keeping with contemporary times in the view of modern students of constitutional jurisprudence survived for 125 years. Although the experience is of moment, its significance is largely historical. After all, there were only two examples of the use of the legislative contempt power over out-of-chamber publications by either House of the Congress over 150 years. Similarly, as we will see, no cases of this nature appear to have arisen in the state courts during the period before *Marshall v. Gordon* and *Jurney v. MacCracken* held that such application of the contempt power by houses of the Congress might be beyond their constitutional powers. In Beck's study of the 108 citations for contempt approved by a congressional chamber, only one case – *Marshall v. Gordon* – involved out-of-chamber critical publications.[203]

---

[200] Jurney v. MacCracken, 294 U.S. 125 (1935); Marshall v. Gordon, 243 U.S. 521 (1916).

[201] 294 U.S. at 147–148, 150.

[202] Bridges v. California, 314 U.S. 252 (1941); Craig v. Harney, 331 U.S. 367 (1947) and Pennekamp v. Florida, 328 U.S. 331 (1946).

[203] In 1871, there was still a third attempt by the Senate to use the legislative contempt power to punish an editor for publication of a treaty still being held secret. while it considered its response. The Senate sought to punish two editors, White and Ramsdell, for their publication of a secret treaty between the United States and Great Britain. The contempt citation was not for the publication but for White's refusal to disclose the source of the leak. As we have seen, the contempt citations in the *Duane* and *Nugent* cases similarly related not to the publication but to the failure of Duane

Nevertheless, the fact that the power existed at all for this lengthy period made its existence a source of important concern because of its potential to act as a "chilling" factor on free discussion of congressional and legislature affairs in the press.

A final note: It is not without relevance when one considers the role of the constitutional guaranties of free speech and press with respect to other repressive doctrines used for the suppression of anti-establishment speech to observe that none of the Supreme Court decisions on the matter relied on the guaranties of free speech and press to support the Court's conclusions on the outer constitutional limitations of the legislative contempt power.

3. The State Experience

In the interregnum between the Revolution and the adoption of the Constitution, at least two states – Maryland and Massachusetts – had constitutional provisions expressly recognizing the contempt powers of their Legislatures. But, in neither state was the grant of power general. The two Constitutions limited the legislative use of the contempt power to meticulously defined circumstances. The Maryland Constitution limited application of the contempt power to cases involving "disorderly or riotous behavior," "threats to, or abuse of their members," or "any obstruction to their proceedings." It also recognized the power to punish by imprisonment the arrest or assault of their members during any sitting or going to or return from the House, or upon their officers in the execution of any order or process.[204] The Massachusetts Constitution was much the same.[205]

It is striking that neither of these Constitutions contained any recognition of the contempt power to punish out-of-chamber critical publications, unless the reference to "threats to, or abuse of their members" may be construed to deal with critical speech generally. The Massachusetts Constitution limited the Legislature's contempt power to the punishment of "disrespect" or "disorderly or contemptuous behavior in its presence." By 1820, no fewer than ten additional states had comparable constitutional provisions.[206] However, as with the earlier constitutions, none of these included a provision expressly

to appear and to the failure of Nugent to answer questions. Hence, it is accurate to say that in the entire history of legislative contempt from Colonial times until modern times, the only judicial cases that actually involved a citation for contempt for an offensive out-of-chamber publication were *Moore* in 1758, *McDougall* in 1759, and *Marshall v. Gordon* in 1916.

[204] Md. Const. Art. XII (1776).
[205] Mass. Const. pt. 2d, ch. 1, §3, arts. X and XI.
[206] *Marshall v. Gordon*, 243 U.S. 521, 536 n.1 (1917).

empowering the legislature to proceed for contempt for out-of-chamber critical publications, except to the extent that such a general term as protecting
the legislature against "abuse" may be construed to include the punishment
of out-of-chamber criticism.[207]

The earliest of the state cases involving out-of-chamber criticism of the
legislature and some of its members is *Cheatham v. Tillottson*, decided in
New York in 1808.[208] Although it did not involve use of the contempt power,
it illustrates the breadth of remedies then available for establishment officials
to punish editors for anti-establishment publications.

Cheetham v. Tillottson grew out of the unsuccessful attempt of the New
York State Senate to prosecute Cheetham, editor of the *American Citizen*,
for charging that rampant corruption had secured passage of a controversial
banking bill. After a grand jury had refused to indict for contempt of the
legislature and Cheetham continued to print his claims, several State Senators
sought other remedies. Sen. Tillotson, in particular, brought two civil libel
suits and prevailed in both.

The *Cheatham* litigation tells us a little about the times, but nothing about
the use of the contempt power to punish critical out-of-chamber speech.
However, perhaps the refusal of the grand jury to indict for contempt of
the legislature and Tillotson's resort to civil libel as an alternative remedy
portends the decline of the doctrine. Similarly, although there are a number
of state decisions involving the exercise by legislative houses of their contempt
powers, the cases involve direct contumacious conduct, not out-of-chamber
critical comment.[209]

As for the full extent of legislative contempt in the states in general and
whether it included out-of-chamber critical publications, no state cases considering the issue appear to be available. The sole reference found is an
1818 newspaper account. Although this reports the adoption by the Maryland
House of Delegates of a resolution directing its Sergeant-at-Arms to arrest
a local editor for an alleged contempt of the House, it also noted that the

---

[207] Ga. Const., art. I §13 (1798); N.H. Const. pt. 2, §§22, 23 (1792); Ill. Const. Art. II, §13 (1818); Ind.
Const. Art. III, §14 (1816); Me. Const., art. IV, pt. 3, §6 (1820); Miss. Const., art. III, §20 (1817);
Mo., art. III, §19 (1820); Ohio Const., art. I, §14 (1802); S.C. Const. art. I, §13 (1790); Tenn. Const.,
art. I, §11 (1796).

[208] Cheetham v. Tillotson, 2 Johns. Cas. 63, 1806 N.Y. LEXIS 155 (1806); 3 Johns. Cas, 56, 1808 N.Y.
LEXIS 12 (N.Y. 1808).

[209] E.g., Johnston v. Commonwealth, 4 Ky. (1 Bibb) 598 (1809 Ky. LEXIS 159) (1809), Hiss v.
Bartlett, 69 Mass. (3 Gray) 468, 1855 Mass. LEXIS 59 (1855) (expulsion of a member); Burnham
v. Morrisesey, 80 Mass (14 Gray) 226, 1859 Mass. LEXIS 315 (1859) (refusal of summoned witness
to answer questions and produce documents) (imprisonment for 25 days); Yates v. Lansing, 9
Johns. Cas. 395, 1811 N.Y. LEXIS 211 (1811).

resolution was rescinded the following day.[210] To what extent there were other instances of the attempted exercise of the legislative contempt power is simply not known.

In sum, notwithstanding the paucity of litigations to illustrate the application of the power, it is clear that until *Jurney v. MacCracken* in 1935 or for about 150 years, American jurisprudence continued to recognize the power of either house of the state legislatures to punish out-of-chamber critical publications under its contempt powers. Notwithstanding state or federal constitutional guarantees of freedom of speech and press, legislatures during this period could constitutionally fine or imprison offending persons. They could do so without any need to obtain grand jury approval of a presentation or indictment, or any need for a criminal trial with all the normal protection offered the accused and conviction by a petit jury. However, this is the law in the books. As for the reality, the doctrine has become moribund, as evident in the federal experience with its single unsuccessful attempt, *Marshall v. Gordon*, to utilize the doctrine in the 250 years since the *McDougall* case.

D. Binding Over of Defendants to Assure Good Pretrial Behavior

The jurisprudential foundation for the criminal law including criminal libel (as well as for the law of blasphemy discussed in the next chapter) was the societal concern for the preservation of the domestic order and prevention of breaches of the peace. Accordingly, in the early days of the New Republic, it was entirely consistent with the repressive jurisprudence of the times for the courts after the arrest and institution of proceedings of persons accused of commission of libel to take steps pending trial to prevent further recurrences. As best that one can tell from the inadequate reports, courts routinely did so on the mere assertion of the prosecutor without requiring any proof of probable cause that the remedy was reasonably required to prevent a repetition of the alleged offense. Thus, as an alternative to imprisonment before the trial, courts were empowered to require the defendants to post bonds for good behavior with the courts, often requiring additional sureties to assure the defendant's compliance. Failing the ability to obtain such sureties in the amount required, the defendant remained in jail, sometimes for months, until the court and prosecutor were ready for trial. In the meantime, further critical comment was stifled for the time being.[211]

---

[210] *See American Watchman*, Feb. 7, 1818.

[211] *See generally* Williams, Preventive Justice and the Rule of Law, 16 Mod. L. Rev. 417 (1953); (Note) "Preventive Justice" – Bonds to Keep the Peace and for Good Behavior, 88 U. Penn. L. Rev. 331 (1940); Rosenberg, note 17, at 18–19.

As with the other repressive doctrines of the times that have been examined, the power of a judge before trial to bind a defendant over for good behavior in libel cases was derived from the understanding of American judges of the scope of judicial authority under the English common law.

Rosenberg reports that as early as the 17th century in the very new Colonies, "courts commonly assessed good behavior, or peace bonds, bonds against people considered likely to cause trouble with their tongues. Bonds could even be used before there had been any formal determination of criminal guilt or innocence." Indeed, Rosenberg goes further, stating: "According to *Dalton's Country Justice*, a commonly used seventeenth-century handbook for justices of the peace, a bond could be declared forfeited without any actual breach of the peace... 'using wordes or threatenings, tending to or inciting to the breach of the peace' was enough."[212]

As we have seen, Blackstone was the authoritative legal reference in the Colonial era and in the Early American Republic. In his *Commentaries*, Blackstone devoted a chapter to the exploration of the law of preventing the commission of crimes and misdemeanors.[213] He explained:

> This preventive justice consists in obliging those persons, whom there is *probable ground* to suspect of future misbehavior to stipulate with and to give full assurance to the public, that such offense as is apprehended shall not happen; by finding pledges or securities for keeping the peace, or for their good behavior.[214]

On binding over for good behavior, Blackstone asserts "A man may be bound to his good behavior for... [among other causes] words tending to scandalize the government, or in abuse of the officers of justice, especially in the execution of their office."[215]

Although Blackstone carefully restricted the use of the doctrine to cases in which "probable ground to suspect of future misbehavior" had been shown, the reported American cases give no indication that the courts were in fact requiring such proof. Indeed, there does not appear to be a single case that

---

[212] *See* Rosenberg, note 17, at 19.

[213] Blackstone was not oblivious to the dangers of punishment before conviction. He expressly limits the doctrine to those cases where "there is probable ground to suspect of future misbehavior." He further advises that the magistrate administering the process: "if he commits a man for want of sureties, he must express the cause thereof with convenient certainty; and take care that such cause be a good one." 4 Blackstone, note 3, at 248, 253.

[214] 4 Blackstone, note 3, at 248. Emphasis added.

[215] 4 W. Blackstone, note 3, at 253. In support, Blackstone relies on the statute of 34 Edw. III, c. 1 adopted in 1360.

so much as mentions the existence of the requirement. It was the routine approval without proof of probable cause of requiring the posting of pre-trial bonds for good behavior that renders the doctrine so pernicious in the frequent partisan prosecutions for criminal libel.

The first American case involving binding over after the Revolution was the 1782 clash between Eleazer Oswald and Chief Justice McKean, which has been earlier reviewed in detail. When Oswald criticized McKean's conduct in fining and lecturing two Army officers, McKean caused his arrest for a "seditious, scandalous, and infamous libel." For his release, Oswald was required to post a £750 bond for "good behavior." As noted, the matter died when the grand jury twice refused to indict.[216]

The next reported case was *Respublica v. Askew* decided by the Pennsylvania Supreme Court in 1792. *Askew* involved a criminal libel prosecution for libeling a witness for giving testimony. On the defendant's submission, he was fined £10 and ordered to give security himself in the amount of £200 and provide two sureties in the amount of £100 each for his good behavior for one year.[217] However, this was an instance in which the good behavior bond was imposed *after* conviction. It did not present the more difficult question of the power of the court to impose its requirement of a good behavior bond *before* conviction.

The third reported case also involves Chief Justice McKean, the 1797 Cobbett-McKean controversy that like the others has already been discussed. McKean required Cobbett to post bond immediately after his indictment, citing the *Askew* decision as his authority, but without referring to his similar action in the *Oswald* case. It was Cobbett's alleged violation of the bond that led to the ultimate judgment against him, not the libel prosecution. Neither in the summary report of the decision in *Askew* nor in Chief Justice McKean's opinions in *Oswald* and *Cobbett* is there any discussion of a judge's authority to require such a bond. Nor is there any reference or discussion of the need for proof of probable cause of threatened repetition as a prerequisite for such an order.

However, it is a different matter in the follow-up decision in the *Cobbett* litigation confirming that under Pennsylvania law an action in debt in favor of the state will lie for forfeiture of a good behavior bond. McKean had resigned from the Court to become Governor and Edward Shippen was now Chief Justice. Counsel for Cobbett challenged McKean's authority to impose the

---

[216] *See supra* text accompanying notes 23–26.
[217] Respublica v. Askew, 1 Yeates 186, 1792 Pa. LEXIS 35 (1792).

bond on Cobbett in apocalyptic terms. Counsel was William Lewis, described as "a giant of the Philadelphia bar."[218] He exclaimed:

> If the chief justice . . . is allowed to bind [a libel defendant] to his good behavior, it is holding a rod of scorpions over his head to be used in the case of the smallest peccadillo . . . ; it is the most dangerous inroad upon the liberty of the press which we thought had been established; it is a violent usurpation. . . . If such things can be done, well may we exclaim, with the defendant *"Poor Pennsylvania!"*

Chief Justice Shippen was not unsympathetic, explaining that the Court also had doubts about the validity of the process: "We thought that, if not authorized by express law, it might be oppressive and ought to be prohibited." However, after careful consideration of the authorities, the Court was of the opinion that the procedure is "regular and legal. The authorities leave an amazing discretion, but so the law is."[219]

Aside from authority, there is a further important issue. It is striking how Blackstone's emphasis on the importance of requiring proof of probable cause was uniformly ignored. Nor does it appear ever to have been argued by defense counsel. This is unique in the otherwise unbroken obeisance to Blackstone displayed in the other 18th- and 19th-century decisions following English common-law authority as stated by Blackstone in other areas of repressive doctrines, such as criminal libel, judicial and legislative contempt of court, and blasphemy.

McKean failed to recognize that the decision in *Askew*, a post-conviction case, did not deal with the fundamental issue in the *Oswald* and *Cobbett* cases, which involved pre-trial bonds. Binding over without prior proof of probable cause in either of those latter cases before conviction involves serious risks of dampening free speech analogous to a prior restraint. After conviction, as in *Askew*, however, the bond is imposed as punishment for the offence. Such a decision is no precedent for requiring a good conduct bond before the trial, as in *Oswald* and *Cobbett*, where by definition there has been no determination as yet that any offense had been committed. Binding over prior to conviction, and without a showing of "probable cause," is the imposition of punishment first, trial later.

However relevant this distinction between pre-trial binding over and post-conviction binding over may be as a matter of legal analysis, it does not seem

---

[218]   *See* G. S. Rowe, note 16, at 112.

[219]   Commonwealth v. William Cobbett, 1 Am. J. 287, 291, 296–297 (1800). *See also* note 226. The reporter adds an interesting note. "I understand that a different decision of this important point was made in *Virginia* in the case of *Callender.*"

to have been raised in any of the subsequent cases or to have played any role in the subsequent development of the law.

Finally, the American judges did not restrict the practice of binding over to libels of the government or the "officers of justice" as stated by Blackstone. Instead, the courts imposed the procedure to defendants in libel actions generally. Thus, as Chief Judge Tilghman said in a 1809 litigation involving Duane: "I will not say that there are not circumstances in which surety for good behavior might be exacted in cases of libels before conviction; on the contrary, I have no doubt that there are occasions on which it may be proper and necessary to insist on it."[220]

The following year, Judge Martin, while sitting in the Territory of Louisiana, referred to Tilghman's opinion, adding: "It is true the chief justice declared his opinion, that, as a general rule, it would be better not to require it. But the defendant has for a long time persisted in the practice [of which he was accused], and it is time to put a stop to it. It is better to prevent than to punish crimes."[221]

The experience in the various prosecutions for criminal libel in the federal courts, both at common law and under the 1798 Act, confirms that binding over in libel proceedings was a common occurrence. In at least seven prosecutions, bonds for good behavior were required pre-trial.[222] In not one did the court appear to make any inquiry into the existence of probable cause. As the Red Queen expounded to Alice, "Sentence first, verdict later."[223]

The partisan prosecutions of John Daly Burk, the editor, and James Smith, the owner, of the outspoken Republican New York *Time Piece* for criminal libel under the 1798 Act illustrate the chilling effect of pre-trial binding over. Upon indictment, Burk and Smith were required to post pre-trial good behavior bonds of $4,000 each. When Burk proposed to run still more attacks on Adams while awaiting trial, Smith became concerned about the possible violation of his bond. He withdrew his support of the paper, and the paper closed.[224] As a result of the good behavior bond, the Federalist prosecutor had complete success in his attempt to shut down this leading New York Republican newspaper without the necessity of a trial.

---

[220] So reads Judge Martin's opinion in Territory v. Nugent, 1 Mart.3 (La. Terr. 1810), *citing* Commonwealth v. Duane, 1 Am. L. J. 180, 1 Am. Dec. 497. However, his citations are in error.

[221] Territory v. Nugent, 1 Mart. 103 (La. Terr. 1810) (Martin, J).

[222] The numerous criminal libel cases involving partisan use of pre-trial binding over include the prosecutions of Benjamin Franklin Bache, John Daly Burk, Dr. James Smith, William Duane, William Durrell, Anthony Haswell, James Bell, Abijah Adams, and Thomas Collier.

[223] Lewis Carroll, *Alice in Wonderland* 96 (Norton ed. 1992).

[224] *See* J. M. Smith, note 186, at 204–220.

The second *Cobbett-McKean* controversy litigation occurring in 1797 illustrates still another unattractive dimension of the binding over process. Although this case has been described at length earlier in this chapter, it is useful to retrace the aspect of the litigation that shows the baleful usefulness of the binding over power in silencing offensive speech. With the institution of the criminal libel prosecution of Cobbett for defaming the King of Spain and the Spanish Ambassador, Marquis de Yrujo, the case was set down for trial at the next term. By order dated August 17, 1797, Chief Justice McKean (about to become the father-in-law of the Marquis de Yrujo) held Cobbett on a $2,000 bond together with two sureties for $1,000 each, for Cobbett's good behavior until trial at the next term of the Court of Oyer and Terminer, November 26, 1797. As described earlier, the grand jury subsequently refused to indict, bringing the underlying criminal libel prosecution to an end.[225]

However, McKean was not to be thwarted. In November 1797, the Attorney General instituted an action in debt against Cobbett for $2,000 on his bond in the previous proceeding, asserting that he had violated the terms of the bond required by McKean's August 17 order. Cobbett, an Englishman, first tried to remove the case to the federal courts and get away from McKean. This failed. The Supreme Court of Pennsylvania with McKean, sitting as Chief Justice, held that the action involved a recognizance in a Pennsylvania criminal proceeding and hence was not subject to removal. The matter then went to trial.

At the trial, the Attorney General asserted that from August 24 to November 16, 1797, Cobbett had published a series of articles in *Porcupine's Gazette* with the intent "falsely, slanderously and maliciously" to defame the government of the United States and its officers and good citizens as well as the Pennsylvania Government and its officers and good citizens. At the trial, he presented what was reported as

> thirty-five different malicious, scurrilous, and abusive publications in the Porcupine's Gazette . . . defaming, ridiculing and reflecting on the general government of the Union, the principles of republican government, the people for adopting those principles, Mr. Thomas Jefferson, Mr. James Monroe, &c. The King of Spain, the French and Spanish nations and ministers thereof

and a series of Pennsylvania figures including former Governor Thomas Mifflin, Benjamin Franklin, and Alexander Dallas.

---

[225] Rosenberg, note 17, at 77; Cobbett, note 16, at 87; 1 G. Spater, *William Cobbett: The Poor Man's Friend* 99 (1982). Francis Wharton, *State Trials* 322–332 (1845).

After argument whether the Court could proceed in the absence of a criminal conviction for the allegedly libelous publications and whether the proceeding was the equivalent to a libel trial without grand jury indictment, the Court ruled that this was merely a civil action on the forfeited bond, with only money damages to be recovered. Accordingly, action by a grand jury as in a criminal case was not required. The Court further held that the jury had the right to determine law and facts. It stated in its charge that if the jury concluded that the publications were libelous "and if they view them in the light we do, they will have no hesitation in pronouncing them to be such.... Libels ... manifestly tend to breaches of the peace, and good causes of forfeiture of recognizance to keep the peace or good behavior." With such a charge, the jury not surprisingly so held.[226]

In the unfolding story, the Commonwealth followed up on its success in the earlier proceeding against Cobbett with an action in debt for violation of the bond for $1,000 against Benjamin Davis, one of Cobbett's sureties. The Commonwealth satisfied its burden of proof of violation of the bond by presentation to the jury of bound copies of the 1797 *Gazette* containing the libelous matter. The jury rendered a verdict for the Commonwealth. On a writ of error, the High Court of Errors and Appeals affirmed the judgment.[227]

Chief Justice McKean's earlier attempt to punish Cobbett through the criminal libel laws could not prevail over the protections afforded criminal defendants in a free society, including the necessity of a grand jury ready to indict and a petit jury ready to convict. However, in the extensive number of remedies available in the repressive jurisprudence of the times to punish dissenting speech, McKean found another remedy to achieve his objective. His power to require a pre-trial "good behavior" bond and a ready procedure to forfeit the bond provided still another way to punish Cobbett. He, thus, avoided the barrier presented in attempted prosecutions for criminal libel. This civil remedy may be contrasted with McKean's successful punishment of Oswald a decade earlier by use of criminal contempt after, as in the case of Cobbett, a grand jury refusal to indict had blocked his attempt to trial the critic for criminal libel.

Although successful in his campaign to punish Oswald and Cobbett, McKean failed in his campaign against a third editorial critic – William Duane.

---

[226] Respublica v. William Cobbett, 3 Yeates 93; 1800 Pa. LEXIS 56, *18 (Sup. Ct. 1800). A different but not inconsistent account appears at 1 Am. L. J. 287 (1800). That report states: "Although you are the judges both of the law and the fact, we can not help saying that we think these publications are libelous." 1 Am. L. J. at 298. *See also* note 219.

[227] Respublica v. Benjamin Davis, 3 Yeates 128; 1801 Pa. LEXIS 3 (Sup. Ct. 1801).

The comparable attempt to punish Duane for his continued attacks on Mc-Kean and his son-in-law, Marquis de Urojo, while awaiting trial in the 1809 prosecution for criminal libel failed. The prosecutor and McKean had failed to place Duane under bond prior to the trial for criminal libel. Thus, when Duane's counsel brought on a *habeas corpus* proceeding to get him released, the new Chief Justice Edward Tilghman granted the motion, noting the absence of any good behavior bond.[228] These celebrated Pennsylvania controversies involving McKean and three of the most outspoken editors in Pennsylvania illustrate vividly the important role of pre-trial good behavior bonds in the political libel cases that characterized this period in America history.

Republican judges at common law presiding over criminal libel cases involving Federalists were no more gentle than the Federalist judges. In Connecticut in one of the celebrated criminal libel cases against Federalists instituted under federal criminal common-law jurisdiction by a Republican District Attorney, defendant Thaddeus Osgood, an aspiring ministerial candidate, was jailed pre-trial by the Republican federal judge for allegedly libeling Thomas Jefferson in a sermon. Unable to find sureties to assure his good behavior, he remained in jail until two prominent Federalists – David Daggett and Tapping Reeve (himself a defendant in one of the companion cases) – posted bond for him and obtained his release prior to trial. Subsequently, the prosecution was dropped and Osgood released.

The 1803 controversy between James Thomson Callender and Richmond attorney George Hay illustrates a further dimension to binding over in libel litigation.[229] As readers may recall, Hay had been one of the lawyers defending Callender in the criminal action against him under the Sedition Act. Two years later Callender and Hay had a falling out and were involved in a personal quarrel. Callender complained to the Mayor of Richmond, who, acting in his capacity as a magistrate, bound Hay to appear at the next court for the city and in the meantime to keep the peace.

The next day, Hay filed a complaint against Callender and Henry Pace with the Magistrates of Henrico County alleging that Callender and Pace had published several infamous and scurrilous libels against him in the *Recorder*. He moved for an order requiring Callender and Pace to show cause why

---

[228]   *See* G. S. Rowe, note 16, at 369.

[229]   The Jan. 14, 1801, Philadelphia *Evening Post* and the Jan. 15, 1803, *Adams Centinel, Gettysburg Pa.*, both carry a reprint from the *Virginia Gazette* reporting in detail on the litigation. *See* Rosenberg, note 17, at 105–106.

they should not be bound to their good behavior as persons not of good fame, even though prior to indictment.[230]

At a hearing before the Magistrates, counsel disagreed on whether the Magistrates had cognizance of the matter, and if so, whether relief was justified. Hay's counsel, a Mr. Marshall and Mr. Rind, asserted that a Virginia statute derived from the English law[231] gave the Magistrates the power to bind over anyone not of good fame. They offered a bundle of issues of the *Recorder* showing that Callender was "a vile calumniator and malignant slanderer," that he had slandered "Mr. Madison, Mr. Giles, and almost all respectable men in the State to such an extent as to have justly incurred the character of a libeler and consequently that of a person of bad fame."

Although there had been no prior arraignment or indictment for criminal libel, the Magistrates held that they had jurisdiction. They approved the recognizance of Callender and Pace and bound them to keep the peace and maintain good behavior in the amount of $500 each and two sureties. Pace complied; Callender failed and was committed to prison and remained there for two days. On January 3, 1803, the Court of Review composed of five Federalists and three Republicans found no statutory power for the Magistrates to require the posting of the bonds. The proceedings of the Magistrates were declared to be illegal, and Callender and Pace were discharged.[232]

This unsuccessful attempt at binding over appears to be the only instance of such an attempt against a defendant who had not already been arraigned or indicted for alleged criminal libel. Fastening on this point, Duane in the Philadelphia *Aurora* bitterly denounced

> this alternative legal avenue enabling a single magistrate to bind dissenting critics with respect to prospective speech without the necessity of indictment.... We are convinced that no circumstance which has happened since the revolution will attract the public notice more than commitment of Callender to jail.... This extraordinary attack on the freedom of the press [binding over editors to keep the peace and prevent them from publishing what they pleased, which was never proposed during the Adams administration] was reserved to the present day.

Three years later, Pennsylvania returned to the center of our stage. Thomas McKean, now Governor, formally proposed that the Pennsylvania Legislature

---

[230] Several years earlier, Hay, legal commentator as well as prominent lawyer, had published a pamphlet advocating the use of good behavior bonds. *See* George Hay, An Essay on the Liberty of the Press shewing that the Requisition of Security for Good Behavior from Libellers Is Perfectly Compatible with the Constitution and Laws of Virginia (1799 rev. ed. 1803).

[231] *Cf.* 34 Edw. III, c.1 (1360).

[232] *See* Rosenberg, note 17, at 107.

adopt the system of good behavior bonds for which Hay had argued in his controversy with Callender. The proposal was caught up into the factional division among the Pennsylvania Republicans. The radical Republicans led by Michael Leib and William Duane opposed McKean's proposal, as did the Federalists in the Legislature. They succeeded in defeating the proposal.[233]

In Virginia, John Taylor led the attack on the procedure of binding over pre-trial. He urged the Legislature to repeal any law justifying the imposition of such bonds. Although the Legislature took no action, the inherent unfairness of such procedures in criminal and criminal libel litigations resting on an assumption before the trial that the defendant was indeed guilty was apparently increasingly recognized.

Pre-trial binding over in criminal libel prosecutions does not seem to play any role in the later libel cases, although it still survives in the case of other crimes. Thus, Massachusetts authorizes the imposition of security on a person accused of any crime, even before indictment, requiring him or her "to keep the peace or for their good behavior" when the court has "just cause" to fear that a crime may be committed.[234]

Similarly, in another area not involving free speech, some states such as Connecticut concerned with physical violence on the part of the defendant have accepted the use of bonds in the interest of protecting persons at risk during the interval before trial. Thus, in addition to special provisions when the court "has reason to believe" that the defendant is "drug-dependent," Connecticut statutes generally authorize "conditions of release [that] will reasonably assure . . . [that] the safety of any other person will not be endangered."[235]

As with the doctrines of criminal libel, blasphemy, and contempt of court or contempt of the legislature for out-of-chamber speech, now entirely or in overwhelming measure restricted, the 21st-century law of binding over is of minor interest. Criminal libel has virtually disappeared, and binding over in such cases with its serious implications for freedom of speech has, of course, disappeared with it.

E. Breach of the Peace

Finally, the historic common-law doctrine punishing "breach of the peace" whether actual or constructive by "tending to make others break it" has served as still another establishment weapon for suppression of dissenting speech. In

---

[233] *See ibid.*, at 107; G. S. Rowe, note 16, at 372–373.
[234] Mass. Gen. Stat. Ann. Ch. 275, §§1, 3 (1958).
[235] Conn. Gen. Stat. §§54–64a (b) (1), (2) (2004); Conn. Super. Ct. Rules, ch. 38–10 (b).

his *Commentaries*, Justice Story advises that the doctrine is not unconstitutional under the First Amendment, explaining that notwithstanding the right to speak freely without prior restraint, a speaker may "not injure any other person in his rights, person, property, or reputation; and so always *that he does not thereby disturb the public peace*, or attempt to subvert the government."[236]

The leading cases in this area are the decision of the New York Court of Appeals in *People v. Most* in 1902[237] and the decisions of the U.S. Supreme Court in *Cantwell v. Connecticut*[238] in 1940 and *Terminiello v. Chicago* in 1949. In decisions 40 to 50 years apart, the two courts reached dramatically different conclusions.

In the *Most* case, John Most, a leading anarchist, was the editor of the anarchist publication the *Freiheit* or "Freedom." On the same day that President McKinley was shot, he published an article "advocating and advising revolution and murder." He was promptly prosecuted under section 675 of the New York Penal Law for seriously endangering the public peace and convicted. The statute provided that "a person who wilfully and wrongfully commits any act *** which seriously disturbs or endangers the public peace for which no other punishment is expressly prescribed by this Code, is guilty of a misdemeanor."[239] On appeal, the Court first found that the publication and its instigation of revolution and murder "necessarily endangers the public peace" and accordingly was covered by the statute. It then considered whether a conviction violated the state constitutional guaranty of freedom of the press. The Court commented:

A breach of the peace is an offense well known to the common law. It is a disturbance of public order by an act of violence, or by any act likely to produce violence, or which, by causing consternation and alarm, disturbs the peace and quiet of the community [citations omitted]. It may be committed by written words, as a libel has been indictable for time out of mind because it tends to provoke violence; or even by spoken words, provided that they tend to provoke immediate violence.[240]

[236] 4 Blackstone, note 3, at 142. Emphasis added. Similarly, he notes that in criminal libel, "The tendency which all libels have to create animosities, and to disturb the public peace, is the sole consideration of the law." *Id.*, at 150.

[237] People v. Most, 171 N.Y. 423, 64 N.E. 175 (1902). Ten years before, Most had been convicted for unlawful assembly. People v. Most, 128 N.Y. 108, 27 N.E. 970 (1891) (meeting in which speaker made threats of violence and revolution).

[238] Cantwell v. Connecticut, 310 U.S. 296 (1940).

[239] 171 N.Y. at 427; 64 N.E. at 177 (asterisks in the opinion of the court).

[240] 171 N.Y. at 429.

It noted that actual breach of the peace as well as an act seriously apt to endanger it were distinct offences in New York, both at common law and by statute. It then upheld the constitutionality of the conviction under the statute. The Court noted that while the New York Constitution guaranteed the freedom of every citizen to "publish his sentiments on all subjects, *being responsible for the abuse of that right,*" it excepted the abuse of that right by "those who publish articles which tend to corrupt morals, induce crime or destroy organized society." Although government cannot abridge the freedom of the press, the legislature may control and the courts may punish the "licentiousness" of the press.[241]

In the early days of the Republic, this understanding of the law derived from Blackstone was the generally accepted view of the limited scope of the constitutional guaranty of freedom of speech and press. For the New York Court of Appeals in 1902, despite the elapse of more than a century after Independence, the law had not changed a whit. Indeed, for support, Justice Vann speaking for the Court went back 100 years to Chancellor Kent's opinion in the *Croswell* case, which has been discussed at length in Chapter 5. He also relied on Justice Story's *Commentaries* on the Constitution. The conviction was affirmed.

Unlike *Most,* which involved political issues, the decision of the U.S. Supreme Court in *Cantwell v. Connecticut*[242] 40 years later turned on religious prejudice. In *Cantwell,* the Supreme Court was faced with the use of the doctrine of breach of the peace to punish a father and two sons who were members of Jehovah's Witnesses and engaging in soliciting support for the group. In an area heavily populated by Roman Catholics, they were calling from house to house and asking the person responding as well as pedestrians for permission to play one of their records on their portable phonograph. The record describing a book, *Enemies,* included an attack on Roman Catholicism.

Two persons gave permission to play the record, and this was done. There was no claim that there was any intention to insult or affront the hearers. Nor was there any showing that their behavior was noisy, truculent, overbearing, or offensive or that the playing disturbed residents, drew a crowd, or impeded traffic. Nevertheless, the matter on the phonograph was highly offensive, not

---

[241] Emphasis in the original. 171 N.Y. at 431. Readers will note that 100 years after St. George Tucker pointed out that "licentiousness" of the press was a conclusory term and not of any use for legal analysis, Judge Vann of the Court of Appeals was still turning to it in an effort to support the Court's decision. *See* Ch. 4, note 178.

[242] Cantwell v. Connecticut, 310 U.S. 296 (1940).

only to Catholics but to all persons respectful of religion. One of the persons hearing the phonograph record testified that he was highly offended and felt like hitting Cantwell or throwing him off the street.

Although the Court recognized the existence of the doctrine of breach of the peace involving acts or statements likely to provoke violence and disturbance of good order, even if not so intended, it made plain the need for substantial limitations on its application in order to satisfy constitutional standards. Thus, on the facts in *Cantwell*, the Court found that a case satisfying the requirements of the doctrine had not been presented. It concluded:

> in the absence of a statute narrowly drawn to define and punish specific conduct as constituting a clear and present danger to a substantial interest of the State, the petitioner's communication, considered in the light of the constitutional guarantees (freedom of religion and freedom of speech) raised no such clear and present menace to public peace and order

as to render the defendant liable to conviction of common-law breach of the peace.[243]

Terminiello v. Chicago[244] decided in 1949 by the Supreme Court grew out of a near riot. Father Terminiello, a suspended Catholic priest, spoke at a meeting of 800 people called by the right-wing extremist Gerald L. K. Smith under the aegis of the Christian Veterans of America. Terminiello denounced alleged Communists, including Zionist Jews, Eleanor Roosevelt, Henry Wallace, and Henry Morgenthau. There were shouts within the hall of "Kill the Jews" and "Get rid of the Jews, niggers, and Catholics." Outside the hall were more than 1,000 angry and turbulent persons protesting the meeting. A cordon of police tried to maintain order, but they were unable to prevent several disturbances. One person was convicted of disorderly conduct for offensive public speech.

Terminiello was charged with violating a Chicago ordinance forbidding any breach of the peace. The trial judge charged the jury among other things that "breach of the peace" consists of any "misbehavior which violates the public peace and decorum" and that "misbehavior may constitute a breach of the peace if it stirs the public to anger, invites dispute, brings about a condition of unrest, or creates a disturbance, or if it molests the inhabitants in the enjoyment of peace and quiet by arousing alarm." Terminiello was convicted and fined $100.

---

[243] *Ibid.* at 308–311.
[244] Terminiello v. Chicago, 337 U.S. 1, 4–5 (1949).

Although Terminiello's counsel had not objected to the charge, the majority of the Court held that the charge permitting "conviction of petitioner if his speech stirred people to anger, invited public dispute, or brought about a condition of unrest" did not meet constitutional standards. Concluding that a "conviction resting on any of those grounds may not stand," the Court reversed his conviction. It explained:

> Speech is often provocative and challenging. It may strike at prejudices and preconceptions and have profound unsettling effects as it presses for acceptance of an idea. That is why freedom of speech, though not absolute [citing Chaplinsky[245]] is nevertheless protected against censorship or punishment, unless shown likely to produce a clear and present danger of a serious evil that rises far above public inconvenience, annoyance, or unrest.

The four dissenters held that because defense counsel had not objected to the charge, the issue was not before the court.

In *Chaplinsky v. New Hampshire*,[246] on which the majority of the Court in *Terminiello* relied, the Court set the outer limits of the breach-of-peace doctrine. *Chaplinsky* involved the alleged violation of a New Hampshire statute forbidding any person from addressing "any offensive, derisive or annoying word to another person who is lawfully in any street or other public place" or "call him by any offensive or derisive name." While distributing Jehovah's Witnesses' literature on the streets of Rochester, N.H., Chaplinsky had condemned all religion as a racket, had accused the City Marshall of being "a God damned racketeer" and "a damned Fascist," and denounced the whole government of Rochester as "Fascists or agents of Fascists." He was convicted for violation of the statute, and the case came before the Supreme Court.

The Court had little difficulty in upholding the conviction. Speaking for the unanimous Court, Justice Murphy stated:

> it is well understood that the right of free speech is not absolute at all times and under all circumstances. There are certain well-defined and narrowly limited classes of speech, the prevention of which and punishment of which have never been thought to raise any Constitutional problems, These include the lewd and obscene, the profane, the libelous, and the insulting or "fighting" words – those which by their very utterance inflict injury or tend to incite an immediate breach of the peace.[247]

[245] Chaplinsky v. New Hampshire, 315 U.S. 568 (1942).
[246] Ibid.
[247] Ibid. at 571–572.

Although the doctrine of breach of the peace survives, it is apparent that its scope and significance have been seriously limited.

F. Conclusion

Thus, it has taken the Supreme Court almost 150 years to complete its refashioning of the constitutional guaranty of freedom of speech and press. However, in the end under its enormously strengthened standards for barring interference with freedom of speech, the repressive doctrines inherited from the English that became part of the jurisprudence of the New Republic have been severely restricted. The offenses remain on the books, but the occasions on which they may be constitutionally employed seem to be negligible. There are few situations indeed that can meet the demanding requirements of the "clear and present danger" standard.

8

Still Other 19th-Century Doctrines for Suppression of Anti-Establishment Speech

The Law of Blasphemy and the Slave State
Anti-Abolition Statutes

A. Introduction

As the 18th century gave way to the 19th, the widespread criminalization of anti-establishment speech cast a wide shadow on the jurisprudence of the times. The Sedition Act of 1798 and the even more draconic common-law doctrine of criminal libel, which serve as the primary focus of this volume, provide a vivid insight into this unhappy period in American jurisprudence. However, to understand how the American society of the time including so many of the Founding Fathers – veterans of the Revolutionary War or the Constitutional Convention – approved of such criminalization and its use, party against party in the political struggles of the period, one should go further. It is essential to understand that criminal libel did not stand alone. It was only one, certainly the most important but only one, of a half dozen doctrines available in the jurisprudence of the times for suppression of anti-establishment speech.

Chapters 7 and 8 seek to place the experience with criminal libel in its larger jurisprudential context by considering these other doctrines that also served to suppress what may be characterized as anti-establishment speech. Chapter 7 examined the various other repressive doctrines employed by Federalists and Republicans alike when they were in power to suppress dissenting political points of view. These included contempt of court and contempt of the legislature for out-of-chamber criticism of the judiciary and legislature, pre-trial binding over for good behavior in criminal libel cases, and breach of peace.

This chapter considers two additional doctrines criminalizing dissenting speech. It starts with a review of the established common and statutory law of criminal blasphemy as still another area of the law at the time suppressing dissenting views of a major establishment institution: the Christian church. It concludes with a review of the statutes throughout the antebellum South criminalizing public discussion of the legitimacy of slavery or its abolition. Although not partisan political speech, the experience in both areas provides still other examples of the limited scope of constitutional protection of freedom of the press and religion as perceived by the courts of the times. The constitutionality of the common law and statutory criminal blasphemy law grounded on Christianity was uniformly upheld notwithstanding the federal and state constitutional guaranties of freedom of religion. This parallels the experience with the comparable jurisprudence of the common law and statutory law criminalizing libel or the statutory law criminalizing the discussion of the legitimacy or abolition of slavery. Not one court in all the cases involving these issues held the prosecution unconstitutional, notwithstanding the constitutional guaranties of freedom of speech and press.

B. Criminalization of Blasphemy Under State Common and Statutory Law

1. Introduction

The crime of blasphemy is still another example of the large number of legal doctrines during the first half century of the Republic that served in various areas to silence anti-establishment speech. The criminalization of blasphemy, of course, involves very different societal values and political policies than those underlying criminal libel and allied doctrines or the circulation of anti-slavery materials. Blasphemy does not involve issues in which security of the state is perceived to be at stake, at least not directly at stake. However, as with criminal libel and the anti-abolition statutes, it rests at least in part on similar concerns of anticipating and preventing breaches of the peace. Further, the blasphemy cases tested the scope of the state constitutional guaranties of freedom of religion and free speech in very much the same way as the criminal libel cases and the anti-abolition statutes tested the perimeters of the state constitutional protections of freedom of speech and press.

The criminalization of blasphemy was a firmly embedded feature of state jurisprudence that persisted until well into the 20th century before finally succumbing to modern constitutional decisions vigorously expanding the reach of the federal constitutional guaranty of freedom of religion and free speech. As such, it has received its fair share of academic discussion as a feature of the

American law.[1] However, it also deserves attention along with the anti-slavery statutes as companion legal doctrines reflecting American societal suppression of anti-establishment speech. Both help explain the near-universal acceptance of the criminal libel during the earlier decades of this period.

Although not involving political speech, the common-law crime of blasphemy and the numerous criminal statutes codifying the common law of blasphemy that were accepted throughout the nation in the period under discussion, thus, provide still a further illustration of breadth of the criminal remedies during the period available to punish dissenting speech.

It also provides a striking constitutional parallel to the experience with criminal libel. The existence of the freedom of religion and free speech provisions in almost all contemporary state Constitutions and in the First Amendment to the federal Constitution[2] were of no avail. They provided no more shelter for defendants accused of blasphemy (or for that matter, defendants accused of violation of its related doctrine, the so-called Blue Laws prohibiting certain business activities on Sundays) than did the comparable provisions assuring freedom of speech and press for persons accused of criminal libel.

2. The English Criminal Common Law of Blasphemy

The twin principles that "Christianity is part of the common law" and that blasphemy was criminal were accepted parts of the English common law. In *Rex v. Taylor* in 1676, Lord Chief Justice Hale in a much quoted passage denounced the defendant, saying:

> Such kind of wicked blasphemous words were not only an offence to God and religion, but a crime against laws, State, and Government, and

---

[1] *See generally* Leonard W. Levy, *Blasphemy* (1993) (hereinafter Levy, *Blasphemy*); *Blasphemy in Massachusetts: Freedom of Conscience and the Abner Kneeland Case: A Documentary Record* (Leonard W. Levy ed. 1973) (hereinafter Levy, *Blasphemy in Massachusetts*); Banner, When Christianity Was Part of the Common Law, 16 Law & Hist. Rev. 27 (1998) (hereinafter Banner); 2 *Works of James Wilson* 425 (J. Andrews ed. 1896); 2 Zephaniah Swift, *System of the Laws of Connecticut* 321 (J. Byrne 1795) (hereinafter Swift); Joseph Story, Christianity a Part of the Common Law, Am. Jurist 9 (1833) (hereinafter Story, Christianity); Note, Blasphemy, 70 Colum. L. Rev. 694 (1970); Anno, Validity of Blasphemy Statutes or Ordinances, 41 A.L.R. 3d 519 (1972).

[2] Readers will recall that until 1833, it was not clear whether the provisions of the Bill of Rights applied to the states. Then in *Barron v. Baltimore*, the Supreme Court held that they had no application. 32 U.S. 243 (1833). This was the law for 100 years. Then, the Supreme Court reversed ground, relying on the adoption of the 14th Amendment. In *Gitlow v. People* in 1925, it held the states bound by the federal provision on freedom of speech and in *Cantwell v. Connecticut* in 1940 bound by the federal provision on freedom of religion. Gitlow v. People, 268 U.S. 652 (1925); Cantwell v. Connecticut, 310 U.S. 296 (1940).

therefore punishable...; for to say religion is a cheat, is to dissolve all those obligations whereby the civil societies are preserved, and...Christianity is parcel of the laws of England; and therefore to reproach the Christian religion is to speak in subversion of the law.[3]

Followed in *Rex v. Woolston*,[4] the doctrine became firmly established as English law. In the chapter of offences against God and religion in his *Commentaries*, Blackstone, thus, summarizes:

blasphemy against the Almighty, by denying his being or providence; or by contumacious reproaches of our saviour Christ. Whither also may be referred all profane scoffing at the holy scripture or exposing it to contempt and ridicule. These are offenses punishable at common law by fine and imprisonment, or other infamous corporal punishment for christianity is part of the laws of England.[5]

3. Blasphemy Law in the Colonies and the New Republic

The English common law, including common-law blasphemy, formed part of the legal system of the 13 Colonies. However, the Colonial law of blasphemy soon outgrew its venerable common-law roots. As early as 1700 in Virginia and Pennsylvania and 1702 in Maryland, the Colonies began to enact statutes criminalizing blasphemy. Although the Pennsylvania statute was mild, the Maryland statute provided for savage punishments.[6] Other colonies followed suit. Blasphemy law – both common-law and statutory – was an established part of the Colonial legal system at the time of the Revolution.[7]

---

[3] Rex v. Taylor, 1 Vent. 293, 86 Eng. Rep. 189 (K.B. 1676). For other cases echoing and re-echoing this principle, *see* G. Nokes, *History of the Crime of Blasphemy* (1928).

[4] Rex v. Woolston, 94 Eng. Rep. 655 (K.B. 1729).

[5] 4 William Blackstone, *Commentaries on the Laws of England* 59 (1769 repr. 1992) (hereinafter Blackstone). When the American courts wanted an authoritative reference to the English common law of blasphemy, they invariably turned to Blackstone. *See, e.g.* Updegraph v. Commonwealth, 11 Serg. & Rawle 394, 1824 Pa. LEXIS 85, at *7 (1824); Commonwealth v. Kneeland. 37 Mass. (20 Pick.) 206, 213, 1838 Mass. LEXIS 35 (1838). Newspapers did much the same. *See* Providence *Patriot & Columbian Phoenix*, Dec. 15, 1827 (blasphemy in the English common law defined by Blackstone, pointing to the quotation in the text).

[6] Penn. Laws of 1700, 1 Sm. L. 6 *enforced* in Updegraph v. Commonwealth, 11 Serg. & Rawle 394, 1824 Pa. LEXIS 85 (1824); Md. Laws 1723, collected in *The Laws of the Province of Maryland* (J. Cushing, compiler 1978).

[7] At the same time, Americans appeared to be interested in the English law of blasphemy. Thus, the American press widely reported the conviction of Mr. Carlisle, a London bookseller and Deist, of the crime of blasphemy in publishing *Paine's Age of Reason* (of which there were said to be 20,000 copies scattered over the country). After indictment, he was confined in King's Bench Prison for want of sureties for his £1,000 bail. This story appeared in the New Bedford *Mercury*, Dec. 10, 1819; Newburyport *Herald*, Dec. 7, 1819; and *Columbian Centinel*, Dec. 4, 1819. A related account

With the Revolution, as readers have learned, 11 of the states had adopted statutes receiving their Colonial law including the law of blasphemy as well as the law of criminal libel, whether resting on common law or Colonial statute, as the law of the new state. Following the pattern of the Colonial statutes criminalizing blasphemy, codification of the law of blasphemy continued after the Revolution, with statutes enacted in Massachusetts in 1782 and Rhode Island in 1798. Criminalization of blasphemy, increasingly based on statute rather than on the English and Colonial common law,[8] was an established part of the law of the land. It comfortably coexisted with the state constitutional guarantees of freedom of religion and free speech.

There was isolated and ineffective dissent. Apparently alone at the time, St. George Tucker's discussion of blasphemy in his popular edition of Blackstone's *Commentaries* not only recognized that the adoption by Virginia of its 1776 Bill of Rights containing a provision protecting freedom of religion introduced a serious constitutional question, but speculated whether it had not in fact abolished "blasphemy as a civil offense."[9]

The doctrine of blasphemy is closely associated with a companion maxim that "Christianity is part and parcel of the common law."[10] As points out, that maxim borrowed from Blackstone was heard so often that a commentator writing in 1902 could refer to the crime of blasphemy resting on the maxim as a matter "decided over and over again."[11] However, as Justice Story pointed out, the legal significance of the maxim in the 19th century was limited, aside

---

appears in the *Connecticut Courant* of Nov. 30, 1819, reprinting a story in New York *Evening Post* headed as London, Oct. 15, upholding the result. The defendant was ultimately convicted and sentenced to three years in jail and a fine of £1,500 in Nov. 1821. *See* H. Bonner, *Penalties upon Opinion* 39–43 (1913). *See also* a report on the 1820 indictment for "seditious and blasphemous libel" of Joseph Swann, one of leaders of the so-called Macclesfield riots; no report is available indicating whether a trial ensued and, if so, the outcome of the trial.

[8] The distinction between the common law and statutory foundations of the doctrine is vital. The common law and the maxim that "Christianity is part of the common law" with which it was associated became irrelevant when the prosecution was based on the statute. Whatever the relation between Christianity and the common law, the statute was now determinative.

[9] In his 1803 edition containing his editorial notes to the Constitution and laws of the United States and Virginia, St. George Tucker annotates the passage quoted in the text. He goes on to assert: "This, as a civil offence, seems to have been abolished by the provisions contained in the bill of rights, etc., together with the other offenses against religion already noticed in this chapter," referring to a prior note listing the U.S. Constitution and Bill of Rights provisions and the Virginia constitutional and statutory references dealing with freedom of religion. 5 St. George Tucker, *Blackstone's Commentaries with Notes* at 59, 59n, 44n (1803 repr. 1969) (hereinafter Tucker).

[10] Even the Supreme Court paid its respects to the dictum. *See* Vidal v. Philadelphia, 43 U.S. 127, 198, 2 How. 127, 198 (1844) (the maxim recognized as part of the common law of Pennsylvania). *See generally* James McClellan, *Joseph Story and the American Constitution* 118–159 (1971).

[11] Banner, note 1, at 27, *citing* Arthur A. Barber, Christianity and the Common Law, 14 The Green Bag 267 (1902).

from its role as the foundation of blasphemy law. Thus, in his opinion in *Vidal*, Justice Story stated:

> We are compelled to admit, that although Christianity be a part of the common law of the state [Pennsylvania], yet it is so in this qualified sense – that its divine origin and truth are admitted – and therefore, it is not to be maliciously and openly reviled and blasphemed against, to the annoyance of believers or the injury of the public.[12]

Whatever the limitations in the scope of the maxim, it plays little role in our discussion. Although the importance of the maxim as the foundation of the common law of blasphemy is unchallenged, we are concerned with blasphemy, and particularly its development as a statutory doctrine, not with the maxim. As for blasphemy, the leading commentators of the period – Blackstone, James Wilson, Zephaniah Swift, as well as Story – all agreed that blasphemy was a common-law crime.[13] Similarly, as we will see, Chancellor Kent similarly recognized blasphemy as a common-law crime in New York. His decision to this effect in the *Ruggles* case was followed by courts in Alabama, Arkansas, Delaware, Pennsylvania, North Carolina, South Carolina, and Tennessee.

However accepted the doctrine, and notwithstanding the celebrated 19th-century cases upholding the doctrine involving some of the leading jurists of the period, Levy has sniffed at what he perceives as its fading significance. Thus, Levy observes that there were only ten prosecutions in the entire 18th century in contrast to the much more vigorous enforcement during the previous century.[14] In addition, the declining level of statutory punishment in the event of violation in some jurisdictions provides further support for the view that the societal evaluation of the seriousness of the crime was substantially abating. Thus, the savage penalties provided in the early 18th-century Maryland statute described above contrast sharply with the milder penalties in the later statutes.[15]

---

[12] Vidal v. Philadelphia, 43 U.S. (2 How.) 127, 198 (1844), *citing* Updegraph v. Commonwealth, 11 Serg. & Rawle 394, 1824 Pa. LEXIS 85 (1824).

[13] 2 *Works of James Wilson* 425 (J. Andrews ed. 1896); 2 Swift, note 1, at 321; Story, Christianity, note 1.

[14] *See* Levy, *Blasphemy*, note 1, at 264–267. In addition to Levy's extensive collection of blasphemy decisions, there appears to be at least one additional case. Moses Goddard was reported to have been convicted for blasphemy in Springfield, Vt., in early Oct. 1790. Springfield, Vt., *Western Star*, Oct. 12, 1790.

[15] A 1788 newspaper account of the visit to Philadelphia of the "famous, or rather infamous, *Jemimah Wilkinson*, a person who professes that she is our Lord and Savior Jesus Christ came [sic] into our world a second time" illustrates a possible change of community attitude. However, *see* very different attitudes reported *infra* in notes 22 and 25.

Notwithstanding the weight of this view, one must recognize that during this period the blasphemy law continued to be enforced. It continued as a living reality, far from the suggested image of a legal fossil. In fact, it seems a vigorous a part of the jurisprudence comparable to the experience in the preceding century. Although 18th-century blasphemy prosecutions including two after the Revolution[16] may have continued at a slower pace than in the 17th century, blasphemy prosecutions in the first half of the 19th century did continue and in significant numbers.[17] Furthermore, the states continued to enact statutes criminalizing the practice.[18] Prosecutions, some of them attracting considerable note, not only continued but without apparent decline. Thus, building on the work of earlier scholars, the author has identified no fewer than 20 blasphemy cases in the first half of the 19th century,[19] or twice as many as the number reported by Levy for the entire

---

The newspaper commented: "Had Jemimah Wilkinson made her appearance a century or two ago, she would then have been capitally [sic] punished, but to the honor of the present age, . . . the mildness of our laws and the good sense of the people are such that no injury or even insult has been offered to any of them" *New Jersey Journal*, May 28, 1788.

[16] These include State v. Wilkinson (N.J. 1788) (failure to prosecute), *New Jersey Journal*, May 28, 1788; and defendant name unavailable (Dauphin Cty., Pa. 1799) (conviction), cited by Levy, *Blasphemy*, note 1, at 407.

[17] Banner's collection of the cases may be found in Banner, note 1, at 31–32n.

[18] Mass. Acts and Resolves, Act of 1782 ch. 8 (July 3, 1782); R.I. Laws 1798, sec. 33.

[19] The 20 19th-century cases include four prominent cases reported in the official law reports that dominate the literature: People v. Ruggles, 8 Johns. 290, 1811 N.Y. LEXIS 124 (Sup. Ct. 1811) (Kent, Ch. J.) (conviction); Updegraph v. Commonwealth, 11 Serg. & Rawle 394 (Pa. 1824), 1824 Pa. LEXIS 85 (1824) (conviction reversed); Commonwealth v. Kneeland, 37 Mass. (20 Pick.) 206, 1838 Mass. LEXIS 35, (1838) (conviction); State v. Chandler, 2 Del. (Harr.) 553, 1837 Del. LEXIS 63 (1837) (conviction). In each of these, the defendant was convicted in the trial court.

In addition, there are press and other reports of 11 convictions for blasphemy and five instances of acquittals or jury disagreement of the following defendants: Commonwealth v. Eli Hamilton (Mass. 1808) (pillory for four hours and costs and imprisonment until sentence performed); Commonwealth v. Caleb Jephtherson (Mass. 1811) (pillory for one and one-half hours); Commonwealth v. Filland, *American Advocate and Kennebec Advertiser*, Sept. 19, 1818 (Mass. 1818); State v. Benjamin R. Allen (Conn. 1818) (imprisonment of 12 months), *Massachusetts Spy or Worcester Gazette*, Oct. 21, 1818; Commonwealth v. Murray, (Mayor's Court, Philadelphia, 1818), *National Messenger*, Nov. 17, 1818; Providence *Gazette*, Nov. 28, 1818, Franklin *Gazette*, Nov. 21, 1818, reported in Updegraph v. Commonwealth, 11 Serg. & Rawle 394, 404, 1824 Pa. LEXIS 85 (1824); People v. John W. Hinckley (N.Y. 1819) (imprisonment of three months), *New-York Columbian*, Sept. 1, 1819; People v. Oliver Story (N.Y. 1820) (imprisonment of four months), *Berkshire Star*, July 6, 1820; Commonwealth v. defendant name unavailable (Pa. 1822), *Farmers' Cabinet*, Mar. 16, 1822; State v. William Cannon (Conn. 1826) (imprisonment of six months and $100 fine), *American Mercury*, Aug. 29, 1826; Commonwealth v. Sharp (Pa. 1829), New Bedford *Mercury*, Feb 2, 1829; State v. Granger (Conn. 1829) (conviction), Baltimore *Patriot*, Sept. 9, 1829.

The acquittals were Ebenezer Darrow (Vt. 1804), Windham *Herald*, Oct. 11, 1804 (acquittal by reason of insanity); Lydia Profet (N.Y. 1820) ("coloured" fortune teller "pretending to discover" the location of stolen goods), *New-England Palladium*, Feb. 4, 1820); State v. Bell, 6 City Hall Records, N.Y. City (N.Y. 1821), 3 *American State Trials* 558, 561 (J. Lawson ed. 1915) and People v. Porter, 2

18th century.[20] Furthermore, as will be seen, cases were brought and convictions obtained and upheld against constitutional challenge until as late as 1941.[21]

Far from disappearing, civic outrage at episodes of blasphemy still ran at fever pitch in many quarters in the nineteenth century. Thus, in an editorial note entitled "Two Great Toms," the Newport *Mercury* in 1802 bitterly assailed Tom Paine and Thomas Jefferson:

> There is no man known in the U. States, who has blasphemed so openly and wickedly as Tom Paine. The Christian would shudder at hearing his expressions repeated. [Noting his selection by Jefferson as "his most favored friend," the editorial continued] Perhaps the President does not know that Blasphemy is a crime which the laws of Maryland punish severely. First offence, "bored through the tongue and fined 20 £. sterl. – for the second offence, he would be branded in the forehead with the letter B and fined 40 £. sterl. – and for the third offence, suffer death. Such, people of Maryland, is the respect paid by your President to your laws, and your religion!"[22]

The very language employed in the press reports of some of the blasphemy cases similarly vividly conveys the serious nature of the offence, at least as seen by some observers at the time. Thus, in the newspaper account of the blasphemy conviction of *Filland* in Massachusetts in 1818, the editor declined to specify what was actually said. Instead, he reported only that the blasphemy for which Filland was convicted was "perhaps the most horrid ever uttered from the lips of a mortal."[23] Similarly, a newspaper report of the blasphemy conviction of *Samuel Sharp* in Pennsylvania in 1829 notes that he was convicted for "expressions . . . too abominable to be published."[24] In like fashion, an account of a blasphemy case in New London, Conn., in

Park Crim. Rep. 14 (1823). The jury disagreement occurred in defendant name unavailable (Mass. 1822), *Independent Chronicle* and Boston *Patriot*, May, 4, 1822.

[20] Whether this actually indicates an increase in the rate of blasphemy prosecutions is another matter. Levy's collection was a remarkable achievement in the light of the greater barriers to research of the earlier periods of the American experience. These barriers suggest that there were not many more 18th-century cases still undiscovered. One must also keep in mind that as late as 1750, there were only 12 papers in all the Colonies in comparison to the 239 papers in 1800. *See* E. Latham, *Chronological Tables of American Newspapers, 1690–1820* (1972).

[21] Oney v. Oklahoma City, 120 F.2d 861 (10th Cir. 1941) (conviction); Lynch v. City of Muskogee, 47 F. Supp. 589 (E.D. Okla. 1942) (conviction). *See also* State v. Mockus, 120 Me. 84, 113 A. 39 (1921) (conviction).

[22] Newport *Mercury*, Dec. 21, 1802.

[23] Report of Commonwealth v. Filland (Mass. 1818), *American Advocate and Kennebec Advertiser*, Sept. 19, 1818.

[24] Report of Commonwealth v. Sharp (Pa. 1829), New Bedford *Mercury*, Feb. 2, 1829.

1818 suppressed the terms used and described the defendant's "conviction of blasphemy – a horrid offence! The proof of which was revolting to every spectator. Sentence, imprisonment 12 months. Let the profane beware! For the transition is easy from profane swearing to this horrid enormous crime."[25] Still other accounts of blasphemy convictions include such observations as "the odious and detestable crime of Blasphemy, a crime which surpasses all in the black catalogue which emanates from human nature in its most depraved state."[26]

Even as late as 1921, the Supreme Judicial Court of Maine in upholding the blasphemy conviction in *Mockus* after specifying the alleged blasphemies[27] apologized that "It is a most embarrassing task to spread these words on the printed page."[28]

However aghast the editors of these accounts appear to be at the nature of the crime, the courts, no doubt reflecting moderating tempers in the society, seem to have had a somewhat different view of the severity of the offense. In the *Sharp* case (1829), the defendant was fined only $22 and costs. Similarly, in the *Filland* case (1818), the account mentions only that he was fined, without troubling to mention the amount. Another Pennsylvania conviction (1822) during this period saw the defendant fined only $5 and costs, although adjudging imprisonment for three months in the case of nonpayment.[29] Finally, in the celebrated *Updegraph* case (1824) discussed below, the trial court after conviction sentenced the convicted defendant to a fine of only five shillings and costs.[30] These modest punishments compare with the sentences of 60 days' imprisonment in the *Kneeland* litigation (1838) and the one year's imprisonment in the New London prosecution (1818).

4. The Blasphemy Statutes

The law of blasphemy in the New Republic was for the most part statutory law. Although it was everywhere accepted that blasphemy was part of the

---

[25] *Massachusetts Spy or Worcester Gazette*, Oct. 21, 1818, copying an account in the Norwich *Courant*.
[26] *Poulson's American Daily Advertiser*, May 14, 1805 (Commonwealth v. Caleb Jephtherson, Worcester, Mass.).
[27] Mockus, a Lithuanian immigrant leftist speaking to other Lithuanian immigrants, was convicted of such blasphemies as "Religion, capitalism, and government are all damned humbugs, liars and thieves"; "All religions are a deception of the people"; "There is no truth in the Bible. It is only monkey business." These were in addition to slurs on the Virgin Mary.
[28] 120 Me. at 87, 113 A. at 40.
[29] Commonwealth v. Unknown Defendant (Pa. 1822) (not reported). Only a newspaper account is available. *See Farmers' Cabinet*, Mar. 16, 1822.
[30] Updegraph v. Commonwealth, 11 Serg. & Rawle 394, 1824 Pa. LEXIS 85 (1824).

common law of the states, having been part of the common law of the Colonies and of England, almost all the states either had "received" Colonial statutes criminalizing blasphemy or had adopted new blasphemy statutes of their own.[31]

Thus, Pennsylvania at the time of the *Updegraph* case in 1824 was still operating under the Colonial statute criminalizing blasphemy that had been adopted in 1700. This early Act provided:

> Whosoever shall, wilfully, premeditately, and despitefully [sic] blaspheme or speak loosely and profanely of the Almighty GOD, CHRIST JESUS, the HOLY SPIRIT or the SCRIPTURES of TRUTH and is legally convicted thereof, shall forfeit and pay the sum of ten pounds . . . or suffer three months imprisonment at hard labor . . . for the use of the . . . poor [of the county in which such offense shall be committed].[32]

The Maryland statute of the same period defined the offense in similar terms,[33] and, as we have seen, provided for dreadful penalties, including boring of the tongue, plus a fine of 20 pounds sterling for the first offense, branding with the letter B, and a doubled fine for the second offense and death without any benefit of clergy for the third.

The Massachusetts statute adopted in 1782 was still in force six decades later at the time of the celebrated *Kneeland* case (1842) discussed below. It provided:

> If any person shall wilfully blaspheme the Holy Name of GOD, by denying, cursing, or contumeliously reproaching GOD, his Creation, Government, or final Judging of the World, or by cursing, or reproaching JESUS CHRIST, or the HOLY GHOST, or by cursing or contumeliously reproaching the Holy Word of GOD, that is the Canonical Scriptures contained in the Books of the Old and New Testaments, or by exposing them, or any Part of them, to contempt or ridicule; which Books are [specifying every biblical book from Genesis to Revelations], every person so offending, shall be punished by Imprisonment not exceeding Twelve Months, by sitting in the pillory, by Whipping, or by sitting on

[31] States with statutes criminalizing blasphemy included Maine, Massachusetts, New Hampshire, New York, Pennsylvania, Rhode Island, and Vermont.

[32] Penn. Laws of 1700, 1 Sm. L. 6.

[33] "Curse him [God], or deny our Savior JESUS CHRIST to be the son of GOD, or shall deny the Holy Trinity, the Father, Son and Holy Ghost, or the God-Head of any the three persons, or the Unity of the God-Head, or that shall utter any Prophane Words concerning the Holy Trinity, or any of the Persons thereof." *The Laws of the Province of Maryland, Acts of 1723*, ch. 16 (J. Cushing, compiler. 1978).

the Gallows, with a Rope about the Neck, or binding to the good Behavior, at the Discretion of the Supreme Judicial Court... according to the
Aggravation of the Offence.[34]

The Rhode Island statute of 1798 simply referred to the "crime of blasphemy"
without further definition,[35] providing for a fine not exceeding $100 and
imprisonment not exceeding two months.

5. The Blasphemy Litigation

The role played by the law of blasphemy in the new nation is best described by
retracing ground familiar to scholars and examining the four celebrated cases
of the period decided by some of the leading judges of the times. The four leading cases were *Ruggles* (1811) in New York, *Updegraph* (1824) in Pennsylvania,
Kneeland (1836) in Massachusetts, and *Chandler* (1848) in Delaware.[36] Each
upheld the constitutionality of the state statute before it, notwithstanding the
guaranties of freedom of religion in their state constitution. In addition, there
are reports of at least eight other less prominent cases during the first half of
the 19th century involving blasphemy. Of these, convictions were obtained
in five. Litigation was episodic, but blasphemy prosecutions and convictions
continued for about 100 years until World War II. So much for the contention
that legal concerns with blasphemy were fading away. Until the U.S. Supreme
Court finally spoke out in the *Cantwell* case in 1940,[37] the courts had little
difficulty in accepting the coexistence of the crime of blasphemy along with
the federal and state guaranties of religious liberty.[38]

---

[34] Mass. R.S. ch. 130, §15. This statute is much the same as the New Jersey statute as to the substance
of the offense, but the more modern New Jersey statute provided simply for punishment as a
misdemeanor omitting reference to whipping, pillory, or the gallows.

[35] R.I. Laws of 1798, §33. A newspaper account some decades later explained that although the statute
did not define the offense, for purposes of the law, blasphemy was defined by the English law,
referring to Blackstone. Providence *Patriot and Columbian Phenix*, dated Dec. 15, 1827, containing
a despatch from an "Investigator" for the *Patriot*. *See* text accompanying note 17.

[36] People v. Ruggles, 8 Johns. Cas. 290, 1811 N.Y. LEXIS 124 (Sup. Ct. 1811) (Kent, Ch. J.) (conviction);
Updegraph v. Commonwealth, 11 Serg. & Rawle 394, 1824 Pa. LEXIS 85 (1824) (conviction
reversed); Commonwealth v. Kneeland, 37 Mass. (20 Pick.) 206, 1838 Mass. LEXIS 35, (1838)
(Shaw, C.J.) (conviction); State v. Chandler, 2 Del. (Harr.) 553, 1837 Del. LEXIS 63 (1837)
(conviction).

[37] Cantwell v. Connecticut, 310 U.S. 296 (1940).

[38] Oney v. Oklahoma City, 120 F.2d 861 (10th Cir. 1941); Lynch v. City of Muskogee, 47 F. Supp.
589 (E.D. Okla. 1942); State v. Mockus, 120 Me. 84, 113 A. 39 (1921). *See* Commonwealth *ex rel.*
Brown v. Rundle, 424 Pa. 505, 227 A.2d 895, *cert. denied*, 387 U.S. 937 (1967).

The Maryland Court of Appeal was the first state appellate court to hold a blasphemy conviction
unconstitutional under the freedom of religion clause in the state constitution. State v. West, 9
Md. App. 270, 263 A.2d 602 (1972).

In these 19th-century cases, blasphemy law departed from the criminal libel jurisprudence in one important respect. As we saw in the great criminal libel cases, constitutional law played a negligible role. It was not always argued by counsel, and when it was, the judges, such as Justice Chase in *Callender* and Justice Paterson in *Lyon*, gave it short shrift. By contrast, many judges in the blasphemy litigations, including such respected judges as Chancellor Kent in New York and Chief Justice Lemuel Shaw in Massachusetts,[39] seriously considered whether the blasphemy litigations ran afoul of the *state* constitutional guaranties with respect to freedom of religion.[40]

The first of these cases was *People v. Ruggles*. In 1811 Ruggles was indicted under the New York common-law doctrine of blasphemy. It was charged that he did "wickedly, maliciously, and blasphemously utter, in the presence and hearing of divers good and Christian people . . . 'Jesus Christ was a bastard and his mother must be a whore.'"

In the trial court, after a jury trial, the defendant was convicted and sentenced to three months' imprisonment and $500 fine. On appeal, Chancellor Kent said that

> the single question is, whether this be a public offence by the law of the land. After conviction, we must intend that these words were uttered . . . with a wicked and malicious disposition, and not in a serious discussion upon any controverted point in religion. The language was blasphemous . . . in a legal sense; for blasphemy, according to the most precise definitions, consists in maliciously reviling God, or religion, and this was reviling Christianity through its author. . . . Such words uttered with such a disposition were an offense at common law. . . . Such offenses have always been considered independent of any religious establishment . . . They are treated as affecting the essential interests of civil society.

[39] Referring to him as "that great judge," Holmes, for example, said of Shaw: "Some, indeed many, English judges could be named who surpassed him in accurate technical knowledge, but few have lived who were his equals in their understanding of the grounds of public policy to which all laws must ultimately be referred. It was this which made him, in the language of the late Judge Curtis, the greatest magistrate which this country has produced." Oliver Wendell Holmes, Jr., The Common Law 106 (1881, repr. 1945).

[40] Barron v. Baltimore, 32 U.S. 243 (1833). Although the courts hearing blasphemy cases prior to *Barron* could have appealed to the federal Constitution as outlawing blasphemy, none did so. In *Updegraph*, the Supreme Court of Pennsylvania, apparently the solitary court referring to the federal constitutional guaranty, held that it was not in conflict with the doctrine of blasphemy.

The federal freedom of religion clause had not yet been held applicable to the states. This did not occur until Cantwell v. Connecticut, 310 U.S. 296 (1940). Further, this decision rested on the 14th Amendment, which was not adopted until 1868. *See* 310 U.S. at 303 (Roberts, J.).

... nothing has prevented the application or the necessity of this part of the common law. We stand equally in need ... of all the moral discipline, and of those principles of virtue which help to bind society together. The people of this State, in common with the people of this country, profess the general doctrines of Christianity ...; and to scandalize the author of those doctrines is not only ... extremely impious, but, even in respect to the obligations due to society, is a gross violation of decency and good order.

Chancellor Kent then went on to conclude that the prosecution was not in violation of the state constitution. The New York constitutional protection of freedom of religion did not forbid judicial cognizance of those offenses against religion that "strike at the root of moral obligation, and weaken the security of the social ties." In any event, the Chancellor noted that the litigation fell under the shelter of the proviso of the New York Constitution that the guarantee did not "excuse acts of licentiousness or justify practices inconsistent with the peace and safety of this State."[41]

In New York, *Ruggles* was followed in June 1821 by the case of *People v. Jared W. Bell* providing further insight into the evolution of blasphemy law in the first half of the 19th century. *Bell* grew out of a spirited argument over the Hartford Convention a few years earlier in which much violent language was used. In the language of the indictment, the defendant "contriving and intending to scandalize and vilify the Christian religion, as received and publicly professed in the state and to blaspheme God and our Lord Jesus Christ" shouted out that "God Almighty was a fool" and that "Jesus Christ was a fool" "for creating such men as composed the Hartford Convention." Bell was indicted for blasphemy and tried. The Recorder hearing the case ruled that "The case of Ruggles has settled the law on the subject; the facts are for the jury." However, the Recorder then went on to give his own opinion of the facts, stating that "it was hardly possible that he [the defendant] could have uttered the words laid in the indictment.... If the jury should believe that he did not and that the prosecution originated from mistake or malice [on the part of the prosecuting witness, a political opponent,] it would be their duty to acquit him."

The jury thereupon found the defendant not guilty. The editor of the trial note observed that although the "words charged were most profane, but the jury evidently considered the prosecution a political one."[42]

---

[41] People v. Ruggles, & Johns. 290, 293, 296, 1811 N.Y. LEXIS 124, 4–7 (1811) (citations omitted).

[42] People v. Jared W. Bell, 6 City Hall Records, N.Y. Cty, (Gen. Sess. N.Y, 1821), 3 *American State Trials* 558, 561 (J. Lawson ed. 1915).

In 1824 the Supreme Court of Pennsylvania in *Updegraph v. Commonwealth*, considered the constitutionality of the defendant's conviction under the 1700 Pennsylvania statute. The defendant was a member of a debating association. In the course of debate over a "religious question," he was alleged to have said that the Holy Scriptures were a mere fable and contained a great many lies. He was indicted and convicted.

On appeal, the Supreme Court warmly expressed its outrage over the defendant's behavior, stating:

> That there is an association in which so serious a subject is treated with so much levity, indecency, and scurrility existing in this city, I'm sorry to hear, for it would prove a nursery of vice, a school of preparation to qualify young men for the gallows and young women for the brothel, and there is not a skeptic of decent manners and good morals, who would not consider such debating clubs as a common nuisance and disgrace to the city. From the tenor of the words, it is impossible that they could be spoken seriously and conscientiously in the discussion of a religious or theological topic; there is nothing of argument in the language; it was the outpouring of an invective so vulgarly shocking and offensive, that the lowest grade of civil authority ought not to be subject to it.[43]

The Court summarily rejected counsel's argument that the federal[44] or state constitutional protections of freedom of religion had been violated. Among other matters, it noted that Justice James Wilson, a former member of the Constitutional Convention, had asserted that blasphemy was a punishable offence notwithstanding the constitutional provisions, and further that it was not a dead letter because rare.[45] This, however, was all dictum. The Court reversed the conviction on procedural grounds; the pleading was defective, having failed to have alleged that the blasphemous language had been spoken "profanely" as required by the statute.

In the following decade, the Supreme Judicial Court of Massachusetts similarly faced the issue of the constitutionality of the conviction of Abner Kneeland, editor and publisher of the Boston *Investigator*, for violation of the reenacted 1782 Massachusetts statute providing for criminal punishment of blasphemy.[46] In his newspaper, the defendant had uttered an allegedly "scandalous, impious, obscene, blasphemous, and profane libel" that the god

---

[43] Updegraph v. Commonwealth, 11 Serg. & Rawle 394, 399; 1824 Pa. LEXIS 85 (1824).

[44] This 1824 state decision foreshadowed the 1833 decision of the Supreme Court of the United States in *Barron v. Baltimore*.

[45] James Wilson, 2 *Lectures on Jurisprudence* 245 (J. D. Andrews ed. 1896); 3 *id.* 112.

[46] Commonwealth v. Kneeland, 37 Mass. (20 Pick.) 206, 1838 Mass. LEXIS 35 (1838), *See* 13 *American State Trials* 450 (J. Lawson ed. 1921). *See also* Leonard Levy, *The Law of the Commonwealth and*

of the Universalists was "nothing more than a chimera of their imagination." After trial and conviction,[47] the defendant was sentenced to three months imprisonment and appealed.

The Supreme Judicial Court upheld the conviction. Chief Justice Shaw, one of the most admired 19th-century judges,[48] writing for the majority, stated:

> It seems now somewhat late to call into question the constitutionality of a law, which has been enacted more than half a century, has never been doubted, though there have been many prosecutions and convictions. It was itself a revision of the colonial and provincial laws to the same effect. It was passed shortly after the adoption of the [state] Constitution; nor was the matter raised or discussed in the 1820 Constitutional Convention, nor in the recent revision of the Massachusetts code of laws.

He defended the coexistence of the constitutional provisions relating to freedom of religion and freedom of speech and press and the blasphemy statute by explaining that the anti-blasphemy statute applied only to a defendant who wilfully meant:

> with a bad purpose to calumniate and disparage the Supreme Being and to destroy the veneration due him. It does not prohibit the fullest inquiry, the freeest discussion for all honest and fair purposes, one of which is the discovery of truth. It does not prevent the simple and sincere avowal of a disbelief in a supreme being.

Chief Justice Shaw pointed out that other New England states including New Hampshire, Vermont, and Maine all had similar blasphemy statutes notwithstanding their own constitutional provisions protecting freedom of religion and freedom of speech and press. He concluded by noting that in *Ruggles*, the Court of Appeals of New York had also held that the freedom

---

Chief Justice Shaw 43–58 (1957). A documentary record of the case is available in Levy, *Blasphemy in Massachusetts*, note 1.

[47] This was Kneeland's fourth trial in these proceedings. His first trial in the Boston Municipal Court in Jan. 1834 resulted in a conviction and a sentence of three months' imprisonment. On re-trial before the Supreme Judicial Court in Nov. 1834, the jury could not agree, although it was reported that 11 jurors had agreed on conviction "in ten minutes." At a re-trial in the Supreme Judicial Court, the jury again could not agree with one juror again refusing to find the defendant guilty. On the fourth trial in Nov. 1835, he was convicted. A motion for new trial was heard in Mar. 1836, but Chief Justice Shaw's opinion on behalf of a majority of the Supreme Judicial Court denying the motion did not appear until Apr. 2, 1838. Justice Morton dissented holding that the court's instructions to the jury were in error. Kneeland's sentence was reduced to 60 days' imprisonment. *See* Commonwealth v. Kneeland, 37 Mass. 206, 225, 246 (1838). *See also* Levy, Blasphemy in Massachusetts, note 1, at 269, 310.

[48] See *supra* note 39.

of religion and speech provisions of the New York Constitution had not abrogated New York's criminal common law of blasphemy.

It may be helpful to note that the Supreme Judicial Court was deciding the *Kneeland* case only a few years after its decision in *Commonwealth v. Blanding*. In *Blanding*, the Court had sustained a conviction for criminal libel notwithstanding the defendant's invocation of the state constitutional protection of freedom of speech and press. The Court had justified its result by distinguishing between liberty and "licentiousness" and asserting, following Blackstone's view of the common law,[49] that the constitutional protection of free speech and free press was directed only at preventing prior restraints.[50]

A newspaper account of this period illustrates aptly how contemporary opinion readily dealt with the apparent possible conflict between blasphemy prosecutions and the constitutional assurances of religious freedom. After contrasting the Rhode Island statute on religious freedom[51] and the Rhode Island statute on blasphemy,[52] a Providence paper in December 1827 readily reconciled the two:

> So long as a man chooses to keep his atheistical opinions in his own breast, he has a right so to do, and in Court he shall not be interrogated on the subject, nor shall he be required to make any profession of faith as a qualification for office, but when he chooses to advance opinions which are thus subversive of all our social institutions, the Same legislature which enacted the act relating to religious freedom provided also for his punishment.[53]

The last of the four celebrated blasphemy decisions is *State v.Chandler*,[54] decided in Delaware, a year after the decision in *Kneeland*. In *Chandler*, the defendant was indicted under the common law of blasphemy for asserting "in a loud voice" that "the Virgin Mary was a whore and Jesus Christ a bastard." He

---

[49] *See* 4 Blackstone, note 5, at 151.

[50] Commonwealth v. Blanding, 20 Mass. (4 Pick.) 304, 1825 Mass. LEXIS 74 (1825).

[51] The paper described at length the Rhode Island statute on religious freedom: 1. No man compelled to attend or support any religious worship. 2. No man shall suffer because of his religious opinions. 3. All shall be free to profess their religious beliefs and that shall not affect their civil rights and capacities.

[52] The paper noted that Rhode Island by statute had provided that every person committing the crime of blasphemy could be fined not exceeding $100 and be imprisoned for not more than two months. R.I. Act to Reform the Penal Laws, §37. The paper pointed out that the statute did not define the crime, but "we turn for its definition in the common law" referring to the Blackstone passage on blasphemy and "finding that denying the being or providence of God is blasphemy punishable at common law by fine and imprisonment."

[53] Providence *Patriot and Columbian Phoenix*, Dec. 15, 1827, containing a dispatch from an "Investigator for the Patriot."

[54] State v. Chandler, 2 Del. (Harr.) 553, 1837 Del. LEXIS 63 (Del. 1837).

was indicted under the common law of blasphemy.[55] Although his counsel had placed his main defense on the unconstitutionality of blasphemy law under the Delaware Constitution,[56] he was, nevertheless, convicted. The trial court sentenced him on each of the two counts to a $10 fine, ten days' solitary confinement, and sureties of $400 for good behavior for one year after discharge from imprisonment.

On appeal, the Supreme Court of Delaware affirmed, citing *Ruggles* and *Updegraph*. It ruled that it was "Long perfectly settled by the common law that blasphemy against the Deity in general or a malicious and wanton attack against the christian religion for the purpose of exposing its doctrines to contempt and ridicule is indictable and punishable." Rejecting Jefferson's repudiation of the common law blasphemy doctrine, the Court contended that "The religion of the people of Delaware is *Christian*." However, at the same time, it recognized that although the maxim "Christianity is part of the common law" was misunderstood, it was, nevertheless, applicable where the speaker was insulting or subverting. Thus, the highest courts of four states upheld the constitutionality of the blasphemy laws.

As the society grew more secular, there were fewer prosecutions for blasphemy. Nevertheless, they did continue, with blasphemy convictions occurring, as noted, until well into the 20th century.[57] Not until the Supreme Court decision in 1952 in *Joseph Burstyn, Inc. v. Wilson* was the crime of blasphemy at last held to be barred by the federal constitutional provisions of freedom of speech and press and freedom of religion.[58] A Kentucky trial court as early as 1894 had anticipated *Joseph Burstyn, Inc.* and had struck down blasphemy as unconstitutional under its state Constitution.[59] In 1970 in *State v. West*, the Maryland Court of Appeals relying on the Maryland Constitution became the first state appellate court to do so.[60]

Thus, neither the federal nor the state constitutional guaranties of freedom of speech and press and freedom of religion stood in the way of the various prosecutions for blasphemy for over 150 years. In this respect, the experience matches that under the libel laws. Although, in the blasphemy cases, the

---

[55] In Delaware, the state Constitution itself provided for reception of the English common law, subject to the provisions of the Constitution, as part of Delaware law. Del. Const. art. 25 (1776).

[56] Del. Const. art. 1, §1 (1792) ("no power shall, or ought to be vested in or assumed by any magistrate, that shall in any case interfere with, or in any manner control the rights of conscience").

[57] E.g., State v. Mockus, 120 Me. 84, 113 A. 39 (1921); Oney v. Oklahoma City, 120 F.2d 861 (10th Cir. 1941). *See* Lynch v. City of Muskogee, 47 F. Supp. 589 (E.D. Okla. 1942).

[58] Joseph Burstyn, Inc. v. Wilson, 343 U.S. 495 (1952).

[59] Kentucky v. Moore (Ky. Trial court 1894), C. Moore, *Behind the Bars*: 31498, 290–291 (1890) reprinting the report in Freethought Magazine, *cited by* Levy, *Blasphemy*, note 1, at 511.

[60] State v. West, 9 Md. App. 270, 263 A.2d (2d) (1970).

courts took the constitutional challenge much more seriously than the judges dealing with criminal libel, the outcome was the same. With both repressive doctrines, the 20th century was well advanced before a single appellate court judge, let alone an appellate court, held that that the constitutional provisions barred criminal prosecutions for either blasphemy or criminal libel. The solid body of experience upholding the constitutionality of the blasphemy laws provides even further support for acceptance by American jurisprudence of the constitutionality of criminal libel laws as well.

Notwithstanding the ineffective role of constitutional guaranties to shut down prosecutions during the 19th century, blasphemy's days as a lively part of American jurisprudence were coming to their end by reasons of profound changes in the society. As observed in other contexts,[61] the weakening of the influence of Puritan values in the law as well as the increasing secularization of the society and the decisive role of the jury[62] help explain the decline.

Notwithstanding the collapse of public support for criminalization of blasphemy and the Supreme Court decision in *Joseph Burstyn, Inc.*, blasphemy has not vanished entirely from the American scene. Blasphemy statutes, unconstitutional or not, still remain on the statute books of six states, including Massachusetts, Michigan, and Pennsylvania. Further, a Pennsylvania film producer was recently denied incorporation because his proposed corporation had a blasphemous name; in that matter, an action seeking to have the Pennsylvania statute declared unconstitutional has been filed.[63]

6. The Contrasting Experience with the "Blue Laws"

The form of judicial response to the so-called Blue Laws provides an interesting contrast to the continuing unanimous judicial support for the blasphemy laws. As early as *Bloom v. Richards*, decided in 1853, the Supreme Court of Ohio, a jurisdiction accepting as did all others the constitutionality of blasphemy laws, had no doubts that a statute seeking to outlaw conduct contrary to

---

[61] *See, e.g.*, Cornelia Dayton, *Women Before the Bar: Gender, Law, and Society in Connecticut 1639–1789* (1995) (discussing the declining role of Puritan values as contributing to changing dimensions of the role of women in the legal system in the 18th and early 19th centuries in Connecticut, including fornication, rape, divorce, and abandonment, among others).

[62] Juries were reaching broader parts of the community. The community itself was changing. Increased immigration, population mobility, increased heterogenity contrasted with the more static 18th-century society.

[63] Kalman v. Pedro Cortez, Pennsylvania Sec'y of State (E.D. Pa. 2009). *See* Sarah B. Gordon quoted in "A Man's Existentialism Construed as Blasphemy, *New York Times*, Mar. 21, 2009, A12, col. 1.

the Christian ideal of those times relating to conduct on Sunday, the Christian sabbath, "is directly prohibited by the Constitution." Although protection of Christianity against blasphemy was constitutional, other state action primarily directed at the punishment of conduct contrary to Christian principles was unconstitutional. Thus, the Court said flatly that: "The statute . . . prohibiting common labor on the Sabbath could not stand for a moment as of this State, if its sole foundation was the Christian duty of keeping that day holy and its sole motive to enforce the observance of that duty."[64] Instead of viewing the statutes as expressing support for Christianity, the courts were ready to accept the contention that the "blue law" statutes reflected instead the concern of the Legislature over the length of the work week. On this basis, entirely free of religious connotation, the Court held the statute constitutional. Other courts dealing with the "blue laws" similarly sidestepped the issue of unconstitutionality under the freedom of religion clause of the state Constitution by relying on the police power of the state.[65]

7. Conclusion

The unanimous outcome of the celebrated blasphemy cases of the period upholding the constitutionality of criminal punishment for violation of the traditional doctrine in terms borrowed from Blackstone provides a fascinating parallel to the comparable experience with criminal libel. The blasphemy statutes were supported by concern that the conduct involved constituted a serious threat to the preservation of good order. The offensive language not only had its direct impact tending to promote violent reactions among persons exposed to it, it was also perceived to have serious long-run effects by undermining the very fabric of society. In these respects, the justification for the blasphemy laws was much the same as the criminal and criminal libel laws. Both doctrines represent subsets of the repressive jurisprudence of the English common law developed to support the English monarchy and the church that became the law of the Colonies because of their English affiliation. With the Revolution and Independence, the law of the Colonies,

---

[64] Bloom v. Richards, 2 Ohio St. 387, 391, 1853 Ohio LEXIS 207 (1853).

[65] Specht v. Commonwealth, 8 Pa. (Barr.) 312 (1848), 1848 Pa. LEXIS 86 (1848); Philips v. Gratz, 2 Pen. & W. 412 (1831), 1831 Pa. LEXIS 13 (1831); City Council of Charleston v. Benjamin, 2 Strobh. Law. Rep. 508 (S.C. 1848); Cincinnati v. Rice, 15 Ohio 225, 1846 Ohio LEXIS 178 (1846) (without discussing constitutionality although vigorously argued by counsel for both parties); Commonwealth v. Wolf, 3 Serg. & Rawle 48, 1817 Pa. LEXIS 10 (1817). Cf. Commonwealth v. Lesher, 17 Serg. & Rawle 155 (Pa. 1828) (jury challenge because of religious conviction against the death penalty).

including these counter-Revolutionary features, became the law of the new states and ultimately the law of the New Republic.

C. Suppression of Anti-Slavery Speech

1. Introduction

The final major area of suppression of free speech and press in the first half of the nineteenth century includes the statutes in virtually all the slaveholding states criminalizing discussion of the legitimacy of slavery. Although occurring some decades after the period of intense political controversy featured by the partisan manipulation of the criminal libel law, the statutes criminalizing discussion of slavery or abolition and the cases under them are, nevertheless, still relevant in presenting insight into the jurisprudential thinking of the times.[66] In addition, they corroborate the predominant role of states' rights rather than free speech as the fundamental motivation underlying the opposition to the Sedition Act by the Jeffersonian South during the earlier struggle between the Federalists and Republicans at the turn of the century.

The Southern statutes prohibiting challenges to slavery had several components. They did not stop with the criminalization of anti-slavery speech. Some of the slave state statutes, as in Maryland and Virginia, also included provisions seeking to prevent the use of the mails for the distribution of newspapers containing articles advocating the abolition of slavery. Furthermore, a number also prohibited the submission of petitions to the legislatures dealing with slavery, its abolition, or slave emancipation. As we will see, these repressive measures were matched in some measure in federal law and practice. On the legitimacy of petitions respecting slavery, the slave state representatives and sympathizers in the House of Representatives were able to force the adoption in 1837 of a "gag" rule prohibiting the filing of anti-slavery petitions with the Congress. The "gag" rule survived until 1844, when John Quincy Adams after a herculean effort was able to bring it to an end. As for the mails,

---

[66] For general discussions of this area, *see* Clement Eaton, *The Freedom-of-Thought Struggle in the Old South* (1940, repr. 1964) (hereinafter Eaton); Russel B. Nye, *Fettered Freedom: Civil Liberties and the Slavery Controversy 1830–1860* (1963) (hereinafter Nye); Michael K. Curtis, *Free Speech: "The People's Darling Privilege": Struggles for Freedom of Expression in American History*, ch. 5 (2000) (hereinafter Curtis, *Free Speech*); Curtis, The Curious History of Attempts to Suppress Antislavery Speech, Press, and Petition in 1835–1837, 89 Nw. Univ. L. Rev. 785 (1995) (hereinafter Curtis, Curious History); Curtis, The 1859 Crisis over Hinton Helper's Book, The Impending Crisis: Free Speech, Slavery, and Some Light on the Meaning of the First Section of the Fourteenth Amendment, 68 Chi-Kent L. Rev. 1113 (1993) (hereinafter Curtis, The 1859 Crisis).

as we will see, indulgent federal administrations actually encouraged federal Postmasters to respect the repressive local statutes.

Although lacking the venerable legal antecedents of the sedition laws, the anti-abolition statutes are manifestly much closer to the criminal libel experience than the blasphemy decisions. Unlike blasphemy, criminal libel and the anti-abolition measures involved sensitive political areas in which political, moral, and even economic concerns ran deep, human passions ran high, the potential for violent aftermath was strong, and security of the state was perceived to be at stake. However, a common element united all three. Each presented potential incitement of breaches of the peace.

At the outset of the discussion of the slave state statutes buttressing slavery by criminalizing express or implied criticism, it is important to note that although the statutes were common, the number of prosecutions were few, and the actual convictions even fewer. Even then, in several celebrated cases in which convictions were achieved, matters were ultimately resolved not by imprisonment or other punishment as provided in the statute, but alternatively by the convicted defendant simply leaving the state.[67] Although one may be tempted to explain this anomaly by noting that the defendants in some of the cases resolved by "banishment" were not radical abolitionist incendiaries but clergymen seeking to preach what they believed to be teachings of Christianity, this is not a fair description. Thus in the *Burritt* and *Garrison* cases, there was no acquiescence in exile for ministers. Instead, the defendants were publishers of Northern origins abandoning their newspapers and other property and fleeing to safer jurisdictions out of fear for their person and freedom.

2. The Experience in the Slave States

a. Anti-Abolition Statutes

Commencing with adoption by Georgia in 1804 of a statute "to prevent the Insurrection of Slaves" making unlawful any communication with a slave "tending to incite slaves to sedition, tumult, or disorder,"[68] numerous states in which slavery played a significant role enacted comparable statutes, including

---

[67] The Georgia jurisprudence, which was not involved in any of the leading cases of this type, provides an interesting comparative parallel. Unlike the statutes of other states such as North Carolina where convictions ultimately resulted in "exile," the Georgia statute actually provided for "banishment" as the sole punishment for the first offense. It went on to escalate the penalties to long-term imprisonment for the second, and death for the third offense. *See* Ga. Laws, Act of May 19, 1804 (1804).

[68] Ga. Act of May 19, 1804.

Alabama, Louisiana, Maryland, Mississippi, North Carolina, South Carolina, Tennessee, and Virginia.

Although Georgia and South Carolina enacted such statutes shortly after the turn of the century, the balance of the slave states did not follow suit until the 1820s and 1830s following a series of violent slave outbreaks and an intensification of radical abolitionist activities.[69] The concern with the possibility of bloody slave insurrection following Denmark Vesey's abortive slave insurrection in South Carolina in 1822, Nat Turner's revolt in 1831, and the increased reports of slave conspiracies created an atmosphere receptive to the enactment of such statutes. The increase in the Southern activities of abolitionists, particularly the widespread circulation in the South of David Walker's incendiary *Appeal to the Colored People of the World*, appears to have outraged much Southern public opinion, and adoption of criminal statutes by the states theretofore lacking such statutes quickly followed.[70]

Walker's *Appeal* was the leading abolitionist handout, with three large-scale printings. It advocated militant resistance and immediate emancipation and was viewed as a call to immediate slave revolt. Possession of copies of the *Appeal* appears and reappears in the accounts of the cases and was a precipitating factor leading to prosecution and conviction under the statutes criminalizing anti-slavery speech.[71]

---

[69] *See* the Message of the Governor to the Legislature of Virginia, reported in the Salem *Gazette*, Dec. 20, 1831, reporting on the death of 61 persons in a slave outbreak in Southampton, Va., in Aug. 1831) ("there is too much reason to believe those plans of treason, insurrection and murder, have been designed. Planned and matured by unrestrained fanatics in some of the neighboring States, who find facilities in distributing their views and plans amongst our population, either through the post office or by agents sent for that purpose throughout our territory.") *See also* the Pittsfield *Sun*, Sept. 10, 1835, reporting that an abolitionist named James F. Otis was arrested in Virginia "and came within a hair space of being *Lynched*."

[70] David Walker, *Appeal to the Colored People of the World* (1829) (hereinafter *The Appeal*). The *Appeal* was reprinted in 1831 in *The Liberator*, William Lloyd Garrison's abolitionist newspaper.

On Aug. 28, 1830, the *Farmers' Cabinet* reported a report that a Wilmington, N.C., insurrectionary conspiracy involving a bartender named James Cowan and others had been uncovered. Cowan is said to have had a large number of Walker's "incendiary pamphlets and to have made use of his profession for their "more efficient distribution."

[71] Aptheker collected a number of such episodes. One was the report of Governor Forsyth of Georgia to the Legislature that the pamphlet had been distributed in the state and that the Savannah police had seized sixty copies. A number of 1830 episodes and prosecutions centered on possession or circulation of *The Appeal*. These included Elijah Burrritt in Milledgeville, Ga., discussed below; the discovery of 30 copies in Richmond in the home of Thomas Lewis, a free black; the arrest and conviction in Charleston, S.C., involving Edward Smith, discussed below; the conviction in Louisiana of James Smith, discussed below; and the imprisonment in 1829 or 1830 of two missionaries to the Cherokees, Worcester and Butler, for possession of *The Appeal* and admitting colored children to their school. *See* Herbert Aptheker, *Abolitionism: A Revolutionary Movement* 98–99 (1989) (hereinafter Aptheker).

The Southern movement toward criminalization of anti-slavery speech and press was also intensified by a greatly increased use of the mails by abolitionists in 1835. For example, a Northern newspaper without disclosing its source reported in the fall of 1835 that "It is said that the number of incendiary pamphlets received at the Charleston Post-Office amounted to 300,000."[72] Another newspaper account reported that a box intercepted at the Philadelphia Post Office contained 2,000 copies of abolitionist pamphlets addressed in bundles to persons throughout the South.[73]

Curtis comments that "by 1835 the assumption that abolitionist publications would lead to slave rebellions was so obvious to many Northerners and Southerners that it needed no demonstration."[74] This should be no surprise. After all, rebellion is what the *Appeal* explicitly called for.

Although all the statutes were directed against the dissemination of anti-slavery ideas to slaves or free blacks, the statutes spoke in somewhat different voices. Although Alabama, Georgia, and Maryland referred to "insurrection," Mississippi spoke of "seditious" publications, Louisiana referred to language tending to "produce discontent" or "excite insubordination," and South Carolina addressed "inflammatory discourse" "tending to alienate the affection or seduce the fidelity" of slaves. Finally, North Carolina criminalized the circulation of any "pamphlet or paper . . . the evident tendency whereof is to cause slaves to become discontented with their bondage . . . and free negroes to be dissatisfied with their social condition." Every statute criminalized any questioning the legitimacy of slavery as an institution.

The Maryland, Tennessee, and Virginia statutes had particularly interesting provisions. In addition to provisions criminalizing anti-slavery communications, these Acts also imposed administrative responsibilities on the judiciary. The Maryland statute, for example, directed the judges each year to charge the grand jury in their jurisdictions to "cause to be summoned before them at all terms . . . all the postmasters . . . in their respective communities and to examine them particularly touching the subject matter of this act." It supplemented the provision by making it a felony for any free black to call

---

[72] The Pittsfield (Mass.) *Sun*, Sept. 10, 1835.

[73] Salem *Gazette*, Sept. 1, 1835, reprinting Philadelphia *Inquirer* account. *See also New-Hampshire Sentinel*, Sept. 3, 1835, reprinting Boston *Daily Advertiser* report of the Philadelphia *Inquirer* description of the affair.

[74] *See* Curtis, The Curious History, note 66, at 802–803. Curtis supports his comment with quotations from Chancellor Kent (self-preservation demands on the part of the white population dwelling in the midst of such combustible materials, unceasing vigilance and firmness") and John Quincy Adams (he "saw the abolitionists as making every possible exertion to kindle the flame of insurrection among the slaves.") 2 James Kent, *Commentaries on American Law* 254 (1836); 9 John Quincy Adams, *Memoirs* 254 (1877).

for or receive any abolitition newspaper or pamphlet at the Post Office.[75] The Legislature was, thus, not only seeking to conscript Postmasters (who even in those early times were federal, not state, employees) to join in implementing the objectives of the statute, but establishing a unique enforcement mechanism to assure that they had done so.[76]

Although the statutes may be seen as substantially uniform in their objectives, the punishments that they provided in the case of violation differed wildly. The 1831 Alabama statute was the most severe. It provided for the death penalty for "seditious papers . . . tending to produce conspiracy or insurrection . . . among the slaves or colored population." The earlier Georgia statute also specifying "insurrection" provided that on conviction, the defendant shall be "declared guilty of a felony, and banished from this state forever [but in the event of return and being found within the state] "shall suffer death without benefit of clergy." The South Carolina statute of 1805 adjudged the crime a "high misdemeanor" and provided for punishment [apparently without any limitation of time] but "not extending to life or limb . . . as may be adjudged." North Carolina provided for imprisonment for not less than one year, the pillory, and a whipping at the court's discretion. Although Maryland provided for confinement from 10 to 20 years, Virginia was much less severe, authorizing imprisonment not exceeding one year and a fine not exceeding $500.[77]

b. The Slave State Decisions
Although the repressive statutes were virtually universal in the slave holding states, there do not seem to have been many cases. References have been found to no more than 15 legal proceedings under all the statutes and a mere four at common law involving criminal libel, some of which apparently did not extend beyond the indictment stage.[78] Although some are officially reported,

---

[75] Maryland Acts of 1842, ch. 272, §§ 1, 3.

[76] In an interesting sidenote, censorship of the mails revived after the Civil War with the enlistment of postal workers to suppress the circulation of obscene materials in the Comstock Act of 1873. 17 Stat. 599 (1873).

[77] See note 64.

[78] In addition, there is a report from New Orleans of the arrest and detention of Robert Smith, a free black, for "circulating a dangerous pamphlet among the slaves." Baltimore *Patriot*, Apr. 1, 1830. (The pamphlet appears to be David Walker's *Appeal*). It is not known whether the matter led to an indictment or trial.

A number of these decisions have been found through searches of the contemporary newspapers. With this search finding numerous cases in addition to those mentioned in the previous literature, there is a strong likelihood of newspaper reports of additional prosecutions that have not yet been identified.

most are available only in limited, and perhaps distorted form, from newspaper accounts. It is surprising that records on more cases are not available. This, after all, is the period of the growing intensity of the national struggle over slavery that was dominating the political landscape. Tempers ran so high that physical assaults between Northerners and Southerners over slavery were occurring on the floor of the Congress.[79] In some slave states, tensions were so high that vigilante committees were organized and unlawfully employed violent means to suppress abolitionist activities.[80] Some vigilante committees were the products of mob action. Others were formed by "conservative" elements to seize and destroy abolitionist materials, in part to dissuade more violent actions by mobs. Whipping, tar and feathering, and forcible expulsion of slavery critics from Southern communities, lynchings, and near-lynchings provide other examples of the vigilante aspects of slave state responses to anti-slavery agitation. In brief, the history of the antebellum South is full of incidents, not only of the use of the law to suppress the dissemination of abolitionist materials, but also of mob and vigilante action. Although historians provide the larger picture of the full panoply of the efforts of the South to

---

[79] The brutal caning on May 22, 1856, of Sen. Charles Sumner of Massachusetts by Rep. Preston Brooks of South Carolina on the floor of the Senate has been prominently reported. Sen. Sumner was attacked with a heavy walking cane and rendered bloody and unconscious. As a result he was absent from the Senate for several years. It is of interest that the House voted down a motion to expel Brooks. However, he resigned and was triumphantly reelected. Brooks became a Southern hero with a town in Florida and a county in Georgia named in his honor.

[80] Salem *Gazette*, Aug. 7, 1835 reprints the report of the Clinton, Miss., *Gazette* of the discovery of a "horrible conspiracy" for a slave uprising contemplating the "total destruction of the white population of all the slave States" from "Maryland to Louisiana" under the leadership of two "steam" doctors, Cotton and Saunders. The account further reports the organization of a local vigilante "committee of investigation" in Madison, Miss. Having found the evidence of the conspiracy "perfectly conclusive" and the guilt of Cotton and Saunders "placed beyond a doubt," the Committee ordered their public execution by hanging, which occurred in Livingston, Miss., on July 4, 1835. A second vigilante committee was active in the neighboring town of Clinton, Miss. In all a total of five white men and 10 to 15 black men were executed after trial "conducted in a manner that would not do discredit to the most dignified judicial tribunal of the country."

The Newport *Mercury*, Aug. 29, 1835, reports an account in the Nashville *Republican* headed "An Abolitionist caught!" A young man named Amos Dresser, a New Englander and a graduate of Brown, was "taken in the act of distributing some incendiary tracts and pamphlets among the negroes.... He was taken before the committee of vigilance – tried, and found guilty, and sentenced to receive 20 lashes on his bare back, and quit Nashville in 24 hours under penalty of more severe punishment." The sentence was "immediately" carried out. Another person was arrested on the same day, and "the city was under a vigilant patrole [sic]." Dresser provided his own account of his experience. The Narrative of Amos Dresser (1836), *reprinted in* 1 *Slave Rebels, Abolitionists and Southern Courts: The Pamphlet Literature*, Series IV, 251–265 (Paul Finkelman ed. 1988) (hereinafter Finkelman, *Pamphlet Literature*). *See also* Aptheker, note 71, at 103–104 noting that pamphlets about this incident were printed in New York in 1836 and in Ohio as late as 1849. Aptheker also reports a similar vigilante incident in Georgia in 1836 involving a Princeton Theological Seminary student named Aaron W. Kitchell.

stamp out challenges to slavery, these are beyond the scope of this volume, dealing only with the legal dimensions of this unhappy history.[81]

As readers will recall, some statutes speak of "conspiracy," "insurrection," or "rebellion." The defendants in most of the cases, however, do not involve revolutionaries. The most prominent involved ministers unable to reconcile slavery with Christianity, as in the *Gruber, Bacon, Worth, Vestal, Crooks*, and *McBride* cases.

In the *Gruber* case arising in Western Maryland in 1819, the defendant was a Methodist Episcopal minister preaching by invitation at a Methodist camp meeting on the grounds of a Frederick landowner to an enormous audience of 2,600 to 3,000 persons, of whom 300 to 400 were blacks. His sermon addressed to the Christian conscience led to his indictment and prosecution. Counsel for the prosecution included one of the most distinguished lawyers of the times, Luther Martin, longtime Attorney General of Maryland, albeit in the twilight of his career. Defense counsel was led by Roger B. Taney, already recognized as a rising star and ultimately Chief Justice of the Supreme Court for three decades. By stressing the lack of proof that Rev. Gruber had intended to violate the law, Taney and his colleagues obtained an acquittal from the jury.[82]

---

[81] The case of Rev. Charles T. Torrey is instructive. Torrey, a member of the Peace Society pledged against any form of violence, attended a "Slaveholder's Convention" in Annapolis, Md., as a reporter for anti-slavery newspapers. When he was observed "taking notes," it became suspected that he represented some abolition paper and this "caused evident excitement in the convention.... [T]he excitement among the people had become so great, that the 'strange reporter' was seized, and forcibly taken out of the gallery. His situation was every moment becoming more perilous, when fortunately, the police intervened and he was conducted to jail on a charge of being an incendiary. But for this timely interference he would, so I hear, have been lynched." *Farmers' Cabinet*, Jan. 21, 1842.

According to one account, he was ultimately discharged under security that he would stay out of Maryland. *Berkshire County Whig*, Jan. 27, 1842. Another reports that he was discharged on posting $1,000 bond (his own for $500 and two sureties for $250 each) for his appearance at the April term and for "good behavior." The magistrate is reported to have said that he had been tenderly dealt with as a stranger and that a Maryland citizen would have been committed for trial. *Farmers' Cabinet*, Jan. 28, 1842.

The same issue of the *Farmers' Cabinet* contained a further report of the episode by the New York *Commercial Advertiser* based on an account of the episode by the Baltimore *Sun*. The *Commercial Advertiser* inquired "whether there is any such thing as personal safety and freedom in citizenship of the United States – whether the constitution under which we profess to live is really anything more than a dead letter. A more flagrant violation of personal right, so far as principle is concerned, has never been presented in this country – not even in the worst cases of Lynch law that have occurred in Arkansas or Mississippi."

[82] David Martin, *Trial of the Rev. Jacob Gruber Minister in the Methodist Episcopal Church at the March Term, 1819, in the Frederick County Court for a Misdemeanor* (1819) (hereinafter Martin), reprinted in Finkelman, *Pamphlet Literature*, note 80, at 7; Eaton, note 66, at 131–133; P. Finkelman, *Slavery in the Courtroom* 158–161 (1985). *See also* W. Lewis, *Without Fear or Favor:*

In Milledgeville, Georgia in the spring of 1830, the publisher of the Milledgeville *Statesman*, Elijah Burritt, who had come to Georgia from Connecticut, was arrested and charged with the possession of 25 copies of Walker's inflammatory *Appeal*. Fearing violence, Burritt fled, leaving behind his possessions and family, and returned home to Connecticut.[83] Burritt came from a prominent Connecticut family. His older brother, Elihu H. Burritt, became internationally prominent for his worldwide advocacy of international law. The arrest was at the direction of the Milledgeville town authority, following a public condemnation of the Walker pamphlet by Georgia Governor Troup.[84]

Although Burritt denied that he was an abolitionist, some of the prosecutions did involve avowed abolitionists. Curtis reports that in 1831 North Carolina Governor Floyd charged that Northerners such as William Lloyd Garrison were spreading sedition among the slaves.[85] In the same year, a Raleigh, N.C., grand jury indicted Garrison, the publisher of the Massachusetts-based abolitionist newspaper *The Liberator* for circulating the paper in Wake County. The outcome of the case, if indeed it ever went to trial, is not known.[86] Aptheker reports still another case of which little is known. He states without attribution that in New Orleans in May 1830, a man named James Smith was convicted and sentenced to one year's imprisonment for circulating the *Appeal*.[87]

At much the same time, an Alabama grand jury indicted R. G. Williams, a New Yorker associated with another abolitionist newspaper, *The Emancipator*. The paper had attacked slavery as contrary to God and nature that had plunged "2,250,000 of our fellow countrymen into the deepest physical and moral degradation."[88] The Governor moved to extradite Williams from New York for trial for violation of the Alabama statute carrying the death penalty. Governor Marcy of New York refused, noting that Williams had not been in Alabama and was not a fugitive.[89] As far as is known, Williams was never tried.

A Biography of Chief Justice Roger Brooke Taney 76–79 (1965); C. Smith, Jr., *Roger B. Taney: Jacksonian Jurist* 178–180 (1973); B. Steiner, *Life of Roger Brooke Taney, Chief Justice of the United States Supreme Court* 72–76 (1922); S. Tyler, *Memoir of Roger Brooke Taney* 123–132 (1970).

[83] Elihu Burritt, *Thoughts and Things at Home and Abroad, with a Memoir* ix (M. Howitt ed. 1884) ("He was obliged to fly for his life to the north. All he had gained by severe industry for years was thus confiscated").

[84] See P. Tolis, *Elihu Burritt: Crusader for Brotherhood* 8, 84–87 (1968) (hereinafter Tolis); M. Curti, *The Learned Blacksmith: The Letters and Journals of Elihu Burritt* 118n. (1937) (hereinafter Curti); *Connecticut Courant*, Mar. 13, 1830.

[85] See Eaton, note 66, at 125–126.

[86] See Curtis, The Curious History, note 66, at 62 nn. 91, 92.

[87] See Aptheker, note 71, at 99.

[88] See Curtis, The Curious History, note 66, at 805–806.

[89] See Curtis, Free Speech, note 66, at 203–204.

In the *Barrett* case in 1839, a Virginia prosecuting attorney moved in Circuit Court for rules against Barrett and ten other defendants to show cause why informations[90] should not be filed against them for violation of the 1836 Act. He produced affidavits that "Barrett had circulated and the other defendants had signed a memorial to congress stating that "slavery and the slave trade as at present existing in the district of columbia where congress has sole jurisdiction ought not so to be, as a sin . . . a foul stain on our national institutions, and contrary to the spirit of republican institutions." With Barrett's consent, the court adjourned, referring a series of questions to the Virginia Supreme Court. The Supreme Court ruled that the offence was a felony and could not be prosecuted by information. That seems to have been the end of the case. Whether it was dropped or whether the prosecuting attorney was unsuccessful in an attempt to have the grand jury return an indictment is not known.[91]

The *Bacon* case in 1848 involved a Virginia minister who was preaching at Christmastime in his own church to his own congregation on the duty of Christians. He noted Jesus' condemnation of the money changers in the Temple as "thieves and robbers." He then asserted that there were thieves and robbers in the church that day for it "was worse to take a human being and keep him all his life, and give him nothing for his labour, except once in a while a whipping or few stripes."

As with Rev. Barrett, Rev. Bacon was tried under the Virginia statute criminalizing the assertion "that owners have not right of property in their slaves."[92] The jury found him guilty. However, although the statute authorized imprisonment not exceeding one year and fines not exceeding $500, the jury fined him only the very odd sum of $49.62 ½. The defendant, nevertheless, moved for a new trial. His counsel argued that to constitute a crime, there must be intent and that there was no evidence showing an intent to violate the law. This was the very argument that had enabled Taney to win an acquittal for Rev. Gruber 30 years before.

The court granted a new trial, holding the evidence insufficient to constitute a violation of the statute. Although as the court noted, the remarks were understood to refer to slaveholders, the words slave or slaveowners were not

---

[90] As discussed earlier, criminal prosecutions in a number of states could be instituted by the prosecutor's filing of a so-called information as an alternative to the voting of an indictment by a grand jury. The latter interposed a democratic restraint on the scope of the prosecutor's discretionary use of his authority.

[91] Commonwealth v. Barrett, 36 Va. (9 Leigh) 665 (1839).

[92] Bacon v. Commonwealth, 48 Va. 602, 1850 Va. LEXIS 43, 7 Gratt. 602 (1850). *See* Eaton, note 66, at 21–22; Curtis, The 1859 Crisis, note 66, at 1127, 1132, 1134–1135.

mentioned, nor had he challenged as a matter of law, as distinct from religion, the right of owners to property in their slaves. Although counsel in his argument had also made brief reference to the freedom of speech provision of the Virginia Constitution, the court did not refer to it.

By 1850, the political climate had become more strained, and even ministers preaching the gospel became seen as dangerous agitators. North Carolina experienced two episodes of prosecution of abolitionist missionary ministers. Johnson vividly describes the setting for the *McBride* and *Crooks* cases,[93] involving two Methodist missionary preachers "uncompromising and outspoken in attacking the institution of slavery." This led to public outcry, with a local minister, for example, reported as inquiring: "I ask, with such public teaching, if men can feel that they are safe from the assassin's knife, from the incendiaries' torch?"[94]

The trial, conviction, and pronouncement of a savage penalty by the trial court against Rev. Jesse McBride ensued. He was sentenced to 20 lashes, the pillory for one hour, and imprisonment for one year.[95] However, as occurred in so many of these cases, the actual outcome of the litigation was very different. McBride appealed to the Supreme Court and while the appeal was pending was released on $1,000 bond.[96] At this point, the case was settled. In return for a pledge to leave the state, McBride and his bondsmen were released from all claims. He left in May 1851, and Rev. Crooks, after threats against his life, followed suit a few months later.

State v. Worth arising eight years later involved still another North Carolina prosecution of missionary ministers.[97] On the eve of the Civil War in 1859, Rev. Daniel Worth, a Wesleyan minister who was the brother-in-law of the Governor, and his colleague, Rev. Alfred V. Vestal, were conducting abolitionary missionary activities. Contrasting with the tense experience of Rev. Crooks and Rev. McBride, the opposition to Rev. Worth and Rev. Vestal was not violent, and the two ministers are reported to have expressed gratitude for "such quiet and peaceable lives." The scene changed dramatically with John Brown's bloody raid on Harper's Ferry, leaving the area in "tremendous ferment." Worth was promptly arrested for allegedly violating the 1854 North Carolina statute, charged with circulating Helper's *The Impending Crisis in the South,* and exciting Negroes to a "spirit of insurrection, conspiracy, or

---

[93] Johnson, Abolitionist Missionary Activities in North Carolina, 40 N.C. Hist. Rev. 295, 298–301 (1963) (hereinafter Johnson). *See also* Eaton, note 66, at 138–140.

[94] Greensborough *Patriot*, Sept. 28, 1850, *cited by* Johnson, note 93, at 310–320.

[95] With the only proof against Rev. Crooks his association with McBride, he was never tried.

[96] Greensboro, N.C., *Patriot*, Sept. 28, 1850.

[97] Curtis, Free Speech, note 66, at 289–296; Curtis, The 1859 Crisis, note 66, at 1159–1168.

rebellion."[98] Although Rev. Worth was convicted and sentenced to a term of one year's imprisonment, he, too, in the end escaped punishment. Before the case could be heard on appeal, the case was resolved in a manner strikingly reminiscent of the experience of Rev. McBride. Rev. Worth's counsel was successful in having Rev. Worth's bond reduced. Worth promptly left the state, and the matter came to an end. Rev. Vestal was not indicted, and he, too, left the state.[99] The following year on the brink of the Civil War, the North Carolina Legislature amended the statute, making the first offence for publication of an "incendiary" book on slavery punishable by death.[100]

Although the North Carolina legal processes did not continue to their formal conclusion in either matter, it should be recognized that the prosecution had achieved its purpose in instituting the litigations. All four ministers had fled the state. Anti-slavery speech in North Carolina had been suppressed, and anti-slavery activity in the state by the Methodist missionaries eradicated. In much the same way, a number of the criminal libel cases brought by Federalist prosecutors against publishers of Jeffersonian publishers or printers had resulted in the offending newspapers ceasing to publish for months or in some cases permanently.

What is the significance of these legal developments? On the one hand, there are only 18 cases and a mere three convictions. Further, only one of those convicted actually served their terms. On the other hand, the overhanging presence of the statute on the books and the isolated prosecutions must have produced significant deterrents to active anti-slavery agitation in the South. Chilling discussion through the threat of punishment is an important dimension of repressive legal doctrine.

Are the 15 cases under the state statutes that have been located really all that in fact occurred over half a century? Are there further cases not yet discovered? These are fair questions to which there is no answer. Moreover, one must acknowledge that little is known of some of the cases that have been identified other than summary references in contemporary newspapers. Accordingly, one cannot feel confident that the 15 cases available fully and fairly represent the experience of the period. Notwithstanding concern about the possible incompleteness of the data, scholars have no choice; whatever the limitations, they are compelled to deal with the materials available, particularly because they are so uniform in both their analysis and outcome.

[98] N.C. Rev. Code, ch. 34, sec. 16 (1854), revising 1830 N.C. Sess. Laws, ch. 5, at 10–11.
[99] See Eaton, note 66, at 211–212; Johnson, note 93, at 295–301.
[100] 1860 N.C. Sess. Laws, ch. 23, at 39 (1860). See Curtis, The 1859 Crisis, note 66, at 1166 n.317.

One is further encouraged to do so because it likely that the few cases that did make their way into the official reports were the more important ones of the period.

The cases found were concentrated: Virginia leads the list with six[101] and North Carolina with five.[102] In addition, Alabama,[103] Georgia,[104] Louisiana,[105] and Maryland[106] had one each. Further, when one reviews the actual outcome, the record becomes even more limited. Notwithstanding the intensity of the struggle over slavery and statutes suppressing anti-slavery advocacy in virtually all the slave states, only one defendant in the 16 prosecutions was actually imprisoned.

In addition to these cases arising under the statutes criminalizing antislavery advocacy, there were four more prosecutions with three convictions involving comparable abolitionist activities that were brought under commonlaw criminal libel; these are reviewed later in this chapter. This comprises the sum total of our knowledge with the legal and extra-legal nature of slave state reaction to the dissemination of anti-slavery agitation. Throughout, it is plain that the constitutional guaranties of free speech and press played no role during the period, as in the experience of the Early Republic under the criminal libel and blasphemy laws.

In any event, while ministers were physically in the state and delivering sermons in local churches, the abolitionists were attempting to operate through the federal mails. This helps explain both the call of the Southern legislators upon the Northern legislatures and governors to extradite the publishers and printers indicted under the Southern state statutes and the Southern focus

---

[101] Commonwealth v. Barrett, 36 Va. (9 Leigh) 665 (1839); Bacon v. Commonwealth, 48 Va. (7 Grattan) 602, 1850 Va. LEXIS 43 (1852); Commonwealth v. Curry, Alexandria *Gazette*, June 17, 1850; Commonwealth v. Janney, *National Era*, July 11, 1850; Commonwealth v. Crawford, *National Era*, Aug. 27, 1850; Commonwealth v. Underwood, *Liberator*, Aug. 28, 1857, Nov. 19, 1857.

[102] State v. Worth, 52 N.C. 488 (1860); State v. McBride, Raleigh *Register*, Oct. 23, 1850, *North State Whig*, Washington, N.C., Nov. 13, 1850; State v. Crooks, Raleigh *Register*, Oct. 23, 1850. A fourth case of this nature was the Rev. Vestal matter, in which Vestal, an associate of Rev. Worth, was the subject of charges but never indicted; like Worth, he settled a pending North Carolina prosecution by leaving the state. Still another North Carolina case is the 1831 case involving the publisher of *The Liberator*, of which the outcome is not known.

[103] State v. Williams (Ga. 1830) (never tried).

[104] State v. Burritt (Ga. 1830) (under 1829 statute), *Farmer's Cabinet*, Mar. 27, 1830 (indictment). See Curti, note 84, at 118n.; Tolis, note 84 at 84–87; *Connecticut Courant*, Apr. 13, 1830; *Farmers' Cabinet*, Mar. 27, 1830.

[105] State v. Smith (La. 1830) (convicted).

[106] State v. Gruber (Md. 1819). *See* Martin, note 82. *See* 5 Oliver Wendell Holmes Devise, *History of the Supreme Court of the United States*, Carl B. Swisher, *The Taney Period, 1835–1864*, 95–98 (1974).

on Postmasters and interception of abolitionary materials in the mails. It also may explain the limited number of prosecutions.

c. State Utilization of Federal Postmasters to Impound Anti-Slavery Newspapers

As noted, Virginia was one of the three states that had enacted statutes charging grand juries with the supervision of the Postmasters in their districts to assure the interception of anti-abolitionist newpapers. Although there appears to be virtually nothing in the literature about the actual consequences of such provisions, Clement Eaton does provide a vivid example that would indicate that they did have some effect. Eaton reports that when a Lynchburg, Va., subscriber to the anti-slavery New York *Sun* complained in 1859 that he was not receiving his papers, Horace Greeley, the publisher, investigated and found that the missing newspaper copies had been intercepted and impounded by the local Post Office.[107]

The ability of the slave states to use the local Postmasters, notwithstanding their federal status, as part of the effort to silence anti-slavery agitation rested on a lengthy period of benign federal approval. With a slave owner, Andrew Jackson, in the White House, the Executive Branch of the federal government played an important role in the suppression of anti-slavery agitation. We discuss this subsequently in the section dealing with the federal experience.

d. Slave State Statutes Jailing Free Black Seamen on Ships Entering State Ports: An Ugly Episode from America's Unhappy Past

The Southern attempt to blockade the flow of anti-slavery agitation from the North was not restricted to the seizure of abolitionist newspapers and publications shipped on vessels entering Southern ports or delivered to Southern Post Offices. It included slave state statutes preventing free black seamen on ships entering ports within the state from circulating among the resident slave and free black communities.[108]

In the traumatic atmosphere following the suppression of the early slave insurrections in the South, it was widely believed that free black seamen from

---

[107] Eaton, note 66, at 211–212. *See also* Akhil R. Amar, *The Bill of Rights* 160 (1998).

[108] Although lacking a complete review of the legal challenges, Philip M. Hamer provides by far the fullest discussion of this unhappy episode. *See* Hamer, *Great Britain, the United States, and the Negro Seamen Acts, 1822, 1848,* 1 J. Southern Hist. 3–22 (Feb. 1935) (hereinafter Hamer, *Negro Seamen Acts*). *See also* 1 Charles Warren, *History of the Supreme Court of the United States* 623–627 (1928) (hereinafter Warren, *History*); Alan F. January, The First Nullification: The Negro Seamen Acts Controversy in South Carolina, 1822–1860 (unpublished Ph.D. Dissertation, Univ. of Iowa 1976) (hereinafter January); Donald G. Morgan, *Justice William Johnson: The First Dissenter* 192–202 (1954); 1 William W. Freehling, *Secessionists at Bay 1776–1854,* 254 (1990).

the Caribbean had encouraged the conspiracies. In response, the coastal Southern States enacted statutes intended to prevent free black seamen on ships entering their ports from mingling with local blacks.[109] These statutes were not limited to American ships from the North. They included foreign shipping and foreign black seamen as well. Their enforcement, thus, had international, as well as domestic, dimensions.

The South Carolina statute was enacted in December 1822 in the wake of the Denmark Vesey slave insurrection in Charleston. It was particularly brutal providing that all free black seamen on ships entering South Carolina ports were to be confined in jail while their ships remained in port. When the ship was ready to leave, the Captain could obtain their release, but only on reimbursing the jail for the expenses of their detention. If the Captain failed to do so, he was subject to fine and imprisonment, and the black sailor was to be deemed an absolute slave and sold by the State.[110]

Hamer reports that the Act was then immediately implemented with the jailing of free black seamen on several ships entering South Carolina ports. He reports that the Captain of one of the ships, an American ship, brought suit in the South Carolina state courts alleging its unconstitutionality. The lower court, however, held the Act constitutional, and the South Carolina Supreme Court affirmed. Other ship Captains unsuccessfully memorialized Congress for relief.[111]

With the statute being enforced against free black English sailors from the Caribbean sailing on British ships, the British Minister, Stratford Canning, protested to Secretary of State John Quincy Adams. Adams quietly interceded with the South Carolina authorities, and prosecutions ceased briefly. When the South Carolina Association, a Charleston group composed of "the most influential members of the tidewater gentry" organized to enforce the statute,[112] learned of the lack of enforcement, they were able to bring it to an end, and the statute was again enforced.

---

[109] When Florida sought to enter the Union in 1845, its Constitution empowered its legislature to pass laws "to prevent free Negroes, mulattos, and other persons of color from immigrating to this state, or from being discharged from on board any vessel" in any Florida port. This gave rise to strenuous debate in the Congress, but in the end, Florida was admitted with the disputed clause intact. See January, note 108, at 291–292.

[110] Act of Dec. 21, 1822, 7 S.C. Stat. 461 (Cooper & McCord 1840). In 1823, the Act was amended to provide that if the Captain failed to collect the imprisoned seaman, he was to be released and ordered to leave the state and never return. However, if he did return, he was to be seized and sold as a slave. The Act continued to be further amended. Act of Dec. 22, 1823, Act of Dec. 20, 1825, and Act of Dec. 19, 1835, 7 S.C. Stat. 463, 466, 470 (Cooper & McCord 1840).

[111] See Hamer, Negro Seamen Acts, note 108, at 4. The case is not reported, and Hamer provides no citation or other support for the assertion, which does not appear elsewhere in the literature.

[112] See January, note 1, at 155.

In August 1823, when Henry Elkison, a free black seaman from the Caribbean and a British citizen, was jailed under the statute, the British Consul in Charleston immediately instituted suit, challenging the constitutionality of the statute. In *Elkison v. Deliesseline*, Supreme Court Justice William Johnson, a Charleston resident, sitting on Circuit in the South Carolina Circuit Court held the statute unconstitutional as in violation of the foreign commerce clause and the terms of the treaty with Britain.[113] The decision "threw Charleston into a flame which extended into Virginia."[114] There was a storm of protest in the press. Johnson defended his position repeatedly, sometimes under his own name, sometimes under a pseudonym.[115] The South Carolina Senate made the State's position clear. The "duty to guard against insubordination or insurrection," it declared, is "paramount to *all* laws, *all* treaties, *all* constitutions." The decision was ignored, and South Carolina continued to enforce the statute.[116]

This unhappy chapter of American history elicited an unattractive comment by Chief Justice John Marshall. When he learned of Johnson's decision, Marshall wrote to his colleague Justice Story, observing "Our brother Johnson, I perceive has hung himself on a democratic snag in a hedge composed of thorny States-Rights in South Carolina." He went on to congratulate himself, expressing his satisfaction at his own avoidance of the issue in an earlier case presenting the same issue in the comparable Virginia statute. This was *Wilson v. United States*, decided by Marshall while on Circuit in Virginia

---

[113] Elkison v. Deliesseline, 9 F. Cas. 493, 1823 U.S. App. LEXIS 242 (C.C.D. S.C. 1823) (No. 4336). Because Johnson denied the writs sought by the plaintiff on other grounds, Johnson's conclusion was dictum. Three months later, the Supreme Court accepted much the same view of the limitations of state power in *Gibbons v. Ogden*. 22 U.S. (9 Wheat.) 1 (1824). As noted by Justice Johnson in his opinion, South Carolina Attorney General James Petigru declined to represent the state in the matter. 9 F. Cas. at 494, 1823 U.S. App. LEXIS at *6.

A Charleston newspaper reprinted the arguments of counsel for the state extensively, *e.g.*, *City Gazette*, Oct. 18, 1824, Dec. 13 and 15, 1824; some were reprinted in other Southern papers, *e,g.*, *Chronicle and Georgia Advertiser* (Augusta, Ga.), Dec. 25, 1824. In Massachusetts, numerous newspapers published accounts of Justice Johnson's opinion, *e.g.*, *Register* (Essex, Mass.), Aug. 28, 1823, reprinting an account in the *Daily Advertiser* (Boston, Mass.), that in turn cited an account in the *Daily Advertiser* (New York) and *Gazette* (Haverhill, Mass.), Aug. 26, 1823, and *Inquirer* (Nantucket, Mass.), Sept. 9, 1823. Twenty years later, an abolitionist journal reprinted the Johnson opinion: *The Emancipator* (Boston, Mass.), Jan. 12, 1843.

[114] Union (Washington, D.C.), Mar. 13, 1851, *cited by* Warren, *History, supra* note 108, at 625n.

[115] *See* Donald G. Morgan, Justice William Johnson on the Treaty-Making Power, 22 Geo. Wash. L. Rev. 187, 193 (1953) ("Seldom, if ever has an American judge suffered from his townsmen so sustained and acrid a volley of criticism and abuse"); Hamer, *Negro Seamen Acts*, note 108, at 7.

[116] Emphasis in the original. S.C. Sen. Res., Dec. 8, 1824, 4 McCord (Law) 480 (S.C. 1828). *The Patriot* (Baltimore), Oct. 1, 1823 ("the editor of the Charleston Mercury states that the act of the South Carolina Legislature, so far from being suspended since the trial of Elkinson [*sic*], proceeds in operation more vigorously, perhaps, than before").

several years earlier.[117] The Chief Justice wrote "We have its [the North Carolina statute's] twin brother in Virginia; a case has been brought before me in which I might have considered its unconstitutionality, had I chosen to do so; but it was not absolutely necessary, and *as I am not fond of butting against a stone wall in sport, I escaped on the construction of the* [Virginia] *act*."[118]

Notwithstanding the express delegation of power to regulate interstate and foreign commerce to the federal government in the Constitution,[119] states' rights had triumphed over federal supremacy in the very first instance of "Nullification" in the Early Republic. Justice Johnson had, indeed, butted his head against a stone wall. Much upset, Justice Johnson wrote to Secretary of State John Quincy Adams that the Constitution of the United States had been "trampeled on" by South Carolina's defiance of the decision. President Monroe and Adams were concerned, but since Elkison had been discharged when his ship left late in August 1823, they took no action.

In April 1824, following the complaint of another British captain over the seizure of four of his seamen, the British Charge d'Affaires acting under instructions from the British Foreign Minister formally complained to Adams. After discussion with Monroe, Adams requested an opinion from Attorney General William Wirt. Later in the month, Wirt issued his official opinion to President Monroe. He concluded, as Johnson had, that the South Carolina statute was in violation of the Constitution. Noting that the case involved British seamen, he also concluded that the statute violated the treaty with Britain as well.[120]

President Monroe wrote to the Governor of South Carolina urging repeal of the statute. Instead, the Governor reaffirmed the policy and continue to enforce the statute. Monroe was in the twilight of his second administration

---

[117] Wilson v. United States, 30 F. Cas. 239, 1820 U.S. App, LEXIS 179; 1 Brock. 423 (C.C.D. Va. 1820).

[118] Letter, John Marshall to Joseph Story (Sept. 26, 1823), 9 *Papers of John Marshall* 338 (Chas. F. Hobson ed. 1922). Emphasis added. The letter is also available in 1 Warren, *History*, note 108, at 626–627. *See* R. Kent Newmyer, *John Marshall and the Heroic Age of the Supreme Court* 434 (2001) ("This flip statement . . . seems to validate the view of John Marshall as a thoroughly political judge who cynically traded principle for expediency").

A few years later, Chief Justice Marshall did indeed "butt his head against a stone wall" in the Georgia Cherokee land confiscation controversy. Although Marshall had held the Georgia action unconstitutional in *Worcester v. Georgia*, 31 U.S. (6 Peters) 515, 1832 U.S. LEXIS 459 (1832), Georgia ignored the decision. *See* Newmyer, *id.*, at 447–450. President Jackson chose not to interfere. In a remark incorrectly attributed to him but which fully described his attitude, he is quoted as saying "John Marshall has made his decision; let him now enforce it." In consequence, Marshall's decision in *Worcester*, like Johnson's decision in *Elkison*, also became a nullity.

[119] U.S. Const., art. 2, §8, cl. 3.

[120] Letter, William Johnson to John Quincy Adams (July 3, 1824). *See* 31st Cong., 1st Sess. App. 1661 (1850); 1 U.S. Op. Att'y Gen. 659 (1824). *See* 1 Warren, *History*, note 108, at 625 n.2.

and did nothing further. John Quincy Adams, who soon succeeded Monroe, was similarly not prepared to challenge South Carolina and to precipitate a major political confrontation. With its nullification policy unchallenged, South Carolina continued to ignore the decision in the following decades.[121]

With British black seamen on entering South Carolina ports continuing to be confined, the British Consul in Charleston continued to litigate, and the British Embassy continued its pressure against the President and Secretary of State. However, all efforts were unsuccessful in bringing the controversy to an end.

Calder v. Deliesseline, heard in the South Carolina courts at much the same time as *Elkison*, involved the seizure and imprisonment under the statute of a British ship's mate, a free man of color, and four sailors who were slaves. The trial court upheld the conviction of all five seamen, thereby upholding the validity of the Act. On appeal, the South Carolina Court of Appeals ordered a new trial, holding that the statute did not apply to the four slaves. It is not clear whether the new trial was ordered for the mate as well.[122]

In early 1831, the British minister complained once again to the Secretary of State, now Martin van Buren, about the continuing detention of British seamen. This communication was forwarded to the new Attorney General, John M. Berrien, formerly U.S. Senator from Georgia. In his Opinion of March 25, 1831, Berrien "dissented" from Wirt's opinion and advised President Jackson that the statute was valid.[123]

Later in the year and again in the following May, Bankhead, the British Charge d'Affaires, wrote to Secretary of State Edward Livingston protesting against the continued imprisonment of British seamen under the South Carolina statute. Livingston sought still another opinion from the Attorney General, now Roger B. Taney. In an opinion and supplemental opinion, Taney expressed his view that the statute was constitutional, relying on the familiar states' rights contention that the state's power to protect itself against slave insurrection was one of its reserved powers and, therefore, not subject to the "supremacy clause." At the same time, he advised that it was "highly probable" that the Supreme Court would find the statute null and void.[124]

---

[121] *See* 1 Warren, *History*, note 108, at 626–627.

[122] Calder v. Deliesseline, 16 S.C. Law (1 Harp.) 186, 1824 WL 903 (1824).

[123] 2 Op. Att'y Gen. 426 (1831).

[124] Official Opinions, Atty. Gen. Roger B. Taney, May 28, 1832, and June 9, 1832. It is of interest that the opinions were omitted when the official compilation of the opinions of the Attorney General was published perhaps because they were so controversial. *See* Carl B. Swisher, *Roger B. Taney* 151–158 (1935); H. Jefferson Powell, Attorney General Taney & the South Carolina Police Bill, 5 Green Bag 2d 75, 89 (2001).

President Jackson took no action. Like Monroe and Adams, Jackson was not ready to precipitate a national crisis over South Carolinian "nullification" on the issue. Moreover, because he was a Tennessee slaveowner and was elected President in 1828 by a solid bloc of electoral votes from the South, it is far from clear where his sympathies were on this issue.

John Quincy Adams kept the issue on his agenda. In 1842 sitting in the House of Representatives, he was able to persuade a badly divided House to request President Tyler to provide the Congress with numerous documents pertaining to the South Carolina statute, including the British protests and the *Elkison* opinion. President Tyler complied fully except for the opinion. He gave an odd explanation: "I am not informed of the existence of any official opinion of the late Judge Johnson on the unconstitutionality of the South Carolina statute."[125]

The continued enforcement of the South Carolina statute caused domestic, as well as international, difficulties. When the statute was enforced against Massachusetts seamen, the Massachusetts Legislature expressed its outrage and authorized the Governor to appoint a representative of the state to negotiate with South Carolina to obtain the release of any Massachusetts prisoners. In response, the Governor in 1844 sent former Congressman Samuel Hoar to South Carolina to investigate and institute suit on behalf of imprisoned Massachusetts citizens to test the constitutionality of the statute. When Hoar arrived and disclosed his business, the Governor called a special session of the Legislature. "This stirred up the hornet's nest . . . [and] a string of red-hot resolutions," climaxed by vote of 117 to 1 in favor of a resolution ordering the agent out of the state.[126] Mob violence threatened, and Hoar and his daughter who had accompanied him were forced to flee. In the Congress, Representative Palfrey from Massachusetts informed the House of the incident and condemned the South Carolina statute and the expulsion of Mr. Hoar.[127]

The British Consul in Charleston, George B. Matthew, continued his aggressive assault on the statute, retaining prominent counsel, James Petigru. Petigru was the former Attorney General who had refused to defend the statute in *Elkison* and was then the United States District Attorney for South Carolina. In an opinion submitted to Mr. Matthew, Petigru concluded that the statute was unconstitutional as well as in violation of the British treaty. Petigru then made still other challenges to the statute in 1853 on behalf of detained British seamen. In *Ex Parte Manuel Pereira*, an action seeking a

---

[125] H.R. Exec. Doc. No. 119, 27th Cong., 2d Sess. (Mar. 2, 1842). *See* January, note 108, at 286.
[126] *Morning News*, Dec. 14, 1844.
[127] *Daily National Intelligencer* (Washington, D.C.), Dec. 1, 1848.

writ of habeas corpus to free Pereira, an imprisoned seaman, was filed in the South Carolina courts. The trial judge denied the remedy, thereby upholding the constitutionality of the statute. On appeal, the South Carolina Court of Appeals dismissed the suit as moot, the seaman having been released in the meantime.[128]

Then, in *Roberts v. Yates*, Petigru chose to bring a suit in the federal courts against the Sheriff for trespass and damages as a result of detention and imprisonment under the allegedly unconstitutional statute. District Court Judge Robert Budd Gilchrist held in *Roberts v. Yates* that the law was valid and constitutional, and the jury found for the defendant. He did not refer to either *Elkison* that had been decided in the same court or to *Gibbons v. Ogden*. Although an appeal to the Supreme Court was then expected, this never took place.

A new consul, Robert Bunch, had been appointed to replace the contentious Matthews. A new British strategy emerged. Concluding that litigious action would not be productive in the stormy atmosphere, Bunch adopted a conciliatory approach, stressing the areas of common interest with Britain a major purchaser of Southern cotton. He dropped the appeal in *Roberts* and brought no further lawsuits.[129] After several years of cultivation of the South Carolina political leadership, he was at last able to reach an acceptable accommodation of the problem, as British consuls had typically been able to do in the other coastal states.[130] The South Carolina statute was amended in 1856 to enable the ship captain to post a bond enabling the free black seamen in the crew to remain on board while the ship was in port. Alan January reports that Charleston was declining as a port with British shipping being diverted to Savannah to avoid the difficulties presented by the onerous South Carolina statute. He suggests that these economic pressures also contributed to the modification of the state's theretofore adamant position.[131] The protracted controversy was at last at an end. In 1857, not one British seamen was imprisoned.[132]

[128] *Ex Parte* Manuel Pereira, 40 S. C. Law (6 Rich.) 149, (S. C. Ct. App. 1853) (*per curiam*).

[129] Robert v. Yates, 20 F. Cas. 937, 1853 U.S. App. LEXIS 573 (C.C.D. S.C. 1853) (No. 11,919). *See* William H. Pease and Jane H. Pease, *James Louis Petigru: Southern Conservative, Southern Dissenter* 138–142 (1935) (hereinafter Pease).

[130] *See* Laura A. White, The South in the 1850's as Seen by British Consuls, 1 J. S. Hist. 29, 34–35 (Feb. 1935); Philip M. Hamer, British Consuls and the Negro Seamen Acts, 1850–1860, 1 J. S. Hist. 160–167 (May, 1935) (hereinafter Hamer, British Consuls).

[131] *See* January, note 108, at 228.

[132] Act of Dec. 20, 1856 §3, 12 S.C. Stat. 491 (1874). *See* Pease, note 129, at 141; Hamer, British Consuls, note 130, at 166.

Louisiana had a comparable statute and an energetic enforcement policy that also gave rise to litigation.[133] In *The Cynosure*, decided in 1844 by the Federal District Court in Massachusetts, the plaintiff, a free person of color imprisoned under the statute, sued the master of the ship for damages and for determination of his wages for the voyage. In denying any claim for damages but holding that the expenses paid to Louisiana were not to be deducted from the mariner's wages, the court held the Louisiana statute unconstitutional.[134]

Fifteen years later in still another case involving the determination of mariners' wages, the Federal District Court in Massachusetts had again to face the issue of the validity of the seizure of seamen of color under the Louisiana statute. Citing the decision in *The Cynosure*, the Court in *The William Jarvis* agreed that the statute was unconstitutional under the commerce clause. The Court also relied on *Gibbons v. Ogden*, but like *The Cynosure* did not refer to Justice Johnson's decision in *Elkison*.[135]

With Louisiana's continued enforcement of its statute against Massachusetts residents, the Massachusetts Governor, not discouraged by Hoar's expulsion from South Carolina, sent another Massachusetts representative, Henry Hubbard, to Louisiana. This produced the same unhappy result. Like Hoar, Hubbard's mission caused "great excitement" and threats of violence, and like Hoar, Hubbard, too, was forced to flee.[136]

Southern intransigence had continued for 40 years. Only with the Civil War and the triumph of the Union Armies did the destruction of the institution of slavery bring the end of the black seamen's acts along with the other trappings of slavery.

e. State Common-Law Prosecutions to Stifle Abolitionist Activists: Criminal Libel and Public Order

In addition to the statutes in the slaveholding states criminalizing challenges to slavery, the controversy over slavery saw the law used in still other ways to suppress abolitionist speech. Criminal libel and common-law criminalization of activities threatening public disorder all were utilized in the effort. Although there were only a few such cases, they occurred not only in the South and slaveholding border jurisdictions, such as Maryland and the District of Columbia, but also in the North, demonstrating the nationwide hostility to the radical abolitionists.

---

[133] 1842 La. Stats. no. 123.
[134] *The Cynosure*, 6 Fed. Cas. 1102, 1844 U.S. Dist. LEXIS 20 (U.S.D. Mass. 1844) (No. 3,529).
[135] *The William Jarvis*, 29 F. Cas. 1309, 1859 U.S. Dist. LEXIS 12 (D.Mass. 1859) (No. 17,697).
[136] *See* Hamer, *Negro Seamen Acts*, note 108, at 22–23.

The Dr. Reuben Crandell Case. The use of criminal libel to suppress partisan political speech and the slave state criminalization of anti-slavery communications have a fundamental identity. They are variant forms of suppressing dissenting or anti-establishment speech. The two sister doctrines actually coalesced in the 1836 criminal prosecution in the District of Columbia of Dr. Reuben Crandell (also spelled Crandall). According to a newspaper report, it became known that Crandell was in possession of "inflammatory publications . . . [and] had tampered with the slaves. A mob collected, and it was with great difficulty the officers of Justice could get him locked up in prison and keep him out of the hands of *Judge Lynch*."

Tempers ran high. During the night, several black houses were "demolished" and a brothel burned. The following morning, an angry crowd gathered around the jail and threatened Crandell. Francis Scott Key, a leading attorney and author of the *Star Bangled Banner*, and others then addressed the crowd. When they were assured that the law was "ample to protect them from the 'machinations of the incendiaries'" and that "punishment of the culprit was sure," the mob dispersed.[137]

Crandell was indicted for his circulation of the publications of the American Anti-Slavery Society attacking slavery in the District, where it was lawful. This allegedly constituted an offence under the common law for "publishing malicious and wicked libels, with the intent to excite sedition and insurrection among the slaves and free coloured people of this District."[138] Following indictment, the defendant was incarcerated for eight months awaiting trial.

Counsel for the defense, among other matters, compared the prosecution to the experience under the "odious" Sedition Act of 1798, which they was denounced as "tyrannical, oppressive, unconstitutional, and destructive of

---

[137] *See* The Trial of Reuben Crandall, M.D., Charged with Publishing Seditious Libels, by Circulating the Publications of the American Anti-Slavery Society, Slavery, Race, and the American Legal System 1700–1872, in 2 *Slave Rebels, Abolitionists and Southern Court, Pamphlet Literature Series IV*, 367–428 (Paul Finkelman ed. 1988).

Finkelman reports that Crandall (*sic*) was the brother of Prudence Crandall, the Connecticut school teacher who had admitted black children to her school and was prosecuted under a hastily enacted Connecticut statute prohibiting the education of colored persons not inhabitants of Connecticut. Crandall v. State, 10 Conn. 339 (1834); Act of May 24, 1833, ch. 9, 1833 Conn. Pub. Acts 420. *See* P. Finkelman, *Slavery in the Courtroom* 139–143 (1985).

[138] United States v. Crandell, 25 F. Cas. 684, 1836 U.S. App. LEXIS 287 (C.C.D. D.C. 1836) (No. 14,885).

Extensive descriptions of the Crandell case may be found in Finkelman, *Pamphlet Literature*, note 80, at 317–444. This contains reprints of several Library of Congress contemporary pamphlets containing detailed descriptions of "The Trial of Reuben Crandell, M.D. with Publishing and Circulating Seditious Seditious and Incendiary Papers, etc. in the District of Columbia, with the Intent of Exciting Servile Insurrections." *See also* P. Finkelman, *Slavery in the Courtroom* 164–170 (1985).

the liberty of speech and of the press." Counsel further charged that the prosecution was applying "the well known principles of the common law to the
same improper and unconstitutional end." Aside from this brief reference,
counsel did not further challenge the common-law doctrine. Unlike the Federal courts, the District of Columbia did not lack common-law jurisdiction.
A Congressional Act had "received" the Virginia and Maryland law as part of
the District law.[139]

Counsel argued that while in Crandell's office, one of Crandell's acquain-
tances had picked up and borrowed a number of pamphlets, some of which
were endorsed "please read and circulate" in Crandell's handwriting. The
acquaintance subsequently left a borrowed document at a store. This being
the only proof of Crandell's "circulation" of anti-slavery documents, counsel
argued that the prosecution had failed to prove its case. After a trial lasting
ten days, the jury apparently agreed, and Crandell was acquitted.[140]

The Garrison Litigation. Another prominent episode of this nature were
the legal steps in Maryland that succeeded in driving the noted abolitionist
William Lloyd Garrison from the state and silencing his attempts to promote abolition in Maryland. Garrison was prosecuted for material appearing
in his newspaper, *The Liberator*, concerning a particular slaveowner, Francis Todd. Although the *Crandall* prosecution involved the application of
an anti-slavery suppression statute, the *Garrison* case was a criminal libel
case, turning on the truth or falsity of the personal allegations about Todd.
Although the prosecution shared the same political and tactical objective of
punishing abolitionists, the specialized issue underlying the *Garrison* prosecution means that it lacks the jurisprudential significance of the *Crandell*
case.

Writing in his Baltimore newspaper, *The Liberator*, Garrison vigorously
attacked Francis Todd, a New England shipowner. As part of the abolitionist
campaign demonizing slavery, Garrison's article charged that Todd's ship
had carried a "cargo of slaves for the New Orleans market" and that they
had been "chained in a narrow space, between decks." After describing the
conduct, he condemned slavery, asserting that men:

> who have the wickedness to participate therein for the purpose of heaping
> up wealth should be sentenced to solitary confinement for life; they are

---

[139] 2 Stat. 103 (1801), United States v. Hudson & Goodwin, 11 U.S. (7 Cranch) 32 (1812).

[140] For Key's argument for the prosecution, *see* A Part of a Speech Pronounced by Francis S. Key,
Esq. In The Trial of Reuben Crandall, M.D. before the Circuit Court of the the District of
Columbia at the March Term thereof, 1836, 429–434 in Finkelman, *Pamplet Literature*, note 80,
at 429–434.

enemies of their own species, highway robbers and murderers and their final doom will be, unless they speedily repent, to occupy the lowest depths of perdition.

Garrison was tried for criminal libel. The prosecution is reported to have "'proved very clearly'" that "the slaves were not being carried to the New Orleans market but for a "humane master who had already purchased them and that on the voyage they were neither in chains nor harshly treated." In about 15 minutes, the jury convicted Garrison, and the Court sentenced him to a $50 fine and costs. Garrison could not, or more likely would not, but in any event did not, pay the fine. He was, accordingly, imprisoned for seven weeks until Arthur Tappan, "financial angel of the Abolitionists," paid the fine and obtained his release. Garrison thereupon abandoned his abolitionary missionary work in Maryland and returned to Massachusetts. Todd then brought a civil action in Baltimore against Garrison seeking damages for the same libel. Garrison did not appear, and the jury awarded Todd $1,000 damages.[141]

As we have seen, David Walker's incendiary pamphlet *Appeal to the Colored People of the World* played a prominent role in provoking enforcement proceedings. The *Appeal* was featured in at least two other cases. Aptheker reports that in March 1830, Edward Smith, a steward on the Boston ship *Columbo*, was found to have a copy of the *Appeal* in his possession. He was speedily indicted, tried, and convicted of "criminal libel," in all of six days. He was sentenced to a year in jail and a fine of $1,000.[142] There may be a question on some of the details of the episode, as reported by Aptheker. Although contemporaneous newspaper accounts agree on Smith's conviction and sentence, they date the episode as occurring in May, not March, 1830 and report that the offense was for "circulating Walker's seditious pamphlet," not its mere possession. Finally they do not make clear whether the charge rested on the common-law crime of criminal libel as reported by Aptheker or the South Carolina statute, or the common-law crime of disturbing the public order.[143] Aptheker further reports that two missionaries to the Cherokees were imprisoned in 1829 or 1830 for possession of the *Appeal* and admitting black children to their school. Again, he does not inform us whether the prosecution rested on the Louisiana statute or the common law.

In addition to these cases involving Walker's *Appeal*, Aptheker reports two other successful criminal libel prosecutions in the state courts punishing

[141] *See* 14 *American State Trials* 291–298 (J. Lawson ed. 1972 repr.); Curtis, Free Speech, note 66, at 199–201; Aptheker, note 71, at 100.

[142] *See* Aptheker, note 71, at 99.

[143] Salem *Gazette*, June 8, 1830; *Republican Star and General Advertiser*, June 8, 1830.

persons challenging slavery. He asserts that there is evidence that George Rye of Woodford, Va., was convicted and fined for "sedition" in 1837.[144] He concludes with a report that a New Orleans journalist and abolitionist, Milo Mowrer, publisher of the *Liberalist*, was jailed in 1830 for circulating "a seditious and inflammable handbill among the colored people" but lacks other details.[145] As with the other cases, whether these cases in fact involved criminal libel or rested on an allied doctrine is not clear.

The cases appear intended to serve two purposes. The primary objective, of course, was the suppression of anti-slavery speech. In addition, it was expected that the institution of criminal prosecution against the local agitators would deter any mob resort to lynch law as a more effective alternative to bring about such suppression. Hence, whether or not the defendant in these and similar cases actually served his term of punishment or paid his fine was of secondary historical significance. The crucial matter was the extent of the impact of the litigation on the dissenter's ability to continue to assert freely his unwelcome ideas challenging one of the central institutions of the local society. Thus, in *Garrison* as in a number of prosecutions, the repressive legal process in the end had been successful in driving the defendant from the state and thereby achieving its objective of silencing the offending critic. Further, as noted, persons challenging slavery were driven out of state by vigilantes and unorganized mob action through tar and feathering, riding out of town on a rail, and threat of mob violence.

Five years after the *Edward Smith* affair, Charleston, S.C., experienced another incident involving the importation of anti-slavery pamphlets by Northern steamers. The steamer *Columbia* from New York on August 1835 landed "an immense number of papers and pamphlets of the *Abolition Incendiary* order – 3,000,000 it is said . . . and deposited in the post office for circulation. Such was the excitement occasioned . . . that a mob assembled at midnight, *composed of the most respectable persons*" broke open the postal bags and seized the pamphlets. The following evening with 3,000 persons present, effigies of the prominent abolitionists Arthur Tappan and William Lloyd Garrison and a person identified only as Dr. Cox "were consumed with the vile documents at their feet."[146]

As reported in the New Bedford *Mercury* quoting a Southern source, a few days later, a public meeting elected a vigilante committee of 21, who promptly

---

[144]   *See* Aptheker, note 71, at 105.
[145]   *Ibid.*, at 101; Nye, note 66, at 154n.
[146]   *New-Hampshire Sentinel*, Aug. 13, 1835. Emphasis added. The story was headed "Capt. 'Lynch' in South Carolina."

made an arrangement with the (Charleston) Postmaster that no seditious pamphlets, or other incendiary publications, were to be forwarded from the Post Office to the addressees. The Committee was reported as immediately taking steps to intercept and "take charge" of the mail on another incoming steamer, the *Wm. Gibbons*.[147]

Mob anti-abolitionist measures were not confined to the South. The following month, Philadelphia had a similar experience with vigilanteism. As the Philadelphia *Inquirer* reported, while a mail boat was unloading its contents, "a large wooden box apparently filled with dry goods, and directed to a responsible individual of this city was *accidentally* forced open when it was found to be filled with *incendiary pamphlets and newspapers*, such as the '*Liberator*,' '*Human Rights*,' and the '*Slavey's* [sic] *Friend*' . . . in packages" addressed to persons in several slave states. As in Charleston, S.C., a Philadelphia vigilante committee was formed to respond to the situation before it erupted in mob violence. The committee met with the addressee, who disclaimed all interest in the box and gave his consent to the committee to dispose of the materials. "[A]bout a hundred of our most respectable citizens" took possession of the box. After debating on the best measures to be taken "to allay the excitement which was rapidly increasing," the contents of the box consisting of two thousand abolition newspapers were removed, "torn into pieces," and scattered in the middle of the Delaware River. The newspaper expressed its view "that the course pursued was the proper course . . . and adopted with a view to the peace and quiet of the city, and the security" of the addressee.[148]

In the same month, the governing council in New Bedford, Mass., adopted a resolution responding to the excitement among a portion of the population of reports of "the circulation or supposed circulation of pamphlets and papers of a seditious and inflammatory character, addressed to the colored population, to a degree seriously to disturb the tranquillity and good order." It called on the Mayor to respond with measures "to allay the excitement . . . and for the preservation of public peace and order." The Mayor responded by requiring the police to prevent any "meeting of colored persons, or free" and pronouncing a 10:00 P.M. curfew for such persons.[149]

---

[147] New Bedford *Mercury*, Aug. 14, 1835. The Southern source for the story further stated: "The prompt and energetic manner in which the Committee have preceded – the high character and standing of the gentlemen who compose it – and the complete confidence reposed in the entire co-operation of the Postmaster in any measure which may concern the safety of our community – should quiet the apprehensions of our citizens, and induce every individual to give their countenance and support to the constituted authority."

[148] Salem *Gazette*, Sept. 1, 1835; *New-Hampshire Sentinel*, Sept. 3, 1835.

[149] New Bedford *Mercury*, Aug. 21, 1835.

f. Limits on Slave State Jurisdiction to Respond Fully to the Circulation of Abolitionist Pamphlets and Newspapers

A grave deficiency in the ability of the slave states to suppress the circulation of abolitionist pamphlets and newspapers arose from their inability to obtain jurisdiction over the Northerners responsible for the documents. William Lloyd Garrison's second indictment for abolition activities in violation of Southern law provides a useful insight into this important dimension of the problem. A decade after the Maryland litigation that drove him out of the state, Garrison faced prosecution in North Carolina shortly after the Nat Turner revolt in August 1831 with its slaughter of a number of whites. According to a newspaper report in the Raleigh *Star*,[150] the Post Office in Raleigh received copies of Garrison's Boston *Liberator* "containing the most illiberal and cold-blooded allusions to the late supposed insurrection among our slaves." The newspaper "found its way into the hands" of the Attorney General, who promptly secured a criminal indictment of Garrison and Isaac Knapp, editor and publisher of *The Liberator*. The prosecution rested on the North Carolina anti-abolition statute enacted the previous year.[151] The Act made violations a felony, punishable by whipping and imprisonment for the first offence and death without benefit of clergy for the second.

Garrison was in Massachusetts, and trial could not proceed in South Carolina until he had been apprehended and extradited. The Raleigh *Star* was skeptical that the Massachusetts "Executive" would consent to Garrison's surrender, and it never did. It is not without significance that immediately below the *Star*'s account of Garrison's indictment was a story about Nat Turner, "the ringleader in the recent murderous insurrection," as its further contribution to whipping up local indignation.[152]

This was political posturing. As was obvious from the start, the indictment was doomed to futility. As described by the Boston *Courier*:.

> It can be of no avail. The editor has committed *no offense* in North Carolina and the Executive of Massachusetts cannot . . . be called on to surrender him. The circulation of the "Liberator" may be extremely dangerous or [*sic*] the South, but we are not aware of any law, which can stop the publication, so long as it does not disturb the peace in this State.[153]

---

[150] Raleigh *Star*, Oct. 13, 1830 *reported* in the Salem *Gazette*, Oct. 21, 1831; *Eastern Argus*, Oct. 28, 1831.

[151] An Act to Prevent the Circulation of Seditious Publications, ch. 5, 1830 Sess. Laws, 10.

[152] *Eastern Argus Semi-Weekly*, Oct. 28, 1831, reprinting Raleigh *Star*, Oct. 13, 1831.

[153] *Eastern Argus Semi-Weekly*, reprinting dispatch from the Charleston *Mercury*, quoting from an article in the Boston *Courier*, Nov. 22, 1831.

The Charleston *Mercury* commented bitterly:

> The paper is admitted to be "extremely dangerous"... and the people of the South are obliged to endure it, simply because the incendiaries reside in other sections of the Union. If there be no law in Massachusetts to arrest this evil, one should be passed without delay. It is an act of common comity, to say nothing of patriotism and humanity, which the non-slaveholding states owe to those in which slavery exists.[154]

Similarly moved by increased abolitionist activities in circulating "incendiary newspapers and pamphlets," Gov. Swain called on the North Carolina Legislature in the fall of 1835 for further action on "incendiary" and "seditious" abolitionist publications. He noted the passage of the 1830 statute criminalizing circulation of such publications in North Carolina, but pointed to a loophole in the statute: "The public safety imperiously requires the suppression of these wicked and mischievous publications, injurious alike to the best interests of the master and the slave. This, I apprehend cannot be effected without the co-operation of the Legislatures of the States from which these missiles proceed." He urged the Legislature to adopt a resolution calling on Northern states "to adopt such measures as may be necessary to assure our safety, and calling on the Legislatures of all the States to enact such penal laws."[155]

The North Carolina Legislature immediately responded adopting a series of resolutions with "almost entire unanimity." The resolutions included an appeal to the North: "Our sister States are respectfully requested to enact penal laws prohibiting the printing within their respective limits of all such publications as may have a tendency to make our slaves discontented with their present condition, or incite them to insurrection." Another resolution directed to the federal government asserted "we confidently rely upon the Congress of the United States in passing such laws as may be necessary to prevent the circulation of inflammatory publications through the Post Office Department."[156] In addition to North Carolina, the legislatures of a number of other Southern states called upon the Northern legislatures to enact statutes protecting the Southern states from such "incendiary" and "seditious" publications.[157]

Although no Northern legislature responded, the Southern appeals did meet with some sympathetic Northern response. Thus, the Town Meeting

[154] *Ibid.*
[155] New Bedford *Mercury*, Dec. 3, 1835.
[156] *Connecticut Courant*, Jan. 11, 1836.
[157] *See* Curtis, *Free Speech*, note 66, at 182–191.

in Newport, R.I., met in September 1835 to consider "the attempts, now being made by the abolitionists, calculated to produce insurrection in some of the States in that Union." After "sincerely deplor[ing] the evils of slavery" and approving emancipation if accompanied by repatriation, the Meeting resolved:

> in the opinion of this meeting, the bitter denunciations which the aboli-
> tionists incessantly pour out upon the Southern slave proprietors, calling
> them pirates, man-stealers, robbers and murderers! are as unjust as they
> are foul and indecent . . . the freedom of the press will be best secured
> by guarding it against such abuses as these abolitionists have prostituted
> it to.[158]

In a similar vein, Dr. Porter of the Andover Theological Institute, describing himself as one who "deeply deplore[d] the existence of slavery," advised

> If such [the anti-slavery] societies choose to advocate their own principles
> through the press, let them keep strictly within the limits of truth and
> sober arguments, and send their publications, not to servants, but in the
> most honorable and open manner to their masters. All inflammatory
> statements, addressed to the former, or tending to excite them to rapine
> and bloodshed, if they do not subject their authors to indictment at
> common law for misdemeanor, certainly deserve the reprobation of an
> enlightened community.[159]

In response to what historians report to be the widespread hostility in the North to abolitionist activities, the Massachusetts Anti-Slavery Society felt it necessary to respond. Describing itself as an abolitionist group and including such leading abolitionists as William Lloyd Garrison and Isaac Knapp of *The Liberator* among the signatories, the Society issued a "public declaration and disavowal" repudiating the "attempt . . . to fix upon Abolitionists sentiments and intentions which they abhor." It defended its activities calling slavery sinful and calling for its immediate abandonment to be confined to the peaceful exercise of constitutionally guaranteed freedom of speech. The declaration and disavowal went further:

> It is intimated, that we [the Massachusetts Anti-Slavery Society] are guilty
> of circulating incendiary publications among the southern slaves. We
> utterly and indignantly deny this calumny, and call for proof. . . . We
> should consider any action of this kind as far worse than useless as

[158] Newport *Mercury*, Sept. 19, 1835.
[159] Salem *Gazette*, Aug. 13, 1833 *citing* the Boston *Daily Advertiser*.

highly dangerous, – and as little less criminal than murder . . . if it can be shown, that any person connected with our cause, has ever circulated inflammatory tracts among the slaves, or with a view to be read by them – we will publicly denounce him as a foe to the peace of society, and to the best interests of the oppressed.[160]

Although the Southern appeals were for statutory intervention, Massachusetts Governor Everett, a Whig, proclaimed that relief was available in the common law. In his inaugural message, after speaking of what the newspaper account described as " the acts of outrage and violence which had recurred in various parts of the country," Governor Everett observed that "the right of the Southern States to their slaves" was recognized in the Constitution:

Every thing that tends to disturb the relations created [by the Constitution] is, at war with its spirit; and whatever, by direct and necessary operation is calculated to excite an insurrection among the slaves, has been held, by respectable legal authority, an offence against the peace of the Commonwealth, which may be prosecuted as a misdemeanor at common law.[161]

Although several Northern Governors including Everett in Massachusetts and Marcy in New York were sympathetic to the Southern appeals, no Northern legislature responded.[162] However, as Governor Everett had noted, the criminal common-law offense of committing a breach of the peace was available, and as we will see, some Northern prosecutors made use of it.

g. Northern State Common-Law Prosecution of Abolitionist Agitation

Unlike the Southern states that could not obtain jurisdiction over Northern abolitionists circulating pamphlets and newspapers in their states, the Northern states not only had jurisdiction, but a legal weapon as well to deal with abolitionist activities conducted within their borders. As Governor Everett had suggested, local common-law criminal prosecutions for breach of peace were available. Thus, in March 1832, several years before Everett's appeal, Judge

---

[160] *New-Hampshire Sentinel*, Aug. 27, 1835.

[161] *See* Curtis, Free Speech, note 66, at 189, 201–202.

[162] In Feb. 1836, bills and resolutions criminalizing "all libellous publications having a manifest tendency and design to disturb the peace of any of the States, by exciting the slaves to insurrection" were introduced in the Rhode Island legislature, but after discussion were postponed until the next session. New Bedford *Mercury*, Feb. 26, 1836. No action was ever taken.

Thacher (also spelled Thatcher) in the Massachusetts Municipal Court[163] had charged a Massachusetts grand jury:

> to publish books, pamphlets, or newspapers, designed to be circulated here or in other States of the Union, and having a tendency to stimulate the slaves to rise against their masters, and to effect their emancipation by fire and the sword, is an offence against the peace of the Commonwealth, and may be prosecuted as a misdemeanor at common law.... [N]o supposed freedom of speech or of the press will screen the author or printer from the penal effects of the deed[164]

He elaborated:

> Some time since, a pamphlet was put into my hands, the author of which I am informed has since deceased, which contained enough inflammable matter ... to set all the States south of the Potomac into a blaze. However unwise and unjust may be the system of domestic servitude, it is not for us to put into the hands of the slave the sword and the brand.[165]

A New Hampshire newspaper commenting on Judge Thatcher's charge added: "If this opinion is correct, George Storrs is liable to prosecution in any county in this State."[166] As readers have learned, Storrs was an active abolitionist clergyman delivering lectures and addresses on slavery in New Hampshire and Massachusetts. The account further reported that while preaching in New Hampshire, he was arrested as a common vagrant but acquitted.[167]

---

[163] Peter Oxenbridge Thacher (also Thatcher) was a judge of the Municipal Court from 1822 to 1843 and has been admiringly described as the "best criminal law lawyer in Massachusetts." *See* Josiah H. Benton, Jr., *A Notable Libel Case – The Criminal Prosecution of Theodore Lyman, Jr. by Daniel Webster* 34n. (1904).

   A newspaper account of this period provides an insight into Judge Thatcher's personality. The *Eastern Argus Semi Weekly*, June 15, 1932, reports that many years previously when Thatcher (*sic*) was in the Congress, he was challenged by Blount, a North Carolina congressman, to a duel for words spoken in debate. "The Judge ... after adjusting his wig and revolutionary hat [replied] I always consult my wife, on matters of importance, well knowing that she is a better Judge of family affairs than myself. If she consents to take the choice of becoming a widow, or having her husband *hanged for murder*, I certainly will fight Mr. Blount. Tell him not to be in a hurry; it will not take more than three weeks to receive her election."

[164] *New-Hampshire Sentinel*, Apr. 20, 1832; *Vermont Gazette*, Apr. 17, 1832. The *Sentinel* concluded that Judge Thatcher's "sentiments are correct. The *hair-brained* Editor of the *Liberator* [William Lloyd Garrison] ought to be checked in his course."

[165] *New-Hampshire Sentinel*, Apr. 20, 1832.

[166] *New Hampshire Patriot and State Gazette*, Apr. 4, 1836; *Vermont Gazette*, Apr. 17, 1832.

[167] The *Portsmouth Journal of Literature and Politics*, Jan. 9, 1836, reports this episode under the heading "Infamous Outrage under Lynch Law. The newspaper proclaimed its neutrality on the issue of slavery, balancing freedom of speech against the "security of the *persons* of our *white* population." It concluded that "No matter what doctrines the Clergy inculcate from the pulpit

Aptheker adds that he was then forbidden by police authorities to speak in New Hampshire.

Storrs was subsequently arrested again in Massachusetts as "a common railer [sic] and brawler" while speaking on slavery, slaveholders, and abolition. Reports differ whether he was preaching or addressing an anti-slavery society. He was convicted and sentenced to imprisonment at hard labor for three months and ordered to pay the costs of the prosecution, taxed in the amount of $15.65.[168] Storrs appealed, but the outcome of the appeal is not reported.

As for Storrs, he continued his abolitionist activities. An admiring article on the more prominent abolitionist Orange Scott, another Methodist minister, reported on Scott's active role fighting slavery at Methodist conferences. The paper noted the welcome given to Storrs and "his frequent companion, the impetuous George Scott."[169]

The Essex *Gazette* later in 1836 published an extract from a report in another paper on a "great Anti-Slavery Meeting in Rhode Island." It stated that the meeting had reaffirmed its dedication to the cause "undeterred by legislative enactments or ecclesiastical denunciations, *by prosecutions at common law*, or persecutions without law."[170] Apparently, although only two accounts of prosecutions at common law have been found, those cases, and perhaps others not yet identified, played a more significant role in the society of the time than the limited number would, otherwise, suggest.

At much the same time, the New Bedford *Mercury* published an article on anti-slavery societies.[171] The article concluded by upholding the power of the Massachusetts Legislature to criminalize the publishing of papers and pamphlets tending to instigate slaves in other states to insurrection and violence. It asserted that the matter was "put beyond question" for the United States by several English common-law cases.[172] It contended that the English common law was a "doctrine which our ancestors had brought to this country as their

---

or statesmen proclaim in the halls of legislation – if they are to be silenced and imprisoned by brutal force, and lawless MOBS, and the ringleaders escape with impunity; there is a real end of our Republican institutions! Liberty can have no existence in the pestilential atmosphere of that Hideous MONSTER, the MOB!"

[168] Essex *Gazette*, Apr. 23, 1836. *See also* Aptheker, note 71, at 105).

[169] *See* D. Matthews, Orange Scott: The Methodist Evangelist as Revolutionary in *The Antislavery Vanguard: New Essays on the Abolitionists* 88 (M. Duberman ed. 1965).

[170] Letter in the Concord (N.H.) *Herald of Freedom*, reprinted in the Essex *Gazette*, Nov. 26, 1836. Emphasis added.

[171] New Bedford *Mercury*, Sept. 18, 1835.

[172] It referred to the 1788 convictions of Lord George Gordon in England for libelling the French Ambassador and the Queen of France, the conviction of John Vint ten years later for a libel on the Russian Emperor Paul, and the 1803 conviction of Jean Peltier for libel in London of Napoleon Bonaparte (Lord Ellenborough).

birth right" and accepted as part of the legal system of the American states. The anti-abolitionist author[173] went further, not only upholding the power of Massachusetts to punish such abolitionist conduct, but contending that Massachusetts had the duty to do so.

3. The Federal Experience

a. Anti-Slavery Petitions in the Congress

As noted, Virginia had instituted a prosecution in 1809 in the *Barrett* case, charging that participation in the circulation of an anti-slavery petition to the Congress violated the Virginia statute criminalizing anti-slavery communications.[174] This effort on the state level was matched by the efforts of Southern Congressmen to cause the House of Representatives to refuse to accept anti-slavery petitions to the Congress. During the seven years from 1837 to 1844, these efforts met with success. Skirting the constitutional injunction that "Congress shall make no law respecting . . . the right of the people . . . to petition the Government for a redress of grievance,"[175] the House of Representatives operated under a rule providing that although anti-slavery petitions were to be received, they "shall without being printed or referred, be laid upon the table [without further action]."[176] After unsuccessfully struggling for several terms of the Congress to eliminate the rule, former President John Quincy Adams, then serving in the House, was at last successful in leading the Northern and Western members to overturn the rule in 1844.[177]

b. Jacksonian Approval of State Interception of Anti-Slavery Newspapers in the U.S. Mails

The efforts of the Southern states to intercept and impound abolitionist newspapers in the mails depended on the cooperation, or at least the benign neglect, of the federal government, which controlled the postal system. President Andrew Jackson, a Tennessee slaveowner, sympathized with the Southern states. He looked upon abolition mailings "as a wicked plan of exciting

---

[173] "Abolition . . . is one of the most unfortunate delusions that ever afflicted this country." New Bedford *Mercury*, Sept. 18, 1835. The substance of this comment appears in other papers of this very period as well. *Compare* the Pittsfield *Sun*, Aug. 6, 1835 ("the misguided and wicked zeal of the Abolitionists").

[174] *See supra* note 91.

[175] U.S. Const. amend. I, cl. 5.

[176] 12 Cong. Debates 4052–4053 (1836).

[177] *See* Curtis, Free Speech, note 66, at 175–181.

the Negroes to insurrection and massacre."[178] He fully supported the policy of Postmaster General Amos Kendall, who had earlier been a Kentucky newspaper publisher. Echoing a view that according to Curtis was widely held in the North as well as the South at this time, Kendall asserted that the Southern states had the reserved powers to act as they were doing with respect to slavery. Kendall asserted: "It has never been alleged that these laws are incompatible with the Constitution and laws of the United States."[179] The Jackson administration defended its actions, asserting that it was doing no more than supporting Southern Postmasters seeking to perform their duties in accordance with the local laws.[180] While Kendall avoided directing Northern Postmasters to refuse to send the mailings of the anti-slavery society into the South by public mails, he encouraged them to impose such an embargo. In his August 22, 1835, letter to the New York Postmaster, he condemned abolitionist literature: "their revolting pictures and fervid appeals addressed to the senses and passions of the blacks, they are calculated to fill every family with assassins and produce at no distant day an exterminating servile war." He gave his blessings to Postmasters examining the contents of newspapers and refusing to distribute them, stating: "As a measure of great public necessity therefore, you and the other Postmasters who have assumed the responsibility of stopping these inflammatory papers, will, I have no doubt, stand justified in that step before your country and all mankind."[181] Similarly, Kendall wrote to the Postmaster at Richmond, who had detained "a variety of pamphlets and papers on the subject of slavery" that while he could not sanction the action, he would not condemn it.[182]

In his December 1835 annual message to the Congress, President Jackson called for a law prohibiting circulation through the mails of the Southern states, of "incendiary publication, intended to instigate the slaves to insurrection." Southerners, however, were distrustful of any extension of federal powers. Sen. John C. Calhoun, instead, introduced a bill seeking to reenforce state laws. His bill would have prohibited any Deputy Postmaster from

---

[178] At his death, Jackson owned 150 slaves and unlike Washington and others did not emancipate any in his will. When a young man, he advertised for one of his runaway slaves, offering to pay not only a reward but adding a bonus of $10 for each 100 lashes that the person apprehending the slave applied up to a maximum of 300 lashes. *See* Jon Meacham, *American Lion: Andrew Jackson in the White House* 302–303 (2008) (hereinafter Meacham).

[179] Report of Postmaster General Amos Kendall (Dec. 1, 1835), Cong. Globe, 24th Cong., 1st Sess. App. 9 (1835), *cited by* Curtis, The Curious History, note 66, at 806–807. *See also* Eaton, note 66, at 200.

[180] *See* Curtis, Free Speech, note 66, at 156, 175.

[181] New Bedford *Mercury*, Sept. 4, 1835, quoting unidentified New York papers.

[182] Salem *Gazette*, Aug. 14, 1835.

knowingly receiving and mailing or delivering any "pamphlet, newspaper, handbill or other . . . representation touching the subject of slavery directed to any person or post office, where by the laws thereof, their circulation is prohibited." Although a version of Calhoun's bill passed the Senate, it died in the House.[183]

Congress ultimately enacted the Post Office Act of 1836. This made criminal any *unlawful* detention of the mail by a Postmaster. However, this did not interfere with the enforcement of Southern anti-abolition statutes directed at Postmasters. In 1858, Attorney General Caleb Cushing issued an opinion that "it cannot be unlawful to detain that which it is unlawful to deliver."[184]

John Quincy Adams bitterly condemned the actions of Jackson. A newspaper account of his eulogy of James Madison in September 1836 reports:

> In discussing the Alien and Sedition laws, [*sic*] observed that they were not suited to the temper of the times, but that they were not infractions of the Constitution [and] much less obnoxious than propositions which have since been made by a Chief Magistrate with the view to prevent the circulation of Incendiary Pamphlets.[185]

However, while there was significant Northern opposition to the complicity of the Jackson administration in the Southern campaign to prevent the use of the United States mails for distribution of abolitionist documents, it was also accompanied by anger at the acts of the abolitionists. Thus, the *Salem Gazette* said:

> We repeat, again and again, our conviction of the impossibility of preventing discussion, without a subversion of the free principles of our government – But this conviction does not lessen the ABHORRENCE with which we regard the distribution of incendiary or inflammatory publications among the blacks of the South, or the dissemination among them in any other way of sentiments intended to excite them to insubordination, to sedition, or to violence. Every person who engages in such an undertaking is a foe to public order, the enemy of his country and of mankind.[186]

---

[183] See Meacham, note 178, at 304–306; William W. Freehling, *Prelude to Civil War: The Nullification Controversy in South Carolina, 1816–1836*, 346–347 (1966).

[184] Act of July 2, 1836, ch. 270, 5 Stat. 80, 87; Yazoo City Post Office Case, 8 Op. Att'y Gen. 489, 494 (Mar. 3, 1857). *See* Curtis, The Curious History, note 66, at 835–836.

[185] The *Connecticut Courant's* report on Oct. 8, 1836, reprinting an *Argus* report dated Boston, Sept. 28, 1836.

[186] Salem *Gazette*, Aug. 14, 1835.

4. Ineffectiveness of Constitutional Guaranties of Freedom of Press to
Invalidate the Southern Statutes Suppressing Anti-Slavery Publications

Although anti-slavery statutes were enforced in a number of celebrated cases
throughout the South, the singular fact is that as best one can tell from the
accounts of the cases available, the constitutionality of such statutes in the
face of the federal and state guaranties of freedom of speech played no role
in any of the litigations. Counsel seemed not to have argued the issue, and
the courts enforced the statutes apparently unconcerned with their possible
unconstitutionality.

Without exception, the laws of every one of the slave states under examination were subject to state constitutional guaranties of freedom of speech and
press. Nevertheless, in none of the cases involving these statutes did counsel
or the court even refer to the state constitutional guaranties or to the federal
constitutional provisions in the period prior to 1833, when the Supreme Court
held in *Barron v. Baltimore* that they did not apply to the states.[187]

It is indisputable that in the Early Republic, the still undeveloped American constitutional jurisprudence – federal and state – provided no protection
for these fundamental rights. It constitutes a sharp contrast to modern constitutional doctrine that has accorded expanding scope to the protection of such
freedoms since their emergence as accepted constitutional law commencing
after World War I.

The absence of constitutional challenge to the statutes criminalizing anti-
slavery and abolitionist advocacy also provides some basis for better understanding the nature of the federal constitutional discussion surrounding the
enactment of the Alien and Sedition Acts. As discussed earlier, so much of the
opposition to the Sedition Act had been centered in the Jeffersonian South.
The constitutional arguments raised in the Congress to the proposed Act had
indeed included, among others, strenuous contentions that it would violate
the federal guaranties of freedom of speech and press. However, as pointed
out, these played a role secondary to the arguments based on concepts of
federalism attacking the Act as beyond the powers of the national government. There was an evident Southern concern that such a statute based on
the implied powers of the Congress might serve as a precedent for a similar
aggressive use of national power to interfere with slavery. Many of the critics
of the proposed Sedition Act further suggested that the Act was unnecessary because the states had the power to deal with criminal libel under the

---

[187] Barron v. Baltimore, 32 U.S. 243, 1833 U.S. LEXIS 346 (1833).

common law. In this manner, the critics had conceded that the various state constitutional protections of free speech and press matching the comparable federal guaranties did not bar such repressive legislation. Thus, when in the decades thereafter the same states widely enacted statutes criminalizing speech, it is no surprise that their possible unconstitutionality under the state Constitutions played no role in the judicial decisions in the cases under the statutes that subsequently ensued.

D. Conclusion

The uniquely American experience with the Southern criminalization of challenges to the legitimacy of slavery and the venerable Anglo-American criminalization of Christian blasphemy present a number of points of interest. Most important of all, they present additional demonstrations of the unattractive, repressive dimension of the American jurisprudence of the times. Along with criminal libel and related doctrines, these additional illustrations show the remarkable breadth of the early American society's utilization of criminal law to suppress anti-establishment speech. At the same time, their continued vitality for decades after the adoption of the federal Bill of Rights and comparable provisions in virtually all of the state Constitutions shows the slow pace in these early years of the Republic of the emergence of the constitutional protections that more than 150 years later have made common-law criminal libel no more than a legal fossil.

A final word of caution: As a matter of the statutory law in the decades under examination, the numerous statutes criminalizing blasphemy throughout the nation and those penalizing anti-slavery expression in virtually all the slave holding states appear to demonstrate a degree of vitality in these areas that may not exist. After all, a meticulous collection of every case involving these statutes that can be identified in the primary and secondary sources yields only scattered prosecutions and few convictions.

Further, an examination of the type of defendants involved and, with rare exceptions, the extremely mild sentences imposed would appear to confirm the relative lack of importance attached to the vigorous enforcement of the statutes. Thus, ministers conducting serious discussions of the implications of Christianity with respect to slavery represented a significant number of the anti-slavery defendants and received sentences that in at least one case was no more than a fine of $49.62 $\frac{1}{2}$ and costs. Similarly, the typical blasphemy defendants were either ranting "crazies" unlikely to attract significant public support or drunkards in their cups, receiving sentences appropriate for what apparently were seen as minor breaches of the peace. By contrast, with the exception of such early Sedition Act prosecutions as the three Newark, N.J., drunks mocking President Adams at the parade in his honor on his journey through the town, the criminal libel trials typically involved highly partisan political expressions by opposition newspaper publishers and printers, leading in many cases to severe sentences of imprisonment and fines in amount significant for the times. Even more importantly, they resulted in the shutting down of the papers of the defendant publishers so often as to lead strongly to the conclusion that such a devastating outcome was the very point of the indictments in the first place.

Whatever the limitations of the blasphemy and anti-slavery prosecutions, the reality remains. Notwithstanding ostensible constitutional protections, the anti-slavery and blasphemy criminal statutes were part of the law of the land of the time, and the successful prosecutions continuing well into the 20th century in the case of blasphemy leave no doubt that the doctrine even at this relatively recent time could not be dismissed as obsolete. The fact that these prosecutions in areas other than criminal libel continued to take place and persisted for almost 150 years in the case of blasphemy and until the Civil War when the slave society was destroyed demonstrates the persistence of the repressive doctrines inherited from the English and incorporated into the jurisprudence of the New Republic.

There is a fundamental identity in the 19th-century jurisprudence of the slave state statutes criminalizing anti-slavery communications and the cases enforcing the common law or statutory crime of blasphemy. Both involve efforts of the established society to suppress dissenting speech. In this respect, they are closely related to much the same earlier experience with criminal libel, contempt of court and legislature for out-of-chamber publications, binding over, and breach of the peace. All are dramatic examples of the jurisprudence of the times suppressing anti-establishment speech in vital areas. Similarly, they illustrate the severe limitations of the constitutional jurisprudence of the time in implementing the guaranties of freedom of religion, speech, or press. None of these doctrines, particularly criminal libel, can be isolated and discussed *in vacuo*. They can be properly understood only when examined together in full historical context as closely related aspects of the jurisprudence, particularly the constitutional jurisprudence, of the times.

9

Conclusion

A. Introduction

The modern reaction to the Sedition Act of 1798 is one of shock and surprise: how could the democratic New Republic founded with all the aspirations expressed in the Declaration of Independence, the Constitution, and the Bill of Rights have accepted so repressive a statute? In a society apparently dedicated to freedom of speech and press, the Act authorized criminal punishment of political critics ridiculing or contemptuous of the Adams administration.

How was it that the Revolutionary American society that had fought a desperate war for Independence, thrown aside the monarchy, and with limited exceptions rejected the concept of the established church could have accepted such pernicious measures of the English criminal common law so contrary to the fundamental political values of the New Republic? How was it that the Congress enacted the statute? How was it that in not one of the numerous federal decisions upholding punishment of Jeffersonian editors and supporters or in any of the even more numerous state decisions did a single judge – whether sitting in the federal or the state courts, whether a Federalist or a Republican – ever express doubt over the constitutionality of the proceedings in the face of constitutional guaranties of freedom of speech and press in the federal and state Constitutions?

This review of the jurisprudence of the Early American Republic in which criminal libel and other repressive legal doctrines formed a significant part of the accepted law serves to explain this surprising development. Far from being an anomaly, the Act was entirely in keeping with the substantial body of repressive jurisprudence received by the new American society from its Colonial days. The governing law was the jurisprudence of the English Crown that had been the law of the English Colonies. It was a highly repressive jurisprudence with a series of ugly doctrines, of which criminal libel was one, governing public speech and press and criminally punishing critics of the English monarchy and other institutions of the English establishment. The 1798 Act did no more than codify the existing common law. Indeed, the Act was, at least in form, less restrictive of freedom of speech and press than the prevailing law of the time.

Many excellent histories have discussed the Act and the political context in which it arose, but they do not deal with this challenging issue. In seeking to provide an explanation, this volume goes beyond an analysis of the legal and political issues involved in the use of the doctrines of criminal libel by the Adams administration against its Republican opponents. Instead, this is a legal scholar's comprehensive overview of the extensive body of repressive jurisprudence of the times of which the Sedition Act and common-law criminal libel constituted only one part. It seeks to contribute to a fuller understanding of how the Act could have been accepted by the Congress and President, and at the outset overwhelmingly approved by the new American society. Further, it helps explain why after the expiration of the Sedition Act, common-law seditious and criminal libel flourished and even intensified for 15 years in the states after the expiration of the Act and the triumph of the Jeffersonians in the national arena. Although the Sedition Act, no doubt, is the most prominent example of this repressive jurisprudence, as we have seen, it constitutes only one dimension of the entire jurisprudence of the New Republic that forms the subject matter of this volume.

Although the English common law protected what it called "freedom of speech and press," this concept had a very different meaning to the lawyers and judges than it does today, or indeed to many people of the time. As noted, it then meant no more than the prohibition of any "prior restraint." Everyone was completely free of governmental restraint to say what he or she pleased, but could be held criminally liable for any statements in violation of any of the repressive doctrines of the times. Thus, notwithstanding the vaunted English freedom of speech and press, a speaker could be fined or jailed if he had ridiculed or brought the protected institutions of the state – the monarchy, the courts, the Parliament, and Christianity – into disrepute. In sum, this formidable body of repressive doctrines constituted a powerful arsenal of common-law crimes to prevent free discussion of controversial measures challenging any of the established institutions of English society.

Accepting the historic doctrines of the English common law, American jurisprudence from its very beginning was, accordingly, a repressive

jurisprudence with legal doctrines in fundamental conflict with the political principles of the newly independent 13 states and the New Republic. This
unfortunate heritage was such a thoroughly accepted part of the American
law that it took 150 years of constitutional evolution widely expanding the
scope of the constitutional guaranties of freedom of speech and press and of
religious discussion before these repressive doctrines so incongruous in the
new democratic Republic were at last thrown aside and become part of an
unhappy history.

Under this repressive jurisprudence inherited from the Colonial law and
incorporating the monarchical objectives of the English common law, people
were jailed, not only in the early days of the Republic but over the country's
history for 150 years thereafter, for expressions of dissenting opinion ridiculing
or holding in contempt the institutions and representatives of the established
order.

In this process, the constitutional guaranties of freedom of press and freedom of religion were no obstacles. The judges were lawyers, and their decisions reflected a lawyer's understanding of the English law.

The English common law – which had become the American law – was
the law in which every American lawyer was raised and which he practiced,
before and after the Revolution. It was the law of the land, in America as in
England, however inconsistent it was with the revolutionary political structure. It constituted the jurisprudential universe that governed legal thinking,
with Blackstone the ultimate authority. It governed their thinking as lawyers,
and it implicitly governed their thinking as members of the Constitutional
Convention and, later, as members of the judiciary.

Lawyers played a leading role in drafting the new federal and state Constitutions. They naturally expressed themselves in the legal language and terms
of art to which they were accustomed in their law practices and in which
they had been educated. When litigation developed, the judges applying the
new Constitution and the new law were thus faced with familiar terms, such
as "freedom of speech and press" that were terms of art that had taken on a
specific meaning in the English law. In applying these doctrines, every one
of the American judges of the time faced with formulating decisions involving these doctrines in dozens of cases in the various areas embraced within
this jurisprudence *without exception* gave those familiar terms the very same
meaning as the terms had in the repressive English system. To the lawyers
(and hence the judges), "freedom of speech and press" meant no more than
a prohibition of any prior restraint.

From the very first decision in 1790 Massachusetts, every court facing the
constitutional issue – whether state or federal, Federalist or Republican in

their politics – enforced the repressive jurisprudence. The new state and federal Constitutions had made no change whatsoever in the historic common-law doctrines. Historic criminal libel and blasphemy (and contempt of court and of the legislature for out-of-chamber publications too) remained fully in force in their rigorous common-law form. The lawyers and judges of the time, thus, saw the issue as a professional matter and shared a professional view of the meaning of the constitutional guaranties of freedom of speech and press and religion.

However, the lawyers and judges did not constitute the full political world. There were other participants not trained in the law. In the formulation and ratification of the Bill of Rights, those other delegates came from many different occupations and knew little of the traditional learning of the lawyers. However, the terms were familiar to all, however much they may have differed in the meaning they gave to them, whether as terms of art as perceived by the lawyers or as popular phrases of use in everyday speech. Thus, they apparently agreed on the language without realizing the dramatically differences in meaning that it may have had to the two groups. This appears to be the most likely explanation of how the profound differences in perceptions of constitutional meaning arose. In fact, historians tell us that the most intensive review of the debates in the ratifying conventions yields no indication of any kind that the issue was ever the subject of discussion. The very familiar terms were apparently accepted on their face. The participants seemingly "knew" what they meant. This apparent unanimity thus masked a profound misunderstanding.

The Republicans led by Jefferson and Madison read the constitutional terms very differently from the so-called legal view. As argued by the Republican spokesmen of the times, the constitutional guaranties represented the implementation of the Revolutionary principles. These had repudiated the hereditary English monarchy and its institutional trappings and replaced the Crown with a Revolutionary form of government: a Republic resting on representative democracy in which the need for public debate of public issues, the policies and performance of public officials, and the qualifications of candidates for public office was vital. For them, the legal view that the guaranties were simply a continuation of the traditional common-law doctrines that made up English law and that had developed in support of the English monarchical system was utterly unacceptable. It was incompatible with the Revolutionary principles on which the new American government had been founded.

But what of the Republican lawyers? How did they reconcile Republican doctrine with the accepted common-law meaning of the critical terms in the

Constitution? In the struggle over the passage of the Sedition Act, this problem was largely overshadowed by their primary challenge to the constitutionality of the Act as beyond the powers delegated to the national government. This was a matter of states' rights for which the common law provided no answer and therefore no inconsistency.

More critically, Republicans, of whom Macon and Gallatin are prominent examples, argued in addition that the Sedition Act was unnecessary. They emphasized that remedies to deal with libels were already available under the laws of each of the states. In each, common-law seditious and criminal libel were part of their jurisprudence. In so doing, they were acknowledging that state prosecutions based on historic common-law criminal and seditious libel were constitutional under their own state Constitutions. Because these all contained guaranties of freedom of speech and press and religion, they were, thus, fully accepting the "legal" view of constitutionality and conceding that the terms had for American constitutional law the very meaning they had for the English and Blackstone.

Thus, as a professional matter, the lawyers and judges of the time shared a professional view of the meaning of the constitutional guaranties of freedom of speech and press and religion. Accordingly, when Madison and Jefferson spoke so eloquently of the constitutional claims of the First Amendment in terms of the Revolutionary ideals of the New Republic, this was political discourse irrelevant for legal proceedings, and it is in legal proceedings not in public debate, that constitutionality is determined in the immediate case.

For scholars as well as lawyers, the inescapable reality is that *every* judge considering the issue for 150 years agreed that in these respects the Constitutions of the country – federal and state alike – reflected the English legal inheritance, not the political ideals of the Revolution.

For the lawyer, the issue of the meaning of the Constitution or the law, as Holmes and Hughes have taught,[1] is what the judges say it is. All else is argument and in the end irrelevant for determining the state of the law at the time. As uniformly expressed by American judges in federal and state constitutional decisions for 150 years, constitutional guaranties of freedom of the press and freedom of religion meant no more or less than as had earlier been set forth in English common law, of which Blackstone was almost as uniformly accepted as the ultimate authority.

---

[1] *See supra* Ch. 5, note 108.

The Revolutionary values that led to the establishment of the new independent American society were thereby unceremoniously frozen out of any role in the new American jurisprudence. In consequence, Blackstone – the authoritative source of English law – became the authoritative source of American constitutional law. Whatever criticism modern scholars have levied on the limitations of Blackstone's scholarship is irrelevant. For the lawyers of his time, Blackstone was the unquestioned authority. A glimpse of the role of Blackstone at the times under examination is provided by Chief Justice Marshall's celebrated opinion in *Marbury v. Madison*, in which he quotes from Blackstone no fewer than four times.[2] American independence meant a radical change in the political system, but in the respects under examination, no change whatsoever in the American legal system. Almost sight unseen, English law with its repressive doctrines had triumphed over the political aspirations of the Revolution.

Although the implications of this professional legal perspective have been largely ignored or dismissed by historians, it represents the working law of the time and for the succeeding decades. As Chief Justice Taft declared more than 125 years later in *Ex Parte* Grossman:

> The language of the Constitution can not be interpreted safely except by reference to the common law and to British institutions as they were when the instrument was framed and adopted. The statesmen and the lawyers of the Convention who submitted it to . . . ratification were born and brought up in the atmosphere of the common law, and thought and spoke in its vocabulary . . . [W]hen they came to put their conclusions into the form of fundamental law in a compact draft, they express them in terms of the common law, confident that they could be shortly and easily understood.[3]

Chief Justice Taft's comments echoed the view advanced 125 years earlier by a Virginian lawyer, George Taylor, who was a cousin of John Marshall. In language strikingly like that of Chief Justice Taft, Taylor said in 1798:

> [Among] the persons who framed the amendments to the Constitution of the United States . . . was a great proportion of lawyers, whose peculiar study had been the common law. Perhaps everyone of them had read and maturely considered Blackstone's Commentaries. . . . Certainly every one of them was acquainted with the laws of his own state, where

---

[2] See Marbury v. Madison, 5 U.S. (1 Cranch) 137, 163, 168–169 (1803).
[3] *Ex Parte* Grossman, 267 U.S. 87, 108–109 (1925).

the terms "freedom of the press" had precisely the same meaning as in England.[4]

Although the repressive jurisprudence of Blackstone prevailed in every case in the courts, this was the "law on the books." It did not reflect the reality of daily political life. From the very establishment of the Republic and continuing for 150 years before the repressive jurisprudence was at last held unconstitutional, the nation was in every sense a free society in which political debate was vigorous and dissent from established policy flourished. Enforcement of the pernicious repressive jurisprudence, while continuing with a strong record of indictments and convictions from juries, was so episodic, and, on occasion, so quixotic, that it had little deterrent effect.

Some scholars point to the repudiation of the legal doctrine so widely evident in the political life of the times as demonstrating that all the historic English common-law repressive doctrines commencing with the Sedition Act of 1798 itself were unconstitutional. However, for a period of 150 years, these doctrines were deemed constitutional by the judges and enforced. Scholars must deal with the reality that for 150 years, Americans were indicted, prosecuted, and convicted and went to jail for statements violating the historic doctrines.

It was not until World War II, or shortly thereafter, that the repressive earlier American law was swept aside, and the older English jurisprudence of centuries ago so repugnant to American ideals and standards was at last expunged from the American scene. Until the middle of the 20th century, no federal or state court had failed to uphold the constitutional validity of any of these repressive doctrines. The strength of these doctrines is evident in the fact that they were not gradually abandoned. On the contrary, they had survived in place for 150 years without vital modification. Then when the doctrines were at last repudiated, they were simply swept away and typically by unanimous decision. At long last, the incompatibility of the traditional legal view and the accepted political values of the society became so profound that the historic legal doctrines repudiated by the march of political events simply collapsed.

In the climactic decision on libel, *New York Times Co. v. Sullivan,* Justice Brennan tried to explain the evolution. Meticulously avoiding full discussion of the legal precedents and the historical roots of the American common-law doctrine, Justice Brennan, instead, rested the Court's decision on the

---

[4] Va. Rep. 137 (George Taylor, Dec. 21, 1798), cited by H. Jefferson Powell, *A Community Built on Words: The Constitution in History and Politics* 57 (2002).

political response of the American society, stating: "the attack on its [the Sedition's Act's] validity has carried the day in the court of history."[5] In focusing on the modern consensus in the maturing American society that the repressive historic law was out of keeping with contemporary American values, he brushed aside the unbroken jurisprudential acceptance of common-law seditious libel for the preceding 150 years.

The Supreme Court's midcentury decisions sweeping away the historic restrictive jurisprudence of the preceding centuries and substantially restricting criminal and criminal libel are a landmark achievement in American constitutional jurisprudence. It is a triumph in the struggle to bring historic constitutional doctrine into accord with the accepted modern values pertaining to freedom of expression.

B. Let Us Call the Roll

Criminal and Civil Libel Involving Public Persons: Virtually dead, thanks to the 1964 decisions of the Supreme Court in *New York Times Co v. Sullivan* and *Garrison v. Louisiana.*

Contempt of Court for Out-of-Court Speech: Dead, thanks to the 1941 decision of the Supreme Court in *Nye v. United States.*[6]

Contempt of the Legislature for Out-of-Court Speech: Dead, thanks to the 1935 decision of the Supreme Court in *Jurney v. MacCracken.*[7]

Binding Over to Assure Good Conduct: Severely limited by federal and state statutes restricting their use and requiring proof of probable cause.

Blasphemy: Dead, thanks to the 1935 decision of the Supreme Court in *Joseph Burstyn, Inc. v. Wilson.*[8]

Anti-Slavery Speech: By 1865, after four years of warfare and hundreds of thousands of Union dead, the Union Army's ultimate battlefield success, and the subsequent adoption of the Thirteenth and Fourteenth Amendments rendered obsolete the laws of the Southern states making challenge to the law of slavery a criminal offense, and in some states a capital crime to boot.

In this manner, the entire body of the complex repressive jurisprudence inherited from the English monarchical legal system that had dominated

---

[5] Justice Brennan was adopting the argument advanced by the distinguished counsel for the *New York Times:* former Att'y Gen. Herbert Brownell and Herbert Wechsler (Brief for the Petitioner, 1963 XX 105981 *48) ("the verdict of history surely susttains [*sic*] the view that it [the Sedition Act] was inconsistent with the First Amendment").

[6] Nye v. United States, 313 U.S. 33 (1941).

[7] Jurney v. MacCracken, 294 U.S. 125 (1935).

[8] Joseph Burstyn, Inc. v. Wilson, 343 U.S. 495 (1952).

American constitutional law for 150 years was at last rooted out of American constitutional jurisprudence. This history provides scholars with a fertile opportunity for reflection on the appropriate standards that should guide constitutional interpretation.

This concludes our detailed examination of the origins, evolution, and ultimate demise of the repressive jurisprudence of the Early American Republic. Through its extensive review of the origins, full dimensions, and ultimate rejection of this jurisprudence, this study of the experience as seen by a legal scholar, as distinct from a historian or political scientist, provides a dimension, heretofore unavailable, to a full explanation of how it was that the same Revolutionary society that overwhelmingly supported the Bill of Rights could have accepted a statute such as the Sedition Act criminalizing critical discussion of public officials and the government. With criminal libel and the Sedition Act recognized as one part of an overall repressive legal system, this study similarly contributes to a fuller understanding of the acceptance by the Revolutionary society of such other repressive doctrines – so surprising to modern Americans – as the law of blasphemy, contempt of court and contempt of the legislature for out-of-chamber publications, and binding over without proof of probable cause.[9] Further, it provides an explanation how this repressive jurisprudence was the law of the land, accepted by all courts and all judges for 150 years.

---

[9] See *supra* Ch. 5, note 108.

Table of Cases

Index